Memorial Book of the Community of Siedlce
(Siedlce, Poland)

Translation of
Sefer yizkor le-kehilat Shedlets

Original Book Edited by: A.Wolf Yassni (Jasny)

Originally published in Buenos Aires 1956

JewishGen
מרכז עולמי לגנאלוגיה יהודית
The Global Home for Jewish Genealogy

A Publication of JewishGen, INC
Edmond J. Safra Plaza, 36 Battery Place, New York, NY 10280
646.494.5972 | info@JewishGen.org | www.jewishgen.org

MUSEUM OF JEWISH HERITAGE
A LIVING MEMORIAL TO THE HOLOCAUST

Memorial Book of the Community of Siedlce (Siedlce, Poland)
Translation of *Sefer yizkor le-kehilat Shedlets*

Copyright © 2022 by JewishGen, INC All rights reserved.
First Printing: March 2022, Adar II 5782

Editor of Original Yizkor Book: A.Wolf Yassni (Jasny)
Project Coordinator: David Aron Mink
Layout and Name Indexing: Jonathan Wind
Reproduction of Photographs: Sondra Ettlinger
Cover Design: Rachel Kolokoff Hopper

Printed in the United States of America by Lightning Source, Inc.

Library of Congress Control Number (LCCN): 2022931517

ISBN: 978-1-954176-33-1 (hard cover: 484 pages, alk. paper)

About JewishGen.org

JewishGen, an affiliate of the Museum of Jewish Heritage - A Living Memorial to the Holocaust, serves as the global home for Jewish genealogy.

Featuring unparalleled access to 30+ million records, it offers unique search tools, along with opportunities for researchers to connect with others who share similar interests. Award winning resources such as the Family Finder, Discussion Groups, and ViewMate, are relied upon by thousands each day.

In addition, JewishGen's extensive informational, educational and historical offerings, such as the Jewish Communities Database, Yizkor Book translations, InfoFiles, Family Tree of the Jewish People, and KehilaLinks, provide critical insights, first-hand accounts, and context about Jewish communal and familial life throughout the world.

Offered as a free resource, JewishGen.org has facilitated thousands of family connections and success stories, and is currently engaged in an intensive expansion effort that will bring many more records, tools, and resources to its collections.

Please visit https://www.jewishgen.org/ to learn more.

Executive Director: Avraham Groll

About the JewishGen Yizkor Book Project

Yizkor Books (Memorial Books) were traditionally written to memorialize the names of departed family and martyrs during holiday services in the synagogue (a practice that still exists in many synagogues today).

Over the centuries, as a result of countless persecutions and horrific atrocities committed against the Jews, Yizkor Books (Sefer Zikaron in Hebrew) were expanded to include more historical information, such as biographical sketches of famous personalities and descriptions of daily town life.

Following the Holocaust, the idea of remembrance and learning took on an urgent and crucial importance. Survivors of the Holocaust sought out other surviving residents of their former towns to memorialize and document the names and way of life of those who were ruthlessly murdered by the Nazis. These remembrances were documented in Yizkor Books, hundreds of which were published in the first decades after the Holocaust.

Most of these books were published privately, or through landsmanshaftn (social organizations comprised of members originating from the same European town or region) that still existed, and were often distributed free of charge. Sadly, the languages used to document these crucial histories and links to our past, Yiddish and Hebrew, are no longer commonly understood by a significant percentage of Jews today. As a result, JewishGen has undertaken the sacred responsibility of translating these books into English so that the culture and way of life of these communities will be preserved and transmitted to future generations.

In 1986, a group of farsighted JewishGenners started a project to pool their efforts together in groups based upon their ancestors from each town and donate money to get the Yizkor books of their ancestral towns translated into English. As the translated material became available, it was made accessible for free at www.JewishGen.org/Yizkor. Hardcover copies can be purchased by visiting https://www.jewishgen.org/Yizkor/ybip.html (see below).

It is our hope that the translation of these books into English (and other languages) will assist the countless Jewish family researchers who are so desperately seeking to forge a connection with their heritage.

Director of JewishGen Yizkor Book Project: Lance Ackerfeld

About the JewishGen Press

JewishGen Press (formerly the Yizkor Books-in-Print Project) is the publishing division of JewishGen.org, and provides a venue for the publication of non-fiction books pertaining to Jewish genealogy, history, culture, and heritage.

In addition to the Yizkor Book category, publications in the Other Non-Fiction category include Shoah memoirs and research, genealogical research, collections of genealogical and historical materials, biographies, diaries and letters, studies of Jewish experience and cultural life in the past, academic theses, and other books of interest to the Jewish community.

Please visit https://www.jewishgen.org/Yizkor/ybip.html to learn more.

Director of JewishGen Press: Joel Alpert
Managing Editor - Jessica Feinstein
Publications Manager - Susan Rosin

Notes to the Reader

The images in the original book were reproduced from photographs from the time of the first edition. These reproductions were already of poor quality, being pre-war and at least 30 or more years old. As a result the images in the book are not very good and the best achievable.

A reader can view the original scans of the book on the websites listed below.

The original book can be seen online at the Yiddish Book Center website:

https://www.yiddishbookcenter.org/collections/yizkor-books/yzk-nybc313988/jasny-a-wolf-sefer-yizkor-li-kehilat-shedlits-li-shenat-arba-esreh-le-hurbanah

or at the New York Public Library Digital Collections website:

https://digitalcollections.nypl.org/items/b3f90050-9a24-0134-6d42-00505686a51c

To obtain a list of Shoah victims from Siedlce (Siedlce, Poland) the reader should access the Yad Vashem web site listed below; one can also search for specific family names using family name option. These lists are continually updated by Yad Vashem, so it is worthwhile to periodically search these lists.

There is more valuable information (including the Pages of Testimony, etc.) available on this website: https://yvng.yadvashem.org/

A list of all books available from JewishGen Press along with prices is available at: https://www.jewishgen.org/Yizkor/ybip.html

Acknowledgements

The translation of Sefer Yiskor L'Kehillat Shedletz from Yiddish to English has taken over four years. A few chapters were translated before I took over the project, but the bulk of this 813-page book was waiting to be done. I owe an incredible amount of gratitude to Ted Steinberg who did the translation as a mitzvah for the Jewish community, not for material returns. Now the story of the Jews of Siedlce from mid-17th Century to its destruction in WWII, is available to the English-speaking world. The Hebrew chapters were translated to English by Mira Eckhaus, who also formatted the obituary. Special recognition goes to Helen Yomtov Herman who told us that we skipped over the chapter that her mother had written. Research revealed that the Table of Contents had erroneously omitted the chapter "The Destruction of Siedlce" page 648. Thanks to Helen, we translated the chapter and corrected the Table of Contents.

Thanks also to Lance Ackerfeld, director of the Yiskor Book Project for JewishGen, who was there to always point us toward the next step.

And most of all, thanks to JewishGen which has taken on this immense project of facilitating the translation of over 1000 books of the memory of European Jewish communities written by the survivors and witnesses. Through JewishGen's efforts, we have these eye-witness accounts of the Shoah for the world to see.

David Aron Mink

Philadelphia

February 2022

Credits and Captions for Book Cover

Front Cover Photographs:

Kaddish Goldstein, who made an Aliya to Eretz Israel at the turn of the 20th century, page 159 [308]
Victims of the pogrom, page 58 [114]

Front Cover Background Photograph: *Coneflowers* by Rachel Kolokoff Hopper

Front and Back Cover Color and Texture by Rachel Kolokoff Hopper

Back Cover Photographs from Top Left:
The first Zionist group: Row above from the left: Moses Greenfarb, Simcha Rubinstein, Niadoshviadosh, Kahana, Tuvklapper. Second row from the left: Niadoshviadosh, Genya, Moshe Temkin, Himelfarb, Rossenwasser, the photographer Rozovski, Mrs. Ladau, Mrs. Weidenzweig, Berl Mintz, page 180 [345]

Berl Kahane, page 25 [43]

Avrahamele Rosenberg, page 294 [556]

A "Mizrachi" children's home in the name of Rabbi Reines, page 196 [364]

Avraham Wasserzug, page 136 [269]

The teacher Rabbi Israel Kuzmir, page 153 [299]

GeoPolitical Information

Siedlce, Poland is located at 52°10' N 22°18' E and 55 miles E of Warszawa

	Town	District	Province	Country
Before WWI (c. 1900):	Siedlce	Siedlce	Siedlce	Russian Empire
Between the wars (c. 1930):	Siedlce	Siedlce	Lublin	Poland
After WWII (c. 1950):	Siedlce			Poland
Today (c. 2000):	Siedlce			Poland

Alternate Names for the Town:

Siedlce [Pol], Shedlitz [Yid], Sedlets [Rus], Shedlits, Shedlets, Sedl'tse, Sedlce

Nearby Jewish Communities:

Zbuczyn 8 miles SE
Mordy 10 miles ENE
Mokobody 11 miles NW
Sokołów Podlaski 16 miles N
Łuków 18 miles SSE
Łosice 18 miles ENE
Seroczyn 19 miles SW
Węgrów 20 miles NW
Liw 21 miles NW
Stoczek Łukowski 21 miles SW
Kałuszyn 21 miles W
Drohiczyn 22 miles NE
Miedzna 22 miles NNW
Stok 24 miles SSE
Międzyrzec Podlaski 24 miles ESE
Sarnaki 27 miles ENE
Dobre 29 miles WNW
Sterdyń 29 miles N
Siennica 29 miles W
Żelechów 30 miles SW
Parysów 30 miles WSW
Radzyń Podlaski 30 miles SSE
Adamów 30 miles S

Jewish Population: 11,440 (in 1897), 14,793 (in 1931)

Map of Poland with **Siedlce** indicated

TABLE OF CONTENTS

Folk Stories of Siedlce

Destruction of Siedlce

Inhabitants of Siedlce in the entire world

Obituaries

Dedication

I dedicate this translation to all the Martyrs of Siedlce and also to my mother, Sylvia Pseny Mink. I never knew of her extended family until after she died. Going through documents, postcards, and photos I learned about her life in Siedlce and about her extended family who was murdered. The trauma about that part of her life was too painful for her to share with her family. It is the responsibility of we who are the living descendants of Siedlce to ensure that their stories will continue to be told, that the memories of those whom we have lost, will stay alive.

David Mink
Philadelphia
February 2022

Memorial Book of the Community of Siedlce
(Siedlce, Poland)

54°06' / 22°56'

Translation of
Sefer yizkor le-kehilat Shedlets

Editor: A. Wolf Yassni (Jasny)

Published in Buenos Aires 1956

Acknowledgments

Project Coordinator:

David Aron Mink

Principal Yiddish Translator:

Theodore Steinberg

Our sincere appreciation to Yad Vashem for the submission of the necrology for placement on the JewishGen web site.

This is a translation of: *Sefer yizkor le-kehilat Shedlets*
(Memorial book of the community of Siedlce),
Editor: A.Wolf Yassni (Jasny), Buenos Aires 1956 (H, Y 813 pages).

Please contribute to our translation fund to see the translation of this book completed.

JewishGen's Translation Fund Donation Form provides a secure way to make donations,
either on-line or by mail, to help continue this project. Donations to JewishGen are tax-deductible for U.S. citizens.

The Great City Shul

Monument for fallen Russian soldiers on the spot of the City Shul shown above

[Page X]

The Holy Ark of the Siedlce Shul

[Page XI]

A Word from those Responsible
for the Siedlce Yizkor Book in Argentina

Translated by Theodore Steinberg

At the end of the bloody Second World War, after the sad reality of the tragic killing of six million Jews had hit us, although we could not believe, or did not want to believe, that in the midst of a civilized world such a misfortune was possible; and when, among the ruins, there appeared small remnants of our unburned brothers and sisters, and, among them, some from our hometown of Siedlce–then the people from Siedlce in Israel, as also in Buenos Aires, understood that their first responsibility was to confront with their fraternal hep the sacrifices of a murderous world and to help, as was required, in different lands and to comfort the victims.

The people of Siedlce in Argentina also understood that along with those who remained alive, the sacred memory of our destroyed holy community of Siedlce should be eternized for all generations and receive redress, the Torah followers and the people of deeds, the simple people, of every type and form who characterized our city, as well as many other cities and towns in Poland; that there should be a symbolic monument that wind engrave in memory for generations not only their tragic destruction but also their beautiful Jewish lives.

Thus arose the thought of issuing this Yizkor Book, which we are bringing out for all Siedlcers throughout the world.

The labor of bringing out the Yizkor Book was not so easy; we dealt with formidable technical and financial difficulties, and at the realization of the plan, we approached Siedlcers in different countries. Finally, our brethren in Israel assumed the difficulty duty of assembling and editing the material for the Yizkor Book. Congratulations!

[Page XII]

The financial burden, as also the publication of the book and everything connected to it, was assumed by the Siedlcers in Argentina; this required three years of strenuous labor, which we did with the intention of making it excellent.

We offer special thanks to all the Siedlcers in Argentina who wholeheartedly supported us and made possible the publication of the Siedlce Yizkor Book, and we will have satisfaction, when all Siedlcers throughout the world will understand and recognize that we felt a sacred historical mission and a responsibility toward our martyrs.

Finally we want to extend our congratulations to our proofreaders, the brothers Menashe and Moshe Constantinowski, for their professional and accurate work. We consider them, together with the editor in Israel, A. V. Yasni, as partners in this gigantic sacred work. May blessings come to them!

[Page XIII]

Introduction

by the Editors

Translated by Theodore Steinberg

With great sorrow we take the step of publishing the book "Yizkor Lik'hilas Siedlce." This kehilla, this community, where we were raised and grew up, exists no longer. A horrible, vicious hand destroyed it.–With the "Sefer Yizkor" we will introduce into history the life of the holy Siedlce community and its tragic end.

For hundreds of years on the soil of Podlask in the state of Poland there was a Jewish settlement. It grew. It developed and created a unique Jewish life with synagogues, beis–medreshes, religious institutions, Talmud Torahs, and yeshivas–suitable for an observant way of life. Every new spiritual direction in Jewish life found an outlet there. Chasidic devotion and raptures entered the heart of the simple Siedlce Jew and imbued him with deep faith in the Creator of the world. A network of Chasidic prayer houses bound Siedlce to the rabbinic courts of different cities in Poland.

The Jewish national revival that stormed through the Diaspora–found in Siedlce a ground prepared with Jewish feelings and thoughts. The first stirrings of Zionist thought struck deep roots there. In this settlement grew up R. Yehuda Ha–Chasid, the fantastic dreamer and mystic, who saw in his fantastic world the nearing of the end–redemption–and went to Eretz Yisroel in anticipation of the messiah. The Jew. Siedlce experienced the development from R. Yehuda Ha–Chasid's messianic redemptive thought to the modern Love of Zion movement, from the agricultural settlements to Herzl's political Zionism. To all of these stages of renewal of Jewish national thought, Jewish Siedlce made its rich contribution and helped propel Zionism to its goal as a great mass movement.

[Page XIV]

We all have in our memories the images of the great manifestations of the revival and building of our old–new homeland–Eretz Yisroel: the Lag B'Omer celebrations and torchlight parades, the Keren Kayemes bazaars in which our young people showed their enthusiasm and took with them most of the population of Siedlce, the mass support for each new aliyah, and the mass sorrow and protest at the time of the bloody events in Eretz Yisroel in 1920 21, 22, 29, and 36.

Impulsive was the Jewish community and cultural life in Siedlce out which grew the Zionist movement with all its variations. The "Mercaz" of the General Zionist Organization, like the trunk of a tree, developed branches of various Zionist groups, from the very religious to the socialist–Zionists. Among the whole variety of pioneer youth organizations, training farms, and pioneer kibbutzim, a special branch from the trunk was the Zionist cultural activities: Hebrew schools, evening classes, lectures, discussions, libraries, and the great part in the library taken by "Ha–Zamir" and "Jewish Art."

Parallel to the Zionist movement was the Jewish socialist workers movement–the "Bund," which bound up the Jewish national revival with life in the Diaspora, and the "Poalei–Tzion" [Zionist Labor], which made a bridge between workers and Zionists. Both parties brought revolutionary spirit into the life of Siedlce's Jewish masses, built economic and professional organizations and led the political battle of the Jewish laborers. In that spirit of the people, the socialist parties created the folk schools, homes for children with a Yiddish basis, organized courses and lectures, and enriched the spiritual life of Siedlce's Jews.

This relatively small Jewish settlement produced writers, poets, journalists, who in their creations mirrored the Jewish life of Siedlce. When Jewish life went haywire, Siedlce created its own Yiddish press, which roused, warned, and motivated community activities, which grew and branched out.

[Page XV]

Jewish Siedlce had its philanthropic institutions and pillars of social help, like: "Ezras Y'somim," [orphans' home] "Moshav Z'keynim" [old people's home], "Bikkur Kholim" [for visiting the sick], "Linas Ha–tzedek," "Beis Lekhem," "Taz," "B'ri–us" [various helpful agencies], a Jewish hospital, and others.

The artisans and the merchants, both large and small, formed credit unions, charity foundations, and fought for economic rights for Jews. A significant part in Siedlce's Jewish life was played by the religious community organization, which upheld and maintained strict religious standards, the rabbis, and so on.

The Jewish lives of the nearly 20,000 Jews in the settlement were multicolored and multifaceted. The greatest majority lived through honest labor, with their firm ethics and morals–Jewish morals. But then, from time to time, bitter, evil actors brought ruin and destruction into this Jewish life. In pain and sorrow we recall: the Czarist pogrom against Jews in Siedlce that brought ruin on Jewish existence and took three score Jewish lives; the excesses at the time of the Polish–Bolshevik war; the various later trials of alleged traitors, which incensed the Polish government; the antisemitic provocations that were made with the intention of destroying Jewish economic life.– The culmination of all of these attempts to uproot the Jewish people came the great destruction that the German hordes brought upon the Jewish population of Poland.

The Siedlce Jewish settlement was razed. Crazily were our dear fellow citizens killed–dying as martyrs, remaining true to their Yiddishkeit.

The Jewish community life of almost four hundred years, their spiritual ascent, their battle for life, their outstanding labor and aspirations for more beautiful and better lives–all of these we will eternize in this Yizkor Book. Let this Yizkor Book be a monument on the unmarked graves of our martyrs. Let this Yizkor Book provide material for the historian who will compose the coming great history of the thousand–year Jewish residence in the state of Poland.

* *

[Page XVI]

The publication of "Sefer Yizkor Lik'hilas Siedlce" that tells the four–hundred–year story of this community was made possible thanks to the great efforts of our friend Yitzchak Kaspi, who for years studied there development of Jewish life in Siedlce and gathered a mass of documentary material about the settlement. His work formed the foundation of this book. A large contribution presented the book with the memoirs of the martyr Yitzchak Nachum Weintraub and the work of the tragically deceased B. Mintz about the Jewish credit bureau in Siedlce. The material from Yitzchak Nachum Weintraub and B. Mintz were preserved by David ben Yosef (Pasowski) and transferred to the Yizkor Book.

The section dealing with the tragic time of the ghetto was written by survivors who themselves had suffered terrible tortures. We present them exactly as they were written. In them can be found omissions and repetitions that we leave for the discretion of the future historian, who will investigate the material.

We feel obliged to express our thanks to Professor A. Wolf Yasni, who spared no labor in editing the various manuscripts and helping with his wise advice.

A special thanks and congratulations to our friends and fellow townsfolk in Argentina who assumed the burden and worries of putting out this book and to all who took part in this great labor. The Siedlce committee in Israel, especially our friends B. Vyman, Yisrael Mendelssohn, Moshe Steinberg, and A. Bar–Chaim (Berenhaltz).

[Page 3]

A History of the Jews in Siedlce
The Origins of Jews in Siedlce

by Yitzkhak Kaspi

Translated by Theodore Steinberg

Sources and Literature

Scant are the sources for the history of the Jews in Siedlce. In the archives of the town are few documents about the almost four hundred years of Jewish life in Siedlce. Although Jewish life in this capital city of Podolia was rich in historical events, until the Second World War, no Jewish historian undertook to study the life of the Jews of Siedlce. Not a single book gives any idea about how a Jewish settlement developed in this area.

Understandably, the Poles had a different attitude toward studying the history of their city. First of all, there is a group of Polish historians who deal with the history of all of Poland, including, naturally, Siedlce. So, for example, Belinski and Lipinski treat the city in their co–written work "The History of Poland." In "The Slavic Geographical Kingdom of Poland," there is interesting information about the city. Siedlce is also mentioned in a group of encyclopedias, such as "Powszechna," "Podreczna," "Nelson," and "Britannica," from which I have taken information for the present work. All of this information is related to the earlier history of Siedlce.

[Page 4]

In the thirties of the twentieth century a special journal appeared in Warsaw dedicated to the study of the history of Podlesie. Siedlce, as the capital of the area, there received appropriate treatment. But the Jewish settlement in the city was intentionally overlooked. Polish historians, as we see, in the following years written widely about Siedlce. There is, indeed, a long bibliography of historical works about the city.

The first work about Siedlce was a brochure in Russian by the editor of "Gubernskiya Vyedomosti" [Regional Government News], in which he showed a tendency to be rather colorful. He says little about the Jews[1].

A. Khozonovkski, in a number of issues of the "Podolia Gazette," published sections of this brochure as if it were part of a monograph from Shtrumpf, which confiscated by the press authorities in Warsaw, who said it was because Subotkin, the current governor, was angry because he had not been shown the brochure. Shtrumpf was actually the son of the converted book dealer in Siedlce Shtrumpf[2].

In 1912 a second book about Siedlce appeared in Russian, "Historical Statistical Survey." The authors were S. D. Koshinski and H.T. Tilinski. This book provided much statistical information about Siedlce that appears in our work.

Tadeusz Monyevvski published, under the name "Siedlce," a guidebook to the city, which appeared in 1929 through the Podolia Museum, which was named after M. Aslanovitsch. We have used the general information in "Siedlce" in the first chapters of our monograph.

We have also used the material from the following historical publications: "Ksiega Pamiatkowa Siedlcam 1844–1905," written from a definitely Polish–Christian perspective; "Kalendarz diecezji podlaskie czyli Siedleckiej 1929" ("Calendar of the Podlaskie Diocese, for Siedlce, 1929), which contains chapters on Christian life; V. Lapinski's work, "Wolka Wyklady religii w dzienniku polskim w gimnazjoch Siedleckim I Bielskim" ("Lectures on religion in the Polish Daily News on secondary education in Siedlce and Bielski").

[Page 5]

In all of these works there is no mention at all of Jews. First in the purely statistical publications about Poland do we find information about Jews, which we have used. Such information is in "Rocznik statystyczny kvolestina polskiego" ("Statistical yearbook of the Polish Kingdom") of Wladislaw Granski, which appeared before the First World War, from Gebetner and Wolf Publishing, and in the publications of the Polish Office of Statistics, which was published in independent Poland.

Also Antoni Winter, in his work, "Patshantki Shedlitz" (Siedlce, 1939), mentions Jews. This same little book handles in an interesting and condensed form older Siedlce up to the end of the eighteenth century. Winter does not mention in his work that Chmielnitzki destroyed the town.

About Jews, the writer states, in Koczinski and Tilinski's names, that the Countess Oginska sold the Jews of Siedlce twenty–eight stores that she had built in the old city hall[3], which had real significance for the development of Jewish life in Siedlce.

A significant contributor to the history of Siedlce was made by the local Polish press: "Tygodnik Podloski," ("Polish Weekly") published 1905–06; "Szitshe Padlyasha"–1924–25; "Platzyavka"–1926–29, as well as the aforementioned journal Podlyasha published in Warsaw in 1927–28. All of these newspapers at different times published valuable articles and notes about the history of Siedlce. We have used these articles.

These materials involve the communal development of non–Jewish Siedlce on whose canvas was superimposed the Jewish life of the city.

Jewish Siedlce belonged, unfortunately, among the not overly popular towns in Poland. It is not even mentioned in the rich Responsa literature. Also old record books were not preserved. Possibly they were destroyed in some of the conflagrations with which Siedlce was blessed. There are four exceptions, record books that existed until the final destruction of Siedlce's Jews, namely: the record book of "Bikkur Kholim Hakhadashah," of the "Mishneh Fellowship," of the "Shas]Talmud] Fellowship," and the record book of the "Pirchei Shoshanim" [Lily Flowers].

[Page 6]

The first of these had already at the time at the time of the outbreak of the Second World War covered ninety–six years. From this record book we have quoted the petitions (translated into Yiddish) that provide a picture of Jewish community life from that time. When we note the sources of the history of Jewish Siedlce, we remember with awe the chronicler of the Jewish community, the holy R. Yitzchak Nachum Veintroib, who lived in Siedlce for over sixty years, and his investigations into the history of Jewish Siedlce extend back a further hundred years.

Veintroib would every day about the actual events in Jewish life in Siedlce. He was active in the life of the community. He knew it well, which enriched his huge archive, which he looked after until the Nazi dominion. At the beginning of the Second World War, the archive was buried, together with his relatives, under the ruins of his house. R. Y.N. Veintroib, already an older man of eighty years, continued his writing in the ghetto, until the critical day when, together with the remnant of the Siedlce ghetto, he was, on Chanukah of 1943, taken away to the death camp of Treblinka and was there tortured. Veintroib had published in the "Siedlce Wochenblatt" a small part of his archive. Thus a small part of his valuable work about Jewish life in Siedlce was preserved.

His recollections of the pogrom he published in the "Siedlce Wochenblatt" in 1923. In 1939 he published new sections about that bloodbath. Veintroib is a trustworthy source for the history of that tragic chapter, because he himself survived the pogrom. As a member of the community council, he served as a protector for the Jewish victims of the pogrom. He therefore could say in his recollections, "I am the man who has known afflictions under the rod of His wrath" (Lamentation 3:1). Using his chronicles of Siedlce's rabbis, rebbes, and cantors, we have reconstructed the appearance of Jewish Siedlce in the nineteenth century.

Because of the scarcity of source material for the Jewish history of Siedlce, we were forced to use a variety of chronicles that were that were published in their time in the Siedlce Jewish press.

[Page 7]

For the history of the workers' movement in Siedlce, we used the work of Yehoshua Goldberg that he published in the "Siedlce Wochenblatt" under the title "Spring in Siedlce." Goldberg wrote his work on the basis of the testimony of the participants in the workers' movement at that time. The testimony belonged to these people: A. Veinapple, Kh. Goldenberg, and M. Yedvob.

We should also recall the editor of the "Siedlce Wochenblatt," Asher Liverant, who deserves thanks for having put out a book about Siedlce that provides a historical reflection of Jewish life in the city in the past. In his editorial office, in a large closet, along with the back files of the newspaper he kept a compilation of materials and documents of historical Jewish life in Siedlce. Liverant hoped that a day would come when he could rework those materials and publish a book. His untimely death negated his plans. His collected materials disappeared, along with the Jewish life of Siedlce.

Editor Liverant also worked to assure that the "Siedlce Wochenblatt" would give space to historical articles. He urged people to record their memories. He never let go of an article or an episode that had relevance to Siedlce's past–even if it was not the Jewish past. Later on, in 1910, he gathered together the materials which had interested Dr. M Shteyn, who later converted. These materials Liverant sent to the editor of the "Yevreskiya Starina" in Petersburg. On the basis of this material, Sh. Goldshteyn published in his fourth volume his interesting work about Siedlce, which we have used for our monograph. From that work we have cited the privileges that the Countess Oginska gave to Siedlce's Jews. The original documents stating the privileges were destroyed together with the Jewish community, and the only written evidence of the documents is found in Goldshteyn's work.

The work that is being published was put together with hard work, with extraordinary exertions.

[Page 8]

It is necessary to thank the national and university library on Har HaTzofim in Jerusalem. Only in such a huge treasure of books could one fine what was needed to tell the history of Jewish life in Siedlce. Between times, I have published my work "Megillas Paros Shedlitz B'Shnas 1906," along with other smaller works. I have been encouraged to do further work on the history of the Jews in Siedlce.

May this modest work furnish material for the great historical work on exterminated Polish Jewry, which needs yet to be written.

Old Siedlce

In order to get an idea about the history of the Jews in Siedlce, it is first necessary to understand the historical development of the city–how it was founded, how it grew, and how it became one of the largest provincial cities in the Polish state.

Old Siedlce was founded as a village. Testimony tells us that the oldest street or quarter on the east side of the city was officially connected to Siedlce on October 31, 1931. The quarter was called Stara–wioska (Old Village). From there they began to build the town, which was given the name of Siedlce. It appears that until the first half of the sixteenth century, Siedlce was divided in two parts: New– and Old–Siedlce. In the seventies of that century, New–Siedlce began to attain the status of a city and Old–Siedlce in time lost the second half of its name, Siedlce, and took on the status of a village. Hence the name Stary–wioska[4].

The Origin of the Name

The origin of the name Siedlce (or Shedlitz, in Yiddish) is, according to Brinker's Etymological Dictionary from the Polish language (pp. 491–492), a derivation from the Polish root "siodlo," which means a settlement.

[Page 9]

There is also a legend that the name was given at the time of a visit to Poland by the Italian queen Vana in 1531. [It is not clear what he is referring to. There was no Italian queen named Vana. The queen of Italy in 1531 was Isabella of Portugal.] Travelling through the area, she rested at the spot where the city of Siedlce now stands and was struck by the beauty of the surroundings, so that the queen exclaimed, "That is a great siedliska [Polish for habitat]][5]. It is difficult to say what pleased the queen, because the whole area around Siedlce is just clayey and wet. This legend has no historical foundation, because the fact is that in documents that come from the time before the queen's visit we already encounter the name of the town as Siedlecz, Siedlce, or Siedlcza. The name Siedlce also belonged to the wealthy man to whom the town belonged–Daniel Siedletzky. He was the owner of the village since 1511[6]. The vacillation concerning whether to call the place a town or a village, as in the case of Siedlce, also marks the history of other places.

Hypotheses About the Rise of the City

Also, the date when Siedlce was founded has not been established. Because of the frequent conflagrations that beset the city, archives and documents that might have held confirmation about the founding were destroyed. Dr. St. Wansawski, who researched the history of Siedlce, stated an opinion that has little historical grounding, but it cannot be discounted. He holds that Siedlce was founded at the end of the thirteenth century by inhabitants of three villages—Siedleyen, Sokolow, and Lukow–who were found in the Jendvzejewo area.

Due to certain circumstances, the inhabitants of those villages abandoned them and came to the vicinity of Siedlce and there established outposts with the name of their home towns.

The emigration of the Jendvzejewo residents must have come as a result of the wars that King Boleslaw the Bashful led against the Yotvingian tribes who came from the Lithuanian steppes and led plundering raids against Poland from east of the Niemen[7].

[Page 10]

Wansawski's theory, however, conflicts with the historical facts, because Lukow in the Jendvzejewo area is first mentioned only in the sixteenth century and there are references to the Lukow in the neighborhood of Siedlce already from 1244[8]. Wansawski's hypothesis that Siedlce must have been founded in the thirteenth century, although it is not factually grounded, can be combined with the theory of a second Siedlce scholar, Grichowski, who also says that Siedlce must have been founded in the thirteenth century. Grichowski bases his opinion on Jablonowski's work on Podlaskie, which in the thirteenth century definitely began to colonize the left bank of the Bug and Narew Rivers. But Grichowski maintains that the Podlaskie colonization took place mainly through Masurians from the region around Czechonow, Makow, Ostrow, and Livow. Moreover it is possible that the founders of Siedlce were Masurians. But it could also have been emigrants from Little Poland or Greater Poland. This hypothesis Grichowski bases on a list of places that bear the name "Sheldlitz" or "Siedlce." Mostly one finds these names in the former Krakow and Sandomir voyevodeships. Fewer of the names come from Greater Poland and Mazower regions[9]. But Grichowski's theory is no more than a hypothesis based on factual historical material. Let us therefore deal with the factual documents about the origins of Siedlce as a city.

The First Documentary Information About Siedlce

The first information about Siedlce as a city comes from the first half of the fifteenth century and bears the date of 1448. This is an authorization from the Krakow bishop Zbigniew Aleshnitzki giving the priest from the Lukow parish, to which Siedllce then belonged, permission to receive tithes from the village of "Siedlesz"[10]. It seems that Siedlce was then so small that it did not even constitute a parish.

Further information comes from the sixteenth century, from 1503, 1504, 1509, 1510, 1511, 1512, and 1524. From these notices we learn the owner of the village of Siedlce was, as we have already said Daniel Siedletzki[11], who was having a boundary dispute with a certain Mikali Zalivski.

[Page 11]

In 1531, Siedlce, along with eight other villages, belonged to the Prussian parish. Only in 1532 did it become a parish unto itself. This was not because of the growth of Siedlce, but thanks to the religiosity and influence of the then owner of Siedlcel, Stanislaw Siedletzki, who wrote a letter to the Krakow bishop Piotr Tomitzki, asking that he take into account the difficulties of communication and the frequent floods of the "Rudnik," a river that later became known as the "Helenka." After the bishop received a recommendation from a special commission that he had appointed to evaluate Siedletzki's argument, he agreed to recognize the village of Siedlce as an autonomous parish[12].

Soon St. Siedletzki decided to build a church by the name of St. Stanislaw. The place where the church stood remains unknown, because it was completely destroyed in a fire. There are indications that it was built on **Stara–wiesh**, where in 1848 the city hospital was built. Evidence is: bones and fragments of gravestones which are occasionally unearthed there. (At the beginning of the "New Times" in Poland, graveyards were found near churches.) But there is a version that deserves notice that says that the old church of 1532 was destroyed and a new one was built and a new wooden one was built on Starawiesh, there were later stood the shrine of the Countess Aginska. In the cemetery records is written that the bones of the Alendzki family–the later owners of Siedlce–were later transferred from the old to the new church. Note that the current church by the name of St. Stanislaw, which was built in 1740, is the third one with the same name. The first was built when Siedlce was a parish[13].

The transformation of Siedlce into a church parish had a historical outcome. Thanks to that event, the town grew and expanded.

[Page 12]

Some years later, in 1557–as it is related–King Sigismund Augustus visited the village and elevated it to the status of a city[14]. By that time Siedlce already figured in the official lists of the Polish kingdom. Thanks to Alendzki, Siedlce received rights of citizenship and a city board of directors.

Accurate information about the size of Siedlce at that time we receive from a "Register of Taxes in 1552." Siedlce belonged to Stanlislaw Siedletzki and was granted forty–nine economic accommodations for its fifty houses. If we estimate there were six inhabitants per house, then Siedlce had three hundred inhabitants.

In another register, "The Collection of Taxes from Siedlce and its villages in 1580," it appears that twenty to thirty years after Siedlce became a city, they inhabitants of Siedlce who paid taxes were enumerated: the mayor, twelve bakers, one sword maker, four street merchants, seven beggars, three well diggers, four furriers, ten shoemakers, one locksmith, two smiths, and two weavers. The district's occupied area, according to this source, comprised 25 wloka [an Old Polish measurement that equaled approximately 44 acres]. The oldest part of the village of Starawiesh paid taxes, according to this register, on twelve wloka; outside that area lived–two street merchants and one beggar[15]. From this we can see that at the end of the sixteenth century, Siedlce and Starawiesh existed separately as a city and as a village. Siedlce was one of the youngest and smallest cities in Poland at that time. Warsaw, which in 1596 became the site of the palatial residence, had ten thousand inhabitants.

On the Trail of Jewish Life

The first information about Jewish life in Siedlce comes from the fifties of the seventeenth century.

Maneusz Maniewski, in his book about Siedlce, provides a short and dry piece of information, without giving a source: "In 1650, Siedlce was destroyed by the Tatars, during the revolt of Bogdan Chmielnitzki"[16]. Comparing this date to those of the well–known persecutions of the time, we can see that Maniewski's dates are exact.

[Page 13]

In the Jewish sources,, particularly in the book "Yeven Metzulah" ("The Abyss of Despair") of R. Nathan (Nata) Hanover, the great chronicle of the catastrophe of his time, neither Siedlce nor Starawiesh is mentioned as having suffered from Chmielnitzki's attacks, although in "Yeven Metzulah" there is not a single mention of Lublin and the settlements in the Lublin voivodeship. Only in one chapter, "Persecutions of the Scoundrel"[17] does Hanover speak about three small towns, without mentioning their names, that were destroyed by the Hetman. But a second chronicler of the decrees, R. Shmuel Feivush bar Nosan Feitil of Vienna in his book "Teet Hayeven" ("Clay of the Abyss")[18], relates about the attacks on the three communities that are spoken about in "Yeven Metzulah" that Chmielnitzki attacked "Weglub," "Starawiesh," "Magrub," and "Patlish." In the first city, according to "Teet Hayeven", there were forty heads of households. In the second there were fifty, and in the third and fourth there were a hundred each. The Jews of these communities must have fled to Nachal to find protection.

Contemplating these places, we can identify them as: Weglub–Vengrov; Starawesh–Starawiesh, a village near Siedlce or Siedlce itself; Magrub–seems to be a shtetl that must have been called Makarov; Patlish–is surely Podlashe, the area where the three villages are located. However, in another spot in "Teet Hayeven" he speaks about a settlement called "Podlasze."

Our assumption about the cities is strengthened because the historian, Dr. Yakov Shatzki, in his critical–historical footnotes to the Yiddish translation of Hanover's book[19] identifies in the same way that we do the aforementioned communities that are mentioned in "Teet Yavan" in connection with the slaughter at Nachal–as with our assumption. But Shatzki does not stress that **Starawiesh** is the same as Siedlce, which is easy to understand. What is not easy to understand is the distance from our Starawiesh to Nachol, which is quite far, in the vicinity of Podolia. How could the Jews have fled with communication conditions as they were then?

[Page 14]

All we can say is that "Teet Hayeven" is full of exaggerations and ambiguities.

Comparing this information with the chronicles of "Teet Hayeven" shows us that Maniewski's information about Chmielnitzki's attack on Siedlce is confirmed. Maniewski formed his report from Church sources. There is also information that that Jews could be found in Siedlce a hundred years before the persecutions, that is, in 1557, and perhaps even earlier.

Our first definite information about Jews in Siedlce comes from the fifth decade of the sixteenth century. This information comes from the history of the Jewish cemetery in Siedlce, which was investigated by Dr. lM. Shteyn (who later converted to Catholicism). Dr. M. Shteyn in 1910 found a document from the end of the eighteenth century (1798), according to which the Countess Oginska gave the Jews land for a cemetery. Here is the document in Polish:

[The Polish document is presented.]

[Page 15]

And here is a Yiddish translation:

Alexandra, from the Countess Czartoryskich, Oginska, the great Hetman from the great Lithuanian countess.

Taking into account the suggestion and the strong appeals from the community and the entire Jewish township, my residents of Siedlce, I give through this decree an assurance to the community and the township of Siedlce that the place by the Jewish school where in the past there were graves–should remain free from buildings and habitation, with these conditions: first–that no Jews, under any pretext, should be buried there except in authorized graves; second: to prevent uglification of the city, this cemetery should be planted with linden trees; third: in order [at this point the document is damaged]…this place should be surrounded by an attractive and high fence put up by the community and the Siedlce township, and this should for now and always be the order. If the community and the Siedlce township should fail to meet these conditions, which are in the decree, then this decree of mine will be dissolved and invalid. As a token of this, I sign this decree with my own hand, with the usual seal.

Presented in Siedlce on the 22nd of March, 1798.

Alex. Oginska.

Dr. M. Shteyn, on the basis of this document, dealt with the history of the Siedlce cemetery in conjunction with the antiquity of the Jewish presence in Siedlce.

The oldest cemetery in Siedlce was near the one–time horse market, near the city school. When this cemetery came into existence is not known. From old times until the Second World War, a monument stood there with an illegible inscription. At least one can date the monument from the year 1630.

[Page 16]

In the later suburban cemetery, which was located near the Jewish hospital, near the city market on Ogrodova Street (later, Shenkevitsh Street) there remain several monuments that cover the period 1740–1822, although there can be no doubt that people were buried here before 1740.

The last cemetery, which was located near the road to Warsaw, was purchased by the Jewish township in 1826; the contract of sale was found in the administrative office of the Padlosh voivodeship. The leaders of the Jewish township who purchased the placer were: Yosef Zlotofirski (?), Dovid Grinberg, and Moyshe Nussboym. They paid 420 Polish gulden. The sellers were the Christian Matteus Skolimovski and his daughters. It is interesting that the Jews endorsed the notary's paper in the Polish language, and Skolimovski and his daughters signed with three crosses because they did not know how to write. The oldest inscription on a tombstone from this last cemetery comes from 1827, but in the archives of the Jewish community, among the documents relating to the purchase of a place for a cemetery, papers were found that established the existence of this cemetery before 1807. There can be no doubt that people were buried there before 1826.

On the basis of these cemetery documents, Dr. Shteyn came to this conclusion: the last cemetery existed since 1807. The earlier ran a century before that, that is, since 1707. The first served for a hundred fifty years, that is from 1557[21]. That was 111 years after the first information about Siedlce. Properly said–from its first establishment.

Unfortunately no materials, neither documents nor archives, remain that would have clarified the history of the Jews of that time. It could be that the number of Jews in the city was so small that they played no obvious role in the

[Page 17]

in community life of Polish Jews, but all that already in the second half ot he sixteenth century there was a Jewish settlement in Siedlce.

Siedlce in the Seventeenth and Eighteenth Centuries

In the course of the seventeenth century Siedlce suffered many fires, which destroyed not only the wooden houses–but also their contents and the town documents. It went so far that on the tenth of December in 1635, the Polish king Wladislaw IV, following the request of the Siedlce furrier, gave him a certificate of privilege. Actually it was a renewal of a previous privilege from King Sigmund III, which had been destroyed by one of those fires[22].

At the same time the city of Siedlce was given as a dowry through the owner of the town, Tomas Alendski, whose daughter, Johanna, had married the Volin voivode Count Michael Czartoryski[23].

In 1678, the town owner received from the central power a permit to repeal a road tax of one groschen for every horse and cow that was brought to the Siedlce market. The income was supposed to be used for fixing the roads.

Another fire, the largest in Siedlce's history to that time, completely destroyed the city in 1693. As in the earlier fires, all files and information were lost. Thus we do not know Siedlce was nor how many inhabitants it had[24].

At the same time Count Czartoryski married his daughter Alexandra to Oginski from the Lithuanian aristocracy, and as himself had received the town as a dowry from his father–in–law Alendski, so he gave it as a dowry to his only daughter, who was mentioned in an earlier chapter.

With Siedlce in the hands of Countess Oginska, an epoch began of prosperity and well–being for the city. This energetic and aristocratic woman undertook measures to attract inhabitants and colonists and also showed sympathy for the Jews.

[Page 18]

Her first actions were the building of several large buildings, thanks to which a variety of high–ranking guests who passed through the town could be put up. In these buildings she also set up a variety of administrative offices, and in later years there was also a welcoming kitchen where the needy could get food in bad times. In the period between the two world wars there were in the buildings: the post office and the women's gymnasium, named for Queen Jadwiga, where there was, it seems also in earlier times, a theater.

Among the important guests who then visited Siedlce, was King Stanislaw Augustus Poniatowski, who visited in 1783. In honor of the event an immense triumphal arch was built on the border between Siedlce and Starawesh (Old Siedlce). The arch had a main entrance and two smaller aisles, which were called "gloves." This was one of the most beautiful monuments in Poland, and it stood until 1942, when the Germans destroyed it. They found that the passageway of the arch was too small for the heavy mechanized artillery that they were bringing from Prussia to the Russian front. Thus the German vandals tore down the arch.

The town owners also planted a walking garden of twenty–three acres with many useful facilities, and near the garden they put the well–known palace, built in Renaissance style.

To the Countess Oginska is also attributed the building of the city hall, known as the "old city hall." Many people also called the building "Jozek" or "Lesser Jozek." This was an original three–story building in the old style with an octagonal tower, two thirds of which was made of brick, and higher up of wood. On the top of the tower was a life size figure of a man. He bore on his shoulders a huge globe made of copper. The statue was made to resemble the faithful valet who was called "wozek" or "Jozek," so that is what people called the tower.

[Page 19]

The "Jozek" building

In the years 1875–1887, the wooden part of the tower was freshly renovated. In the copper globe a document was found, written in Latin on parchment. It said that after the fire, the town was rebuilt in 1784, thanks to the special efforts of the Countess Oginska. To prevent fires that could be caused by lightning, Adam Kukel, the chief "engineer" of Countess Oginska, installed a lightning rod. The celebration of its completion came on September 4, 1784. The testimony of many witnesses is attested in the document by signatures. The chief poet of Countess Oginska, Franciszek Karpinski, composed a special poem for this momentous occasion.

But not five years after finding the document, on February 2, 1887, another fire broke out in Siedlce. The city hall was completely burned. Jozef Zenkowich rebuilt it and installed a new lightning protector. The costs were again borne by Countess Oginska[25].

[Page 20]

The Beginning of the Organized Jewish Community

In 1765, Siedlce numbered 631 Jews[26]. The rabbinic chair of the Siedlce community was occupied by the famous R. Meir, the author of the "Netiv Meir"–notes on the Talmud. He went to his eternal rest in the cemetery next to the Jewish school. As Dr. Yakov Shatzki[27] explains, in the eighties of the eighteenth century there were rabbis from Siedlce in Warsaw. Jews earned their living in business and lease–holding, and things went well for them. As far as we can guess, there were a few very wealthy people in the town. One of them was R. Chaim Greenberg, who, in 1790, left a will in Hebrew, to divide up his inheritance. The will can be found in the Siedlce mortgage bureau[28].

In the Podlasie museum, which was located in Siedlce, there is a typical document in which we read that on the first of January in 1797, Countess Oginska sold to a certain Itzkavitch, for 2,700 Polish guilder, a building holding several stores, that she had had built. Information that we have from other sources tells us that the same countess, in order to find financing for renovating the city hall, ten years earlier, on the first of April, 1787, sold to the Jews twenty–eight buildings. The price for each building was between 300 and 2,500 Polish guilder[29].

It is hard to determine when an organized Jewish community life began in Siedlce, due to the lack of documents. One must assume that the Siedlce community existed in an organized form in the second half of the eighteenth century. A later document informs us that in 1794, the community was required to build a house with a dwelling place for the rabbi and a room set aside as a yeshiva. The earlier document about a place for the Siedlce Jewish cemetery, which the Countess Oginska had approved, speaks specifically about the Jewish community, to whom the land was given over.

[Page 21]

All of this shows that in the nineties of the eighteenth century, the Siedlce Jewish community was a regularly acknowledged institution. Such rights could not be established in a single decade. One must therefore assume that the Siedlce community existed long before it was required to build a house and establish a cemetery and before it received the right to represent the Jewish population before the Countess Oginska.

The document of 1794 that gives the community the right to build a house with a dwelling for the rabbi and a yeshiva has the following text:

Alexandra z Xiążąt Czartoryskich Ogińska Hetmanowa (Wielka) W. X. Litewskiego, Dóbr Siedleckich Dziedziczna Pani.

Ponieważ Żydzi obywatele Moi Siedleccy tak gminni jakoteż Bratctwo swoie maiący dla ozdoby Miasta ułożyli Dom wymurować, w którym iedna strona kosztem składki powszechney tychże gminnych na pomieszkanie dla Rabina, druga zaś Domu tego połowa kosztem samego Bratctwa na Szkółkę do nauki ma bydź wymurowana; zapobiegaiąc przeto wszelkim za Czas dalszy trafiać się mogącym Inkonweniencyam, takowe czynię raz na zawsze postanowienie. Iż ponieważ Bractwo samo składa fundusz na wymurowanie Szkółki, przeto nikt prawa nadal mieć nie może wdzierania się do teyże Szkółki lub do ławek w niej będących, toż tylko samo wspomniane Bractwo się zarządzać y wstęp wolny do ławek ma sobie zachowany. Inne zaś cechy jako to krawiecki y wszystkie iakie tylko są żydowskie w Mieście Moim Siedlcach, ponieważ swoie oddzielne mają Szkółki, do tych się udawać, y do dawnych Ustaw stosować powinny.

Na dowód czego takowe Ustanowienie, raz na zawsze trwać maiące przy zwykłej Pieczęci Rękę Moię własną podpisuję.

Dan w Siedlcach, Dnia dwudziestego ósmego Stycznia, tysiąc siedemset dziewięćdziesiątego czwartego Roku.

　　　　　　　　　　　　　　(30　　*Alex. Ogińska*

[Page 22]

Here is the Yiddish translation:

"Alexandra, from the Countess Czartoryski, Oginska, the great leader of the Lithuanian territory, the heir to the court of Siedlce.

Because the Jews, my citizens of Siedlce, those of the community and the fellowship, will, for the beautification of the town, construct a house, one side to be paid for by the collection of funds from the community for a dwelling for the rabbi; the other half of this house at the expense of the fellowship for a school (for learning); in order to avoid any misunderstandings in the future, I set down now and forever these conditions: because the fellowship alone provides the funds to build a school, therefore in the future no one will have the right to occupy this school or the benches therein. Only the aforementioned fellowship and its administrator grant free access to uphold it. Other entities, like the tailors and such other Jewish fellowships in my city of Siedlce because they have their own schools, should go there and be obliged to observe the old statutes. As evidence that these conditions should be for now and forever, I have signed and sealed this with my own hand. Issued in Siedlce, the 28th day of January, 1794, Alex. Oginsaka."

As can be seen in this document, the Jewish settlement in Siedlce had, in 1794, not only had an organized and legally recognized community, but also fellowships and guilds. The fellowship that would, according to the document, open a school–one must assume that this meant either a cheder or a yeshiva–was surely the Talmud Torah fellowship.

The Jewish Settlement of Siedlce after the Division Of Poland

In 1793, the collapse of the Kosciuszko Rebellion was followed by the second division of Poland. The country was divided among Russia, Austria, and Germany. In 1796, Siedlce was in the hands of the Austrians, who set up headquarters there.

[Page 23]

Three years later, Countess Oginska died. After her death, the town reverted to the Czartoryskis. Soon negotiations began between the Austrian power and the old–new landlords. In July of 1804, Count Adam Czartoryski exchanged Siedlce for other territories.

According to the demographic study of Prof. Y. Mikulski published in installments in "Szitshe Podlaskie" in 1934, Siedlce grew quickly, especially at the end of the eighteenth century, thanks to being located at a crossroads.

"The first of these roads," writes Mikulski, "went between the settlements: Liv, Wengrow, Lukow, Lublin, or along the length of the Bug River southward; from Wengrow, the dirt road went north as far as Danzig (there is still a reminder in the Wengrow marketplace– the so–called "Gdansk Stone Building"); the second path united Warsaw with Lithuania and simultaneously led through Liv, Wengrow, Sokolow. As time passed, after the construction of the rail lines from Warsaw to Vilna and from Warsaw to Brisk, Wengrow gradually lost its good fortune as the junction point to Siedlce."

Siedlce was not long attached to Austria. Two years later, after Napoleon had created the duchy of Warsaw, after the outbreak of the Austrian War in 1809, one of the fiercest battles was fought in the area of Siedlce. Siedlce itself was liberated by the Polish army, which was under the command of Josef Dembrowski. After the peace treaty, when Podlaskie was united with the duchy as a new department, Siedlce became the capital of the new quarter and an important city in the department.

At the Congress of Vienna in 1815 it was decided to create from the existing Duchy of Warsaw the so–called Kingdom of Poland. A pact was created with Russia, and the Siedlce Department was converted into a Podlaskie Voivodeship with Siedlce as its capital. It remained such until 1840, until the liquidation of the Podlaskie Voivodeship and the creation of the Siedlce Gubernia.

[Page 24]

From this tumultuous epoch, from the second division of Poland until the liquidation of the Podlaskie Voivodeship, in 1840, very few documents about Jewish life in Siedlce survive from which to learn how Jews lived From one document that turned up from 1812 from R. Noson Dovid Gliksberg, we see something about the license to charge for kosher meat in Siedlce, which was, it appears, a very good business, since for a single year the licensee paid twenty–seven thousand Polish zlotys to succeed an earlier licensee who lived in a different city. The go–between for this transaction was the later R. Bunim of Peshischa. The contract was written in Hebrew. The translation from Hebrew to Polish was made by the then official translator, who lived in Warsaw. We provide a Yiddish translation of the Polish copy of the contract:

"The undersigned declare that an agreement has been decided between us, the undersigned from one side and the Jews Avraham ben Dovid, Kalman ben Moyshe, and Yakov ben Yitzkhak, about the license to charge for kosher meat in the city of Siedlce for the period of one year, that is, from March 1, 1812 until the end of February in 1813. This agreement was decided on today among us, for which the above–named licensees have committed to pay for charging for kosher meat for the city of Siedlce for this year the sum of twenty–seven thousand Polish guilder. And in accord with this agreement the licensees have deposited a sum proportional to this sum for two months, and also for another month, the sum of six thousand, seven hundred and fifty Polish guilder. The rest of the amount two will be paid in two installments. (It appears that another contract was written in which all of these details were spelled out.) Thus, there are among us clear terms, that is, between the undersigned and the licensees, if, God forbid, an enemy should enter the country (as in 1812 there was the historic war between Russia and France), the price of the contract for the licensee of 27,000 guilder for the year will be null and void without blame. The licensees will owe nothing more than 20,000 guilder, and the deposit and the monthly sum will be reckoned according to 20,000 guilder per year.

[Page 25]

And as the licensee will reckon on twenty thousand guilders, the licensor will accept that for the year without more payment.

All of the above details in the contract, aside from the price of the license, remain in effect without regret. And neither side can make any claim on the other.

However, if the country remains peaceful and no enemy invades, the contract for 27,000 guilder will remain in effect.

On the basis of this contract, which will be sealed by a notary, every claim or exception is settled, and the licensor has to right to confirm it with a notary even without our instruction, and as a token I sign under this agreement, in Siedlce on the 28th of February, 1812.

Simcha Bunim of Voidislow

(as representative of H. Eisenberg)

I, the undersigned, accept, together with the others, this agreement, which my representative as decided, upon which I attach my name.

Yakov Eisenberg.

I confirm that this accords with the Hebrew original. In Warsaw, the second day of October, 1812.

M. Bochner (official translator from the tribunal of the judiciary)"

At the same time, in 1816, there was a blood libel trial. The community of Warsaw intervened on behalf of Siedlce[30]. In 1831, in the well–known November uprising, Siedlce was known for the Igan Battle (two or three kilometers from the city). The headquarters of General Diebitsch were in Siedlce. For a certain time, the Grand Duke Constantin was also there. He was the brother of the czar and chief of the Russian army.

[Page 26]

And at the same time, in the Igan Woods, there played out the great battle under the command of the generals Bem and Franzinski.

Fifteen years later, long after the rebellion had been put down, the neighborhood of Siedlce experienced the battles of Potocki. He was captured by the Russians together with a group of rebels and they were hanged in the center of the city. Also active in the rebellion against the Russians was the merchant Yizchak Greenberg, who was consequently known as "Khrabie [brave?] Potocki."

In 1841, the Russians proceeded to build a prison. The work lasted three years. The prison was built especially for political prisoners, and at first it was not so large. Over time, other buildings were added until it became one of the most severe central prisons in independent Poland. Between the two world wars it overflowed with political prisoners, mostly communists.

After the unification of the Siedlce gubernia with the Lublin gubernia, according to an order of August 9, 1844, Siedlce was reduced to a county seat, and it remained so until 1866, when the gubernia was renewed and Siedlce again was raised to the status of a regional capital.

Czarist Russification and Polish Anti–Semitism

After the second unsuccessful Polish rebellion, in 1863, the then governor Gorki, with help from the trustee Aputin, began intensive activities to Russify Siedlce. The government did everything, even changing the city's external appearance in an effort to eliminate anything Polish.

A writer from that time, Swietochowski, published his feelings. He provides a clear picture of Siedlce at that time, though he is not stingy with anti–Semitic venom. He writes (on page 9):

"A mix of national uniforms hostile to us on military men and civil officials. These ignorant, drunken types, raised in the spirit of eastern culture, speak a foreign language, which strikes us with violence. For a relatively few inhabitants of the city, there are a large number of institutions, bureaus, centers, barracks for the army; everywhere one sees many Russians.

[Page 27]

Poles have been totally ejected from government posts. The Russians have begun massively to bring in Jews from the thankless east. The unfortunate small number of Polish citizens live in terrible poverty, relying on agriculture and small businesses, from renting out small rooms on their ground floors to the families of Russian officials"[31].

From a chronicle that appeared in "Novoratshniki Siedlce" in 1873, we see characteristic details about Siedlce at that time. Understandably, the description does not lack anti–Semitism:

"Behind the gubernia building (later the bishop's palace, in front of the city park) a square with benches was laid out. In the square, arrangements were made for a new campus. This campus will have a cannon, which will be fired to let the populace know when it is noon. The city hall in 1873 should be renovated, on all its levels, because they are threatening to collapse, so they must be torn down and totally rebuilt.

"A little while back, drozhkies used to go there. It is unfortunate that the concourse is open to Jews, who can be recognized by their disorder, which they have brought even here."

Further on comes the following characterization of community life:

"A scornful emptiness, a frightful nothingness. Looking over the nauseating sleepiness, over the miserable powerlessness, it is difficult even to think that a part of these people are educated, know the responsibilities of the community which they will not carry out. These people are significant. They would like to know how to direct others. That which should come from their own initiative they seize upon and then….play cards, they spend time with Molly or with Esther (names of Siedlce's bar girls from that time), or they go to worse places.

[Page 28]

The reason is the solitariness and the smallness of their way of life. There are family areas, but there are no community areas. Our daughters don't read, aside from Dumas' romances. They are partial to no other language aside from the language of love.

"We have no other entertainment aside from dance, which perhaps pleases the women and the fervent young dancers; but it leaves the older men with an aftertaste of nausea. If a couple go off together, which seldom happens, they trudge through the city mud for half an hour, drink tea for a quarter of an hour, and the other twenty minutes are spent in gossip. The aristocrats promote for ladies the card game 'Bezhik' and for men 'Preference.'

"I should now present a panorama with gifts of the growing light or a magic–bird that will soon cover the whole world and is made of various layers in order to delight and sanctify a well–known charlatan. People from the world of work lose to the dishonest lotteries and hope to win a month's wages in an hour. There are, too, provincial towns that stand near Siedlce. In Lukow there are evenings when the whole town and its surroundings come together. Frivolities and entertainments are arranged that we don't even want to think about.

In Siedlce there are about 500 houses, but who knows ? Maybe half of them are taverns adorned with Esther and Molly, Wolf and Kamp. So, too, with the taverns that are behind the Szczal Gate.

"In Podlaskie there is no industry. The only business is shop keeping, which lies in the hands of those who are hostile to us. Either the citizens are poor because they can barely feed themselves or they are the most backward capitalists in the world. The towns are inhabited almost entirely by clerks. Three quarters of them are clutched in the hands of the Jews."

From these descriptions, colored with anti–Semitism, we get an idea of Jewish life in Siedlce at the time: the number of Jews grew. Most of the Jews came from the east.

[Page 29]

They were later branded as "Litvaks." Jews struggled to accommodate themselves to the new conditions, dealing with Russian clerks, entering new professions, and occupying themselves with the usual Jewish occupations in the Polish shtetls: running taverns, beer halls, and so on.

Siedlce's Jews in the Nineteenth Century

The number of Jews in Siedlce in the first quarter of the nineteenth century and their percentage in the larger population was thus:

Year	Jews	Christians	Others	Percentage Of Jews
1827	2,908	1,508	25	65

As can be seen, the Jews comprised almost two–thirds of the city's population. but even in 1827 they did not have undue weight in the city, and their influence waned in the course of the nineteenth century, as later tabulations will show.

From 1827 on, the figures and statistics regarding Jews are precise and detailed, because in the 30's of the nineteenth century there were already rules requiring the registration of newborns. Births were recorded in the gubernia city of Siedlce by the civil service, on the basis of the civil law of the Polish kingdom from 1825[32].

From a list of births in 1837 that the Siedlce managing committee published a hundred years later, we find the names of Jews who lived in the city in the eighteenth century and whose families later grew in size.

Synagogues and Beis–Medreshes

For the ten years beginning in 1851, Siedlce was under constraints to build a shul. The old shul, which had been made of wood, burned down in the great fire of Hoshanah Rabbah night.

[Page 30]

In 1851, Siedlce had been without a shul for five years. A new shul–this time made of brick–was begun in 1856. In 1870[33], a fire broke out again and destroyed the roof and the aron–kodesh. The work continued for several years and was completed in 1876. This shul was huge and beautiful, in the style of those shuls that had been built in Poland in the eighteenth century. Externally the building looked magnificent. First of all, it was the tallest building in the area at that time–four stories high. On the east and west sides were two windows, close to the roof, in the form of the two tablets of the law. The entrance was furnished with a large anteroom, which led to the right–to a small prayer room, known as "the tailors' shul." To the left was the entrance to the women's section, which formed part of the ground floor on the north and south sides and part of the second story of the shul. From the right and left of the anteroom, steps led to a balcony one floor up.

Arriving in the shul's interior, one encountered a great hall, in which were table and benches for 800 people. In the middle was a reading platform that was reached by four or five steps. The eastern wall, with the aron–kodesh, was adorned with musical instruments made out of copper. The aron–kodesh , which was itself a work of art, was built into the wall itself. In front there were two lions, with various scenes from the Tanakh painted around. It is hard to know who the architect of the shul was. The aron–kodesh was made by one

Y. Zwibak and his two sons. At the time of the fire of 1870, the aron–kodesh was partially damaged. The part that could be salvaged was later used for the reconstructed shul[34].

This shul also served as the official representative of the community. Honored guests of the community were taken there–both Jews and non–Jews. Official community celebrations were held there, as were celebrations of national holidays.

The city shul was destroyed by the German murderers during the Second World War on Christmas night, the 25th of December, 1939.

[Page 31]

The Germans set fire to the shul while refugees from other cities who had nowhere else to go were inside. In the morning, the Germans forced the Jews to confess that they themselves had set fire to the shul[35].

Also the city beis–medresh, which was located near the shul, was there at the beginning of the nineteenth century, as was the Mishneh Havurah that shared the building.

Aside from the general prayer houses, there were in Siedlce also from older times "workmen's shuls" like the "tailor's shul" and the "butcher's beis medresh." Workmen's prayer houses were created on the basis of craft specialties as counterparts to the organized Polish guilds that then existed in Poland.

Each of these prayer houses had its own record book, which served, first of all, as a rule book and a way of remembering important events that took place during the existence of the havurah. We know that in the record book of the Mishneh Havurah there was a ruling: The record book had to be in the hands of the "arbitrator," who would be elected every erev Shavuos. The "arbitrator" was chosen by a secret ballot, and he chose a secretary, whose job was, if a member of the Mishneh Havurah passed away, to send notices to all the members who were enrolled in the record book letting them know that they were required to study a chapter of the Mishneh "for the raising up of the soul."

In 1878, the idea arose to establish privately a beis–medresh. This was the idea of the Siedlce big shot and patron, R. Yisroel ben Yehiel Greenberg, who twenty–five years later also built a Talmud Torah. The beis–medresh was known in the city as "Yisroel Yehiel's beis–medresh." Yisroel Greenberg had purchased a place at the corner of Dluga (later: First of May Street) and Pusta Street. The czarist governor was opposed to establishing the building, especially right on the street. The government committee did not approve of the site. R. Yisroel Greenberg was forced to put up in front a door, ostensibly for a restaurant. Later the door was made over into a window. Eventually permission for the beis–medresh was granted.

[Page 32]

The beis–medresh cost 6,000 czarist rubles and opened in 1879. Greenberg was moved to create the beis–medresh because he was a fierce misnagid; as a big shot, he did not care to pray in the city beis–medresh, and he did not want to pray in one of the many Chassidic prayer houses that then existed in Siedlce–so he established with his own money a misnagid prayer house[36].

War Between the Chassidim and Misnagdim

Beginning in 1750 and for a hundred and fifty years after, a war played out between Chassidim and Misnagdim. We know of several zealots on both sides who established their interesting characters. The Misnagid R. Meir Nisn, the progenitor of the many–branched Nussbaum family (he died in 1810), was a great scholar and a learned man. He translated into Polish the book "Bekhinas–Olam." In his time he conducted a polemical argument with the Peshischa Rabbi R. Simcha Bunim. It is also known that at the same time he conducted disputes with another of his opponents–R. Kalman Chassid. Already known as "Chassid," R. Kalman was a scholar, a religious Jew and Talmudic genius[37].

Apparently R. Simcha Bunim of Peshischa had in Siedlce passionate adherents. Such we know was R. Zisha of Siedlce, who was chosen by a secret gathering of Chassidim to travel to the wedding of the grandchild of the rabbi of Apt, Rabbi Yehoshua Heschel, which was to take place in Astilla. This mission was connected with rumors that had been spread that the rabbi of Apt was about to declare an excommunication on R. Simcha Bunim because a group of rabbis, led by R. Yakov Shimon Deutsch (who later lived in Zhelekhow), found that Peshischa branch of Chassidism was in violation of Jewish law. This group had decided to send five students from Peshischah who would be able to debate with their opponents. The delegation was comprised of the following: a wise man, a Talmud scholar, a Chassid, a wealthy man, and an eloquent person; R. Zisha of Siedlce was chosen as the wise man; the other four delegates were– R. Feivele Gritzer, an elderly Chassid who used to travel on contracts from Lublin; R. Yissachar Hurwitz as the rich man, a son–in–law of the then well–known Warsaw dowager Frau Temerl; as spokesman, R. Eliezer Ber of Grachawitz; and as Talmud scholar the then well–known Warsaw genius and later rabbi of Ger, R. Itsch Meir[38]. So R. Zisha of Siedlce was among such a group of people and was trusted for such a mission, which shows that he was renowned in the Chassidic world of the nineteenth century.

[Page 33]

In the nineteenth century the Misnagdim had the upper hand in controlling the Siedlce community. The rabbis were all from the Misnagid side. And aside from the rabbis, the town preacher was an influential person in Jewish Siedlce. The preacher would often study a lesson with the public and deliver a sermon. After the preacher there was the town cantor, whose influence on the public hung on his cantorial abilities. If the cantor was a good prayer leader, with a sweet voice, his influence could be large. Understandably, the choice of a cantor was the cause of much debate for the community. Often it was tied up with arguments and dissatisfaction on one side or the other. One side held that the cantor should be a God–fearing man and a scholar. The other side held rather that the cantor should be a fine singer with sweet voice. For decades the cantors in Siedlce were the subjects of argument.

Thus it happened that from 1818 on the cantor in Siedlce who were Misnagdim, opponents of Chassidism. Such a one was R. Shmuel Dovid Semyotitscher (who died in 1861). After him came his successor, R. Reuven Kantor. The cantor R. Yakov Zalman Rubinshteyn of Slutzk was also a Misnagid. When he was left without a pulpit–as people said–because the city's shul burned down in 1874, he left Siedlce and went to Lithuania, because he could not stomach Poland because of its Chassidim. He remained there for a year, until the shul was repaired. When he returned, he brought with him the Lithuanian Misnagid spirit, because a dispute had broken out in the city . R. Yakov Zalman, lacking the strength to fight, abandoned Siedlce.

[Page 34]

The preachers, too, were for many decades Lithuanian Misnagdim. Since in the nineteenth century Chassidism had also penetrated into Siedlce, there was also a great deal of conflict in the preaching of both sides.

A fervent Misnagid was the preacher R. Manis. His salary was a few score groshen a week, all told, which even in those times only lasted him for a couple of days in the week. On the other days he fasted. He wrote a book of insights on the Torah. He must have died in 1835[39].

He was succeeded as preacher by R. Yisroel, who was known by the name R. Yisroelke the Preacher. The Chassidim truly hated him. The Chassidim went after him so much that on Hoshanah Rabbah evening in 1851 he fled from the city.

At the same time, the rabbinical chair in Siedlce was occupied by a Misnagid rabbi, R. vi Hersh Weingarten, who was persecuted by the Chassidim. R. Zvi Hersh died in 1818. He wrote a number of books, which were burned up in the fire, except for "Maram Zvi," which was published posthumously in 1900 in Zhitomir.

His sons and grandsons were great rabbis: R. Mordechai Menkes, the author of the book "Ma'amar Mordechai," on the tractates Pesachim, Bezah, Megillah, Baba Kama, Baba Mezia, Shavuos, Hulin, Pirkei Avos, with his insights (Zhitomir, 1900)–was a great–grandchild of R. Zvi Hersh. A son of R. Mordechai –R. Duber–was proud of his great–great–grandfather. In his book of responsa, "Anaf Avos," on the four sections of the Shulchan Aruch (Zhitomir, 1900), he writes of his pedigree: "Unworthy that I am, the son of the righteous Rabbi, Our Teacher, Mordechai, may his memory be a blessing in the life of the world to come, the author of the book 'The Light of Mordechair', on the Talmud and its commentators, the grandson and son of the faithful gaon, famous in his generation , Our Teacher Zvi Hersh, may his memory be a blessing in the life of the world to come, the head of the Beis Din in the holy congregation of Siedlce in Poland[41].

The quarrels ended, as I said, after a hundred and fifty years, because other winds began to blow on the Jewish street–the arriving Haskalah movement–and slowly extinguished the flickering fires between the Chassidim and Misnagdim.

[Page 35]

The opposing sides recognized that the Haskalah was the hateful to both of them.

A certain play about the battle between the Chassidim and the Misnagdim comes to us in the description by the famous writer Heinrich Heine, who visited Poland in 1822. He came to Siedlce after visiting Mezrich. It appears that during his visit he stopped in no other city. He does not call Siedlce by its name. He just refers to it as a city near Mezrich. We know that the writer came from Warsaw.

At that time there was no train that went around the city, so he must have gone through Siedlce. There can be no doubt that the city he speak about is Siedlce.

Heinrich Heine was not terribly enthusiastic about the outward appearance of the Jews of Siedlce, with their dirty caps, beards, and their "jargon." Therefore he speaks with appreciation about the spiritual life of Polish Jews. In describing the Jews of Siedlce–he describes Polish Jews in general. About this interesting characterization by Heinrich Heine of Siedlce Jews, and therefore Polish Jews, the historian Graetz paused to emphasize the spiritual physiognomy of the Polish Jews, or, more precisely, of the Misnagdim.

Since 1858–1867, the rabbinical chair in Siedlce was occupied by a Misnagid rabbi, Rabbi Yisroel Meisels, a son of the famous Warsaw rabbi and Polish patriot Rabbi Duberish Meisels. While in Siedlce, Rabbi Meisels busied himself and published an important book of responsa–"Tiferes Zvi." After his father's death, in 1870 he produced the "Sefer Hamitzvos" of Rambam with his father's commentary under the title "Be–urei Ha–Radom." (Radom is an acronym for Rabbi Dov Verish Meisels.) After leaving Siedlce, Rabbi Yisroel Meisels went to Warsaw, and then because of his father's concerns he went to Krakow, where he became a rabbinical judge[42].

R. Yisroel Meisels died in 1876. In Krakow a large beis–medresh was established in his name, and on his grave was placed a monument, on the right side of which was inscribed the following text. The text contains an acrostic on the name Yisroel Meisels. Each line ends with the word Yisroel–the rabbi's name.

[Page 36]

The monument reads like this: [the text is in Hebrew]

Zion, for the soul of our father the rabbi, the gaon, the faithful, the righteous, the famous, the holy, Yisroel, head of the Beth Din of Siedlce, The rabbi, the gaon, the renowned in all corners of the land Duberish Meisels, may his memory be a blessing.

> Let wailing be heard in the borders of Israel
> Lament, our brothers, the house of Israel
> The rabbi and hero fell today in Israel
> Alas! for the rest of days will flicker the light of Israel
> We are left to sigh for the shepherd of the rock of Israel
> His works are known throughout the diaspora of Israel
> Day and night he labored in the Torah of the law of Israel
> He sat in Midian and judged Israel
> His sun shone there to light up for the children of Israel
> His spirit died for God and found the honor of Israel
> The secret will dwell on high with all the holiness of Israel.

The day his pure soul left, the fourth of Marcheshvan Israel mourns heavily[43].

Also the later rabbi, R. Baruch Lifshutz, author of the book "B'ris Yakov," was a Misnagid. Alter Droyanow, in his big collection of jokes, tells that one time a famous Chassidic rebbe came to Siedlce; as was common, the Chassidim brought offerings to him to get blessings and to get his advice. In the morning, R. Baruch Mordechai came to the rebbe. The rebbe, seeing that he had such an important guest, went to the rabbi and asked:

"What has troubled you to come to me?"

R. Mordechai answered him, "I wanted to see with my own eyes how a religious person can take something for nothing."[44]

The Haskalah Movement

Unfortunately, because of a lack of source materials, we have no information about the effects of the Haskalah in Siedlce.

[Page 37]

From an anonymous pamphlet attributed to a certain Radominski[45], it seems that in Siedlce, already in 1819 there were in the local elementary school twenty–six Jewish students, among whom several excelled and received awards. From another source[46], we are made aware about a group of female students who finished an elementary trade school. Among them was one named Hinde Greenberg, who also received an award for scholarship.

From these facts we can see that in Siedlce there were Jewish parents who sent their children to study in school together with Christian children. If we consider the strongly conservative conditions that ruled the Jewish family in a provincial Polish town like Siedlce, we must realize that in Siedlce there lived at that time enlightened people [Maskilim] who were interested in the broader education of their children.

More indication about Maskilim and the Haskalah are available from the later years of the nineteenth century, which we speak of later.

The Development of the Jewish Hospital System

A Jewish hospital on a very low level, but a hospital nevertheless, existed in Siedlce in the early years, even before the nineteenth century. It was located in the area where later, in 1890, the Jewish hospital was built–between the second cemetery and Pienkne Street on one side and the city market and garden, which bordered the so–called "alleys" on the other. In a letter from August 29, 1844, the supervisory council of Siedlce addressed the synagogue council with a letter that had been sent to the community head of the month.

According to the existing ordinance, the Jewish community is allowed to form a committee of several persons respected in the city. Each person should have served in turn for a month. Consequently such a person was called the "community head of the month." The exchange of letters took place between the "community head of the month" (also called the "dozor") and the government. The government carried out its correspondence with the "dozor" through the mediation of the Siedlce administration. The letter says[47]:

"Whereas the council has already met and whereas the order of 3/2 1842 gives him the supervisory power over the poor folk of the Jewish faith, therefore should the dozor provide an account of all the funds for the Jewish hospital."

The response of the dozor to this message, written in October of 1844. is respectful; in the answer he says:

"Responding to the reminder concerning the funds, I state: The Jewish community of Siedlce has long intended to build a hospital for Jews. The necessary arrangements for it have been made, and we need a suitable spot and enough funds. A spot is available, but the funds, thanks to the last dozor, were squandered and are now insufficient. Previous dozors did not commit to build the hospital but were satisfied with the longtime overcrowded hospital, but it is now fitting to undertake the project."

This copy of the document is not signed, and it is not possible to determine who were the dozors who signed the letter.

In the correspondence there are also details about a certain Leibtsche Lichtenberg, who is praised for his private underwriting the building in which the Jewish hospital was located, without which it would have fallen on the community.

This giving away without obligation the building with the "foul" place–as it was reported–did not find favor with the government. In another letter from the dozor to the government, which was written on July 13, 1846, the dozor writes a report to the magistrate in which he speaks about an auction to lease the garden near the hospital. The conditions on which the garden can be leased (which was spoken about at this point as a foul place) were thus:

"It will be leased for one ruble and fifty kopeks per year. The auction must bring in half the sum, 75 kopeks as a deposit.

[Page 39]

From this deposit the auctioneer can take nothing. The fee must be paid in half–yearly installments. Free entry and passage through the place to the hospital and the cemetery. If during this time it is decided not to build a new hospital, this contract will be annulled."

Under these conditions it is signed–"representing everyone: Sh. Wishniaw," who was then the secretary of the community.

As can be seen from this correspondence, a kind of hospital already existed. Means were gathered to build a better one, And in the auction, too, we can see hints about building a new hospital on the spot. The old so–called hospital was in fact a wreck, Its status as a hospital was later officially suspended. On December 30, 1868 the Siedlce magistrate informed the dozor that the house near the cemetery would remain in the estate of Yudel Lichtenberg for ten rubles and ninety kopeks. There he speaks of a house and not a hospital.

The history of the later and new Jewish hospital began in 1869. In connection with Russian government orders, which bore the name: "Statute on the conduct and dress and separation of the Jews and their wives." Dated July 19, 1851 and first published on March 3, 1871, , the police chief Modroch sent a copy to the dozor to proclaim it three times in the shul. According to the order of the government committee, the dozor had to influence the Jews to cut off their sidelocks and to wear their hair in the Christian style. The wives should remove their wigs and by March 10, 1871 should appear neatly and by March 15 should exchange their clothes for clothing prescribed in the order. Otherwise they would be held responsible. The order was not supposed to affect rabbis.

In the city there were some Jews who would not abandon their traditional clothing. Therefore they were punished by the government with a fine.

[Page 40]

The money from the fines the government placed in the Polish Bank. In 1869, it amounted to 11,551 rubles. The Jewish township, with the dozor Yisroel Ber Liverant, took the step that the accumulated money from the fines should be given to the community for the purpose of building a hospital. These efforts lasted more than twenty years until the request was fulfilled. The correspondence between the Jewish community and the central governmental organization in Petersburg, through the mediation of the Siedlce magistrate, paints an interesting picture of how Jewish community life appeared in the second half of the nineteenth century.

The Jewish community in its letters revealed a building plan and showed that it had chosen a spot for the hospital near the city market at Pienke corner. They laid out a plan to build a structure that would hold twelve beds, with the possibility of expansion to fifteen.

The government committee responded to the letter as follows: the architect of the government committee, Modziewski, has estimated that the proposed hospital should have at least twenty rooms as well as auxiliary facilities, such as: a kitchen, washrooms, stables, and so on. The main building should cost 14,000 rubles and the auxiliary facilities–2,500 rubles. Installation, linens, furniture, dishes, and instruments–1200 rubles. Altogether 17,700 rubles. The government also determined that the chosen spot was too small and was not suitable for such an institution because it was in the center of town and near the market. The township was instructed to buy another site.

Four years passed until the Jewish township again raised the issue of the hospital. It was the 23rd of August in 1877. The dozors H. Zivula and Sh. Greenberg asked the magistrate to renew the efforts toward a Jewish hospital and made the same proposal as earlier, but the response from Petersburg was no less negative than before.

In a letter of 31 August, it was said that the project was already considered earlier and the governmental body asked the dozor to show exactly what was required to realize the project, but nonetheless they repeated the same thing to the dozor.

[Page 41]

In the letter there was also a "gift" for the township secretary Shoyme Vishnye, because he had allowed the township to proceed in the same way, for which he received a strong rebuke. The dozors at the same time decided to put forward another candidate for the post of secretary.

On August 18, 1873, then later on December 6, 1877, the magistrate, in the name of the Petersburg government, demanded that the dozor should set forth the intentions of the Jewish organization about a permanent fee for the hospital under the "personal responsibility of the dozors and the secretary."

The next development in the hospital affair was this: the magistrate, at the beginning of 1880, proposed to foreclose the horse market in front of the shul and move it to Pienke Street (later Market), and also to take the community's spot in order to enlarge the proposed market. This proposition called forth strong dissatisfaction in the Jewish population, because in that era, community life revolved around the market. Many Jews had their houses and shops there.

On April 16, 1880, the dozor was again asked to show when the cemetery would be shut down, for that was a necessary consideration for the hospital project. The hope to be able finally to build a Jewish hospital was real and the Jewish leaders became more active. The dozor presented the authorities, together with an application to build a hospital, a resolution with 233 signatures from the Jewish township that recognized the necessity of the hospital and committed to pay 1445 rubles annually. This time the project was forwarded to Petersburg, to the Minister of the Interior for approval.

It was four years later, on April 3, 1884, that the project was returned with a note from the Governor General saying that the technical committee had found in the plan technical flaws and that the sum of 1445 rubles would only be a portion of the total expense, and the rules for such institutions required that the whole cost be covered, so that the sum was too small. Signed:—Gorka.

The project, with the governor's addendum, was on April 22, 1884 forwarded to the dozor by the magistrate, who called attention to the fact that the site chosen by the township was not suitable for a hospital because it was in the center of the town next to the projected market, bordering that site: exchange the site, which was needed for the market, for the estate of a certain Boyelski. (On this site later on stood the military hospital, and then in independent Poland the military recruiting office [PKO]).

On January 31, 1885, Yisroel Ber and Binyamin Liverant committed themselves to underwrite the hospital on the township's site for a sum of 125, 104 rubles, which they guaranteed with their houses and possessions.

The changes in the building plan because of the technical difficulties, as well as the technical cost estimates, ended the earlier project. Consequently, things dragged out for another four years, and only in 1888 were all the necessary documents and permissions gathered together in order to obtain the final permit. These documents included:

1.   technical improvements with a statement that, because of a shortage of resources, they would begin by building one structure. (The earlier plan had envisioned two buildings.) The new project was approved by the government engineer Morzhewski on March 10, 1888.
2.   a certificate witnessed by 279 signatures of donors headed by the dozors: A. Kaminski, Y.M. Lubelski, B. Kahana, and the current rabbi, Rabbi Graubard, about building only a single building with ten beds (the earlier plan had projected 50 beds), as well as a commitment to pay 2,147 rubles and 50 kopeks to maintain the hospital.
3.   a signature from the dozor A. Kaminski from July 1, 1888, representing the entire Jewish population, that it does not desire and will not desire in the future to approach the government with any request for a subsidy or for underwriting the hospital. This time the plan was successful. The plan was well worked out.

One more time the magistrate tried to impede the carrying out of the plan.

[Page 43]

His reason was the same–the place was too small and not appropriate for a hospital. On February 28, 1890 the dozor was ordered to call a meeting in the morning at the rabbi's, with the participation of the leading citizens, to consider the question of changing the location chosen for the hospital, because the site was technically and hygienically not suitable for a health facility, and in connection with that, what would be involved in buying a different building, a more suitable one.

From the minutes of this meeting, we see that twenty–three citizens met: Yudel Arzhel, Mordechai Heinsdorf, Sender Baxenboim, Moyshe Goldhtern, Neteh Zilberzweig, Yisroel–Ber Liverant, Fishl Frenkl, Shmuel Brukarzh, Neteh Rubinshteyn, Yakov Slushni, Moyshe Kelmeson, Yisroel Richter, Yosef Zayantz, Gedaliah Shapiro, Avigdor Solnitza, Binyamin Liverant, H.D. Lichtenfacht, Meir Yonah Rozenzweig, Yakov Greenshpan, Wolf Oppenheim, Zalman Kamyenne, Kalman Yabkiob, No report of the meeting remains. It appears that the meeting rejected the magistrate's proposal, because they were ready to build.

Berl Kahane

[Page 44]

Quite characteristic is the application from the Jewish township to the governor on December 18, 1890. In the application, the township asks: whereas the Jewish hospital is ready to open, they should invite a doctor of the "Jewish faith," who would be able to speak Yiddish to the patients. Justifying the rightness of this request, the community suggested Dr. Rosenthal, who was popular in the town because of his industriousness, his optimism, and because he had treated the Jewish poor everywhere. Their request was fulfilled, but characteristic were the arguments that the Jews used so that they could have a doctor in the hospital who could speak Yiddish to the patients.

The hospital was completed at the end of 1890. On September 5, 1891, the governor, by means of the magistrate, told the dozor–whereas the hospital would soon open, the governor requested that five candidates–citizens familiar with hospital matters–should be nominated so that one of them could be made the curator. The magistrate suggested the following candidates: Mordechai Heinsdorf, Itzl Arzhel, Yisroel–Ber Liverant, Noson Zilberzweig, and Avraham Kaminski. The dozor, however, preferred other candidates: M. Heinsdorf, Binyamin Liverant, N. Zilberzweig, Hershke Zelnik, and Itzl Arzhel. On October 4, 1891 the magistrate announced the curator for three years would be Alter Slushni. Such was the protectorship over Jewish affairs: ask for and receive their suggestions and then do whatever they wanted anyhow. The second curator, Avraham Kaminski, was then appointed by the community itself. From 1902 until 1926, the post of curator was held by Y. N. Weintroib. In order to secure the income of the hospital, fifteen stores were opened.

In 1892, a cholera epidemic broke out in Siedlce. The hospital was turned into an epidemic health center. On December 31, 1892, Dr. Rosenthal announced that from the first of January in 1893 the hospital would return to normal function.

[Page 45]

A History of the Jews in Siedlce (cont.)

The "Shas Society" and the "Visitors of the Sick Society"

In 1839 a Shas Society [Shas is an acronym that refers to the Talmud] was established in Siedlce. Twelve years later, in 1851, a record book was created for the society. As Y.N. Weintroib[48] explains, twelve rules were included in the record book. Some typical rules were:

Section 1) Each member is responsible for learning a page of Gemara every day in the beis–hemedresh, early in the morning, "for great is the Talmud that has no limit to it";

Section 2) No one should learn his page of Talmud alone, but only with the group, together, as the sages say: "an author to his friends"*, and at a table, on the east side and the south side of the Holy Ark;

[[*A note is added here saying that the editors could not locate the source of the quotation and offering alternatives from Ethics of the Fathers and the Talmudic tractate B'rachos]]

Section 3) Every society member must pay, for the good of the society, at the beginning of each month, four groschen, and if he does not pay, he will be expelled from the society;

Section 4) Whoever is prevented from coming to learn even one day shall pay a fine of a groschen, and whoever transgresses two of these rules shall pay a fine of five groschen.

Section 7) New members can only be accepted at the completion of reading the Talmud, once every seven years, or when new officials are chosen, but not more than three and only with the agreement of a majority;

Section 8) The membership fee for new members is not less than eighteen zlotys and pastries for the whole society, and never, never allow scholars to join the society;

Section 9) There should be no relatives among the leaders and trustees of the society;

Section 10) When people celebrate having finished a tractate, they can supply a feast only with the permission of the majority, and for a great celebration the leaders must make a feast without asking the group, and each member must give not less than one zloty for the necessities of the feast.

[Page 46]

From such a celebration, which occurred on the twenty–second of Adar in 5638 [1878] , we learn the following details:

The entire day, which was a Monday, was counted as a holiday. All the members of the Shas Society wore their Shabbos clothes. At seven in the evening, they all gathered in the town's beis–medresh. Admission was accorded to holders of entrance cards, which were called by the Hebrew term "letters of invitation"; the beis–medresh was nicely decorated with lamps, lights, and silver menorahs. By the entrance and over the windows were inscriptions: Faith–Zera'im, Ethics–Mo'ed, Husband–Nashim, Salvation–Nezikin, Wisdom–Kidddushim, Knowledge–Tehoros. [The Hebrew words are the names of sections of the Talmud.]

At nine in the evening, the governor, Dmitry Moskvik, arrived, accompanied by his retinue: Vice–Governor Petrov, Police Chief Dornovo, and other highly placed guests. The celebration began with the singing of Cantor R. Avraham Chaim Ephron and the choir, and with the playing of R. Leibush with his son Yontsche and their band. Psalm 30 was recited. The governor drank a L'chaim to the czar and then to the whole community, after which people answered the governor's questions about the service of the cantor, that he received 250 rubles a year. The governor asked that the cantor be given 50 rubles more per year. He was happy as he and his retinue left the beis–medresh. The feast went on for the entire night, with the participation of three hundred people. The dozors then were: Shimon Greenberg, Zvi Zebula, Yisroel Dov Liverant. The trustees of the Shas Society: Feivel Boym, Zvi Yosef Tcharnobroda, and Dovid Shimon Hacohen Greenberg.

The "Visitors of the Sick Society"

During the course of the nineteenth century, the Jewish settlement in Siedlce created a whole array of mutual help organizations, charity organizations, and so on. Because of a shortage of source materials, it is difficult to paint a picture of how these organizations operated what their activities were and the bases of their existence.

[Page 47]

For one such organization, the "Visitors of the Sick Society," which was established in 5604 (1843)–their record book has been preserved. From this record book we get an idea of how Jewish community life appeared at that time.

First of all we must emphasize the name of the organization–"The New Society for Visiting the Sick." From this we infer that before this society there had already existed a group to visit the sick. Second, it confirms our assumption, stated earlier, that Jewish community life began to form from the working class, which is further attested by the record book of the "Society for Visiting the Sick," which records in the introduction that this society was formed by shoemakers, who started "The New Society for Visiting the Sick" for mutual aid–to visit individual sick people daily.

The external appearance of the record book: a quarto format with two hundred pages bound in dark green leather. The language is Hebrew in the rabbinic style of the 18th century, but with many errors. The title page is ornamented and similar to a particular pattern.

In the introduction it is said that the undersigned have taken on the responsibility for the mitzvah of visiting the sick, "which is one of the greatest pillars of the world." The signatures were sealed on 7 Adar, 5604. (As is well known, 7 Dar is the anniversary of the death of Moshe Rabeinu). The signatures give only the first names and the fathers' names; no family names are mentioned in the record book.

On the second page are listed the following eighteen rules of the society ([49][although the text incorrectly says 79]):

1.   If a member of the society becomes, God forbid, ill, it is required that two men from the Visiting the Sick Society should visit him and stay with him throughout his illness. If one should fail, God forbid, without good reason and not go, he must give the leader a half zloty for the treasury (of the Society) and the leader must send someone to spend the night with the sick person.

2.   If a member of the society is ill and, God forbid, has no money for a cure, the leader must lend him money for a cure, money from the treasury, and when he recovers, he must pay back the money in weekly installments, according to his means.

[Page 48]

3.   If a member of the Society dies, mercy be upon us, the whole Society must pray for him for thirty days, every evening and morning. If the deceased has no children, one of the members must say Kaddish for him for a whole year.

4.   If a member of the Society has a son, he must give 18 groschen for the benefit of the Society, and if he has a daughter, he must give 9 groschen.

5.   If a member gets a new suit of clothes made of taffeta, he must donate 18 groschen for the benefit of the Society, and if he gets a new suit of clothes of lesser fabric, he must give 9 groschen.

6.   Two members of the Society must go every week to collect money that members of the Society have pledged.

7.   Every time a vote must be taken, two shoemakers must be chosen: one a leader and the other a supervisor, to assure that everything is in order.

8.   A vote must be taken every year on the 18th of Adar.

9.   The person chosen through an election to be a leader can take no other position for three years. If during those three years he fulfills his duties appropriately and later he wants to give for the welfare of the society whatever the monthly leader asks of him, he will be treated like all the other members in regard to places of honor.

10.   Every 18th of Adar, all the members will assemble for a vote. The procedure for the vote is thus: each person will be given a ballot; the monthly leader writes the names and puts the ballots in the ballot box. He takes out six ballots and then replaces them in the ballot box. These six choose the leaders of the Society.

11.   The electors can choose four leaders: a treasurer, someone to maintain *[Page 49]* the record book, three auditors, and three supervisors, who will oversee matters so that the Society will function in an orderly manner, which will be assured by the electors, and they should be certain that everything that is required will be recorded in the record book clearly and distinctly.

12.   The electors should not delay the appointment of a note taker for more than three days. But if they want to delay longer, they should not appoint a note taker. They should hold a new election according to the above provisions.

13.   If the Society want to write a Sefer Torah (if it is needed, as shown in section 7*) every member is required to contribute what the leaders determine. If one does not wish to donate what the leaders have determined, the leaders and the members should meet to impose a fine.
(*Editor's note: They see no such provision in section 7)

14.   Non–members of the Society who wish to join should notify the monthly leader and he should present this to the membership. After consideration, if he is chosen, he must pay the entry fee and take care of other matters. The entry fee cannot be less than six guilden, aside from cakes and pastries for the members.

15.   Everyone who belongs to the Society is required to give the sexton eighteen groschen compensation for calling the Society together.

16.   The monthly leader has two votes on every question that will be determined by majority vote. Whether for imposing a fine on a member who violates a rule that is laid out here or because the members will have realized that someone should be fined or if someone has rebelled against the leaders, the fine will be imposed according at the discretion of the monthly leader, and also he will collect the fine from the accused.

[Page 50]
       All should be recorded so it will be remembered.

       17.   When there is an election in the Society, as described in rule 10, there must be added to those who are elected, up to eighteen people, taking care of rule 7. And if the Society should grow and become more prosperous, the electors, at the time of the election, have the right to choose one shoemaker as a leader and one as a supervisor.

      18.   If a member of the Society becomes, God forbid, ill, the whole Society shall assemble in the beis–medresh and recite Psalms for him so that the blessed Name should take pity on him and send him a complete cure.

The first minutes of the elected leaders, supervisors, treasurer, and keeper of the record book are written on the third page of the record book. And it is attested by four signatures of electors who chose the directors. Such minutes were written every year after the elections.

After the first minutes, a new rule was added–a nineteenth, which declares: if a new member is enrolled in the Society and he pays the entrance dues, half goes to the treasury and half to the leaders, who have the right to do with it according to their discretion. According to the new rule, an event book should be created, and the treasurer is forbidden to reveal any of its details without an order from the leaders.

The crisis in the Society began in its fourth year. The members began to neglect their duties. On the first of Marheshvan in 5607 (1847), the following remarks were written in the record book:

"Although we established a 'Visiting the Sick Society' and each one committed when he joined the Society to give weekly whatever he felt he could and to spend the night with each sick person from the Society, according to the rules in the record book, but now, because of our transgressions, when times are bad, the members of the Society have stopped their donations and there is nothing left with which to aid the ailing. whether for cures or whether for other needs, therefore we have undertaken to strengthen the Society anew and to see that each person must give, week by week, that for which he is responsible, according to what was decided at the time of his admission to the Society.

[Page 51]

There should be no delays, not even a single week. Each one must spend a night with a sick person, when he is summoned by the leader. Otherwise he should pay someone else to spend the night and not find various excuses. But if, during the course of an entire month he should not give what is dues from him or he will not go to spend the night with a sick person when he is summoned, he will be expelled from the Society.

If one regrets that he has not donated or that he has not spent the night with a sick person, he must pay a fine, according to the leader's discretion. When someone is expelled from the Society, he cannot neglect what he had earlier pledged, neither through Jewish law nor through any other method, and no attention should be paid to his pleas."

In 5612, there is written in the record book a rule that shows that in the life of the Society arguments began to arise on the subject of honor. This rule goes thus:

"We see that there has a arisen a discussion and a conflict among the leaders over who should receive the pastries and brandy on the day of an election and who should oversee the elections. Because such arguments are sinful, in order to forestall disagreements among the leaders and the other members, it is decided that whoever is chosen as the first leader should provide a place for the cakes and brandy and for the election, and if he has no appropriate place in his home, he can choose a place in another member's house, and all the leaders and supervisors are forbidden to complain."

In the life of this Society there were several other longer pauses, but each time the Society renewed itself. The last time the Society renewed itself was in 5670, at which time it took on new leadership.

[Page 52]

The Appearance of Siedlce in the Nineteenth Century and the Number of its Inhabitants

The already mentioned Prof. Y Mikulski gives an accounting of the growth of the city during the nineteenth century.

Year	Number of Inhabitants	Number of Jews	Percentage of Jews
1821	4441	2908	65.5
1840	6471	4359	67.4
1855	7263	4804	66.1
1878	11931	8156	68.3
1897	15131	10094	66.7

The weak growth of the population in the nine years between 1846 and 1855 was, according to Prof Mikulski, because in 1845 the Podloski Gubernia was merged with the Lubliner. Siedlce ceased to be a Gubernia city. That resulted in the departure from Siedlce of several administrative offices and, with them, all the people who had interests in those offices[50].

In the thirties of the twentieth century maps of Siedlce from 1811, made by a certain Vattar, were found. They give us an idea of the construction of Siedlce at the beginning of the nineteenth century and of the building out of the eastern section of the town, that is, the area of the old city hall. Another map, from Colonel Winter, from 1829, focuses on the western part of the town, that is, the area of the prison. It seems that these are the oldest maps of Siedlce.

From these maps we can see that Florianski Street was built very badly. On that street there were altogether six wooden houses. Behind these houses were the so–called "pig–fields" with a "puddle" in the middle of the street.

[Page 53]

Sienkiewicza Street did not exist then. At that spot there was a city garden. (Hence its old name–Ogradowa Street–before it was called Sienkiewicza.) There were also no traces of the later hospital on Starawiesch. From the east side up to the shrine of the Countess Ogrinska, was a small garden, and by the shrine was a lake, which lay in the direction of the later gymnasium named after the Hetman Zhulkowski. There also was a broad horse ground that belonged to the palace. On the site of the later Teatralner Street there was a long, wooden, conspicuous theater, and behind that, another lake, which led to Posta Street; a hundred and thirty years later, the location of the lake was private property.

A large lake could also be found on what was called then, and later, Blagia Street. Not far from the spot was the building of the Pawshechner Shul. The length of the lake, which ran the length of the street, extended, according to Moshtow, for several fathoms. I somewhat smaller lake was on the other side of the area, where later on a Folk School was built. Beyond the lake there were city gardens on one side, from the right side until the slaughterhouse, and on the other side–the clayworks.

Of Jotka Street there was a portion–from Dluga to Broworna–that went further toward Prospect, which then had no name but then became known as the co–called "Jewish Brewery," because of which the street was later called "Broworna."

On the site of the later city hall (which was destroyed during the Second World War) and the firehouse the neighboring square–the site was then a horse market, so that the street, which before had been called Starynek, was given the name–Kanski–Rynek.

Warsaw Street, later Pilsudski, after the Second World War, during the rule of the Polish People's Democracy–"General Swierczewski"–at that time was known by the name of General Ruzhynsky out of gratitude, because he had saved the town from the Russians.

[Page 54]

The general's later deeds, however, persuaded them to change the name of the street. Brick houses then existed in the city. Between 1811 and 1829 there were nineteen or twenty, naturally not counting the town square with its buildings. The later, well–known tax office, the church, the later home for the priests, the town hall–an old brick house where later there was a club–and then a row of brick houses.

The Warsaw Highway was constructed in 1920.

On a map of the third and last Jewish cemetery–established in 1825–Kierkucki Street was called "The Old Warsaw Road," from which we can see that there was a road from Siedlce to Warsaw before the highway was built, through Kerkutzki Street. Actually, Warsaw Street went thus: Kerkutzki Street was the direction of the train line up to the village of Piaski. Then the road went to the Jalawitsch Woods, where houses were later built for the foresters, cut across a bridge over the stream and went on to Alt–Igan. From there, it went through the villages of Dombrowski and Tychy–to Warsaw.

The town market, between the prison and the Jewish hospital, was totally missing from both maps. On that spot there was the so–called town trench, which went in a straight line through the streets: Pilsudski, First of May Street, and then linked up with Okopawa Street. Then the trench cut through the location of the later cathedral and the built–up area between the cathedral and the Polish Bank.

Palna Street did not exist, but on the site of the later Glukhi Street there was a winding road that was a continuation of the Kerkutzki Street in the direction of the Old Warsaw Road. This street, or path, as it should be called, began near the second cemetery, on Shenkewitsch Street.

[Page 55]

Jewish Siedlce at the End of the Nineteenth Century

In 1894, Jewish Siedlce took part in an Enlightenment [Haskalah] publication in Yiddish that had the goal of fighting fanaticism in the three towns: Byala–Podolsk, Siedlce, and Janow.

The publication was called "Anti–Fanaticism." Its creators were: the Hebrew teacher Sholem Ratshin from the nearby town of Byala–Podolsk, together with a group of maskilim from the area, among them a certain Miss Saltzman from Siedlce. The character of the publication can be determined from its name–"Anti–Fanaticism". It was to conduct the work of enlightenment for the Haskalah and to fight against the fanaticism that flourished on the Jewish street. Although the Haskalah had established positions in Jewish life, the aforementioned journal was not published in Siedlce itself but in the neighboring town of Byala–Poldolsk, But Siedlce played a major role in the publication.

"Anti–Fanaticism" required no print shop, no administrative or technical personnel, because the newspaper was written by hand, by Ratshin himself, who made three copies. It was distributed in the towns of Siedlce, Byala, and Janow–one copy in each town.

The editor, Sholem Ratshin, was a Chekovian character. A zealous maskil, a proponent and enthusiast for Hebrew, whom the Orthodox had persecuted, agitating against him. They, the Orthodox, considered him a heretic and his newspaper a heretical publication. The maskilim, on the other hand, considered it a source of "wisdom"…they would read it with great curiosity and pass it from hand to hand.

Only three issues of "Anti–Fanaticism" appeared, and none of them still exist. Of the contents and existence of this remarkable journal, we know only from memories that appeared in "Polish Life." Following the example of Chekhov, we should print a poem that appeared in the first issue of "Anti–Fanaticism".

[Page 56]

The poem is called "Yisrolik"[51]. This "creation" illustrates the literary level of the periodical.

I have been homeless,
And now I am so as well.

Whoever has read my story
Knows how great is my strength.

Many rivers of blood
People have drained from me,
Yet I know full well
How great is my power.

How many troubles have I encountered
In the course of my life,
But I have never been ashamed
That the name "Jew" is my due.

Bathing in my blood
Over the smallest things,
Because they can never change
My name of Jew————[52]

At the end of the nineteenth century, the Siedlce Jewish writer Y. N. Weintroib told his memories of Siedlce's R. Avraham Nusboym, who was a friend of Alexander Tzederboym, the editor of "Ha–Meylets" ["The Tribune"], where Nusboym would publish correspondences. He also wrote for Polish newspapers. Nusboym even translated into Polish the poem "Tzion, halo tishalo" by R. Yehuda Halevi and the "Shemonah Prakim" of the Rambam. Also Yitzchak Lipetz and Kalman Galitzki, two well–known maskilim in Siedlce, wrote correspondences in a variety of papers.

About societal and cultural aspects of Siedlce at the end of the nineteenth century, we get an idea from two articles that were published in "Ha–Meylets," both in 1900, the first in February and the second in May. In order to provide a full picture of the economic and spiritual life of Siedlce's Jews at that time, we present the articles not in their chronological order.

[Page 57]

Z. Zchuchis in his article from "Ha–Meylets" in July of 1900 describes the economic life of Siedlce:

"Everything depends on luck, even a city! It happens that a secluded shtetl, as big as a person's hand, containing few inhabitants–its name may appear in the papers. It also happens that a large, populated city, known for its commerce, never appears in the list of the cities and is never cited in the papers, neither for good things nor for bad…Among cities with such bad luck must be reckoned Siedlce, one of the governmental centers in Poland. It is not mentioned often in the press, neither for good nor for bad, so I decided to visit there and publish my impressions. According to the census, a number of Jews live in Siedlce, eighteen thousand. Among them are, thank God, some who are wealthy who can do much for existing institutions and also influence their brothers, those who are poor in spirit and in goods. So might suppose the reader who is far away, but things are not so.

Let us just consider the material situation of the population. Lately the material situation of the whole world has gotten worse. Earnings are small, and in Poland there has been a lull in business and industry. So, for example, in the city of Siedlce there is no industry and no business, aside from small merchants and workers that we know from every city and shtetl, who subside on their backbreaking work. Everyone in Siedlce who gets a bit of money opens a little store, lays by a little merchandise and sells it on credit. Understandably, he gets no income thereby. But what should the poor fellow do, since he has no other option? There are in Siedlce more merchants than customers, and there is no building that does not house a business. The battle for existence is awful. If someone walks down the street, a merchant will fall on him and drag him into his shop, and a second into his.

[Page 58]

The pedestrian is astonished. The people with money in their pockets are usurers. And the citizens, having no options, are compelled to pay interest, which leads to interest upon interest.

So it is no wonder that in a short time they are bankrupt, so that they cannot exist."

Z. Zchuchis, in "Ha–Meylets," wonders about the more well–to–do Jews, with good resources, why they do not concern themselves with bettering the situation of the less fortunate. They could provide salvation for many destitute families. And they would also profit:

"If they understood, they would start to build factories. There is a broad field and a labor supply for a factory. Thousands of Jews would be able to find work. Is it not to be laughed at that in a governmental center like Siedlce there is not a single factory? Every Jew loves to imitate another. If a single Jew were to try to establish a factory and were to succeed , many Jews would follow suit. Just think of those merchants who sprout like mushrooms after a rainstorm…

…Also the moral situation is no better than the material. Charitable institutions that should moderate the situation of the needy do not exist in the whole city. If there is an organization called "Visiting the Sick" or "Charitable Loans," they are in disorder. The supervisors give no accounting and no one demands it of them. Is there, then, no such institution as a "G'milus Chasidim," especially at the present moment when the situation is so bad? Can one believe, as I say, that such institution do not exist? That if one becomes impoverished, he must starve to death. He has no prospect of a loan, except from the bloodsuckers. The truth is, there are a few goodhearted people who open their hands to help, to rescue the fallen and impoverished, but one swallow does not make a summer…How far the rich of Siedlce are from their brothers, their own flesh and blood, whose need does not touch them, we can demonstrate thus:

[Page 59]

Let us consider the published list of donors to the cause of the poor in Bessarabia who suffered from the drought–there we find not a single person from Siedlce! Not a kopek did they give! Why would the people of Siedlce distance themselves in such a way and isolate themselves from the larger world and ignore what was going on under their very noses?"[53].

Z Zchuchis ends his description with these critical remarks.

A little later there was published in the same paper ("Ha–Meylets," number 240, 11/2/1900) another critical article about Siedlce. The writer, Mordechai Krosunski, seems to have been a maskil, a Litvak, who visited Siedlce, described in "Ha–Meylets" the educational system that existed in the city at that time. He writes:

"They upheld already outdated customs. They held by the old ways of life and every early custom remained unchanged.

A Talmud–Torah building for poor children, such as exists in every town–no such thing, even though there are pushkes on the walls of every shul with the inscription 'a donation for the Talmud–Torah. ' Perhaps there is some mystery there…but there is no Talmud–Torah, and the young men grow up, to put it simply, without Torah and without learning.

Governmental schools, elementary and middle schools, are like those in all towns, but Jews have nothing to do with them. For the Jewish students, who make up five percent of the student population, there are only two local schools.

Further on, the writer characterizes the Jewish economy in Siedlce and comes to the conclusion that this is a result of the irrational educational system that existed in Poland at that time. Krasunski continues in his flowery style:

"The writer of these lines visited all sixty of the 'cheders' that exist in the city, and in none of them did he find a single student who knew Tanach.

[Page 60]

At the same time, the Lithuanian students in the town learned Tanach, because people engaged with these students. In one 'cheder' in which fifteen– and sixteen–year–olds from the wealthier neighborhoods were learning, I saw, to my great joy, the book of Isaiah. In answer to my questions, they said that last summer they had studied only as far as chapter four.–'And what prophetic books did you study after last summer? ' I asked. 'Only this book and nothing else… '

'How is that possible?'

"In the first week of the term we studied two chapters and in the last week of the term we studied another chapter…"

The teacher, who was present during this conversation, responded briefly and said that the study of loshon kodesh [Hebrew] had not been undertaken by the parents, and he himself was afraid of studying Tanakh, lest people say that he was a heretic…

Thus the Jews treat education, and that is the basic reason for the lack of responsibility for a good and useful thing. The study of Talmud is widespread, but as long as it lacks order and system, it is aimless. Except for a small portion of students, who excel in Torah, the rest are ignorant of Torah and empty of knowledge. They are faithful to all the traditions of their religion, but they have no deeply rooted examples except for habit…

Comparing this characteristically maskilic critic of Siedlce with the aforementioned judgment and the memories, we see that both articles, which appeared simultaneously, present Siedlce as an industrialized city unwilling to establish economic undertakings. M. Krosinski also discusses why no Talmud Torah building existed in the town and he surveys the prevailing educational system.

About the Talmud Torah building, the critic is correct, because at that time in Siedlce the Talmud Torah was in ruins. P. Dromi, who considered the Talmud Torah of that time when Krosinski published his article, tells us that at 71 Pyenkne Street, the same street that contained the Skerniyev Chassidic study house, there was a half–ruined house where there were four teacher who taught children.

[Page 61]

At that time, such was the Talmud Torah. The names of the teachers were: Yossl Tchetver–he taught the youngest children; the second was Avraham Ratinievitsch, known as "the Bubbe," because his wife, Esther Masha, was a midwife–he taught elementary Chumash; the third was Baruch Leibl Strussman, who had taught there for thirty–eight years–he taught Beginning Gemara; the fourth was Moyshe Mordechai Kirschenbaum, who was called Moyshe Mordechai with the Eye, because he was blind in one eye–he taught the older students Gemara and Tosafos. Over all, sixty students studied there. These students were poor. The Talmud Torah was supported by the congregations that used to collect a payment of a few kopeks each month. Also on special occasions, like weddings or circumcisions, people made donations. Even so, there was never enough to pay to teachers their poor wages and they often went hungry.

Three years later, after the publication of the articles in "Ha–Melitz," Siedlce acquired a real Talmud Torah building. The opening of this great building came on Thursday, the third of Elul in 1903. And as we already explained in an earlier chapter, it was supported by money given by the R. Yisroel Greenberg. The building cost 4,000 rubles. The dedication was magnificent. The rabbi of Siedlce, R. Shimon Dov Ber Analak made a speech about current affairs. The chazzan with his choir sang several chapters of Psalms. Later on there was a memorial service for the donor of the building, who had died in the meantime, and who had twenty–five years earlier built a beis–medresh. The widow of R. Yisroel Greenberg, who had financed the completion of the building, was given a "Mi Sheberach."[54].

The Talmud Torah building contained about fifteen rooms and was three stories tall. When the Polish government took over school and educational matters, the Talmud Torah was under the supervision of the general school people.

[Page 62]

Thus was the institution obliged to meet all the standards of hygiene and pedagogy. The Talmud Torah contained ten classes. There were times when two or three classrooms were parallel, since there were no more than eight classes, and two were used for community meetings. Thanks to the dozor R. Yisroel Gutgelt, who had ruled that the school should get a large percentage of the taxes on kosher slaughtering, the school could meet its budget.

After the First World War, the site was modernized. Secular studies were incorporated. Students learned the vernacular, Hebrew, arithmetic, drawing, history, geography, natural history, and other subjects. For the first time, there was a charge for tuition. There were about 400 students in the school.

Despite all the reforms, the school was still like an old–time cheder. The students worked from eight in the morning until seven in the evening, with an hour break in the afternoon, summer and winter. There was no summer vacation, nor walks for pleasure or nature walks. In the cheder the rabbi ruled with his whip. And even when secular studies were introduced, they took up only two hours of the day.

The Talmud Torah was managed by a group of trustees who were not elected by secret ballot nor by a council of parents, and were not nominated by the community. Among them were often the aforementioned businessmen Yisroel Gutgelt, Monish Ridel. Moyshe Chaim Levin, Moyshe Zagan, Sender Kantor, Henech Shteynberg (Kalushiger), Shloyme Shmuel Abarbanel, Yehonatan Eiberschutz, Velvel Orlovski, Yishayahu Zelikovitsch, Eliezer Shlifski, Yoysef Tcharnay. N. D. Glicksberg was for many years the chair of the group.

In 1922, Y. Gutgelt financed the opening of a locksmith workshop in the Talmud Torah. The donor's intention was that young men, after they finished the Talmud Torah, should be able to learn locksmithing. Until 1925, the workshop which was led by Yoysef Barg, was associated with the Talmud Torah.

[Page 63]

However, because none of the trustees were concerned about the students having a trade, the workshop stood nearly empty. It only served as a means for the building to make up for its large deficit. Thanks to the efforts of several businessmen, the building committee decided to convert the workshop into an independent institution. From then on, the workshop was occupied, but it existed only a short time until it was closed.

Speaking of the Talmud Torah, one should also mention the yeshiva, to which young men came who had finished the Talmud Torah and whose parents or guardians were interested in allowing their children to learn more Torah. The students in the yeshiva worked under a "supervisor," who would "declaim" a lesson from the Talmud and translate it. The students would repeat the lesson. Nothing besides Talmud and commentaries was studied in the yeshiva. On Fridays they would "review" the portion of the week. Prophets and Writings were considered not worth studying. Apparently this yeshiva was established in Siedlce in the seventies of the nineteenth century.

Actual evidence of the existence of the yeshiva we have from Fishl Dromi, who was himself a student of the yeshiva around the year 1900. He recounts that on Pienkne Street, in the house of R. Hershl Shlifka, the yeshiva operated under the leadership of R. Yisroel Drogotshiner, who was known by his familiar name of R. Yisroelele, a fanatical Jew who in his day sent out a appeal known as the "Souvenir of Faith," subscribed to by many rabbis, saying that people should not read newspapers. He would pray with three sets of tefilin–Rashi and Rabbeinu Tam–and at morning and afternoon prayers he would put on Rabbeinu Shimshon tefilin. Interestingly, R. Yisroel Drogoshiner brought from Kovrin a teacher named R. Yitzchak Tenenboym to study Russian with the students, but God forbid, no Hebrew, because that was considered heretical. After that, when the building secretary Chatkes went to Warsaw, Yitzchak Tenenboym took over as secretary. He was replaced as Russian teacher another Lithuanian Jew named Sheplan, a brother of the then popular healer Sheplan.

[Page 64]

R. Yisroel Drogoshiner left Siedlce after the pogrom. He was replaced as head of the yeshiva by R. Dovid Yitzchak Mendzezhenski Chasid. When the Talmud Torah was quartered in its own building, it was above the yeshiva, which had existed as a self–standing institution, until it was decided to convert it into a continuation of the Talmud Torah and it no longer existed as an independent yeshiva.

It is appropriate to note that after the year of revolution–1905–and after the pogrom, the idea arose in Siedlce's Orthodox circle to reform the educational system. This aspiration was expressed in a recommendation given by the then rabbi of Siedlce R. Shimon Dov Analik to a certain R. Leib Hutner in Warsaw. The letter, which can be found in a private archive[55] recommends: to consolidate the existing schools under the supervisory council that would collect tuition from parents. This council should pay the teachers' salaries and also have pedagogical oversight over both teachers and students, should select the students and assign them to the teachers, and so on. The rabbi made these recommendations several weeks before his death, when he was already ill and he left it as his testament.

He wrote: [the text follows in both Hebrew and Yiddish]

"Many people have long come to the conclusion that it is necessary to create in all cities special committees to oversee teachers and students. These committees should oversight over the schools. Their purpose should be to examine the students and separate them appropriately for the teachers. The parents should pay tuition to the committee, and the committee should pay the teachers. I have learned that the rabbi, the scholar, R. Leib Hutner, may he live long, the son of the great rabbi R. Yoryself Zindel, may he live long, from Warsaw, has the ability to effect these measures, which have long existed successfully in Warsaw. He already does much to promote Torah life, and the need is great. I have known him for a long time, the esteemed Rabbi Leib. He acts as the Torah demands. Therefore it is right to help him in all ways, and this should be made known to the Jews. Parents and teachers will see the benefits that will quickly accrue, and the Jews will be happy. Signed: today, Tuesday, the ninth of Kislev, 4667 [1907], in the holy congregation of Siedlce.

Sh. Ber ben Meir, may his memory be a blessing.

In Jewish Siedlce, as in most cities and towns in Poland, people looked with disdain on craftsmen. Handworkers were considered inferior to teachers, who, until marriage, lived at their parents' expense or on the kindness of others.–After marriage they would live at their in–laws' expense. The craftsman was considered inferior to a shopkeeper or to a moneylender. People mocked a craftsman, calling him an "angel keeper" [in Yiddish a pun–craftsman="bal–melakhah" and angel keeper="bal–malakh"]. A butcher was called derogatory names. People jokingly said that a butcher attracts two pigs through one hole. [An explanation follows, but since I do not understand the intricacies of butchering, I have no idea what it means.]

[Page 66]

The same attitude applied to tailors. Butchers and tailors were regarded as something less than human. At the beginning of the twentieth century, this attitude changed. Jews recognized that productivity was important. The Zionist and Pioneer movements also helped, because they regarded labor as an ideal in life, as did the Jewish socialists, who put the working class at the head of the table in community life.

We will consider at length the chief labors that occupied the people of Siedlce.

Construction Workers

The first trade that Jews adopted in Siedlce was construction and related skills, such as : bricklaying, carpentry, and locksmithing.

These trades developed because Siedlce, as a government city, had a government administration. The bureaucrats required places to live, and houses became a source of income, so people undertook building. The frequent fires, about which we have already written, destroyed houses, which were then rebuilt, thanks to the city's credit bureau, which for this purpose gave credit to every householder, who had only to ask for building credit. The bureau made no distinction between Jews and gentiles. Consequently, Jews built and Jewish master craftsmen, with their children and their laborers, could earn a living. And among these laborers there were always some Poles.

Around 1902, when the Jewish workers began to organize and fight for better working conditions, the Christian workers saw that they should not be completely dependent on the Jewish master craftsmen; they could themselves become masters, take their own orders, and become self–sufficient. They did not join the fight of their Jewish comrades. The Christian building workers organized themselves into a union and began to fight against their former breadwinners–the Jewish builders.

[Page 67]

The Christian union began to take orders and fulfill them. However, thanks to the city–president Dombrowski, who was liberal to the Jewish population, the Christian union did not achieve its goal. Dombrowski summoned to his home several Jewish masters, advised them to go to the government and to remind them about an ordinance from 1816 concerning the rights of unions. The city–president also tried to work on the Christian master craftsmen, so that they would accept into the union the Jewish masters. This intervention had no effect on the Christians. Their union was endangered. According to the rules, a union had to have at least ten members. Since there were not ten members, the Christians found Christian craftsmen from the area around Siedlce, so that they ended up with ten and preserved their union.

The Jewish masters were not organized but acted individually. This lasted for several months, until an answer was received, but meanwhile the Christians replaced the Jewish masters in their accustomed jobs.

In 1912, at the suggestion of the bishop of Chelm, Yevlogi, the government of Siedlce moved to Chelm and the building boom ended. The bureaucrats left their apartments, so that there were now empty apartments and no tenants.

Butchers

Butchering was the most widespread trade in Siedlce. Even in the nineteenth century, boots from Siedlce were known throughout Russia. Merchants would come to Siedlce from deep inside Russia, stay for a few weeks, and return home with great transports of boots.

The master butchers were divided into two categories: one was called "Urzhendawa," that is, craftsmen who would work on orders from clients and excel in good work. And "work at home" craftsmen, or "small masters," who would get their material from large merchants and do their work at home."

[Page 68]

Before the First World War, there were in Siedlce about 150 of the first type and about 200 of the second, that is, about 350 proficient butchers.

The situation in the trade was satisfactory. All the butchers and their employees were able to sustain themselves honorably. The greatest commotion in the trade came in the winter months. At that time the contracted transports that had been agreed upon in the summer were sent out.

Every butcher felt that he had an economic support under his feet. Even if he had money problems, he could come for help to the office of S. B. Minin and Arzhel. They would give money or discount the coming bills for inventory. So things went until the outbreak of the First World War in 1914.

Boot Leather Cutters

This trade was tied up with shoemakers. The fate of the shoemakers was the same as the fate of the leather cutters.

This trade had the same two categories that were mentioned earlier–the "Urzhendawa" and the "commercial," who worked for export. Around 1910 there were 34 leather–masters and 80 workers. With the outbreak of the First World War, there was a falling off of demand, but the military orders provided work.

After the war, the number of leather–cutters increased. This happened because unemployed journeymen opened their own shops. Competition grew. Seventy–five percent of leather–cutters were unemployed.

Tailors

On the eve of the First World War, there were 35 master tailors in Siedlce, in five categories. The first and most prestigious category were the military tailors, who were called "colonels." Because many military men were quartered in Siedlce, these five tailors made a good living, though there was something of a lull in the summer months, when the military men were away on maneuvers.

[Page 69]

The second category of tailors–12 Jews and one Christian–worked for Polish landowners and clerks. They also had a good income.

The remaining three categories were: 5 ladies' tailors, 9 old–clothes tailors, and 4 village tailors. The number of tailor employees, both qualified and unqualified, amounted to 65. This number does not include female tailors and sewers.

The status of this trade was good. Not only was there no unemployment but there was a shortage of workers. Consequently Siedlce would get apprentice tailors from the poorer villages.

The Zionist Movement Before the First World War

For the Jews of Siedlce, as it was for most religious Jews in all the cities and shtetls of Poland, the longing for Eretz Yisroel filled their hearts for generations, long before the arrival of Khivas Tzion and the Zionist movement. Already at the end of the seventeenth century Siedlce's R. Yehuda the Chasid arose as the head of a messianic movement that sought through various means to make aliyah to Eretz Yisroel.

The name of R. Yehuda the Chasid, of this remarkable religious personality, was firmly bound up with the city of Siedlce. We have no certain information about his childhood years, and we also do not know whether he was born in Siedlce or whether he settled in the city. Form all of our sources that touch on the life of R. Yehuda the Chasid it is clear that this messianic dreamer lived in Siedlce and from there in 1699 began his journeying to Eretz Yisroel.

Many historians, including Sh. A. Haradetzki, incorrectly hold that R. Yehuda the Chasid was from Shidlowietz rather than from Siedlce[56]. In the sources his home town is called "Siedlce near Gorodno." Siedlce, it should be understood, cannot be confused with Shilowietz, which has nothing to do with Grodno (Gorodno). Shidlowietz is in the Kielce Woiwodship, and Siedlce is much nearer to Grodno.

[Page 70]

That R. Yehuda was from Siedlce is shown also by the fact that he was accompanied by people from the poor shtetls around Siedlce and went with them to Eretz Yisroel. Thus, for example, one of his students was R. Gedaliah from Semyatitch, a shtetl close to Siedlce, about forty kilometers away. In the book "Seek the Peace of Jerusalem"[57] that R. Gedaliah wrote, he mentions a Chasid named Zalmen Beilar, who was called Bialer, who was apparently from Biala–Podolsk. Biala is near Siedlce. It is therefore beyond any doubt that R. Yehuda the Chasid was from Siedlce. We will therefore in the history of our Siedlce community include the activities of R. Yehuda the Chasid and his pilgrimage to Eretz Yisroel.

His leaving Siedlce and his journey were the result of a messianic movement that began in Poland spread to Germany, Moravia, Austria, Hungary and went as far as Italy. Because of the confusion that followed, this movement also attracted followers of Sabbatai Zvi, led by Chaim Malach. The aim of this movement was to bring redemption by refining the morals, doing penitence, prayer, fasting, and asceticism. We must consider that this movement arose fifty years after the decrees of 1648 and 1649.

R. Yehuda the Chasid left Poland at the end of 1699, together with 120 followers. On the way, as they went through various countries, he gathered more followers. His camp eventually numbered 1500 souls. About 500 died on the journey. The remaining 1000 arrived in Eretz Yisroel. Their camp was called "Chevra Kadisha" (Sacred Fellowship). Some of them had traveled from Poland to Moravia. From there they sent messengers to Germany. R. Yehuda the Chasid himself, together with three companions, came to Frankfort–am–Main and there on Shabbos Ha–Gadol he gave a sermon that caused a great awakening. He also went into the women's section holding a Torah scroll and preached to the women.

[Page 71]

His sermons were full of admonitions to lead a moral life, and he said that the world was ready for redemption. In Frankfort he raised a great deal of money for his expenses. Shmuel Oppenheimer, the advisor to the emperor's court in Vienna, gave much help to the pilgrims–he gave them passports and fitted two ships to take them to Constantinople. Some of the pilgrims, led by R. Yehuda the Chasid, went through Venice. A second group, with Chaim Malach, the follower of Sabbatai Zvi, went through Dniester, on the Black Sea, to Constantinople.

What happened later to the pilgrims has nothing to do with our history. Our only purpose was to show the relationship of R. Yehuda the Chasid with Siedlce.

But R. Yehuda was not the only one; there were cases when Jews from Siedlce left their home town, their source of income, their close relatives, and went far away–to Eretz Yisroel. Older Jews who decided to go to Eretz Yisroel without the assent of their wives, sons, daughters, and grandchildren left their wives, tore apart their family life, but would not let their journey be interrupted.

In the middle of the nineteenth century a learned Jew from Siedlce, a shochet named Avraham Avraham's, went up to Eretz Yisroel. He was born in Siedlce in 1801. When he was 36 years old, he left Siedlce and emigrated to London. There he became a shochet. He wrote several books about the laws of ritual slaughter. His most popular book was "Bris Avraham"–a commentary on the Shulchan Aruch "Yoreh De'ah," the laws of ritual slaughter. He also published an autobiographical work "Va–yiskor le'Avraham." In 1879, Avraham's left London and went to Jerusalem, where he built a house, and shortly thereafter he turned the house over to a fellowship called "Mishkenos Yisroel" as a prayer house. Avraham's died in Jerusalem in 1880.

As soon as the Bilu Aliyah began in 1882 [a student movement for agricultural settlements in Palestine that began after the pogroms of 1881], the thought of Jewish settlements in Eretz Yisroel spread in Siedlce and the surrounding communities. A group of Jews from Mezrich in 1883 went to Eretz Yisroel and proceeded to establish there the colony Yesod Hamalah, on the west bank a river.

[Page 72]

The experiences of these pioneers, the hardships they underwent in realizing their dream, the sacrifices they made to fever, hunger, before Baron Rothschild assumed responsibility for the existence of the colony, the shortage of water–all of this reverberated in the hearts of Siedlce's Jews, who thirstily absorbed the news that came from nearby Mezrich.

The dignified Khibas–Tzion movement had already established a foothold in Siedlce. At the movement's first conference, held in Katowice in 1884, the delegates from Siedlce were R Moyshe Goldberg and Yehoshua Goldfarb. In the city there was a chapter of "The Committee for the Support of Jews who Work the Land in Syria and Palestine," which was also known as the "Odessa Committee," although in fact it was an affiliate of the Khivas–Tzion, which was officially outlawed in Russia. Gradually the Khivas–Tzion circle grew. To it belonged most of the Chasidic young people, who drew close to it through nationalistic Haskalah writings. In secret meetings, ostensibly engagement parties for a young men and women or weddings, word spread about Khivas–Tzion ideology. They sang the popular song of Levinzon:

[quotes from "The Flower," which is actually by Eliakum Zunser]

Ahad Ha'am's polemic against the Chovevei Tzion [another Zionist movement] found a good reception in Siedlce. When he founded his secret organization "B'nei Moyshe," it included several Siedlce Jews.

[Page 73]

In any case, the name of Yehoshua Goldfarb was known as a member of the "B'nei Moyshe."

At that time the rabbi of Siedlce was the already mentioned R. Shimon Dov Analik, who was noted for his strong opposition to Zionism, just as he was opposed to Chasidism. An ideological struggle broke out among the Jews of Siedlce. In Zionism alone there were three factions: "Khivas–Tzion" "Political Zionism," and the spiritual center. There was a particular conflict between orthodoxy and Zionism. And opposing all of these movements was the Bund, whose activities in Siedlce began at the same time as Zionism and which regarded Zionism as a bourgeois movement.

There were discussions that more than once ended with fisticuffs. But the Zionist movement sank deep roots in Siedlce. It was an organization whose activities had a wide appeal among the masses. The Colonial Bank spread money and actions around.

In letters in "Ha–Melitz" from that time, signed with the pseudonym "Yehudi," the Zionists' efforts in Siedlce were criticized.

At that time there also appeared in "Ha–Melitz" letters entitled "Poor Thoughts," under the pseudonym "Yehudi," which sharply criticized Zionistic activities in Siedlce and lamented the weak activities of the Colonial Bank. Yehudi also wrote about the sermons that Rabbi Analik delivered against Zionism[58].

When we compare the letters of Yehudi with the memories of Fishl Dromi, we can come to the conclusion that not everything that appeared in "Ha–Melitz" was absolutely true. It is possible that the widespread actions of the Colonial Bank were feeble, but in Siedlce they were no more feeble than in other cities in Poland. This shows the continuing development of Zionism in Siedlce.

When the Keren Kayemes L'Yisroel was established in 1901, the Zionist movement in Russia was in jeopardy.

[Page 74]

The Keren Kayemes stamps could not be distributed, and funds could not be collected openly. But the Zionist activists risked their freedom and began to distribute Keren–Kayemes pushkes, which were smuggled in from Cologne (Germany), which was then the headquarters of the Keren–Kayemes. The pushkes were smuggled across the Russian border to Bendin, From there, a devoted activist named A. Liver, took the pushkes to Siedlce. One time, a transport that had been sent to Siedlce fell into the hands of the police. It appears that the work that had been done in Siedlce satisfied the central bureau of the Zionist movement, because Dr. Yechiel Tchlenov, the president of Keren Kayemes, sent a letter of appreciation, which was found in the Keren Kayemes office.

The Zionist organization in 1901 established a library, which a couple of years later was given the neutral name of "Ha–Zmir." This shows that in Siedlce the Zionist movement soon after its beginning had created favorable ground for its activities.

Community Libraries

Yitzchak Lipietz's Secular Library

A library existed in Siedlce from the end of the nineteenth century. The owner of this library was Yitzchak Lipietz, a book dealer, who would sit between minchah and ma'ariv in the assembly room and study with the everyday Jews the portion of the week. Lipietz was a maskil, a writer of popular books and commentaries, someone who knew current Haskalah writings, medieval Jewish poetry, and Jewish philosophy. He had collected about a hundred books and lent them to readers for a weekly payment.

At that time in Jewish Siedlce, modern ideas were beginning to circulate. This was a national movement. Already a workers' movement was developing.

[Page 75]

This community movement urged its adherents to read books, so the circle of readers expanded.

Thus was created the foundation for the rise of several libraries, which could not happen for two reasons: the czarist regime regarded libraries and the reading of books as forbidden things that could endanger the foundations of the reactionary, anti–Semitic regime. In order to start a library, according to the law, people had to obtain permission, which they could not get. The second condition that prevented the arrival of libraries was Jewish orthodoxy. The religious sector in Siedlce considered the reading of any books aside from Gemara, books of Halacha, and responsa as heresy. Even the reading of Tanakh was regarded with suspicion. A reader of a secular book was persecuted, and such a thing as a library was an outlandish phenomenon.

So Yitzchak Lipiets would distribute his books in secret.

In 1900, a group of young maskilim, led by Yoysef Rosenvasser, founded a secret community library. It attracted Zionist and nationally inclined elements. This library had to withstand many vexations and had to serve different generations. Its directors had to worry that the government could learn of its existence and confiscate the books. There was also a fear that those involved with the library could be arrested. Nevertheless, the founders nurtured the library with dedication and fidelity. They would purchase books with their own money. The library received a great deal of support in the form of books and money from the already mentioned Russian officer Baron von Kleist. [I remember no such mention.]

On March 15, 1904, the oft–mentioned activist Y. N. Vayntroyb received governmental permission to start a library. The permission was granted to Vayntroyb's son–in–law Mordechai Meir Landoy, who was himself a community and Zionist activist. The library, according to political restrictions, could not be legally considered a community institution. In a brochure that appeared on the library's twenty–fifth anniversary, in 1926[59], was printed the text of the permission, which we offer in Yiddish translation:

[Page 76]

Ministry of the Interior
Siedlce Region
Chancellery
March 15, 1904
Number 1631
Siedlce

Permission

In the name of the third section, chapter 2, 14th volume of the codex concerning publication and censorship, the current permission is granted to the citizen of Siedlce, resident of the shtetl of Orleh, quarter of Belz, district of Grodno, Mordechai–Meir Landoy, the right to open and maintain a secular library with Russian, Polish, Yiddish, German, and French works that will be approved by the censor, on the condition that Landoy will take upon himself according to the law the full responsibility for maintaining the stock and he is responsible for following all existing and possibly forthcoming laws and orders regarding book handlers and secular libraries.

In significance thereof we give to Landoy this permission, which is signed and sealed.

Stamp–tax is paid
Governor Voikov
Head of the Chancellery Chveshtshenko

Thus began a new chapter in the developmental history of the library, which was, at that time, the only cultural institution in the city. Gradually the members of the library began to divide themselves into study groups for Jewish history and Tanakh. There was also a secret Zionist group and a drama circle. At that time the library held 1200 books. The library's popularity grew, and the founders, themselves Zionists, directed the library in an impartial way.

[Page 77]

But because those years were tumultuous and in the Jewish streets there were struggles between two parties–both illegal–the Zionists and the socialists, the socialists sought to gain control of the library. There were a number of struggles, but the library remained neutral.

The czarist government did not lose sight of the library and often sent policemen to conduct searches and to confiscate forbidden books. Such were considered the socialist and Zionist publications. Understandably, when they were informed about such searches, people removed such books until after the danger had passed.

The Jewish Revolutionary Movement Around 1905

Siedlce, as we have written elsewhere, had no large industrial base. Understandably, then, Siedlce also lacked a large proletarian sector. In hindsight, a change arrived in 1900.

At that time a great movement began in Siedlce. It came after a huge fire that wiped out an important portion of the city. The burnt–out householders, after they received their insurance payouts, or, as they were called, their "firecash," were determined to rebuild their destroyed wooden or brick houses. Thus there arose a social class of contractors, who undertook the labor for the homeowners. The contractors were known as "padryatchkes" (from Russian, meaning "initiators" or "providers"). These people carried out the work with hired laborers, who were called "associates." The growth of building jobs led to the increase in other trades, such as: masons, locksmiths, carpenters, and housepainters. These tradesmen worked in the city as long as there was work; when the work paused, or when there was a quarrel between contractors, the workers went to neighboring towns or big cities: Warsaw, Brisk, Bialystok, and Lodz.

[Page 78]

They worked there and on holidays they would come home to Siedlce, to their parents and relatives, to celebrate the holiday together. The return to Siedlce after working in other places for some months, encountering other workmen and their impressions that they shared– this was something to experience! On holidays, Siedlce boiled like a kettle.

This is how the life of Jewish workers in Siedlce seemed at the beginning of the 20th century: When parents determined that their child had a "bad head," and were disappointed that they could not make him a student, that child, who had not yet even had a bar mitzvah, was given to a craftsman as an apprentice. The master received a certain sum of money for teaching his trade and kept the young man with him for four years. Truthfully, though, the young man learned little. The master's wife ruled over him. The poor young man had to carry out the master's bidding, whether it had something to do with his trade or not, such as: carrying water, doing the shopping, rocking the children, and so on. In short, he was a hewer of wood and schlepper of water. At the end of four years, the apprenticeship ended; he was "released from apprenticeship." The apprentice received a new title, a "year–young man." As a reward for his work, he received a small sum of money for the year. After that year, the "year young man" became a "season young man"–that is, he would be paid for a half year, and only after working for several "seasons" would he become a "week man."

The workday for such a worker in summer went from sunrise to sunset, and in winter until late into the night. When Shabbos or a holiday was over, the worker would change from his Shabbos clothing into work clothes and hurriedly go to his work in order to make up the time that he had lost by stopping early on Friday. There was no lunch hour and no rest time–certainly not. Relations between masters and their workers was rough and unpleasant.

[Page 79]

The Bund and the P.P.S. and their Effect on Siedlce's Jewish Workers

At that time, around 1900, there were already activities from the "General Jewish Workers' Alliance of Poland, Russia, and Lithuania" [the Bund]. On the Polish streets the P.P.S. [the Polish Socialist Party] was active, and it also did work among the Jews. Both groups had begun to grow and organize activities in Siedlce, and they led a propaganda campaign against the czarist regime and a battle to improve the living conditions of workers.

The leader of the Bund was Avraham Yablon, a carpenter who had come from a religious family. He was a grandson of Chaim Shloymo Yablon, a well–known grocer in Siedlce. Yablon worked several years in Warsaw and had there joined the "Bund." He became well–versed in the party's literature and became involved in Warsaw with the propaganda for the Bund and active in the illegal organization. Avraham Yablon was the founder of the Bundist organization in Siedlce.

The leader of the Jewish group in the P.P.S. was Avraham Kadish. In later years he went to America, where he lived until around 1947. In his last years he developed a love for Eretz Yisroel. Part of his possessions he donated for the establishment of a cultural center through the Histadrut [General Organization of Workers] in Acco (Israel), in memory of his home town, Siedlce.

Nest to him was Yudl Mastboym, a young man, barely seventeen years old, the son of Itzl Mastboym, himself a rebellious type. The writer Yoel Mastboym, Yudl's brother, says this about his father the rebel: "My father used to put his hands on the buffet at the tavern and tell himself or listen to the heroic stories of Christians and Jews in the rebellion against the 'lords,' hear a curse on the Russian czar from the peasants or curse him himself. He would shock the peasants by informing them

that Moyshe Rabbeinu was a socialist and the "Pan Jesus" was a mentsch"[60]. The whole Mastboym family, aside from Mrs. Mastboym and her son Yoel, were active in the revolutionary movement.

[Page 80]

Yudl Mastboym's revolutionary activities are described by the lawyer A.M. Hartglass in his introduction to the Hebrew translation of Yoel Mastboym's "The Red Life":

That must have happened in 1906. The revolutionary himself was not brought to the court proceedings because he was lying ill in jail. His defense, two famous lawyers–Bernzan and Makovsky (the latter was the justice minister in independent Poland before the Second World War) conducted the defense of "Smaluch," which was the pseudonym of Yudl Mastboym (who, when he was small, would look for buttons in the gutters). Makovsky–Hartglass says–undermined the accusation and repeated that the Russian Empire trembled before "Smaluch." This provoked laughter from the judge. Then Yudl Mastboym was sentenced to hard labor for life in Siberia[61]. He was sent away and no one knows how his life ended.

The mood for revolution grew among the Jewish workers in Siedlce. Edelshtat's song "In Conflict" was very popular. Here is how it begins:

> We are hated and pursued,
> We are plagued and followed
> And all because we love
> The poor, languishing folk.
> We would be shot, hanged,
> We are robbed of our lives, of
> our rights,
> Because we long for truth
> And freedom for poor people…

The Bund's influence grew quickly. The party gained many adherents, mostly religious young people, half maskilim, middle class young men, dressed in Polish–Jewish style–a "vented" kaftan, opened behind to the waist and a small cloth hat on the head. Many of them in time became craftsmen. Women also belonged, most of them seamstresses, who were taken up with the movement. The "chaverim," as they were called, often held secret gatherings, at which they discussed political questions and sought solutions for bettering the lives of the poor.

[Page 81]

The P.P.S. also increased propaganda among Siedlce's Jews. Characteristically, the more Polish party included the Chasidic young people, who did not even know any Polish. To the P,P.S. also belonged the slaughterhouse workers and such strong characters. They were impressed that the P.P.S. was not concerned with theories but only with practical terrorist actions. The most active members of the P.P.S. were Moyshe Kalmanovitsch (known as "Gabbai," because his father was a zealous Chasid and gabbai in the Kotzk prayer house", Yisroel Zimmerman ("Badchan") Michael Agresboym, Moyshe Chasid ("Chasid"), Mendel Radzinski, Avraham Federman ("Schnitzer"), Asher Levita, Yosl Schloss, Chaim Serkhei (known as "Ketsche"). They all worked under the leadership of Avraham Kadish.

The activities of the Bund were led by Eliyahu Vira, Tuvia Kagan, Shaul Zubrovitsch (known as "Vyetrok" because his home was full of talk [This involves a Russian pun.], Shloyme Stolovy, a student in the fourth level of the gymnasium, Moyshe Lies, Yakov Ratinyevitsch, Zalmen Burshteyn, and Yakov Liverant.

Both parties–the Bund and the P.P.S.–conducted their activities conspiratorially. When the number of associates had greatly increased, they began to gather in the "People's Tearoom," which was located in a big house at the edge of the market. The "People's

Tearoom" was "project" of the local czarist government and was established in 1902. This was supposed to be a kind of "cultural center" for the czarist functionaries and also a place to divert the masses from the secret revolutionary movements. There one could get hot water, also known as "kipiotek," and, on request, flavorings. Sugar one had to purchase. There one could read the official Russian–government newspapers, play dominoes, engage in conversations, and so on.

So the czarist "cultural house" became a meeting spot for the members of the Bund, who gathered there and held discussions and conversations. The situation, however, became known to the police, who spied on the place and conducted searches and made arrests.

[Page 82]

A History of the Jews in Siedlce (cont.)

The Conspiratorial Activities of the Bund

Because of the newly developed situation, the organization was compelled to provide a secret apartment. One of the Bundists–Meir Vica–had rented a dwelling, a room with a kitchen, on a roof from the homeowner Mendel Liverant. The house was located on Pzhechadniya Street, across from the police station. Furthermore, the house had a second advantage: the courtyard cut through to another street, Pienkne Street. They figured that in case of a search, people could escape through the back street. In order not to attract the attention of the neighbors, they brought into the dwelling a few poor furnishings, like the furniture of a new tenant, and in front they put a sign for a book bindery–Meir Vica's profession.

In this apartment, the leadership of the Bund met to arrange the organizational work. Most of the members of the Bund had no knowledge of the existence of this secret apartment, in which the activists gathered late at night. There was an agreed–upon way to knock on the door. Before the door would be opened, one had to say the password.

The Bundists had to consider the question of their proclamations and literature. They decided to use hectography for their announcements. The assignment was given to three members of the Bund: Zalmen Burshteyn (Fritzl), Yakov Liverant, and the already mentioned Ratinyevitsch. They worked in the stamping factory of Yakov Lerner. When Lerner was occupied in the city, the three journeymen prepared a hectograph and carefully took it to the secret apartment. There they copied proclamations that were distributed among the workers. The proclamations clarified the crushing economic conditions of the workers, their lack of political rights, and their lost freedom. The workers were called on to struggle under the banner of the Bund. The hectograph was fully in use, since they published not only leaflets but also brochures that were bound in oilcloth covers and passed from hand to hand.

[Page 83]

The workers would devour this material thirstily. They believed that this propaganda material came from Warsaw.

A characteristic story involves the party member Yakov Liverant, who was called "Pentak." He was the custodian of the party's literature, which he hid in a recess in his parents' home. On the first of May there was an alarm in the city that the police were conducting searches. Liverant's father, knowing that in the recess there was illegal Bundist literature, took it out and burned it. Shortly thereafter, Liverant went to find the published material, for which he had risked his life, but he found nothing. He went angrily to his father in the smoking room and demanded the material. His father told him that for his sake, and for the sake of the whole organization, he had destroyed the material. Pentak did not want to hear this, stood his ground and again demanded the literature. Then he invoked "sanctions" against his father: he stood in the shop and interfered with business. When a customer came to buy cigarettes, he would denigrate the product. The conclusion was thus: Moyshe Yehoshua Liverant went to the Bund and pleaded with them to intercede with his son. The organization's judgment was that he should pay a fine, which he paid to the Bund out of shame.

In Y. Lerner's stamping factory they also secretly made the party stamp, which was a globe with the words "General Jewish Bund of Russia, Lithuania, and Poland, Siedlce." In the center of the stamp–two hands giving shalom Aleichem–the symbol of unity.

The organization continued to grow, so that Mendel Liverant's room was too small. People could not go to the "People's Tearoom" because of police tricks, so the organization created an "exchange." The organization was divided into groups of five to ten members. At appointed times–particularly Shabbos afternoon–people went out into the street, into Warsaw Street–the section from the hospital to the military square.

[Page 84]

There the members of the Bund gathered. They walked here and there. Literature was distributed there and the organizer of the group would enlighten the members about the status of the worker class and its duty to fight for a better life. These walks ended with the posing of questions, which the agitator tried to answer. Some of the agitators had the great confidence of the members, and what they said was taken as the ultimate truth. Such agitation finally gave rise to the first strike in the city.

The Organization of the Stamp Workers and the First Strike

As a result of socialist propaganda, whether from the Bund or from the P.P.S., intense relations developed between the owners and the workers, merchants and employees. In addition, the maidservants were taken up by the agitation that had promised to free the working men from a foreign yoke.

There was a heavy influx to the Bund from the building trades, among which was also the carpentry trade. Among the Bund activists were two carpentry workers–Meirl and Liess. Also Avraham Yablom, the founder of the Bund in Siedlce, was a carpenter, and although he worked in Warsaw, he had great authority in Siedlce. He would often visit his home town and locate among his fellow tradesmen zealous and spiritual Chasidim, such as: Itsche "Kepl" (Gelbard), the sons of Chevel (Glazman), Alter Shmuel Yoseles (Yablon), Avraham's cousin), Yishayahu Brenovitski, Leibush "Kop", Leibl "Kozeh" (Sheynboym), Yankel Marcusfeld, Dovid Tchutchikel,(Maltchinski) and Alter Malach (Zilberboym). Carpenters active in the Bund were: Noah Skolker, Chaim Mordechai Stankevitsch, Mattis, and others.

The workers' experiences among the building trades were the same as among the shoemakers: they worked for eighteen hours a day. On Thursdays and the days before holidays they worked the whole night, and in wintry conditions. When Shabbos was over they immediately after havdalah went back to work. The situation was such that the carpenters were the first to go on strike.

[Page 85]

Organized and methodical were the preparations for the strike. The organization had planned meetings of ten to fifteen people at which the significance of the strike was explained. Then it was put to a vote. Almost everyone favored the strike. The last meeting, which was held on the second day of Pesach, was conducted in the same way as all the others: passwords and patrols from the city along the way to the meeting–in the hall of the "Piaskes," on Lukaver Way. There all the workers from the carpentry trades, after speeches from the leaders, unanimously voted to declare a strike of all the carpentry workers in Siedlce.

During chol ha–moed, the workers used to come to the bosses to figure out the prospects for the whole season and to discuss work for the coming season. This time, the carpentry workers gave no clear answer to the bosses about further work. In the city people had already talked about the coming strike and soon after Pesach the bosses of those trades received the following demands: 1) a twelve–hour workday; 2) an hour and a half for lunch and an half hour for breakfast ; 3) work from hour to hour; 4) better conditions. These demands, topped by the Bund's stamp, ended with a comment that no worker would show up for work if the demands were not subscribed to. And there were separate demands for the apprentices: not being required to do housework, not to be insulted, learning the trade, and others.

At first the bosses belittled the whole thing: "Do I know what's going on? Those guys are being foolish, sending summonses, threatening with 'srikes' [sic]. Who asked them?" The bosses agreed that none should submit to the demands. But the season was looming, and the workshops stood empty. Some of the bosses dealt with the leaders of the organization and accepted the demands. For others, the strike went on. There was a bloody battle with some tough guys from the trade who were strikebreakers, but their strength did not help. The first strike of Siedlce's workers ended in victory.

[Page 86]

It was hard for the bosses to get used to the idea that the workers could have an opinion about the workshops. After the strike, there were still conflicts and fights. For calling out at work, "Lunch, comrade," a carpentry boss threw a plane [woodworking tool] at the worker Yehoshua Hablen and broke his nose. The workers made a judgment against him and he was forced to pay a fine to the organization. Hablen ended up with a crooked nose, of which he was as proud as he would have been of a war wound.

The successful strike of the carpenters greatly increased the prestige of the organization. It attracted sympathizers and adherents. It was already too crowded in the secret apartment of the Bund. The overflow went out to the street, from the hospital corner to the military square. The agitators came there and explained to the workers their economic and political situation.

The agitation worked. There were new strikes. The painters went on strike. Because that trade included Poles, the strike was led by the P.P.S. and the Bund. After the painters, the leather and needle workers went on strike. The strikes ended with victory for the workers. In Siedlce people began to work a 12–hour day with a break for lunch. Also, earnings went up. The Bundist organization became prominent in the city. But the czarist secret police also became interested.

Arrests and the Bund's Illegal Activities

It did not last long, The government followed the clues to the "conspiratorial apartment" of the Bund. This came a short time after the carpenter's strike in the spring of 1903. In the middle of the night, the gendarmes came, led by Ratmistzh Bialapoldski, with police led by the police chief Shedever, and secretly entered the dwelling and conducted a thorough search.

[Page 87]

The czarist police dismantled the floor and there found the whole archive, which consisted of illegal literature and a hectograph. The owners of the house, the "master bookbinder" Meirl Liebfreund" with his "apprentice" Tuviehleh Kagan, were arrested and taken to the well–known Siedlce prison.

After the first political arrests cam more arrests. In the course of a single week, these members of the Bund were arrested: Yankel the "Bubbe's" (Ratiinievitsch), Max (Shoyme Stolovey), Moyshe Liess, and the "Langer Kiveh." At Moyshe Liess' place they found illegal literature. The hiding place of the literature was revealed by an informer. After being confined for a year, Moyshe Liess was released. He arrived home sick with the final stages of tuberculosis, and he died shortly after. His death called forth a great outpouring in the city. All the parties took part in the funeral. The comrades honored his parents' request that there not be songs nor speeches. Everyone expressed his honor for the deceased in a different way: when the wagon arrived, the comrades unharnessed the horses and themselves pulled the wagon to the cemetery. At the grave, delegates from each party laid garlands of flowers.

The Siedlce prison where the political prisoners were confined had a reputation in the criminal world. At that time, on the eve of the Revolution of 1905, there was a special section for political criminals. Thirty–some persons were imprisoned there, including well–known political prisoners from Russia. Even Dzherzhinsky, who later led the G.P.O. [known in the West as OGPU] is supposed to have been confined there. The regime there was easy. The political prisoners enjoyed privileges. Those from the intelligentsia gave talks to the general population and created new activists. Those who left the prison were educated.

The arrests of the real Bundist leaders in Siedlce did not hinder the movement. Instead it soon called forth new strong leaders: Esther Mastboym, the sister of the writer Yoel Mastboym, Itshele Stalav (a stamp worker), Yehudit Liverant (a milliner), Herschel Liverant (a baker), Yehoshua Shpiegelman (an upholsterer), and Yisroell Chrushtshel.

[Page 88]

Thus the movement grew, and so it needed a leader. The Warsaw committee of the Bund sent to Siedlce a representative named Boris. Boris, a tailor, settled in Siedlce and became the leader of the Jewish workers. He was a type of everyday person who became prominent at that time, with little education but with an extraordinary understanding of political matters. He led the larger and smaller meetings of the party. Belonging to the political circle that formed in Siedlce were: "Kostek" (Chaim Shleiffer), Goldenberg, "Max" (Mordechai Yedvob, a locksmith), "Yntchek" (Avraham Vaynapple, a painter), Bobek (Moyshe Dovid Grossman, a tailor), Chaim Zishele (Ratinovitsch), Matisyahu Shlifki (carpenter), Ruzhke Srevrenik (seamstress), Reizele Friedman, Freida Zhelekhovska,(sewer), tall Rivkeh dark Yehudit (Felicia), the "Skinny Shaya" (Khrenovitzki, a carpenter), and old "Malach" (Zigelboym).

The political circles met in the private dwellings of the Bundists. The larger assemblies gathered in a field outside the city or in Alter Bultz's orchard. Alter Bultz was an older man, a tailor with a long, old–fashioned beard. In winter he worked as a tailor and in summer he kept an orchard, and consequently he was always in need. He was one of the truest and most devoted comrades of the Bund. He did all the party's errands and considered himself the sexton of the Bund. When there were gatherings of the Bund in his orchard, he stood on guard, and if he heard something, he bade everyone to get away quietly. He alone would stand by the exit to the orchard and not run away.

In the winter of 1904, larger meetings were held openly in the synagogue or the beis–medresh. The workers would take over the houses of prayer and hold their meeting. Often fights would break out with those who were praying or with the gabbais, who did not want to give in to those meetings.

[Page 89]

Aside from the already mentioned workers who directed the activities of the organization, there were also in Siedlce so–called "cabinet–socialists," intelligent sympathizers who supported the Bund with money and organized the "red cross" (a committee to help political detainees). Among these sympathizers, a special place was held by an esteemed bookkeeper who was employed by the wealthy firm "S.B. Mintz." This bookkeeper had gathered around himself a circle of sympathizers and adherents of the Jewish–Socialist movement. These intelligent, middle–class young people in capes, most of them bookkeepers wearing pince–nez on their noses, made quite an impression on the city. It is appropriate to give their names: Yankele "Diplomat" Goldshtern was an assistant bookkeeper at the Mintz firm; Avraham Ziglvachs, an employee at a manufacturing business. He came to Siedlce from Lublin. To this group also belonged the "B'nei Slushneh"–Meir Alter's and Meir Avrahaml's, who was a perpetual student. Meir Alter's was a singer, an amateur, and had a bicycle shop that employed Polish workers. Because of his Polish workers, in addition to the Bund, he sympathized with the P.P.S and wrote documents for the Jewish P.P.S.

By the first of May in 1904, Siedlce had a broadly developed workers' movement with different parties and directions that had already aped in the city. The Zionists had also assumed a visible position. Siedlce had become "a city with a name." All the parties sent speakers and agitators: Zionists who spoke Hebrew and Bundists who wore shirts with tassels. At the Bundist center every day was lively. People conducted heated discussions on various issues and agreed to celebrate the first of May with a demonstration.

The police heard about these plans and arrested the leader Damanski with his son and his assistant Stempinski; from the Bund– George and Fritzl "Pentak." Despite this repression, the parties were not stopped from celebrating the first of May with a demonstration.

[Page 90]

The First of May Demonstration and the Bloody Gathering in the Woods

On the first of May, early in the morning, groups of workers appeared in different streets with red markers in their lapels. They ordered the shopkeepers to close their stores, for their own sakes. The shopkeepers understood what was meant and shut up shop. In the workshops, too, people put aside their work. In the streets, military patrols soon appeared with rifles and bayonets. The military ordered the stores to reopen. At noon the street became silent. The military patrols left. The party organizers took advantage and at that moment brought everyone out. Soon Warsaw Street was filled with a world of colorful workers. Red flags flew, and the street was filled with workers' songs and slogans. First came the P.P.S., which was made up of workers, peasants, Jewish youth from Chasidic homes, and the slaughterhouse workers. The procession went through a number of streets. It was the first time Siedlce had seen such a strange picture. The cavalry showed up and with drawn swords dispersed the demonstration. There were no deaths. The effect on the city was extraordinary.

In the summer of 1904, the Bund declared a "May walk" in the historical Igon Woods. The Bundists secretly gathered in the woods, where, in 1831, the Polish rebels had fought the czarist army. For the simple workers, there was called a May walk. When everyone had gathered, Avraham Yablon declared that they had come together to consider the difficult workers' situation and the remedies that should be adopted in order to better the lives of the proletariat. Later, a "Litvak" spoke about the political situation in relation to the Russian– Japanese War.

Two soldiers who happened to be passing near the woods noticed the gathering and notified the authorities. It was not long before the organization's "patrols" notified the people that the dragoons were on the way.

[Page 91]

(Dragoons were a special unit of the czarist cavalry.) The dragoons surrounded the woods, as strategy dictated.

At first there was panic among those gathered there, but soon Yablon quieted them down, calling on them to search their pockets to be sure they had nothing suspect and then to remain quiet while awaiting the enemy. The foreign agitator fled through side paths, while the mass of people waited peacefully for the outcome. The army approached. The commander of the cavalry, Kosakov, approached the group with a drawn revolver, drawing forth curses and cries. One bold woman went up to the officer and announced that this was not a political gathering but just a May celebration. The officer seemed to quiet down and ordered the cavalry to encircle the crowd with a chain, but soon came the following orders: "Swords out! Strike them on the head." There was terrible chaos. If one could run away, one did. But they were surrounded by the horsemen, who struck their victims with their swords, accompanied by Russian curses.

Then the city's police chief, Shedever, arrived with a company of policemen. A large group of the assembled, including the injured, were seized. Under a double cordon of police and cavalry, the arrested were led to the prison–the wounded to the prison hospital. At the prison gate, the arrested were beaten mercilessly. Before the arrested were brought to the prison, an alarm went through the city that all those in the forest had been seized, so thousands of Siedlce's Jews gathered at the prison, desiring to see the prisoners.

On the same day, a long table was placed in the prison yard, around which were seated: the gendarme's legal advisor V. Bilitsh, Vice–Governor Voikov, Prosecutor Skariatin, Police Chief Shedever, who was known in the city as "Avrahamkele Goy," the city doctor Savitzky, the city surgeon Dovid Schwartz, and the dozor Avraham Kaminski. Around them loitered secret agents and police. Each of the prisoners was summoned to the table and examined.

[Page 92]

All of them gave the same answer about the gathering: "It was not a political meeting, only a May celebration." Dozor Kaminski stated that everyone from Siedlce should immediately be free to leave. But the outsiders, from the surrounding towns, those without proper documents, were held. The wounded were taken to the hospital.

The following were victims of the military ambush of the gathering: 1) "Yellow Stellman"–a young man from Lukow, who received a sword cut on the palm of his hand;2) Grishke Ish–a student from the government gymnasium, who received a severe wound from a sword on his neck and that reached his tongue. The best Siedlce doctors treated him with utmost care. Finally they were able to save him; 3) A young woman's ear was severed; 40 Golde Ette Sima's, a young party member, was stomped by a horse and wounded on her head and chest. For years after that she was ill and then died of cancer. Aside from the sword wounds, there were scores of lesser wounds. All received medical treatment at the Jewish hospital.

The events in the Igon Woods upset the whole Jewish population of Siedlce. The brutalities of the czarist government created sympathy for the revolutionaries. Respectable Jews helped the wounded. People gathered funds and equipment for them. Good–hearted wealthy women visited the hospital and brought gifts. The following people took special care of the wounded: the hospital director, Yitzchak Nachum Vaintroyb; the adjutant Dr. M Shteyn; his assistant, the student Abramovitsh; and the surgeon Aaron Gron.

Self–Defense Against Pogroms and the War with the Underworld

In the city, the esteem of the Bundist organization grew stronger. People began to reckon with them at all levels. The strikers from different crafts took strength from the party and people began to respect them.

[Page 93]

The party organization became the deciding factor in all community and private disputes. In addition, the czarist government began to take the organization into account as a strong factor. They began to "look through their fingers" at their activities and to avoid provoking the masses. The organization became a second government in the city. People came to them with accusations of injustices, thefts, and different personal quarrels. The party conducted courts, recovered stolen goods, and even reconciled quarrelling husbands and wives.

People from nearby towns often came to the Siedlce Bund, asking them to intervene in private disputes. The comrades guarded their organization's reputation and did not allow the Bund to be involved with private matters. In the summer of 1905, people began to speak forcefully about a pogrom against Jews that was being prepared by the "Katzapes" [the Russians]. In Siedlce, self–defense measures were taken by different factions working together. People said that the self–defense brought together cold people and hot weapons, such as: switch–blade–knives, brass knuckles, clubs with "wire–souls," and so on.

Early one morning in the summer of 1904, a delegation came to Siedlce from the shtetls of Partchev and said that in the shtetl a demonstration was being prepared, to which all the peasants from the surrounding towns would come. They were expecting a pogrom. A group of comrades from the self–defense group decided that they were prepared to travel to Partchev in order to protect the Jews from a pogrom. Also Jewish members of the P.P.S. declared their readiness to defend the Jews in small towns.

The Siedlce self–defense group arrived in the shtetl. Everyone flocked around at news that these new guests had arrived. These defenders were accommodated behind the village with the horse dealers. The young men could not understand how they came to be with the horse dealers, but on the next day the matter became clear.

A lawyer lived in the shtetl–Adler. He invited the young men and began to talk with them. The lawyer indicated his satisfaction that these young men were prepared to protect Jewish honor and life.

[Page 94]

"But in Partchev there is no danger of a pogrom, because the peasants in the surrounding villages live at peace with the Jews"–so Adler explained to the defenders. From his continuing speech it was clear that they were involved in a dispute that had broken out between the horse dealers and the peasants. The dealers had acquired horses in an unkosher way from the peasants, who wanted to get even with these "merchants." The lawyer advised that they not get mixed up in such an affair, because it could bring no honor and the Jews would reap trouble.

The defenders returned to Siedlce. There was an uproar in the organization over the matter. They initiated an investigation into who had led the defenders into such dangerous territory. It appeared that this bit of work had been led by a son of a horse dealer, a member of the organization. He was quickly expelled from the party. Some wanted also to reckon with the horse dealers, but the party preferred to avoid a fight.

The battle that the organization waged against the underworld took on a more serious character. At that time, in all the larger worker centers, a battle began between the organized workers and the underworld (procurers, thieves, etc.).

Siedlce also had an underworld gang. There was no lack there of brothels and procurers with "brides." From time to time would come travelling gamblers and housebreakers from the Minsk area (Novominsk). The organized workers, like warriors for the right, saw in the underworld activities a huge transgression against humanity and massed to get rid of this social filth.

In Siedlce, the war against the underworld began in the following conditions:

In the town there were preparations for a Catholic celebration to lay the foundation stone for a new church. Noblemen and rich peasants from the area came; so, too, did thieves and housebreakers from Minsk. The organization knew of this matter and undertook a battle with the underworld.

[Page 95]

A certain Yossele "the Prince," who had picked the pocket of a nobleman, was detained by the organized workers. A fight ensued, and Yossele was so battered that he had to be hospitalized.

After this victory over the underworld hero, the workers went after the secret brothels, expelled the women, and destroyed the houses. There was a brothel in Siedlce that was called "Moscow House." It got this name because the owner was a retired soldier. His house, which existed legally, served the officers of the local garrison. The workers left this house going up in smoke.

In Siedlce itself, the underworld gang was too weak to fight with the workers, but the punks sought vengeance against the Siedlce workers, who came into the little shtetls. A Siedlce craftsman could not be sure about his life. The Siedlce organization, for its part, sought vengeance against the merchants from the small shtetls, who had to come into the government city. The streets were watched by the workers, and the merchants were not allowed into the city. Finally a delegation from the little shtetls came to the Siedlce organization and they came to an agreement.

The organized workers also tried to reform members of the underworld and set them on a virtuous path. Women workers struck up acquaintanceships with prostitutes and tried to convince them to leave their filthy way of life. They offered them more moral work. Some of the underworld figures threw off their ugly occupations and became adherents of the "do–gooders," as the punks called the organized workers. The battle between the workers and the underworld took on a whole new complexion at the time of the strike in the mechanized shoe factory of the Seber brothers, which was called "Koshetzes."

"Koshetzes" is what people in Siedlce called a certain category of market merchant who were considered worthless. They knew how to curse, insult, and hit you over the head. (The nickname "Koshetz" actually comes from the Polish word "Kosh," a basket that one stands with in the market.) The Seber brothers had a mechanical shoe factory which employed a couple score workers.

[Page 96]

People in the Bund had long discussed whether there should be a strike in this factory. They were simply afraid of the consequences, knowing the brutal recklessness of the Koshetzes. Finally the party leaders decided, and they sent demands to the Seber brothers–owners of the mechanized shoe factory. The shoe manufacturers responded to the demands with vulgar threats. The organization decided to get into it with the "Koshetzes."

They had let the Warsaw section of the Bund know that one of the Seber brothers was travelling to Warsaw on business. The Warsaw workers met the shoe manufacturer and executed a sentence on him. The "Koshetzes" in Siedlce therefore decided to break up the workers. They went out into the street and happened upon two leaders of the Bund, "Kostek" (Chaim Goldenberg) and Fritzl (Zalmen Burshteyn) and attacked them murderously. Fritzl was taken to the workers' headquarters with a bloody head. Kostek managed to escape. To help the Siedlce Bund, comrades from Kalushin arrived. A great battle ensued. The Koshetzes saw that they were dealing with a much stronger force. They entered into negotiation with the organization of the Bund and they came to terms. The Seber brothers accepted the demands and the war with the underworld came to a halt.

In the eyes of the populace, the organization had done a lot. The battle with the underworld, the clearing out of theft, robbery, and prostitution strongly improved the image of the workers' movement, which gained many followers. The Bund and the P.P.S. became bolder in their actions and revolutionized Siedlce.

Terrorist Activities of the P.P.S. Battle Organization and the Military Dealing with the Jews

The revolutionary year 1905 entirely changed the character of the workers' movement in Siedlce. On the ninth of January (the twenty–second, according to the European calendar) in Petersburg, under the leadership of the priest Gapon, who later appeared to be a provacateur in Petersburg, a demonstration was held with holy pictures [icons] to the Czar's Winter Palace. Their slogans were very tame–"Work and bread" for the great number of unemployed who lived in the czarist capital.

[Page 97]

The demonstration was met with a fusillade from rifles and guns and ended with hundreds of dead and thousands of wounded. This bloodbath that the czarist rulers caused among the workers, called forth in all of Russia a powerful revolutionary wave. The workers' movement in Siedlce was also moved to take action against the czarist government. The battle group of the P.P.S. ("Boyavka"), on the advice of its central committee and on the vote of its local organization, undertook to commit assassinations against czarist operatives.

The first assassination, an unsuccessful one, happened just before Shabbos, in May, 1905. The already mentioned Mendel Radzinski and Michael Agresboym "Chasid" attacked an officer near Prezeh's Orchard. The victim escaped with a slight wound to his hand, but the attackers were captured. "Chasid" was sent to Siberia and was killed there. After this unsuccessful attack there was a whole series of assassinations of gendarmes and police leaders. In the center of the city, on what was then known as Warsaw Street, a gendarme was killed by several revolver shots. At the same time, May 23, 1905, near the city club, a bomb was thrown at the aforementioned police chief Shedever. He was lightly wounded. Unlike the first attack, when Radzinski and Agresboym were captured immediately, in subsequent assassinations there was no evidence that Jews were involved.

Quiet reigned for a short time. One Shabbos night in November of 1905, a czarist policeman was shot.

There was another half year of relative quiet, and then on May 30, 1906, the city was shocked by an attack which was simultaneously conducted against President Morovitsch, Council Member Chveshtshenko, and Police Secretary Moravski. They were set upon by several unknown persons, who shot them. Morovitsch was killed and the other wounded, Chveshtshenko seriously.

[Page 98]

The climax of the assassinations was the bloody attack on the eve of Rosh Chodesh Elul, 1906 against the police chief Galtzev, who had assumed the position after the murdered Shedever. Galtzev had participated in a commission on sanitation together with the Polish doctor Savitzky nad the Jewish surgeon Schwartz. They had gone on an inspection to the soda water factory of Shmuel Yoysef Goldshtern. As they were leaving the factory, which was on Pienke Street–a totally Jewish neighborhood–a bomb was thrown. The police chief was blown apart on the spot. The Jewish surgeon Schwartz was wounded and died several days later. Only the Polish doctor Savitzky survived. This time, too, the leaders of the bomb attack were not captured. At the inquiry, the surviving doctor said that as they were leaving the factory, a short while before the explosion, someone came up to him and said in Polish that he should quickly take cover.

Galtzev was a liberal person and more than once had convinced the governor to work for the good of the Jews.

After the assassination, an old tailor named Ch. M. Friedman, was arrested. He lived on the second floor of the house where the attack was planned. The suspect spent a long time in prison. Eventually he was freed. In all probability, no Jews were involved in this attack.

Shortly after this murder, soldiers appeared on the streets of Siedlce, dragoons from the Lubavitsch regiment who were quartered in Siedlce. Infuriatingly, they opened a "blind" volley right in the Jewish streets. Six Jews were killed, four men and two women: Shloyme Zalmen Goldshtern, Itta Miriam Matshelinski, Yitzhak Milgroym, Dovid Matselinski, Mrs. Suknevitsch, and Baruch Mordechai Morgenshtern. About forty other Jews were either slightly or severely wounded.

[Page 99]

This bloody reckoning with the Jews of Siedlce was not the first. The czarist army had, before this bloody shooting on erev Rosh Chodesh Ellul, 1906, more than once dared to terrorize the Jewish populace, with the excuse that they were acting against the revolutionaries.

Thus, for example, the Jews of Siedlce had survived two bloody days–Thursday, August 11, and Tuesday, August 16, 1905. The army had surrounded the Jewish quarter and shot, allegedly, at the "revolutionaries" and "socialists." The Bundist activist Yakov Yablon was shot. Eyewitnesses said that the attack of the army began before night, while Jews filled the beis–medresh to say the afternoon prayers. Several Jews who had been frightened by the shooting went into the beis–medresh for protection. The murderously aroused soldiers broke into the beis–medresh and with the butts of their rifles struck right and left. Finished with this bloody piece of work, they exited and then fired through the windows into the beis–medresh–sixty Jews were wounded. After this bloody event, iron shutter were made for the beis–medresh to provide protection against shooting through the windows.

The governor of Siedlce, Volozhin, had demanded from the leaders of the Jewish community, from the dozors (Y.N. Vayntroib, Hershke Zelnick, and Moyshe Temkin) who had come to ask for protection for the Jewish population–had demanded that they should give him, the governor, a list with the addresses of the revolutionaries. In his conversation with the dozors, the representative of the czar treated them condescendingly and adopted a despotic tone. Y.N. Vayntroyb says in his memoirs that the governor warned that he had prepared threatening letters so that if anything happened to him, to the governor, not a single person would remain alive in Siedlce. That is why the threatening regiment had been brought by Volozhin to Siedlce. The governor gave the delegation a little time in order to call a meeting in the home of the rabbi so they could decide about betraying the revolutionaries.

[Page 100]

After the three dozors had communicated with the rabbi of the time, Rabbi Shimon Dov Analik, a larger gathering was called of the prominent members of the community, who sought a way to escape their predicament without betraying any Jews. The result of the meeting Vayntroib later delivered to Volozhin, that no one in the Jewish community knew who the revolutionaries were and if any of them were in Siedlce. Truly, he said, there had been assassinations, but the attackers were, it appeared, outsiders and probably not Jews, who had come to Siedlce and, did their deeds, and fled. No one knew who these people were. Understandably, this answer did not please the governor.

Preparations for the Pogrom Against the Jews

After the assassination of Galtzev, the atmosphere in the city became more suffocating. It felt as if something stirring. Military patrols with bayonets on their rifles traversed the city. The stores, which used to be open until late into the night, had to close their doors at eight o'clock, according to an ordinance. In the Orthodox Church they held memorial services for the dead and preached sermons against the revolutionaries. It was often said that the Jews were the only revolutionaries. It was no longer a secret that people were preparing for a pogrom against the Jews.

The word among the Jewish populace became more oppressive when changes from the administrative power became known. Among other things, Lieutenant Colonel Tichinovsky was named as head of what was then unhappily known as the "Okhrana."

Tichinovsky had belonged to the Black Hundreds of the "true Russian people," who were involved everywhere in organizing pogroms against Jews. He was an old Russian officer who had taken part in the Russo–Japanese War in 1904 and had become a lieutenant colonel. His hatred for Jews and for revolutionaries was all–consuming. At that time he published a pamphlet called "How to Put Down the Revolution," in which he advocated using the army to subdue the revolution.

[Page 101]

Because the pamphlet was written in such a brutal style, it was confiscated by the Russian government.

This member of the Black Hundreds lived well with Jews. He had "his Jews, who lent him money on interest…"

This Lieutenant Colonel Tichinovsky was the chief organizer of the pogrom in Siedlce in 1906, which only became known later, when the secret report about the Siedlce pogrom to the Governor General in Warsaw was made public.

On Friday, the seventh of September (the seventeenth of Elul, 5666), the tenor of the town became more oppressive. The patrols with their rifles at the ready were strengthened. Jews hesitated to show themselves in the streets. It was the same the next morning, on Shabbos. Few Jewish stores opened up on Saturday evening. Police roamed the streets and made it known that the government permitted stores to stay open until eleven.

At nine in the evening, a volley of rifle fire was heard, and from time to time was heard again. People who lived near the new city hall, known as the "City Clock Tower"–said that they saw a red flag unfurled from a tower of the city hall. This served as a signal that the pogrom should begin. And truly, at that moment it began. People who survived those bloody days and who during the pogrom watched through cracks in their shutters later related that they noticed soldiers stationed on all the streets, posted at equal distances from each other. They shot into the windows of Jewish homes. This shooting was accompanied by noise, clamor, and the wild screaming of drunken soldiers

Tichinovsky

The Beginning of the Pogrom

[Page 102]

The City Clock Tower

. From time to time–witnesses testified–isolated shots were heard from the houses. People were ostensibly shooting at the army. It later came out that these shots came from Russians posted on the roofs and in the attics playing the role of Jewish revolutionaries who were fighting against the army. This was supposed to indicate that there was no pogrom in Siedlce but that they army was putting down an armed Jewish revolution.

The shooting lasted throughout Saturday night.

At about midnight, Tichinovsky had the police summon the city rabbi, Rabbi Sh. D. Analik, and the two dozors, Y.N. Vayntroib and Moyshe Temkin. Temkin arrived with a bruised face, thanks to being murderously attacked by an officer. Temkin had been saying Psalms when the shooting began.

[Page 103]

The officer stormed into his house with a group of soldiers and claimed that people in the house were shooting at the military patrols– and then viciously beat him. The Jewish representatives who were brought to the police building beheld a dreadful scene: at tables loaded with food and drink that had been stolen from Jewish businesses and homes sat Tichinovsky with his staff. He was drunk as he gave orders about which streets should be taken. Between orders, they guzzled wine and sang the czarist hymn "God Save the Czar."

Soldiers receiving orders to fire

When Tichinovsky was informed that representatives of the Jewish community had arrived, he screamed at them, "Why are the Jews shooting at the army? There are already many dead soldiers"–he fumed. "Therefore"–Tichinovsky went on–"I have ordered them to shoot all Jewish revolutionaries." Using this excuse, he again repeated the well–known demand: "Give the government a list with the addresses of the revolutionaries."

[Page 104]

The commander addressed the delegation in a brutal, insulting tone. He said that if the revolutionaries were not turned over to him, he would wipe out the whole Jewish population in the city, and first–he said–he would should the delegation

The representatives, having no way out, told Tichinovsky that they were prepared, with the army's help, to go find the revolutionaries. To this end, they asked, they asked to have several hours, because they began to think they might find a contingent of Jewish revolutionaries who were fighting against the army. They also thought that if soldiers had been killed, as the lieutenant colonel maintained, they should go through the city and see what was going on[63].

Tichinovksi agreed to give the delegation two hours only. After this time they must–he ordered–provide a list of revolutionaries.

With heavy hearts the Jews left the police station; having nothing substantial to give to the murderous Tichinovsky–they did not hurry to return.

People burglarized the Jewish houses

[Page 105]

When Tichinovksi became aware that more than three hours had passed and the Jews had not come to him, he sent the police to bring them in. The representatives came to Tichinovsky with broken hearts. On the whole way back to the station, they saw how Jewish businesses had been broken into by the unruly soldiers, who stole goods and got drunk on the liquor. The sidewalks and walls were sprinkled with blood. Sofas were placed on the streets, and on them sat drunken officers who gave orders to steal and murder.

Tichinovsky, seeing Wayntroyb and Temkin, shouted bitterly, asking why they had taken more than their two hours. When he heard that they still had not brought a list of revolutionaries, the lieutenant colonel, he drew out his gold watch and warned that if in a half hour they had not satisfied his demand, he would kill all the Jews.

Y.N. Wayntroyb worked up his courage and asked: whether the chief of the "Okhrana" would be satisfied with a list of only Jewish revolutionaries or whether it should include Poles. Tichinovsky understandably answered that he wanted the Poles as well. To this the Jewish representatives responded that they did not know the Polish community and they did not know who the Polish revolutionaries were, so that this was actually a matter for the leaders of the Polish community. Tichinovsky then ordered that to the four Jews–Rabbi Sh. D. Analik, Y.N. Wayntroyb, M. Temkin, and the community secretary Tchotchkes, should be added the city–president, the churchman Stsipia–del–Campo, and three prominent Poles. These people would be responsible for indicating the revolutionaries who "were shooting" at the czarist army."

The Jewish delegation left Tichinovsky and went to the city rabbi to report what was happening in the city and about the crazy order from the chief of the "Okhrana." The rabbi received the Jewish representatives with shock, and with sorrow he listened to their report of the bloodbath that had been organized by the government itself.

[Page 106]

The rabbi, Rabbi Shimon Dov Analik, was a great personality and strongly gave his advice. He regarded all of Yisroel as being of the highest rank. Before he had arrived in Siedlce he had been the rabbi in Sharky, Ostrow, and Tiktin. He had a firm character and his conscience was crystal clear. Thanks to these qualities, the rabbi of Siedlce was greatly beloved and respected by the community. He was a great scholar and a sharp misnagid, but even so he tolerated the Chasidim, who also showed him great honor. He had written two books: "The Sayings of Rashad," which contained all sorts of notes and sermons and touched upon the rules of Hebrew grammar, was published in Warsaw in 1912. There was also his composition "Oreach Mishpat." a commentary on the "Choshen Mishpat." When he died, other manuscripts were found. The leader of the Jews of Siedlce saw how his community would be slaughtered by the barbaric czarist soldiers, who received their orders from higher up. And he, the rabbi, the fearer of Heaven, the man of influence, could not help his unhappy community. Rabbi Analik felt all this so deeply that he passed away several months after the pogrom.

* *

When the rabbi heard the tragic report that Y.N. Wayntroyb had delivered, he was completely broken. After consulting with the dozors, it was decided that those present should go to General Engelky, the representative of the governor, and report the bloodbath that had been arranged to him. The community leaders, together with the rabbi, believed that the representative of the czar in Siedlce, the governor, would be embarrassed by the actions of the pogromist Tichinovsky.

On Sunday morning, the delegation made its way to General Engelky. After they reported on the conditions in the city and recounted the actions of the Russian army, branding them as anti–Semitic, the general became furious and ordered that he was arresting the Jewish delegation because they were…spies.

General Engelky declared further that after such "chuzpadik" behavior on the side of the Jews, they deserved to be shot. He ordered the arrest of the Jewish delegation.

[Page 107]

He immediately notified Tichinovsky that the leaders of Jewish Siedlce had come to complain about him. In order to terrify the Jewish delegation even further, Engelky permitted the representatives, at their request, to write farewell letters to their families, on the condition that the letters be brief.

After the Jews had written their letters, they were taken under a strict guard to the police, where they found Tichinovsky. The hero of the pogrom approached the prisoners wrathfully and yelled: "Instead of going to find the revolutionaries, you went to the general to report on me. Soon you'll be shot as spies." The delegates were led to the wall of the police building, with the soldiers lined up before them–one for each representative–a soldier holding a rifle. It appears that this was a species of bestial play by the pogrom leader, the chief of the czarist Okhrana. He did not give the order to shoot, and instead he said to the Jews that he would free them on condition that they should compile over the next several hours the desired list.

Meanwhile, it was Sunday night. The shooting died down. However, fires broke out in all corners of the Jewish quarter. The czarist soldiers thus destroyed Jewish houses. Five houses on Prospect Street were burned, five houses on Sokolov Way, four houses on Yatke Street, ten hospital stores and the shops of Shmuel Solarsz and Berl Rosen.

On Monday morning, cannon shots were heard. This was the Rembertov Artillery, which had been specially brought to the city. They shot the houses of Breina Tshistaka (47 Pienke), Rochel Grach (75 Pienke), Moyshe Eliyahu Salnitze (91 Pienke), and the house of Esther Ratinovitsh (34 Alene). The same day, at six in the morning, they sent out a military patrol to bring the rabbi, Wayntroyb, Temkin, and the community secretary Tchotchkes. The same scene repeated itself. The drunken Tichinovsky addressed them despotically: "See!" he growled. "I've already brought in cannon. If I need more, I'll bring them from Rembertov.

[Page 108]

If I don't hand over the revolutionaries, I'll make a ruin of Siedlce."

The community heads could no longer be dominated. They sprang up, saying that it was a calumny when the chief said that there were Jewish revolutionaries in the city. When the army had searched all the Jewish houses, aside from distraught citizens, with their wives and children, no revolutionaries had been found. If you want, you can shoot us. One of the delegates ripped off his caftan and showed that he was prepared to be shot. This bold gesture worked somewhat. The murderer Tichinovsky retreated a bit and responded that he was giving the Jewish representatives some soldiers and they would together go to seek out possible revolutionaries.

On Monday, September 10, at about ten in the morning, accompanied by an officer with soldiers, they left the place where Tichinovsky remained and went into the city. They heard the officer reproach Tichinovsky. They heard that since the "action," the soldiers had gone for more than twenty–four hours without being relieved and they were hungry and tired. Tichinovsky responded in an aggressive tone: "The battle is underway. Out of loyalty, men hold up for twelve days, but they hold up!"

A house on Pienke Street shot through by a cannon

After being in the city for several hours, the delegation returned to the commandant and reported that they could not discover any revolutionaries. The pogrom–commander blew up again and ordered the Jewish representatives to be lined up against the wall and finally shot. At that very moment, in came the officer Stoyanov, whom the commander of the Dubnow Regiment had sent to discover the cause of the shooting. Stoyanov went up to Tichinovsky, spoke to him softly, and asked what was going on. Tichinovsky explained the purpose of the "action," which was "to uncover the revolutionaries and put down the revolution." One of the delegates, who heard the words of the officers,, called out in a loud voice that over the course of several hours they had combed the city looking for revolutionaries, but they had found none. Stoyanov recognized that something bad was afoot and announced that he was prepared to go out with the delegation to find revolutionaries.

About Stoyanov it was said that he was interested in political questions, that he was highly esteemed in the regiment. When the regiment went out on summer maneuvers, he left the lieutenant colonel in charge. At the time of the pogrom, Stoyanov spent a whole day going through the streets and silently and intently observing everything. In several cases he saved Jews from death. Later on there arose about him a variety of legends. For instance, Jews said that during the pogrom he rode a white horse through the streets and shouted at the soldiers: "Don't kill–or you'll be court–martialed"[64].

While the delegation, with Stoyanov, were in the streets, a shot was heard from a nearby house. The officer and then the delegation went quickly into the house and began to search. Aside from starving and shocked Jews, they found nothing. They went up to the attic and there they found a Russian in civilian clothing. He lay by a window and shot into the street.

[Page 110]

As it later came out, in the special inquiry that the officer conducted, the shooter was a policeman decked out in the civilian clothing of a Jew. He was stationed in the attic of a Jewish house and shot his rifle as a provocation. Styoyanov, in front of the delegation, expressed his irritation with the military commander who had arranged the provocation. The officer arrested the Russian and turned him over to the police. But people regarded the whole incident with indifference. The officer Stoyanov then went with the delegation and discovered several similar situations. Then he expressed his opinion that the whole thing had truly been a type of provocation.

After the officer had communicated with the commandant of the Dubnow Regiment and had given a detailed report, the commandant, Ultimativ, ordered Tichonovsky that if he did not put an end to the murders, his regiment would attack Tichinovsky's pogromists. Tichinovsky was afraid and ordered an end to the shooting.

* * *

On Monday night, September 11 (1906), the mass shooting stopped, but isolated rifle shots continued. Tichinovsky never stopped boasting that he had put down the "revolution." At the same time, he regretted that the number of murdered was only thirty–one Jews rather than hundreds. His desire to bring in the army to help, in order to raise the pogrom to a whole new level–came to nothing, thanks to the intervention of the officer from the Dubnow Regiment. The commandant of the Dubnow Regiment sent patrols into the streets to stop the shooting of Jews, thanks to which the shooting ceased.

That same evening, Wayntroyb was again called to Tichinovsky. As the Jewish leader later conveyed in his memoir, he found the lieutenant colonel in a half–crazy state. In his dwelling at 14 Oleyna Street, he was running around in his socks and yelling: "I have completed my work. If you want to escape from the city, show it by giving me the names and addresses of all the revolutionaries. If not, I'll bring in more cannon and all the Jews will be shot."

The proud and fine leader, Y.N. Wayntroib, answered the bloodstained murderer: "You should be sorry for having spilled so much innocent blood, after having killed so many innocent people." After that, Wayntroib left Tichinovski's home. That day the rabbi had telephoned the governor and asked permission to bury the dead. Permission was given on condition that there should not be mass participation at the burial and there should be no eulogies. Jews began to emerge from their hiding places. They encountered a fearful pogrom landscape: more than a score of dead and hundreds of wounded, destroyed houses, vandalized businesses.

Some of the wounded from the pogrom

It was clear that the following twenty–six Jews were killed during the days of the pogrom:

1.   Meir Wolf, 33, killed by the officer Balechov on Sunday morning, the second day of the pogrom.

[Page 112]
        Balechov actually wanted to murder Meir Slushny, a bicycle maker who lived in the same house, but when he encountered Meir Wolf, he killed him.

2.   Nahum Slushny, 18. He was killed by the same Balechov. When the officer saw that he had not killed the man he had intended, he began to search for Meir Slushny. Because that man was out of the city, he found a different Slushny and murdered him.

3.   Avraham Miltshak, 19, shot on his way to the the police.

4.   Yitzchak Weinberg, 45, first beaten up and then shot on Pienke Street.

5.   Yehoshua Rosen, 3. The child was killed in the hands of his mother, while his parents were being led to jail. On the way, the child was struck by a soldier and later died.

6.   Yehuda Lifshitz, 18. First he was wounded as he stood by his parents in their store. He was taken to the hospital. On Sunday night, as he sat in his bed, a bullet came through the window and wounded him severely. He died several days later in Warsaw.

7.   Sholem Dov Feder, 76. When the pogrom broke out on Saturday evening, the old man headed for his home. Soldiers in the street split open his head.

8.   Sarah Solarsz, 70. Killed by a bullet that came through the window of her dwelling. The child whose hand she was holding was wounded.

9.   Blume Burshteyn, 40. She was taken from her dwelling on Sokolov Street and shot in the courtyard.

10.   Avraham Rafal, 22. A Jewish soldier home on leave. He stationed himself in front of his parents when soldiers entered their house, so the soldiers shot him.

[Page 113]

11.   Yehoshua Stochowski, 19. First the killers wounded him, then shot him.

12.   Stochoweiski, a child, died of wounds.

13.   Moyshe Zalman Dietent, 45.

14.   Dov Matchelinski, 25.

15.   Yoysef Goldshteyn, murdered, 30. Was a guest of a Siedlce family.

16.   Gavriel Sonnshein, 20. Wounded earlier. When he was being brought to the hospital, a patrol shot him.

17.   Mendel Teyblum, 34. First the soldiers put out his eyes, then shot him.

18.   Mordechai Yoysef Miller, 40. A teacher. He was cut into pieces by swords and bayonets.

19.   Tov Shlarsz, 30.

20.   Dvorah Feygnboym, 17.

21.   Shvientzientziantzikamien [??] 18. Both fell at Dvorah Feygenboym's house.

22.   Sheindl Weynshteyn, 34. Murdered in her shop in the hospital building.

23.   23–24 Chaim Yakov Liberman, 30, and Channah Liberman, 52. A mother–in–law and son–in–law shot together by soldiers.

25.   Shraga Ratinievitsch, 22.

26.   Jan Baritz (Christian). Watchman at the hospital, struck and killed by a bullet.

Together with the six victims who had already been killed, there were 31 Jewish and 1 Christian fatalities.

How the Pogrom Against the Jews of Siedlce Was Organized and Prepared

The pogrom in Siedlce was the last in a series of pogroms after the publication of the October Manifesto of the last Russian czar, .. The Manifesto of October 17 (the 29th, according to the European date), had promised freedom and equality for Russian citizens, and for the Jews it brought pogroms that flowed like bloody waves over almost all Jewish settlements in czarist Russia, and in Poland reached Bialystok and Siedlce.

[Page 114]

It became clear to everyone that the pogroms had been organized and prepared by czarist agents, because according to the words of the czarist minister Pleve, the revolution had to be drowned in Jewish blood. That sentiment was expressed at the time of the Siedlce pogrom, which was a military pogrom against Jews. The effect of the bloody events in Siedlce were extraordinary, especially because the revolution was in decline and in Russia the legislative parliament, the Duma, had become active. The czarist government was therefore interested in immediately coming up with a justification for the murderous events in Siedlce.

Victims of the pogrom

[Page 115]

This justification found its expression in the lying report about the events in Siedlce which was presented by the general governor Skalon to the war minister. The report states:

On September 8 (Old Style), on a variety of streets in Siedlce were heard simultaneous revolver shots coming from revolutionaries directed at patrols, pedestrians, and riders. The alarmed army began to fire back at the houses from which the shooting had come. The shooting had lasted all night and began again at two in the afternoon on the ninth, becoming more intense in the evening. On Sunday the garrison was strengthened by the arrival of the Dubnow Regiment and the 48th Cadre Battery. Because of the persistent from the attics, which lasted until the morning of the tenth, six cannon shell were shot at the houses. Then the shooting of the revolutionaries ceased and the army returned to making searches.

This fallacious report from the highest levels of the czarist government in Poland–Governor–General Skalon–was issued after the governor general had in his hands the true report, which told how the czarist government in Siedlce had organized and prepared the pogrom against Jews. This secret report would perhaps never have seen the light of day, except for a fortunate accident, which was that at that time the secret agent and collaborator with the Warsaw "Okhrana"–Bakai–had gone to the side of the revolutionaries.

Bakai, who had been brought into the revolutionary movement by the social–revolutionary activist Burtzev, was in the chancellery of Governor–General Skala\on when a special messenger from the Siedlce Ohrana brought in the accurate report on the pogrom in Siedlce. The messenger trustingly told Bakai that he had been ordered to hand over the report to a trusted member of the governor general's chancellery.

[Page 116]

Bakai convinced the messenger that he–Bakai–was actually the "Okhranik" on duty in the governor's chancellery to whom the secret document should be given.

As soon as Bakai had the report in his hands, he made a copy, which he turned over to the social–democratic faction in the Duma. Soon after, Bakai disappeared from Russia. The representatives of the revolutionary camp thus received the document, on the basis of which they could openly identify the murderous deed of the czarist government.

The secret document that was given to Governor General Skalon contained a report from the Siedlce gendarme Rotmistch Pietochov about the events in Siedlce on the 8th, ninth, and 10th of the September (Old Style) of 1906.

For the first time in the history of czarist Russia that contained so many anti–Jewish pogroms organized by the government, it was officially established that the pogrom was organized by government officials and not by the crowd, which had been the official government version of pogroms.

The report, dated the 22nd of September 1906, covered five sheets.

Pietochov said[65]:

On the 11th of August 1906, I was called to the police committee, where I found Police Colonel Virgalitsch, Captain Pototski, Alec Grigorov, the representative of the Siedlce police captain Protopopov and the head of the "Okhrana," Lieutenant Colonel Tichinovsky. It was a conference about how to conduct in Siedlce mass house searches. Such searches had been ordered in a telegram by the ruler of the area. Lieutenant Colonel Tichanovsky ordered that people should single out several important people from the city, even if they themselves played no part in the revolutionary movement, except that they would not give the government names and addresses of revolutionaries. Tikhanovsky proclaimed that he intended to put them in prison as "hostages" and to let them know: if an assassination would be carried out against anyone that they knew, the detained would pay with their lives.

[Page 117]

He also said that he would take on all responsibility. To the question of how the condemned would be killed, Lieutenant Colonel Tichinovsky posed a question to the police chief, asking whether he could point out a policeman who would agree to pose as a madman and shoot or poison those confined in the prison.

"We must answer the terror of the revolution with stronger terror"–he declared.

At the same time, we assembled again–so says Pietochov in his report–the district gendarme committee, where they devised the plan to encircle the whole city and conduct house–to–house searches, and while the searches were underway, firemen should be prepared and doctors should be stationed in the hospitals. This was Tichinovsky's request. He undertook to notify the hospitals. When asked the purpose of these preparations, Tichinovsky explained that there would surely be dead and wounded, because no mercy would be shown and arms would be employed.

The dragoon officers, when they heard these intentions, rubbed their hands together with joy and openly said: "We'll make a little pogrom and show no mercy." There was soon such talk among the soldiers. It was clear to us that Tichinovsky and the dragoon officers would create a bloodbath on all of Siedlce's Jews. All attempts to restrain Tichinovsky and his followers were of no use. He, Pietochov, and Colonel Wirgalitsch went several times to the governor to warn him of the danger. In a conversation with the police chief, Tichinovsky said: "Captain Pietochov does not intend that we will arrest people. Those who are known for their revolutionary activities will surely not be found among the arrested."

The first night, September 8, when the first shooting erupted in Siedlce, Tichinovsky, in order to encourage the army, called out a group of trumpeters and the singers of the regiment, and while the guns were shooting, when human blood was flowing, when houses were in flames, the singing of the soldiers could be heard. When alarms spread that Tichinovsky might be targeted for killing, he went to his squadron so that they could make for him a proper "memorial service" and bathe him in blood up to ears.

[Page 118]

Pietochov tells further how the pogrom progressed. He also blames together with Tichinovsky the current Governor–General Engelik and also Governor Volozhin, since they were in charge of the district.

From all the materials and documents that were revealed soon after the pogrom in Siedlce, it became clear that the bloodbath visited on the Jews of Siedlce, like the pogroms in other cities and towns in czarist Russia, was systematically prepared by the army and led by the local army representatives, as in Siedlce it was led by the almighty leader of the "Okhrana," Lieutenant Colonel Tichinovsky.

Just before the outbreak of the pogrom, in a designated area, notices were distributed that were signed by the "Society for a Reformed Order, also known as Saint Nicholas." Hundreds and thousands of these notices were distributed[66]. So, too, in Siedlce these incendiary notices were distributed with their well–known nonsense from the "Protocols of the Elders of Zion," with the secret talks of the leading rabbis of the Jewish people and their overall plan to exterminate the Christian world.

Here is [some of] what these rabbis of the Jewish people are supposed to have said:

It is now nineteen hundred years that we have been fighting against the Cross, and our people will not falter or stop. If we are scattered throughout the world, that is so that we can rule the whole world. Our power grows from day to day. At our disposal is now the Golden Calf that Aaron the priest made in the desert, and it is the true god of our time. Only when we have sole control of gold will we assume domination.

The "Berliner Tageblatt," which published the notice and condemned its contents, wrote that the incendiary notice was the work of ultra–Slavic clergy who supported the Black Hundred "Union of the True Russian People."

[Page 119]

Such notices were distributed in the army in the area around Siedlce and in Siedlce itself. Thus was the ground prepared for the pogrom, and the army undertook to organize it in Bialystok style, but in a different form–only with the participation of the government and without assistance from the civilian mob, from thieves and robbers.

The city was divided into districts, at the head of which wee placed the officers of the dragoons, who were known for their as pogromists, Black Hundreds. The most successful and honest officer in the regiment was Baron von Kleist. He had a positive attitude toward Jews and even sympathized with the Zionist movement; and, as we have mentioned, he donated a large number of books to the library in Siedlce. But this baron did nothing to prevent the pogrom.

The leaders of the precincts were the officers: Balichov, Vestolov, Alexandrov, Musaratov, Baron Bialer, the aforementioned Baron von Kleist, and Sumarakov.

After the Pogrom——Trials of the Victims

When the czarist bandits had finished their bloodbath, at which they were so good, and when the lying report was made public, people in government circles began to consider how to disguise the outrageous action of murdering and robbing innocent Jews. The government thought the best way out was to make the victims their scapegoat, to put the "guilty" Jews before a court and judge them according to "objective" standards. Before, during, and after the pogrom, the police had arrested six hundred Jews. In the course of time, a large number of the detainees had been freed, but nearly four hundred remained under detention. The local government intended to initiate a trial against these Jews for treason.

According to "Die Welt" of September 19, 1906, the Zionist Action Committee went to the Russian Minister of the Interior Stolyopin, to the Minister of War Rediges, and to the Minister of Justice, Shtsheglovitov, Count Von Baden, and to the kings of England and Italy–with a request to intervene so that the detainees would not be put before a court martial, which was known to condemn innocent people to death.

[Page 120]

The London "Times" reported that the Vice Foreign Minister of England had met with a Jewish delegation, which gave him details about the Siedlce pogrom and raised horror about its outcome. The British Vice–Minister consulted with his ambassador in Petersburg and asked him to work for the good of the detainees.

After all of these interventions, nearly 250 of the detainees were released, but more than a hundred and fifty Jews remained in prison. The government declared that these Jews had shot at the army patrols. These unfortunates had to appear before a military court martial. Then the community turned to Baron David Ginzburg of Petersburg. They received a response that said the baron had visited Prime Minister Stolyopin, who had authorized him to send an order to the army in Siedlce that justice should be ensured. According to this report–Ginzburg shared–it turned out that there would be no court martial, though some of the detainees would be sent to Siberia.

Soon an "Aid Committee for the Victims of the Disorders in Siedlce" was created. (The government did not permit the committee to be called by its rightful name: "Victims of the Pogrom.") Sympathetic telegrams arrived from all over. The Polish community and press responded with particular warmth. All of the Polish newspapers took up collections. Some of those papers collected large sums of money. The committee was also associated with the YIKO in Petersburg and "Alliance" in Paris.

From a report[67], we see that according to the material that the Aid Committee gathered, the suffering from the Siedlce pogrom affected 440 craftsmen's families, 416 merchant families, 380 workers' families, 130 families of independent professions, and 186 families without stated professions. In total, 1502 families numbering 7306 individuals. The damage amounted to 344,584 rubles. The money that was raised amounted to a hundred and twenty thousand rubles.

[Page 121]

Poles were also represented on the committee. Its members were: lawyer St. Zonderland–chair, A.D. Tchotchkes–secretary, Rabbi D.B. Analik, Y.N. Wayntroyb, Father Szipia–Del–Campo, M. Mintz, lawyer, Alexei Chzhnovski, Asher Arszel, city mayor Karsak, and N.D. Glicksberg.

A few days later the committee received a telegram from Baron Ginsburg, Feinberg, and lawyer Shlozberg asking for the appointment of a couple of people to deliver a report about the process of the pogrom, about the court martial, and about the detainees to Stolypin, and also to assign responsibility to the guilty.

The following delegation traveled to Petersburg and held meetings on these issues: lawyer Winaver, lawyer Schlossberg, lawyer Warshavsky, lawyer Sheftel, Feinberg, Vovelberg, Fishbeim, and the Siedlce deputy in the Russian Duma Dimsha (a Pole). On the agenda were two questions: 1) aid for the victims, and 2) a memorandum to the government. The memorandum was put together by lawyers Fishbein, Luria, Warshavsky and was sent to Minister of the Interior Stolypin, with a copy to Baron Ginsburg, who quickly intervened with Baron Knal, who was Stolypin's closest aide. Baron Ginzburg requested that the Minister of the Interior would meet with a delegation of Jews from Siedlce. This audience took place. Stolypin had already read the memorandum and his conclusion was: he could not believe that the army had carried out the pogrom. He promised: to carry out a quick investigation, no court martial would be held, and the hundred and fifty Jews would be released.

The Memorandum to the Russian Prime Minister Stolypin

Premier Stolypin was given the following memorandum by the delegates of the "Citizens of Siedlce:

Excellency,

We approach you on the issue of the events in Siedlce on the days of September 8–10, 1906. We do not wish to describe the horror or indicate the names of the perpetrators and complain about them. We wish only to establish the facts that cannot be denied, so that His Excellence can prepare the appropriate consequences:

On the 21st of August, an unknown person threw a bomb at Commandant Galtzev, which caused, to the great sorrow of the whole community, his death. After that, the military garrison began to torment the inhabitants. Soon after the assassination of the police chief, an order was given to shoot into crowds, which caused the death of many innocent people. Two hundred people were arrested, but the assassins were not taken. After these events, the military patrols tormented the citizens so much that they trembled before the military and hesitated to be seen in the streets.

Living conditions became increasingly bad. Representatives of the inhabitants went to the mayor and complained about the bad behavior of the army, but total silence dominated in the streets. The governmental administration responded, "Be prepared." Truly, preparations were made to preserve order in the future, as appears in the following facts:

> 1. The governor gave command of the city into the hands of the lieutenant colonel of the 39th Lubovsk Norwegian Regiment, Tichinovsky.
> 2. Several days before the misfortune, a staff was raised over the clock tower, which served, as we saw later, as a signal for the beginning of the pogrom.

[Page 123]

> 3. The military officers openly collected information about the city plan, its streets and houses.
> 4. The Siedlce garrison–according to the semi–official governmental organ "Warshavski Dnievnik"–prepared a plan for besieging the city and realized the plan.

Thus did the military and civilian powers simultaneously prepare for a siege of Siedlce, but we were given no knowledge of the situation. What is more, the garrison commandant saw no need to report to the populace about the developing situation, about the danger that awaited the populace, about the extraordinary plans, and about the appointment he himself had made. Everything was held in secret, because the citizens were seen as open enemies and evil people. To the question of whether the outbreak of the events was pre–planned, the government and the garrison must answer in the greatest detail:

Excellency,

We ask permission to indicate to you that if there was indeed a revolution in preparation, the local government had at its disposal a garrison of five thousand soldiers that could have prevented an uprising through searches and stronger surveillance of strangers, very few of whom were in Siedlce. But according to the announcement of the garrison commandant, the outbreak of the citizen uprising came first and was followed by the uproar in the city caused by the army. According to the official announcement, the so–called "revolutionaries" actively opposed the army for 36 hours, so that the Siedlce garrison had to call for help to the Dubnow Regiment and the 48th Artillery Battalion.

When, on the morning of September 9, a delegation appeared before the commandant at his command, together with the city president, members of the city council, and the gentlemen lawyer Zanderland, Tortshinski, Farminski, Dr. Shavelski, and others, the commandant announced that he would reduce Siedlce to a shambles if by one o'clock the revolutionaries and their arms were not turned over to him. Clearly stated: he proclaimed a destructive war against the inhabitants. It was impossible to satisfy his demands. They could not comply because what he demanded could not be found.

[Page 124]

When the delegation went to the governor, he was incapable of giving a definitive response. Lieutenant Colonel Tichinovsky at the same time repeated again his threats and without cause arrested the whole delegation. On the declaration by the delegation that they did not know who had shot and from where the shots had come, Tichinovsky pointed to several houses and permitted members of the delegation to search the houses so they could see the "revolutionaries" for themselves. In these particular houses, they found only an old man and two women. This was conveyed to the commandant. He had not counted on this, and the shooting continued. Finally the poor houses were shot to pieces.

During this whole time that these war activities continued, the city was cut off from the world. No one was allowed to enter Siedlce. Permanent residents who had left the city in anticipation of the misfortunes and wanting to return, uneasy about the fate of their families, were forced to remain in the train station. The telegraph office was closed to the community.

And what appear to be the losses of these 36 hours of "war"? According to the official count, the army suffered no wounded or killed. On the side of the populace, 31 were brought for burial in the Jewish cemetery and 3 to 5 in the Christian cemetery. According to official news, 150 people were injured and according to other accounts–300. Two hundred were arrested, though none were guilty of revolution, because none of them were armed. A check on the dead and injured showed that the wounds came from rifle butts and bayonets. Since people had not dared to leave their homes, one must conclude that the soldiers had broken into dwellings.

During the shooting, soldiers would attack Jewish homes, and in each when the door was not opened, it was broken down with the help of iron bars. Immediately after breaking into a dwelling, the soldiers ordered the inhabitants to turn over revolutionaries, and thereby they extracted greater or lesser amounts of money. Anyone who was bold enough to stand up to them was beaten unmercifully. During the searches, those in the houses were tormented with all sorts of beastly, inhuman actions by the soldiers. We will describe only a single case:

[Page 125]

A young Jew, the father of six children, Meir Wolf, was assaulted in his apartment while he was praying. In the presence of an officer he was tortured–he was thrown from wall to wall until he had no strength left. We should note that no weapons were found, neither on the victim nor in his dwelling.

Of the 1025 houses in the city, several hundred were shot up. The Jewish hospital was also shot up. In the whole city there was not a single house that was not struck by bullets. If one added up all of the bullets that were fired, one would see that the number was greater than the number of inhabitants. These facts speak for themselves. But the garrison was not satisfied with that and called in reinforcements: cannon! Why was this necessary? It appears that this was a penalty for the sins that had not been committed. The government tormented the populace, whose suffering was like that of a man who is condemned to death though he is free of sin, though he never lifted a finger. The soldiers went wild, murdered unarmed men, raped women, stole property, and burned houses.

The version that the arsons and the robberies were carried out by civilians–Is totally wrong. It is impossible to believe that during these events civilians could be seen on the streets. The idea that civilians burned the destroyed houses is also unbelievable. If there were activities by a foreign enemy, the army should have stood up to such an enemy and not allowed a pogrom.

Altogether 59 stores were robbed, 11 houses and 12 buildings were destroyed by fire. Numberless private apartments were robbed and destroyed. The losses in property and money amount to over a million rubles.

[Page 126]

The tragedy of the event is the destruction of the rights of people and the triumph of injustice.

In the time since our journey from Siedlce to Petersburg, both the Jewish and Christian people of the city live in trembling over the next day. From you, Excellency, we await actions that will calm down the unfortunate people of Siedlce.

Excellency: Basing ourselves on your letter, we come not to beg for mercy but for the re–establishment of truth and rectitude.

Signed–

> Alexei Brzhanovsky
> Dovid Tchatchkes
> Stanislaw Zonderland[68].

It is appropriate to note who the signers were of this bold memorandum to the all powerful Stolypin. The first–Alexei Brzhanovsky, was a member of the community committee to help the victims of the pogrom. He was a Pole, a man of education and high ethics, an aesthete and a great Polish patriot. He loved truth and fought for what was right. Dovid Tchatchkes was the secretary of the Siedlce Jewish community. The last signer–Stanislaw Zonderland, was a lawyer, a converted Jew, who was always found among Jews. Zonderland had converted so he could pursue a juridical career. He was from that type of convert who did not want to lose contact with Jews. Every Pesach he would give "Ma'os Chitim" [Passover charity] and secretly he gave charitable donations to the Jewish poor. He cherished a Tanach that was written on parchment and that he had inherited from his grandfather. More than once had he lobbied for Jews, because he was not simply satisfied with his wealth.

The Czarist Inquest–Commission

A short time after the delegation had submitted the memorandum [The Yiddish says "the memorial"], after the audience with Stolypin, an inquest commission came to Siedlce and called witnesses.

[Page 127]

Both Jews and Poles were called as witnesses, and they described the murders by the army; widows and orphans testified against individuals who had murdered their husbands and children. After two weeks in Siedlce, the commission returned to Petersburg.

It appears that people at high levels of the czarist bureaucracy were not too happy with the results of the commission's work, because soon a second inquest commission was sent. Again there was a process of witness testimony and confirmation. While the commission was at work, the government began to release the arrested Jews, who were still in prison, so that before Chanukah in 1907 all the detainees had been freed, with the exception of one or two whom the government held as confirmed revolutionaries. The liberation of the detainees was the only satisfactory outcome of the bloody pogrom.

Since the findings of the inquest commissions were dismissed, Y. N. Wayntroib was sent to Petersburg. Again Baron Ginzburg intended that this representative should have an audience with Stolypin. Thus Wayntroib and the baron were taken together to Stolypin. The premier listened to Wayntroib's speech and, according to the account in the "Tiedzhen Polski," responded:

From the perspective of the government and community interests, as well as because of questions raised in Europe, we have developed a desire for detailed knowledge of the matter. Thanks to both official and private information, he will arrive at the naked truth. Because current knowledge is disjointed, he must, in order to make a firm decision, await the final report of the inquest.

Stolypin affirmed in a later declaration that, according to the most up–to–date information that he had received, people in the days in question had used to many weapons and that the arrests of the delegation by the "Ohrana"–chief was simply and undoubtedly incorrect.

The guilty parties should be punished. As for the army, men had indeed stolen– so said the czarist premier–although according to the official reports, it did not seem so widespread as reported in private sources.

[Page 128]

According to these reports, the robberies were limited to trivial things, for example: pieces of soap, cigarettes, etc. The bestial behavior of the army toward the populace should be ascribed to the provocation toward the soldiers that was caused by revolutionary activities. As in all of Poland, there existed without doubt in Siedlce revolutionary parties. According to the reports, the number of revolutionary shots aimed at the military certainly amounted to at least a thousand. The fact that no revolutionaries with weapons had been captured could be explained by saying that the revolutionary activists had hidden themselves at the appropriate time. Thus did Stolypin excuse the pogrom activities of his subordinates.

The facts that would demonstrate the intentional preparations for the pogrom he ignored–these were military matters that were practiced everywhere in case of the outbreak of disorder. Such steps were taken in Petersburg.

Over all–so Stolypin concluded–the state of war could not be separated from the revolutionary activities. But he would try to ameliorate the state of war by imposing more supervision of soldiers by officers. He, the minister, knows the Poles and believes that they can live together. He believes that it is necessary to create certain reforms with the aim of coming to an understanding[69].

The Interpolation in the Second Russian Duma

The already mentioned lawyer St. Zonderland, who was at that time a deputy in the second Russian Duma, did not rest until he had introduced an interpolation, which was devised by the legal commission of the Siedlce Aid Committee and subscribed to by the Polish "Kolo," into the Russian Duma. In the meantime, the second Duma was dissolved, and the interpolation was not considered.

[Page 129]

But it ended up being good propaganda. Each deputy received a copy. Although the interpolation had the same contents as the earlier cited memorandum, we present the full text because of its historical significance:

On the basis of paragraphs 33, 58, and 59 of the rules of the Imperial "Duma," we have the honor to request the introduction to the assembly of the "Duma" the following declaration:

The last two years have been punctuated by serious events carried out particularly against the Jewish population, as also against students and against the general intelligentsia. In Kingdom Poland, such events have not been lacking, but suddenly in the last days of August (8–10–Old Style) came terrible excesses–the well–known "Siedlce Pogrom," which differed markedly from similar occurrences that went by the same name. The city of Siedlce, which has a population of 25 thousand with a large percentage of Jews, was in 1906 administered by then–Governor General Engelky. On August 8 (O.S.), 1906, the police chief Galtzev was suddenly murdered. The murdered man had shown sympathy for the local Jewish population and one should therefore dismiss the idea the Galtzev's killer, who was not discovered, came from the Jewish sector.

On the day of the assassination, the army conducted a "small pogrom," that cost the lives of six people and affected scores of buildings. Because of the murder of Police Chief Galtzev, Siedlce was put under a special guard ("Ohrana"), at the head of which was Lieutenant Colonel Tichinovsky.

Foot patrols and horse patrols filled the streets. People were ordered to close up their businesses and homes at 8 in the evening. After that hour, people were forbidden to show themselves in the streets, etc. The city was seized by a terrible panic. On the 22nd of August, several citizens and representatives made their way to Governor General Engelke with a request to make conditions easier in the city, which he promised to do, but at the same time a high beam was raised over the building of the police commission, though no one understood its purpose. But it's purpose was to raise an alarm, to serve as a military signal for an alarm.

[Page 130]

Early on the 26th of August 1906, the foot– and horse–patrols (without any cause from the inhabitants) were reinforced and held up their provocations. The horse patrols rode with loaded rifles and unsheathed swords, but at the same time the patrols, in the evening, began to assure the merchants that from that day on they were permitted to stay open later than 8. Nevertheless the streets in the evening remained empty and the inhabitants stayed, as they had been doing, at home. That same evening, according to an order from the leader of the "Okhrana," the city was besieged by the army. No one was allowed in or out. Telegraphic communication was also prevented. According, in all probability, to already prepared orders, around 9 in the evening revolver shots were heard in the city center, near the main patrol. After these shots, which were repeated in other parts of the town, military volleys began to thunder from the 29th dragoon regiment and from the Lubow infantry regiment. This shooting spread to all the major and minor streets and lasted almost without a break for three nights and two days, that is, the 8th, 9th, and 10th of September in 1906 and ended with a large number of cannon shots. An eyewitness of these events, one of the signatories of this interpolation, can [trans. note: the text says "cannot," but that makes no sense] surely testify to the horror, pain, murders, terror, and the sea of suffering that befell the peaceful and guiltless population of Siedlce during those 48 hours. The whole population remained without bread and water, staring every minute at death, hiding from the bullets in their cellars or, if they were able to get there, in the towers of the city jail. The whole time, the savage military burned and robbed. The details of this pogrom, which caught the amazed attention of people not only in our country, in our kingdom, but also in other countries, received full confirmation in the original in the report of Police Captain Pietochov was sent there by the Governor General of Warsaw on 27th September 1906. (A copy is attached.)

[Page 131]

It is impossible to recount every aspect of the horrible pogrom. We must therefore present a number of facts and try to sum up the whole of the pogrom in Siedlce:

The soldiers, many of them led by officers, broke into private dwellings and businesses and, threatening beatings and shootings, carried out their plunder. Anyone who put up the least resistance, the soldiers beat unmercifully. They killed and wounded men, women, children, and the aged. Thus they killed Meir Wolf, the father of six children, whom the soldiers, with officer Balichov in charge, found praying in his dwelling. They tortured the children, dragging them through around the rooms, hitting them with the butts of their rifles. Chana Liebhaber, 50 years old, and Chaim Lieberman, 28, who refused to give ransom, were harmed by the officers and the soldiers, who, taking the injured to hospital, simply killed them. Ratinievitsch, who emerged injured from his burning house, the soldiers brought to the hospital, where, seeing that he was still alive, they killed him with a rifle. The director of the Jewish hospital Jan Baritsch, was killed in the hospital courtyard while carrying out his duty, caring for the wounded and the murdered. Mendel Tayblum, 34–forced out of his home on Warsaw Street, had his eyes put out and was later shot. Mordechai Miller, 40–taken from his home, he had no money to redeem himself–was hacked to death by sword. In the same way 32 other people of various ages were killed, from age 4 to 76, including 7 women, 15 heads of household, and children, not one of whom died accidentally in the street. All were shot, stabbed, slashed with swords in their homes or while they were being taken to the hospital. Eighty people, including seven women, severely wounded by bullets, swords, and rifles, were taken to the hospital. This does not include the slightly wounded. Hundreds of people were left without a roof over their heads and without what was needed to survive even for a day with small children.

[Page 132]

Together with the bloodletting, the savagery of the drunken soldiers showed itself in the burned out houses and businesses and the destroyed, ruined possessions. The homes and businesses of Greenberg, Rosen, Solarzh, Liverant, Stoloveh and others were burned and looted, as wee all the businesses in the market. According to the report of Captain Pietochov, and also according to other witnesses, the soldiers used for their destructive work kerosene that they were given. Cannon fire severely damaged the houses of Ratinievitsch, Grad, Rosenberg, Tchistaaka, and others. Also, hundreds of houses on all the major and minor streets were damaged by rifle fire.

In the walls of many dwellings (for example, at Rabbi Analik's, Dr. Bichovski's, Dr. Dayanovski's, and others) scores of bullets could be found. The soldiers shot not only private buildings but also community buildings like the Catholic church, the Jewish school and beis–medresh, the building of the Polish school, the landworkers' credit organization, the Jewish hospital, and others. In front of the hospital were wounded the surgeons Maria Glazavska and Yehuda Lifshutz, who died a few days later from his wounds.

It is impossible to count up the cases of robbery. Many businesses and private homes were robbed. One can form an idea of the thieves from the report of Captain Pietochov. He provides a decree from the Siedlce garrison on September 30, 1906, number 97, on which is written "not for publication." In this decree, all section leaders were ordered to conduct thorough searches of the entire garrison and to confiscate stolen items.

Altogether, the savagery of the excesses can be illustrated by the fact that the soldiers used thirty thousand bullets. "They didn't economize on bullets." The strength of the wasted energy was so great that after the 24th of September (O.S.), that is, well after the pogrom, on Stadalne Street, Victoria Radzhikovska was shot without provocation while she was sitting quietly by her table in her own home. One of the signers of this interpolation, Zonderland, with another prominent citizen, on the 5th of October, at 6 in the evening (well after the pogrom) was pursuing an important matter when a military patrol encountered us,

[Page 133]

They drew their swords and took us prisoner. By a miracle, along came an officer whom we knew and who saved us from certain death.

All of these facts are enough to show that Siedlce had become the victim of an organized pogrom without the least provocation by the people of the city. A pogrom that was conducted in collaboration with the civil government. The organizers of the pogrom had to find a pretext in order to justify their actions. This pretext, which was fabricated and had nothing to do with fact, was that Siedlce was full of armed revolutionaries who were preparing an uprising. These revolutionaries shot at the army and actually–on August 26 they shot at a military patrol at the central command. All of these arguments were undercut by the facts. If the siege of the city with the help of two artillery divisions lasting 48 hours, the cutting of the telegraphic communications, and the searches throughout the entire city did not uncover a single arms cache and not a single revolutionary and not a single armed civilian–this was clear evidence that there was not a single revolutionary in the city; and if there was not a single killed or wounded soldier, it is clear that no one was shooting at the army.

Moreover, the local investigation demonstrated that no one shot, not at the patrols and not at the command center, because the traces of bullets in the walls and windows of the command center could not have come from external shots. Thus those first random shots were, undoubtedly, a provocation. That the military–organs had not the least factual basis for maintaining that there were armed revolutionaries in Siedlce is shown by the following:

On the morning of September 9, Lieutenant Colonel Tichinovsky called in several prominent citizens, among whom was one of the undersigned, Dep. Zonderland, and he ordered them to give him within two hours the arms and the revolutionaries or he would destroy the city. All attempts to convince him that it was impossible to fulfill his command proved fruitless.

[Page 134]

Then those who had been summoned, watched over by guards, amid the unceasing shooting, made their way to Governor–General Engelky with the request that the shooting should cease and women and children should be allowed to leave the city. The governor–general refused to give a prompt answer. Lieutenant Colonel Tichinovsky responded, "Then I will do all that I promised." Soon Tichinovsky and Engelky spoke on the telephone. Officer Grabowsky appeared in Engelsky's courtyard with a contingent of soldiers and announced to the delegation that according to the orders of the "Okhrana" they were being arrested. He led them back to Lieutenant Colonel Tichinovsky. In front of police headquarters Tichinovsky awaited us together with his retinue and gave us a "fair welcome": "Instead of going to search for revolutionaries"–he ground his teeth–"you went to interfere with General Engelky. In less than five minutes, not one of you will remain alive."

They lined us up by the wall. Before each of us stood a soldier with a rifle at the ready pointing at our hearts, waiting for the order from the "Okhrana." Lieutenant Colonel Tichinovsky repeated his prior order concerning uncovering weapons and revolutionaries, pointing to the houses on Pienkne Street, from which people had allegedly been shooting. Then the detainees, under guard, were taken to the indicated houses, in which they, along with the officers and soldiers, found nothing aside from two old men. All of these events lead to the conclusion that everything that happened was organized by the Siedlce military and civil powers, as indicated in Pietochov's report and also in the reporting of the "Warshawski Dnievnik"[70].

Soon after the pogrom, on September 12, the inquiry began. All of the citizen witnesses and also Deputy Zonderland were examined five times, namely: by the Warsaw assistant governor–general, by representatives named by the minister of the interior, by those appointed for extraordinary events by the Warsaw governor general, and by civilian and military inquest judges.

[Page 135]

The failure of these inquests to believe the populace convinced several residents, among them Dep. Zonderland to make two visits to the Minister of the Interior with a report (a copy is attached). The minister, acknowledging the particular truths of the matter, assured the deputation "that the guilty would not escape punishment." But the result was quite otherwise: instead of punishment, for their activities the guilty–Lieutenant Colonel Tichinovsky–received a letter of thanks (published in the newspapers) from the Warsaw governor general. In this way, the punishment–worthy injustice aroused no opposition. Only one military policeman was punished by a military court for robbery, but for their terrible overstepping of military discipline, for their clear passivity in tolerating crimes, and for not assuming responsibility on the basis of paragraphs 345 and 346 of the penal code–neither Lieutenant Colonel Tichinovsky nor Governor General Volozhin received punishment.

Thus we propose that the Duma should inquire from the Ministers of the Interior, of War, and of Justice:

1.   Whether they have taken steps, and what they may be, for those who are guilty in the described events to take responsibility;

2.   Whether they have taken preventative measures, and what they may be, so that civil and military powers will not allow pogroms, whether through activities or passivity, against the general population and particularly pogroms conducted by the military.

This interpolation was brought to the interpolation–committee without prior discussion about its contents.

Self–Defense

From the bloody pogrom events in czarist Russia shines out one sterling word–self–defense: the self–protection of the Jewish people against the murderous actions of the czarist government. Understandably, self–defense became a valuable activity in the affairs of the Jewish revolutionary parties in the revolution of 1905.

[Page 136]

But not less was the effect of Bialik's fiery words concerning passivity and allowing oneself to be slaughtered that the great writer had presented in the publication of his "B'ir ha–harugah."

Had the Jews of Siedlce prepared a self–defense? Had self–defense been ready at the moment it was needed?

We know that self–defense existed and just before the pogrom it had been revived under the leadership of Hersh Chaim Geliebter. Those belonging to the self–defense group were: Boyarski, Yudel Mastboym, Yosef Smaleh, Elphraim Vilk, Avraham Sarnatzki, Yakov Brenner, Mottel Wisotski, Yakov Stalovi, Aybkorn, Berek Shtandman, Yakov Moyshe Krasitzki, Chaim Dembowitsch, Meir Saltzman, Yakov Salarzh, Yablon, and Wishnieh.

Eyewitnesses testify that the self–defense group showed no activity. Before the pogrom they disappeared and were not visible in the city. But it was clear that the group did not know what to do, because the pogrom was not made up of gangs but was a military operation of trained soldiers, well–armed with rifles and cannon.

What was the attitude of this self–defense organization after the experience of the pogrom?

The organization "Ha–t'hiyah", which taught the democratic popular wing of the Zionist movement, made a point in its program about active participation in political life (the fight against czarism, self–defense activities). In Siedlce, "Hat'hiyah" was one of the strongest organization of the province. With the help of "Ha–t'hiya" members and members of "Dvorah" (an academic women's organization, mostly students from the women's classes in Warsaw University and students from the dental school), weapons were smuggled from Warsaw to Siedlce when they thought a pogrom was being prepared[71].

From the memoirs of the Bundist activist A. Litvak we know that at the end of June, 1906, in an issue of the "Volkszeitung" there was a meeting of the Bund's central committee. On the agenda was the question of self–defense. A. Litvak explains:

[Page 137]

Self–defense at that time was at an impasse. This was just after the pogrom in Bialystok, in which the soldiers from the local garrison had participated. Thus had begun a new round of pogroms, all with the army's participation, just as in Bialystok. The Siedlce pogrom, which broke out a couple of months later, was entirely conducted by the army. What can a civilian self–defense corps do in such pogroms? When pogroms were conducted by a mass of hooligans, even by the half–organized Black Hundreds, our self–defense corps could have an effect. Sometimes they could forestall a pogrom, so it would not even begin. Sometimes, by keeping it from spreading as it usually did, they could minimize its bloodiness. But what could our self–defense corps do against the army that carried out its bloody work under orders? To stand up like accidental revolutionaries against disciplined and organized riflemen would only bring unnecessary sacrifices. And if they had to do something…what was their alternative?

In the discussion, a proposal emerged: The Bund should issue a proclamation with a clear warning, that in case of a military pogrom, they would use dynamite to blow up the city. Before such a catastrophe, even the army commanders would pause. Who made this proposal I do not know, perhaps I myself. In any case, I strongly supported it.

Many of our comrades argued against it, from a practical standpoint: we could not carry out such a thing. It would make us look laughable and would prompt severe repression. Lieber raised political motives against it: with such a tactic, he said, we would arose the whole non–Jewish population against us. Even those who are currently opposed to the pogrom, or hold themselves neutral, would tomorrow become our bitter enemies. The only victors would be the czarists, who themselves would not spare the non–Jews. They would even provoke us, so that in this or that city hundreds or thousands of innocent Christians would suffer, with the result that there would arise the bitterest war between Christians and Jews that they could inspire. If we should insist on this course of action that has been set before us, our area would repeat what had happened in the Caucusus, where the czarists had inflamed the Tartars and the Armenians against each other. They shot at each other while the czarists enjoyed the carnage from a distance…

[Page 138]

Lieber's reasoning made a strong impression on all of us. But I did not withdraw entirely. I proposed that we should not blow up the whole city, only the governmental buildings, and we should do it so that no civilians should be harmed. I was also not supported in this proposal–who knew if an explosion could be so localized. The situation was quite difficult, and in my mind I wondered: should we allow ourselves to be slaughtered without resistance?…

No proposal was put up for a vote, and the question remained formally open. Several weeks later, I published in an issue of "Glock" (the illegal journal of our Warsaw committee, in the summer and fall of 1906–in all, their were three issues) under the name of Levy, an article in which were several subtle defenses of my second proposal. No one paid attention to my article: the Siedlce pogrom was the last in that period and the whole question soon became irrelevant[72].

Y. Greenboym, considering this period of pogroms, asserts:

In Siedlce there was no attempt, and would be no attempt, made at self–defense. One shot in self–defense would have brought forth a crescendo of shooting against the city.

The events in Siedlce did not create Jewish confidence in self–defense. All of the youth circles of Poland gave up on the idea of self–defense[73].

In Jewish circles in Siedlce a report went around about the wife of the Russian officer Uriel. People said that she was a member of the social revolutionary party and she had organized in her home a gathering of the terror groups where they discussed the question of transforming themselves into self–defense forces[74].

[Page 139]

A History of the Jews in Siedlce (cont.)

The Repercussions of the Pogrom in Siedlce

The three–day–long pogrom in Siedlce was a link in the chain of anti–Semitic pogroms that the reactionary czarists had organized in Russia. The pogroms aroused the liberal world in Russia and beyond its borders. Journalists from foreign and Russian newspapers came to Siedlce to see the tragic outcome. Correspondents came from the "Neue Freie Presse," the "Daily Mail," the "Echo de Paris," the "Gazzetta Faranga," and Warsaw's "Der Veg," the only daily Yiddish newspaper in Poland. The uniqueness of the events were portrayed for weeks and months.

The young artist Maurycy Minkowski (killed in an automobile accident in Buenos Aires in 1930), who had almost completed the Arts Academy in Cracow, came to Siedlce in the company of the young journalist Noah Prilutzki. At the train station they were amazed at seeing hundreds of bewildered Jews sitting with their packs and waiting for a train in order to escape the city. With this as his inspiration, the artist created the pictures "Refugees" and "After the Pogrom," which had an extraordinary success in international shows.

Y.L. Peretz also came soon after the pogrom along with the young writer Menachem Boreysho in order to console the city. Peretz long bore the difficult impressions that the city had made on him[75].

The Russian Duma (Parliament), the Social Democrat Tzeretely spoke out against the regime, against the nightmares it created in Siedlce and Bialystok. The Russian press, too, even though they operated under firm censorship, wrote confidently about the participation of the regime in organizing the pogrom.

The well–known and influential newspaper of that time, the "Petersburg Statement," wrote: The regime is obliged to seek and find those who are truly guilty of these murders, not excluding their own agents, who lay the entire blame on the Jews.

[Page 140]

The English "Times" emphasized: "It is difficult to publish sympathetic feelings for a regime that helps perpetrate a barbaric slaughter. There is ground for believing that Stolypin is upset that the events in Siedlce help his enemies to undermine him."

In regard to the pogrom, the French newspaper "Aurore," the paper of Clemenceau, wrote: "We regret that we believed Stolypin merited being called a liberal prime minister." The "Berliner Tagblatt" sharply attacked the czarist prime minister: "Stolypin's accomplishments in Russia have been shattered. Will he and his be silent about the events that will also probably take place in Warsaw (There were rumors about preparations for a pogrom in Warsaw–Y.C.)–will he also lose his foreign reputation?"

The Yiddish press reacted strongly and sharply: "Glas Zhidowsky" (in Polish), under the editorship of the lawyer a Hartglass, and the government, as a penalty, had shut down the paper; "Dos Yiddishe Volk" in Vilna, from the 13th of Tishre, 1907, in its lead article had written, "The slaughter in Siedlce has ended, as all slaughters of Jews have ended: with the coming of commissions of 'inquiry,' after which comes a message blaming everything on the revolutionaries, while the pogromists fight for higher reasons, and so the story goes."

"Der Yiddisher Arbeter," the organ of Tz. K. of the Poale Tzion in Austria reacted in number 32 from 1906 in this language: "How long will Europe regard with equanimity the system led by the czar's underlings? How long will the Jews of Europe see the murders of Russian Jews and be silent after the official excuses of the government because the Jews of eastern and western Europe are absolutely without influence? It is high time that the czarist regime should once and for all cease to exist."

"Der Neier Veg," number 18, from 5 (18) September 1906 wrote: "Unable to stifle the revolution by the barbaric and devilish means it has heretofore used, it now tries to fight with new weapons that have never before been used in any country or in any revolution– the government treats the country as a camp of fiends, as a foreign army, which has declared war and will destroy the country. The government makes a ruin of the land, creates everywhere a state of war, sends out punitive expeditions, murder, death, robbery, takes captives, as if there were a bloody war between two devilish peoples."

[Page 141]

"Di Velt," the organ of the Zionist Action Committee (published in Cologne in the German language), devoted much space to the Siedlce pogrom. This central Zionist mouthpiece brought news and depicted the situation of hundreds who had been arrested before and after the pogrom. The arrested were accused of trying to overthrow the czarist government.

"Ha–tzefirah," number 251, from the 24th of Kislev 1906, carried a report by the Siedlce maskil K. Galitzki. He recounted that the local committee to support the victims of the Siedlce pogrom had collected 1200 rubles. The money had been sent to Petersburg to the central committee for the victims. The article also describes the attitudes among Siedlce's Jews after the pogrom:

The Jews of Siedlce gathered in the city's beis–medresh to pray. They read the Torah portion "Va'yakhel" {[This is not the name of one of the weekly portions. Rather, it is a passage following the story of the golden calf that is related to repentance–trans. note]. The cantor said a memorial prayer for the martyrs. After the prayers, the rabbi eulogized the fallen.

Also in the city synagogue, the official city cantor, R. Yosef Tiktinski, arranged a prayer service. Also those in attendance wept bitterly.

A gathering to protest the bloodletting was also organized. The protest resolution called for equal rights for all Jews in Russia.

The Effects of the Siedlce Pogrom in America and England

The first alarming news about the Siedlce pogrom appeared on one day, September 10, 1906, in all Jewish newspapers. The "crying heads" told about the frightful experiences of Siedlce's Jews. However, these descriptions of the bloody events in Siedlce bore the seal of the czarist information office.

[Page 142]

The correspondents of the American press bureau "The Associated Press," it seems, received their information about the Siedlce pogrom directly from the czarist government circles, or they had been influenced by these circles. They received the impression that Stolypin and the Warsaw governor general wanted them to.

So, for instance, at first in the New York "Forward" the pogrom was described in such a manner that it gave the impression that the army in Siedlce was fighting against Bundists and revolutionaries. First A. Litvin, the Forward's special correspondent, warned the one should treat with caution the news from the "Associated Press." In particular, people's eyes were opened by the news that appeared in the American papers, that Dr. Paul Nathan, the chair of the "Union of Aid for German Jews" had wanted to visit Siedlce and the Russian government had not given him permission to go to the city. This fact emphasized to everyone that the Russian government held back the true story of what had happened in Siedlce.

Already on September 12, 1906, the "Forward" wrote under the heading "In the Civilized Countries, People Remain Silent":

The Jewish people could have thousands slaughtered and lose whole towns, and the civilized world would not come to help. Our local American republic acts like all the rest: President Roosevelt mixes in everywhere, but when it comes to killing the killing of thousands of Jews, he remains silent. The government in Washington takes on Cuba, but when numberless Jews are killed, when our brothers fall like sheep, not a voice is raised.

The well–known author Yakov Dinenzon writes in a column in the "Yidishe tageblatt" on September 25, 1906:

Is it not time that a fine hero should be found in Europe or in America, someone like your Roosevelt, who would have the diplomatic wisdom and dexterity to interfere in anywhere and bring an end to the terrible war in Russia and make peace.

But I doubt that your Roosevelt will test his luck and his wisdom once more.

[Page 143]

But I do not doubt that without such a fine hero from abroad, the battle in Russia will not come to a quick end and the horrors of Russia will spread around the world.

Meanwhile we have blood, iron, and fire, pogroms, military trials, hangings, and slaughter in the streets.

In Siedlce, what goes on in the streets? How many killings? How many orphans? How many cripples and new Jewish beggars? Siedlce! Now you are mentioned in all the newspapers, but until now no one spoke about Siedlce.

The "Morning Journal" of September 10, 1906, wrote the following about the incoming news of the pogrom:

The pogrom was not unexpected. Two weeks earlier, on August 24, the European newspapers printed dispatches that police and soldiers in Siedlce were planning a pogrom and that Jews were fleeing from the city. Jews were preparing themselves for the pogrom.

All of the Jewish newspapers in America celebrated in particular the heroic bearing of Siedlce's dozors–Y.N. Wayntroib, M. Temkin, community secretary D. Tshatchkes, and the Siedlce rabbi D.B. Analik–for their intervention with the governor of Siedlce and the murderer Tichinovsky. Also the Russian newspaper "Birzhevi–ya Vyedomosti" printed an article called "Siedlce's Heroes" and stressed the proud bearing and high courage of the Jewish leadership in Siedlce.

After the pogrom in Siedlce, the Jewish community leaders and openly liberal opinions were disturbed in anticipation of further pogroms organized by the government against the Jews. As we have already said, there were fears of such a pogrom in Warsaw.

The current leader of the P.P.S in Galicia, Ignace Dashinski, telegraphed the London "Times" from Cracow that the Russian government had brought in special soldiers who knew how to make a fine slaughter ("Judisches Tageblatt, September 16, 1906).

[Page 144]

On the next morning, the same newspaper reported that Dr. Paul Nathan, the chairman of the "Union of Aid for German Jews" had sent the following alarming telegram:

A letter from Warsaw reports that Russian and Polish officers from liberal circles believe that a slaughter is imminent for the Jews of Warsaw. Jewish soldiers report as the commanders of their regiments who are quartered in Warsaw made speeches to their troops in which they declared the czar had chosen a day for reckoning with the Jews. In short, since the czar wants them to kill the Jews, the commanders distributed ninety thousand rubles among the soldiers.

The telegrams from Dazhinski and Nathan revealed the intentions behind the proposed danger. The pogrom in Siedlce made the danger even starker by saying that the czar's devilish plan would be carried out in Warsaw. However, no pogrom took place in Warsaw, but daily murders took place there, as Yakov Dinenzon rightly noted in the "Yidishe tageblatt" in his article "Regarding the pogrom in Siedlce."

When, after the Siedlce pogrom, it became known in other countries that the czar planned to hold military trials for two hundred people among the victims of the czar's army, the Jewish community leaders–David Alexander (director of the "Board of Jewish Deputies" in England), Claude Montefiore (chair of the Anglo–Jewish Association), and Leopold Rothschild (vice–president of the Organizational Bureau) published the following letter in the London "Times":

As representatives of the Jews in England, we protest the newly–planned battle against our unfortunate brothers in Poland. We hold fast that it violates the limits of propriety that characterize the civilized world that those who committed such atrocities against the Jews of Siedlce should sit as judges against people whom they arrested to cover up their own misdeeds. We ask with pounding hearts that those arrested should receive at the very least impartial trials. From a telegram we have learned that two hundred people were arrested in the confusion and that their fate is in the hands of army judges who have already been chosen. We hope that the voices of civilized lands will prevent this terrible miscarriage of justice.

[Page 145]

Siedlce Jews in America and Their Help for the Victims

At that time there were in America approximately 140 immigrants from Siedlce whose families were still in their hometown. The news in the papers about the pogrom against Siedlce's Jews gave the immigrants a horrible shock.

Several activists among the Siedlce group in New York began to plan an aid program for the pogrom's victims. On the same day, a meeting was organized at which it was decided to call for a mass gathering to found the "Siedlce Pogrom–Relief Committee." At this gathering, which was poorly organized, there were few people from Siedlce, and the sum that was collected there amounted to about a hundred dollars. A second mass meeting was organized, which was held on September 13, 1906. From a note in the "Forward" under the headline "Siedlce in a River of Blood," we can see who spoke at the meeting. In the note, we read:

A huge mass meeting is called by the Siedlce branch 53 of the "Arbiter Ring" this Thursday, the 13th of September, at 8 in the evening. Where the following speakers will address the crowd: B. Feygenboym, Dr. Gurewitsch, M. Katz, Dr. Sh. Feskin, Ab. Goldberg, and many others. Come in masses to show sympathy and consolation for the widows and orphans.

We find a report about this mass meeting in the "Yidishes Tageblatt" of September 14, 1906:

Last night at the Terrace Lyceum, 205 East Broadway, a mass meeting was held, called by the Siedlce branch 53, over the terrible pogrom that occurred in Siedlce. Despite the powerful storm that occurred last night, the huge hall was packed with people, who shed many tears as a variety of speakers described the great misfortune that befell Siedlce's Jews. Many pledged donations to the aid fund for the unfortunate people of Siedlce.

[Page 146]

For several months, the Siedlce group in New York tried to raise a meaningful sum for aid, but the amount they gathered was very small. The directors of the collection then decided to go the "American Jewish Committee," which was led by the well–known millionaire Jacob Schiff. This group had gathered a huge sum to aid pogrom victims in Russia. Some of the money was sent to London in case of a pogrom–which was a frequent phenomenon in czarist Russia–so that help could be conveyed quickly. The Siedlce representatives wanted some of this money to be sent to the victims of the Siedlce pogrom.

According to Sh. Tcharnabrode in his memoirs, which were given after his death to the YIVO in New York, the lawyer Louis Julian (Slushne), a son of Yoel Julian (Slushne), the chair of the Siedlce "Pogrom Relief Committee," went on behalf of the committee with a letter to Jacob Schiff proposing a meeting between him and the committee. Jacob Schiff quickly responded to letter, saying that he was prepared to meet with the committee.

Jacob Schiff warmly received the delegation, which consisted of three people: the committee chair, the already mentioned Julian (Slushne), his son Louis the lawyer (who was not a member of the committee), and Harry Green.

As soon as the Siedlce committee arrived, Schiff remarked that he knew why they had come to him and he had already done what they wanted. He showed the delegation a telegram that he had received from Claude Montefiore. This was a response to Jacob Schiff's telegram that they should send a meaningful sum for the pogrom victims in Siedlce. Claude Montefiore told Schiff that they had sent seventy–five thousand rubles to Baron Ginzburg in Petersburg, with the proviso that the Baron should send the money to Siedlce.

The Siedlce "Pogrom Relief Committee" rejoiced over Jacob Schiff's answer that such a sum had been sent.

[Page 147]

The help of the American committee revived the Siedlce group. The committee members became even more fervent in their efforts.

Emigrants from the pogrom came to New York, fleeing from Siedlce. They no longer wished to remain in the city that oppressed them to death. Those who arrived declared that irresponsible do–gooders had taken over the Siedlce committee, and they put their own financial welfare first. This news made a strong impression on the committee members in New York. The matter went so far that the New York "Pogrom Relief Committee"decided not to send funds to Siedlce, but to use it for grants for the newly arrived immigrants. But when the relief committee went to the Yarmalawski Bank, where the money was located, the bank refused to hand over the money, with the warning that the money was intended to be sent to Siedlce. When negotiations with the bank produced no results, it was decided not to put any more funds into that bank and that any money yet to be collected should be used for grants for the new immigrants, whose number in America–particularly in New York–was growing from day to day.

The "Pogrom Relief Committee" was dissolved in 1907. It had done much for the victims of the pogrom. Despite the malevolent warning about the activities of the Siedlce committee in helping the pogrom's victims, one must stress that the committee provided sums of money for the reconstruction of ruined houses and burned buildings, stolen merchandise, and grants to buy passage for emigration to Copenhagen, America, o Eretz Yisroel, where the emigrants from Siedlce had begun to go. From the assembled funds, a total of a thousand rubles was designated fir the opening of the "savings and loan," which in later years became the "Udzhalovi Bank," one of the largest cooperative banks in Poland. The descriptions of the immigrants had been exaggerated and smelled of gossip.

[Page 148]

The Siedlce Pogrom in Folk Song and in the Light of History

The pogrom in Siedlce had no Bialik, who could publish artistic accounts of his sorrow and fury over the form of Jew–extermination (the military pogrom) that the czarist government had developed. But the people themselves considered the horrible murders of Siedlce's Jews.

In the course of long years–almost a whole generation, until Hitler's extermination of the Jews–the bloody misfortune lived in the people's memories. Parents told their children about those nightmarish days. The people created a song that was sung to a melancholy tune.

The song consisted of 12–14 stanzas and told in rhyme what had happened in the city. Sadly, no one wrote down the text of the song, and so from oral memories of those who lived through the pogrom, we can present only six stanzas:

On Shabbos evening, after their meal
the Jews wrung their hands in fright.
They never could have imagined
how terrible would be that night.

In attics and basements we sat hidden,
afraid for our very souls.
The Labovsk swine[76] ran wild in the courtyards.
Destroying our lives was their goal.

The feathers, they all went a–flying
as in winter comes down the snow;
our gold, silver, diamonds, and jewelry
off with the bandits did go.

Yitzchak the well–known butcher[77]
tried to defy the toughs–
they hit his head with their rifles
and ran off with all of his stuff.

[Page 149]

Just listen, Abraham the goy,[78]
don't think that it will be so.
You ordered the deaths of children
and the cost of children's blood you will know.

In your own little town,
be sure you look around–
lest someone throw a bomb.

The pogrom in Siedlce received attention in historical accounts, which appeared in later years. The great historian and martyr Shimon Dubnow unfortunately described the murders in Siedlce in his latest history of the Jewish people, but in several spots he included errors. Thus, for instance, Professor Sh. Dubnow calls the pogrom's organizer "Tichanovitsch" rather than his correct name, Tichanovsky. Dubnow writes:

————The head of the security police in Siedlce, Tichanovitsch, planned a bloody military pogrom (8–10 September)–casualties included 30 killed and 150 injured Jews. The pretext was a provocative shooting at soldiers, after which the army opened a wild volley in the streets and bombed Jewish houses. A second agent from the local "Okhrana," a police official, delivered an official report that the Jews had no pretext for a pogrom and that it was entirely a planned police action; nevertheless, the guilty Tichanovitsch was not punished, but instead received thanks from the Warsaw Governor General "for his efforts in restoring order"[79].

In 1916, in Prague, Czechoslovakia, a brochure was published in German in which the author, Avraham Greenberg, described the Siedlce pogrom. The author did not cut down on exaggerations[80].

The historian of the Polish workers' movement–Stanislaw Martinowski–in 1936 published in Lodz, in Polish, a work in which he dealt with the 1906 Siedlce pogrom.

[Page 150]

In 1947, the writer of the present work published, for the fortieth anniversary of the Siedlce pogrom, a Hebrew monograph about the events in Siedlce[81].

The End of the Pogrom Heroes

The murderer Tichinovsky died after great suffering a short time after the pogrom. While he was handling his revolver, a bullet was discharged and hit the pogrom hero, from which he developed blood poisoning. For a while he lay unconscious. He would cry out that the Jewish dead, his victims, would not allow him to rest. When he regained consciousness, he told his colleagues–the officers closest to him–that he feared assassination from the Jews, and he begged them that if anyone actually killed him, they should take vengeance on the Jews with a second slaughter. A short time thereafter, this evil man gave up his unclean ghost. A short time before his death, it became known that Czar Nicholas II at issued an "imperial thanks" and gave gifts to a number of Black Hundred heroes who excelled in conducting pogroms and slaughters against the Jews of Russia. Tichanovsky was singled out.

Tichanovsky had received a welcoming telegram from the Black Hundreds in Yelisavetgrad (South Russia). He responded to this telegram with thanks: "I thank the loyal Russian men. Bayonets are mightier than rags."

Governor Volozhin left Siedlce in 1912, when the district was dissolved. He went to Chelm, and from there–to Petersburg, where he assumed the position of head of the Police Department. Finally he became the head of the Holy Synod.

At the time of the revolutionary storm in 1917, Volozhin and his wife, Madam Dolgorukov, who had come from an aristocratic background, fled to France. These czarist notables in 1932 lived in the Riviera town Boulogne–sur–Mer and survived by running a spice shop.

The czarist government later persecuted Pyetuchov for his report to Skalan about the pogrom.

[Page 151]

As a punishment, he was sent from Siedlce to Riga. A couple of years after the pogrom, a judgment was made against him for three rubles of army funds. Thus did the czarist government get vengeance against Pietuchov for his report to Skalan about the Siedlce pogrom, which had caused the government such trouble.

Zionist and Cultural Activities After the Pogrom

After the pogrom, all activities of the Jewish community were directed toward helping the victims, taking care of the orphans, appealing to Petersburg, and so on. Then was established the "Esras Yesomim" (Orphans' Aid), which later developed into a major organization to aid orphans. Slowly the Zionist movement came back to life, as did the activities of the socialist parties that existed illegally in Siedlce. At that time, a group of Poale Zion was organized in Siedlce.

How the Zionist activities in the summer of 1906, before the pogrom, appeared, we can see in the description in the memoirs of Shimon Tcharnobrode.

In his memoir, Tcharnobrode says:

It was in the summer of 1906. Zionist work in Siedlce was feeble. Aaron Menachem Gurewitsch was the Zionist leader in town. The only Zionist activity was that every Shabbos Mr. A.M. Gurewitsch would speak about Zionist and general Jewish questions.

Although I was then very young, I was a member of "IIa–tekhia" (a democratic–Zionist youth organization). I went to hear his talks. But I was quite unhappy about the feebleness of the Zionist activities that took place in Siedlce.

One time on Shabbos, in the summer of the Siedlce pogrom, I heard that there would be a talk by Mr. A.M. Gurewitsch. I went to hear the talk. After the talk, I approached Gurewitsch with a question: Why was Zionist activity so pathetic?

[Page 152]

Mr. A.M. Gurewitsch responded that he was glad to hear that I was dissatisfied with the state of Zionist work and he advised me to think of activities.

In the summer of the Siedlce pogrom, I threw myself heart and soul into Zionist work. Zionism, the Zionist movement, became my ideal…In fact the organizational work got a good start, but in the middle of his Zionist activities, A.M. Gurewitsch [trans. note–Sometimes he says "A.M." and sometimes "M.A."] had to leave Siedlce for Odessa for a Zionist gathering that M.M. Usishkin had called on his own initiative. Because of czarist prohibitions, this gathering was held illegally in a summerhouse near Odessa.

M.A. Gurewitsch received an invitation to the gathering and so went to Odessa[82].

As we noted earlier, the democratic–Zionist organization "Ha–tekhiah" smuggled weapons into Siedlce when it became known that the government was preparing a pogrom against the Jews. "Ha–tekhia" wanted to create a real self–defense organization.

**

Soon after the pogrom, an exodus from the city began. Mainly people headed for America, but a certain group of Zionist and Poale Tzion members went to Eretz Yisroel. The so–called Second Aliyah to Eretz Yisroel was then under way, comprised of idealists; not everyone, however, could withstand the harsh conditions of the journey, so some returned. But some struck deep roots in the life of Eretz Yisroel.

The emigration of Siedlce's young people to Eretz Yisroel made a strong impression, as did the letters they sent, in which they described their lives as farmers in the Galilee or Judea. The impression became even stronger. The Poale Tzion published their Poltava Platform, which strengthened the Zionist influence among the masses. One of the effects in the city was the strengthening of ties to Eretz Yisroel through the involvement of the bank Sh. B. Mintz and Yehoshua Goldfarb, who was born in Mezrich. The two partners had opened bank offices in Siedlce with branches in Mezrich, Byala Podolsk, Lukow, and Sokolow.

[Page 153]

About Yehoshua Goldfarb we know that he was born in 1867. His father, R. Moyshe, took part in the Khivas Tzion movement and was among the founders of "Yesod Ha–ma'alah" [a settlement in Palestine], and by profession a brewer. Yehoshua also belonged to the "Khov'vey Tzion." As he grew older, he was a member of the "Benei Moyshe." From Siedlce he went to Eretz Yisroel, and there, together with Zev Gluskin of Warsaw, founded the wine business "Carmel" and was also among the founders of "Menucha ve'Nakhalah"–the creators of Rekhovot.

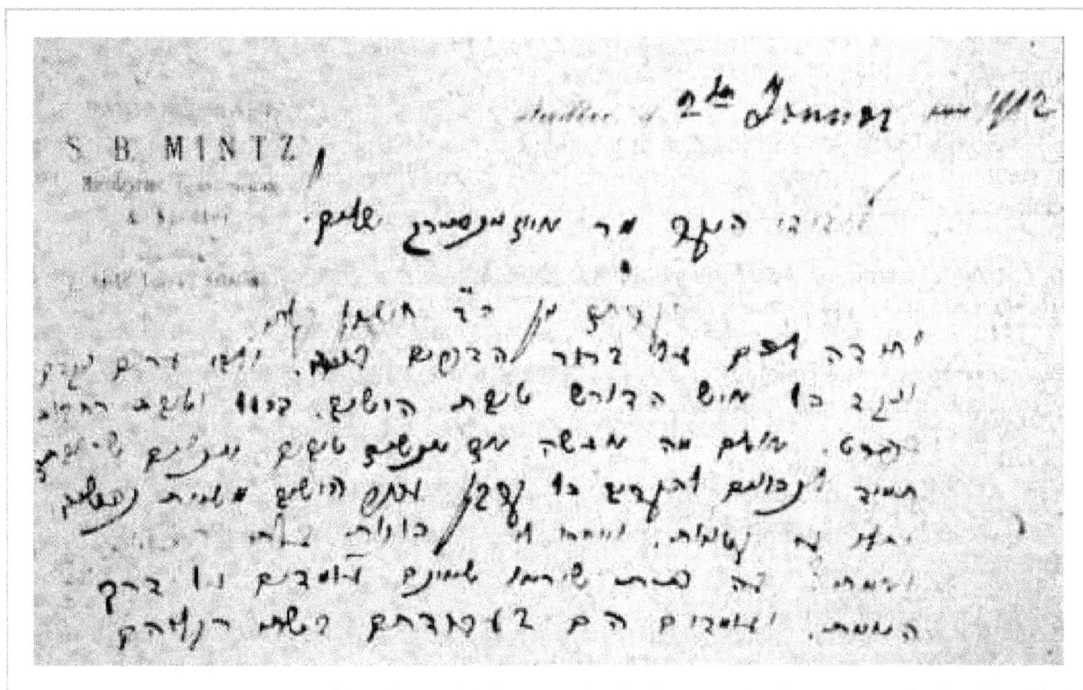

The letter from Shimon–Ber Mintz to Rekhovot

At first, Yehoshua visited Eretz Yisroel as a tourist. Later, in 1909, he settled in Rekhovot and was active in local community life and became involved with the colony's committee. A while later he moved to Tel Aviv and founded a business by the name of "Kadmas Ha–aretz," which bought property around Tel Aviv. At the time of the First World War, Goldfarb lost all the money that he had left in Poland. In Eretz Yisroel, he helped to fund the large Tel Aviv bank "Kupas Am," which planted an almond grove in Rekhovot.

[Page 154]

Before and during the First World War, as long as Siedlce found itself under the domination of the czarist government, there was no possibility of discussion of greater Zionist activity. The most work went into organizing meetings and lectures that were laboriously prepared by Greenboym, Hartglass, and others. Such gatherings were held conspiratorially or under other pretexts so that the Russian government would not seize them. With the end of the czarist regime, the Zionist movement became livelier. It moved from being a small circle to a mass movement.

Before the outbreak of the war, a group of Zionist young people came to Eretz Yisroel. Among them was the later–to–be leftist Poale Tzion leader Yosef Slushni. For various reasons, whether because of illness or economic problems, some of them went back to Siedlce. Yosef Slushni also came back and undertook broad business activities.

* *

At that time a new boom took place in Siedlce's Jewish life. The workers' parties, the "Bund" and the "Poale Tzion," which had been illegal, began to show lively activities. The only place where this openly Jewish community life was on display was the aforementioned library and the "Ha–zamir" Society.

The "Ha–zamir" Society came into existence in the difficult years after the pogrom. In those dark days of great apathy and indifference toward community life, in August of 1908 a small group of wise people, lovers of literature and music, gathered and founded a society under the name of "Ha–zamir" [The Nightingale], which a short time later was changed to "The Literary–Musical Society of Jewish Arts." It is strange that the creation of such a society occurred in such difficult times.

For the opening of "Ha–zamir", the writer Tchemerinsky (R. Mordechayele) was brought in. The atmosphere was dignified.

[Page 155]

The following comprised the first committee: Kalman Golitzky, Matityahu Mintz, Yitzchak Eliyahu Zucker, Avraham Ziglwaks, Moyshe Volovsky, Berl Mintz, and Yosef Rozenzumen. The committee had developed a broad set of activities involving music and literature. There was a chorus, a drama section, and an orchestra. They also arranged readings by Kalman Golitzky and lecturers who were brought in from Warsaw.

The activities of this cultural institution were influential in the community life of Siedlce, and "Ha–zamir" helped to strengthen the spiritual and national life of the depressed population of Siedlce.

The czarist government watched the community closely and began to persecute it. The early signs were obvious. Meetings were not permitted. The local society was told that its hall would be closed. Only thanks to the intervention of Y.N. Wayntroib did the society continue to exist.

In 1912, "Ha–zamir" changed its name to "Jewish Arts." The following were added to the society: M. Mandelman, Berl Tcharnabrade, and Asher Liverant, Genia Halbershtam, Tirzeh Zucker, Rochel Edelshteyn, Bronia Goldberg. Thanks to these people, the society developed quickly.

At the same time, the aforementioned library also developed. It was founded in 1900. By 1912, the number of books had more than doubled to more than 2,500. However, it lacked a systematic catalogue and a list of subscribers. In order to broaden the activities of the library, a project was instituted to unite the library with "Ha–zamir," which had already changed its name to "Jewish Arts" According to its by–laws, the society could incorporate a library, so that the existing library in the name of M.M. Landau transferred to "Ha–zamir." Under its new custodians, the library flourished. First, it had a larger location, and in its first two years, until the outbreak of the First World War, the numbers of readers increased to over three hundred.

[Page 156]

When the war broke out, the military government threw the library out and requisitioned their building. Thankfully the books were taken care of by the committee, like an eye in the head [that is, they were treasured]. The hard times and the concern for their continued existence tore the library workers from their work. There was a danger that the library would disappear, but thanks to the energy and concern of a group of devoted guardians from the cultural organization, the library remained unhurt. Keep in mind that no purchases were made, because there was nothing available to buy, which meant that a sum of money remained. This meant that during the German occupation, a fine location for the library could be found on what was then Warsaw Street.

The First Jewish Periodical Publication in Siedlce

In December of 1911, the first published periodical appeared in Siedlce. "The Shedletzer Vort" ["The Siedlce Word"]–that was the name of the small, thin booklet, as big as a small little prayer book. "The Shedletzer Vort" was considered a rarity in those days, when it was not so easy to distribute a newspaper in Russia, especially in Yiddish. Therefore this little booklet had a special charm, despite its poor appearance.

This publication was thanks to the travelling loner, the ailing Avraham Gilbert (cousin of the well–known writer Sh. Gilbert) who arrived in Siedlce with a small press and some printing type, in order to open there a publishing house and derive a little income. It could be that Avraham Gilbert came to Siedlce because of his brother Moyshe, the Siedlce resident, Russian teacher, and overall active member of the "Agudas Achim," an organization that at that time played an important role in the cultural and community life of the city. Moyshe was a man of talent and used to write songs, parodies, humoresques, fables about local concerns.

[Page 157]

He often appeared with his creations at concerts and evening events that were organized by the "Agudas Achim." He had a large following in the local community. From sheer delight, people often carried him around on their shoulders.

Because he had no work and no income, Gilbert struck upon the idea of issuing a weekly paper. He brought the printing equipment with him, along with printing type, and he knew how to write…

Gilbert confided his plans to Dovid Neumark, a religious frequenter of the beis–medresh who later became a Bund activist and an editor of the Bundist publication–the "Folkszeitung" [the "People's Newspaper"]. (Today in New York is works at the "Forward" and "Der Vekker.") Neumark told the secret plan to Fishman, who later wrote a book of stories called "Summer Days" (Warsaw, 1938) and "Homeless Jews" (Shanghai, 1948). The three of them came to an agreement and decided to publish a Siedlce newspaper.

The birth of the journal was accompanied by great labor, because he had too little printing type and he had to do all the work himself. He could not even think of taking on an assistant because his finances would not allow him to.

Despite these circumstances, the "Shedletzer Vort" was born. Neumark treated "Ha–zamir." He printed a story by A. Maidanik, a translation from Hebrew. Avraham Gilbert was represented by two poems and Y.Kh. Fishman with his first tale, "A Chasidic Story," under the pseudonym Y.Tz. L'vavitsch. Itsche Altshuler also wrote a short article.

It took two weeks to print the paper, because there was only enough type for half a column, and each column was printed twice. In the second issue, which appeared in 1912, he was assisted by Yakov Tenenboym and Yehoshua Goldberg. He printed a kind of local poem under the name "Siedlce Panorama," which was quite successful. It provided descriptions of well–known Siedlce personalities.

[Page 158]

The "Sedletzer Vort" was liked by its readers, but not by the czarist government. The police arrived at Gilbert's pathetic publishing house and confiscated the forbidden materials.

Avraham Gilbert, lost the courage to continue, and his pioneering spirit was taken over by Yakov Tenenboym, who had participated in the second issue of the "Shedletzer Vort." Yakov Tenenboym was by profession a country doctor. Although he was absent–minded, his writing was sharply funny, impactful, satirical, and flashy. When Tenenboym became interested in Journalism, he was already about thirty years old and had five children. Everybody wondered when Tenenboym became a journalist and had the idea to put out a weekly paper.

The writing was very difficult for Tenenboym, especially because he alone had to fill three–quarters of the paper. He brought Y.H. Fishman into the work. Fishman, then about twenty years old, at first was unwilling to do the work, but eventually he became involved in the writing. He and Tenenboym would sit all day, and often into the night, working on the paper.

Because of his journalistic work, Tenenboym neglected his medical practice. It appears that the ailing did not wait for him.

Tenenboym also approached his offended friend Yehoshua Goldberg about working with him on the paper. Goldberg was about the same age as Tenenboym. They were friends since childhood, but they had a falling out when they began working in journalism…because Yehoshua had brought into Tenenboym's room his poem for the journal, but he put the manuscript onto the table and not handed it to

Tenenboym. There was a kind of literary jealousy between them. Tenenboym envied Goldberg because of his talent. Yehoshua had already published poems in a Warsaw literary magazine.

[Page 159]

At the same time, Yoel Mastboym showed up–Yehoshua's young friend, who had begun to write. Goldberg edited the "Shedletzer Vokhenblatt" for three years. There he wrote sketches and feuilletons that described life in the city. His feuilletons, "From the Tales of Siedlce" and the cycle "My Teachers" were sources of Siedlce folklore, which, sadly, have still not been put into book form.

With Goldberg's help, Tenenboym later began to put out a new paper that was called "Siedlce Life." The editorial was by the lawyer A. Hartglass, who at that time lived in Siedlce. Hartglass was not invited to take part in the work, but it happened that he wanted to participate. He announced his desire to write for the paper. Naturally the editors happily welcomed him. He wrote his article in Yiddish, but his Yiddish was full of errors. It was called "Our Defects," and criticized the Russification of the Jewish intelligentsia. As an example, he cited an advertisement for the earlier newspaper by a reader named Yagodzinsky. The advertisement was written in Russian.

Y.Kh. Fishman also published a story about the bad luck of the former rabbi of Siedlce, R. Yisroel Meizels, the son of the famous Warsaw rabbi Berish Meizels, who had been the official rabbi of Siedlce (1858–1867). We wrote about him in an earlier chapter.

After the second issue, there was, as is customary among Jews, a rift: Goldberg and Tenenboym left and put out another paper, the "Shedletzer Viderkol" [the "Siedlce Echo"]. (All subsequent publications bore the first word "Shedletzer.") The first issue appeared in a large format, on yellow paper with nice graphics. IT was printed by Yehoshua Lichtenfacht. Tenenboym, as always, had filled the paper with articles and notices that filled all the pages. The articles and notices filled both sides of the pages, and their focus was the face of the city.

[Page 160]

Before the publication of the second issue, a sensation was created when the lawyer A.M. Hartglass submitted an article that drew the attention of all the Jews in Siedlce because of its sharp attack on the anti–semitic article by Dr. St. Wansowski in "Glos Podloski." St. Wansowski was then profoundly anti–semitic and called for a war against the Jews. (Later he became a liberal and supported the Jews.) His article was called "The Uplifted Weapons." As he argued against Wansowski, Hartglass found it necessary to make certain observations about the Jewish population, about their behavior at certain times. These observations upset Tenenboym. In the same issue in which Hartglass' article appeared, Tenenboym printed a long critical article arguing with these observations about Sidelce's Jews.

Hartglass would not let this go, so he immediately sent a longer response in which he demonstrated that Tenenboym was mistaken.

Tenenboym had already prepared an array of pamphlets against prominent people and community leaders, but he had nowhere to publish them. It appears that someone had intervened and the police arrived at his print shop, confiscated the remaining copies of the "Shedletzer Viderkol," and strongly warned him not to continue publishing the journal. Tenenboym also faced a trial, but his father Chaim–Michael intervened. He did whatever he could…and he protected his Yankel from a judgment.

Gilbert, too, seeing what had happened to Tenenboym, published a third issue of "Shedletzer lebn," and thus ended the first period of the Jewish press in Siedlce. Gilbert resigned and left Siedlce and went to Switzerland to heal his ailing lungs. It is a shame, a true shame, that no trace remains of these publications. Y.H. Fishman writes about all these publications in his unpublished memoirs[84].

Aside from the newspapers, A. Gilbert and D. Neumark published a small book of poems, "Die Nachtigall" ["The Nightingale"], which contained mostly poems by Gilbert.

[Page 161]

The Time of the First World War and in Independent Poland

The First World War broke out, as is well known, on August 1, 1914. In Siedlce was quartered the north–west headquarters of the Russian army, led by General Danilov. General Danilov, it appears, was not anti–semitic, and at the behest of Rabbi Rubenshteyn, made efforts to stop the expulsions of the Jews from the eastern front. Since this matter concerns Siedlce, we will discuss it further on.

Rabbi Rubenshteyn, the former rabbi of Vilna and senator in the Polish senate, describes in his memoirs[85] his visit to Siedlce at the beginning of the First World War and his meeting with General Danilov:

Pesach was approaching–so says Rabbi Rubenshteyn–and people were concerned about getting matzo to the Jewish soldiers at the front. In this cause, Rabbi Rubenshteyn went to General Danilov and asked him for permission to take matzos to the front.

General Danilov's quarters were in a military train. His train car stood by a special platform of the Siedlce train station. No civilian could approach it, except with great difficulty. Rabbi Rubenshteyn had identification papers from Duke Tamanov. On the basis of these papers, Danilov, by telephone, allowed Rubenshteyn to visit him. After the army security had checked out Rabbi Rubenshteyn's papers, he was taken to the train.

Danilov's adjutant led Rabbi Rubenshteyn to the welcome car. From there he was taken to Danilov's private living quarters on the train, which were decorated like a luxury dwelling, ornamented with mirrors and pottery and doors made of polished glass.

The rabbi stated the purpose of his visit. At first the general was doubtful about whether it was necessary or important to bring matzos to the Jewish soldiers in the midst of combat. He also had doubts about whether it was possible.

[Page 162]

Transport, Danilov said, was beset by many problems. The trains were needed for carrying soldiers and ammunition. Every village had lost its normal peacefulness and private comforts. The Greek Orthodox soldiers–he said–would also not receive their religious "treats."

After Rabbi Rubenshteyn explained the importance of matzos for Jews, the importance of the mitzvah, which was much more important than the Russian custom of eating sweets for Easter, Danilov agreed that it was not fitting to force Jews to eat chametz on Pesach, and it would not be proper. Nor would it be wise to upset the religious conscience of soldiers in the trenches when they felt themselves face to face with death. Danilov responded: "Nu, gut [translator's note: I doubt that the general said "Nu, gut"] send the matzos. Give me instructions and I will order that the matzos should be taken at the right time and should be divided in the proper way among the Jewish soldiers."

The staff commander also dealt with the rabbi's second request, that the army should send the matzos by military trains and the "Jewish Committee Concerning Matzos" should be freed from paying transport feels. The committee had saved up scores of rubles for this, an amazing sum in those hard times.

When the rabbi had finished his discussion of the matzos, the general spoke with him about other things. His courtesy greatly impressed the Vilna rabbi. The general paid several compliments to the record of the Jewish soldiers, who impressed him with their service. The courteous behavior of the general gave the rabbi courage to raise other Jewish matters. He set before him the anti–Jewish incitement, he described the woes of the "homeless," their being sent to Siberia without trials after baseless accusations of espionage.

General Danilov responded that his duty was to worry about what the army needed at the front and to preserve order behind the front.

Rabbi Rubenshteyn left the general, and when he arrived at home, he sent a telegram with new questions about how to care for the matzos.

[Page 163]

Once again the rabbi telegraphed the general and asked for a second audience.

This time, too, the general was very courteous and agreed to meet the rabbi in two days.

In a second case–explains Rabbi Rubenshteyn–he came to Siedlce with a delegation from Warsaw in order to intervene with General Danilov and ask him to introduce the Jewish delegation to the head of the general staff Alexeyev, to whom the delegation wanted to complain about military and civilian authorities who created such sorrows for the Polish Jews. Their chief request was: people should not exile the "homeless" in Warsaw, and the aid committee, which had raised sums of money from the royal committee in Petersburg, should cease abusing the Jews. The delegation also knew of a plan to deport the Warsaw Jews that the local powers had devised, and they wanted to touch upon the issue.

On the same day, a telegram arrived in Siedlce at the address of Rabbi Rubenshteyn that said that there was also an order to deport the Jews of Lithuania. The expulsion was supposed to encompass all the districts in the region: Vilna, Gradno, the length of the Nieman and the area from Kovno to Bialystok. The delegation, led by Rabbi Rubenshteyn had the assignment to confer with General Danilov, who was headquartered in Siedlce, and to have him nullify the decrees of Jewish expulsion from Warsaw and the right bank of the Nieman.

The night before the audience, General Danilov ordered that Rabbi Rubenshteyn be found in Siedlce in order to request that Rabbi Rubenshteyn should come to him without the rest of the Warsaw delegation.

When Rabbi Rubenshteyn conveyed his requests to the general, Danilov said that the orders about the Nieman were not in his jurisdiction. But he promised that he had already gone to the general of the tenth district and inquired why he had not carried out the orders of the head of the general staff to cease oppressing the Jews, but General Ratzkevitsch answered that in his jurisdiction he made the decisions and in the tenth district he could do what he wanted, because he was responsible for security. Be assured–Danilov told the rabbi–I would not allow such things.

[Page 164]

The Nieman was the boundary between the front and the hinterlands–the Rabbi went on–and Jews were being driven out from the shtetl of Trok and from the areas on the right bank of the river, which was under the control of Your Excellency.

Impossible–the general said–the Jews are hysterical and they are fantasizing.

The Vilna Rabbi assured him that he had received a telegram from the Vilna community that clearly stated that all the Jews from those areas, including the Jews of Trok, which was near Vilna, were awaiting expulsion.

The general became upset, and in order to counter Rubenshteyn, he sent a telegram to Duke Tumanov, asking him whether it was correct that an order had been issued to expel the Jews from the right bank of the Nieman. In just a moment, even before the audience ended, Tumanov's reply arrived. He confirmed the news. He said that the order had been issued by General Ratzkevitsch.

As soon as the answer arrived, Rabbi Rubenshteyn took heart and began again to argue: It is impossible that the expulsion of Jews from a shtetl only a few kilometers from Vilna should not include the Jews of Vilna, who would also be expelled. Can they issue such an order without your knowledge!

Danilov became furious with General Ratzkevitsch and said: "Vilna is always under my control–the Jews will not be expelled!" Danilov assured him that the Jews of Warsaw would also not be expelled.

As later became obvious, General Danilov did a lot for the Jews in that area in his capacity of commander at the front.

* *

On August 12, 1915, the Russian army began to evacuate Siedlce and retreat from Poland. The Hebrew daily paper"Ha–Tzefirah" gives the following description of how the city was handed over to the Germans:

[Page 165]

The police left the city on Wednesday, August 11, 1915, and the militia took over the post office. At night shooting was heard and flames appeared. Government buildings were burning and the depot blew up.

After midnight the Cossacks arrived in the city. They tore the doors of the largest stores in Siedlce and stole merchandise. Several of these thieves broke into the dwelling of a rich man and forced him to hand over all of his money. Later on, another group arrived, searched around and took another 1250 rubles. The Cossacks spent the whole night going from house to house and stealing.

On Thursday, at 10 in the morning, a German patrol arrived in the city. Then the Germans entered the city from all directions[86].

After the Germans occupied the city, a civilian committee with a German governor managed Siedlce. The electric station, which was founded in 1906 and was destroyed in the war, was relaunched by the Germans, first as a private concern and in 1918 it was turned over to the city. The total electric output was very little, consisting of a single machine of 75 horsepower.

Thanks to poverty and hunger, a typhus epidemic broke out in the city. In the Jewish population, which was undernourished, there were many deaths. Religious people in the city sought a charm to halt the epidemic. They believed that people should hold a wedding in the ceremony and conduct a burial for "sacred papers" and torn holy books that had been stored in the "genizah" of the city shul and in the beis–medresh. Both activities, which are noted down in the Jewish Hand–Encyclopedia[87] and in a folklore collection , in "R"shimoys"[88], were carried out. In the former case, a wedding was conducted in the cemetery of the Kerkutzka Street cemetery (the last cemetery) between Yidl the "Tzenerkop" [something like "with the head of a teenager–not a compliment], who was a well–known porter, and a mute girl. As for the burial, many Jews took part. Socres of wagons and stacks of ruined documents were brought for burial.

[Page 166]

 Of the nine doctors who lived in the city on the outbreak of the war, only three remained. Several had been drafted into the Russian army as combat doctors, while others, together with the nurses, had been evacuated to Russia.

Although in the city and in the surrounding areas there had been no major battles, even in the early days many sick and wounded had arrived. From the twelfth of August until the fifteenth of September, 38 wounded soldiers from the German and Austrian armies lay in the city hospital, two officers and 111 Russian soldiers; 32 of them died.

Regarding the attitude of many Poles in Siedlce toward the Jews, we can see this in an article that was published in an American newspaper. The author, M. Zeidman, gives many details that demonstrate the evil attitude of the Poles toward the Jewish citizens.

Yidl the Tzenerkop–who carried the board for washing the dead

At that time, masses of Jewish refugees streamed toward Siedlce ("the homeless"). These "homeless" were driven out of Brisk, Kobrin, Pinsk, and Grayevo. The newspaper explains:

The organization that had been founded to help the Jewish unemployed also helped the refugees; to this end they instituted a tax on meat and schmaltz. The tax raised, in its first month, twelve hundred rubles. Soup kitchens were also established[89].

[Page 167]

An accurate picture of Jewish life in Siedlce under the German occupation in the First World War can be found in a report published in the Yiddish press in America by two women from Siedlce, Bracha and Chana Kagan–daughters of the Siedlce butcher Hershel Kagan[90]–the two women left Siedlce and by various means arrived in Rotterdam, then took the ship "Norttdam" to New York. The immigrants were invited by the club of Siedlce immigrants to report about the situation of Siedlce's Jews. Later the report ws published in one of the Yiddish papers. The report, which can be found in the Sh. Tcharnebrode Collection of YIVO in New York. We give a characteristic description of that time with certain stylistic and orthographic changes:

Sisters and brothers from Siedlce!

It has been a short time since I left Siedlce, from the place where I lived together with your parents, together with your dearest and most beloved. For the whole time since the outbreak of the war, it has been 31 months of sorrows and troubles. Now I stand before you and will give you greetings from everyone with whom I lived.

But what shall I tell you about?

How can one say in words all the troubles of 31 months? There were troubles the like of which the world does not know. The worst inquisitor could not dream them up. They were inhuman troubles, that no human language can express. No words have been created for such pains and horrors.

How can one convey the weeping of women whose husbands and children were taken by battle?

How can one convey the sorrow of broken, destroyed peaceful homes, on which people worked hard and strained for their whole lives?

How can one find words to describe the devastation of children whose fathers were killed in the war and whose mothers died of disease?

How can one convey the moments that people live amidst the agony of death for weeks and months?

[Page 168]

How can one present the times when people are caged on all sides and receive the worst news about death and devastation?

How do you anticipate the time when the enemy pursues you from the outside and inside you are frightened by terrible reports?

It is awful when one begins to recall all the images, images of blood and marrow, of young and old, of women, men and even young children; these are images that slice into the deepest part of your heart and create new wounds. These are images that pile one atrocity atop another, and all together torment mercilessly, although you want to forget them immediately; but how can one forget such images, when it all continues even now?…

It is difficult for me to describe the different images pervaded by such horror. They contain pain that cannot be eased. The only thing you can do is give a little bread and thereby mitigate some of their hunger pangs.

People of Siedlce!

Can you imagine what they are going through, lacking even a piece of bread? Can you understand what it means: weak old men, pale young women have to work and dig the earth just to get a piece of bread? Can you grasp how deep the pain is when old religious Jews permit themselves to work on Shabbos just for a piece of black bread?

Hunger!!! That is the main horror there. At four in the morning (because it is not permitted to go out earlier), you can see on the streets men with ashen, melancholy faces in whose eyes burns the fever of hunger. They head for the lines where, beginning at 8 o'clock, they will receive a half pound of black brad, baked with potatoes. They hurry there! They have left at home their starving children, who have waited from the day before, or even the day before that, for a piece of bread. And there is already a line of a hundred men, women and children. The door of the store is locked, the windows are closed, and the line keeps growing. extending to other streets. Then a window opens, through which the bread is given and the whole mass of people move forward.

[Page 169]

There is pushing and shoving. They know that if they are not among the first, they won't get bread. Often, very often, more than half return home sorrowfully, desperate and hopeless. Therefore they are ready to turn on each other in order to get bread, but now along come the whips of the Germans and more than one woman or man or child remains lying wounded and bloodied in the street…

The horrible epidemics–typhus and tuberculosis–rule free and wide over those weakened by hunger. And how awful is the situation of the sick. People would always sell their last piece of clothing to help the ill, but now they are afraid to summon a doctor, but as soon as a sick person develops a fever, they are required to remove the patient from the house and send him to a special hospital for infectious diseases outside of the city. The house is closed up, and no one is allowed to see the patient in the hospital, and often no one knows what happened to the corpse. Usually the corpses are burned. Consequently, most of the time people decide to remain at home without medical help or to go to the regular hospital.

The jails are packed with "lawbreakers" who steal bread or other products in the city.

How awful, how horrible is the treatment of the prisoners! They get almost nothing to eat! They are disinfected and forced to perform hard labor. It seldom happens that anyone leaves the jail. Death rules there!

People of Siedlce!

It is difficult for me to convey all the prior and current sorrows of our dearest and most beloved. I can only say that hunger is the worst manifestation of recent times.

Do you know what hunger entails? You cannot feel it, you can only understand. Whoever has not seen the evidence of hunger in Siedlce, when hundreds of women go to the local leaders and one cry–"Bread"–can be heard, cannot understand that all other issues disappear, become as nothing under the single cry for bread, which takes first place and cries out for an answer when no answer can be given.

[Page 170]

The eyes of all your beloved on that side of that ocean turn to you. You are the only people from whom they can now expect anything. You have the duty to help them and you must help them.

This description of Jewish life in Siedlce after the outbreak of the war pertains to the first period of fighting. Later on, things improved a little. The military rulers began to give orders for shoes, which restored employment in the shoe factory. At the same time there was a shortage of workers because so many shoemakers had been mobilized over the past year, until the Russians had lost the city.

A similar situation existed among tailors. The tailor workshops worked on military demands.

When the front got near Siedlce, conditions changed radically. The Russian Cossacks tormented the tailors. They would order garments, but instead of paying, they would take the mended uniforms and beat the tailors and the members of their household with whips.

When the city fell into the hands of the Germans, the situation of the tailors was not better than those of other crafts. The shoemakers were in a bad way. They had lost their workshops, had been put to hard military labor, serving in the hospital or in the prison for two marks a day.

The normal commerce of the city barely existed. But smuggling existed. A number of Jews received their income from smuggling into the city products from the villages. The German rulers fought strongly against smuggling, but quite a number of Jews got their income from smuggling, and some even became rich.

But most of the Jewish population in Siedlce at the time of the German occupation in the First World War lived in need. In order to alleviate the need of the Jewish population in Siedlce, a soup kitchen was opened that fed a thousand people.

[Page 171]

The "Bri–os" Society opened an infirmary for walk–in patients and also paid home visits, treated tubercular children with summer–camps, and the "Ahi'ezer" Society helped the poor population with money and goods. Until the end of the First World War, there was in Siedlce a many–faceted Jewish social life, that took care of the religious, cultural, and social needs. The only official legal government institution–the Jewish Kehillah–was still in the hands of the so–called "dozors." They based themselves on an older and undemocratic system, a leftover from czarist rule.

Activities of the City's Philanthropic Institution

With the help of the "Joint," Jewish philanthropic institutions were active during the war in Siedlce. The most notable were "Ezras–Y'somim" and "Moshav–Z'keynim."

There was a story behind these two organizations.

"Ezras–Y'somim" began its activities in 1906, soon after the pogrom, when organized help for orphans whose parents had been murdered was required. The creators of this organization for orphans were themselves young.

A growing number of young people were taken with warm feelings for the orphans, and so was born the idea of creating an institution that would organize on–going help for these still–living victims of the czarist pogrom. A group of young people took the initiative to create an "Ezras–Y'somim" and took their idea to the Siedlce kehillah, which provided a certain amount of money for the project.

They took a room on Dluga (later First–of–May) Street, number 22. They bought beds, kitchen equipment, while donors provided other necessities. And so the "Ezras–Y'somim" came into being, providing a home for twelve children.

The number of orphans slowly grew.

[Page 172]

The room became too small. The "Ezras–Y'somim" moved to a bigger apartment in the community building.

At the same time, there existed a "Moshav Z'keynim" [a dwelling for older people], that took care of lonely older people. This was a kind of "poorhouse" in a small house. The few old people were cut off, the beds were filthy, and the food that was given to the old people was not suited to them. Jewish women used to bring them a little food so they would have something to eat.

In 1909, R. Ephraim–Fishl Frankel bought a house on Ogradova Street (later Shenkovitsch). In this house, which was originally bought only for the Moshav–Z'keynim, the ground floor was devoted to the "Ezras Y'somim" and the first floor–for the Moshav–Z'keynim. R. A.F. Frankel also put up a beis–medresh on an empty lot that he owned at 14 Kilinski.

This building for "Ezras–Y'somim" and Moshav–Z'keynim solved the problem for only a short time. The administrators of the two institutions quarreled. The Moshav–Z'keynim maintained that the house was bought only for them, and "Ezras–Y'somim was taken in only provisionally, and as the Moshav–Z'keynim grew, its leadership held that the "Ezras Y'somim" should leave. On the other side, the "Ezras–Y'somim" was not comfortable in the small building. In the meantime, the number of orphans grew steadily. The "Ezras–Y'somim" could not dream of leaving the building, because they had no other place.

During the war, "Ezras–Y'somim" really helped the orphans who arrived with the refugees. The number of children grew. The building was too small, but they could not think about enlarging it or about finding another place. Their financial situation was too straitened and both institutions relied on subsidies that they received from the kehillah and from central philanthropic organizations.

Also the Moshav–Z'keynim had to broaden its activities and take in needy old people.

[Page 173]

A History of the Jews in Siedlce (cont.)

Community and Cultural Activities During the German Occupation in 1914–1918

The difficulties of economic life during the occupation did not stifle cultural and community life. In fact, there was a revival in these areas. The Germans took over the czarist government as "spreaders of culture." They even sent out a special call to Jews in Yiddish and called on the Jews to find against the czarist overlordship, which created only pogroms for Jews. The arrival of the Germans created new perspectives for Jewish community and cultural life. Community life, which had been stifled under the czarist rule, bubbled like a new spring under the free conditions brought by the Germans.

As soon as the Germans had taken Siedlce, social and cultural activities began in all facets of Jewish life. Religious young men organized a study circle with the aim of studying Tanach with workers. Their goal was to bring knowledge of Tanach to the workers. Almost all such workers in the city would come each evening to the lessons. Although the organization had a strongly religious character and encouraged its members to submit their tefillin once a year for inspection, it still aroused the anger of the Ger Chasidim, who regarded the group with great suspicion, assuming that it was spreading heresy. They reported to the police that the group was disloyal both to the government and to the Jewish Torah, and the police disbanded the group.

At the same time, two workers clubs opened in the city: the "Workers' Union"–which was unaffiliated–and the "Workers' Home," from the Bund. There no one studied Tanach.

The religious young people did not give up. They formed a fellowship called "Mikra," with the same goal as the study circle. A Jewish scholar named Lifshitz would learn with everyone each evening between afternoon and evening prayers. A "Beis–HaTalmud" was also created.

[Page 174]

Permission for the "Beis–HaTalmud" was issued in the name of the Siedlce rabbi at the time, R. Chaim Yehudah Ginzburg, who was charged by the government with keeping order and for the rabbinic seminar.

The name of Rabbi Ginzburg lent the "Beis–HaTalmud" prestige. The rabbi was not a native of Siedlce. He was born in Magelnitz in 1856. His first rabbinic office was in the shtetl of Glavatschov, in the Radomir Voivodeship, where he served as rabbi for six years. From there, he returned to his birthplace, Magelnitz, where he served as rabbi for fourteen years. In 1908, a year after the death of Siedlce's famous Rabbi Sh. D. Analik, Rabbi Ginzburg took his place. He served as rabbi there for 22 years, until May 9, 1930, when he died.

Rabbi Chaim Yehuda Ginzburg was an expert in Talmud, in rabbinic decision making, and in all of rabbinic literature. He was considered one of the most important rabbis in Poland, but he was also very modest and was liked by everyone.

The students at the "Beis HaTalmud" received permits to be in the streets after ten in the evening, which was then forbidden under the German supervision. The "Beis–Hatalmud" did not concern itself with political matters, only with studying Talmud and other religious books. Eventually there came a split–some of the members wanted to study secular subjects as well. This raised a storm among the religious students. The conflict spread to the streets, and the Ger Chasidim came out against this institution. They held that in the "Beis–HaTalmud," which was located at Kilinski 28, lessons were called to order by a bell and on the floor were spittoons, just like in non–Jewish schools. These uproars led to a split. Some–the very religious–created the "Shlomey Emuney Yisroel" organization, which later changed its name to "Agudas Yisroel," while the progressive wing created a new society called "T'vunah." "T'vunah" was a national organization. Its statutes allowed it to open branches in other cities. The organization took advantage and opened around ten branches in different cities in Poland. A little while later its headquarters moved to Warsaw. Only a branch remained in Siedlce.

[Page 175]

"T'vunah" was basically unaffiliated and its goal was "knowledge and reverence for Hashem," as it proclaimed in an announcement; the organization also dealt with secular studies, with learning languages, like Polish, German, and Hebrew. They arranged separate concerts for men and women.

Eventually "T'nuvah" also experienced a split over attitudes toward Zionism. The majority had decided to join the "Mizrachi" Party. Those who disagreed joined the "Shlomey Emuney Yisroel. In this way, new parties came into being on the streets of Siedlce. From an earlier time, the Zionists and the Folkspartei had existed.

The organization of the religious part of Siedlce Jews into two parties–"Shlomey Emuney Yisroel" and "Mizrachi"–called forth conflicts and there were even scandals regarding meetings. The "Shlomey Emuney Yisroel" once brought Dr. Carlebach and Dr. Cohen to lecture at an open location. The speakers were interrupted by members of the Zionist organization. Levi Gutgelt and the brothers Baruch and Mordechai Yaffa were consequently fined 100 marks each by the police. Dr. Carlebach and Dr. Cohen did not finish their lectures in the original site but, accompanied by two police guards, were taken in a droshke to party headquarters, where they finished their talks.

"Dos yidishe folk" (Vilna), number 30, from 1917, describes this incident and argues with the "Yidishe vort," the organ of Shlomey Emuney Yisroel," which tried to present the incident in a different light.

At the same time, the Zionist organization renewed its activities. Hartglass, M.M. Landoy, Levi Gutgelt, brothers Mordechai and Baruch Yaffa Geldman, and others revived the Zionist movement.

Already during the First World War the Zionists conducted a strong propaganda campaign for Eretz Yisroel. In Siedlce, a Jewish student appeared along with the "homeless."

[Page 176]

The student appeared in Zionist circles and proposed forming a Jewish legion that would fight against the Turks and make Eretz Yisroel a Jewish country. This was even before Jabotinski had formed the Jewish legion.

This idea possessed many Jewish young people in Siedlce, who organized themselves covertly. The student himself, whose name remains unknown, took his plan to the lawyer Gruzenberg in Petersburg. Gruzenberg responded that organizing a legion could bring shame to the Zionists in Turkey. But the young Zionists organized a "march" to Eretz Yisroel, though nothing came of it.

In the first year of the war when need and hunger were so terrible for both Jews and Poles and thousands of unemployed roamed the streets of Siedlce, young Zionists communicated with the landowner from Zhelkower (several kilometers from the city) about working in his fields. These young people wanted to learn about agriculture, so that after the war they could go up to Eretz Yisroel. In a wagon pulled by horses, a group traveled to the landowner's property. They were assured of a good welcome from the czarist police, who still had power in Siedlce. The police stopped the young pioneers near the Raskash bridge as suspected "revolutionaries." Before the detainees were brought before an inquest, they tried to destroy their coins that were marked with P.A.P. (Palestine Workers' Fund). Only after the landowner had intervened was the group released[91].

The Jewish young people did not work for long because of the great pressure of unemployed Poles on the landowner. He had to break the contract with the Jews and replace them with Poles.

After the Germans took control of the city, the Zionist movement became legal. One could see people openly carrying Keren Kayemes pushkes in the streets.

The Balfour Declaration that was promulgated on November 2, 1917, had a great impact in Siedlce.

[Page 177]

A large gathering was held. One of the speakers was Mordechai–Meir Landau, a son–in–law of Y.N. Wayntroyb. Young Landau was so emotional about this great historical event that during his talk, as he recited the words of R. Yehuda Halevi's poem "Tzion ha–lo tishali," he had a heart attack, became very ill, and died a short time later[92].

Even before the Balfour Declaration was issued, the Poale Tzion party was becoming stronger in Siedlce, although it had conducted illegal activities in czarist times. The Poale Tzion secured a location and opened the Workers' Home. The party benefitted from having Yosef Slushni in its ranks. In his young years he was involved in the Zionist movement and belonged to the "Tze–irey–Tzion" faction.

After he was forced to return from Eretz Yisroel to Siedlce, as we related earlier, in 1916 he joined the Poale–Tzion party and soon became quite active. He worked hard at organizing the professional trade unions.

On May 1, 1917, Slushni led a workers' demonstration in the city park. Police dispersed the demonstrators, and Slushni was injured and arrested. Soon after he was put on trial and sentenced to two months in prison.

Cultural and School Activities

The Hebrew evening courses and Jewish gymnasium

At the instigation of the Zionist activist L. Gutgelt, brothers Mordechai and Baruch Yaffa, M.M. Landau, Wolf Tuchklaper, and the student Galanski[93], on chol ha–moed Succos in 1915, a meeting was called. Taking part were students from the highest classes in the Russian gymnasium, Chasidic young men, and people with maskilik tendencies. The meeting decided to open evening courses.

[Page 178]

The Hebrew evening courses drew the spiritual force of the "Tze–irey–Tzion" party, Zionist organizations like "He–Hachlutz" and "Ha–Shomer Ha–Tza'ir," numerous self–education circles, the touring and sports clubs, and many others. The courses existed for many years. Statistics show that several thousand young people learned the Hebrew language in these courses, acquired knowledge of Jewish history and of Hebrew literature.

The teachers and students in the evening courses were ruled by the slogan:

"We have our lips [i.e., our language]–who can prevail against us?"

At the same time that the Hebrew evening courses were established, two sisters–Yehudis and Branislava Halbershtam–arrived in Siedlce. They, together with Yadwiga Bialer, opened a school for girls with four classes. These energetic women were held back by none of the economic difficulties that beset the school's founding, and they endured for several years. In 1922, Yehudis Halbershtam decided to continue her studies and returned to her hometown of Warsaw, where several years later she completed her degree and became a teacher in the women's school of Frau Dickshteyn. Her leaving Siedlce resulted in the closure of the school there.

The first "reformed" school in Siedlce was opened in 1915, thanks to the initiative of Monish Ridel. Before that there were in the city kheders of the old type: in a small, stifling room the rabbi with his whip taught his students from early in the morning until late at night. No one taught them how to write. With the opening of the "reformed" school, traditional schooling took on a new form.

The reformed school "Torah v'Da'as" [Torah and Knowledge] had four classes. For two hours of the day, students learned writing, reading, arithmetic, and drawing. The students wore uniforms. The success of the teacher in the class or his loss of the class after the lesson was determined by how the students stayed in their seats. The "reformed" school existed only a few years and was closed by the police. When Ridel went to the authorities, he was told that the school was closed because the students wore hats with blue and white crowns.

[Page 179]

In addition, the literary–cultural–musical society "Jewish Arts" ("Ha–Zamir") grew. The cultural revival of Jewish Siedlce at that time found expression in an article that Kalman Levartovski (later "Ba–Levav") published in the Hebrew daily newspaper "Ha–Tzefirah" (Warsaw) He wrote:

Our quiet and modesty city all at one time changed its outward appearance, as if went from one owner to another. As soon as it was freed from the Russian threat, young people began to arrive. Young people from Chasidic homes started Hebrew evening classes. It took a lot of strength and travails, because even today Chasidim regard such things with a jaundiced eye, as if they were transgressors and sinners, because they started an institution to teach Hebrew. But nothing stopped them. The classes are developing nicely. Nearly two hundred students from every level of society are studying there.

The intelligent youth have revived "Ha–Zamir," which was established in the city about eight years ago, though the Russian authorities interfered with its activities, until it almost ceased to exist. Recently these culturally inclined young people revived "Ha–Zamir." First they recruited many new members. With their help, they obtained a new location, larger than the old one. They put in a reading room and a room for playing chess. Altogether "Ha–Zamir" has become a central spot that is necessary for every young person who has spiritual desires. Although "Ha–Zamir" has not yet done a small part of what a cultural institution must do–for example, organizing lectures about Jewish history–we hope that soon the institution will be firmly established and undertake what has to be done.

Last Tuesday (the thirtieth of Kislev), the directors of the Hebrew evening classes arranged a Maccabee evening. The evening opened with a Hebrew reading by teacher E. Goldfarb that set the tone for the gathering.

[Page 180]

Next Hebrew and Yiddish songs were sung by a choir. A variety of compositions were read in Hebrew and Yiddish. Finally there was an entertainment called "Air Mail." Most of the letters were written in Hebrew. German officers came to the entertainment, including high–ranking individuals, like for example, the city's vice–governor, who asked for one of the organization's officials in whose name the license had been granted. He shook him by the hand and expressed his pleasure at the evening[94].

Such were the Germans during the First World War.

At the same time, four homes for children were opened in the city: "Herzlia" by the Zionist organization, a children's home named for Rabbi Reynem by the "Mizrachi,"

At the same time, four homes for children were opened in the city: "Herzlia" by the Zionist organization, a children's home named for Rabbi Reynem by the "Mizrachi," the Large Children's Home by the "Bund" and the Dinezon Children's Home by the Folkists, who also opened a school for 150 children. In the school, the basic language was Yiddish.

The library under the aegis of "Jewish Art" also developed, and the number of readers increased. By the end of the First World War there were more than 600, as the following table shows:

Number of Readers in 1913–1918

Year	Men	Women	Total
1913	153	110	263
1914	184	119	303
1915	305	184	489
1916	375	225	600
1917	322	251	573
1918	372	266	638

"Jewish Art" also established a dramatic division under the direction of Yakov Tenenboym, who in recent years had taken a leading role in the cultural organization. The following pieces were performed: "Seven after a Horse" (a comedy in three acts by Y. Tenenboym, directed by the author). The premier took place in 1917 in the society's building. The play depicted the life of a coachman and stood out for its good humor.

[Page 181]

Jewish Siedlce in Independent Poland

The Germans occupied Siedlce until 1918. When revolution broke out in Germany, Kaiser Wilhelm was compelled to abdicate and flee to Holland. In all of Poland, not just Siedlce, the Germans were disarmed and expelled by the followers of the later army commander and marshal of Poland–Jozef Pilsudski.

Jews from Siedlce also joined Pilsudski's legions. Here are the names of those known to have joined Pilsudski: Mottl Feinboym, Yakov Feldman, Moyshe Rosenblatt, Yishayahu Wisocki, Yantl Weinappel, Feyvel Nizack, and Abraham Mroz.

In November, 1917, this group was joined to ther 2nd legion regiment, which was quartered in Ostrow–Komanow. The group from Siedlce served in the 8th battalion. Later the group was joined by Zalman Freilich, a former legionnaire from Siedlce who had been interned in a German prison camp for refusing to swear allegiance to the German army. He was later released with a whole group of Pilsudski legionnaires who had been arrested by the Germans for the same infraction. The Jewish legionnaires from Siedlce took part in the disarming of the Germans, which was directed from Nawaweiski Street in Warsaw.

That same Zalman Freilich came to Siedlce. He was sent on a secret mission to the local leaders of the P.A.W about carrying out the disarming of the Germans. Another Siedlce legionnaire, Moyshe Rosenblatt, received an order to go to Lomzhe for the same purpose.

On November 11, 1918, the independent Polish government was established. The Jews hoped that the Polish people, who had been dominated for a hundred twenty–five years, would know in freedom how to treat the Jewish citizens, who, along with the Poles had fought for Polish freedom–these hopes almost immediately dissolved. The Polish Jews were bloodily disappointed. Renewed Polish life began with excesses and pogroms against the Jews.

[Page 182]

The more secure the Polish government became, the greater grew the anti–Semitism. Polish civil organizations were formed for the purpose of destroying Jewish economic existence. Such specially founded cooperatives and societies as "Razvay," "Blawat," and others were also formed in Siedlce. These societies in their rivalry with Jewish merchants and shopkeepers stopped at nothing, whether kosher or not kosher [legal or illegal].

The extermination politics of the Polish government and the economic boycott of the civilian societies went in the direction of not having any business dealings with Jews, including not providing opportunities for work. Governmental positions were given to Poles, even if they were not specialists in the areas. The anti–Semitic slogan "Your own is sacred" was everywhere in non–Jewish Poland. In Siedlce no Jews were accepted as governmental or communal clerks. In the whole communal labor force there was but one Jewish tax collector. Jewish building contractors found no work. Poverty grew among the Jews.

Anti–Semitic agitation was rife in the government, claiming that at the time of the Russian overlordship the Jews favored the Russians, but soon after the outbreak of the Russian–German War, they suddenly became Germanophiles, although thanks to denunciations by the Poles during the war, the Russians hanged many Jews, sent others to Siberia, or put them in jails, and during the German occupation hundreds of Jews suffered in German prisons or prison camps or forced–labor camps, where many of them died or became disabled.

A special place in the anti–Semitic agitation was taken by the accusation that the Jews were enemies of independent Poland and were opposed to the national interests of the Poles. This poisonous incitement was fundamental to the Polish people and to the army. The fiery declaration and protests of the responsible Jewish organizations did not help.

[Page 183]

Understandably, according to every military or diplomatic pronouncement of the Polish government, the Jews were considered guilty. It was common knowledge that it was dangerous for a Jew to go out in the street, especially for one wearing traditional Jewish clothing. Traveling on a train was a hardship. For such "pleasures," many Jews paid with their lives. People received death blows and people were often thrown from the train in the middle of the journey. Jews with beards were set upon in the streets and forcefully shaved or had their beards plucked out. Then they used bayonets to carve phrases on the victims: "Long live Poland" or "So dies the rabbi." And people were forced to sing "How Beautiful."

Jews were dragged to do military work. Any officer or soldier could seize any Jew for work, without regard for age, on Shabbos or holidays, on the street or at home or in the beis–medresh, during or after prayers, without regard for profession: a doctor, a rabbi, a counselor. So it happened in Siedlce Asher Arzhel and Yisroel Gutgelt, both counselors. Gutgelt had put up the largest sum in Siedlce for war loans, but that did not save him from his fate. Both Jewish representatives were seized for work, and they went through all the usual Jewish suffering–having their beards plucked, receiving savage blows. Their shoes, their clothing, and whatever they had with them was taken. They were forced to sing and proclaim the well–known slogans. They were released after two or three days.

All of the protests and speeches against this injustice were of no help. The request to regulate the system of work seizures was also ineffective, obligating them to willingly supply the required number of workers.

Requisitioning locals for the army clearly marked the preference for requiring mostly Jewish dwellers and locals from Jewish society. It did not help to point out other locals who were more suited to the work. Jewish deserters were sought out not only in public but also in community areas and beis–medreshes. The intention was clear: to destroy Jewish community life.

[Page 184]

In the spring of 1920, when the war between Poland and the Soviet Union broke out, persecution against Jews erupted throughout Poland, and Siedlce was not excepted. On orders from Commandant Krapowski and his assistant Bayer searches were conducted in Siedlce in all Jewish, political, cultural, and workers' institutions, including even the neutral "Jewish Arts." The Zionist Bureau and the Mizrachi Organization. The funds of the Keren Kayames were confiscated. The sites of the societies were shut down. Many of the Jewish activists were arrested. The arrested, including the Bundist activist Slushni, were sent to Dombye–a concentration camp near Cracow.

With the retreat of the Polish army, the camp grew worse. A couple of days before the Polish army evacuated Siedlce, all men between 17 and 40 were forced to leave. Thus opened a broad expanse of blackmailed Jews. Each military "official" used all his power in abusing and extorting money from Jews. They were not choosy–they included those released from military service, younger than 17 and older than 40–so that any Jew who had not come across with money was taken into the military just as he was. Every protest was met with sharp anti–Semitic jokes, such as, "You can complain to Rabbi Samuel or you can go to your representative Morgenthau." There were some who told them to go to the Sejm commission to get them to investigate the events in Pinsk. This was a reference to the Jewish "chutzpah" that had demanded the Polish Sejm to send a commission to investigate the murders of 22 Jewish youth committed by the Polish army in Pinsk.

In such conditions, the Jews of Siedlce were convinced not to show their faces in the public and to close their businesses to unfamiliar customers. The anti–semites and agitators in the Polish army used this report, that the Jews shut up their shops, to claim that it was because the Jews would not sell merchandise to the retreating Polish army.

[Page 185]

This created an atmosphere like that before the Siedlce pogrom in 1906–Jews hid them in attics, in cellars, and those who could escaped to the woods.

News arrived from nearby that conditions in the camp were worse than in Siedlce. Finally the Polish army left the city.

After the occupation of Siedlce by the Red Army, the terrorized Jews began to emerge from their hiding places.

The sudden appearance of Jews in public was immediately interpreted by the anti–Semites as sympathy for the Bolsheviks. In fact, the Jews had no cause for such sympathy, except, perhaps, because the Bolsheviks had not harmed or abused them.

The prices of new goods increased from day to day. The lack of merchandise and the expense in the city forced the Jews to go to the villages to buy food at amazing prices. The merchandise in all the stores, without regard for quality or quantity–from ladies' hats to toys–was like make–believe. Whether one needed or not, it was sold. The Red Army paid with Soviet rubles according to a predetermined price, which was actually quite distant from the true worth of the rubles. And if the merchants would not sell, the goods were confiscated.

In this situation, when the merchant had to take a price based on the actual value of the Soviet ruble, there appeared so–called "friends," who "explained" to the Red Army soldiers that the Jews wanted to exploit them. This continued from August 7 to 10.

On that day there arrived in Siedlce a hundred bedraggled Jews, men and women, young and old, from Lukow and Adamow. They explained that the Polish people had threatened them with reprisals for their alleged sympathy and help for the retreating Red Army. And the Soviet Army had encouraged them to flee, assuring them that the returning Polish army would slaughter them, as had happened in Ukraine and in White Russia.

[Page 186]

Several hours later, the Red Army gave the same advice to the Jews in Siedlce. The fear of the oncoming Polish army afflicted the Jews, and a large number joined the chaotic retreat of the Red Army, Jews of different classes and ages. So fled the workers who had been employed by the Red Army, a rabbinic authority with his ten–year–old son, young people eligible for the army who feared that they would not be sent to the camp, older Jews, and anyone who found himself outside the city.

After being in Siedlce for seven days, the Red Army left the city and the Polish army arrived. They brought with them captured Bolsheviks and…fleeing Jews, bruised and beaten up, stark naked, looking barely human. The first soldiers broke into Jewish dwellings, breaking, stealing, and destroying.

Prominent Poles in the city, who feared a repetition in Siedlce of the events of 1906 (the Siedlce pogrom)–because of its effects on international Polish politics–released a statement to the Polish people in which they affirmed the loyalty of the Jews at the time of the occupation by the Russian army. The announcement, however, had no effect on the military powers–no Jewish delegation had been sent to the Polish high officials or to the army leader, Jozef Pilsudski, or to Prime Minister Wincenty Wintos–more effective were the false reports that were spread saying that the Jews had greeted the Bolshevik army with…bread, salt, and flowers.

The socialist Roman Baski provided the following details in the Polish socialist paper "Robotnik" that we cite according to "Ha–Tzefirah"[95]. It shows clearly how confusion arose about the Jewish populace and that a Jewish delegation had met the Red Army with bread, salt, and flowers.

Roman Baski writes:

On Thursday, August 10, the police abandoned Siedlce. A citizens' patrol was organized in the city to take over the duties of the police. In the course of the day, rifle shots were heard, accompanied by cannon fire.

[Page 187]

These were the last Polish soldiers who, while evacuating, shot at the Bolshevik lines.

At eight in the evening, the last Polish soldiers left Siedlce for Warsaw. Silence ruled the town. Each minute awaited the arrival of the Red legions. The city leaders and councilmen assembled in the city hall.

Suddenly a car arrived and stopped in front of the city hall. From the car emerged two prominent Polish government officials. It appeared that they had been delegated by the Polish government. They were Mukhnatzki and Stamirowski. They asked for the Soviet delegation for an armistice, with whom they had been assigned to do business.

The members of the city government responded that no Soviet delegation for an armistice was in the city, though they expected the imminent arrival of the Bolshevik army in Siedlce.

The Polish delegation decided to wait.

They quickly prepared a white flag and put it on their automobile. At the same time, they sent a group of militia men to the Mezritch highway in order to alert the arriving Bolsheviks about the Polish delegation that awaited them in Siedlce. but it so happened that the Bolshevik army entered Siedlce by way of the Mard highway, so that the militia men who had been sent to the Mezritch highway returned to the city after the Bolsheviks were already there.

The sending of the militia outside the city was not without consequences. By chance, this group contained a majority of Jews, so that a report spread that the Jews had gone out to greet the Bolsheviks. Then people with vivid imaginations described the meeting with bread, salt, and flowers. It could not be otherwise–if they went out of the city, then of course they took with them bread and salt, even though no one saw either bread or salt.

[Page 188]

Somewhat different is the matter of the flowers, which has its own story: the Bolshevik regiment that was quartered in Siedlce had a band that played day–in and day–out in the open air. Once it was Shabbos, the only Shabbos when the Bolsheviks were in Siedlce and the band was playing a waltz or a march, some Jewish serving girls, who were carried away by the music gave a few flowers to a trumpet player. That was the basis for the rumor about giving flowers to the Bolsheviks. And this is the foundation for all the slanders that existed about the Jewish populace.

The Jews of Siedlce were again witnesses of how each day soldiers sang anti–Semitic songs, and with the help of the peasants dragged into the city hundreds of Jews who were beaten up, abused, naked, worn out, many on the verge of death. They were thrown into prison, without medical help and without a drop of water. There the unfortunates, despite officers, officials, and diplomatic officials, were viciously tortured.

The detainees in the prison later related that in that vicinity all the Jews were in no better a position and that on the roads and in the fields lay many murdered Jews. Others were drowned in the Bug, among them: Hershel Suchadalski, Yitzchak Shteynberg, Moyshe Janodzhinski, a 70–year–old teacher, bothers Shmuel and Yitzchak Wayntroyb. There were also corpses with their eyes put out and cracked open skulls. They could no longer be recognized.

The Jews in Siedlce itself also suffered hellish pains. As if by a sign, armed bands, directed by a mob, broke into barricaded Jewish homes, viciously beat young and old, including women, who were raped. Many men were seized at work. They were forced to herd cattle and bear heavy loads. After four or five days, some returned home, beaten, abused, naked and barefoot. Some never returned home. They were killed barbarically and thrown into pits along the roads. Among the tortured were: Yechiel Richter, 67, Bunem Friedman, and Mendel Dickshteyn.

[Page 189]

The Accused at a Court Martial

At the same time, the court martial, within twenty–four hours, passed judgment and executed many Jews from Siedlce and the surrounding area. Among them: Avraham Greenshpan, Shoyme Shpiegelman, Yisroel Sarni, Moyshe Nitke, Hersh Warshawski, Moyshe Blumberg, Noson Fille, Yehuda Gwiazde, Moyshe Weizman, Hershel Popowski, Hersh Obfal, Pinchas Weissberg, Yosef Shteynberg, Moyshe Mendelssohn, Chaim Goldberg, Yisroel Ribak, Matisyahu Mandelboym, Ovadiahu Goldman, Avraham Galawski, and others. For many minors, the death sentence was changed to ten years hard imprisonment. Among these: Elkhanan–Mordechai Nautshitshe, Moyshe Gutgold, Zaltzshteyn, and others. The first to be shot were brought to the Jewish cemetery. The rest remained to be buried in the woods, where they were shot.

All those who were sentenced were denied any defense; many of them, not understanding Polish, did not know what they were being asked and what they were charged with.

The operating courts martial and the death sentences for Jews were met with approval by the Polish newspaper "Courier Poranni." The Polish newspaper tried to glorify the sentences of the military tribunals and presented the Jewish victims as collaborators with the Bolshevik army. They were especially interested in Greenshpan and presented him as a Warsovian who came to Siedlce to serve as secretary of the Bolshevik committee. The truth was that Avraham Greenshpan was the son of a Siedlce merchant, Feivel Greenshpan. He was a Zionist and even a member of the Zionist council. He worked as a clerk and a magistrate in Siedlce. The story that Avraham Greenshpan was the secretary of the Bolshevik committee was a made–up slander that had been formulated by the city leader and later town elder in the Siedlce circle–Kaczlotsch.

In the lying report from the "Courier Poranni," whch was reprinted in "Ha–Tzefirah"[96], we read:

The Bolshevik followers who were seized with weapons when the Polish army returned to Siedlce were put before a court martial. There were about 400 of them.

[Page 190]

These were Jews. Most of them were not from Siedlce but were deserters from the Polish army who went over to the Bolsheviks and fought against us.

On its first day, the tribunal handed down ten death sentences for participation in armed action against the Polish army.

The death sentences were carried out against five of the condemned. For the other five, the death sentences were commuted to hard labor, because the condemned were minors.

Among those shot was a Greenshpan, a graduate of the Warsaw Business School. Greenshpan arrived in Siedlce a day before the arrival of the Bolsheviks in the city, and he was the secretary of the local communist community for as along as they were in the city.

A Report by A. Z. Hartglas About Terror Against Jews

As reported in a communiqué, a gathering of Jewish members of the Sejm was called over the situation that had developed in Siedlce. After a three–day journey, the Sejm deputy, lawyer A. Hartglas, who had been chosen by the Siedlce circle, arrived in the city.

Thanks to his efforts, patrols appeared in the city and stopped the bestial activities of the undisciplined soldiers. The kidnapping of people at work diminished. But there was still danger in going outside of the city.

The conditions of the detainees continued to be awful. They lay in narrow, filthy rooms with indescribable agony from their wounds, without medical aid, hungry, thirsty, and naked. No one knew what awaited them, whether they should say their final confessions [vidui].

Thanks to the efforts of Deputy Hartglas, it was arranged that the city's public kitchen and from the Jewish residents, food would be provided for the 2,000 or so detainees, but something else was needed: when the food was brought, the prison authorities let loose the starving captive Bolsheviks, who seized the provisions.

[Page 191]

Deputy Hartglas investigated everything that had befallen the Jews and delivered a report to the organization of Jewish Sejm deputies. The report, which we copy from the Hebrew daily "Ha–Tzefirah" of September 3, 1920, says the following:

The general impression in the city on August 23 was very mournful. Jewish stores were locked up from fear of thievery that had progressed to murder. There were cases where people were tortured. Some gave up their money and possessions under threat of terror, even after the arrival of the Bolsheviks. When the Polish army returned, there were outrages in the city. People cut the beards of Jews while the army stood by.

When the Polish army abandoned the city, an order was issued that citizens ages 17–40 should leave Siedlce. Consequently, many Jews hid in cellars and attics out of fear, so that they would not be torn from their families. When the Bolsheviks came to Siedlce, the Jews tried to creep out of their hiding places and to show themselves in the streets, which allowed certain elements of the Polish population, particularly among the working class, to offer their own explanation for this phenomenon.

Despite the slanders of the "Zhetshpaspalita," no Jewish delegation offered the Bolsheviks a welcome. The Bolsheviks showed no evil intentions. They did not steal but paid for everything, equating a Polish mark with a Soviet ruble.

When the Bolsheviks were in the city, the workers' circles, Polish and Jewish, adopted a sympathetic stance. The P.P.S. in Siedlce on August 14 made a proclamation in which they declared their agreement with the Bolsheviks and called on them for help against the Polish bourgeoisie. (A copy of this proclamation was given to the Ministry of the Interior.) The Jewish communists, overall, did not behave badly. They never denounced a Christian to the Bolsheviks.

[Page 192]

On the other hand, Polish citizens from the workers' circles incited the Bolsheviks against the Jews, accusing the Jewish merchants of profiteering. They brought Russian soldiers and the Bolshevik army to Jewish houses. Aside from that, the followers of the Bolsheviks behaved boldly and violently ripped hats off the heads of people without concern for religion. These people then incited the Polish army against Jews.

The Bolshevik "Revcom" (Revolutionary Committee) was at first composed of the following: 1 Pole from Russia, 1 Jew and 1 apostate from Russia, who later replaced the Pole. The regional commissar was a Pole, a former clerk in the Siedlce magistrate's office. Also the provisional commissar was a Pole–a former Siedlce councilman–and the commandant of the city was a Pole from Russia. The representative of the provisional commissar and leader of the commission was a Pole from Siedlce. At the head of the cavalry was the Pole Lukowski from Siedlce. The Red militia consisted of a hundred men, mostly Poles–train workers and watchmen.

The militia tortured citizens and robbed them. The Jews who were employed by the Red militia mostly fled before the Polish army arrived. The Polish militia remained and joined up with the citizen guard. In general the Bolshevik committee had Jews from the workers' circle and half–intelligent Poles.

After the arrival of the Polish army, a tumult broke out among the Jews. Jews had arrived from Kotzk, Zhelekhow, and Parczew and spread the word from the Bolshevik commander of Lukow that the Jews would be murdered. This news seemed accurate. A week earlier, on August 6, the priest Halbershtam, had informed the rabbi, that a pogrom against Jews was being prepared. If it came to pass, the church building would be open so the Jews could take shelter there. Because of this alarm, Jews began to flee from the city into the woods. In particular the Jews from 17–40 who had not left the city according to the earlier order ran, along with the Polish soldiers who feared being held responsible.

[Page 193]

In addition many Jews found themselves outside the city when the Bolsheviks left. These Jews were away from the city in the villages because of hunger and they wanted to buy from the peasants permission to plant potatoes. They increased the confusion.

When the Polish army was in the city, they immediately began to beat up on the Jews, rob them and take other awful actions against the Jews who had left the city and had now returned. People killed Jews on the roads and in the villages. In Brashkow they killed the teacher Jagodzinski, an old man of 70. Thanks to a miracle, the Jew whose children were studying with the teacher survived. The bodies of twenty murdered Jews were found in the woods around Siedlce..

When I was in Siedlce, people brought from the Golitz Woods four corpses. A clerk from the district court who saw them said that they were so beaten up that they could not be recognized. Among the dead was the Jew Suchadalski, who had fled from the general confusion. The murderers claimed that the killings occurred because the Jews were seized with weapons. This was the source of the legend about 500 armed Jewish communists. Now the talk is of more than a thousand armed Jews.

On August 25, according to the court decree, the Zionist Avraham Greenshpan was shot along with deserters, because he had worked with the Bolsheviks.

I intervened on behalf of the Jews with the city commander H. Pr. Juzwi, who took over the army on August 25. The commander truly devoted his energy to restoring order. He sent out groups of officers to restore order and he began to come to an agreement with the magistrate and the Jewish community to work openly so that the evil period could be considered over.

Food was needed, but not money, because the boycott against Jews went on to such a degree that Jews were pushed out of the lines at food stores and the police could do nothing. No one would sell to the Jews. It appears that hatred for the Jews increased, as one could see from the announcement that was openly issued on August 8 and the revisions that were issued on August 21.

[Page 194]

The revisions were signed by the city president H. Koshlatch, a courteous and upright man, though no friend of the Jews, and there can be no doubt that the revisions were made to clarify the meaning. It is interesting that in the interval between the release of the announcement and the making of the revisions, Prime Minister Witos came to Siedlce and opposed the issuance of the announcement that the Jewish–Polish council had requested.

On August 27, I received news that the excesses against Jews and the kidnapping for hard labor in Siedlce had come to an end.

We give here the above–mentioned announcement and the revisions that were made to it:

"To the inhabitants of Siedlce:

Again the fortunate moment for which we have been waiting has arrived: the hateful army has left our city. On this day we should celebrate with all the solemnity and joy before the whole Polish people. However, these first moments have been desecrated by attacks on Jews. The Polish people, who more than once have brought freedom to other people, must not do this. Truly, there are among the Jews some who hate us, but with full determination we make known that the Jewish citizens support the existence of the Polish kingdom. We urge all the inhabitants of our city not to desecrate our great holiday by falling on other citizens, our neighbors. It is necessary to take a stand to calm down the disturbed atmosphere. One must act with integrity and appropriate speech to the more rancorous so that quiet will exist among the citizens. Any attacks or atrocities against citizens and their property should be avoided. No one should make up his own justice. Every criminal will be uncovered, and those guilty of every attack on the Polish kingdom and on any citizen, those guilty of taking others' property or of atrocities, will meet justice. To punish the crimes committed by our enemies, whether Jews or Poles–there are on earth appropriate examples, and in heaven there is a God.

[Page 195]

Poles! Be true sons of your heroic parents and ancestors, who bore freedom and rectitude, and if you see someone mistreating citizens, your neighbors, go immediately to the authorities whose job it is to preserve peace and order in our city.

Henrik Pczedetzki–Bishop of Poldlocz
A. Chzhanowski–Chairman of the School Board

M. Shimanski–Commander of the Citizen Guard
Edmund Kozhlatch–President of the City of Siedlce
Siedlce, August 18, 1920."[97]

Aid For The Victims

In the course of several days, about 800 victims came to the Siedlce Aid Committee, which had been organized by the "Joint." They brought written certificates with not less than two witnesses, legally attesting to the torture, barbarity, damage in money, objects, inventory, merchandise, clothing, linens, and the like. It all amounted to a sum of around 11 million marks.

Here is an account:

Damages	Before the Departure of the Polish Army	After the Return of the Polish Army	Total
In cash	75,235 marks	1,002,345 marks	1,077,580
In jewelry	53,800	636,630	690,430
Merchandise	822,500	2,090,686	2,913,186
Orchards, gardens	880,100	49,200	929,300
Workshops	62,100	58, 300	120,400
Inventory	368,300	1,105,000	1,473,300
Clothing, shoes, linen	491,360	3,197,989	3,689,349
Totals	2,753,395	8,140,150	10,893,545

Total damages in Siedlce were 10,893,545 marks[98].

[Page 196]

The Siedlce committee, despite its efforts with the central committee in Warsaw, lacked the power to make good even the smallest portion of the losses; not even the poorest could attend to articles of the greatest need cheaply on the streets. A significant number of Siedlce's Jews and Jews from the surrounding areas were hungry, barefoot, and naked. It was heart–rending to see the desperate condition of the Jews, among whom there were some who before the disaster had been wealthy. Daily they besieged the office of the committee, ran from one member to another and departed without aid, because the committee was helpless. Small grants were given for products and clothing, about 200,000 marks, aside from the standing subsidy for the public kitchen. This was like a drop in the ocean. We should mention with gratitude the Siedlce association in New York, who sent five hundred dollars.

The American committee could in no way satisfy the requests of Jews in the ruined shtetls and villages to purchase for the High Holidays at least a few talesim and Torah scrolls the replace those that had been destroyed.

The Jewish population was reduced to poverty. In order to provide the poorest at least with bread, potatoes, and aid–as winter approached–in the midst of need they put out a call for colossal sums. The committee wanted to raise even the necessary sums to mount a defense for the scores of trials, so that a lawyer could rescue people from death sentences and scores of years in prison. It went so far that on Yom Kippur in 1920, during religious services, prayers were halted and money was gathered for the defense of the accused.

How the Bolshevik Order Appeared in Siedlce

The Warsaw "Ha–Tzefirah" of 1920 (number 183), wrote that the Jewish press was not permitted to send its correspondents into war territories.

[Page 197]

"Ha–Tzefirah" therefore used material from the Polish newspapers, on the basis of which it described for its readers how life appeared in the short time that the Bolsheviks occupied the Polish cities. The Hebrew paper took no stand on the facts reported in the Polish papers–it had no power to control the news and to investigate it. There are, consequently, a number of errors that resulted from a particular point of view.

The broadest report came from J.Sh, the correspondent of the Polish Socialist "Robotnik" (the paper of the P.P.S), who travelled with the journalist entourage. About Siedlce he writes:

The Bolshevists arrived in Siedlce on Tuesday, August 6, 1920, in the middle of the night. The next evening appeared order number 1, in three languages–Russian, Polish, and Yiddish–signed by the chairs of the revolutionary committee–Alperovitch and two committee members: Pawlik and Pankevitsch. The order stated:

"In accord with the order of the political section of Division 3, a revolutionary committee has been designated for Siedlce, consisting of the following: president–Comrade Alperovitch–and members–Comrades Pawlik and Pankevitsch.

The whole army around Siedlce was in the hands of the revolutionary committee and all working comrades and all Soviet people in the area must report to them. All leaders, councilors, and magistrates are relieved of their duties, and all clerks must suspend the work of their offices until all matters can be handed over to the Soviet army.

Anyone who violates these orders will be punished with the full severity of war– and revolution–time."

The Polish version was in garbled language…

On the same day an order was issued to the army that was camped in Siedlce.

[Page 198]

This order was signed by the head of the military division and the commandant of the city, the commandant of the division–N. Yesierski–and the military commissar–Kolykov. Yesierski shared in his order that in accord with the orders from the division leader, he would begin from that day to fulfill the function of leader of the local military–division and city commandant. Further, he shared, "the city of Siedlce is declared to be in a state of siege. If the people, who are well known, conduct anti–Soviet agitation, they will be severely punished. They will be shot." And so on. This order, too, was written in poor Polish.

Two days later, "Order Number 2" was issued by the revolutionary regional committee in Siedlce. The most interesting part of this order was the warning–to the political and professional organizations to register immediately with the leader of the "Revcom," H. Pawlyuk.

Order Number 3 from the revolutionary committee, on August 14, was published only in Polish and Yiddish. The order threatens and more severe punishment for all who deal in financial speculation and raise prices. Large and small merchants are warned to sell goods for the same prices that existed before the Polish army abandoned the city. It was also forbidden to decline to accept banknotes issued by Poland or to accept them at a lowered value.

Aside from these orders, the Siedlce revolutionary committee made the following announcement: "To the working masses." The announcement said:

Finally the hour has come when you will no longer be exploited. The bosses will no longer take the results of your overworked energies and then throw you the crumbs. The camp of the workers' army brings you freedom from the yoke of the bourgeois regime and has no claims on your territory. This is not the camp of the czarist army and the bloodthirsty aristocracy.

At this time, when a workers' regime will be fashioned on this earth, a regime made up of Polish workers–no footprint of the Russian army will be found on Polish land.

[Page 199]

At the same time as this announcement, a second announcement appeared in the name of the provisional revolutionary committee of Poland, that was called "Polrevcom." This announcement indicated that a provisional committee for Poland had been established and had taken the rudder of the government in its hands and taken on this task: until a stabile government of workers and peasants could be formed, to lay the groundwork for the coming soviet order of the Polish socialist republic. To this end, the army, through the revolutionary committee, would take over the aristocratic–bourgeois government and would guarantee the integrity of the Polish earth– and so on.

In the short time of their governing, the revolutionary committee dealt with political matters. They named a "director of the city economy," a commissar who had to lead the city. This office was given to a certain Lewandowski. He began his activities by publishing an order about cleaning the streets and squares. which was to be done by the owners of the stationary properties.

It appears that the revolutionary committee believed that it would remain, if not forever, in any case for a long time. As evidence we have not only the published orders and announcements, but the sketched out projects for orders that we have seen. These projected but unpublished orders address stable administrative power, dividing up responsibilities, forming commissions for immoveable properties, and so on.

The revolutionary committee also concerned itself with providing intellectual content for the inhabitants of Siedlce. Under the direction of the political division of the revolutionary council, two issues of a wall poster appeared with the name "Warshawianka." The first issue, on August 16, hotly denounced the establishment of "Polrevcam" in Bialystok and contained a short article about the delegation from capitalist Poland. The second issue, and the last, was published on August 17, the day before the retreat of the Bolsheviks from Siedlce–announced in huge letters that the "workers'–government of Poland is moving to Warsaw.

[Page 200]

The workers' government brings to the proletariat freedom from the chains thrown on them by the capitalists and social traitors of the P.P.S." This issue of the "Warshawianka" also contained a biography of Markhlewski that said:

The president of "Polrevcom," Comrade Y. Markhlewski, came from a family of distinguished noblemen. He is a brother of the well–known Professor Markhlewski. Even in his early years, Comrade Markhlewski cut his ties with his aristocratic–bourgeois surroundings and allied himself with the revolutionary movement of Poland and Germany. Comrade Markhlewski wrote many books on theory that deal particularly with questions of agriculture in Poland and Germany.

With this issue, the short life of "Warshavianka" came to an end. On the next day, with the appearance of the morning stars, the Bolsheviks left Siedlce in confusion.

* *

The Polish newspaper "Dwa Grosze" (a Jew–hating rag) published a photocopy of the first issue of "Warshawianka," which showed only that part of the paper that was printed in Yiddish. That Jew–hating rag always distorted the facts in this way, in order to incite the masses against the Jews, implying that they were the Bolsheviks. All the other newspapers acknowledged that the "Warshawianka" had been printed in two languages, in Polish and Yiddish.

According to "Dwa Grosze," the text of the Bolshevik newspaper read as follows:

Workers of the world, unite.

Warshawianka

Organ of the Polish division of the revolutionary council of the 16th army, August, 1920.

The waves of the world revolution of workers have flooded all of Poland. The mighty Polish proletariat is awakening and taking steps to create a workers government.

Long live the socialist revolution.

Long live the workers' council.

[Page 201]

A History of the Jews in Siedlce (cont.)

Meetings

At a meeting of all the workers' committees in Siedlce, the representatives of the "Bund" and the "Poale–Tzion" declared that they recognize no government aside from the workers' regime, which they will defend. The representatives of the P.P.S declared that the entire politics of their party is phony. The workers' regime will free Poland from the oppressors' yoke.

The meeting voted to unite all the professional unions in a strong association.

The "Dwa Grosze" provided the following commentary to the photocopy that it had published:

This example of the Jewish, Bolshevik "Warshawianka" demonstrates two facts: 1) the Bolsheviks had no intention of negotiating with our peace delegation. Their Intention was–to seize Warsaw and install the Jewish–Bolshevik regime, with whom Soviet Russia would make peace. In other words: The Jews in Warsaw would make an agreement with the Jews of Moscow over how to rule over the people of Poland and Russia. To aid them, the Jews would use the "Shabbos Goy," the few bloodthirsty types, like Dzherzhinski and Fruchniak. 2) The Bolshevik newspaper demonstrates that the Bolsheviks have found friends among us, the Poale Tzion, the Bund, and the P.P.S.

The Polish government should use this information to make the proper decisions.

In the midst of this raging from the anti–Semites, the Jewish deputy organization of the Polish Sejm (in the persons of Y. Greenboym, H. Farbshteyn, A. Hartglas) presented a petition to the Polish prime minister about the killing of Jews in Poland.

The petition does not deal exclusively with the events in Siedlce but goes into the general situation of the Jews. But it was known that the petition was written by the well–known Deputy Harglas after his visit to Siedlce and on the canvas of his experiences in that city. Although in the document he mentions other cities in Poland, that does not diminish the local significance of the historical document, which we present from the Hebrew translation in the daily newspaper "Ha–Tzefirah."

[Page 202]

The petition reads:

The outrages of the military personnel against the Jews, which have lasted already a year and a half, with only small breaks, grew stronger in the first days when the danger of the Bolshevik invasion increased. The increase in the outrages was especially felt with the increase in agitation against the Jews, which was led by the announcements from the army that were spread by the government, by way of the publication of "Szolniesz Polski" ("The Polish Soldier"–a newspaper that was designed for the military–Y. Kaspi). These announcements are propaganda that Jews and Bolsheviks are one and the same.

When Dep. Hartglas informed the current War Minister and former vice–minister General Sosnkowski about this situation, the minister expressed his astonishment and promised an investigation. Nonetheless, the anti–Jewish agitation continued. Not only did it not stop, you should understand, but it increased as the Bolshevik threat increased. The Sejm deputies saw with their own eyes how the police spread the reports. General Sosnkowski's intervention had the result that the anti–Jewish announcements in Warsaw were not distributed, but copies of the same announcements were distributed in other Polish cities through the ""Szolniesz Polski."

Under the influence of this agitation, the anti–Semitic spirit increased, and instantly the outrages and robberies also increased, led by the army. The Jewish populace, seeing the danger that was encouraged by the government, took in the needy victims, in order to do their civic duty. A Jewish committee was established to defend the government. The Jewish young people, and particularly the students, as a body willingly joined in the military work. The female students took up sanitary work. This voluntary work service by the Jews for the welfare of the government was soon transformed into required work by the government.

[Page 203]

The military powers had prevented the Jewish committee from working to found a hospital for wounded soldiers. The idea of Jews the right to establish such a hospital was put in doubt. Jewish nurses were systematically prevented from entering the laboratories of the Red Cross. There were also cases when Jewish volunteers were not accepted into the army.

The growing anti–Semitic spirit permeated society into the provinces. Under the mask of the need to assure peace in the state during the crisis, the government in many cases arrested Jewish community workers without regard for their political leanings. Communists sat in prison, as did socialists, Zionists, and those without a party. Various Jewish institutions and associations were shut down, even those of an economic and cultural character. Such facts were openly known in the whole area of Congress Poland–in Wlodawa, Nasielsk, Zambow, Mlava, and Mezritch. The government in Galicia dismissed requests to establish Jewish associations on the pretext that those are institutions that serve exclusively Jews (Oswiecem, Rzeszow, Cracow).

When the enemy began to approach Modlin, the military governor of Warsaw, General Latinek, issued an order to evacuate the Jewish populace from the areas near the fortress: Novy Dwor, Zakroczym, and Pamjerowek. The Jewish deputies who asked the government about this matter received the answer that the order applied not only to Jews. However, it is an established fact the printed order read "Jews, Germans, and Russians" and in reality from these places applied it only to Jews. The apartments and goods of the Jews, who lost their homes, were immediately plundered by the soldiers and the crowds of the Christian population who remained in the places.

At the same time, the Minister of War decided to instruct the publishers to circulate the pamphlets, which had been held in secret, about removing Jewish soldiers from the military locations so that the number of Jews who worked there should not exceed five percent.

[Page 204]

There was also an order create a camp in Jablonna for a Jewish work battalion. All military units were told to withdraw Jews from their ranks and send them to Jablonna in order to establish exclusively Jewish worker units.

On August 15, they began to carry out this order. Jewish soldiers were withdrawn from their formations in which they had long served. An exception was made for soldiers who were in the first row at the front. In many places the Jewish soldiers had their uniforms torn off and under strict guard they were sent to Jablonna. There they were held like detainees. Jablonna was not only a concentration point for soldiers who had been mobilized for military duty but also for those who had volunteered, even the Jewish personnel from the legions and who had gone through the camp in Szetszifjorna (interned by the Germans before the liberation of Poland–Y. Caspi) and were decorated for defending Lemberg and other places.

The attention paid to the needs of these arrested soldiers was beyond criticism. For days at a time they received no necessities, and until the last minute they received not even straw mattresses to sleep on, despite what the official report might say.

Around the camp were placed guards from Poznan ("Poznantchikes"–violent anti–semites who entertained themselves by cutting the beards of Jews–Y. Kaspi), They treated the detainees badly. As a result of this treatment, the arrested were beaten with deadly blows; aside from the Poznan military guards, policemen served as overseers. As it turned out, there was a guard for every prisoner.

After many intercessions over four weeks, finally word came to dissolve the camp at Jablonna, but even so the soldiers were treated with special rules that overrode the normal army. The Jewish soldiers were not returned to their former military groups, but they were sent to other divisions.

[Page 205]

There they were treated as though they were guilty of military infractions.

As the retreat of the Bolsheviks began, people started to spread alarms about supposed Jewish treachery. Intelligence from general headquarters reported that in Siedlce an armed Jewish division had been seized and that it had fought on the side of the Bolsheviks, and that in Bialystok the Polish army had fought with the local Jewish populace, which had aided the Bolsheviks. After a thorough investigation, which was made on the spot, it became clear that in Siedlce not a single armed Jew had been captured. The announcement by the representative of the local Polish community, which spread the day after the Bolsheviks left, said nothing about a Jewish group. It did say that without exception the Jewish community had conducted itself with extreme loyalty.

Also about Bialystok it became clear that there was no fighting with the Jewish populace. On the contrary–the representatives of the Polish populace on the citizens' committee could find no fault with the behavior of the Jews.

The legend about Jewish treachery that was spread by general headquarters circulated throughout Poland, and everywhere the Jews were accused of treachery.

Investigations in various places had shown that the participation of the Jewish populace in the Bolshevik occupation government was less than that of the Polish population, among whom not only the socialists but the members of the right took positions with the Bolsheviks. So it was in Milawa, Biala Podlaska, Lomzhe, Pultusk, and elsewhere. Under the Bolshevik government, the Jews, aside from those in the villages, suffered more than others, because from the Jews a greater contribution was demanded in the form of goods sold according to prices determined by Soviet currency and according to an artificial rate of valuation. The Bolsheviks imprisoned and removed from their homes both Jews and Christians. In many places the mobs joined the Bolsheviks in stealing from the Jews. In Wysokie Mazowieckie, where the Polish population took a passive role in the Bolshevik offensive, the Jews organized an armed defense, which kept the Bolsheviks out of the city.

[Page 206]

The Prime Minister, at the time of his visit to Siedlce, promised to receive a delegation from the Jewish populace. At the same time, a Polish announcement appeared whose goal was to weaken the effect of the first announcement from the Polish community. After the Prime Minister's visit to Plotzk, the official Polish telegraph agency published a half–official piece that claimed that the Jews in Plotzk had helped the Bolsheviks, had poured boiling water on the Polish soldiers, and held secret telephone conversations with the enemy. The governing committee in Plotzk disavowed these slanders, but the Polish telegraph agency published only a few of these denials.

In the last days of August there was a conference in Tarnow, at which one of the speakers was Deputy Brill–a member of the party of the Prime Minister. In accord with the Prime Minister's stand on the question of Jewish treachery, the deputy called for peace. The Prime Minister neither stopped nor disagreed with his words. Before the Prime Minister had assumed his high position, the Jewish–Polish council had decided that it was necessary to issue an announcement to the Polish populace, and the government was obligated to distribute this announcement, which had to be certified, because the Jews were citizens. To this point, the announcement had not been published because the Prime Minister had promised to sign it because of the facts that had been determined in Siedlce and in Plotzk.

It is not to be wondered at that the army, which was poisoned by tales of Jewish treachery, about Jews who poured boiling water on Polish soldiers, the army which in the course of months had incited through announcements and posters against the Jews as Bolsheviks– had agreed that the outrages against the Jews, which had lasted for a year and a half, should not be punished, this army that had indicated its every victory with the blood of murders, terror, and robbery against the Jewish people.

[Page 207]

In Siedlce, soldiers made Jews herd animals, then, outside the city, after robbing them–they killed them. In this fashion seven Jews were murdered, among them Richter–an old man of 66, along with other people fifty years and older. Aside from them, in the surrounding areas, in villages and on the roads, more than ten Jews were murdered, among them the aged teacher Godzhinski, a man of 71. In the city, many Jews were robbed. Several Jewish young women were raped. In the nearest village, Gwatzhenitza, the Torah scrolls in the synagogue were ripped up and the Jews were forced to rip up the remaining pieces. The Jews who were forced to herd animals and were not then killed were forced to beat each other, to spit in each others' faces, to lick up the blood of the wounded, and so on.

In Mardi, the Jew Shteynberg was murdered and several women were raped. In Dragitszin the Jews were forced into the river and many of them were shot in the water. Some were given the opportunity to escape from drowning, but the peasants of the area were called on to beat up those who fled. In Laszitz many Jewish girls were raped. The majority of local Jewish residents were robbed. The soldiers who did the stealing were urged on by an officer, who shouted in a loud voice that such theft was permitted for twenty–four hours and now the robbing could continue. The local police mocked the Jews who were begging for protection. In Wiszkow, the Christian people were called on to indicate Jews about whom they had complaints. In Gawrolin, the Jew Rutenberg was shot without a trial at the instigation of a Christian who was a business competitor. In Laskaszew (Laskerow), a young Jewish woman was shot in a similar way. In Luncki, near Plotzk, two Jews were shot without trial. In Lukow the soldiers shot without a trial twelve Jews who had returned from Mezritch.

[Page 208]

Before being shot, they were forced to dig their own graves. In Jagodna, three Jews were killed in the same way. In Dzhiwali the soldiers, at the urging of the watchman, shot a Jew who lived there.

In Pultusk, Jartzi, Makow, Wengrow, and Zambrow, people beat and mocked the Jews. In Otwock the soldiers daily rapaed Jewish young women after September 12. In Glinianka the soldiers, without a trial and in defiance of an officer, shot 21 Jews and raped a number of women. Before shooting them, the soldiers made mock of them. In Komarow, near Ostrow, a peasant from Lomzhe hanged a Jew. In Malkin, six Jews were shot without a trial. Among them was a man of 71–Eliezer Katczer. The Jewish women were raped. In Dobra, near Minsk–Mazowiecki soldiers shot a Jewish woman because she would not open the door when they came to rob her. In Skochadalia the Jew Platkowski was shot without a trial. In the neighborhood of Sokolow, in the villages and on the roads, sixteen Jews were shot. In Koemia, near Kaluszyn, sixteen Jews were shot after being forced to dig their graves. The sixteenth was killed by having his head smashed with a rake. In the nearby village of Mikas, three Jews were killed in the same way. In Rizhin, 30 Jews were killed, while the rest were tormented. Their clothes were taken from them and they were thrown into an icy pit.

Even in Visoko–Mazowieck, where a group of armed Jews had fought off the Bolsheviks, losing 11 fighters in the process, even there the members of this group were beaten and tormented, even though they had been taken prisoner by the Bolsheviks and had escaped. And all of these places to a greater or lesser extent were subject to armed groups of thieves.

The above deeds are far from encompassing all the crimes that were committed against the Jews. We have no information about many places, especially from the area around Lublin, where the followers of Petliura and the Bolshevik soldiers rampaged. It is known about Zamosc (the new city) that masses of Jews were robbed and women were raped.

[Page 209]

One young woman, who defended herself, had the fingers cut from her hands. And in Wladowa, Jews were buried alive, and so on and so on. We also lack detailed information about the area of Bialystok, where scores of Jews were killed on the roads in the woods.

There can be no doubt that most of these atrocities resulted from stories that had been spread about the Jews' treachery. Giving these stories the appearance of truth, hundreds of Jews had been arrested. Jews who had fled and then returned were arrested and imprisoned, accused of treason. From among the soldiers who had escapade from Bolshevik captivity, the Jews were selected out and put in jail under suspicion of treason.

A few Jews who had worked for a few days for a salary as clerks for the Bolsheviks, as both Jews and Poles had done during the Austrian and German occupations, were shot according to the legal sentences on charges of treason (like the story of Greenshpan in Siedlce). No consideration was given to whether these Jews could be judged by a quickly–set–up court in agreement with the first point of an order from the council for the defense of the government that was published on August 9. In the same place and at the same time, one could find free Christians who worked together with the condemned Jews in the employ of the Bolsheviks and even of the Bolshevik commissars who remained after the retreat of the Bolsheviks. Some of them even received documents in which the government recognized their service to the Bolsheviks as a civic deed that undermined Soviet rule in Poland.

In Plotzk, the tribunal condemned to death Rabbi Shapiro, a man who had nothing to do with politics, on the charge that he led the movement of the Bolshevik army. No one heard the testimony of witnesses (Jewish and Christian) who came to the court, and at the time of the first inquiry, they confirmed his innocence of the charges.

[Page 210]

In such ways, stories about Jewish treason were manufactured, along with other signs that they were factual. Thus the environment grew in which new reports about Jews were fashioned.

Jewish publications could not show the groundlessness of these accusations because the mouth of the Jewish press was closed by the censor. At the same time as the Polish press gave out fabricated articles from Plotzk and Bialystok about Jewish treason and incited against the Jews–the Jews were forbidden to defend themselves. Jewish newspapers were punished for printing an article from "Narod" (a nationalistic Polish newspaper–Y. Kaspi) about Jablonna.

In the same way, lies were spread everywhere, but the truth was suppressed. Hatred for the Jews, who were presented as criminals, was instilled deep in the Polish masses.

Because of the above–stated facts, attested by the undersigned–the Sejm should decide:

> 1.   To appoint a commission with the participation of representatives from the Jewish national deputies to throw a light on all of these facts that have been described.
> 2.   To bring to justice all those who are guilty of issuing illegal orders and who are guilty of spreading false reports and committing the illegal actions that are described above.

This petition was signed by Y. Greenboym, A.M. Harglas, and H. Farbshteyn.

The Jewish National–Council in Protection of the Jewish Population

At the of 1918 a conference was held in Warsaw to plan a Yiddish national convention in Poland. Participating in the conference were 498 delegates from 144 cities and shtetls in Poland.

In the central Jewish National–Council, which was chosen at the conference, M. Laterman from Siedlce served as a representative from the handworkers' organization.

[Page 211]

The Jewish National–Council intervened many times with the government about events and outrages that occurred in the city. In the report of the current Jewish National–Council and Sejm organization[100], we find sections about interventions on behalf of the Siedlce Jewish community.

At the beginning of 1919, a petition was introduced in the Sejm about the murders and robberies among the Jewish population in Siedlce. The petition contained a trove of informational material. In the course of the summer months, Siedlce devised a protocol against outrages against Jews, with the participation of soldiers from Haller's army. These outrages were a result of the agitations and incitements by the Polish press.

At that time in the eastern regions there were many homeless people who had fled from Russia. Because the Polish government wanted to expel these people from the eastern regions, the club had to intervene in order to protect the refugees from expulsion. Thanks to the club's intervention, the escapees from Brisk and Minsk were allowed to remain in the area of Siedlce and Wysokie–Mazowieckie. Approximately 152 families were saved from Brisk, to which they could not return because the city had been devastated.

In the course of 1920, there were outrages in Siedlce. Not a single month passed in which nothing untoward occurred. In January and March the army went on a spree. Also in April and July, people beat up Jews. In August, Jews were even murdered, and in December the military committed outrages.

In November of the same year, the Sejm–club of Jewish national deputies protested that in the election lists for the city council in Siedlce, only Polish citizens had been named and that the elections were scheduled for Shabbos.

[Page 212]

Thanks to the intervention of the club, the election was moved to Sunday. Furthermore, the club of Jewish national Sejm deputies intervened in the following incidents: in July, 1921–against the terrible outrages against Jews in which soldiers from Silesia participated; in October, 1921–against attacks by Christian civilians against Jewish funerals in Siedlce; in May, 1922–against ongoing anti–Jewish outrages that were led by the army.

The activities of the Jewish National–Council were felt in Siedlce at the time of the elections for the first Polish Sejm in 1922. The attempts to undercut the Jewish community in the Sejm election came to nothing. Then a nationalist minority bloc tried to elect a Jewish deputy, but no Jewish deputy was elected from Siedlce because no one from the Jewish list received enough votes. The greatest number of votes went to the bloc of the nationalist minority.

The votes for the Jewish list were thus divided:

Number 16–national minority bloc:	7852
Number 4–"Bund":	763
Number 20–Folk Party:	405
Total	9020

After the Polish–Bolshevik War

After the difficult experiences of Siedlce's Jews at the time of the Polish–Bolshevik War, Jewish life in Siedlce began to return to normal. Jews tried to return to their occupations. Around 1921, there was a renewal in the garment industry. Orders began to come in from Poles, especially from Galicia. The devaluation of Polish currency stirred the development of the profession. The prices of raw materials went up, thanks to inflation. Finally the situation stabilized. In 1930 the number of Jewish tailors reached 600.

[Page 213]

From the building industry, which in czarist times had employed many Jews, in Independent Poland they were almost entirely ejected.

The First World War had reduced almost the entire industry to nothing. No houses were built. The Jewish construction workers were thrown out of their industry. Later, in Independent Poland, when there was a resurgence of building through individuals or government and community institutions, no Jews were allowed to work on them. In New Siedlce (Novo–Siedlce) which had begun construction in 1924 and where hundreds of houses soon appeared–not a single Jewish construction worker was employed. The economic–extermination policy of the Polish regime had led, in relation to the Jewish population, to the attempt to eject the Jews from their economic positions. For the working Jews of Siedlce, it pulled the ground out from under their feet. Jews tried to enter other professions, and in Siedlce they set up a knitwear industry.

Until 1921, there was no knitwear undertaking in Siedlce. Knitwear used to be brought in from Warsaw and from Lodz. Soon there were five workshops, which employed sixty workers. The season for knitwear work was in the month of Elul and lasted until Purim. The demand at that time was very great. For the whole summer, the factories stood empty.

According to the first census in Independent Poland from December 9, 1921, Siedlce, with its surrounding towns, had a population of 31,687. But the population was growing, so that in 1924, the number had increased to 35,219, according to the following table:

Jews	Christians	Total	Percentage of Jews
18,963	16,256	35,219	53.8

Together with the ongoing extermination–policy of the Polish government in relation to Jews, in Siedlce there was strong anti–Semitic agitation.

[Page 214]

Deputy Sadzewicz began to put out a local inflammatory newspaper under the name "Przyjaciel Narodu" (Friend of the Nation), whose editor was a fervent anti–Semite, Wladislaw Shalatkowski. He conducted anti–Jewish incitements in the style of the Polish Jew–devouring official press, writing that Jews are "nomadic rodents" etc., giving the Polish population false and tendentious information about Jewish life, aims, and hopes. Later, when the "Siedlce Wochenblat" began to appear, every innocent notice in the paper was purposely distorted and explained as an assault by Jews on Polish interests. The anti–Semites claimed that the Jewish paper in Siedlce was supposedly edited by "Litvaks," the mortal enemies of Poland.

The difficult situation of the Jews of Siedlce, their tragic environment during the Polish–Bolshevik War, did not kill off community activities. As life began to return to normal, the communal and political organizations began to resume their activities. "Jewish Art" revived. The "Bund" and the leftist "Poale Tzion" extended the school system for Yiddish instruction, which M. Mandelman writes about in his memoirs.

The activists in "Jewish Art" resumed their cultural work. They began to appeal to the Polish powers to return the site of "Jewish Art." After long negotiations, they succeeded. Also, the sections devoted to drama, music, and the chorus resumed their activities. The musical division had an especially difficult time because during the Polish–Soviet War, Soviet soldiers took many of their instruments.

The library of "Jewish Art" did not interrupt its activities throughout the difficult time of the Polish–Bolshevik War.

[Page 215]

It actually increased the number of readers and the number of books, as the following tables show:

Number of readers in the library, 1919–1925

Year	Men	Women	Total
1919	431	416	847
1920	270	226	496
1921	243	188	431
1922	312	223	535
1923	316	235	551
1924	300	171	471
1925	302	172	474

Number of books read, 1921–1925

Year	Hebrew		Yiddish		Russian & German		Polish		Total	
	#	%	#	%	#	%	#	%	#	%
1921	1513	15.9	5408	57.0	94	1.0	2479	26.1	9494	
1922	1376	9.8	7057	50.3	206	1.5	5403	38.4	14042	
1923	699	7.1	3875	39.3	146	1.5	5137	52.1	9857	
1924	987	8.5	5400	46.7	161	1.4	5026	43.4	11574	
1925	1790	16.6	4786	44.2	123	1.1	4121	38.1	10820	

In 1922 the library had 6928 books, and in 1924 it purchased another 285. Thus in 1924 the library had:

Language	1923	Purchased 1924	Total
Hebrew	1377	64	1441
Yiddish	1196	162	2158
Russian	1424	——	1424
Polish	2052	59	2111
German	79	——	79
Totals	6928	285	7213

[Page 216]

The year 1926 marked the half–jubilee of the existence of the library. The date was considered a great a great holiday by all sectors of the population. The library then owned almost eight thousand volumes. A community–wide committee was formed in the city which proposed a great academy for which it sought new subscribers. To honor the anniversary of the library, a publication was issued in 800 copies presenting historical material about the founding and development of the library. This cultural celebration also resounded among people from Siedlce around the world. Particularly interesting was the report from Yosef Rosenwasser, the founder of the library. Rosenwasser was then in Berlin and sent for the celebration a moving letter. He wrote

…My joy at your news is boundless. Ach, God! My dear only child (the library) still lives, for which I made so many sacrifices, for which I was excommunicated by the Skver Chasidim and forced to leave my dear home and my noble child.

The library of "Jewish Art"

The library of "Jewish Art"

[Page 217]

The only consolation is that my child, brought up with such difficulty, still lives and is in such good hands. This gives me the strength to forget my sorrows. I must also tell you that I am not the only one deserving of thanks. There are many others who should be thanked. First of all, Baron Georg von Kleist, who was the main person who helped with advice and actions to raise "the child." Others were: Zev Tuchklaper, Asher Liverant, Yehoshua Goldberg, Moses Greenfarb, and many others whose names I cannot remember…

The anniversary committee also released the following announcement to the Jews of Siedlce:

It has been 25 years since the founding of our Jewish library in Siedlce, which is now associated with "Jewish Art." A quarter of a century ago, a small group of enthusiasts with modest strength laid the foundation stone for this building which has grown into an exquisite book–treasure of over 8,000 volumes–one of the finest Jewish libraries in Poland.

The library has undergone many transformations during this time. Many were the dark forces that sought to bring troubles on this treasure. But they did not count on the self–sacrifice of the library supporters and the obstinacy of the true readers–and the library, with no external support, has grown into a splendid beacon for all local, conscientious Jews.

For a quarter of a century, this library has been the only source of light and education for the thirsty Jewish young people in Siedlce. And today more than ever, those who desire knowledge flow to us. Who has not drunk from this source? Every one of us who has sought peace and quiet, and those who have not–for all of us, this source has been a fountain of life in the springtime of our lives. And if someone from among our thousands of readers grows wings and then flies away into the greater, broader world, that is where he received the impulse.

That is why the days from April 10 to April 18 have been declared the anniversary week of the Jewish library, and it is a great holiday for the Jews of Siedlce. And now the thousands of readers, along with thousands of potential readers, and all who will become readers, are celebrating.

[Page 218]

But Jews are accustomed to have an accounting even on holidays. Our joy is always mixed together with a serious thought. Now at the time of the anniversary we have to consider the future of the library.

Now, in the week of celebration, we call to life all local conscientious Jewish strength to help on one hand to transform this holiday into a demonstration for our library and on the other hand–to create for it a better future through financial contributions.

Our library must continue and be supported through all of the city's institutions–Jewish and non–Jewish–whose job it is to spread knowledge and education.

We must make it possible for our library to have its own location that can hold all its treasures and assure its future development. We must enable the library to grow bigger and more beautiful. We must also make the library more accessible to the greater Jewish population and increase the number of readers.

We must therefore ensure that the library will truly be the crown of Jewish Siedlce.

If we want to get this done, then our joy will be deserved, creative, the joy of a job well done–a holiday for the people of the book.

Long live our serious cultural holiday.

Committee to Celebrate the 25th Anniversary of the Library of the Association "Cultural Arts" in Siedlce.

This committee included the leadership of "Jewish Art" and the people–H. Goldberg, M. Grabia, M. Zhebrowicz, Y.L. Liveront, Y Rosenzumen, M. Rotbeyn, and Shpielfidl, as well as the representatives from the Zionist organizations with their divisions "He–chalutz," "Ha–shomer ha–tza'ir," from the Jewish Folksparty and its divisions, from the Jewish faculty, from the merchants and handworkers organizations, and a whole array of people from Warsaw, Lodz, Eretz–Yisroel, and New York, and Prof. Arbeter–Fareyna.

[Page 219]

They issued an announcement about the anniversary celebration of the Jewish library and called for help with the activities of the celebration committee, both financial and otherwise[101].

The library existed until September, 1933, when the Second World War broke out [sic–trans. note]. The Nazi vandals destroyed and stole the literary treasures, which from 1926 until the outbreak of the war, had greatly increased, so that on the eve of the destruction the number of books had grown to 12,000.

The Student–Library at the "Mutual Aid"

The Jewish students of the governmental gymnasium formed, around 1924, an organization for mutual aid for destitute students that helped them pursue their studies. It was a secret organization, because no student was permitted to reveal who belonged to it. Along with the organization, a library was created for the studious young people of the middle schools in Siedlce. The library developed and grew thanks to the efforts of the young people who organized various entertainments and lotteries whose proceeds benefitted the library. The book collection at the beginning of the thirties numbered about 4,000 volumes in two languages: Polish and Hebrew. The library existed until 1932. After long negotiations it was shut down, as the Jewish student–library of the "Mutual Aid" was to be given to the Hebrew "Tarbus" school. The "Tarbus" school also took the library of the evening courses, which had existed from 1915 until 1926. Together with the newly bought books, the school owned a great book collection, which before the war numbered six thousand volumes.

Yiddish and Hebrew Books in the City Library

The city library, which was located in the old city hall, formally had a Yiddish–Hebrew section, which was, in fact, never active.

[Page 220]

At the intervention of the Jewish councilmen, they would promise that slowly the section would be revived. But it never happened. The city managers had already taken care that it should be as it was. The city library owned about 800 Hebrew and Yiddish books.

Zionist Activities After the First World War

When the war ended in 1918 and the worldwide "He–Chalutz" movement was founded, there was already a similar organization in Siedlce with excellent activities.

The Zionist organization had leased in Raskazh two acres of land and began to work it as a practice garden. The central committee of "He–Chalutz" sent the agronomist Haykes as an instructor. The number of pioneers was then small–six, in all. They lived a communal life; they lived together in Raskazh, they shared physical and professional labor, and made spiritual arrangements. They learned Jewish history, Zionist history, and the geography of Eretz Yisroel. In short, they hoped to accommodate themselves so they could make aliyah to Eretz Yisroel.

Meanwhile, the Polish–Bolshevik War broke out,, and just like the rest of the community life, "He–Chalutz" petered out.

In the city there was a chapter of "Ha–Shomer Ha–Tza'ir" to which the middle–class youth belonged.

Together with "Ha–Shomer Ha–Tza'ir," "He–Chalutz" rented a room and wanted to establish again the locksmith school that the donor Y. Gutglas had opened at the Talmud Torah and which had been shut down. The pioneers strove to learn a productive craft that they could practice in Eretz Yisroel. But the plan to reopen the school came to nothing, because the Ger Chasidim influenced the donor that he should not support such a thing, giving a school to the young pioneers.

An important move was taken by "He–Chalutz" in Siedlce in 1919. Several hundred books were gathered together along with tools and were sent to Eretz Yisroel.

[Page 221]

When Y.Kh. Brenner was killed in Jaffa in 1921, the news greatly upset Jewish Siedlce. In response to a call from "He–Chalutz," thousands of Jews from Siedlce gathered in the city garden. At that time, "He–Chalutz" had about eighty members. But shortly after, aliyah to Eretz Yisroel was closed down, which had a great effect on "He–Chalutz," and diminished its influence.

In 1923, "He–Chalutz Ha–Tza'ir" was founded, an educational arm of "He–Chalutz," that accepted members up to 18 years old. "He–Chalutz Ha–Tza'ir" was not an agricultural organization. The young people began to learn Hebrew and awaited the opportunity to realize their aspirations.

At that time, the membership of "He–Chalutz" and "He–Chalutz Ha–Tzair" was as follows:

He–Chalutz			He–Chalutz Ha–Tza'ir			Total	Made Aliya
Male	Female	Total	Male	Female	Total		
24	11	35	32	48	80	115	32

At the time of the Fourth Aliyah, which was provoked by the politics of Grabski, middle–class Jews from Siedlce made aliyah. Most of them liquidated their businesses, sold their possessions, and made aliyah. But this aliyah did not last long, because so many Jews did not know how to lead their lives in Eretz Yisroel and thus returned to Siedlce. Some went from Eretz Yisroel to other countries.

Simultaneously, masses of young people began to stream to "He–Chalutz," seeking membership. In the ranks of "He–Chalutz" there developed a discussion between "broadening" or "deepening," that is broadening the ranks according to the circumstances or ceasing to accept new members in order to increase the consciousness of those who already belonged.

[Page 222]

Only 70 comrades then were accepted into "He–Chalutz,", which already numbered a hundred pioneers. The pioneers had done their preparatory work, received certification in agricultural areas, in stone–carving, and in carpentry. Thus there existed in the organization itself methodical labor for Keren–Kayemet and for the "League for Working Eretz Yisroel"[102]

At the same time, the Mizrachi Organization also created "He–Chalutz Ha–Mizrachi," which sent its members to certifying kibbutzim and later to Eretz Yisroel. In the community Zionist organization there was also a "He–Chalutz Ha–Mizrachi."

"The Siedlce Vochenblat" and Other Periodicals

The Zionist movement grew in Siedlce in all its varieties at the beginning of the '20s. At the time of the election campaign for the Sejm and the senate and the city council, people strongly felt the lack of their own press through which to address the Jewish population of nearly twenty thousand people. In Zionist circles, the thought arose of issuing a weekly paper in Siedlce.

In the summer of 1922, the idea began to develop of a regular weekly paper in Siedlce. Efforts were undertaken to get permission to issue a paper. Until the permission was prepared, people issued a series of independent bi–weekly publications.

A group of community activists (Y. Grauman, Asher Liverant, Levi Gutglas, and the already mentioned Yehoshua Goldberg) put out the "Voice of Siedlce" (published in only three issues), every two weeks in June, 1922. Then there was an interval of two months, and on September 1 of 1922 appeared the fourth issue. But the small group of "penmen"–aside from Y. Grauman, who in 1923 emigrated to the United States–were the real creators of the Yiddish Vochenblat in Siedlce.

[Page 223]

From right to left: Levi Gutgold, Asher Liverant, Y. Grauman, and Y. Goldberg

In September 15, 1922 appeared "The Siedlce Newspaper," four sides, in quarto. Y. Grauman was listed as editor and A. Liverant as publisher.

On the first page appeared the following statement from the editor:

We believe that Siedlce and its vicinity deserve to have a regular Jewish paper. at least a weekly paper, which should objectively and comprehensively react to all everyday, economic, and cultural questions and phenomena of local life. Meanwhile, we must, for technical and other reasons, be satisfied with this singular issue, which should serve for us and for you, our reader, as a sample of the forthcoming Yiddish Vochenblat in Siedlce———

In the second column, Y. Grauman published an editorial, "On the Subjects of the Day," about the forthcoming first elections for the Sejm and the senate in Independent Poland–how the Jewish vote can be used productively in the election districts where thanks to abuses in the election organization there was little or no chance to elect a Jewish deputy.

Under the pseudonym "Bergaldi," Y. Goldberg published a satirical poem called "The Cemetery City."

"Yinger" (L. Gutglas" was represented by an article "Be afraid, you from yesterday," which strongly attacked the backwardness of the community leaders.

Standing, from right to left: Menashe Czarnabrada, H. Kartcz, Avraham Shloyme Englander, Itsche
Altschuler, Meir Vyman, Fishl Popovsky, Yehuda Tenenboym
Seated from left to right: Levi Gutgeld, Moyshe Czarnabrada, Yakov Tenenboym, Y. Grauman, Asher Liverant

[Page 225]

In an article, "Downhill," L. Gutgelt shows that slowly step by step, our economic life was rolling downhill; in truth, this was partially a phenomenon caused by the state. In Siedlce this was quite obvious, because the city was impoverished and there were no sources of income.

With a notice about the library in the "Jewish Arts" association, a little local news, a warning against non–kosher meat, a survey of the local Polish press, election matters, announcements and congratulations, such was the paper.

The second issue had a new name, "The Siedlce Vort" [Word]. It appeared on October 1, 1922, with eight pages and the same make–up. On the first page was an announcement that soon would appear the first issue of the regular weekly paper "The Siedlce Vochenblat." Outwardly, this issue is similar to the "Siedlce Newspaper." The "Siedlce Vochenblat" was delayed, and the following issue was called the "Siedlce Tog" [Day]. It appeared on October 12.

The editorial staff of the "Siedlce Vochenblat," with the editor Asher Liverant in the middle, with a glass of tea. Among them are Y.P. Greenberg, Yehoshua Eckerman, A. Kimmel, Bella Finkelshteyn, Avraham, Friedman, Velvel Lev, Kaspi, Dovid Popovsky, and others

[Page 226]

After the successful appearance of the single issue, permission was received from the government to put out the "Siedlce Vochenblat." The Zionist organization intervened to make the thought of issuing the paper a reality. Thus, the Zionists created an organ of their own that served as the mouthpiece for the local organization. This was at the time of the English mandate concerning Eretz–Yisroel in San Remo, on the eve of the Fourth Aliyah.

During 1922 three issues appeared, and in 1923, 38 issues appeared. From then on, the newspaper appeared weekly without interruption until the Second World War, that is, for 18 years.

In issue 2 from 1923 appeared the following message to readers:

In difficult material conditions, with little intellectual skills, with full indifference and partial ignorance about the business, we undertook the "Siedlce Vochenblat." As we have so far, so will we continue to combat every community injustice and misdeed, react to every malfeasance which affects us, the Jews of Siedlce.

The paper struggled for its existence and made attempts to attract advertisements. Siedlce, however, had few business or factory interests, so they were satisfied with congratulations and obituaries. About the financial condition of the paper, we have a second announcement: "To Our Readers," published in the fourth issue of 1923:

The publication of a daily paper, particularly in a provincial city, encountered many strength–sapping difficulties. This is neither the time nor the place to provide details of the great difficulties, both technical and material, that the paper experienced. It is also not the time or place to tell how small the number of initiators was or how few people carried the whole business on their shoulders.

[Page 227]

——————Individual birds, when they receive no straw to build their nests, sing no songs. Although everyone recognizes the importance of our undertaking, few readers feel the basic duty to pay the price of a subscription, putting in danger the existence of our newspaper.

In March of 1925, the "Siedlce Vochenblat" celebrated a milestone, the appearance of its hundredth issue. An editorial in honor of the milestone said:

The publication in a provincial city, without any underwriting, of a hundred issues of a weekly paper should definitely be celebrated as a small holiday in the history of the Jewish provincial press in Poland.——————

We have accomplished the end that our paper has become almost an elementary intellectual staple in every Jewish home in Siedlce, even in the whole province, which has a looser community than the capital, and our paper has begun to penetrate all the Jewish homes.

The "Siedlce Vochenblat," from its first appearance and throughout its existence, served the community's cultural life as well as the development of various cooperative institutions, school and educational institutions, for awakening and continuing the feelings for their homeland among emigrants from Siedlce in other countries and encouraging them to support local institutions. Most important were the services given by the Vochenblatt to the Zionist institutions whose organ it was. But the paper suffered many internal and external disturbances.

For example, it happened that L. Gutgelt addressed in an article the business of the local government and a particular official, saying that he had acted "in the style of the old police" (meaning that he had acted like the czarist police). The official then imposed a large monetary fine on the "Siedlce Vochenblat." When the editors turned to the readership for contributions to pay the fine, and then published a list of donations that came from readers and sympathizers, the same official felt offended and doubled the fine that he had imposed on the paper.

[Page 228]

It happened more than once, especially when the Zionist land policies opposed those of the government, that the Vochenblat was confiscated. More than once–especially at the time of the elections for the Sejm or for local offices–the distribution of the paper had to be undertaken away from the hands of the administration.

The "Siedlce Vochenblat" also survived a ban from the Siedlce rabbinate. The ban was also sponsored by the Orthodox weekly "Our Way." This medieval weapon was used against the Vochenblat because in issue 17, a feuilleton was published called "The Grandiose Sunday Mikveh Gathering," a satire on a gathering that was supposed to compile a list of all the women who observed Jewish laws of hygiene–"Pure Ones among the Daughters of Israel." In the same issue was written:

In the name of the holy gathering, people received permission to send to every home leaflets with a revolting purpose, to make meetings and rabbinical sermons about such matters, so that every mother, when she would teach her own daughter, should do so in a special room, with two observers.

This article convinced the Orthodox leaders of the city to order the rabbinate to forbid reading of the "Siedlce Vochenblat."

The condemnation did nothing to lessen the circulation of the paper, but it had reverberations not only in the city but also in the daily Jewish press, which protested this method of one–sidedness in the rabbinate.

A letter from the handworkers' union to the paper said:

The Jewish handworkers in Siedlce, as part of the citizen democracy, recognizes that the issuance of a condemnation by the rabbinate against the "Siedlce Vochenblat" is reminiscent of a clerical notion from the Middle Ages regarding freedom of speech.

The Zionist committee in its meeting of May 16 decided to express the fullest recognition and belief that the good part of Siedlce was totally on the side of the "Siedlce Vochenblatt."

[Page 229]

"Jewish Art" put out a declaration is which it said:

We protest in the strongest way against the dark deeds of the local "holy ones," who have, under the mantle of religiosity, have spread demoralizing obscene announcements, called evil meetings, and, lastly, have tried, through medieval methods, to stop the mouths of those who have the boldness to react to these methods.

A. Einhorn in the Warsaw "Heynt" of May 25, 1925 wrote an editorial called "Ban":

The ban now stalks the Jewish streets. A few months back it was in Lublin, now in Siedlce, both times against the published Yiddish word.

The provincial pillars who have bear the heavy burden of worry for Jewish souls have begun to make it quite simple: if a Jewish paper writes anything that is not in their spirit, they quickly seize the old sword from its sheath and hack away; they put the newspaper under a ban. Two are now accursed: the "Lublin Tageblat" and the "Siedlce Vochenblat."

It is not a question of these two "victims," which are, after the ban, in just the same shape as they were before. It is a question of the phenomenon itself, which sets before us a sad corner of our community life.

The "Folkstzeitung" (Warsaw) dedicated a long article to the matter.

The "Lodz Tageblat" of May 23, 1925 in an article entitled "Our Ban," reviewed the story of the ban in great detail, how it was issued, and ended the article with the following words:

The fact itself requires no explanation and is an excellent illustration of how certain rabbis besmirch the honor of the rabbinate.

The "Lublin Tageblat" devoted to the ban a long feuilleton, "The Siedlce Ban." The "Tageblat" recalled the ban that had been proclaimed a year earlier, which had in no way harmed it, as though no one knew from whence it came or where it went.

[Page 230]

The paper ended the feuilleton:

For our colleagues we have this advice: "Don't ask after the doctor, but after the sick person." It won't hurt you at all, God forbid. It can only harm small–minded intriguers.

In regard to the frictions and controversies and the ban, the prophecy of the "Lublin Tageblat" was right. The "Siedlce Vochenblat" appeared for eighty years without interruption, until the outbreak of the Second World War, and became a truly regional paper, which provided space for articles from the whole area. Thus, on April 23, 1926, a second supplement began to appear, "Life in Mezritch," which became an independent section of the paper and had its own set of editors.

As we have already said, the "Siedlce Vochenblat" was established by Zionist leaders and writers, and the paper followed this path until its last day. The Vochenblat served all the Zionist factions. Only at certain times, when the Zionist front was not unified–for instance, at the time of elections for the city council, the community, or even at elections for the Zionist congress–the different Zionist factions would separate. Then the paper would serve the general Zionist organization. As for the general Zionist ideal, its position was to be unified.

The paper was in favor of constructive work in Eretz Yisroel. In the area of culture, it propagandized for Hebrew. It is proper to note that from the end of January, 1934, until halfway through 1935–a year and a half–the "Siedlce Vochenblat" published a "Hebrew Supplement," The Yiddish spelling of the of the newspaper was old–fashioned, just like that of the Warsaw "Heynt." When the editors proposed to use a new orthography, L. Gutgelt, whose influence on the paper was significant, was opposed. Only in 1937, two years after the death of editor Asher Liverant, did the "Siedlce Vochenblat" begin to use the new orthography.

[Page 231]

The circulation of the paper was 800 copies, but with time it grew to 1000.

In 1936 the "Siedlce Vochenblat" celebrated its fifteenth anniversary. In a special article dedicated to the great day, L. Gutgelt, among others, wrote:

When one leafs through the fifteen years of the "Siedlce Vochenblat," one sees with how much industry and responsibility it has fulfilled its duty. The "Vochenblat" became, and remains, a paper of battle, a paper that makes no peace with the current situation, a paper with an ideal, a paper that awakens and calls to action. The first articles in the paper opposed institutions that were ruled by shoddiness and corruption. During its existence, the "Vochenblat" fought for the extension of social aid and mutual aid for the purpose of shaping new institutions, strengthening those that existed with the work of the Jewish masses, awakened the consciousness of mutual aid, for education and cultural institutions. A significant chapter for it was the battle with the anti–Semites. The "Vochenblat" was silent about no offense done to Jews and always promoted our rights. As a provincial paper we should fight against sending Jewish life back to the dark Middle Ages. The "Vochenblat" is among the few provincial publications that had to survive searches, trials, and even denunciations over supposed disloyalty.

During its eighteen years of existence, hundreds of writers contributed to the "Siedlce Vochenblat," locals and from elsewhere in Poland and in the larger world. To the editorial circle belonged, in addition to those already mentioned, Yechiel–Pesach Greenberg, who published stories, essays, poems, criticism of the arts; Y. Ch. Eisenberg wrote poems and essays; Y.N. Vayntroyb, whose name has appeared so often here, published memoirs about the pogrom in Siedlce and many biographical articles about Jewish personalities in Siedlce; A. Goldberg and Sh. Rosenbgarten wrote sports in Siedlce; B. Mintz published a monograph about the people's bank; Yoel Mastboym wrote memoirs about his childhood in Siedlce.

Others who worked on the paper were Dr. Dovid Kleinveksler, later a lawyer in Haifa; Peretz Listek, Yosef Listek, Dovid Ben–Yosef (Pasawsky), Avraham, Friedman; the writer of this work, and his brother Leib Srebrnik.

[Page 232]

"Unzer veg" [Our Path], the "Siedlce Tribune", "Dos Vort" [The Word], and "Siedlce Life"

Besides the "Siedlce Vochenblat" weekly papers were put out by all the other active Jewish parties in Siedlce. Two years after the Zionist paper began to appear, the Agudah began to put out a weekly publication called "Unzer Veg" [Our Path], an Orthodox weekly. The paper appeared with some interruption from May 16, 1924 until 1930, with 2 or 4 pages with a circulation of 400. The main editor was Berish Jakobowicz. A committee did the editing: Sholem Yellen, Rabbi Meir Schwartzman, Yehudah–Aryeh Zuker, Aharon Gelkenboym, Yisroel–Meir Kleinlehrer, and Shmuel Ginsberg. The Orthodox weekly represented the Agudah's political views in the Siedlce city council and in the community. Details about "Unzer Veg can be found in the memoirs of Rabbi M. Schwartzman.

In 1926 and 1927, M. Mandelman, Yakov Tenenboym, and Menashe Czarnobrode put out a paper called "Dos Vort" [The Word]. The paper had a folkist coloring and served the interests of the Jewish Folks School, which was then active in Siedlce.

Also the leftist factions published their weekly. In 1930 the Bund's worker Binyamin Kramarzh put out a weekly called the "Siedlce Tribune," which lasted for two years. Dovid Nymark published in this weekly a memoir in installments of the social and cultural life of Siedlce at the beginning of the twentieth century. This paper, with its small circulation, closed down thanks to a lack of resources.

Z Rozenzumen, an activist in the "Poalei–Tzion" of Siedlce and its surroundings, together with A. Friedman, who, because of friction with his colleagues at the "Siedlce Vochenblat, had left the paper, decided to published a new weekly, "Siedlce Life."

[Page 233]

The first issue appeared on October 9, 1935 and it lasted for three years, until the winter of 1938.

Through the initiative of a group of fiction writers–Y.H. Eisenberg, Y.F. Greenberg, and Y. Tenenboym, in January of 1927 a bi–monthly literary journal began to appear under the title "Vortzlen" [Roots]. Its aim was to present young talent, regardless of their orientation. Two issues appeared. An editorial in the first issue said:

We propose to provide a stage for young writers. We take on the burden with full responsibility. We know that the way is difficult, but we have the courage to approach publication with our modest attempts.

Our journal will not serve any particular orientation or formula. Our criterion is–talent, steeped in truth. Our goal–an excellent approach, a conscientious appreciation.

The contents of the first issue: B. Olitzki–poems; Y.Ch. Eisenberg–Shadows; M. Bershling–Poems; a. Vogler–Poem; L. Olitzki– The First Three Rubles; Y.F. Greenberg–Without Anything; Sh.L. Schneiderman–Poem; Y. Tenenboym–The Hatchet; A. Zilberman– Because of a Guy; M. Natish–Poems; about young Yiddish prose H. Levi–Harvest Time; P.G.–Tanach in Yiddish; A. Lehrer–Direct War Poetry; L. Plony–Bibliography and Notes.

[Page 234]

The format of "Vortzlen" consisted of sixteen pages published by Ch. Rosenblat.

I should also point out the effort of a group of young people, graduates of the Hebrew Folks' School "Tarbus" in Siedlce, who in October of 1931 put out a hectographed paper called "Ha–B'ris" [The Covenant]. After the first two issues, the paper was published every two weeks. The paper was the organ of the Hebrew–speaking circle, under the editorship of the Hebrew teacher Hillel Schwartz, with the participation of writers from the school. Hillel Schwartz later made aliyah, became a policeman, and was killed by piece of shrapnel on August 4, 1938 near Ramat–Ha–Kovesh, at the time of the bloody events there.

The first published issue of "Ha–B'ris" appeared on December 6, 1931 and the following contents: An editorial–(H. Schwartz) concerning Chanukah; Y Srebrnik (Y Kaspi): an article about Chanukah as a spiritual holiday; Shomo Reich described in a long literary piece his father's funeral; further:—an article an notice concerning the pioneer movement and the Hebrew language. At the end, a humorous section. It is appropriate to add that the patron of the paper was no other than the editor himself who, from his small salary, cut down on food and warm clothing, devoting his coins to the existence of the Hebrew bi–weekly paper, which lasted for four months.

Community Council and Dedication of the "Ezras Y'somim"

Around 1924, it was possible to believe that life had returned to normal. For the Jewish community, new problems cropped up. There was a lack of open, legal institutions that would undertake and organize Jewish community life. The Polish overseers had not found it necessary to reorganize the Jewish community, although such a demand had been the topic even in 1919 at a conference of the leaders of the Jewish communities in Poland, which was convened by the central Jewish national council.

[Page 235]

A representative from Siedlce was there. At the conference it was proclaimed that the demand of the German occupation government about the organization of the Jewish religious union in the Warsaw General Government and in the decree of the country leader of February 4, 1919 about the changes in the organization of the Jewish communities in former Congress Poland, does not meet in any way the legal demands of the Jewish population.

The Polish regime, which had no interest in broader Jewish autonomy, desired that the community should control only religious functions. The dozors also did not want to lose their power if the community enlarged its framework, and in 1923 Siedlce had the following community budget that illustrates the character of the Jewish community:

Income	
Taxes	33,000,000 marks
Slaughter income	35,000,000
Shops at the hospital	1,000,000
Shops at the cemetery	1,000,000
Bath	180,000

Total	70,180,000
Expenses	
Rabbinate	11000,000
Shul: cantor, sextons	3,000,000
Cantor, beis–hamedresh	240,000
Administration	10,000,000
Talmud–Torah	7,000,000
Ezras–Y'somim	3,000,000
Old–age home	1,500,000
Slaughtering expenses	25,000,000
Total	60,740,000

[Page 236]

The "Agudah," which had a strong religious character, was quite influential in the community at the time. As the rules had established a definite category of voting rights, to which belonged only a particular category of taxpayers, the dozors from the "Agudah" arranged that no taxes should be collected from the general population so that they would not be able to vote.

The Zionists, who had adopted the slogan "Occupy the Kehillah," fought in Siedlce with all their might for control of the community for the purpose of ending the situation and winning the sympathy of the Jewish masses. With their votes they later were able to exercise their wills.

The Jewish community building

[Page 237]

Around 1926, the first more democratic votes came to the community, and new people became part of the governing body. The "Bund" at that time boycotted the community body; in the third decade, however, when the "Bund" changed its views and took part in the campaign for votes, it succeeded in passing several mandates.

The Zionist parties led a battle in the community body to support the Zionist institutions and finally achieved a victory. They also assisted the Yiddishist elements in the battle to receive support for the Folks' School with a Yiddish basis. The Jewish community in Siedlce had set aside certain sums for the Hebrew "Tarbus" school, Hebrew evening courses, the Yiddish Folks' School, and Keren Kayames L'Yisroel. The community later gave a hundred zlotys to every pioneer who made aliyah to Eretz Yisroel.

* *

After 1920, when life began to return to normal, the officers of "Ezras–Y'somim" [the orphan home] began to seek ways to obtain a suitable locale for the orphan home. Then they purchased a small wooden building with a garden, which was in the same neighborhood as the old people's home. The wooden building was pulled down and a special committee was chosen to construct a new building. The committee consisted of: Dovid Rubinshteyn, chair; Monish Ridel, assistant; Bunim Rothenberg, secretary; Yisoel Gutgelt, treasurer; Wolf Barg, steward; Yisroel Zucker; Dovid Kanafni; Alter Kaminski; Eliyahu Levita; and Yakov Yom–Tov.

An announcement issued by the committee said:

Small and narrow is the old home of the "Ezras–Y'somim." The number of children who make their home there is very small, but even so, because of its size they must sleep two, and sometimes three, to a bed.

Even worse is the fate of the greater number of orphaned children who cannot be taken in, barefoot and alone, wandering the streets, living in cellars and attics.

[Page 238]

We must use all of our strength to find for them their necessities and a home. Without capital, without any pre–arranged income, we are dedicated to putting up a large building that must and will soon take in a great camp of about 150 such poor orphans and relieve their suffering.

Truly we rely on your feelings for the fate of these children. We have calculated that along with us, you will understand for whom we are proposing this building; and truly, the recent war years have shown that the fate of our people lacks a firm foundation, that no one has a secure tomorrow. Unfortunately, all of our messages to you have not produced a response.

After about six months, work on building the orphan home was under way, and on December 13, 1926, while the building was in progress, the following accounting was published:

Purchase of land	8,670.70 zlotys
Materials	26,728.71 zlotys
Labor costs	15,218.14 zlotys
Miscellaneous	3,682.83 zlotys
Total	54,300.38 zlotys[103]

In 1927 was the dedication of the building. The orphan home became a jewel in Jewish Siedlce. The number of children who lived there increased to 70. The house had three levels and contained a dining hall, bedrooms and relaxation rooms, a recreation hall, a library, and other features. The poor orphans enjoyed a warm atmosphere. In summers they would go to summer dwellings for vacations. The building that they had left was given over entirely to the old–people's home.

"Ezras–Y'somim" did not have a school for the children. In that situation, the boys learned in the Talmud Torah, the girls in the government school, the "Tarbus," and some in the Folks' School. The writers and community activist Puah Rakovski greatly praised the institution but also criticized sending the children to the Talmud–Torah, where they studied for 12 hours a day.

[Page 239]

When the children grew up and had to leave the home, they were apprenticed to craftsmen in order to learn a trade appropriate for their abilities. They learned: shoemaking, tailoring, locksmithing. Some went into printing and other trades. There were also times when, with the help of the Central Orphan Welfare Agency and "Giant," children from the Siedlce Ezras Y'somim were sent to France, Canada, or the United States.

The building of "Ezras Y'somim"

The "Ezras Y'somim" was financed primarily by the Jewish community, which gave it a yearly stipend. The city governing committee also provided a yearly subsidy. Aside from that, members would pay a yearly fee, and people from Siedlce who lived elsewhere would send contributions. The old–people's home operated in the same way. The financial difference between the two institutions was that the old–people's home had fewer expenses, because "Ezras–Y'somim" needed more for education, clothing, and so on.

[Page 240]

In 1930, "Ezras Y'somim" survived a severe crisis. The institution was shut down. This resulted from the following conditions: After their building was completed, "Ezras Y'somim" had many debts, amounting to about 18 thousand zlotys, on which sum they had to pay interest. After three years, the interest amounted to the colossal sum of 13 thousand zlotys. The situation became so serious that the directors were forced every day to worry about prolonging the borrowing and redirecting of funds. The holders of the debt also insisted that the borrowing should be underwritten by the steering committee members. When the loans were not paid off, the debt holders put a sequester on the possessions of the committee members.

Because of this developing situation twice called for consultations with the prominent citizens of Siedlce. But no one attended. Only five people attended the extraordinary meeting that was called for the 26th of May in 1930.

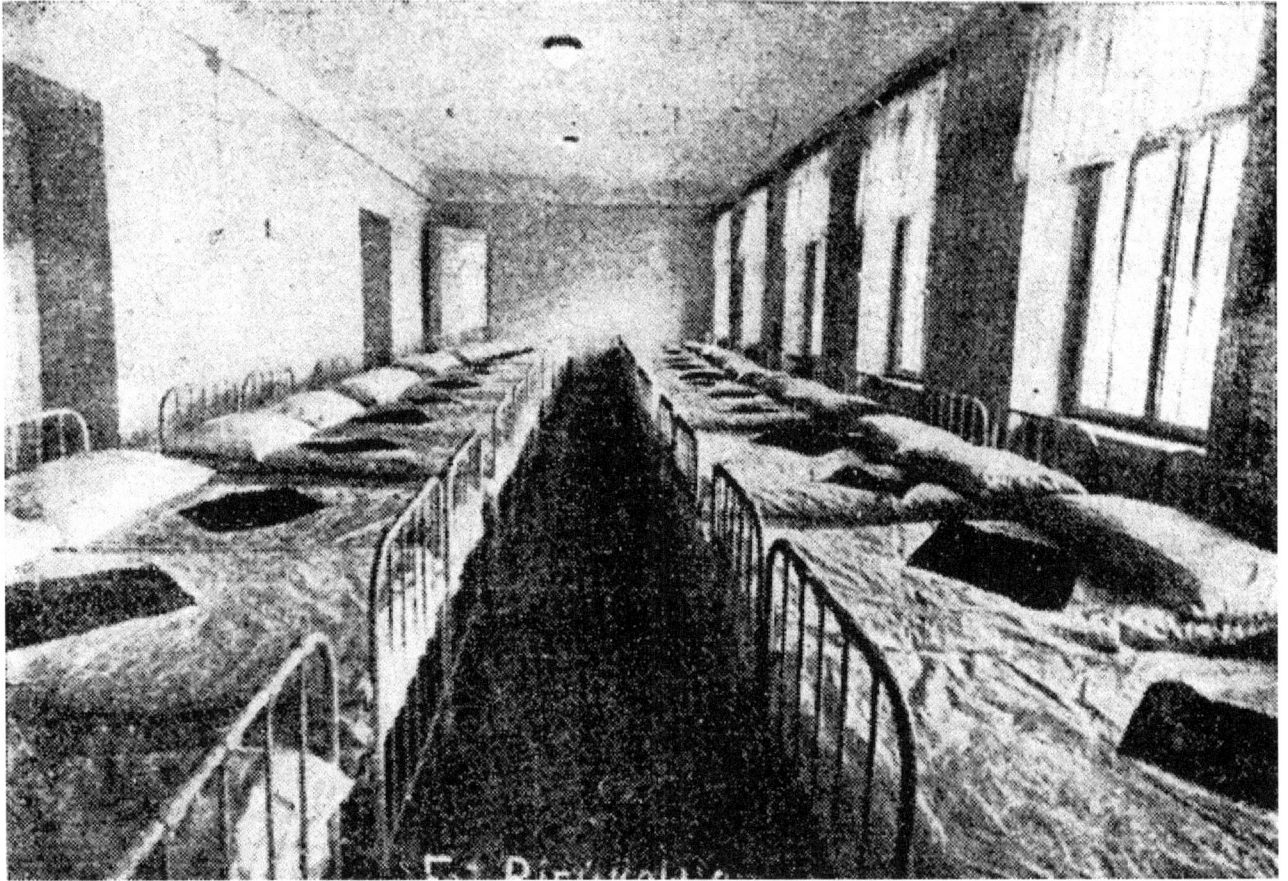

A bedroom for children in Ezras–Y'somim

[Page 241]

The committee therefore issued the following resolution: they declared that since the entire deficit of the "Ezras Y'somim" was left over from the time of putting up the building, and since the building belonged to the entire community of Siedlce, the community should cover the deficit. This proposal was made in the community council, which authorized the community committee to extend a loan of 20 thousand zlotys and thereby cover the deficit. The "Ezras Y'somim" committee went to the "Union of Orphan Concerns" and persuaded them to lend that sum to the community committee for a period of three months at four percent interest[104].

Until this matter was settled, the committee called forth the guardians of the orphans, turned the children over to them, and closed the institution. But the problem was solved and in July the institute was opened again. Thus things went until the outbreak of the Second World War, when the children were evacuated to Minsk (in the Soviet Union). At the outbreak of the Russian–German War (June, 1941), some of the children were taken further into Russia and survived, but some were killed in Minsk.

The Passover seder for the orphan children with the participation of the Ezras Y'somim Committee, led by Asher Arzhel. At the table state the educator M. Stchalke, the teacher Yakovicz, and Asher Arzhel

[Page 242]

During many long years, the following personnel led the "Ezras Y'somim: Alter Kaminski, chair (he left Siedlce in the thirties); he was replaced by Yisroel Gutgelt; Bunim Rottenberg, secretary (the secretaries changed: he was replaced by M. Stczalka); Dovid Kanapni, treasurer; Aaron Yochlin, steward; Yisroel Zucker, Yakov Yommtov, Gittl Fershter, Sarah Czarnabrode, Avraham–Yosef Karnitzki, members. Fishl Dromi (Popowski) represented the community as an ex–officio member.

The Ezras–Y'somim children in the woods of a summer camp

Aside from the "Ezras Y'somim" and the old people's home, Siedlce after the First World War established a whole array of philanthropic organizations. In May of 1925, at the urging of Moyshe Brokarcz and Yisroel Rosenblum, a "Beis Lechem" [House of Bread] was established. Its mission was to provide bread and other foodstuffs to the needy who were too embarrassed to go begging. Every Erev Shabbos and Shabbos, Jews would go to the courtyards with large baskets and call out: "Gut Shabbos, Jews. 'Beis Lechem' is here to distribute challahs, bread for poor Jews." Doors and windows would be thrown open and people would pass out bread and challahs. The baskets would be brought back to the "Beis Lechem" office, where the other products would be divided up.

[Page 243]

A second required institution was founded in December of 1926——the "Toz," an acronym for the Polish phrase "Society for the Preservation of Health" (for Jews).

"Toz" took on the task of watching over the health of the Jewish population, particularly children. It conducted clinics. In its last years, "Toz" oversaw the Jewish hospital in Siedlce.

At the same time there was a "Linas Ha–Tzedek," which was on duty throughout the night. This group provided a doctor in case of need and also lent out medical devices and so on.

The "Bikur–Cholim," which already existed for many years, halted its operations from time to time, but each time it resumed those activities.

After the Bolshevik Revolution in Russia, the Novograd yeshiva came to Poland and opened branches in a variety of cities. Siedlce had such a branch.

The arrival of the Novograd yeshiva in Siedlce drew great attention. It was located in the butchers' beis–medresh. Students would come there to focus on the Talmud. For several hours a day they would study Mussar from two volumes: "Mesilas Yesharim" and "Orchos Tzadikim" (the first volume was by R. Shmuel Dovid Luzzato) [A footnote corrects this, explaining that the book was actually by Rabbi Moshe–Chaim Luzzato.]. Each day, at the time of the afternoon service, it was time to study Mussar. A student from the yeshiva, attended by four younger students, would march in the hall of the butchers' shul or in the courtyard; the older student taught Mussar to the younger ones.

On Thursday evenings–summer and winter–the students did not sleep, but studied through the night. This was called keeping watch.

[Page 244]

A special experience was the "Hitor'ros" [spiritual awakening] that was made on Shabbos after the third meal. The head of the yeshiva would stand before the opened Ark of the Covenant while the yeshiva was entirely dark, and he would preach. The listeners, from their great devotion, would cry out, which signified either repentance or remorse.

There were four divisions in the yeshiva. The fourth, in which the oldest students studied, was called "kibbutz." There were three heads of the yeshiva–R. Leibl, R. Shabbtai, and R. Mikhl Tsikholnik.

The political power of Jews in Siedlce was broad but became weaker. The Polish supervising authority did everything it could to make the city more Polish. They created an artificial Polish majority, as documents later showed.

At the time of the city council elections, on May 29, 1927, nine of the twenty–nine elected members were Jews.

The second census, from December 9, 1931, gave the following figures:

1. Count of the Population

Jews Men	Women	Total	Christians Men	Women	Total	Combined Men	Women	Total	%Jews
7,031	7,762	14,793	10,683	11,400	22,083	17,714	19,162	36,876	41

2. Count by native languages

Yiddish and Hebrew	Polish	Other	Total	% Yiddish and Hebrew
14,601	22,019	256	36,876	39.6

When we compare the results of the second census from the end of 1931 with the figures from the first census from the end of 1921, what strikes the eye is the difference in total populations. In the first census we had 18,963 Jews, but in the second census there were only in Siedlce 14,793 Jews, that is, a decline of 22 percent. And we see that the number of non–Jews grew from 16,256 in 1921 to 19,162 in 1931, that is, an increase of 17.9 percent.

[Page 245]

This change in the population count was not the result of Jews leaving Siedlce in such numbers over the ten–year period. It was the result of the politics of the Polish government, which aimed to reduce the number of Jews belonging to Siedlce. This was necessary for rigging the elections so that there would be fewer mandates from Siedlce. To this end, a number of small towns that had earlier been included as parts of Siedlce were separated from the city and declared to be independent municipalities. At the same time, a number of villages that were inhabited only by Christian farmer workers were assigned to Siedlce. Thus the number of Polish inhabitants was artificially increased.

Jewish life in Siedlce in the last years before the outbreak of the Second World War was over all in decline. When the Polish prime minister spoke in the Sejm, he justified the economic war against the Jews. The anti–Jewish Siedlce paper "Pszyotszel Podlyosze" (number 9 from 1936), contained an article "The Polish Earth Should Burn their Steps." The author of the article, St. Kapetcz, rejoiced that as a result of the prime minister's speech, the Polish Foreign Minister Beck had demanded that colonies be created "to accommodate the overflow of the Jewish population." Kapetcz wrote:

The war against the flood of Jews should be waged by the entire people, by every individual, and through every aspect of community life.

It is clear that the Jews will not leave on their own, so we should establish colonies that can take in 800,000 a year, not just 80,000. They don't leave because it is good for them here. They feel at home here.

[Page 246]

The well–known leader of the Pilsudski camp (Sanatzia), Pulkownik Boguslaw Miedzinski editor of the official "Polish Gazette" and former Postmaster, published in his newspaper in June of 1938 a Jew–baiting libel. The author of the Jew–baiting article had a close connection with Siedlce. He was the husband of Janina Shteyn, a daughter of the Siedlce doctor Moritz Shteyn, the longtime director of the Jewish hospital, researcher on the Jewish past in Siedlce, who later converted to Catholicism. Miedzinski graduated from the Siedlce Gymnasium in 1909 and later studied in the Lemberg Polytechnic and in the Agrarian School of Jagellonian University in Cracow. In his anti–Semitic article Miedzinski repeated the lines which had been disproved already eighteen years earlier, that Jews had greeted the Bolsheviks in Siedlce and so on. He wrote:

The communist idea is deeply ingrained in the Jewish youth. In 1920, when the Bolsheviks came to the region of Siedlce, the whole population aided the Polish army in repulsing the enemy. And what did the Jews do?

The Jewish communists of Siedlce–he continues–took up a voluntary collection for the Red Army. At the end of July, the following occurred: The Polish general headquarters sent a parliamentarian to Siedlce, where the Bolsheviks were. The parliamentarian later travelled in a car with a Soviet flag and surrounded by a Bolshevik escort. When the car with the Polish officer came to Kalushin, the Jews were in the streets and met the arriving troops with an outcry: "Long live Soviet Russia." Quite simply, the Jews thought there was a Bolshevik officer in the car, not a Polish one.

Miedzinski assured his readers–this fact was told to him by an officer who was surely no anti–Semite but had actually belonged to the leftist sector of the P.P.S. He asks: is if possible that such facts should lack evidence? Is it not clear why there is such an uproar when people try to deal with the Jewish problem?

[Page 247]

Not only was Boguslaw Miedzinski an enemy of Israel but so was his wife Janina. The apostate was inspired by Hitler's regime in Germany. Since Frau Janina Miedzinski had taken a position as a work inspector, in February of 1937 she came from Warsaw to Siedlce and gave a talk entitled "The New Work System in Germany," which was a song of praise for the Hitlerian system.

The pogrom that was organized against the Jews of Brisk, in May of 1937, had wide repercussions in Siedlce. An aid committee was formed in the city for the victims in Brisk. It included: Dr. Kh. Bergman, M. Ratbeyn, Y.N. Wayntroyb, Y.A. Zuker, Y. Slushni, M. Saltzman, and B. Zucker. They issued an announcement that said:

Let not our brothers from Brisk suffer from hunger and need! Let us rebuild the ruins of Brisk! Not a single Jewish business or workshop should cease to exist!

Together with all the other cities in Poland, our city of Siedlce must take an active part in aiding Brisk! This includes both material and psychological aid for our victimized brothers and a spit in the face to the deplorable anti–Semitic evildoers!

In addition to material aid, thousands of Jews from Siedlce also took part in travelling to protests against the pogrom. All businesses in the city were closed on May 30, 1937. This indicated the specific Jewish solidarity and togetherness against the anti–Semitic scourge. This solidarity and unified posture of the Jewish population in Siedlce called forth the scorn of the Siedlce Polish and anti–Semitic paper "Zhemia Siedlceke," which published an article entitled "Jewish Protests":

The behavior of the Jews in such a bestial manner, just as Hitler has done, has not prompted an appropriate reaction among the Jews of Warsaw and Siedlce. If for Brisk, the demonstrative closing of stores on Monday was a vocal reaction, how much should the Jews have demonstrated by closing their stores–for hours and days–after Hitler's pogroms?

[Page 248]

After the Polish prime minister Gen. Slavoy Skladkowski had, in his already mentioned speech in the Sejm, approved of the economic battle against the Jews, the divisions were erased between the National Democratic Party (N.D.), which had always been anti–Semitic, and the official government party, the Sanatsiya, which from its beginning had interested itself in the good reputation of Poland and had made a show of friendship with the Jews.

The economic battle against the Jews, their elimination from the Polish economy, had in Siedlce, as it did in other places, took concrete forms. In the Jewish streets, around the businesses, special uniformed picketers roamed and prevented Christians from entering Jewish businesses. When a Christian customer approached a Jewish business, the "picketers" would confront him and ask why he wanted to bury the Polish economy by not buying from a Christian store. It is easy to imagine that this kind of activity affected almost the entire confidence of the impoverished Jewish population of Siedlce. Christian customers stopped patronizing Jewish shops, while Christian shops began to do very well. They used credit and other privileges that the Polish government had given them.

The economic battle also manifested itself in other aspects of life. In November of that year, Christian cabs appeared in Siedlce with signs that read "Christian cab." This development ruined the income source that had benefited scores of Jewish families for a century. In time, Siedlce was also "honored" with an Aryan doctor's union. The Endecja [the aforementioned N.D.] lawyer Chzhanowski also proposed a petition that all the Christian lawyers except for three signed. This petition required excising Jews from the corps of lawyers. The above–mentioned anti–Semitic lawyer was a son of Alexi Chzhanowski, a liberal and a friend of the Jews, whose activities on behalf of the Jewish community we remember from the early chapters of our work.

[Page 249]

With the greatest energy, the local government proceeded to liquidate Jewish business in Siedlce. On August 16, 1938, an order was promulgated by the Siedlce magistrate that took away the incomes of 27 Jewish merchants who had alcoves in the city market. They were required to give up their spots, because supposedly their alcoves were to be renovated. At the same time, it was declared that all merchants who owned businesses, stalls, or tables in the market had to leave their spots on September 1, 1938, because the city directorate would "renovate" the businesses in the market. All spots for food merchants had to be in a particular place, and special shops were established for other merchandise.

The price for such a shop amounted to from 25 to 40 zlotys a month, and because the city directorate needed money, they required rent for a whole year. This order hit the Jewish merchants in the market like a thunderbolt, because the entire income of a small business or a table in the market amounted to about 50 to 80 zlotys. The poor, ruined merchants had to come up with 300 zlotys for their business, because otherwise they faced catastrophe.

And what kind of renovation was undertaken? Before the renovations there were 48 locations, which became 60, but none of the additions went to Jews. Finally, the anti–Semitic government decided that it was necessary to take a radical step in order to destroy the existence of the Jewish merchants. Although the market had, for a hundred years, come together on Tuesdays and Fridays, this custom was nullified, and the market operated only on Shabbos. Jews did not want to desecrate Shabbos, so that the anti–Semitic order destroyed the existence of a large number of Siedlce's Jews.

From economic anti–Semitism, people turned to hooliganism. Physical attacks on Jews in the streets of Siedlce were a common occurrence. On June 1, 1937, a group of Poles, armed with sticks and iron bars, set out on the side streets, and when they encountered a Jew, they beat him. Among those who were assaulted were: Yakov Kroyt, Esther Tarnheim, Hersh Yablon, Bialeshklo, M. Zilberberg, Yitzchak Heler, and two yeshiva students whose names I do not know.

[Page 250]

From then on, attacks against Jews became constant occurrences. A Jew was afraid to leave his house in the evening. Jews confined themselves to their dwellings as soon as night fell. The city garden, which always used to be full of promenading Jews, where there had been entertainments and mass demonstrations–now the garden was bereft of Jews, because of the wandering gangs with deadly intentions. Anti–Semites would lie in wait for passing Jews and beat them up.

Consequently the leaders of Siedlce would fuss over certain guests who would travel through the city, on their way to the Bialoweza Forest. One could often see the German Hitler–ministers–Goering, Goebbels, and Mussolini's minister Count Ciano, who were received with great honor. The Poles little thought that these were their deadly enemies.

On October 19, 1937 the Jewish community in Siedlce protested the incorporation of Jewish banks into the high schools. Jewish Siedlce gave insisted that this was the beginning of an attempt to force the Jews into a medieval ghetto. consequently, the protest was unanimous: businesses closed, workers went on strike, and Jewish students did not appear in their educational institutions.

At the same time, when Jews were being so starkly robbed of their elementary civil and human rights, there were some Jews who really desired to demonstrate their Polish patriotism. The "Siedlce Vochenblat" wrote about them[105]: the recruiting committee for the Silesian Legion enrolled volunteers, but it made difficulties for Jewish volunteers, members of the Jewish combat unit who wanted to be mobilized with the Silesian Legion. The recruiters separated the Jewish volunteers with a variety of justifications. They were sent into Jewish combat units, or they were told that no decision had been made regarding Jewish volunteers. Two Jews did not want to give way and insisted on being enrolled. It seems that the Polish patriots did not want to cause a scandal, so they were enrolled in the volunteer legion.

[Page 251]

Thus Jews wanted to demonstrate their patriotic feelings, though people tried to prevent them.

[Page 251]

A History of the Jews in Siedlce (cont.)

Siedlce's Poles in the Fight Against Anti–Semitism

There was in Siedlce a medical doctor–St. Wansawski, as we have already mentioned. he had been an anti–Semitic voice in the early years of the twentieth century. But in time he became quite liberal and changed his attitude toward Jews. He became the city doctor and the editor of an influential newspaper. When the wave of anti–Semitism hit Siedlce, Dr. Wansawski began to protest against the injustices done to Jews.

Dr. St. Wansawski, who was a freethinker, printed in his newspaper, "Szemia Siedlcka," a series of articles in which attacked the racism and anti–Semitism in regard to the elections for the last Sejm and senate, which occurred in the summer of 1938. Wansawski published a characteristic article in which he wrote:

Poland is declining because of a number of circumstances. A great guilt lies on the Church with its contempt for other faiths and customs. Also guilty is the arbitrariness of the masses–which the new current of the Polish upper class has not abandoned. But Poland is also on the decline because it has not learned how to raise itself above egotistical nationalism. Except for a few individuals, no one thinks of the entire state. No one pays attention to the jumble of interests of the national minorities that exist here. While in Europe, with other neighbors, people have begun to think of the whole country, here the mass of people think only of their own rights, not of their responsibilities. We have not tried to live in peace with our minorities, with their religions, with their cultures. We have ruled over them with pain and strife and battle, perhaps without weapons but with the intention to exterminate them and with contempt. At times of upheaval, we have adopted altruistic slogans ("For our freedom and for yours"), and we have turned to the Jews with fervent calls for unity and aid. But this lasted only a short time, because always quickly return to our old ways–to the defense of our oppressive nationalism.

[Page 252]

 In battle, we rise to the heights of heroism and of selflessness. Today, when we have obtained our independence, we have simply identified the nationalistic ideal with the state, and in the name of the nationalistic ideal we have begun an offensive against the national minorities, and most of all–against the Jews.

In this fashion, Dr. Wanasawski described the anti–Semitic character of Polish nationalism. He ended his article with the following declaration:

As we are today free people, in a prosperous time of the national identity, a swarm of parties and cohorts of a "nationalistic" character are arising, and they ask the question: Who stalks our language, our culture, our customs? And the answer is: the Jew, the Mason.

If they did not exist, they would have to be created so that they could be taken as an object of persecution–as that which is not Slavic. Perhaps people would persecute all brunettes as people who dishonor the Slavic race. Who knows? The spread of "nationalist" ideas with attributes of suffering, bombs, and invective comes so easily because of the lowering of ethical standards after the First World War. People, on the average respectable and not foolish, let themselves be led by young people who create the political climate without themselves knowing what they want but who label each of their successes with the name of "national"–a feudal doctrine of the worst sort that finds adherents not only among the crude young people but also among serious doctors and lawyers. Characteristics that were once regarded as chivalrous have been overthrown and are regarded as evil.

Dr. Wansawski, along with several Siedlce Poles from the free–thinking camp were among the few non–Jews who separated themselves from the anti–Semitic agitation that seized Seidlce, including the Catholic clergy.

[Page 253]

When in August of 1938 the Pope issued his encyclical against racism, the Siedlce Catholic paper "Glos Podolski" quickly provided anti–Semitic commentary on the encyclical. "Glos Podolski" printed articles about Jewish swindlers, Jewish usurers, and reprinted anti–Semitic information from the French press, which explained why Jews were expelled from Middle Europe, especially from Poland, and headed to France. To such clerical anti–Semitism, no one in Poland reacted.

Countering racism, there arose in Siedlce a community of members of the organization "Fun Nev," political detainees of the P.P.S–the revolutionary faction that had its headquarters in the city. In a declaration of this organization from February 12, 1939, we read:

Seeing the danger that accompanies the negation of democratic and humanistic rights of equality and freedom, that were established at the time of the battle for Poland's independence, we declare, we, the first soldiers of Marshall Jozef Pilsudski, the former political detainees, tested through years of battle, penal labor, and hangings for the love of our fatherland, of the ideals of independence and equal rights for people and citizens:

    1.   In all the battles for independence of our fatherland, we knew no divisions based on faith or race.
    2.   We all–under the banner of the P.P.S.–all to whom equality and independence are precious, without divisions between classes, races, origins, or religions, arm in arm, fought for certain victory, and in that battle we were all ready to sacrifice our lives.

3.   We will remain true to the ideals and therefore we will proclaim our thoughts or die in order to realize them and extinguish the anti–democratic urges of race hatred.

We hold that the youth are the future of our fatherland and that only in an atmosphere of brotherhood, equality, and freedom can the true love of our fatherland flourish, which is the basis of its greatness–we address all parents, that they should point their children in the direction of the ideals of equality, brotherhood, and freedom, for which their parents have suffered and died.

Chair: Stanislaw Ruzhanski
Secretary: Wawrzeniec Waltchuk

[Page 254]

The voice of these fighters against racism had little effect, because the anti–Semitic agitation had such a strong following. The actions of the picketers grew more intense, as did the prevention of Christian customers from entering Jewish businesses, and such actions were considered legal by the government. The pickets who observed the Jewish businesses more than once created turmoil, when, for instance, something fell from the window of a Jewish house, like a piece of plaster, or someone stuck out a tongue. When such a picketer would make an outcry, the police would make a show of force.

Also, physical attacks on Jews became a chronic problem.

In the summer of 1938, the German Jews of Polish extraction were expelled to Poland by Hitler's government. The Polish government would not allow them into the country, and they were ordered into a camp in the border town of Zbaszyn. Many of them came to Siedlce. Despite the harsh material conditions, the exiles were warmly received. An ad hoc committee looked after their housing needs and helped them settle. A number of orphan children found places in Siedlce's "Ezras–Y'somim."

Activities of the Community on the Eve of the Catastrophe

At the same time, as dark clouds gathered over the heads of the Jews in Siedlce, the community seemed unaware of the danger that threatened it.

The community elections, the last before the Second World War, occurred in 1936. They showed the splits and fractures in the Jewish community. This time victory went to the progressive elements, which, until 1936, had no representatives in the community organization. At the first meeting of the last newly elected community council, on November 29, 1936, the "Agudah's" representatives announced that they would remain faithful in their opposition to the council as an institution, because their responsibility was to worry exclusively about the religious needs of the Jewish population.

[Page 255]

Therefore the Agudah would primarily see to it that the community should have a rabbi, support the "Talmud–Torah" and the "Beis–Yakov School" and also look after the hospital; and thinking about the commandment of "You will support your brother and strengthen him," the "Agudah" would support the charitable activities of the hospital. All the other factions stressed in their statements that they considered the community to be an autonomous national institution that should benefit all social and cultural aspects of the Jewish population.

The finances from that time show how the activities of the community had expanded. We can compare this document with the balance of community activities in 1923. We can see that the institution had progressed greatly in expanding its activities[107].

INCOME

Taxes from 1936	23,541,27 zlotys
Surplus from 1935	6,945.690
Administrative payments	1,722.75
Slaughtering	27,443.50

Cemetery	4,985.00
Rent from apartments and the mikveh	5,578,18
Passover actions	1,828.55
Interest on late taxes	525.86
Deficit	1,563,61
TOTAL	74,134,61

EXPENSES

Rabbinate	5,200.00
Administration	5,850.
Bureau	1,050.
Shul, cantor, sexton, heat, light	4,234.
Slaughterers and related expenses	14,580.
Cemetery	1,944.21
Retirements	2, 735.00
Administration of community buildings, employees, insurance, labor	2,767.89

[Page 256]

Sick fund	813.89
Social action: winter activities and others	4,794.69
Subvention: Talmud–Torah	6,441.70
Yeshiva "Beis Yosef"	327.00
"Beis–Yakov" School	1,035.00
"Tarbus" School	2,110.50
"Yavneh" School	234.00
"Ezras–Y'somim"	2,076.23
Old Age Home	1,917.15
Jewish Hospital	750.00
"Toz" and summer colonies	718.83

"Linas Ha–Tzedek"	947.77
Va'ad Ha–Kashrus	348.38

Miscellaneous:

Covering the deficit until Jan. 1	2,887,87
The same subvention	632.80
Redemption of promissory notes	2,400.00
Sick fund	5,118.94
Various debts	947.77
Unexpected debts	1,965.82
TOTAL	74,134.41

A Quarrel Over a Rabbi and a Cantor

In 1932 a quarrel broke out among the Jews in Siedlce that was only settled shortly before the outbreak of the Second World War. The quarrel concerned the election of a rabbi to replace R. Chaim Yehuda Ginsburg, who had died.

After his death, there was a contest over choosing a rabbi. The dead man's son, R. Alter–Eliezer Ginsburg, was not considered a candidate. Several rabbinical authorities put forward their candidates. There were parties on every side of the decision, you understand. Each candidate had supporters and detractors, and all had to be evaluated based on their learning and other qualities, as well as on their party affiliations. One rabbi, who was strongly opposed by the Zionist and Mizrachi movements, was Rabbi Eichenshteyn from Chodorov, who belonged to the ruling government party and served the interests of the Polish regime.

[Page 257]

This meant that he opposed the everyday interests of the Jewish commune. In national Jewish circles, Rabbi Eichenshteyn was not considered a representative of the mass of Jews. A variety of rumors circulated about him. For example: that he would receive the rabbinical chair in Siedlce because that was in the interests of the Polish regime. It was also known that a Pole named Czekhowicz, a brother of the Polish finance minister, had broadcast near and far that Eichenshteyn and no other would be the rabbi of Siedlce. Since Eichenshteyn belonged to "Agudas–Yisroel," and since it appeared unlikely that he would be legally elected, his supporters devised a variety of machinations in order to guarantee a majority in the community council elections. The votes of the "Agudah" were assured, as were the votes of several bigwigs.

The forthcoming election prompted heated opposition from the Zionist and Mizrachi parties. Electioneering became very pointed. The national camp accused Rabbi Eichenshteyn of serving the anti–Semitic Polish regime. There were also reports that Rabbi Eichenshteyn would gain the rabbinical chair in Siedlce through bribes that he had distributed. Campaign advertising appeared with citations from the Talmudic writings opposing this action of the rabbi. They also used citations from the Rambam [Rabbi Moses Maimonides], that said:

Any rabbinical judge who is named to his place on the basis of money should not be honored by having people stand in his presence. And it is also required to degrade him and hold him in scorn.

*[**trans. note**–This passage appears in both Hebrew and Yiddish, and its source is cited in a footnote: Halachos Sanhedrin, 3: 9. He also provides a more correct Hebrew version than was used in the ad, thanks to Menashe and Moyshe Konstantinowski.]*

[Page 258]

An excommunication that had been issued in 1909 by some of the great ones of Israel, led by R. Avraham Sochachewer, the Alexander rabbi, and the Ger rabbi, began with the words "In the name of the Lord, the God of Israel."

The excommunication had been subscribed to by 162 rabbis and teachers from various cities and shtetls in Congress Poland. The subjects of the excommunication were referred to as "gods of silver and gods of gold." And the battle between the two sides did not take place only on paper. Blows were also exchanged between the two sides.

The outcome was the Rabbi Eichenshteyn was selected as the rabbi of Siedlce. The Polish official who had supervisory powers over the community confirmed the votes, as did the Woiwode of Lublin and later on the education minister, so that the Chodlover [Rabbi Eichenshteyn] would become the rabbi of Siedlce.

This decision was published in July of 1939, when the catastrophe of the war could be sensed in the air of Poland.

At the same time, there was also a controversy over the matter of a cantor. This occurred after the longtime Siedlce cantor Y.D. Pasowski left Siedlce for Eretz Yisroel. Those who prayed in the synagogue were divided into two camps: one camp supported Cantor Zhupowicz and urged that he should remain as the Siedlce cantor. The second camp–led by the synagogue committee–wanted to engage a different cantor. In this case, they created a competition, and every Shabbos a new cantor would lead the prayers. This controversy ended with the appointment of Cantor Zhupowicz as the Siedlce cantor.

The Zionist organization, as already mentioned, had since 1926 supported a "Tarbus" folk school. On September 3, 1938, a group of energetic workers opened in Siedlce a Hebrew "Tarbus" gymnasium. The first thousand zlotys for this purpose were given by the teachers of the "Tarbus" school themselves. It was proposed to rent a locale, to create a laboratory and to open a preparatory course for graduates of "Tarbus" and of other schools for the second class of the planned gymnasium.

[Page 259]

The Jewish library, too, at that time had not declined.

Aside from the community library, there were in Siedlce also party book collections. On the eve of the Second World War, Siedlce had the following libraries:

The "Bund"	1,200 volumes
Leftist Poalei–Tzion	1,000
Rightist Poalei–Tzion	600
Tze'irey Mizrachi	500
Poalei Agudas Yisroel	400
"He–Chalutz"and Hel–Chalutz Ha–Tza'ir	500

4,200 Books owned in total by the party libraries

The community libraries included:

Jewish Art	12,000 volumes
School libraries	6,000

Hebrew–Yiddish collection in the city library	800
18,800 Books	
23,000 Books in total	

The 23,000 books constituted the premier intellectual and cultural possessions of Jewish Siedlce.

Despite the difficult and deplorable condition of the Jewish population in Siedlice in the last two or three years before the Second World War, Jewish cultural activities did not dissipate.

The Number of Jews in Siedlce Before the Outbreak of the Second World War

The last statistics show that on July 1, 1938, that is, 14 months before the outbreak of the Second World War, Siedlce contained a population of 40,962, and among them 16,180 Jews. In other words, Jews constituted 39.5 percent.

[Page 260]

The last statistics concerning the number of Jews in Siedlce appeared in the "Siedlce Vochenblat" of July 1, 1938, as follows:

Men	19,789
Women	21,173
Total	40,962
Under 7	6,500
7–14	7,000
14–18	2,780
Over 18	24,682
Jews	16,180
Christians	24,782

Siedlce's Jewish Writers and Journalists

Like so many Jewish settlements in Poland, Siedlce produced Jewish writers and journalists, a few of them quite noteworthy. We will provide biographical sketches of the writers and poets who grew up in Siedlce.

Yisroel Chaim Eisenberg

Born around 1900. Well–known poet and essayist. Crippled by illness, he lived in penury and even attempted suicide. Eisenberg worked on the "Siedlce Vochenblat" and on other projects. In the thirties published a drama "Khordos and Miriam." He was among the editors of a bi–monthly journal "Vartzlen," which appeared in only two issues from "Orient" publishers, 1927.

Dr. Yakov Eisenshtat

Son of Moyshe–Abba, born in 1898. At the time of the war's outbreak in 1914, Yakov Eisenshtat was 16 years old and studied in the Siedlce Russian gymnasium. He went along when the gymnasium was evacuated to Volodimir. After graduating from high school, he went to the medical school at Darmater University [trans. note–I can find no references to such a place.]

[Page 261]

In 1918 he returned to Poland and later entered Warsaw University. From there he went to Naples (Italy) and studied medicine in the university there.

In order to support himself, Eisenshtat had to seek employment in a number of jobs.

Yakov Eisenshtat showed great zeal in learning. The famous Italian scholar, professor of psychiatry at the university in Naples, Leonardo Bianchi, took an interest in him, helping him both materially and intellectually. Bianchi took him on as his assistant and gave him opportunities to carry out his scholarly activities, in which he showed great ability. A year after Prof. Bianchi's death, the medical faculty of the university unanimously elected Eisenshtat to the professorial chair of the famous Italian psychiatrist.

At the university's expense, Dr. Eisenshtat traveled abroad and spent an entire year in Leningrad in the clinic of the famous Professor Bekhterev. Together with Professor Bekhterev, Dr. Eisenshtat conducted experiments on the properties of brain tissue, on the possibility of thought transmission [ESP?], on hypnotism, and he created his original theory on thought itself and on the sources of thought.

Y. Eisenshtat published a book in Italian entitled *The Effect of Education on Hereditary Abnormality*. The book had 576 pages, with 59 illustrations and many tables. This important work, which the professor dedicated to his teachers, Professors Bekhterev and Leonardo Bianchi, was the result of 3,000 experiments that the professor conducted on children of various criminals from sanatoriums around Naples. He also undertook a research oriented journey to Switzerland, Germany, Russia, and Austria, seeking out the children of criminal lawbreakers. The author investigated their characteristics on the basis of the research that he had done on the child's family as well as on his individual characteristics.

[Page 262]

He illuminated these characteristics that were hereditary from anthropological and psychological perspectives and often observed three generations: parents, children, and grandchildren. He was interested in the fate of those children after they left their institutions.

This book garnered reviews in many medical journals from different countries. A longer consideration was written by Dr. Konigshteyn in issue 21 of *Warszawskie Czasopismo Lekarskie*. He closes the notice with the following lines: "Eisenshtat's extraordinary book has been recognized throughout the medical world in all countries. It has been totally embraced. In every chapter of this book we see not only a well–educated clinical doctor but also a bold societal reformer and medical teacher. It is fitting that this beautiful work should become an integral part of our literature."

In one of his works, Dr. Y Eisenshtat proposed that the human mind creates electromagnetic waves (similar to the heart's electrical impulses), and these waves can be picked up by other people and even by animals. The experiments that Dr. Eisenshtat conducted in Naples confirmed his theory and attracted the attention of wider scholarly circles.

Dr. Eisenshtat's studies of the so–called hereditary criminals aroused interest in the Italian scholarly world. In these studies, Dr. Eisenshtat showed that even the children who inherited their parents' criminal tendencies could, through certain educational methods, obtain new perspectives and qualities that could change their whole character from shameful criminality. These new perspectives and qualities he could give to the children and thus create for society productive, excellent citizens. And truly Dr. Eisenshtat showed practical results: of the 3,000 criminals and morally abnormal people who were under his observation and treatment in the Naples madhouses and prisons, 92 percent were turned into normal, productive people.

[Page 263]

The Italian press, in discussing Dr. Eisenshtat's methods, said that he brought honor to scholarship and to mankind: "Thanks to Dr. Eisenshtat's investigations–a famous Italian newspaper said–we see a ray of hope and belief in the future of our race. The future of our people is all the more threatened through the immense growth of nervous and spiritual illnesses.

Dr. Eisenshtat later assumed the seat of psychiatry in the University of Naples, and when it became possible, he received Italian citizenship. The royal decree that recognized his Italian citizenship said that he received it for his significant scholarly services.

During the Second World War, Dr. Eisenshtat left Italy and settled in the United States, where he continued his scholarly work.

Kalonymos–Kalman Barlev (Levertowski)

Born in the winter of 1897. His home was a mixture of Chasidism and Enlightenment. He received a religious education. At the time of the First World War he was active in the Zionist movement; he was particularly active as a propagandist. By profession he was a teacher. When "Tze'irei Tzion" was established, he became a member and then became one of the leaders. At the founding conference of "Tze–irei Tzion" in Poland, at Succos of 1919, he became the founder of the people's socialist idea. After the second conference, when the party split–Barlev aligned himself with pioneer activities and became the secretary of the central committee. As the stream of the Third Aliyah became stronger in Poland, in 1921 he went up to Eretz Yisroel. He worked at building the road between Tiberias and Migdal. Together with Y. Ch Brenner he was active in the circle of "Tze'irei Tzion," which influenced the founding conference of the Histadrus in Haifa and of the introduction of the party into "Achdus Ha–Avodah."

[Page 264]

For several years he was active as a worker and teacher in Nes–Tzionah–later as a teacher in Petach Tikvah. At that time Barlev also began writing, and he collaborated on "Kuntres, " on "Daber" and on "Ha–Po'el Ha–Tza'ir." Starting in 1927 he was a regular collaborator on "Daber." Beginning as a reporter–in 1941 he became an editor of the "Daber" publication "Hinei" and co–editor of the afternoon edition of "Daber." He also published many feuilletons under a variety of pseudonyms. He also wrote poems and translations of English poetry.

Barlev died of a heart attack on October 26, 1942.

Alter Gold

Born in 1894 and raised by his grandfather Yosef–Zav Heller, a shochet and inspector who was greatly loved in the city. He worried that his grandson would study Gemara day and night. Alter studied in the Siedlce yeshiva. His studies did not make him happy–Czarist persecutions of the Jews gave him no rest. He left Poland and went to America in 1913. There he quickly joined the "B'nei–Tzion" organization. He became active in Zionist causes and became one of the editorial group of the "Voice of B'nei'Tzion."

In 1915 he organized and led the Siedlce "Relief." He collected funds to help groups in Siedlce. He was mobilized in America during the First World War.

When he returned from the war in 1919, he took an active role in creating an organization to build a temple of music in Eretz Yisroel, as a monument to fallen Jewish soldiers. To this end, he edited and distributed a monthly journal, "The Jewish Soldier." He also edited and collaborated on a variety of newspapers.

Yehoshua Goldberg

Born in 1883. His father, R. Moshe, a lover of Zion, came from Zamocs and was a relative of Y.L. Peretz. Yehoshua received a religious–nationalistic education. He excelled in his studies in cheder. He later studied secular subjects learned languages, read a great deal and showed talent in sculpture, drawing, and writing.

[Page 265]

Already in his early years he published poems in a series of literary publications. During the course of five years he became the editor of the "Siedlce Vochenblat."

Goldberg made pictures, wrote feuilletons and songs that described the life of the city. Under the title "Spring in the City" he published memoirs about the years of the revolutionary awakening (1905). His feuilletons "From Siedlce's Stories" and the series "Teachers" which appeared in scores of issues of the "Vochenblat", are a source of Siedlce folklore.

Yehoshua Goldberg was murdered by the Germans.

Levi Gutgelt

Born in 1896. His father, R. Yisroel Gutgelt, was known by his familiar name–Yisroel–Yossel Enseles. He was a major, well–to–do merchant who dealt in lumber, kerosene, and colonial products, a businessman and a philanthropist, owner of a huge book collection, and a supporter of the Chasidic court at Ger. Although he was one of the leaders of the :Agudas Yisroel," he secretly contributed to the "Keren Ha–Yesod."

Levi received a strongly religious education. He studied in cheder and with the best private teachers. But when Levi grew up, he began to be interested in secular education and languages. He familiarized himself with Enlightenment literature, studied world literature, immersed himself in Jewish history and Jewish problems.

At the time of the First World War, under the influence of the "homeless," among whom were Zionists–Gutgelt became a Zionist. He also became a teacher in the gymnasium of the Halbershtam sisters, where he attended lectures in his long kaftan and round cloth hat, but in school he wore his short clothing and gave his Hebrew lecture, learning with his students with a special fervor. He took no pay for his lectures.

The young Gutgelt did his Zionist work with diligence and devotion. One encountered him everywhere: in Hebrew evening courses, in meetings of the Zionist organization at gatherings for Keren Kayames, in propaganda and organizational activities.

[Page 266]

In 1922, Gutgelt, together with other writers from Siedlce, proposed to put out a Yiddish weekly, which then existed for eighteen years until the outbreak Second World War. Levi Gutgelt later took on an array of leadership positions in the Zionist movement. He was a member of the Zionist party council "Al Ha–Mishmar" faction and helped lead the Tarbus school system, and he never stopped writing for the Vochenblat. For its first five years, he was the actual editor of the newspaper.

Aside from his journalistic work for the local paper, Gutgelt published articles in the central organ of the Zionist organization. In Zionist Siedlce itself, for twenty years nothing was done without his participation.

Levi Gutgelt, along with his wife and child, perished in the Warsaw Ghetto.

Yehiel–Pinchas Greenberg

Born in 1897. He was a grandson of Yisroel Greenberg, the philanthropist and businessman who financed the building of a beis–hamedresh and a building for the Talmud Torah. Starting at age five, he studied in a cheder. At the time of the Polish–Bolshevik War, he fell into the hands of the Bolsheviks. That experience later served as a theme for his book "From the Bloody Field."

[Page 267]

Y.P. Greenberg published his first stories and poems in Weissenberg's anthology. Later he became one of the major collaborators on the local newspapers, such as the "Voice of Siedlce" and the "Siedlce Vochenblat," as well as others. In 1927 he also took a part in the journal "Vortzlen," which appeared in two issues. He published a book, "Blumen" [Flowers], Shtramen Publishers, Siedlce, 1925, and "From the Bloody Field" (Siedlce, 1927. He was killed at the time of the German liquidation of Siedlce's Jews.

Dovid Greenfarb

Born in 1890. Received a religious education. Later he began reading secular literature. Greenfarb wrote and published poetry. He taught violin as a profession. Killed by the Nazis in the Second World War.

M.A. Hartglas

Born in Biala Podlaska on July 4, 1883. His father, Kalman, was an attorney and raised his son in the spirit of Polish assimilation. After Hartglas graduated from the gymnasium in his home town, he studied jurisprudence in Warsaw University. For demonstrating against the production of an anti–Semitic play in the Rasmaytacztcai Theatre in Warsaw, he was imprisoned for three weeks. For another demonstration, he was expelled from the law faculty of Warsaw University. He continued to study as an external student, and thanks to his abilities, he became a lawyer.

[Page 268]

From his earliest youth, he was active in the Zionist movement. He participated as a delegate to the Zionist Congresses–at Helsingfors in 1907 and at the Hague (1907), Carlsbad (1921, 1923) and in Zurich (1929). In Free Poland he was excluded from the legal profession because of his Zionist activities and as vengeance for being chosen as a Jewish delegate in the Polish Constituent Assembly. Hartglas appealed to the lawyer's council and won.

Together with Y. Greenboym and Dr. Y. Ton, led the Zionist faction in the Constituent Assembly and elected also to the second Sejm. In the Jewish circle, he belonged to the radical opposition that was led by Y. Greenboym. Particularly appeared in opposition to the well–known agreement on Jewish–Polish understanding.

He was known as a defender in the well–publicized rehabilitation trial of the Rabbi Shapiro of Plotzk, who had been shot in 1920 as a Bolshevik and a spy for the Russian army. His journalistic activities he began in 1906 in "Glos "Zydowski." He took part in the Zionist press in Polish and Russian, as well as in Martin Buber's "Der Jude." From 1917 to 1920 he edited the Zionist papers "Tygodnik Zydowski" and "Zycie Zydowskie" and published a number of Zionist pamphlets such "Territorium y Narod" (1906), a pamphlet in Polish about the foundations of Zionist land politics in Poland (1918). His first article translated into Yiddish was published in "Shedletzer Lebn" (1912). After 1920 he was a regular contributor to "Heynt." He taught himself to write Yiddish and published articles focusing on questions of Jewish politics in Poland and on Zionist matters. He also participated in many other Zionist productions, including: in "Chodesh" (1921), "From Bygone Days"–about the Polish–Bolshevik War. His books include his speeches (1919–22) and "The Jewish National–Council in Poland" (Warsaw, 1923).

In 1940 Hartman and his wife fled from Nazi–occupied Poland and went to Eretz Yisroel, where he worked for the Jewish Agency as the leader of a division to investigate the crimes of the Nazis during the Second World War. Hartglas feels that his conscience is not clear, because he left his brothers in the German vise, and in despair he tried to commit suicide. He was saved from his despair. When the State of Israel was established, Harglas was nominated to be the leader of the Interior Ministry. Later he became active as the justice advisor in that ministry. He died in Tel Aviv March 23, 1953.

[Page 269]

Avraham Wasserzug

Born in 1901 in Lublin near Wlatzlawek. His father, R. Moshe, was a property owner and simultaneously a strongly religious Jew. He sent his son Avraham to cheders and later to yeshiva. At an early age, Wasserzug received a rabbinical diploma from esteemed rabbis and scholars.

Wasserzug, however, yearned for a secular education. He entered the government school for Jewish religious teachers in Warsaw and graduated in 1925. A year later he came to Siedlce and became involved in Jewish religious and government–folk schools for Jewish students. A. Wasserzug also became involved with literary work. In 1929 he wrote and published a Hebrew play for children about the times of King Saul called "The Musician from Bethlehem." In 1935, for the eight hundredth anniversary of the Rambam, Wasserzug published in Polish a biography of the Rambam called "Maimonides." Wasserzug had prepared an array of works about Jewish thinkers from the Middle Ages. His works were destroyed in the Second World War. The author and his family were killed at the time of the liquidation of Siedlce's Jews in 1942.

[Page 270]

Yischak–Nachum Wayntroyb

Born in 1863 in Terespol to strongly religious misnagdish parents. His childhood was spent in learning Tanach and Gemara with commentaries., first in cheder and later in the Terespol beis–hamedresh. In 1882 Wayntroyb married the daughter of the notable Shimon Greenberg and settled in Siedlce. He became active in the Khivas–Tzion movement, which involved a large number of religious Jewish young people. Because of his talent in community work, Wayntroyb took on a leadership position, not only in the Khivasl–Tzion movement but in all Jewish community matters of Siedlce. He also devoted much time to writing, reading, and studying

Wayntroyb, after he settled in Siedlce, began to record all the events in the city. Over time he collected a great deal of material of historical value. After 1922 he published memoirs in the "Siedlice Vochenblat." In the thirties he also published a cycle of records about the pogrom, that gave a good picture of the history of the Jews in czarist Russia in general and in Siedlce in particular. In depicting pictures and images from Siedlce and events from the past hundred years, he would obtain eyewitness accounts from older people, who told him of their memories of life in Siedlce. Waynbroyt wrote for "Ha–Melitz," "Ha–Tzefirah" and other newspapers; besides what he published, much remained in manuscript.

Since the beginning of political Zionism, Wayntroyb occupied a place of honor in the movement. Because of the attention he drew from both Jews and non–Jews, Wayntroyb was elected to positions in many community organizations.

[Page 271]

During the Second World War, when Wayntroyb was older he experienced all the pains and sorrows of Hitler. With his own eyes he saw the destruction of Siedlce's Jewishness. Among them–his daughter, grandchildren, and great–grandchildren, he lived until December 1943 and was taken with the remnant of Siedlce's Jews to Treblinka, where he died in the gas chamber. His great archive disappeared, and no one knows where it could be found.

Mordechai Temkin

Born in 1891. His father, R. Dov, was a wealthy merchant and a modest man.

Temkin's great–great–grandfather was the father–in–law of the famous national writer Peretz Smolenskin. In the archive of the writer Alter Droyanov can be found a poem that Mordechai Temkin, the grandfather of Mordechai Temkin's father, wrote for the wedding of his daughter Leonora, who married Smolenskin.

Mordechai Temkin's mother derived her pedigree from a rabbinical family. Her older sister married Rabbi Avraham Eiger, the rabbi of Lublin. Thus, members of the Temkin family were Lublin Chasidim.

Until his bar mitzvah, Mordechai Tempkin, like all Jewish boys in Poland, studied the Talmud and its commentaries in cheders, but secretly he would read secular books, particularly literature from the Haskalah. The young Temkin was influenced by his teacher Gurewitsch, who came to Siedlce with a great many Haskalah works.

In his fifteenth year, Mordechai Temkin began to write. Not wanting to trouble his parents, he left Siedlce and went to Watrsaw. There he began to visit the house of the writer Fishl Liakhover, and with the help of the young writer Yakov Warshawski he became a teacher in Mlava, near the Prussian border. Remaining for a year in the village, Temkin amassed a sum of money and in 1907 he went for the first time to Eretz Yisroel.

With a letter of recommendation from the already known F. Liakhover and from Hillel Zeitlin, Temkin joined the editorial board of "Ha–Poel Ha–Tza–ir," which had been established in Jerusalem.

[Page 272]

Y.H. Brenner, who was then the editor of "Ha–Poel Ha–Tza'ir" became close to him and gave him work in the administration of the weekly paper. At the end of every week, one could encounter Temkin with the top administrator of "Ha–Poel Ha–Tza'ir" N. Twersky as they carried bundles of newspapers to the Austrian post office in Jaffa Tower in order to have them sent to subscribers both local and foreign.

Mordechai Temkin published his first poem in "Ha–Poel Ha–Tza'ir": "When I Came to my Country."

The young writer was drawn to education. He began to study in the teacher's seminar of "Ezrah," but because of the yellow fever from which he suffered, he left the seminar and he was forced to leave Eretz Yisroel. In 1911 he returned to Eretz Yisroel, where he remained for the rest of his life.

From then on he was a teacher and published poems in a variety of periodicals in Eretz Yisroel. His first book, "Drops," was published in 1927 by K'tuvim Publishers. His second book, "Poems and Prayers"–by D'var. His third book, "The Book of Poems and prayers," appeared in 1942, also from D'var, with The help of the Bialik Institute. Shortly after, The Bialik Institute put out a new book of Temkin's poems, "The Voice of Balm." Temkin's poems were translated into German, English, Polish, and Yiddish. He also translated a number of works of world literature.

Dr. Moshe Temkin

Born in 1884. His childhood years consisted of contentment and joy. He was raised in the court of his grandfather, who lived like a lord and had his own stable of horses, along with orchard keepers and gardeners. The young Moshe grew up differently from other Jewish children. He learned to ride horses, catch birds and doves, and play in gardens and on roofs.

At age 5 he began to study in cheder and later in yeshiva. When he grew up, he studied European languages with a teacher who came from Paris and Versailles.

When Zionist ideas began to take hold in Siedlce, Temkin threw himself wholeheartedly into Zionist work.

[Page 273]

After the pogrom in 1906, at the time of the Second Aliyah, he went to Eretz Yisroel and worked in different settlements in the Galilee and Judea. There, too, he began his writing career. He served as secretary on the weekly "Ha–Poel Ha–Tza'ir." Shortly thereafter he left his town and came to Hadera where he worked in an olive grove. From there he went to Kinneret in order to work on creating a national farm, on which he later worked as a watchman. His later destinations were Jaffa and Jerusalem, where he gave private lessons and prepared to go to university.

At that time Temkin published his first stories and feuilletons in the newspaper "Ha–Achdus," which was edited by Ben Zvi, who later became president of Israel, and Y. Zerubavel.

In 1911 Temkin began to study medicine in the French University in Beirut. The First World War forced him to interrupt his studies and return to Eretz Yisroel.

During the bloody events of 1920, Temin was one of the founders of the self–defense and a committee member together with Z. Jabotinski, Y. Ben Zvi, Rokhel Yanis, and Von Priesland.

In 1922, Temkin returned to Beirut to study and he received his doctor's diploma. After finishing his studies, he returned to Eretz Yisroel, where he specialized in studying malaria, published articles in "Ha–Sh'loakh," which was edited by Y. Klausner, wrote articles in French about malaria and typhus in the French "Revu Malaria Topicale" and in "Ha–Refuah" and in "Ha–Rofeh Ha–Ivri."

In 1936 his first book, "The Infected Motherland"–a novel–appeared. In 1937 he published several works, such as "Those Who Go to Death Asking about your Welfare"–a novel about the Tel Khai events–"The Young Woman from the Valley," two stories and treatises in pamphlets about Shaul Tchernichovski and Brenner. In "Echo of Jerusalem" almost every Friday he published articles under the pseudonym "Shemen."

Temkin also left a number of works in manuscript.

[Page 274]

Yakov Tenenboym

Born in 1882. In his young years he was a Bundist, later an anarchist, and finally a folkist. He was arrested at the time of the Siedlce pogrom and held in prison for a long period, because the Siedlce police chief thought he was a dangerous revolutionary. Some years later he was an informal doctor and was popular in the whole town. He read and studied a great deal, and in his encounters at public gatherings he demonstrated his familiarity with philosophy. In Siedlce he received the nickname "Nietzsche." He was among the first members of "Ha–Zamir" and the library and was for a long time the chair of "Jewish Art."

His literary activities he began in the second issue of the "Siedlce Word." Later he collaborated on the "Siedlce Echo" and "Siedlce Life."

When the "Siedlce Vochenblat" began publication in 1922, Yakov Tenenboym was a constant collaborator. With the numerous feuilletons that he published, he brought life to the paper. He was one of the editors of the "Vortzlen," which began to appear from "Orient" Publishers in 1927.

Tenenboym was also a lover of Yiddish theater. People enjoyed his performances, particularly in "Mazel Tov" by Sholem Aleichem. He also wrote the following pieces: "Shiva for a Horse," a comedy in three acts that shows the life of a wagon driver in a good–humored way; "The Skeleton," a drama in three acts. He directed the dramas "For our Beliefs" and "God of Vengeance" by Sholem Asch, Basha the Orphan" by Y Nordau, as well as scores of one–actors, among them: "To Go to Ha–Zamir or Not," which were performed at various locations in Siedlce."

His end was tragic. At the time of the liquidation of the Siedlce ghetto in 1942, he was shot along with the medical personnel and the ailing in the courtyard of the Jewish hospital. He was carrying out his duties for the ill.

[Page 275]

Shimon Czarnabrada

Born in Siedlce and traveled to the United States. Community activist and collector of historical material about the Jews in America and in various settlements in Poland. He published in the anthologies "Polish Jews " edited by Z Tigel and issued by the "Federation of Polish Jews in America" and in scores of issues of the Siedlce Vochenblat." He died in New York on November 27, 1945.

Sholem Yellen

He was the son of the well–known Siedlce book dealer R. Moyshe and a grandson of R. Yitzchak Lifshitz, author of "Canopy of Peace,' "Tastes of our Traditions," and other books. Little Sholem grew up in this bookish environment. As a boy he studied in the beis–hamedresh and in a variety of yeshivas. He impressed people with his sharp wit and was considered an elui [a genius], a scholar learned and proficient in "Orthodox polemical literature," such as "The Generation of the Rishonim" by Eizik Halevi. He was also versed in Jewish history.

After 1915, Sholem Yellen became active in community and cultural life. He was among the founders of "T'vunah," and at the time of the split in 1917, he founded in Siedlce the "Shlomei Emunei Yisroel" (later called "Agudas Yisroel").

His literary activities arose when a bitter battle broke out in Siedlce between the Orthodox and the free thinkers..

A group of active businessmen from the "Agudas Yisroel" movement began in 1924 to issue an Orthodox weekly paper under the title "Our Way." Sholem Yellen became the editor and administrator of the paper.

He wielded a sharp pen. He fought with the purest intentions to be persuasive.

In the Second World War he was killed by the Nazis.

[Page 276]

Asher Liverant

Born in 1884. He received a religious education in cheder and yeshiva until he was sixteen. Then he became a fervent member of the Haskalah movement. With a few other activists, he founded the first community library, which over the years grew and grew and became the great library of "Jewish Art." His act was quite bold, given the conditions of the time: the persecutions from the side of the Orthodox and the reactionary politics of the czarist government, which made his community activities seem revolutionary and rebellious.

Asher Liverant taught himself Hebrew and founded in Siedlce a chapter of the community "Dovrei Sfas Ever." He was active on behalf of the "Lovers of Zion" committee from Odessa. When the Keren–Kayames L'Yisroel was created, Liverant was the most active member; later he helped to establish the Hebrew evening courses. He was also one of the founders of the Siedlce Tarbus school.

In 1922 Liverant collaborated on the "Siedlce Vochenblat," later becoming the editor–in–chief. In the paper he called on the Jewish community to fight for the existence of the Jewish minority in Poland and for the independence of Eretz Yisroel.

Liverant impressed with his fine virtues: a desire to learn, constancy, good–heartedness, and understanding for everyone he encountered.

He died on March 11, 1936 after a long, difficult illness.

Moyshe Mandelman

Born in 1895 to Chasidic parents. He received a traditional education in cheders and yeshivas. When he was fourteen, he received a rabbinical certificate. Meanwhile, however, he began in secret to study Hebrew, Tanach, and forbidden books.

A group of writers and members of the dramatic sector

Seated from right to left: Rozensumen, Goldberg, Mastboym, and Tenenboym
Standing from right to left: Mandelman, Saposhnikov, Zigelvaks, and Slushna

Although his father persecuted him horribly–he was exiled from his home for months at a time–nevertheless he studied Russian, Russian literature, mathematics, and natural sciences with studious devotion. He passed whole days secretly in the Jewish library reading Hebrew and Yiddish books. At the same time, he learned watch making as a way to be independent.

[Page 278]

From 1912 on, Mandelman worked in the Jewish library in Siedlce, and during the German occupation he was very active in the development of "Jewish Art."

In 1916, Mandelman joined the Folks Party, worked actively in Siedlce and the vicinity and was elected to the central committee. At the same time, he was one of the enthusiastic builders of the secular Jewish school system. In the fall of 1917, he helped to establish the first Jewish folk school and children's home in Siedlce.

In the summer of 1918 he tore himself away from Poland and went to Kiev (Ukraine), which sparkled with a lively Jewish life. It was a time of Jewish national cultural autonomy in Ukraine, led by a Jewish ministry.

The minister of Jewish affairs, Latzki–Bertholdi, grew close to him, and Mandelman became one of the managers of the of the famous "Jewish Folk Publishers," which over the course of two years of tragic conditions caused by pogroms and political events issued cores of valuable volumes.

Mandelman was also active in the central committee in collecting materials about the pogroms in Ukraine. Several times, at great personal sacrifice, Mandelman rescued these materials from destruction. They were later, at the beginning of the twenties, taken to Berlin under the supervision of the prominent historian Y. Tcherikower.

In Kiev Mandelman studied in the local teachers seminar under the leadership of the famous pedagogue H.Ch. Fialkov and the historian Ben–Tzion Dinur (Education Minister in Israel). At the same time he was also active in the Kiev culture league and in the literary club.

In 1920 Mandelman returned to Poland. He took an active role in organizing in Warsaw the culture league and the "Tzisho" (the Central Jewish School Association), and he participated in the first school convention in June of 1921.

In 1921 he became a delegate of the Folks Party in Baranovicz, where he presided over the whole area of the then popular "Ukrainian Jewish Committee for Repatriation and Emigration." He organized in several places a group of handworker parties, and at the time of the elections for the Polish Sejm in 1922, he represented the Folks Party for the whole region.

[Page 279]

At the party conference at the beginning of 1923, Mandelman was elected general secretary of the Folks Party. Simultaneously he assumed a prominent spot in the central organization of the handworkers' union.

In fall of 1925, at the request of the "Tzisho," he took over leadership of the Jewish school in Siedlce. He also helped to organize the Jewish secular schools in Mezrich, Lukow, and Sololov, towns neighboring on Siedlce.

In the fall of 1929, "Tzisho" gave him the mission to act as travelling proponent for the school ideology and to arrange for the maintenance of the schools. During the next ten years, until the outbreak of the Second World War, Mandelman many times traveled to hundred of cities and towns in Poland and twice to the Baltic, Scandinavian, and southwest European countries. On these journeys, Mandelman delivered hundreds of talks and lectures.

In 1931, after resigning from all of his positions in the Folks Party, Mandelman joined the Bund. He worked also for the Bundist "Folks Newspaper," where he wrote about school and cultural matters. In the years 1938–39, he published in that paper interesting travel impressions of Finland, Sweden, and Norway. His articles also appeared from time to time in the "Tzisho" journal "School System." Mandelman was also closely associated with YIVO since its earliest days. On his travels he collected a great deal of material for the philological–folklorist section of YIVO.

During a short stay in Vilna–Kovno at the time of the Second World War in 1939–40, Mandelman did intense work for YIVO and created significant resources, which became the only income for YIVO.

In spring of 1941 Mandelman arrived in America. He published in the New York "Tog" a series of articles, impressions of the Red Cross. For five years, Mandelman worked on the Jewish Encyclopedia under Dubnow.

In 1946–57, at the request of YIVO, he visited the largest cities in America and Canada.

[Page 280]

Starting in the fall of 1947 he was active in the "Jewish Cultural Congress," organized the chapters in Chicago., Los Angeles, and Detroit, visited scores of other cities in the United States and Canada for publicity and fundraising.

On the tenth anniversary of the Ghetto Uprising in Warsaw he published the pamphlet "Holiness and Heroism, Faith and Trust" through the publisher M.N. Stein, Chicago.

Yoel Mastboym

Born the second of Adar, 1884 in Mezrich, which was then part of the Siedlce guvernia. Received a traditional cheder education. From childhood demonstrated a talent for art, writing, and music.

As a child, he left Mezrich for Siedlce, along with his parents.

Starting at 15, he learned house painting, which for a long time served as his source of income.

In later years Mastboym left Siedlce and settled in Warsaw. There he began to publish his stories. His first story, "Yerahmielke the Shochet," was published in "Der Veg," under the editorship of Zvi Prilutzki. Dovid Frishman recognized the new talent and published his creatios in "R'shafim," which he edited. Mastboym was also active in Warsaw's "Ha–Zamir."

In 1912 Mastboym's first book–"Sketches and Pictures"–appeared from Shumin Publishers in Warsaw. In 1917 he published a dramatic poem, "A Melody."

In the years 1919–22 Mastboym lived in London and worked on "Di Tzeyt." Returning to Poland, he published the works: "Three Generations," "Abroad," "On Foreign Paths," and "Pioneers," collaborated on "Moment," "The Lodz Daily," "The Lodz Folksblat," "Nosz Przeglad,," "Nowi Dziennik," "Chwila." He travelled around Poland and later put out his book "Galicia."

In 1933 Mastboym settled in Tel Aviv. He works for "Ha–Aretz," and issues his works in Hebrew translation: "Khalil Ha–Tzuanim," "B'Mafteach," both translated by Y Koyfman (Tel Aviv), "Dirah shel M'ritah" and "Ha–Khaim Ha'Adumim," translated by A Mitus.

Before the outbreak of the Second World War, Mastboym was in Poland, which he had to flee before Poland was taken over by the Germans. He published his experiences in his book "Sixty Days in Hitler's Poland, published by "Dvar."

Later Mastoym put out the first volume of his novel "Ha–Shloshah"–translated by Y Aliav. The Yiddish original came out in London under the title "Strength from the Earth." The first part of his autobiography, "My Stormy Years," published in Buenos Aires by "Polish Jewry," was translated by Yitzchak Caspi into Hebrew and published by "Yavneh." The second section of his autobiography is "On the Ladder," published in installments in "The Latest News."

Dovid Neumark

Born in 1897. His father, Moyshe–Mordechai, was once a wealthy merchant, but later he became poor and had to turn to teaching.

Neumark learned from his father and in other cheders, Talmud–Torahs, and yeshivas.

At 16 he took to reading "outside books" and gave talks in Hebrew. At about the same time he began to write, sending articles to Yiddish and Hebrew papers. Around 1910, together with some friends, he put out a Hebrew newspaper called "The Young Jew." The writer Meir Karana also participated.

In 1911 he was a co–creator of the first published Yiddish newspaper in Siedlce–"The Siedlce Vort," "Siedlce Life," and the "Siedlce Echo."

Already in 1912 he associated ideologically with the Jewish workers' movement, but not confined to a single party. Only in 1015 did he join the "Bund," in which he remains active even now.

[Page 282]

At the beginning of the twenties he edited the Bundist daily "The Worker's Voice" in Lemberg while at the same time collaborating in the Bundist press of Warsaw. He became a member of several party factions. From 1925 until the outbreak of the Second World War he was the co–editor of the Bundist "Folks Newspaper." Before the war he wrote a large book (320 pages), "60 Years of Zionism," the result of several years of work.

Because of the war's outbreak, the book was not published.

At the beginning of the Second World War, Neumark escaped from Warsaw to Vilna, from there to Kovno, Japan, and in 1941 he came to Canada, where he carried on his journalistic work in the "Forward," and in the Bundist "Our Time," as well as in an array of journals in New York, Mexico, Paris, and Israel.

Chana Safrin

Born in Siedlce. Left the city at the time of the First World War. Published poems in the New York "Freiheit." In her forties she published her book "Nitzachon."

Bracha Stalavi

Sister of Chana Safrin. Published poems in the New York newspaper "Der Tog."

Mordechai Ovadyahu (Gottesdiener)

Born the third of Sivan, 1909. Studied in cheders and on a pioneer agricultural farm in Czenstokhow, received a certificate and became active in "Ha–Shomer Ha–Tza'ir" and in the pioneer movement at the time of the Zionist demonstrations in Siedlce against the bloody event of August in Eretz Yisroel (August, 1929). Gottesdiener was injured by the police. Later he left Siedlce and lived in Vienna and London. There he met Ch. N. Bialik and became his private secretary. He came to Eretz Yisroel in 1931 and began to write for "D'var," "Al Ha–Mishmar," "Ha–Dor," "Ha–Poeel Ha–Tsa'ir," "Moznayim," "Glionot," "Gazit." He signed his articles with a variety of pseudonyms, such as M. Eyin–Ro'I, Y. Ro'ani, M.D. Ahimin, Yakov Ish–Tam, "M.E.R." "Mel–ayin." Collaborated on "Dorot" and "Ha–Doar."

[Page 283]

In the years 1936–47, on "Ha–Olam" as editor of the statistical section of the publication of the Histadrus, Kupas Cholim.

His books, "Adam Ba–Khutz" (Masada, 1940–41) and "Mipi Bialik" (Basada, 1949–50), were well–received by critics. Soon a book of his stories will appear: "Tachana Achas."

Yakov–Hersh Fishman

Born June 2, 1891. He received his education in cheder, later in the Siedlce yeshiva, which was led by R. Dovid–Yitzchak Mendziszetzki.

Yakov–Hersh's father was a Chasid and his mother was an extraordinarily religious woman. His parents were certain that their son would be a great scholar. Already in the yeshiva Fishman began to wrote about community concerns. When the library opened in Siedlce, young Fishman became a "resident" there. Yiddish literature–Mendele Moycher Sforim, Feierberg, Asch, and others–greatly affected him. At the same time, he began to read Hebrew books and learned Russian and Polish.

Fishman in 1911 published his first story in the "Siedlice Vort." Later he participated in the local publication "The Siedlce Echo," edited by Y. Tenenboym. Around 1913, in Warsaw, he published two stories. They were published: one in Alexander Farbe's collection in honor of Chanukah, "Little Lights," and the second in a collection in honor of Shavuos, "Spring." The second story he signed with his real name.

During the First World War, Fishman remained in Siedlce and worked for "Ha–Zamir," and he became active in the literary division. In 1911, he enrolled in the Bund and became active in the professional movement in Siedlce, Bialystok, and later also in Warsaw. In 1919 he left Siedlce and settled in Warsaw. After 1930 published numerous stories. In 1938 appeared a book of stores called "Summer Days."

[Page 284]

At the beginning of the Second World War, when the Germans occupied Siedlce Fishman fled to Vilna, which was still under Lithuanian control. There he issued a large collection called "On the Way." Later he made his way to Japan, where he worked on the Russian monthly magazine "Yevreiskaya Szisn." At the end of 1941 he came to Shanghai. In 1948 he issued a book of stories, "Wandering Jews." In that same year, Fishman emigrated to Canada and there worked on the "Canadian Eagle." Later he moved to the United States, where he is preparing a new book of stories.

Moyshe Fairman

Born in 1905. His father, R. Yosef–Dovid, was a fervently religious Jew, a fanatic and a learned man. Moyshe grew up in a Torah environment. From childhood on he impressed with his good memory. Before his bar mitzvah he had already learned the Talmud. The agadah [the narrative sections of the Talmud] greatly affected the young Fishman and awoke in him the creative spirit of the later novelist.

When he was 15 or 16, he began to be skeptical about religious matters and he started to read and to study everything that he could: Zohar and "Shomer" {penname of Nahum Meir Schaikewitz, a well–known Yiddish writer], Dinezon and Mickiewicz, Shenkewicz and "The Guide for the Perplexed"–everything was food for his spiritual hunger. Together with a pair of friends, Fairman secretly studied with a paid tutor to prepare for a test for the fifth class of the gymnasium. Two years later he passed the test and enrolled in the Poznan teachers' school in Warsaw. While he was still young, he attempted to write. He maintained that this was his inheritance–his grandfather had left behind a manuscript of a book about the laws of slaughtering, and his father had written insights into the Torah. His first work in Hebrew was an interpretation of the Chumash. Later he assembled all the cures presented in the Talmud, organized them according to the illnesses, and published them in a book called "The Cures of Moses." At fifteen he began to write poems. In the Poznan school he wrote poems in Polish.

In 1921, Fairman left Poland for America. In New York he studied education with the intention of working in Jewish pedagogical settings.

[Page 285]

Under the influence of M. Algin, K. Mirmar, and Sh Niger, who were then teachers in the program, Fairman began to write short stories in Yiddish. His first story, "My First Revolutionary Deed," was published in 1922 in "Cinderella" (the journal of the Workers' Circle School). Later he published stories in the "Morgen Freiheit" and in newspapers. To this period belong the stories "In the Shop," "The Little Black Boy," "The Fly," "Getzl," "We Need a Union," "Wandering Souls." "Wandering Souls" won the admiration of critics. Leib Malach, in a publication from Buenos Aires," wrote that only because of the story "Wandering Souls,," it was worth giving a literary prize.

In 1926, Fairman passed an examination at Columbia University and became a pharmacist.

Around 1928 he finished writing a novel in three sections, called "Abie Yedman." He the first volume, he described Siedlce; although the name of the city is never given, one can easily recognize it.

The novel was never published.

After Fairman wrote the novel, he lost interest in it. In 1933 he began to write stories in English, and in 1947 he published a novel in English: "Man's Heart Is Evil."

Meir Corona

Born in 1895 to a distinguished scholarly family that derived its pedigree from generations of scholars, rabbis, and geonim. From childhood on he was distinguished by several attributes. By nine years of age he had already studied by himself Gemara with Tosafos. He was orphaned as a child and raised under the supervision of his grandfather, his mother's father–R. Yosl Mordechilis, a great scholar.

At ten he was sent to study in the Minsk–Mazowitzk yeshiva, which was overseen by the local rabbi. At twelve his grandfather sent him to study in Slutzk, in Minsk Guvernia, in the yeshiva of the famous gaon R. Issur–Zalman Meltzer. There he was called a Polish genius. Under the influence of friends, he began to read Hebrew literature, and in secret he studied Russian and began to write satirical stories in Hebrew. But he did not let that interrupt his yeshiva studies.

[Page 286]

After studying in Slutzk for six years, at eighteen he received rabbinical ordination from his rabbi, R. Issur–Zalman Meltzer.

At the time of the First World War he was in Siedlce. At the end of 1919 he left Siedlce for Israael. He worked as a builder in Haifa. When the "Work Battalion" of Y. Trumpeldor was created, he enlisted in the Jerusalem squad. In Eretz Yisroel he wrote for "Ha–Poel Ha–Tza'ir" and in the battalion journal "Me–Chayenu."

In 1927, Corona left Eretz YHisroel for Mexico. For many years he ran a publishing house, until heart disease in his forties forced him to stop.

In Mexico, his three books of stories appeared: "Heimishe Mentschen," "Tzeitn," and "In the Stream of Life." in manuscript–a completed novel, "Back Home."

Mordechai Corona

Meir's brother, born in 1900. Became active in the Siedlce Poalei–Tzion–Youth Organization. In December, 1918, was a delegate to the conference of the Poalei–Tzion Party, held in Warsaw.

At the beginning of 1920, Mordechai Corona made aliya to Eretz Yisroel. There he took part in the workers movement and was a member of the Haifa Workers Council and a judge in the local Histadrus Court.

In 1925 Corona left Eretz Yisroel and settled in Mexico, where he helped to organize the "League for Building Eretz Yisroel" and was a member of the local Jewish school and president of the pedagogical council.

At the time of the Second World War, he edited the newspaper "Freivelt." Later he was regular collaborator on the Mexican newspaper "Der Veg." He wrote for various periodicals and for the local Poalei–Tzion paper "Dos Vort."

In 1951 he traveled through Europe and Israel. His travel impressions appeared in Mexico a year later in a large book called "From Mexico to Eilat and Back."

[Page 287]

Dov Rozen

Born in 1914. His father, R. Avraham Yehuda, was a well–known grain merchant in Siedlce and a very religious businessman. Dov received a strictly religious education. He studied in cheders and in the Skernievicz study house with the famous scholar R. Asher–Gedaliah Goldberg. At 17, he began to play an active role in "Poalei–Agudas–Yisroel." He left Siedlce and instead of going to study in the Yeshiva of the Scholars of Lublin, as his scholarly father had requested, he went to Warsaw and worked in knitted goods. After a short time he joined training kibbutz for "Poalei Agudas Yisroel" and together with the first group of pioneers from this organization, in the month of Shevat, 1934, he came to Eretz Yisroel. After working for a time in orchards and as a carpenter in construction, he became private secretary to the chief rabbi of Tel Aviv, R. M. A. Amiel, for whom Rozen worked until the rabbi's death. Rozen was also the chief secretary of the "Reshet Ha–Chinuch Ha–Talmudit" (the Talmudic education network composed of a number of yeshivas from Rabbi Amiel's foundation).

Rozen was also involved with publicity work and published articles in the Orthodox press: "Ha–Tzofah," "Ha–Y'sod," "N'tivah," "Sha'arim," and in other collections. Because of ideological differences he left the "LPoalei Agudas Yisroel" and around 1937 he joined "Ha–Poal Ha–Mizrachi." In 1945, for the 200th anniversary of R. Shneur–Zalman of Liadi, Rozen (using the pseudonym D. Zeira) published a pamphlet called "The Master of the Tanya, and in 1950 a second pamphlet (using the same pseudonym) called "Progress Begets Progress."

Since the establishment of the state of Israel, Rozen has worked in a responsible position in the Ministry of the Interior and has published in the journal "Ha–Shalton Ha–M'komi B'Yisrael" articles about work in the local self–managing committees. His short publication, "Oved Ha–M'dinah v'Ha–ezrach," a kind of "Shulchan Aruch" for civil servants, appeared in 1950 and attracted great attention.

[Page 288]

Shlomo Rozen

Born March 17, 1919. Studied in the Talmud–Torah and in the government folk school. He began to write at an early age. His first articles were published in the wall posters of "Ha–Shomer Ha–Dasi" in Siedlce. He became active in the organization. In 1937 Rozen left for the pioneer training camp "Reshis" near Warsaw. He prepared to make aliyah through illegal means, but the Second World War disrupted his plan. In September of 1941 he managed to get to Eretz Yisroel, having made his way through Russia, Japan, China, Singapore, Dutch China, and other countries.

After arriving in Eretz Yisroel, Rozen joined a kibbutz associated with Hao–Poal–Ha–Mizrachi in Kfar Pins. He worked in the saffron fields and the woods of Hadera. In the spring of 1943 he was among the first settlers in Kfar Etzion. He was the director of the greenhouse and was active in community and cultural life. In 1943, his book "Mitoch Ha–Mapolet," where he describes Siedlce and its surroundings at the time of the First World War. Rozen also published article in "Ha–Hod" and in other papers. He fought in the defense of Kfar Etzion, and he fell in battle along with his comrades.

Simcha Rubinshteyn

Born in 1895. Simcha received a strictly religious education. When he grew older, he began to take interest in Hebrew literature and adopted Zionist thought. In 1906, after the pogrom in Siedlce, he made aliyah to Eretz Yisroel, entered a teachers course from "Ezrah" in Jerusalem.

[Page 289]

After several years in Eretz Yisroel, he left, spending time in Turkey, and finally he came to America, where he worked as a Hebrew teacher. He published articles in a variety of periodicals in Hebrew and he assembled Hebrew chrestomathies. He edited a paper for young people called "Ha–Do'ar La–No'ar."

Rabbi Meir Schvartzman

Born the 22nd of Shevat, 1901 in Zagreb. His father was also a rabbi. Rabbi Meir Schvartzman studied in cheders and yeshivas and received a prestigious rabbinical ordination. In 1924 he became a Siedlcer's son–in–law when he married Miss Chava, the daughter of Avraham–Yitzchak Yablan and settled in Siedlce.

For several years, Rabbi Schvartzman was the chief collaborator on the Orthodox weekly "Unzer Veg," and he also collaborated on all of "Agudas–Yisroel's" papers and magazines, such as "Der Jud," "Yidishe Tageblat," "Degelnu," and "Drachenu." He was a gifted speaker and visited many Polish cities. In Siedlce he put together chrestomathies for the students in the "Beis–Yakov" school with the titles "Lilies" and "The Old Grandmothers." There he also organized a group of religious young zealots known as "Fighters in the Wars of God."

Rabbi Schvartzman took a position of leadership in "Agudas Yisroel." He visited the greatest religious communities in Poland, Galicia, and Volhynia, where he organized "Beis–Yakov" schools. He participated in Orthodox congresses and visited many European cities: Vienna, Marienbad, Chernovitz, Iasi, Cracow, Amsterdam, Zurich, Basel, Berlin, Hamburg, Paris, Strasbourg, where he met with all the Orthodox leaders.

In his youth he wrote poems that were published in many Orthodox magazines. Every Shabbos, like a learned Jew, he would study with a crowd.

In 1938, Rabbi Schvartzman settled in Canada. He served as a rabbi in Cornwall and later as the director of the Talmud Torah "Etz Chaim" in Toronto, and in 1948 as a rabbi in Winnipeg.

[Page 290]

Rabbi Schvartzman collaborated on many newspapers in America and Canada, such as "Dos Yidishe Vort" (Winnipeg), "The Canadian Eagle" (Montreal), "Canadian News" (Toronto), "Der Tog," "The Morning Journal" (New York), "Ha–Modiyah" (Jerusalem), and "She–arim" (Tel Aviv).

In 1942 he published a book "Meir Ayney Y'sharim," a collection of interpretations on the Five Books of Moses. By 1950 there were five volumes. In 1945 his book of Hebrew poems, "Buds," was published by Netzach in Jerusalem, and in 1946, his book "Our Holy Days" appeared.

Rabbi Schvartzman is a member of the Orthodox rabbinical association in America and a member of the rabbinical committee in Winnipeg.

Hillel Sh'khori (Schvartz)

Born in 1913 in a small shtetl called Selsz, near Kartuz Bereza. He received a secular education in the "Tarbus" school. After graduation, he entered the Hebrew teacher's academy in Vilna. He graduated in 1931 and soon was hired as a teacher in Siedlce, where he worked until 1933. In Siedlce, Hillel Sh'khori was busy with cultural work, and led a group in speaking Hebrew, for which he would consider problems and methods of Hebrew literature. He began to issue a monthly paper called "Ha–Bris." At first it was hectographed and later printed. He paid the expenses of the paper out of his own pocket.

In 1933, Sh'khori decided to go to Eretz Yisroel. He left his teaching post and went to a pioneer training camp in Grokhov, near Warsaw. Every day Sh'khori did hard physical labor, and at night he edited the daily kibbutz bulletin, wrote propaganda pamphlets and wall posters.

In March of 1938 made an illegal journey to Eretz Yisroel. He soon joined the kibbutz in Ramas Ha–Kovesh, where he worked devotedly. At the time of the bloody unrest in Eretz Yisroel, on August 4, 1938, when Sh'khori and seven companions were returning from work in a nearby kibbutz in their truck, they were attacked by an armed Arab band that ambushed them. Their vehicle was destroyed and Sh'khori and his friends were killed on the spot.

[Page 291]

Menachem Shtern (Morgenshtern)

Born in 1912. His father, R. Avraham, gave him a secular and religious education. He studied in cheders and with private tutors. Later he studied in the government teachers school for teaching Jewish religion (in the Poznan area) and he graduated. In 1937 he emigrated to the United States. He published his prose and poetic creations in the "Tzukunft" and other papers. Most recently he has been active in New York as a teacher of Yiddish and Hebrew.

With this spiritual and social make–up, the great Hitler destruction began for Jewish Siedlce. With the arrival of September 1, 1939, the destruction began.

[Page 292]

Notes and Bibliography

Translated by Theodore Steinberg

1. L. Gutgelt, "Siedlce Weekly," No. 2, 1922.
2. Ibid.
3. Antoni Winter, Poczatki Siedlec, p. 27.
4. Prof. Y Mikulski, "A Bit about the Development of Siedlce, A Demographic Sketch," published in installments in 1934, Zycie Podlasia.
5. A. Winter, Poczatki Siedlec, p. 12.
6. T. Moniewski, Siedlce, p. 6.
7. Gazeta Podlaska, No. 2, 1932.
8. Ziemia Siedlecka, No. 25, 1937.
9. Prof. Y. Mikulski, in his Forward to A. Winter, Poczatki Siedlec, p. 6.
10. T. Piekosinki, Kodeks Dyplomatyczny Malopolski, 1.
11. T. Moniewski, Siedlce, p. 5.
12. A. Winter, Poczatki Siedlec, pp. 13ff.
13. Ibid., p. 17.
14. T. Moniewski, Siedlce, p. 6.
15. A. Winter, op. cit., p. 19.
16. 16. Siedlce, p. 6.
17. Yon Metzulah, Publication of the United Kibbutz, p. 64.
18. Mit Hayon, Viniza Pub.
19. Decrees of 1648. YIVO Library, Vilna, 1938, p. 149.
20. Zydowska Starszyna. Tom. IV, 1911, C. Goldsztein.
21. Glos Podlasia, Nos. 11, 12, 13, 1910.
22. A. Winter, Poczatki Siedlec, p. 21.
23. T. Moniewski, Siedlce, p. 6.
24. Ibid.
25. A. Winter, Poczatki Siedlec, pp. 26–27.
26. According to notes of M. Tcharnabroda in the archives of YIVO.
27. Dr. Y. Shatzki: History of the Jews in Warsaw, vol. 1, p. 127.
28. Y. N. Wayntroyb, Recollections, Siedlce Weekly.
29. A. Winter, Poczaatki Siedlec, p. 27.
30. Dr. Y Shatzki: History of the Jews in Warsaw, vol. 1, p. 278.
31. T. Moniewski, Siedlce, p. 9.
32. Siedlce Weekly, no. 19, 1937.
33. Y.N. Wayntroyb, Siedlce Weekly, No. 24, 1930.
34. Ibid.,
35. According to testimony in my private archives.
36. Y. N. Wayntroyb, Siedlce Weekly, No. 27, 1930.
37. Ibid., No. 39.

[Page 293]

38. M. Unger: Pshischa and Kotzk, p. 17.
39. Y. N. Wayntroyb, Siedlce Weekly. No. 24, 1930.
40. Ibid., No. 36.
41. A. Sh. Hershberg, Record Book of Bialystok, Vol. 1., p. 195.
42. David Flinker–Cities and Peoples in Israel, Warsaw, p. 111.
43. [blank in original]
44. A. Droynov, Book of Jests and Jokes, second edition, Vol. 1, p. 239.
45. Co Watrzymuje Reforme Zydow w Kraju Naszym War, 1920.
46. Dziennik Urzadowy Wojewodatwa Podlaskiego, 1824.
47. This moving letter and the other documents concerning the development of the Jewish Hospital are from the community archives of Siedlce, which were totally destroyed.
48. Siedlce Weekly, No. 11, 1939.
49. Ibid., No. 43, 1926.
50. Zicia Podlasia, published in installments in 1934.
51. Life in Podlosia, No. 19, 1934.
52. The change in the spelling is largely because of Life in Podlosia.
53. Ha–Melitz, No. 149, 1900.
54. Siedlce Weekly, No. 52, 1933.
55. Private archive of Bar–Yudah, Tel Aviv.
56. Sh. A. Horodzki, Avaley Tzion, p. 102.
57. Gedaliah Msemyawitz, "Seek the Peace of Jerusalem," Berlin, 1716.
58. Ha–Melitz, No. 257, 1899.
59.
60. Yoel Mastboym, "My Stormy Years," p. 29.
61. Forward: A. Hartglass, to: Y. Mastboym, Red Life. Hartglass acted as a lawyer in the trial of Yudel Mastboym.
62. Siedlce Weekly, No. 36, 1938.
63. Y.N. Wayntroyb, Siedlce Weekly, No. 43, 1938.
64. L. Gutgelt, Heynt, No. 209, 1931.
65. Y.N Wayntroyb, Siedlce Weekly, No. 4, 1939.
66. "Die Welt," No. 39, 1906.
67. Ha–Zman, No. 185, 1906.
68. Yitzchak Caspi, The Story of the Siedlce Riot in 1906.
69. Tydzien Podlaski, No. 8, 1906.
70. Varshawski Dnievnik, No. 240, 1906.
71. Article from A. Levinson in the collection "Struggles of a Generation," also known as "Beginning of the Movement," p. 15.
72. A Litvak, "What Happened," p. 244.
73. Greenboym, "The Jewish War in Poland, 1905–1912," p. 46.
74. Mastboym, Ha–Aretz, No. 4476, 1934.
75. Mastboym, Goldene Keyt, No. 6.
76. One of the regiments: Dubnow or Lubavich, which conducted the pogrom.

[Page 294]

77. Yitzchak Vaynberg
78. Named for the governor.
79. Sh. Dubnow, The Newest History of the Jewish People, Vol. 3, p. 413.
80. Grunberg, der Grosse Pogrom von Siedlce in Jahre, 1906.
81. Yitzchak Caspi, The Story of the Siedlce Riot in 1906.
82. A.M. Gurewitsch arrived in Siedlce from Vilna in 1904. He founded a Hebrew school and led it. Gurewitsch married the daughter of a Siedlce homeowner, Yakov Lerner. The young teacher began to encourage the Zionist organization.
83. Archive of YIVO in New York.
84. My private archives.
85. Ha–Tzofah, Tel Aviv, Nos. 1521, 1524, 1527, from 1942.
86. Ha–Tz'firah, No. 162, 1911.
87. Jewish Hand–Encyclopedia, p. 59, A. Gitlin Publishing.
88. Lists, New Order, Vol. 2, Yitzchak Caspi, p. 99.
89. Wahrheit, 2/19/1916.

90.   The two sisters later married in America. Both wrote poems. Bracha was the wife of a carpenter. She often published poems in the New York newspaper "Der Tog." Chana, whose family name is now Safran, in 1946 published in America a book of poems, "Nitzachon." Some of the poems had been published in the "Morgen Freiheit."

91.   "Undser Yubel" (Our Anniversary. , Siedlce, 1928.

92.   On the twenty–fifth anniversary of the library of the journal "Jewish Fine Art," in Siedlce, p. 24.

93.   Galanski was a grandson of Avraham Shimon, the Chasid from Kotsk, who shortly was freed. Galanski later belonged to the Zionist club "Gordonia" and later on he converted.

94.   Ha–Tz'firah, No. 228, 1915.

95.   Ibid. No. 186, 1920.

96.   Ibid., No. 184, 1920.

97.   Ibid., No. 190, 1920.

98.   On the basis of material from my private archives.

99.   Ha–Tz–firah, No. 205, 1920.

100.   Published by Y. Greenboym, Warsaw, 1922.

101.   According to documents and material taken from the brochure: On the twenty–fifth anniversary of the library of the journal "Jewish Fine Art," in Siedlce.

102.   "Undser Yubel," Siedlce, 1928.

103.   "Orphans' Aid" in Siedlce–report for 1926.

104.   From a communication from the steering committee for "Orphans' Aid" in my private archive.

105.   Siedlce Weekly, No. 38, 1938.

106.   Ziemia Siedlecka, No. 23, 1938.

107.   Siedlce Life, No. 10, 1936.

108.   Siedlce Weekly, No. 35, 1938.

[Page 295]

The Orthodox Siedlce

by Rabbi Kalman-Eliezer Frenkel

Translated by Mira Eckhaus

We are used to call our land Eretz-Israel homeland (Moledet), because the Israeli nation was born in it; But this word is not too simple, and every country a person is born in, is his homeland, as the sages say: "The beauty of a place is in its inhabitants", that is, from its residents you can know the beauty of the place. And if this is right for a country, it is surely true for a city, where a person was born, raised and educated. In this respect, each of us cherish his homeland. But I will admit and not be ashamed, because as a resident of Siedlce, I have always envied great jealousy in Warsaw, Lodz, and the like. In Warsaw I would have find Jewish merchants with complicated businesses, or in Lodz, the preoccupied Jewish blacksmith, and yet they were involved in public activities, Torah, Hasidism and the like. When I visited there, I always pondered in the words of the Mishnah "Don't say I will change once I'll have time, in case you will not have time", and the Rabbi of Kuczek would interpret the Mishnah: "in case you will not have time" – perhaps your Torah, which you deal with, is desirable to God, although you don't have time, but out of trouble". Meaning, that the city of Siedlce, with all its importance, was a provincial city, with no industry and no great trade and its people had a lot of free time. However, I'm not looking now for bad things but to show the good and the beauty of the city. Now we are busy in building a monument to this ruined and desolate city from its holy residents, so our sons and future generations will know who its residents, Yeshiva students, rabbis and public activists were, who were all slaughtered and killed by the Nazi murderers with the help of local Polish during the World War in 1939-1942. This book that is dedicated to the hollies of Siedlce, residents of Israel, residents who are different in their views, opinions, and each of them, as his ability and mindset and in accordance with his views, came to describe what he saw and found in this city, its businessmen and institutions and the people whom he knew and met in Siedlce. I will talk about the "Mizrachi", that I was one of its founders.

[Page 296]

But I will not fulfil my obligation as a religious Jew if I do not first describe to the reader the rabbis of the city, whether I knew them personally or whether I heard about them. I dedicated the first chapters of my memoirs to the rabbis, Yeshiva students, public activists, merchants and Hassidic of Siedlce, and later to the Mizrachi that was founded at a later time. And I must state in advance, that most of my knowledge of Siedlce is from fifty years ago until 1918, when I left Siedlce and moved to Radzyn. Ever since, thirty-four years ago, I would rarely come to Siedlce, as a passing guest, and I did not know what had formed in it until the Second World War.

The Rabbis of the City

It's been said about the rabbi of Liadi, that once he was asked by one opponent during the period of debate between the Hassidim and the opponents, whether Messiah of Israel, to his arrival we expect every day, will be from the Hassidic people or the opposition people. The rabbi answered them that the Messiah will be from the opponents. The opponent wondered: but the Hassidim always say that your way is the right way, while your honor tells me, that Messiah will be an opponent. The rabbi answered him: The Hasidim respect also a real opponent, but the opponents do not want to respect the real Hassidim, therefore in order for everyone to believe in the Messiah, he will be from the opponents and the Hasidim will believe in him as well.

To the praise of Siedlce I must note that in the last hundred and fifty years, the rabbis who served the city were distinct Hasidim and also distinct opponents and almost all were likable all over the city boulevards, between Hasidim and opponents, and this is a reason to praise the city, which did not differ in the rabbi's views, and if he was a wise student, loyal to his role as the city teacher, master of the city, he was respected by all the members of the community, unlike in other cities in Poland, where also the matter of the rabbinate was being swept away in the dispute between the Hasidim and the opponents. I had not heard of such a controversy during my time in Siedlce. And so, the rabbis who served in Siedlce were once a Hassid and once an opponent, and they were all important to the public, each according to its greatness in the Torah and his deeds.

The first of the rabbis I have heard of is Rabbi Zussia Plotsker, in about one hundred and fifty years ago. Rabbi Zussia Plotsker was a passionate Hassid of the disciples of Rabbi Bunim of Przysucha. A friend of the Rabbi of Kuczek and the Rabbi of Warka. Rabbi Shmuel Shinwar, the author of the book "Ramatayim Tzofim," served as the next rabbi of Siedlce. He also was a Hassid. The rabbi who served after him was Rabbi Israel Meisels, a well-known opponent, the son of Rabbi Doberish Meisels, a rabbi in Warsaw whom the Russians deported to Galicia after the Polish uprising against the Russian emperor (The Phobestania). After him, Rabbi Mordechai Lifshitz, the author of the book "Brit Yaakov", served as the rabbi. He found his rest in Siedlce, in the new cemetery and on his grave was built the tent of Rishon, the tent of Zion.

[Page 297]

The son of this rabbi was the known Rabbi Yaakov Zalman Lifshitz from Kovno. His son-in-law was Rabbi Eliyahu Klatzkin from Lublin, who lived at the end of his life in Eretz Israel and his second son-in-law was Rabbi Yechiel, who was a teacher and served as such in Siedlce in my time. Followed him Rabbi Itzela, a teacher, who served as the rabbi until the last period of the extermination. Rabbi Baruch Mordechai was known as a clear opponent. He was succeeded by Rabbi Yissachar Baarish Grahbard. He belonged to the Hassidim and except for his greatness in the Torah, he knew languages and wisdom and was a man of the world. Later he was called to serve as the rabbi of Benzin, written the book of questions and answers called "Divrei Yissachar". Followed him in the rabbinate of Siedlce was Rabbi Shimon Dov Analik of Tykocin, who was known in the class of Yeshiva students as "Der Schwartzer Iluy". I knew him personally and I will talk more about him. He was a definite opponent, was raised and educated in a circle of opponents. The city Tykocin was known as a fortress of resistance to Hassidism. And yet, I do not know if there was a rabbi so dear to the Hasidim as this Rabbi Shimon. And not only because he adapted himself to the people of the city, was wearing a silk garment all days of the week and on Shabbat Was wearing a shtreimel on his head, as is the custom of the place, but because of his integrity and dedication to public and Torah matters. And although he opposed not only to Hassidism itself but also to national and political views, nevertheless the Zionist people also liked and cherished him, because he was a man of truth, and was willing to give his life for the commandments of the Torah and the affairs of the community. I remember, at the time of the beginning of political Zionism, one of the residents of Mezrich, one of the richest men and public activists, a great and enthusiastic Zionist and a great in the Torah, came to speak at the Beit Midrash and he received permission to do so from one of the community leaders of the city, Rabbi Itzchak Nahum Weintraub, who was then head of the community and he didn't ask the rabbi for his permission. Stickers were posted on the walls of the beit midrash in the "Shul Hoif&$148;, that on a certain day and at a certain time a certain person will speak. At the scheduled hour, the rabbi came down from his house, entered the beit midrash and announced that he did not give permission to speak in the beit midrash on any political matter and the like. Rabbi Itzchak Nahum Weintraub approached him and said to him: Rabbi, we have already given permission and we have already gathered an audience, respecting the people requires that he be allowed to speak. Rabbi Shimon kicked him in the leg and said: In my entire life I have not been defeated by a man; I am the responsible of the Beit Midrash. Tykucin still does not have a rabbi and I can return there. And he did not, in any way, allow the speaker to speak, saying that the beit midrash is a place for prayer and ethics and not for secular matters.

This rabbi wrote two books about the Torah, "Ora Lemishpat" and "imrei Rashad". The last book, in its most, contains his sermons which he recited before his audience. He was a great speaker and preacher for the status of a rabbi. At that time, he taught a daily Talmud class at the Beit Midrash of Shas and was dedicated to public affairs, in general and in detail.

[Page 298]

During the pogrom in Siedlce in 1905, he turned to the substitute of the governor, the regional Russian minister, and demanded him to stop the shooting and the murders in the city. The substitute replied that the revolutionary Jews were firing on the army. The rabbi denied this and demanded that he will go with him to do searches and find the revolutionaries. When he went out and saw the corpses of dead Jews on Warsaw Street (who were Rabbi Mendele Tiblum and one of Alexander followers, neighbors who were both killed on Saturday night), the rabbi took off his shoes and walked in socks in the street. When the substitute of the governor asked him for his actions, he said that he, as a rabbi, was mourning when he saw an ally Jew lying dead on the street. These things affected the substitute of the governor until he turned to the Henzlenik Tikhonovsky, damn him, and said to him: "We went and searched all over the city and did not see or find a single revolutionary who had a weapon to fire in the Russian army and did not see a single soldier wounded. On the other hand, there are dozens of Jewish people killed. People with families, with small children, people who never held a weapon in their hand and did not know how to use it". These words were joined by the battalion minister, Hadovolsky, whom Tikhonovsky had invited from the city of Biala, to come and help the Russian army against rebellious revolutionaries, and then the battalion commander was given the custody of the city and the hateful Tikhonovsky left the city with his men. That was on Monday (the pogrom broke out on Saturday night) evening and the deads have not yet been buried. After the pogrom the rabbi of blessed memory, became sick due to all the trouble and fear and in the middle of his life, while he was 50 years old, he passed away in 8 Shvat, about six months after the pogrom. The city then felt the great loss, when its rabbi was taken from it, its pride and glory. Rabbi Shimon left behind a son, Rabbi Leibel from Grajewo, who served as a rabbi in a town, and his three sons-in-law, that were married to his daughters, all served as rabbis in towns in Poland. One of them is Rabbi Alter Brizman, who served as a rabbi in Kolno, rolled to Russia during World War II and from there came to our country, broken and shattered. Rabbi Shimon rests in the new cemetery next to the pogrom saints and so a third tent was added at the Siedlce cemetery. The third tent, which was after Rabbi Baruch Mordechai's grave, is a markup of rabbi Hershley Rabinowitz, the son of the Rabbi of Biala, a young Yeshiva student, whose followers crowned him as a teacher and a rabbi and he moved to Siedlce. He came in the summer months and on Yom Kipurim he caught a cold and got sick. After Sukkot he died and he was only twenty years old and left behind a widow with small children. His followers built him a tent on his grave. One on the sons of Rabbi Hershley, Rabbi David, later moved to London and was named the Rabbi of Biala. He died there in his youth. The second son, Rabbi Yechiel, lived in Siedlce and was his father's successor. During the war he rolled to Russia and from there to Tel Aviv, to Zvulun street and today he is the rabbi of Biala and Ozarow Hassidim.

[Page 299]

The teacher Rabbi Israel Kuzmir

The tent of Rabbi Shimon Dov was, therefore, the third tent in the new cemetery in Siedlce. The successor rabbi after Rabbi Shimon Dov was a rabbi from Mogielnica, who arrived to Siedlce after a few years, Rabbi Chaim - Yehuda Ginsberg, of blessed memory. He was a Hassidic rabbi and not only a Hassid, but a Hassidic person with all its positives and negatives, and a great wise student in the Polish argumentation method and was dedicated to the city affairs. Here, too, we have seen the greatness of the people of Siedlce. No disputes arose over him, although this rabbi was far from the previous rabbis like far east to west. His predecessors were far more modern than him and also better preachers than him. When I left Siedlce in 1918, he served as the rabbi and only by word of mouth do I know, that after Rabbi Ginsburg served Rabbi Shlomo Eichenstein, Rabbi of Khodoriv, until the days of the extermination and he escaped to Russia and no one heard about him later.

In the days of the rabbi from Mogielnica, well-known Torah figures stood out in Siedlce, some of them merchants who were extreme in the Torah and some concentrated in studying Torah. Among these was rabbi Moshe Hirsch, who used to teach a regular lesson at Mishnayot, and at the same time he was attached to a regular arbiter of the local rabbinate. At that time, or a little earlier, the rabbi from Radix, Rabbi Israel Kuzmir, also joined the Court of Justice in Siedlce (he has a son in Eretz Israel), and this too it to praise Siedlce, whose residents did not go to seek an arbiter from afar but appointed people for the Court of Justice from among their brothers. Another important Torah personality stood out during the period of the rabbi from Tykocin, Rabbi Nachman Lev, who was the rabbi's substitute in the Shas lesson in case the rabbi was busy. But he was too simple and modest to take the position of an arbiter or of a rabbi, though he deserved it because of his greatness in the Torah and his integrity. Rabbi Lev was the son-in-law of Rabbi Avigdor Riddle, a simple Jew but a loyal and honest merchant. Rabbi Avigdor's sons also excelled in honesty. He married his daughters with Yeshiva students with Torah and God-fearing. One of them was Rabbi Nachman Lev. His eldest son was Rabbi Shimon Riddle, a wholesale merchant of flour, an honest and religious man, famous in the city Lamuel, who would leave his trade to perform a mitzvah without receiving any benefit. Riddle had a son in Israel, Mr. Yaakov Riddle. Rabbi Nachman Lev also had sons in Israel. In the last years, rabbi Monish Riddle, who previously was a known Tabak merchant in Siedlce and survived the extermination, also came to Israel.

[Page 300]

There were also Jewish merchants in Siedlce that owned large trading houses and concentrated in studying Torah. Of these, Rabbi Tuvia Karmarez should be mentioned, the son-in-law of Rabbi Avrahamcha Lifshitz, a very distinct wise student, who had a shop for sewing materials on Warsaw Street, that sat all his life at home and studied Torah and only in moments of rest would he enter his shop to look after it a little. He deserved to be a rabbi in one of the large towns because of his greatness in the Torah and the Halacha. And though he lived his life in distress, he did not want to make a living from the Torah. His sons were Torah students, his eldest son, Rabbi Hirsch, and his son, Rabbi Mendel Karmarez, a cigarette factory owner who invented a state-of-the-art machine and received a patent from the Russian government. Rabbi Hirsch Karmarez has a son in Eretz Israel, a rabbi in Kibutz Gvat, where his sons are. Rabbi Mendel Karmarez also has a son in Eretz Israel, Mordechai Cnaani. The son of the latter, Avraham - Hertz, fell on the conquest of Jaffa, in Nisan 1948. Even more astonishing was Mr. Tuvia Karmarez, who was actually far from trade and the like and whose entire essence was only the Torah. He is the brother-in-law of Rabbi Eliezer Lifshitz, a great merchant of tobacco, an enthusiastic Hassid and a great scholar, who also dealt with his trade. But he never came to his store before the fifth hour, after the pray and the regular lesson, and in cases he went to eat lunch, he never returned to his store, but sat and learned in depth. He was among the rich, had a large house, a large trading business and yet was an enthusiastic Hassid, who concentrated in studying Torah. He has a grandson who lives in Hadera, Mr. Isser Rosenberg, who is the son of his daughter, and his daughter's daughter, Mrs. Ehrlich, lives in Kfar Pines.

Rabbi Shmuel David Zeidenzeig was quite similar to Rabbi Eliezer Lifshitz in the city of Siedlce. At the time he was a timber merchant and spent most of the week in Warsaw. But about an hour before he left you could find him at home sitting and reading the Gemara, thinking about the Torah. Also, on his return in the winter days on Thursday afternoon, after greeting the members of his family, he would sit and engage in Torah. He followed his father in this regard, my grandfather. The late Rabbi Yisrael Sinai Zeidenzeig of blessed memory, who had complicated businesses, houses and forests, was a Kock Hassid, who studied in the beit midrash of Baal Chiddushei HaRim of blessed memory. He was also the owner of the Engelsky Hotel in Siedlce, on Feinkana Street. He stayed outside the town for weeks and every Saturday he stayed at the Hassidim's house for hours after the prayer ended and studied Torah with devotion until late in the afternoon and only then returned home for Shabbat meal. His sons-in-law were known as part of the genealogy of the greatest in the Torah and in the Hassidism, among them was my father, may he live long life, who studies his entire days the Torah and worship God.

At the time, there were two famous Jews in Siedlce, Rabbi Avrahamcha Lifshitz and Rabbi Yosef Anzels. Both excelled in philanthropy and Hassidism. Rabbi Avrahamcha Lifshitz was the father of Rabbi Eliezer Lifshitz and the father-in-law of Rabbi Tuvia Karmarez, whom I mentioned above. Rabbi Yossele Anzels had two well-known grandchildren in Siedlce, who were famous in their philanthropy.

[Page 301]

Rabbi Asher-Moshe Galkenbaum and Rabbi Avraham-Yodel Rosen, both partners and their homes were full of Hassidism and Torah and especially excelled with their help to the needy and rebellious. Their wives also excelled in these virtues. Their concern was at the beginning of winter to prepare trees, potatoes and cloths for the poor and their family members and were known for the righteousness of their philanthropy. Rabbi Asher - Moshe Galkenbaum has only one family member left, Rabbi Aaron Galkenbaum, who lives in Bnei Brak and works in the city municipality. Rabbi Avraham-Yodel Rosen came to Eretz Israel with his sons and died here in good health. A similar type was Rabbi Mordechai Heinsdorf or Rabbi Motil-Ephraim, as he was called earlier among Alexander's followers. His commerce place was Borski house, and his house served as the house of the Hassidim's committee. On Rabbi Hillula's day, Rosh

Chodesh meal, holiday and festive, I found there, far from the city on the way to Sokolov, Hassidim eating and drinking. The above mentioned has a son, a daughter and grandchildren in Eretz Israel.

A special person was Rabbi David Mintz. He was a merchant and a Hassid at once. He made a living through a stationery store on Warsaw Street, near the district court. He studied diligently, dipped every day in the Mikveh and was a humble and honest man and never had an idle conversation even among the Hassidim. He studied with intent and his trade was also for the work of God, so that he would have a livelihood and would not need the help of the people, and as soon as he was freed from it, he would return to his work, to the worship of the Creator. The man was lucky because his wife was just like him and helped him in his trade as much as she could, so that he would not have to devote himself too much to his trade. He was called Rabbi David Leibels in Siedlce, after his father-in-law Rabbi Leibel Orzel. Rabbi David's son-in-law is Rabbi Ze'ev (volovil) Soloveitzik, the son of the glory Rabbi Chaim Soloveitzik from Brisk. Rabbi Ze'ev Soloveitzik filled his father's place and was a rabbi in Brisk. During the war he escaped and made an Aliya to Eretz Israel and he now lives in Jerusalem and is known there as the Rabbi from Brisk.

There were also nice types of homeowners in Siedlce who were not among the Hassidic community, but their behavior was exemplary and they are: Rabbi Hirsch - Yosef Tsernobroda, Rabbi Moshe - Abba Eisenstadt, Rabbi Israel Gottgeld, Rabbi Moshe Chaim Levin, Rabbi Gedaliah Orzel, Rabbi Natan-David Glicksberg, Rabbi Fishel Frenkel, Dr. Sheflin, etc.

Rabbi Hirsch - Yosef Tsernobroda was a religious Jew, an opponent, who was praying when he woke up, studied his regular classes and later came to the trading house. He was reliable in his speech as well as in negotiations with people. His brother Berl was dressed like the Hassidim but was known as an educated person to a certain extent. He was the librarian of the library in Siedlce and later one of the founders of the youth club called "Hazamir" (the Nightingale).

Rabbi Moshe - Abba Eisenstadt had a modern home and was a reliable and good Zionist merchant. His son Paltiel Eisenstadt is in Eretz Israel.

[Page 302]

Rabbi Grones Friedman was a wealthy Jewish man and had a home. His trade was mainly with the gentiles, to whom he lent money for houses and estates. He would pray in the large public beit midrash and still would wear silk clothes on Shabbat. He instructed his sons in Torah and Hassidism. His grandchildren are in Israel, the Friedman brothers. Similar persons were Rabbi Gedaliah Orzel and Glicksberg, Hassidic partners. They lived in one house and even though their business was a lending business such as Rabbi Grones Friedman, they were considered very honest traders. Rabbi Gedaliah Orzel was one of the followers of Radzyn and the Rabbi from Radzyn was often accommodated in his house. Glicksberg was for many years the member of the committee of Talmud Torah and a more modern person. But they both instructed their sons in the Torah. Glicksberg's son, a survivor of the Nazi hell, arrived to Israel in recent years.

Rabbi Israel Gottgeld and his partner R. Moshe Chaim Levin excelled in public activism, and after a quarrel between them parted ways with the partnership. Both of them were typical public activists. Rabbi Israel Gottgeld was the son-in-law of Rabbi Yosef Anzels. He received a large amount of money from his father-in-law in Siedlce and also from his father. He had two large houses and did not need to run a business. As he had a lot of free time, he devoted himself to public activism. As rumor has it, he was recently the chairman of the community. His son Levy was among the organizers of the Zionist Organization in Siedlce. He was said to be a diligent and loyal activist, one of a kind, who, because of his activism, forgot to marry in his youth. At the time of the extermination, he was captured among the rest of the Jewish people, may God avenge them. Moshe Chaim Levin was dedicated to the pursuits of Talmud Torah activism together with Rabbi Moshe Zakon who had no sons. Rabbi Moshe Chaim Levin has a grandson in Israel named Binyamin Levin.

I must mention two more Jews, Rabbi Fishel Frenkel, a rich man that built his own special synagogue; And the other is Dr. Sheflin, who was then considered as half a doctor of medicine and also built him a synagogue in his courtyard on Feinkana Street called Sheflin's Beit Midrash. It was interesting to see how doctor Sheflin grows a beard and serves as a doctor. Since most of the doctors were gentiles, people thought he was a specialist and asked him to examine sick people and he also wrote pharmacy prescriptions. These two, like Rabbi Israel Yechiels before them, whom I did not know - built special synagogues with their money for the benefit of the public that were later named after them.

Synagogues for Torah and prayer

In addition to the synagogues that I mentioned above, there were also a tailors' synagogue in Siedlce by the Great Synagogue and a synagogue in Daluna Street, called Petersburg Stiebel and a butcher's beit midrash on the butchers' shops street, apart from lots of Hassidim houses (Shtiblech): for the followers of Gur, Skarenwitz, Alexander, Amshinov Forsov, Biala and more.

[Page 303]

Each synagogue served as a place for the Torah and there were those who had a special Maggid Shiur in the evenings, between Mincha and Maariv and on Shabbat and holidays. The houses of the Hassidim served as a place of Torah for young men, Yeshiva students, who sat and studied, also for the owners of the houses who devoted many hours a day to study Torah. Many old men and young people, who were not among the Hassidim, studied in the great beit midrash Torah and God's worship, and many young people from Siedlce also studied in famous yeshivas abroad.

There was a Great Yeshiva in Siedlce. The Rosh Yeshiva was Rabbi Israel Drogetsner. The second Rosh Yeshiva, Rabbi David Itzchak, was a diligent Torah scholar and a good explainer, who attracted the young people to the Torah and many young people from distant towns were attracted to this yeshiva. The people of the city would provide them with food by the "days": Each homeowner undertook to support one Yeshiva student for one day a week in order to allow him to study Torah. The Yeshiva students were also provided with accommodation. This state of spreading of Torah and God-fearing continued in Siedlce all the days until World War I in 1914, when many adults and young people were taken into the army and a great change came in the private and public life of Polish Jewishness.

Public Activists

At that time the public activism concentrated only on community affairs and charities in the city, such as: an orphanage, a hospital and a house for elderly people. I do not remember the activists of the orphanage, etc., but I do remember the city or community activists, which are Rabbi Itzchak - Nahum Weintraub and Rabbi Moshe Temkin. Both of them were religious in the full sense of the word, early risers to the Beit Midrash. These two devoted themselves to the public affairs of the public in Siedlce. During the previous war, while the Russians were leaving Poland, Rabbi Moshe Temkin, who had medals (badges of excellence) of the Russian Tsar, packed his goods and traveled with his family to Russia. At the end of the war, he returned to Siedlce without property, broken and shattered. On the other hand, Rabbi Itzchak-Nahum Weintraub remained as the head of the community throughout the years. He was a handsome Jew on the outside and inside, properly dressed and one of the Zionist leaders. His son-in-law, Mordechai Meir Landau, was at the time a devoted religious Zionist, a director of a credit bank. He died in his youth in Siedlce and I eulogized him in the name of the "HaMizrachi" at the time.

I do not know what was Rabbi Itzchak-Nahum Weintraub's income and how he could have devoted himself so much to the public affairs. But the fact is, that over the years we have seen Rabbi Weintraub as the head of the community who was devoted to the affairs of the public in faith and pleased the whole community.

[Page 304]

Before I will start to describe the state of the parties or the beginning of the Zionist parties' organization, I consider it my duty to speak of the butchers, the Hazanim (cantors) and the Shamashim (beadles) as the public servants of the community.

At the time, the head of the butchers in Siedlce was Rabbi Chaim Shochat, a Jewish Hassid. At the end of his life, he handed over the butchering to his son Rabbi Shimon Shochat. The above-mentioned has a son in Israel, Mr. Kleinlard, one of the leaders of the Agudat Israel workers in Jerusalem. The rest of the butchers, which I remember in Siedlce were Rabbi Yitzchak Meir and Rabbi Zalman Shochat, the later has a son in Israel.

The Hazanim (cantors). I remember the Hazan from Brisk in my days, a man with a large beard, who was always wearing a cylinder on his head and participated in all the events that took place, a circumcision, a bar mitzvah, a wedding etc., he gave his blessing and received his reward. Followed him, I think, was Hazan Yaakil Rovner, followed by Rabbi Yosef Pesovsky, who made an Aliya to Israel at the end of his life and died here two years ago. The last Hazan, Mr. Zopowitz, also made an Aliya to Israel after the last war.

The Shamashim (beadles). It is also worth mentioning two Shamashim (beadles) that were special persons. The first that I still remember, was Rabbi Isaac, or Eisele Shemesh. He was known as the Shamash of the Beit Din. He was a great Jew in Torah and God-fearing, who added respect to the local rabbinate. And I do remember what I have heard from the late Rabbi Israel Sinai Zeidentseig, of blessed memory, who said that 80 of 90 years ago, during the decree on the cutting the payot and religious clothing in Russia, and Rabbi Eisele was still a young man, who spent his time at the beit midrash, who was dressed like a religious guy at that time, with long payot, and a Russian policeman was coming towards him with large scissors in his hand, he grabbed Rabbi Eisele's hand and cut his payot with the scissors. Rabbi Eisele cried like a baby, because how would he show his face, that looks like those of a gentile with no payot, to all his acquaintance? And the policeman on the other hand, enjoyed his actions and laughed at his weeping. After a few moments, Rabbi Eisele got up, picked up his trimmed payot from the ground, put them in his hand and ran away. What did Rabbi Eisele do? He glued his payot on both sides of his hat and thus did not look like a man whose payot had been trimmed. A few days later, the policeman met

Rabbi Eisele on the street and was amazed at the sight of his eyes, is it possible that these payot had grown long again? So, he grabbed him by the hand and surprisingly Eisele took off his hat along with the payot and mocked at the policeman. And so, no one accounted Eisele as without payot, and only when he would sit in the beit midrash studying and his hat dropped to the right or left side would a payot come out next to his face and the other behind him.

The other was Rabbi Hershel Shemesh. He was an exceptional. He was always elegant in his appearance as one of the richest, but he had a very gentle soul, in Israel and especially in Siedlce. When a rich Jew would marry his daughter, in his house or in a hall, he would set a table full of good things, specific people or the Shamashim would have served the refreshments to the guests and as usual the Shamashim would have eaten and enjoyed the feast openly or secretly and also took dishes from the feast in their pockets for their family members, some of them even provided food for their family members for a whole week through these dishes.

[Page 305]

Hershel HaShamash did not act this way, he never enjoyed the feast and led himself to eat his meal in his house before coming to the feast. He himself never tasted the meal and did not take for his family even if the in-laws asked him to do so. Therefore, he was very reliable on everyone and when he came to the feast, they used to give him the key of the closet or the room in which they kept the groceries. And even if the in-laws and the relatives wanted something, they had to turn to him. He was very reliable in his position and he was proud of his actions. He respected the Shamashut profession. And if there were faithful Shamashim in Israel, then Herschel HaShamash is one of them, if not the leader among them.

At the time they mentioned his daughter who was a member of the PPS, A socialist party in Poland, that used always to shout that the Russian Tsar Nikolai was shoving in her throat. She sat in the prison in Siedlce and once a red flag was found hanging from her room's window.

At that time, in 1944, when I was studying with a well-known teacher, young people came to him and asked him for money to buy weapons for the revolution people. They were wearing black shirts with a steep collar and red belts. Once in winter, as I left the room in the evening, I had to go through Konsky - Rinok, a garden on Warsaw Street, the Konsky – Rinok was full of people and in the middle, someone stood and spoke in front of the audience. The next day, Jewish boys dressed in black shirts ordered to close the shops in the same manner religious Jews were accustomed to walk around on Friday evenings before it gets dark, to warn that shops should be closed and Shabbat candles should be lit. This situation lasted for weeks and months. Suddenly, they ordered in the middle of the day, to close the shops and the crowd would disperse home. I did not understand it then and I do not understand it even now, what they got from it, as most of the shops or ninety-nine percent of them belonged to Jews and the gentiles thought that it is because of a Jewish holiday or some kind of a mourning for Jews, until one clear day, it was Tuesday, a loud explosion was heard in the city and echoes were heard throughout the city followed by gunfire. It was later found out that a bomb had been thrown at the city police chief and he was killed and as a consequence, the police started firing all over. One of the bullets hit Rabbi Shlomo Zalman of Lublin, the son of Rabbi Moshe Shulkis, who passed away some time ago, and his son came from Lublin to build a gravestone on his grave. When Rabbi Shlomo Zalman heard the bomb nearby, he began to run away and one policeman shot him, and that week, on Friday he died of his wounds. I remember the funeral that was arranged for him in Friday evening before in got dark, in order to bury him before Shabbat enters.

[Page 306]

Since then, the government announced a military status in the city and the signal for this was a long pole which was placed on the city clock above the police building. One of the rules of this military situation was that any gathering was forbidden and at certain hours in the evening it was forbidden to walk outside without a special license. This tense situation lasted until the pogroms in Siedlce, which took place in the month of Elul (17 - 18) 1905.

I still remember the outbreak of the pogroms. The governor of the city brought a military unit and trained it for the role of suppressing the uprising of the revolutionaries. On the same Saturday evening, while I was standing on the street, a military patrol passed by us, two Jews stood on Prospektova Street and had a conversation. As a child I asked them naively, how someone is able to kill someone else? Both of them told me that if it is a revolutionist, they are willing to kill even their father or their brothers. I wondered about the discipline and the special training of this organization and as they passed by me, a single shot was heard followed by shots of guns and cannons incessantly, all night, and on Sunday and Monday as well. A fire of houses was also added to it (as they were of wood). It was not clear whether the houses were set on fire due to the bullets or were ignited on purpose. On Tuesday, the pogroms ceased and the dead were buried. Licenses were distributed to all those who wanted to leave the city. Our family also received such a license and of Wednesday we left the city and did not return for months.

At the time, Siedlce was preparing a rescue committee to help the families of those killed and those who had lost their property in the fires and the robbery that the soldiers carried out for two and a half days. There were also cases of rape as was the custom of soldiers who were given a free hand to kill and plunder. In this committee, except for the member of the community, were also Mr. Tzetzkas, who then served as the secretary of the community and the converted lawyer Zonderland, that despite the fact he abandoned Judaism, he was a very respectful lawyer, honest and loyal with financial matters.

The detailed the rest of the details from the pogrom above, in my memoirs about the Rabbi from tikcyn, Rabbi Shimon Analik of blessed memory. The pogrom in Siedlce caused many of the youth to leave the city and some of them even left the country and traveled to the United States, Canada and South Africa. Among those known to me was Mr. Mordechai Rosenbach. I found him in Durban in South Africa, twenty years ago when I visited there. He is very rich, owns a tobacco factory and was very happy to meet a Jew from Siedlce. In recent years he has donated twenty-five thousand lirot to the University of Jerusalem and a sum of fifteen thousand lirot has worked to yeshivas in Eretz Israel. And according to the information I received from him, he is coming to Israel soon.

Zionist work, or rather, Israeli work of Siedlce people .

[Page 307]

Begins in 1689, meaning two hundred and sixty years ago. Rabbi Michal Tikoczynski from Jerusalem, the grandson of the chief rabbi R. Shmuel Salant, tells us about this in his book, and according to Mr. Tidhar in his book "Encyclopaedia to the Pioneers of the Yishuv and its Builders "(Part One, p. 17), Rabbi Yehuda the Hassid from the city of Siedlce and one thousand people from Poland and Russia, made an Aliya in 28 Cheshvan 1700. Five hundred died along the way. He purchased the courtyard for the Ashkenazi community in Jerusalem and built there a synagogue named after him. From the month of Cheshvan, 1720, after the deportation of the Ashkenazi community and the destruction of the courtyards by the Arabs, the place was called the ruin of Rabbi Yehuda the Hassid. And I will copy the words of Rabbi Michal Tykoczynski from Jerusalem in his book as they are, and this is his language: "And the rumor came then in 1689 in the Horodna district and its surroundings, that God began to visit his country and that a considerable number of those who live in the Ashkenazi community (probably there was only a Sephardic community) to gathered in the courtyards of God in the midst of Jerusalem and the late Rabbi Yehuda from the city of Siedlce decided to make an Aliya to the Holy Land together with other great rabbis in Torah, charity and asceticism. Among them was Rabbi Yaakov of Vilna, the father of the late wise Rabbi Zvi. They arrived to Jerusalem and settled in the Ashkenazi courtyard, which was the courtyard of the synagogue from Ashkenazis. When they came, they dedicated themselves to living a life of asceticism in holiness and purity. Some speculate that in their prayers they delayed the end and it was decided in heaven that he will dye, and so a few days after his arrival to Eretz Israel, the Tzaddik Rabbi Yehuda the Hassidic passed away, and a few days later, the rest of the Tzaddikim and the Hassidim that came with him, died too. This tragedy that befell the congregation of the Tzadikim for the return of Zion did not extinguish the passion to Zion that many had. The desire to make an Aliya to Jerusalem did not stop and the Ashkenazi courtyard was expanded and the Ashkenazis also owned houses and shops around their main courtyard and the settlement flourished". So far I have copied from the above book.

Some of Siedlce people did not know that it was Rabbi Yehuda the Hassid who built the synagogue in the Old City of Jerusalem, which is still named after him "the ruin of Rabbi Yehuda the Hassid". I could not find out who was Rabbi Yehuda the Hassid, but even in my time I knew some of the Aliyah members who made an Aliya before official Zionism ... One of them was Rabbi Israel Yosef (I do not remember his last name). I also remember that he was the Gabbay of the Descarnewitz Hassidic house in the city of Siedlce. His son was from the PPS. in those days. Maybe it gave him a boost out of shame, to make an Aliya to Eretz Israel. I remember that he traveled and returned after a year and brought with him packs of moss growing in Israel and distributed perfumes to bless on them on Saturday night and also 8 Tzitzits from the beginning of the fleece were distributed among his acquaintances. After settling his affairs, he returned to Eretz Israel a year later and we have not heard from him since. After him I remember Rabbi Leibel from "Soda Wasser", from street Feinkana, which had a soda and soda pop factory.

[Page 308]

This Jew longed all his life to make an Aliya to Israel. Once he traveled to Israel as a tourist and returned from there. After the Balfour Declaration and the handing over of the mandate to England, he applied to the Ministry of Eretz Israel in Warsaw, which I attended together with the late Rabbi Nissenbaum as the power of attorneys of the "Mizrachi" and asked to be given a permit to make an Aliya to Israel. He told us that he had sold his soda factory in Siedlce and intended to make an Aliya to Eretz Israel and establish a factory there. Rabbi Nissenbaum doubted if an old Jew as he was, is still capable of doing something in Israel. That year there was a drought in Jerusalem because the rains in I came to Israel in 1924, and I have found Rabbi Leibel in Moshav Zkenim in Jerusalem, where he spent the rest of his life.

It is worth mentioning Rabbi Kaddish Goldstein, who liquidated a factory, left his home and made an Aliya to Israel in 1902 and has a grandson here, Mr. Yona Popovsky and great-grandchildren.

Kaddish Goldstein, who made an Aliya to Eretz Israel fifty years ago

[Page 309]

Rabbi Gedaliah Gutgeld evaded his family members, who did not agree that he will make an aliya to Israel. And one evening in 1907, he went out as if to close the shutters of the house and made an Aliya to Israel. Also, he has grandchildren and great-grandchildren here.

In addition, Rabbi Avraham Moshe Weinberg, a Jew from Bar-Torah, the owner of a vinegar factory, was considered amongst the rich people and made an Aliya to Israel among the tourists. He returned and then made an Aliya again, probably without a property. He suffered a lot in Israel. He lived in Tel Aviv and on the night of Shabbat of Parashat Bereshit, while he was sitting and studying in the house of Gur's Hassidim, he had a stroke and he died on the Gemara. His daughters live in Tel Aviv.

Fifty years ago, R. Moshe Mordechai Lifshitz made an Aliya to Israel. He was the son-in-law and nephew of Rabbi Avraham'tzi Lifshitz of Siedlce. Rabbi Moshe-Mordechai Lifshitz has sons in Eretz Israel and if I am not mistaken, the owners of the Lifshitz printing press in Jerusalem are his descendants.

In the old cemetery in Tel Aviv, on Trumpeldor Street, I saw a gravestone with the inscription: "Rabbi Avraham Moshe Bar Yosef of Siedlce, who drowned on the sea of Jaffa on 11 Tammuz 1908, is buried here". I interrogated about him and I was told by Chevra Kadisha in Tel Aviv that his last name was Berlinerblum. They were probably not used to writing the last name on the gravestone here, but his grandson came a few years later, handed his last name and erected a gravestone on his grave. Who the man was I could not find out.

The late R. Yehuda Reinman, whom we all knew in Siedlce as a very religious and devout young man, was a bookkeeper in banks, he married the daughter of Rabbi Mikela Rosenberg Brisker and was a candidate for a position of a rabbi in Siedlce after the death of the Rabbi of Tykocin. Rabbi Yehuda Reinman came to Eretz Israel in 1926 or 1927, and died in Tel Aviv on the 24th of Iyar 1930, leaving behind a wife and two sons. One died of an illness and one fell in Spain while traveling there to help the rebellions. The wife became ill and returned to Poland where she died. Let my words be of remembrance for this noble family, that have no remnant left. The father of Rabbi Yedidya Reinman, Rabbi Leibish Yedidim, as he was called in Siedlce, a Hassidic Jew who was devoted to the work of God (he was the son-in-law of the Rabbi of Zwolen from his marriage to his second wife). This distinguished old man died in Jerusalem a few years after the death of his only son. Also, the son-in-law of Rabbi Leibish Yedidi's, Rabbi Herzl Glickman came to Eretz Israel at that time; Rabbi Herzl was the son of the noble woman Bluma Orex, as she was called in Siedlce. Rabbi Herzl had a cement pipe factory in Siedlce. In Israel, Rabbi Herzl Glickman was for some time one of the settlers in the village of Hittin near Tiberias of the Mizrachi and did not succeed in earning a living here. This family was well known among Radzyn's followers. Rabbi Herzl's brother, Rabbi Moshe Itzhak, was the son-in-law of Rabbi Heshil, who became the Rabbi of Radzyn after the death of the late Rabbi Mordechai Yosef. Rabbi Herzl Glickman lived in Holon near Tel Aviv and died two years ago in Tel Aviv, where he rests. He left a wife, a son and two daughters. He is a member of "Dan" busses company.

[Page 310]

Of Radzyn's followers came to Israel at that time Rabbi Kalman Hoover (?) from Siedlce. At the time, he was known in Siedlce as one of the best teachers. I also studied with him when I was ten years old – for eleven years. He studied with only 4 selected fellows and was a good explainer. I remember that he knew how to teach the boys the commentary on "Akdamot" that is said in Shavuot before the reading of the Torah, to explain the matter of the birth of the moon, the incense matter according to a well-known addition in the Shavuot Tractate. He was weak, suffering from headaches. When he came to Eretz Israel, he settled in Hittin village of HaMizrachi and when I arrived there, I was amazed to see how Rabbi Kalman rides a horse, and he was one of the best farmers. When the people of Hittin dispersed due to lack of water, Rabbi Kalman Hoover settled in Petah Tikva and made a living from a grocery store. He died a few years ago in Petah Tikva. His son Shmuel Hoover settled in the Avraham village of Hapoel HaMizrachi near Petah Tikva, the rest of his sons live in Mexico and are very wealthy.

Another of Radzyn followers, may he live long, Rabbi Itzchak Bronstein, from the Berg family from Siedlce, a great scholar who currently lives in Tel Aviv. The late Rabbi Zalman Gershon Nosovski also made an Aliya from Siedlce. He was considered in Siedlce among the great and distinguished merchants. He was a member of the Biala Hassidim and passed away several years ago. He left behind a wife, sons and daughters. His eldest son Chaim - Dov is a dairy owner. The young son, David, is a clerk in the Department of Commerce and Industry of the Government. His daughter is an activist at the committee for Siedlce in Tel Aviv.

Zionist action in those days. Before I will talk about the history of the Mizrachi in Siedlce, that I was one of its founders, I would not fulfil my duty if I will not mention two people from Tze'irei Zion (Zion Youth), who brought me to Zionism and then to Mizrachi. Both my father's and my grandfather's houses were houses of Torah and Hassidism and the matter of Zionism and Mizrachi were stranger to them. I was then a five- or six-years old boy. I was already studying Gemara. As I was the eldest in the house, my father hurried to teach me a lot of Torah, much more than suitable for my age. When I was two and a half years old, I was led to a Heder wrapped in a tallit. By the age of five I had already started studying Chumash and a feast was prepared in my honor and I had to deliver a sermon (I think since then the fear of the public has disappeared from me). At the age of six I started studying Gemara. My father, as was the custom of the Hassidim at that time, went every year to the Rabbi of Skierniewice for Shavuot and Rosh Hashanah until after Yom Kippur. When I was seven years old, my father took me with him to the Rabbi. Since then, I travelled with him to the Rabbi in all the trips he did, and sometimes also in the winter, for fifteen years until the period of the World War in 1914. And so, I managed to absorb Hassidism to some extent. By the time I was twelve - I had already wrote Hidushim in the Torah. Many Hidushim in the Torah that I wrote, were printed during 1912-1914 in various magazines, like "Shaarei Torah" in Warsaw, Hame'asef" in Jerusalem, "Ohel Itzchak" by Rabbi Kalman of Satmar, "Asefat Chachamim" in Galicia and "Tel Talpiot" in Hungary. in 1913, articles by me were also printed in "HaModiha" by Rabbi Akiva Rabinowitz from Poltava.

[Page 311]

The same learning in depth in the Torah, from the dawn of my childhood, really led to the weakness of my body that has continued since, because I did not know in my youth pleasure or play, apart from writing Hidushim of the Torah or sitting together with Hassidim and receiving newspapers, magazines and letters of questions and answers from genius rabbis of the world at that time. A lot of questions and answers letters are currently with me and I hope I will be lucky to print them. I exchanged letters with the Rabbi of Brezan and Rabbi Yoav - Yehoshua of Konskie. In the questions and answers book named "Shem Olam" by the Rabbi of Voytek, the son-in-law of the famous Rabbi Skidel, about ten questions and answers to me from the years 1912-1914, were printed (The book appeared in 1928 in Riga). Chapters from the Hassidic chapters, which I studied and which I heard, were presented in my book "rumors and evidence", which I printed in 1939 in Jerusalem and in my book "burnt offering of the month", which was printed in 1950. The chapters I heard are mainly included in the book "Imrot", which is now being printed.

But how did I get familiar with Zionism? As I said, I was then about five or six years old. My father traveled to the Rabbi and I went to pray with my uncle at the house of the Gur Hassidim in Siedlce, and between Shacharit and Musaf, during the prayer break, I went up to my grandmother's house to taste something. And here comes Mr. Yshahayahu Zeidenzeig, which is now named Ben Sinai, the brother of my late mother, who is now in Tel Aviv. Veteran Zionist and his friend, Mr. Leibshe Kahana, the son of Berl Kahana, a well-known man in Siedlce, who was a great philanthrope. They both sat in the same room where I tasted on Yom Kippur and sang songs of Zion in Yiddish and Hebrew. The melody and words captured my heart. I remember that I could not taste anymore and my heart was drawn to Zion. Since then, I dreamed of Zion and saw it all the time: in my dreams and when I was awake. And from the moment I heard about the founding of the Mizrachi in Warsaw, I organized and founded the Mizrachi in Siedlce.

The history of the Mizrachi in Siedlce. There was no real Zionist action in Siedlce, as in other Polish cities during the Russian Tsarist period, in which organization of any kind was strictly forbidden. The action was expressed in collection of pennies for the Keren Kayemet and in the sale of shekels. And I still remember that Mr. Paltiel Eisenstadt would turn to me and sell me a Zionist shekel. And only with the German Occupation in 1915, the restrictions were cancelled and various organizations began to operate. At that time, the Zionist Organization in Warsaw and the Histadrut HaMizrachi started operating. I belonged to the Mizrachi group, and began organizing young people under the Mizrachi flag. One day Mr. Nechemia Malin, a clever and a knowledgeable man, invited me and started pleading that I will organize the Mizrachi and suggested that I will contact Rabbi Asher Orzel, a well-known figure in Siedlce, who at the time had a bank, and ask him to serve as the Mizrachi chairman in Siedlce.

[Page 312]

At that time Rabbi Zlotnik, a rabbi in Gabin (now known as "Rabbi Avida" and lives in Jerusalem) – was the speaker on behalf of the Mizrachi. I invited him on behalf of the Mizrachi, to come to Siedlce to lecture on the Mizrachi. I rented the theater hall on Ogradova Street for that purpose.

The Presidency of the first Assembly for the establishment of "Mizrachi Youth"

On behalf of the German government of the Emperor Wilhelm II, two rabbis served then in Poland. One named Karlibach and the other Rabbi Dr. Pinchas Cohen. Both of them had the goal of organizing ultra-Orthodox organizations, as a barrier against the Zionism spirit, that was then blown from the West, especially from England, after the Balfour Declaration. Some young people who were not absorbed in the Zionist spirit, founded an organization called "Tvuna". Apparently, it was an organization for Jewish studies, but it could be recognized that an anti-Zionist spirit is blowing in it. And so, two organizations that oppose each other's opinion were established.

On the one hand, the "Tvuna", in which most of the religious intelligence was united, and on the other hand, the Mizrahi youth organization, which I headed.

Dr. Cohen and Karlibach succeeded in organizing in Poland the Admors (Hassidic leaders) and many rabbis in the organization "Shlymei Emunei Israel" or "the Orthodox Association", who later changed its name to "Agudat Israel". And although there were positive sides to the foundation of "Agudat Israel" in terms of strengthening and establishing religious Judaism, the main goal was anti-Zionism. However, after the defeat of Wilhelm and the recognition of Poland as an independent state, a panic arose within the "Tvuna" members and thanks to the action of the Mizrachi and the young people of the Mizrachi, who began to develop a Zionist action then, they took off the walls of "Tvuna" hall the pictures of Dr. Cohen and Karlibach and the entire organization, with its members, officially moved to the Mizrahi Youth, and thus the Histadrut of the Mizrahi Youth in Siedlce became a strong organization in the social and political sense.

[Page 313]

"Mizrahi Youth" conference in Siedlce,
with the participation of Gnibowski and Y. Greenberg from Eretz Israel

The "Mizrahi Youth" committee in Siedlce

[Page 314]

In 1918, I left Siedlce and since then I have not participated in the work of the organization and only after that, in 1920, when I came to Warsaw to run the Mizrachi Center, I had the opportunity to speak with friends and personalities from Siedlce. I think it is possible to find people from Siedlce, who will be able to write details about the Mizrachi since its inception until the period of the extermination by Hitler, damn him.

In 1924, I made an Aliya to Eretz Israel with my family. I learned from rumors that the Mizrachi movement in Siedlce later developed and attracted hundreds of members. They founded a Mizrahi school and took a position in the city and in the elections of the rabbi in Siedlce. After the late Rabbi Chaim-Yehuda Ginzburg, two candidates appeared, one from the Mizrachi and one from the Aguda.

In the above things, I intended to place a memorial monument for Siedlce, our hometown, so that our sons and grandsons would know and remember the memory of our holy and dear brothers whom the Germans, with the help of the Poles, destroyed in their reign, or the sake of engraving in their hearts the duty and mitzvah to avenge their vengeance, as stated in our Torah: **Remember what Amalek did to you - do not forget!**

[Page 317]

Parties and Social Institutions

Siedlce – The Zionist City

by F. Drumy (Popowsky)

Translated by Theodore Steinberg

In Poland, Siedlce had a reputation as a Zionist city. In the book "The Struggles of a Generation", Avraham Levinsohn wrote: "When the central committee of the organization "Ha–t'khiyah" was founded in Warsaw, the two branches–Siedlce and Bedzin–were the strongest and most active in Poland." Siedlce served the Zionist name very well, because that is truly what it was. All of Jewish communal life in Siedlce was imbued with Zionist activities. Through their representatives, the Zionist organizations played a leading role in communal economic and political areas, such as the city council, the Jewish communal organization, missions to the local government, interventions with the central government, both in czarist times in Petersburg or later with the Polish central government in Warsaw. Zionist cultural activities in Siedlce were rich and many–colored: schools, evening courses, libraries, lectures, readings, friendly conversations, discussion evenings, social gatherings, and sport clubs. The Zionists in Siedlce also made an impression on economic and social–philanthropic affairs and they were active in the associations and unions: the merchants' union, the small businessmen, the craftsmen's union, the credit associations, the merchants' bank, the lending bank,, the charity fund, the orphans' aid, the old people's home, the hospital, "TAZ," the soup kitchen, and so on.

Aside from all of these city and general foundations, the Zionist organizations had their own party groups, which took no second place to the similar community organizations.

[Page 318]

Everywhere the Zionists were the innovators and tone setters. They always offered encouragement and ideas, doing the work for its own sake, not for their personal benefit. Always the interests of the whole and of the individual as part of the whole took first place with them. Consequently their words and demands were always effective and persuasive. Even the strongest opponents of Zionism, when somehow they were in the majority, supported the Zionist proposals. The effect of the Zionist representatives was felt. not only in Jewish circles but also in the non–Jewish world, as in the magistrate's office and the city council.

It is appropriate to recall that when there was a small majority of the Agudah in the community council, they supported Zionist proposals and underwrote with larger sums the Hebrew Tarbus School, the evening courses, subsidized the Keren Kayemes for Eretz Yisroel, and gave travel money for each pioneer who made aliyah to Eretz Yisroel. In the Beis Medreshes, synagogues, and in many of the Chasidic prayer houses donations were given to the Keren Kayemes. In the Great Shul and Beis Medresh, speaking of Zionist matters was regarded as virtuous. On every Tamuz 20 in the city synagogue, a memorial for Dr. Herzl was organized and speakers were invited for the occasion.

The Zionist gathering always filled the halls. It was a special holiday in the city when someone from the central Zionist organization or a representative from Eretz Yisroel visited. For this reason the Zionist leaders were always prepared to come to Siedlice. One of the most frequent visitors was the chair of the Zionist Central Committee in Poland, a deputy in the Polish Sejm, the first interior minister in Israel–Yitzchak Greenbaum. When he left the train station, Jews would come out of the stores and dwellings, and each one told the other that Deputy Greenbaum has come to give a lecture. Always the hall was too small to hold all who would attend. The greatest events in the Zionist world, and in the general world, like the issuing of the Balfour Declaration in San Remo, the opening of the university in Eretz Yisroel, were holidays for the whole Zionist family and for each individual.

[Page 319]

Not everyone could participate in the celebrations that had been organized because no hall was big enough. Hundreds of people had to be turned away without even being able to stay in the hallways. Every level of the population took part in the holiday, because such were the adherents of the Zionist organization: men and women, learned Jews, Chasidim, opponents of Chasidism, the intelligentsia, merchants, craftsmen, workers, the rich and the young.

[picture caption: The Zionist conference in 1933 in Siedlce with the participation of Deputy Yitzchak Greenbaum]

The Zionist organization in Siedlce demonstrated amazing initiative and energy in creating agencies. It was indeed a pleasure to see ow the older, established Jews in the city always worked with the younger despite regular differences of opinion. But they always shared the same purpose, which united them all.

Thanks to this, there were no schism among the Zionist groups. The older members understood the desires of the young and were always full of enthusiasm for the devotion of the young to their work. The young members also knew to value the work of the older and always paid attention their words and their advice.

[Page 320]

In order to participate with the young people in their work, the older would join the young in their meetings for the Keren Kayemes, in the sale of Zionist membership cards, in working for the Tarbus, and so on. Gatherings for Keren Ha–Y'sod were strictly reserved for the elders.

We will present in chronological order the activities of the Zionist movement in Siedlce, beginning with the period of Hibbas–Tzion [an early Zionist movement, from the 1880's].

Early Secret Zionist Meetings in Czarist Times

Zionist work in Siedlce began at the time of the Khibas–Tzion movement. At that time, when the "Bilui" [a movement for agricultural settlement in Palestine] heeded the call "House of Jacob, come, let us go" and went to Eretz Yisroel, in 1884, soon after the Khibas–Tzion Conference in Katowice, in Siedlce, in the dwelling of R. Yitzchak–Nachum Weintraub, z"l, there was a secret gathering to establish a chapter of Chovevei Tzion. A secret meeting in czarist times risked being sent to Siberia. In addition, at that time it was also an enormously bold and revolutionary act to come together and speak about Eretz Yisroel, especially when these were not only young people but family men, Chasidic youth who sat and studied in the prayer houses and bees medreshes, the Intelligentsia, merchants, and craftsmen.

Among those participating in this secret gathering were: the instigator of the meeting–R. Yitzchak–Nachum Weintraub, Moshe Goldberg, R. David Eiziks, Yitzchak–Meir Rapaport, Yehoshua Goldfarb, Moyshe–Abba Eisenstadt, Shimon–Ber Minntz, Berl Kahana, Fishl Frenkel, Shmuel Zucker, and others. Every Friday evening, people would come to R. Yitzchak–Nachum's home to discuss current topics, to read a circular (if one had arrived) and to collect money for settling in Eretz Yisroel. Yitzchak–Nachum Weintraub was, in fact, the father of Zionism in Siedlce. From the first day when he had been married and come to Siedlce, in 1878, until 1942, when his spirit departed, he took every opportunity to demand and awaken the world to Zionism. At his every appearance, he would recall a Midrash from the Sages, a verse from Tanakh, and use the words of his rabbi, R. Shmuel Mahilewer, z"l.

[Page 321]

Also, when he studied in the Ger prayer house with R. Moyshe Goldberg and then R. Yisroel Yechiel's beis–hamedresh and even later in the great city beis–hamaedresh, he always referred to Eretz Yisroel and thus always incorporated Zionist thinking in the broader Jewish world.

When R. Yitzchak–Nachum Weintraub became a great merchant, he never gave up learning every day a page of Gemara and also found time to read books. He read both older and newer literature. He had understanding both for the Jew who studied religious texts and was observant and for the Jew who was totally secular. He often made the time to intervene and calm down the disputes between the observant and non–observant. He invested a great deal of labor and energy in getting the Siedlce administrator to give permission for opening a library in Siedlce, and the observant Jewish merchant, R. Yitzchak–Nachum Weintraub, supported the library with all his might.

He also loved exercise, which he worked at. Early every day, both in winter and summer, he went out happily and chopped wood as exercise.

He never turned down anyone who came asking him for a favor, like, for example, a good deed, offering security at a bank, which he often ended up paying, many thousands. This Zionist activist was attuned to human sorrows. He always listened when someone spoke to him from the heart, when people came to him to have an edict revoked, whether for everyone or for someone in particular. He devoted all his energy to it. We saw him at the time of the pogrom in Siedlce, together with R. Shimon–Ber Analik, z"l, Moshe Temkin, and secretary of the Jewish community council Czaczkes, when he went to intervene with the local government to stop the shooting as bullets were flying around his head.

After the First World War, when the Polish military justice system judged Jews who had been denounced by Poles for supposedly helping the Bolsheviks, R. Yitzchak–Nachum Weintraub hasted with R. Yisroel Gutgold, z"l, on Yom Kippur to the local authorities to counter the accusations.

[Page 322]

There was no organization that Yitzchak–Nachum did not help to get in order. For such things he always found time and was precise. Every event that took place in Jewish life, whether large or small, was known to him. Even in the Second World War, although he was quite old, beaten down and depressed by many misfortunes that befell him, he still wrote and collected material about Jewish life and death in that horrible time. Sadly, however, in the last moments before his departure for Treblinka, he destroyed those materials.

The Second World War, with its horrors, laid a heavy burden on this idealistic Zionist. He survived the first awful tragedy on September 2, 1939 when his daughter, Freyda Landau, together with the Jablon and Saltzman families were injured by the German bombardiers. It was so sad to see how the older Weintraub stood there by himself, digging to extricate them from under the ruins. The second horrible misfortune was the death of his grandson, the lawyer Yosef Landau with his wife and children. He himself later stayed with Shmuel Greenspan until the last action in November of 1942 in Gensz–Barki. Sadly he did merit fulfilling his lifelong wish of going to Eretz Yisroel and of carrying out the vow he made at the funeral of his son–in–law Mordechai–Meir Landau, z"l, that he would take his remains to Israel.

The First Zionist Activists in Siedlce

We have already mentioned the names of the participants in the first Zionist gathering in Siedlce. We should now also acknowledge their activities and personal lives: Moyshe Goldberg, came from Zamosc and became a Siedlcer through his marriage with the daughter of R. Shmuel Brukarsz, an outstanding householder in Siedlce. He studied with Y.N. Weintraub.

[Page 323]

Goldberg was a learned man and a Maskil, at the same time that he was a good merchant. Together with Yehoshua Goldfarb, a bank owner (who later founded the Kupat–Am Bank in Tel Aviv) Goldberg was named as a delegate to the Minsk Zionist Conference in 1903.

Moyshe–Abba Eisenstadt, an outstanding householder in the city, an excellent merchant, devoted Zionist and a son of the Berezan rabbi, Eisenstadt's two children, a son and a daughter who now live in Israel. The son Paltiel, until he left Siedlce for Warsaw, was active in all the Zionist goings–on in the city, and he was also one of the founders of the Hebrew evening courses.

Shmuel Zucker, a brick maker, a Rodziner Chasid and proud nationalistic Jew. For a time he was a member of the city council and sharply reacted to the demonstrations of Poles against Jews. He spent his last years in Paris with his children, and he died after being struck by a car. Also the other participants in the secret meeting were good Jews, charitable men and outstanding community workers.

At the time of the Hibbas–Tzion movement–a young Maskil, Yedidiah Reinman, collected money for the settlement in Eretz Yisroel. He had read a great deal about it, so he sat and taught about it in his Kalabiel Chasidic prayer house. After his marriage to the daughter of R. Michel Rosenberg of Brisk (in Lithuania), he spent some time in the wholesale grocery business in Siedlce. Later, he liquidated the business in in 1924 he made aliyah to Eretz Yisroel. A few years later he was struck by a passing motorcycle, hit his head, and died. Also his wife Sarah and their two sons, Yakov and Noach, came to tragic ends. His wife had devoted herself to disseminating Zionist ideas in a variety of areas.

After the First Zionist Congress in 1897, Zionism began to spread in the different strata of Siedlce and finally became a mass movement.

In 1900, Mordechai–Meir Landau arrived in Siedlce. There he married Frida Weintraub, the daughter of R. Yitzchk–Nachum and he settled in Siedlce. With his Jewish intelligence, worldly knowledge, and organizational abilities, he gave life to the Zionist efforts in Siedlce. His first job was:

[Page 324]

to arrange for a Zionist beis–hamedresh, where the worshippers were educated men and craftsmen. In this beis–hamedresh were: Avraham Wade, Shmuel Wurman, Yoself Zilberfaden, Meir Perla, and Paltiel Sluszne. These people were truly devoted Zionists. One time, when a representative of the central office came to hold a lecture in the city beis–hamedresh, the rabbi, R. Dov–Ber Analik, z"l, being a strong opponent of Zionism, organized a group of fishermen and butchers to come with him. One of them ripped down a chandelier and used it to strike the head of Y. Zilberfaden, who ended up spending a long time confined to his bed. This event had a powerful effect on the members of the Zionist minyan, who consequently worked even harder for the Zionist ideals and increased the ranks of the movement.

In the same year, an underground library was created. The organizers of the library were: the Zionist Yosef Rosenwasser, known as Yossl the Cantor's son or Yossl the Cigarette Man, Zev Tuchklapper, Asher Liverant, Yehoshua Goldberg, Moses Greenfarb, and others. Thanks to the efforts of R. Yitzchak–Nachum Weintraub with the local governor, in 1904 the library was made legal under the name of Weintraub's son–in–law, Mordechai–Meir and the community "Jewish Art, Ha–Zamir." In 1903, at the Pan–Russian Zionist Conference in Minsk (White Russia), Siedlce was represented by two delegates, Moshe Goldberg and Yehoshua Goldfarb.

"Ha–T'khiyah." Hebrew School and the Second Aliyah

In that same year, when the Ha–T'khiyah" was created in Warsaw, led by Yitzchak Greenbaum, Yon Kirshrat, Yosef Shprinsk, Zelig Weizman, M. Hurwitz, Yakov Alszwanger, Noach Priluczki, and others–a branch of the organization opened in Siedlce. It, along with the branch in Bedzin, was considered the strongest in Poland. The leaders of the Siedlce "Ha–T'khiyah" were: M.–Meir Landau, Moshe Zucker, Moses Greenfarb Peretz Kamar, the Niedszwidsz brothers, Dr. Moyshe Temkin, Yishayahu Zeydenzweig, and others. Temkin and Zeydenzweig now live in Israel.

[Page 325]

"Ha–T'khiyah" undertook "selling shekels" [a fund raising project for Zionist causes that involved the sale of coupons], leading meetings for the Keren Kayemes, and other Zionist efforts. In the organization's charter there was also a point about combatting pogroms. To this end, weapons were purchased in Warsaw. At the same time, a group of young people was organized: "Collective of Distributors of Shekels." The leaders were: Fishl Popowski, Elimelech Heinsdorf, Yakov Ridle, all of whom now live in Israel. The "shekels" were distributed among the young people and were to be paid off over the course of a year–a kopek each week. Also the Keren Kayemes collections were made by selling stamps (or collecting kopeks), which were distributed at weddings and other happy occasions.

In 1904, the directors of the beis–hamedresh decided to open a Hebrew school, which we have written about elsewhere. Gurewitsch and Kaplanski, the two teachers who were active in the school, were also active in Zionist affairs. Zionist ideology permeated all levels of the Jewish populace in Siedlce. Gurewitsch stood out. He was a sympathetic, idealistic young man who knew both older and more modern literatures and worked energetically among the masses. He clarified the most complicated matters so that the simplest person could understand. He spoke like a professor, quietly and distinctly, so that he exerted amazing influence on people. After a time, he left Siedlce and became the director of the Hebrew Gymnasium in Vilna.

That period marked a revival of all the Jewish parties. Aside from "Ha–T'khiyah" and "B'nei–Tzion," the "Poalei–Tzion" was also active, under the leadership of Moyshe Pachter, Sarah Kaplan, from Semyoticz, Gavriel Schlechter, M. Steinklapper, who was known as Mottl Chasid, David Urszech, and Lyuba Eisenstadt. The "Bund," too, was quite active. In 1906, at the time of the pogrom in Siedlce, the delegation to the governor was led by R. Yitzchak–Nachum Weintraub, z"l.

[Page 326]

In 1907, at the time of the Second Aliyah, the following went to Eretz–Yisroel: Menachem ben Hillel (Menachem Becker), the brothers Dr. Moyshe Temkin and the poet Mordechai Temkin, who still live in Israel), Peretz Kamar, Gavriel Schlechter, Menashe Goldzack, Sev Tuchklapper, Yakov Temkin and the Mechanic family, some of whom later returned to Siedlce. In the same year, the lawyer Hartglass settled in Siedllce, thanks to whom the strength of Zionism increased. He enlarged the ranks of the Zionists. Although lawyer Hartglass spoke little besides Polish, since he was raised in a Polish–speaking environment, and the older Jewish people understood little Polish, his lectures were well–received because of his simple and comprehensible way of speaking. He had a special effect on "Amcha," and he had particular success among the Chasidim. His later appearances in the city council, in Independent Poland, on behalf of the Jewish faction, always made an impression not only con the Jewish ranks but also among the Poles. Everyone saw in him a powerful, upstanding fighter who would never keep silent about an injustice, even if it affected a non–Jew.

It is interesting to convey the following about Hartglass' activities: During the First World War, a German policeman shot a dog on the street and ordered a Polish student to carry it away. Hartglass, to defend the student's honor, protested that the policeman had dishonored the student with such an order. Hartglass then taken before the war court, where Polish lawyers defended him and later thanked him. When Hartglass was elected to a position in the Polish Sejm and left Siedlce, the local zionists lost a great power. Now Hartglass in in Israel and is active in the Ministry of the Interior, where he heads the legal division.

In 1907, Mordechai–Meir Landau and others created in Siedlce a lending bank, which later took the name "Udzialowi Bank,' led by the Zionist Nehemiah Malin. He was also for many years the leader of the craftsmen. In the craftsmen's union these Zionists were active:

Shmjuel Wurman, Aharon Mardski, Yehuda Wade, Moshe Laterman, Meir Perla, Paltiel Szlushna, and Berl Srebnik, who who were so influential in the craftsmen's union that it nearly became a Zionist craftsmen's union.

[Page 327]

On August 13, 1915, during the First World War, the Germans took Siedlce. The Germans of that time should not be compared to the Germans of the Second World War. The entrance of the Germans troops brought improvements compared to the czarist regime. At that point, an age of creating and organizing a variety of community, cultural, and economic institutions began. Among others, at the end of 1915 the Hebrew evening classes were renewed. These courses attracted hundreds of young people from all levels of the Jewish population. Thanks to them, people began to hear Hebrew spoken on the streets of Siedlce. From time to time there were even social events and lectures in that language. There were also literary–musical evenings that attracted many attendees.

The first board of the Hebrew evening courses

P. Eisenstadt, A.Sh. Englander, Levi Gutgelt, Moshe Ackerman, the brothers Baruch and Mordechai, Yaffe, Asher Liverant, Kalman and Dinah Lewartowski, Esther Gutglick, Alter Geldman, Henech Salzman, the teachers Akiva Goldfarb and Zev Tuchklapper

[Page 328]

The founders of the Hebrew courses were: Paltiel Eisenstadt, Avraham–Shlomo Englander, Moyshe Ackerman, Esther Gutglick, Levi Gutgelt, Alter Geldman, Henech Salzman, Yehudah Tenenbaum, the Yaffe brothers, Asher Liverant, Dinah and Kalman Levartowski. Let me introduce the lives and activities of these generous Zionist who accomplished so much.

We have already mentioned Paltiel Eisenstadt when we spoke about his father Moyshe–Abba.

Avraham–Shlomo Englander, the son of a prosperous Zionistically–inclined man was of delicate health. Even so, when he was not confined to bed, he devoted his time to Zionist causes; he was a member of the Zionist committee, for a time was involved with the

Keren Kayemes, and also worked in the Warsaw central office. In Siedlce, Englander worked with the soup kitchen, was secretary of the community "TAZ," and finally worked as a bookkeeper in the Jewish hospital. For his whole life he hoped to go to Eretz Yisroel, but this was not allowed to him; he died from illness in the ghetto.

Moyshe Ackerman was born to Chasidic parents. His grandfather, a fervent Kotzker Chasid who was known as R. Matisyahu Cossack. Ackerman worked for a time for "He–Chalutz" in Warsaw, and he lived in Israel after 1924.

Esther Gutglick came from Brisk and arrived in Siedlce at the time of the First World War, when the czarist brigades drove the Jews out of Brisk.

Levi Gutgelt, born to very wealthy Chasidic parents, was the son of Yisroel and Sarah. When he was three, his father wrapped him in a tallis and carried him to cheer. When he began to study Chumash and later at his bar mitzvah, his family made big celebrations, meals for children, to whom gifts were given–bags filled with goodies, meals for Chasidim, who danced and rejoiced until late at night. His father hired a tutor for him at home, not wanting his son to study with other children. In addition to the religious tutor, Gutgelt hired for his son two secular teachers: Akiva Goldfarb for Hebrew and Moses Greenfarb for Russian and Polish. Under the direction of Moses Greenfarb, Levvi began to read secular books, understandably without the knowledge of his father. After reading through Mapu, Smolenski, Feierberg, Bialik, and others, he became interested in Zionism. he entered the circle of Zionists and became friendly with Mordechai–Meir Landau.

[Page 329]

Zionist ideology captivated him and later he became the very heart of Zionism in Siedlce. There was no gathering, no meeting, no conference in which he did not represent or argue for Zionism. He was always a member of the board and carried out many labors–and the credit for his work he always attributed to someone else.

Levi Gutgelt was also a man of books. He was the first reader of every newly published bookHe loved to stand in the library and advise everyone about the books they should read. He took time to distribute Hebrew books, and he rejoiced not over his own work but because a book would go home with someone. When the library wanted to purchase books, Levi was the buyer, because people knew that he would bring in the best.

Even in his later years, Levi remained young and always worked with young people, especially with schoolchildren, to whom he gave talks. For a time he taught in the Hebrew classes, and he was the leading speaker, or the only speaker, at every gathering. For a time he was an instructor at the Warsaw Central Committee of the Zionist organization. He was always the escort when a friend would make aliyah to Eretz Yisroel; he would travel with that friend to Warsaw in order to help. He would accompany him to the train station and rejoice that he wold have a friend in Eretz Yisroel. He was always true and generous to every friend.

Levi Gutgelt was also the actual editor of the "Siedlcer Vochenblat" from the founding of the paper. Although the official editor was Yechiel Graman, he soon left for Canada. Gutgelt often filled out the whole paper himself. It was rich in content and reacted to all the events in both Jewish and city life. He also wrote for the Warsaw daily "Heint;" he was one of the founders of the Tarbus School, and with extraordinary generosity he led the work in the educational institution.

[Page 330]

In his last years he was the leader of the "Training Department for Pioneer Aliyah" at the Palestine office in Warsaw. His wife was Tzalbah, the daughter of Yisroel Salzstein. They also had a successful daughter. When the Second World War broke out, Gutgelt prepared to go to Eretz Yisroel. He had already prepared all the necessary documents, but unfortunately he was not successful. Italy had entered the war, and exit from Poland was no longer possible. At the time of the German occupation, he was in Warsaw, as Hillel Zeidman explains in his book "The Days of the Warsaw Ghetto." The Germans expelled him from his home at 40 Elektoralna Street on Yom Kippur of 1942 and sent him to Treblinka. Thus was our dear and beloved friend tormented. He was the heart of Siedlce's Zionism.

Alter Geldman, the son of a scholar, a devoted Rodzinger Chasid, during the First World War, when the Russians left Siedlce, went with them. We know nothing of what happened to him.

Hence Saltzman, a student at the polytechnic, a son of a devoted old member of the Poalei–Tzion–Meir Saltzman.

Yehuda Tenenbaum. His father Yitzchak was a religion teacher in the schools. For a time he was secretary of the Jewish community organization, and his son was a member of "He–Chalutz." He participated in the Zionist projects and meetings. Tenenbaum now lives in Israel on the Azar Moshav.

The brothers Mordechai and Baruch Yaffe, grandsons of Yerucham Shatz from Brisk, came to Siedlce at the time of the First World War as refugees from Brisk. They took an active part in the Zionist and community work in Siedlce. Baruch was a powerful speaker and conducted arguments with the leftist groups in Siedlce. He was a good friend, but always with a serious demeanor. He left Siedlce and became an instructor for the Xionist Central Committee in Warsaw. In 1920 he went to the Zionist Conference in London. He remained there for a while and learned English. From London he made aliyah to Eretz Yisroel and there became the leader of the aliyah training in Tel Aviv.

[Page 331]

His brother Mordechai was always happy and generous to his friends. He participated in all Zionist projects and became active in community projects as well. He eventually had a position in the "Joint" and left Siedlce. Later he made aliyah to Eretz Yisroel and he lives there now in Kibbutz Giniger in Emek, together with his wife Shoshanah and their two sons.

A banquet to honor Mordechai Yaffe on his departure for Eretz Yisroel at the beginning of his work for the Joint

Asher Liverant, son of a Maskil and devoted Zionist–Meir Liverant. Together with Yedidiah Reitman, Asher worked for the Odessa committee, corresponding with Menachem Ussishkin and Yechiel Tchlenow. He was one of the founders of the Siedlce library and was for a long time the librarian. He knew all the readers and knew how to give all of them books according to their tastes. Asher Liverant was also the germanent secretary and recording secretary of the Siedlce Zionist organization. With the development of the Keren Kayemes, Asher Liverant actually took a leading role. He took care of pledges in the beis–medreshes, of distributing pledge cards for the benefit Keren Kayemes, and for gathering funds at weddings and other happy occasions. Asher Liverant was the publisher of the "Siedlcer Vochenblat" since its establishment in and from 1929 he was also the actual editor.

The Keren Kayemes committee led by Yehoshua Ackerman

The Keren Kayemes committee with Avraham Hertzfeld from Eretz Yisroel

[Page 333]

The whole financial burden of the newspaper was on him, although he was in terrible ill–health. In the paper's hardest times, he looked after it, paying no attention to his own material situation at home. His beautiful smile never left his face. He had a very sharp eye and always recognized what the paper should cover, and he immediately published it in the columns of the "Siedlcer Vochenblat." He always strove to be ready to fulfill his dream of making aliyah to Eretz Yisroel, but sadly he never could. In 1943, he died in the Jewish hospital from asthma.

Dinah and Kalman Levartowski, son and daughter of Akiva and Chava–Gittl; Chava–Gittl came from a powerful family. Her father, R. Shmuel Groynem, was a wealthy merchant, for forty years a gabbai in the great beis–medresh. Akiva Levartowski was Radzinerr Chasid whose rebbe was known as an opponent of Zionism, but he was influenced by his children and joined the ranks of Zionists. After a time he even became a member of the Zionist committee in Siedlce. Kalman, in his activities, was thoughtful and insightful. He achieved the goals he had established. He was one of the founders of "Tz'irei–Tzion" in Poland and he worked for "He–Chalutz." In 1920 he left for Israel and he worked on the roads in the Galilee. He became a teacher in the settlements and changed his name to Bar Levv. He wrote for "Kuntras" and, after 1927, for "Davar." He was member of the settlement "K'far Azar." He died in October of 1942, leaving behind a wife, a son, and a daughter.

Dinah was for a time a teacher of Hebrew in Siedlce and later lived in Warsaw. She lives now in Israel.

The Teachers of the Hebrew Classes

The teachers of the Hebrew classes at that time were: Akiva Goldfarb, Zev Tuchklalpper, and David Neimark, the son of a teacher, a Kotzker Chasid. He was very bright, not a Zionist for very long, having gone over to the "Bund." He wrote for the "Folks Newspaper" under the pseudonym "Aryeh." He lives now in America and remaining faithful to the Polish "Bund," he works for the "Forwards" and writes articles opposing Zionism for the Bundist press.

[Page 334]

Akiva Goldfarb was a lover and ardent follower of Hebrew. From early in the morning until late at night, whether at home, at school, in private talks, in Chasidic homes, in Maskilic homes–everywhere he went, he promoted the language. For him, learning Hebrew was an ideal, a holy labor. He had a wife and two children. Even though his wife was not well, he never demanded money for teaching, even though this was his only source of income. He was happy if people just learned Hebrew.

Zev Tuchklapper was one of the first members in the Zionist group in Siedlce. He had been in Eretz Yisroel, then later came back to Siedlce. He was a member of the committee of the cooperative loan society.

Among the Hebrew teachers of the classes were also: Har–Zahav, a great teacher, author of many books on pedagogy. He lives now in Israel. For many years he was the proofreader in the publisher of "Ha–Po'el Ha'Tz'ir." More recently he is in the "B'tei Avot" in Chulin. David Morgenshtern also had a little room where he gave private lessons in Hebrew.

Yehoshua Greenberg and Matisyahu Yaverbaum also tried to promote the Hebrew language. Yaverbaum's son Mordechai and his daughter Sarah are now in Israel. His second son Simcha was a solder in the Israeli army and was killed in a bus accident.

The Activities of "He–Chalutz" and "Tz'irei–Tzion"

In the same year as the creation of the Hebrew classes, "He'Chalutz" was founded in Siedlce. The founders were: Chaim Suchodolski, who was physically weak but spiritually strong, an energetic worker who was in Israel for a short time but returned to Siedlce; the student Gelbard, Adam Levita, Ada Barg ((Mrs. Barg lives now in Israel); Kimmel, who was busy with a variety of Zionist labors, giving lessons for "He–Chalutz Ha'Tza'ir," working for a time as secretary for Keren Kayemes, always yearning to go to Israel but killed by the German murderers; Mottele Greenberg, now in Israel; the student Engelman who gave lessons for "He'Chalutz" about Palestine.

[Page 335]

In 1919, the brothers Bunim and Berl Vyman, owners of a brewery in Roskosz, gave a large tract of land to "He–Chalutz," who created there the first training farm in the Siedlce area. Special actions were undertaken to work the farm. Many Zionists did their training there and then made aliyah to Eretz Yisroel. Along with the workers from "He–Chalutz," new strength was brought by : Alter–Boaz Huber, Melech Heinsdorf, Rochel Tenenbaum (from the home of Riback) and her husband Yehuda, all of whom now live in Israel.

The members of "He–Chalutz" also worked for the Petrikoser landowner, and in later years they formed a "kibbutz" of pioneers from the whole area who took on physical labor both in and outside of the city.

In 1916, Mordechai–Meir Landau organized the first Zionist committee in Siedlce, composed of the following: M.–M. Landau, Y.N. Weintraub, Akiva Levatowski, Yedidiah Reinman (the lawyer), Harglass, and others. In 1917, the educational society "Das" was formed by M. Landau. During the occupation of the First World War it conducted Hebrew–Yiddish folk schools and courses for adolescents.

In 1920 there were two conferences in Siedlce, one of general Zionists and one from Tz'Irei–Tzion. At the general Zionist conference there were delegates from the following cities: Lukow, Mezricz,, Biale–Podlosk, Radzin, Mard, Loszics, Sarnak, Semiatids, Noval–Minsk, and Kaluszin. Participants included the lawyer Alszwanger, Yosef Grawitzki, Y. Itkin (all of whom are now in Israel). A regional committee was elected headed by Berl Weinman (also now in Israel).

At the Tz'Irei–Tzion conference were representatives from all the aforementioned cities. From the central headquarters came Barzilai, who later drowned in the Sea of Galilee in Israel.

Both conferences and the elected committees worked together to strengthen the Zionist movement and the Zionist ideology in Siedlce.

[Page 336]

A Zionist conference in Siedlce in 1920 with the participation of representatives from the Zionist Central Committee in Warsaw

It is incumbent on us to recall one of the outstanding Zionists of that time–our comrade Ellchanan Levin. At first he had trouble speaking Yiddish, but thanks to his genial intelligence he quickly picked up the language and always had a large following at all his presentations, especially when he had discussions with leftist groups. Later, when he was already a lawyer in Warsaw, he was one of the chief leaders of the revisionists in Poland.

In 1922, the Zionist committee decided to publish a newspaper to serve as the community Zionist tribune in Siedlce. The first meeting about the newspaper involved about 20 comrades. Among them were: Yosef and Levi Gutgelt, Nehemia Malin, Yehoshua Akerman, A–Sh. Englander, Bunim Rotenberg, Yechiel Groman, Yehoshua Goldberg and–turning to those who are still alive–Fishl Popowski (now in Israel) and Shlomo Suchodolski (now in America). On the spot, the participants pledged 5 zlotys each, and the paper was given the name "Siedlcer Vochenblat." The first editor was Yechiel Groman and the publisher was Asher Liverant. We have written elsewhere about the role played by this newspaper in the Jewish life of Siedlce.

[Page 337]

In the same year, Dr. M. Shleicher came to Siedlce. He appeared just at the moment when some of our leading personalities had left Siedlce. He was very useful to the movement. For a long time he headed the Zionist organization, was its representative on the city council and the community council, took part in all fundraising activities for Keren Ha–Y'sod, Tarbus, and so on. He devoted great energy to health concerns among Jewish children in Siedlce's schools, was the chair of "TAZ." From Poland he went to Israel and now lives in Haifa.

The Activities of the Tarbus School

In 1926, a Hebrew Tarbus School opened in Siedlce under the direction of the Zionist Committee. We will devote a special chapter to that, but I will recall here several comrades who took an active role in the work for the school:

Asher Orszel, the chair of the school trustees, came from a religious Chasidic family. He himself was a Chasid and traveled to the Parisow rabbi. He was intent on Talmud study, but he also read secular books. He managed a banking house along with his brother Naftali Neugoldberg, and later he was a bulk iron merchant.

A conference of Tz'irei–Tzion in 1920

[Page 338]

Still later he had a factory that made iron plows. Despite his business and factories he devoted much time to community work: he was the founder and director of the "merchants' bank," for many years the director of the community organization, a councilman in the city council and a member of the governmental tax appraisal office. In the tax office, he defended Jewish interests. Many times he would leave his own businesses and hasten to defend a Jew against harsh appraisals. It was simply a pleasure to be in the presence of and hear his words and clever speech. Of all his community labors, the school always took first place.

Yehoshua Ackerman was a devoted Zionist acolyte who came from the Kotzker Chasidim. With true Chasidic fervor he took up Zionist and community work, often to the neglect of his own private affairs.

Yosef Gurgelt, son of R. Yisroel, devoted many years to the development of the school. For a long time he was in charge of its finances, always being sure to pay the teachers on time, even if there were not sufficient funds in the bank. He was also active in the work of Keren Kayemes.

Moyshe Yom–Tov, son of a Jewish grocer, R. Berish, was a member of "He–Chalutz Ha–Tza'ir" and worked on their training programs. He was also active in the league of workers for Eretz Yisroel, but the largest part of his time went to the Tarbus School.

Henoch Ribak and Sholem Salzman, both merchants, prayed in the Chasidic prayer houses and had an extraordinary interest in the work of the school, which they held in high esteem.

Fishl Popowski (Drumy) (now in Israel–Ed. Note: also the author of this chapter!) was one of the founders of the Tarbus School. Popowski worked for ten years as an instructor for the central office of Keren Kayemes in Poland. In Siedlce he was a member of the community council steering committee and for many years a member of the steering committee of "Ha–Zamir." He devoted all of his time to a variety of Zionist activities and undertakings. He took part in open presentations.

We must also recall Dr. Bergman, who was very active in different Zionist labors. At the time of Hitler's Invasion, he rescued himself and came with the Polish troops to Israel. His wife, son, and daughter also came to Israel. His son fell in the War of Independence, and the parents and their daughter went back either to Poland or Germany.

[Page 339]

In 1932 in Siedlce, was founded "He–Chalutz–Ha–Clal–Tzioni." The founders were: Yitzchak Kaspi, Baruch Alberg, A.Sh. Englander, Ridel, and others. "He–Chalutz–Ha'Clal–Tzioni," like other Zionist youth organizations, excelled in collecting for the Keren Kayemes. He taught Hebrew, Zionist history, and matters dealing with Palestine.

When Yitzchak Kaspi left Siedlce and went to Israel in 1933, "He–Chalutz–Ha–Clal–Tzioni" was taken over by Elimelech Feinsilber and Avraham Friedman. With their cultural activities they maintained the Zionist youth, giving talks about Zionist history and Palestine. Friedman and Feinsilber had worker earlier in various Zionist activities.

And finally, we should praise those comrades who at different times took part in all Zionist actions and gatherings. They excelled particularly in organizing the bazaars for Keren Kayemes, as well the activities for Keren Ha–Y'sod, and they participated in the development of the Tarbus School.

Their names are: Miriam Szibuczi, Esther Salzman, Puah Rabinowicz, Sarah Radzinski, Chava Dame, Heniek Wyman, Tzlova Saltzstein, Chava Wakstein, Radashinski, Beilah Finkelstein, Rochel Garfinkel, and for many years Genya Vyman and Yehudis Kwiatek, now in Israel, and many others whose names I have forgotten. All of these comrades whom I have recalled, through their activities gave Siedlce the wonderful nickname of the "Zionist City." Sadly, most of them were killed by the Germans and were unable to fulfill their dream of going to Israel.

[Page 340]

In the Shade of the Kalina Trees
as a Souvenir of My Beautiful Hometown

by Dr. M. Temkin

Translated by Mira Eckhaus

"A man is nothing but a pattern of the landscape of his homeland"
S. Tchernichovsky

The praise of Polish Judaism is not similar to that of Lithuanian Judaism in terms of the Torah greatest and the God-fearing. Nor as that of German Judaism in the abundance of culture and talent for action, or that of Galician Judaism in terms of the state men and the wise scholars, but in the spirit of great innocence, in the holy spirit, which bordered on nobility, as much as exile and the diaspora can be identified with nobility.

Diaspora Judaism had different faces, just as the lands of its dispersal were different: the landscape, the climate, the forests and rivers, the vegetation, the appearance of the sky and the earth, and especially the forms of life and economy, are what left their mark on the glorious tribes of Judaism, because the beauty of a place is for its inhabitants. The human genius sucks from the "locus" genius, in the words of the poet: a man is nothing but a pattern of the landscape of his homeland".

The evidence to that is the difference between the Polish Judaism and the Galician Judaism, despite the family bonds between them. The main characteristic difference between them relates to in the connection of Poland to the extensive Russia, which gave it a material welfare and abundant livelihood. The prosperity of the Polish Judaism a generation ago came out of the abundance and welfare that enabled the Jews of the towns to stagnate, to engage in Torah, in Hassidism, in the correction of the soul and the treats and also to alienate to the rationalism, the education and the wisdom of the gentiles that chewed the original vast Judaism tree and to adhere to the tradition and morality of the fathers, that bound them together in courageous ties, religious ties and the racial destiny. While Galician Judaism lived in poverty and hardship. In Shibush (Buchach), says Agnon, the hardship did not stop from Isru chag Passover until Mar Chesvan", a sister to the poverty of the Lithuanian Judaism, that the "Krupnik" did not stop "from Passover to Passover" (Shetzky).

[Page 341]

The landscape in Poland was also more abundant with trees, forests and rivers, and the contact with the local people was more reciprocal and more humane, and no doubt all of these things had an impact on the lifestyle and the worldview of the Polish Jews. We can find a proof to this in the Hassidism of Poland which was, under the influence of the factors listed above, more noble, gentle and more spiritual, less centralized than that of the Galician Hassidism (Chortkov). The Polish Hassidism referred to the general Israeli population, it was Internal, mental and universal with a vision (Kotzak).

In the Polish town we may have not found the Baserbian people nor the sharp Lithuanian rationalism nor the Galician cunning. There was, however, a precious warmth, the warmth of simple craftsmen with houses, but of an elite race, Torah scholars and innocent men of action. In Galicia, which was granted early political liberation and was subordinate to the progressive kingdom of Austria, no favorable conditions were created for the development of cultural and educational organizations. Poland was the cradle of the modern Hebrew and Yiddish literature; Warsaw was the center of the spiritual activity of Polish Jews. Writers and activists of general value, who spread their ideas across the border, also grew up in Poland and therefore, the distribution of education among the Jews of Poland was different from that in all the Diaspora. In Poland they did not use the education and the secular studies to make a living. In Poland they studied secular studies for their own sake, as they studied Torah for its own sake and not for their benefit, in order to obtain a diploma and welfare, since Polish Jews were generally alienated to education and to the rationalization of life. Therefore, in the Polish Judaism there was no war of fathers and sons, as was in other countries. The transition from holy to secular studies was a natural process that time caused, without severe crises, without hatred and mental difficulties. A guy who became a heretic, cut his payot and capote, walked with girls in the moonlight, had hallucinations about love and did not leave the "stibl" nor the customs of the Hassidim. He did it out of kindness and love of life, he did it for heaven's sake, without hatred and teasing, the old and the new co-existed with enough room to both.

All these actions derived from innocence and loyalty. The cunning and deceit, the history of the life in exile, as if they had been missed, there was no discrimination in their lives. The Hassidic temperament of innocent and truth was introduced into the education, the new tools were filled with old Jewish content.

One fact out of many that I remember is that when I was ten, my mother took me to a wedding at her brother-in-law the Admor in Lublin (Akiva Eiger's grandson). I was already infected by the influence of outside books. Nevertheless, the wedding, which was held in splendor and greatness, made a great impression on me. A spectacle that is all majestic, warmness and devotion. I saw there followers, extremely rich, who danced enthusiastically with the poor and needy, who worn torn and worn out cloths.

[Page 342]

My mother told me about Rabbi Eiger: Once his only daughter was very ill, so his wife came in on Yom Kippur's eve, to arouse him to ask for mercy on her. He answered her angrily: "On Judgment Day, when all the people of Israel have a home of mercy, will I stand and ask for mercy only for my daughter?!"

Such was the generation in Poland. And such were the ancestors of Judaism there. And from this tree grew a new root, a first generation of resurrection and freedom, sons who are loyal to their race, innocent young men who carried in their hearts a kind of passion of holiness and anxiety for precious things, with no purposefulness, who were the foundation and the root of the life in the Diaspora.

This first generation did not disappoint, they were innocent people then. From the moment they became knowledgeable and recognized that the place of a national and Zionist Jew is in Israel and not in the diaspora, they arose and made an Aliya 45 years ago.

The period also helped. This was the period of the awakening of the masses in the vast territory of the Kingdom of Russia, then the first shocks of the disintegration of the tyrannical regime were heard, and the movement of the masses that awoke from centuries of stagnation. The "Bond" appeared on the Jewish Street, which served as the mouth of the poor and the common people and pretended to ease their suffering and find a solution to "the trouble of the Jews" in the ways that led to their assimilation. It did not recognize "the trouble of Judaism" and ignored it. It was a movement of assimilation coming from below, similar to many assimilation movements coming from above. But it was wrapped in hollow rhetoric of materialist dialectics, a kind of a movement at that time, without continuing to weave aspirations. Dreams and longings of the people, without a universal general foundation of all the Jews wherever they are, and therefore did not escape the decree of total destruction and passed from the world, like other assimilation movements. With no name and remnant.

I mention the appearance of the "Bond" in Poland not because the "Bond" was a landmark for the social movement, but because its appearance was a big business, with lots of noise and commotion, which characterizes mass movements. However, the "Bond" was preceded by the Enlightenment and the Zionist movement, especially among the youth.

The desire for education and knowledge among the youth was great. They learned languages, read books alone and in groups and especially in the beautiful city garden early in the morning. A library was founded with the assistance of Mr. Landau, which provided books for those who were thirsty for God's word. In fact, it was a Zionist activity, perhaps unknowingly, because every spiritual and social awakening in those days was fluent in the national channel, and its expression tools were necessarily the circumstances, Hebrew and a Zionist action.

In this innocent period of precious reality, which was the spring term for social ideas and the spring of adolescence, hearts were trained for deeds and actions.

And one day new faces appeared in our city, two Lithuanians, who were marvelous in our eyes.

[Page 343]

One was named Gurevitz and the other Kaplansky and they spoke Hebrew in a Spanish accent. These were the first swallows, the first Hebrew teachers, who opened a "revised room" in our city and they breathed life into our simplistic dreams, and hence the practical Zionist affair in our city began. Because almost all the Jews of the Polish towns were Zionists, especially the masses, by nature, but it was an abstract Zionism, devoted to the heart and now became a reality. It was so great that even a young man like Yoel Mastboim, who was checking other beliefs at the time, would sometimes come to us and tried speaking "Hebrew".

These two people were the living spirit in all the Zionist enterprises, they held history courses and held Hebrew talks, trips, and the connection between the Zionist youth from different places of the city became stronger, which was previously avoided due to distancing and lack of common interest. The highlight was the public gatherings in the synagogue, which were held in great numbers of participants and splendor. It seems that the authority has looked favorably on this new movement of Jews and convened public assemblies, which it has prevented from other movements, and maybe it has seen it as a kind of thunder of the revolution that hovered in the air. The influence of that Hanukkah ball was great, a Zionist ball that opened with the sounds of "Hatikvah" played by wind instruments, with the authority of the government, despite the community leaders, who were mostly haters of Zion, except for Mr. Weintraub, who was prone to Zionism in public.

"Hatchiya" Association was founded, which changed its name with the development of the movement to "Zion's Youth". A meeting center was opened, a kind of a club, first at the Kahwa cafe and then at Peretz Komar, who was also one of the first Zionists in the city who made an Aliya to Israel, although his consciousness was probably not yet matured and he deviated from the Zionist path, he settled in Egypt and the connection with him ceased. Then began the period of speeches, the traveling Zionist emissaries, who visited the cities of Israelis in the diaspora. The best of them were Yosef Shprintsak – of "Zion's Youth", who came from Warsaw to make young people Zionists, and in parallel with the "Bond" there was a split in the Zionism of the youth and our city began to fill with emissaries of "Poalei Zion", the buds of Zionist socialism, that Gabriel Shlechter, who was a honest and simplistic guy, was their leader. At that time, we often saw in our city, strange hairy young fellows, a clear sign of revolution in those days, that spoke about complicated matters. I wonder if one of the listeners or even the speaker himself understood something in this complex issue. It was a kind of dialectic for the sake of dialectics, a kind of a quibble without any real scientific basis. Among these speakers, I remember Ben Zion Yedidiya, a black-haired, lean-fleshed man with a crown of curls, who was a great speaker.

[Page 344]

Following this Zionist activity, other social enterprises were also founded, the Habima Amateur Band, which staged the play" scattered and dispersed" {Mefuzar v'mefurad") by Shalom Aleichem. Literary parties were also held: Y.L. Peretz, Menachem and Bal Makhsoves honored us with a visit in our city and read their works to a large audience, full of admiration.

In this period of the beginning of the awakening of the movements, of liberation of general forces from their indifference, the areas were still blurred. The foundations of the organization were still loose and non-binding. Even the day-to-day Zionist work, which was mainly focused on fundraising, did not satisfy the hunger for action. There was another group with Rosenwasser, the elder of the Zionist community at its head (see the attached photo here), which was engaged in advanced training, reading literature, members' conversations, trips and in social work. It founded "Orphanage", which operated for several years and served as a center for public affairs, and was a place for the investment of social vigor.

This period was also saturated with a lot of explosives. The Polish Socialist Party (PPS), which included many Jewish members, chose, as part of partisan tactics, the field cities as a cushion for terrorist action against the Russian government, and our quiet city, which stagnated, became an inferno of assassinations and bombings of those in power. The Russian bureaucracy in the remote provinces of Poland was known for its hatred of the Jewish population. In general, it was more convenient for it to be redeemed by the Jews and to impose the responsibilities for the terror on them. For three days and three nights, the Jewish community was in danger of extermination. The army, and especially the Wahlini battalion, who camped in the city, took over the city, massacre, robbed and abused and also set buildings on fire. And even cannons were used as an excuse for Jewish revolt. Forty-one Jews were killed and hundreds were injured in this pogrom, the first in Poland, which was the protectorate country.

The good ones in the youth have come to the conclusion, that there is no existence for the people in the diaspora. The first ones to make an Aliya to Israel adjacent to the pogrom, were Simcha Rubinstein, Zvi Glibter from Zamosc (who studied at the gymnasium and did not finish his studies) and myself. Rubinstein and I turned to farming, because as mentioned, we were innocent and even before the 'Hapoel Hatzair" party were founded, it was clear to us that here in Israel, we had to change our lives and make a living from the land and not from other occupations.

[Page 345]

Therefore, we went directly from the ship to the Galilee, to Sejera, which had then a reputation because of a group of agricultural men, who worked there and were headed by Eliezer Ben Shochat. And he was the one who led us in the middle of a Saturday night, so we will not miss even one day of work, to the Moshava Melachamiya and arranged us for agricultural work for the peasants. Rubinstein could not do this job and moved to Jerusalem and entered the "Ezra" seminary and I continued working until the summer. When I had several times a fever, I was advised to go to Judea.

The first Zionist group:
Row above from the left: Moses Greenfarb, Simcha Rubinstein, Niadoshviadosh, Kahana, Tuvklapper
Second row from the left: Niadoshviadosh, Genya, Moshe Temkin, Himelfarb, Rossenwasser, the photographer Rozovski,
Mrs. Ladau, Mrs. Weidenzweig, Berl Mintz

[Page 346]

Pioneering Youth–Movement in Siedlce

by David ben Yosef (Pasowski)

Translated by Theodore Steinberg

Almost all of the Zionist youth groups in Poland had chapters in Siedlce. I will here focus on a few of these youth groups that played a definite educational role in Siedlce Jewish life.

The "He–Chalutz" began its activities even during the First World War, in 1916, and even then busied itself with pioneers of the aliyah to Eretz Yisroel. They set up preparatory opportunities in farming, where the young people were occupied with productive physical labor. Then they established the first pioneering kibbutz in the village of Patrkaz and at the farm of the Vayman brothers, in Roszkosz.

One of the chief functions of "He–Chalutz" was to remove Jewish youth from worthless endeavors and introduce them to healthy, constructive work. Even during war time, the first pioneers from Siedlce went to Eretz Yisroel.

"He–Chalutz" in Siedlce, as in all the Jewish settlements in Poland, grounded Zionist thought in concrete deeds. Scores of Jewish young men and women went up to Eretz Yisroel thanks to the multifaceted educational work of "He–Chalutz." Hundreds of Siedlcers who find themselves today throughout Israel in different important positions in cities and towns owe thanks to "He–Chalutz," to which they belonged, for through "He–Chalutz" they prepared themselves to come to the land.

[Page 347]

Let me also take the opportunity to mention our Siedlcers, pioneering activists, who could not manage to come to their longed–for land and who were bestially killed by the Nazis. I recall one of the most active participants, one of the founders of the He–Chalutz movement in Poland, my friend and companion–Moshe Yom Tov; my friend Benjamin Charney, one of the last pioneer leaders before the outbreak of the war; he died from hunger in Russia; David Furayter, one of the most active leaders in the pioneering socialist youth movement "Freiheit–Dror."

Those of us who are still alive remember the invigorating activism of the pioneering youths, the imposing intensity of the "Tel Chai" academics, with the participation of the choral and dramatic organizations, with their staged recreations of life in Eretz Yisroel; the regional pioneer conventions, the convention of 1930, with the participation of a delegation from the Histadrut in Eretz Yisroel (Siedlce was the center of the Podlasie circle and there was located the Podlozher regional committee of all the Zionist organizations); the pioneering expedition to the village of Krynytsi, to the court of the Jewish landlord Tsinaman. I recall the overflowing, enthusiastic voices at this gathering, the hora dancing around the bonfire in the woods until late at night and the loud singing of Hebrew songs, whose echo carried as far as the houses in the surrounding villages.

Committee of "He–Chalutz" in Siedlce in 1930–33
In the middle is chairman and secretary of the Podlasie district committee, David Posowski (now Yosef ben Yisroel)
[trans. note: he is the author of this chapter.]

[Page 348]

In "He–Chalutz" were organized all of the Zionist youth groups working for Eretz Yisroel. On the committee were representatives from "Ha–Shomer Ha–Tza'ir," "Freiheit–Dror," and "He–Chalutz Ha'Tza'ir." Each group had its own meeting place and conducted multifaceted cultural and educational efforts.

I must also recall the important activities related to mutual aid that enabled comrades to journey to Eretz Yisroel. The "Keren He–Chalutz" created significant funds and underwrote needy olim to Eretz Yisroel. For the olim, these funds were a salvation, because the journeys to Eretz Yisroel were quite difficult, and there were no agencies or "Joint" to help with the expenses.

* * *

Among the youth groups working for Eretz Yisroel, the chief one was "Ha–Shomer Ha–Tza'ir". "Ha–Shomer Ha–Tza'ir" was a purely scout movement that had a magical attraction in its appearance, with its special uniform, accoutrements, and symbols of "chazak v'amatz" [Hebrew for "be strong and of good faith"]. This movement truly enrolled in its ranks the best of the Jewish youth.

"He–Chalutz" with the author Nathan Bistritcki on his visit to Siedlce

[Page 349]

"Ha–Shomer Ha–Tza'ir" in Siedlce was already organized after the First World War–in 1921. The chief founder and leader was Herschel Slushni, and the other leaders were Malkeh Levin, Yehudah Liverant, David Yom Tov, Bunim Czarnebradeh, and others. "Ha–Shomer Ha–Tza'ir" focused on the school youth from the middle school and some from the Folks School. Their nicely decorated meeting places–referred to as nests–were transformed into welcoming homes for brothers and sisters who were prepared to help each other and live and work together. I remember the silent, secret collections of money to help comrades who were not able to pay their school tuitions or to buy books, as well as other forms of aid, which was one of the foundations of this movement.

Impressive were the Lag B'Omer celebrations; the proud marching of the Shomer young people in columns through the streets of the city called forth great respect, even from the non–Jewish population, and enthusiasm from Siedlce's Jewish inhabitants. It was really something to be proud of and to stand by.

Before my eyes stands the little street by Yehoshua Levin's mill where on Lag B'Omer thousands of Jewish young people gathered with joyful pennants and from there march to the Raskosher Woods, where special pavilions had been set up, along with a kitchen. People sang and danced. It was as busy as a beehive. Parents stood around and watched, getting great pleasure and pride from them, and at twilight–the march back to the city in a procession with the singing of pioneer songs from Eretz Yisroel.

"Ha–Shomer Ha–Tza'ir" with its leader and founder Mr. Herschel Slushni

[Page 350]

Every summer, summer–colonies would be organized in the Polish villages around Siedlce. These had a purely scout character and impressed one with their aesthetic appearance and their fine, precise discipline, order, and distinctive teachings, which promoted a longing for Eretz Yisroel.

One of the last summer colonies of Ha–Shomer, which I visited as a guest, was in a Polish village between Siedlce and Zhelekow. The leader of this colony was Yosef Kabtzan, who lives today in Israel. "He–Chalutz Ha–Tza'ir" was a recruiting organization for young people before "Ha–Shomer." [trans. note: The text says "before 'He–Chalutz,'" but I think he means before "Ha–Shomer."]. This movement, which was under the direction of "He–Chalutz," did real education work for Eretz Yisroel. "He–Chalutz Ha–Tza'ir" organized a number of social events, meetings, discussions, and entertainments for young people.

תרצ"ג- 1933

העולים של ההסתדרות ,,החלוץ" צשדלץ

The pioneer emigrants to Eretz Yisroel in 1933

[Page 351]

Members of "Ha–Po'el" on bicycles bound for Eretz Yisroel

In "He–Chalutz Ha–Tza'ir" were found young people, mostly from the Workers Circles and from the "Amcha" families, middle–class homes. In that organization, people were not fussy about who their friends were, and it did not matter which schools they attended. Family pedigree played no special role…One could meet in the ranks of "He–Chalutz Ha–Tza'ir" students from Talmud Torahs, Folks Schools, and young journeymen, apprentices in various trades. "He–Chalutz Ha–Tza'ir" organized conferences and summer colonies and over all conducted multifaceted activities in all domains.

* * *

The Zionist–socialist–pioneer youth organization "Freiheit–Dror," which activities similar to the other pioneer organizations, had its own sports club, "Ha–Poel," which was famous in Poland. In its trip to Eretz Yisroel on bicycles, organized by "Ha–Poel" in Poland in 1932, several Siedlcer sportsmen from "Ha–Poel," members of "Freiheit–Dror," went along. Later on both organizations united with "He–Chalutz Ha–Tza'ir" into a single entity.

[Page 352]

All of these Zionist youth groups together in the time of their glory–from 1930 to 1932–numbered about 2,500 members; about 75 percent of them wanted to go to Eretz Yisroel–a significant factor in the life of the Jewish youth of Siedlce.

The Zionist youth groups would participate in different fundraisers, for Keren Kayames, Karen Ha–Yesod, KPA"Y [Kupat Po'alei Eretz Yisrael], and others. There would be competition among the groups to see who could collect the most and who could take first place.

The strength of the Zionist–pioneer youth could be determined by the solemn parades in closed ranks through the streets of the city at the times of special Zionist demonstrations that happened from time to time at various opportunities.

I remember the colossal and impressive protest demonstration and people's parade in 1929 as a protest against the August unrest in Eretz Yisroel. The line of demonstrators extended for kilometers, over several streets, and it demonstrated that Zionism was a force in Siedlce. Understandably, the chief participants were the Zionist youth groups.

Pioneers from Siedlce participated in pioneer training throughout Poland. And there was such a training center there as well.

Unfortunately, more than once people had to manage or accommodate parents who were obstinate and would not permit their children to go to the preparatory camps and even more opposed travel to Eretz Yisroel. Tragic situations played out among those whose parents would not agree. I have comrades and friends here in Israel whose parents would not write to them and remained angry with them because they left home and went to Eretz Yisroel.

The idealistic pioneer youth, however, were not deterred by hardships. They left their homes and families and came to the old–new Jewish homeland. Thanks to them, the ground was prepared for an independent Jewish state, which is the gathering spot for the remnant who survived Hitler's extermination.

[Page 353]

Pioneers from Siedlce at a preparatory camp in 1925
Top row in the middle is Moshe Yom–Tov, leader of the Siedlce
pioneers

Committee of Poalei–Tzion and "Dror Freiheit."
In the middle is the emissary from Eretz Yisroel, Eliezer Grawinsky

He–Chalutz Ha–Tza'ir with Yehuda Liverant

Pioneers on an outing

The committee of Freiheit

Committee of the Workers Branch

[Page 354]

Memories and Reflections

by Eliezer Bar-Haim (Bernholtz), Haifa

Translated by Mira Eckhaus

(In memory of the pioneering youth movements in our city)

With singing and drums, filled with all - good, a shoe is headed to the wall,
We will bring a handful of golden hearts and dreams
With singing we will carry them in jugs of bloody youth
And the first clusters of lives in baskets of love,
Everything is a gift for the battle and to sanctify Masada!
Open, wall, the gates of your empty archives
And we will preserve in them the grain of our lives to change the battle
For Masada's fields are desolated and are swords-stricken,
And who knows how long the battle will last and how long the days of siege will be
And until the coming of the seven years, until the time of the rains
And dew will fall night after night on an unsecured land
Until the victory scythe will reap the field blessing safely -
Accept the first fruits of our lives – provisions for your hungry warriors
And the springs of our youth - to your thirst!

I. Lamdan – "Masada"

How can the memory of the boys and girls of our unforgettable city, of the young generation, of the fresh and pure pioneer tribe, who without account and "purpose" prepared for the long journey, for the long-awaited leap to tomorrow, to the longed-for land, in which it sought to fulfill its dreams?

The pioneering youth movements were the ones that marked Siedlce, the vibrant city, on its organizations and its parties, with a characteristic mark and a special charm. It was the pioneering youth movements that formed its image. The city of Siedlce did not particularly bring out great leaders. But collectively it had the human material and was great in its quality, and especially the youth, in both early childhood and old age.

In reality at that time, every guy and every girl, every pioneer was like Don- Quixote, seeking adventure and hardship, wandering and dreaming, seeking the truth, having morals and was a fighter for honesty.

[Page 355]

Many may wonder about the attempt I am making, to put on paper and direct my words to distant close friends and remind them of forgetfulness, even though the past is not so far away, it was only yesterday ...

I know the obstacles that stand in this way, I know, that over the years that passed, strangeness and opacity accumulated; After all, we have all managed to grow up and maybe even grow old and not just biologically ...

I know how difficult it is to say, express and in particular write about these topics. And on the other hand, how difficult it is to listen, hear and even read it. But there is no choice, we have to cry and remember those who are missing, the boys who died prematurely, who were an important part of our lives ...

Well, we will put their memory on paper, and I do believe, that there are those who still hear the things that come from the heart, and that there is still attentive ear and it is possible to carve a window to the hearts.

* * *

Because of my age, I was not one of the founders of the youth movement in our city. I joined when everything was almost done, I was only privileged to be among those who continued its operation and to some extent I was able to be among those who still "didn't make up their mind". Well, how was the beginning?

It has been said by the fire: "A number of boys and girls who were still studying, began to ask for the paths of their lives. The atmosphere at school was suffocating. The environment, the house, the street, the company of the adults – emptiness ruled everything. The routine was everywhere. Boredom was all around".

At first, we didn't have a clear and final goal, we grew up as a plant in the field. In our hearts there were expectation and searching for the truth, we were completely independent, we strived for the sun and the beauty, the scouting accompanied us, but did not satisfy us.

As a mighty stream of water, the rebellion erupted, the vibrant youth overflowed and thus we adopted the famous rebellion song of D. Shimonovich:

"Do not listen, my son, to the morality of a father
And to the doctrine of a mother do not hear,
As father's morality is: "line to line" ...
And mother's doctrine is: slowly, slowly" …

And so, in a storm of experiences, indecisions and constant searching, we found the path in life, the pioneering immigration, the self-fulfillment, which was the perfect blend of human redemption from the chains of the current regime, along with the creative and constructive Zionism that promised to build and to be built within it. "... we found the Zionism for ourselves.

[Page 356]

Not a Zionism that told others to make an Aliya and build! We rebelled against the "official Zionism" (and this was the secret of the success of the pioneering youth movements). In this it was the revolutionary and the innovator. Such was its freshness and the magic of its soaring dream, and the strength of its war in reality, in which it made its way to tens of thousands of youths, because it was full of longing and aspirations. It dared to qualify and reach its full goal through enormous obstacles, rebelled against the dear parents, the school, the Jewish Street, the official Zionism. It created the training in inhuman and cruel conditions, and sometimes even in loneliness. It climbed and broke the siege ...

* * *

And who does not remember the great moment of the youth movement, Lag BaOmer day. The poet that can describe the experience of the boys and the girls on this day has not been born yet! Fear and trepidation held us several weeks before the holiday. After all, the preparations for the day were sufficient, but the heart was full of fear. And the nature was watching too ... As freemen we walked down the street. We did not march, we hovered in the air and all the Jews of the city celebrated the new-old holiday. The sky looked different. The sun seemed to come out of its pouch. The birds sang a new song, the trees looked as if they were praying for our safety. The atmosphere in the city was of a holiday. The eyes were glowing and the faces of the people rejoiced. We simply brought the Land of Israel into the midst of the diaspora and turned it into...

I remember when we would get to the nature and the forest. And at once a great camp arose and was created. A camp of small and large tents and within it waving the blue-and-white flag. We left the walls and the dust of the city. And the march? After all, we walked with one breath, with one heartbeat, at a uniform pace that is unparalleled! That day we decided on our future, we swore to overcome the obstacles, to come out of the darkness into a great light.

And in the evening the fire was ignited, a red flame rose and everyone added a branch and listened to the "conversation" of the burning fire, and then with complete spontaneity the singing erupted. A great singing, about the land, about the constructive brothers and the illegal immigrants to Israel, about the torments of redemption, about conquests and struggles.

And without noticing, the hands joined and a circle was formed. The hearts thrilled and we were all suddenly dancing. What a wonder! What a dance! What a rhythm! What a Hassidic enthusiasm! All the hearts merge into one soul. All the dancers - one body, a cohesive camp.

And when we returned home, lots of Jews - children and bent old men – looked at us with excitement, they felt with all their senses, that we are the future, we are the wall, they felt these are the steps of the redeemer Messiah, we herald the gospel of resurrection and victory, we are the symbol of the fulfillment of the longings of all the generations for two thousand years ...

[Page 357]

Then the knees will tremble ... for we know that the moment is sacred: in our soft and young hands the waving flag has been entrusted, we walk with rhythm, with a light heart and with serious consideration...

The Jewish and graceful Siedlce is gone! The popular, serious and naughty city has disappeared ... the city no longer foresaw all these, everything was burned at the stake, everything was burned for the sanctification of God.

* * *

I remember one Saturday evening, while the streets of the city were full of settlers that were walking in the streets and on the sidewalks, there was a general assembly of the "Chalutz" members on all their diversity. The graduates of the youth movements gathered: "Hashomer Hatzair", "Hachalutz Hatzair" "Freiheit" and some that were not related to any party.

The conversation and the debate were about the "mixed training". A serious and poignant debate: in fact, it was a conversation about unification and separation within the pioneering camp, which although we were all sympathetic to the idea and goal, we educated ourselves to uncompromising self-fulfillment and instructed ourselves and others to draw final and decisive conclusions. We were probably already at that time divided about frameworks and tactics, which were not yet so clear. The truth question was: based on which values shall we educate, based on what unify or separate us, shall we educate into life values or frameworks of life forms?

And most surprisingly: although we were still babies in all matters related to politics, we did not yet know how to distinguish between the national kibbutz and the united kibbutz and the members of the groups. We did not know exactly how great was the danger of separation, and yet we knew, remarkably, to explain with vigorous precision the necessity of separation. And we did it with a deep, blind and unshakable faith…

Where did we get the faith and the strength to explain, educate and debate about a world we just dreamed of? Who put us judges on such crucial and material questions such as: the unity of the pioneering youth movements, the unity of the kibbutz movement, the value of the kibbutz and the moshav? Who also gave such proficiency and experience in life, or authority to rule laws and score, for example, who is the "maximalist"? Also, such proficiency and experience in life, or authority to rule laws and set grades, for example, who is the "maximalist"?

Apparently, the faith was so deep and mystical and that the dream was mixed with impeccable self-confidence, and that our confidence was so solid that we will climb to the top of the mountain ... and so, the song was born and we sang it:

> We climb and sing on swords and corpses
> We walk and pass ... and in light and in the darkness
> And we're walking when we know or don't know the way
> We sing and climb! We climb and sing!

[Page 358]

And who knows where we got our fiery faith in the General Workers' Federation and in the overall framework of the labor movement in Israel. It was an unshakable jealous belief, that we are the potters, that this is the way and there is no other. We are the faithful and promising reserves, we are the form wall, we are the future of the nation and the status, for them both – we are the young generation ...

We have bound ourselves in an inseparable connection to the historical destiny, we believed that we would overcome the separate shells and discover the redeeming, common and unifying content, and that one fate awaits us all.

* * *

Indeed, the tragedy is immeasurably great and profound: Polish Judaism, the crown of the Israeli nation that is dispersed throughout the diaspora, has been destroyed. The pioneering movement with tens of thousands of blessed youths within it, with all its reserves that were saved from fire, saved the honor of the nation. It aroused, prepared and positioned itself as the head of the Ghetto Rebels. Only a few, those who were saved from the fire, managed to reach us at a safe shore, in order to tell us the full extent of the disaster and the destruction. Few news came from the youth from our holy and tortured city. But there is no doubt that until the last minute they stood in the front rows within the people and died when their lips were dubbed together with all the victims of Israel:

As long inside our hearts	Our hope has not been lost yet,
A Jewish soul still yearns	Hope is two thousand years old
And onward toward the East	To be a free people in our country
The eye looks at Zion-	The land of Zion and Jerusalem.

In our continuous historical destiny, we often face difficult combinations of conditions and circumstances. But it seems to me, that such a tragedy also the Satan has not yet created. Those young men and women who trained themselves and devoted their lives to a pioneering fulfillment at every hour, day and night, in dream and reality and were already planted in the virgin soil of the homeland - were run over, slaughtered, burned in the diaspora ...

The truth is just that, they were there only by a chance. They simply did not make it on time, whether because of age or because of missions imposed on them or they took on themselves. Each of us, who was privileged to make an Aliya and to see the fulfillment of the great vision, and to have a family in Israel – or otherwise we would also be among the slaughtered, the raped and the burned.

The tragedy is so horrible and heartbreaking, and we are engrossed in forgetfulness ... Even objectively the tragedy and the collapse are doubled and multiplied; After all, we have always said and memorized to ourselves that it was the trouble of the Jews that gave birth to Zionism, which began to lay the foundations for the "national home". But when the trouble of the Jews reached its peak of horrors and it was time for our national home to fill its great role, it was at this time that the resistance and the plot of destruction also reached their peak.

[Page 359]

We probably did not have time to prepare the right tools, we were late and lagged behind in our work. The State of Israel was late on the road and for a brief moment there was a danger that we will be left only with false messiahs. The history laughed at us, apparently, and yet there are no fixed laws in human history ...

There is no forgiveness and the human intelligence will not grasp the absurd processes of the deep catastrophe and the terrible blow that hit us all.

We continue to fly and ride in the train of life. We once burned the bridge that connected us to the past. We rebelled in the "exile", we despised all, we were extreme to cruelty to others and to ourselves; apparently in those days, it was impossible otherwise.

We need today - as breathing air - a serious and sharp turning point. Then, we did not see the mental and moral power of the Jew, that was strengthened and unified by the hands of an exile of many generations. Today we actually need it very much and perhaps most of all it is needed for tens of thousands of teenagers, who were born here, in the Moledet (homeland).

We need a fertilizing integration, to the integration of all the good and treasures we have stored in all the stations of our lives in all generations, and in our generation. We will return to the source and our fertilizing and renewing values. We will cultivate the love of Israel and the love of man among us, for the existence and prosperity of the State of Israel - the desire of all generations.

Indeed, the seed sown with our own hands has not failed, although we have not yet reached all that we dreamed and nurtured ...

We who continue, will erect a monument forever to those who did not get to come, we are the defendants!

May we be deserved to it - and hope we do not disappoint!!

[Page 360]

Organization of Chasidic Youth
and "Mizrachi Youth"

by Avraham Friedman

Translated by Theodore Steinberg

In 1915, when there was a revival among Jewish young people, Chasidic and religious young people were not left out. It became clear that one did not have to study Talmud in the cramped rooms of the prayer houses in unhygienic conditions, by the light of a kerosene lamp, or even with a light, under the supervision and control of the gabbais who took orders from their rabbis.

Scores and hundreds of young men were removed from the prayer houses, and their parents were besieged because their sons no longer wanted to wear sidekicks and soft collars, read secular books, or walked on Shabbos in the city parks, and so on.

The chief influencer of the Chasidic youth movement was Sholem Yellen, a devoted student of Torah and fearer of Heaven, the son of Moyshe Moykher-Sforim, who in his poor home did not have all the facilities for learning; Yellen, together with Aaron Nelkenbaum (now in Israel), Leib Ratbine, and Pesach Rosen, made the first attempt at organizing the religious young people. At first they used the premises of the "Mishnah Society" to study Torah for its ow sake, while in the premises of the "Talmud Torah" they conducted courses in Tanach for religious laborers. The best-known of the Ger Chasidim in Siedlce at that time, R. Leibush Feivel Goldberg, held, however, that the Tanach courses were an insult to the Talmud Torah and ordered them to move. A couple of days later, these courses were forbidden by the government.

The Mishnah Society offices were soon seen to be too small and uncomfortable for the great number of Chasidic-religious young men.

[Page 361]

Then the friends A. Friedman (now in Israel), Yishayahu Zelikowicz, and Yehonatan Eibszicz and they found a large and attractive location in the center of the city at 28 Kilinski, in the building of B. Altenberg. There the society first got its proper name—"Beis-Ha-talmud." In "Beis-Ha-talmud," more than sixty students comfortably learned the Talmud and its commentators, and occasionally they glanced at "The Guide for the Perplexed," "The Duties of the Heart," and other such books. The "Beis-Ha-talmud" also occasionally organized lectures on "Torah and Tradition," led by well-known religious speakers, the "German rabbis" Cohen and Carlebach. One of these lectures in a large movie theater was interrupted by attacks from Zionists and had to be continued in a different location; the speakers were taken there under guard.

A bit later, the young men Sh. Yellen, A. Friedman, and, having come from Brisk, David Zussman saw that not everyone was happy with the education program, because learning Torah was not enough and it was too difficult to live within the four cubits of Torah [a traditional description]. One also had to obtain a secular education. A charter was drawn up for a religious-cultural union under the name of "T'vunah" [Reason], which was legally recognized in 1916 with the right to establish chapters throughout Congress Poland.

"T'vunah" had as its goal: knowledge and awe for God. It found broad appeal, gathering around itself almost the whole of Siedlce's religious youth. In the newly appointed premises of four room with a large hall at 4 Ogrodowa, in the house of Mrs. Slushny, there were more than 200 comrades who daily attended the various evening courses in Polish, mathematics, bookkeeping, and others, as well as lessons in Gemara. "T'vunah" also organized social events and lectures as well as putting out a bi-weekly broadsheet called "Our Cultural Corner." Rabbi Zlotnik from Gambin attracted the young men from the prayer houses with his lectures. The religious organization "T'vunah," which had only existed in Siedlce, quickly became well known, and from the various cities and towns near Siedlce in the province came delegates who asked for our charter and then started such organizations.

[Page 362]

Also in Warsaw a "T'shuvah" organization was begun as an outgrowth of Siedlce's. There was also a central office that had connections with over 15 branches. With the development of "T'vunah," the "Beis-Talmud" closed in 1917.

At the same time, there existed in Siedlce a small circle of "Tz'irei-Mizrachi" ["Youth of the East"] comrades. Rabbi Kalman Frankel (now in Israel), Yoel Kamienicz and others in 1918, after pogroms in the Ukraine, began to influence them with nationalistic ideas, especially among the young people; this kind of thought also seized on the membership of "T'vunah." On four consecutive Shabboses, therefore, there were amazing gatherings for discussions on the topic of "Nationalism and Religion." More than thirty of the comrades spoke and broadly explored the problems involved, both pro and con, and finally, after almost two years of activities, "T'vunah", by a majority vote, yielded to "Mizrachi." The first task was to strengthen the "Tz'irei-Mizrachi", whose first council consisted of D. Zussman, A. Friedman, Y. Eibershitz, M. Karfin, Y Zelikowicz, Y. Falszfan, and Y. Kamienicz.

"Tz'irei-Mizrachi" had, thanks to its nationalistic-political character, a broad field of action. The first duty of the new council was to popularize the work of the Mizrachi program among the middle classes and particularly among the Chasidim. To this end, week by week, well-known speakers were brought in from the Mizrachi center in Warsaw. The first public lecture presented the well-known scholar, Torah scholar and outstanding speaker Rabbi Avigdor Emial, z"l. He was the rabbi in Grayeve, then later in Antwerp and finally was the chief rabbi of Tel Aviv. His two-hour talk about Jews and Yiddishkeit made a terrific impression. Scores of young people joined up on the spot. The same speaker a little later visited Siedlce and was our houseguest; the best thing was that the rabbi's outreach appealed to Chasidic circles.

[Page 363]

My father, R. Kalman Friedman, z"l, who was a Ger Chasid, received no comments from the Chasidim, even though "Mizrachi" was considered supremely unkosher in the prayer houses. Another frequent guest was Rabbi Bradt from Lipne, who is now a rabbi in Tel Aviv and who was even then renowned as an outstanding mass speaker, as was also Rabbi Neufeld, z"l, from Nowy Dwor, who, with his heartfelt spiritual talks commanded the greatest respect. After each lecture, there were sympathizers in the prayer houses and beis-medreshes who were later drawn into the Mizrachi.

"Tz'irei-Mizrachi" also set up an inexpensive soup kitchen to help the post-war poor Jewish population. This kitchen was located in the house of Sh. M. Meizlish, at 22 Ogrodowa. More than once the Polish inspector, Dr. Ritel, published congratulations over the orderly operation of the kitchen. Members of the Siedlce committee traveled to Mokow, Sololow, and Mezritch to organize chapters of "Tz'irei-Mizrachi."

At the beginning of 1919 there was the first members' conference in Siedlce, which undertook major decisions about the course of future projects, establishing there the central office. "Tz'irei-Mizrachi" also understood the necessity of organizing Jewish women and proceeded to found a "B'nos Mizrachi."

The committee of "B'nos Mizrachi" with Rabbi Neufeld from Eretz Yisroel

[Page 364]

At the end of 1919 a small women's group was formed and it was decided lot bring in from Warsaw the young "Tz'Irei-Mizrachi" member and effective speaker Rabbi Elimelech Neufeld, the son of the already-mentioned Nowidwor rabbi, now a worldwide coordinator of "Mizrachi" in Tel Aviv. He was in Siedlce for a few days, and it was his job to nene the first committee of "B'nos Mizrachi". A few weeks later, the same speaker delivered a talk organized by the "B'nos Mizrachi" in one of the largest halls in Siedlce. It was entitled "The Education of Women in National Life." There was a huge audience. The "B'nos MIzrachi" numbered about 60 members, some of them quite active. They were: Freida Nusbaum Dinah Urszel, Sarah Radzinske, Sarah Slawiaticzi, and Malkeh Srebnik.

At the same time there was also established in Siedlce a kindergarten called "The Shelter House for Orphans" in the name of Reines, z"l. It was located in the home of Mrs. Barg, 24 Ogrodowa, in the courtyard.

A "Mizrachi" children's home in the name of Rabbi Reines

A combined committee from Tz'Irei- and B'nos-Mizrachi worked together on the regular activities of the children's home. They made nicely painted little tables and benches as well as playthings necessary for the more than 40 children, who received an excellent education from the accredited kindergarten teacher Feiga Levartowski (whose husband, Marduke lives today in Israel).

[Page 365]

"Tz'Irei-Mizrachi" also attempted to establish "Ha-poel Ha-mizrachi" [Workers Mizrachi]. It was not easy to find qualified artisans who were willing to liquidate their well-established workshops and make allyah to Eretz-Yisroel with the goal of founding a cooperative. They tried to start a group of 8 carpenters for whom all travel arrangements would be made. The writer of these lines obtained passports for them and later, after a large banquet, took them to the Siedlce train station. "Ha-poel Ha-mizrachi" lacked a large following in Siedlce because not all of the crafts were not suitable for Eretz Yisroel and the majority of workers in Siedlce were shoemakers and tailors.

The "Mizrachi" in Siedlce survived through elections so that "Tz'Irei-Mizrachi" did all of its work so that "MIzrachi" would emerge with honor from the elections. To the credit of "Mizrachi" we should note the well organized "Cheder Mizrachi," also known as "Torah v' Deah," at 8 Shenkewitcz, which was formed in 1920. It was led by Ephraim Tzelnik, Eisenbergf (from the hotel), Alter Eisenberg (a manufacturer), and others. All were killed by the Nazis. Those who were not killed were A.D. Gottesdiener and Monish Ridel (now in Israel).

In 1922, I went to Lodz, but my influence continued and had good results. Both of my brothers, Menachem and Zechariah were active in "Tz'Irei-Mizrachi" together with Issur Rosenberg and other who live now in Israel.

[Page 366]

The Jewish National Fund Bazaar in Siedlce

by Avraham Friedman

Beginning in 1930, there were eight traditional bazaars in Siedlce. They were held in the large, beautiful hall of the "Ezras Y'somim", on the intermediate days of Passover, when the larger Jewish world would all go walking through the city, after throwing off the heavy yoke of winter.

Conducting such a bazaar was truly a difficult job. Preparations lasted for three months, with a well devised plan that involved a number of large and small steps. In particular, every year they had to find new attractions to grab the interest of the Siedlce populace so that they would visit the bazaars, so that despite their frequency, attendance at the bazaars always increased.

Activities always began with an advertisement in the newspaper "Siedlce Vochenblatt." Simultaneously, hundreds of letters were sent to domestic and foreign firms inviting them to advertise their products. The soap manufacturer "Stock," the chocolate company "Flutas," and the pen–and–ink company "Pelikan" held prominent spots in the bazaar. Also the large Siedlce firms, like Czibuczki, Rodzinski, and others waited the whole year for the three bazaar days in order to show their goods to the thousands of visitors,

The craftsmen, with their fine exhibits, "WIZO" with its delicate embroidery, were not left behind.

[Page 367]

Almost all of the young people took part in the "home activities," and almost no household failed to have a large or small display.

The opening of the bazaar was marked by a torchlight parade by the well–organized pioneering youth through Siedlce's streets and an advertisement in the movie theater "Szwietawid" which was shown at al three showings that evening. The opening address was almost always delivered by the longstanding leader of the KK"L [Keren Kayemes L'Yisroel, the Jewish National Fund], A. Sh. Englander. After that came a talk by the representative of the Center. A frequent speaker was Avraham Bialopolski (who died in Israel run 1951). Immediately afterward, the kiosks were opened and everyone bought "treasures" until late in the night.

During the days of the bazaar, aside from the trade in material things, the youth groups held lotteries, lectures about the Jewish National Fund, and dance evenings, which the young people took advantage of before beginning their strenuous work. No other party or organization conducted activities during those days, not wanting to come in conflict with the Jewish National Fund.

The concluding words were always delivered by Mr. H. Fishl Popowski (later Dromi, who lives now in Israel), who worked in the central office of the Jewish National Fund in Warsaw and would come to Siedlce as a guest for Passover.

The nicest bazaar was the fourth, which captivated Siedlce with its more than 1400 displays on 8 decorated tables and two splendid kiosks painted with original and Israel–themed motifs. The work was led by the members if "Ha–shomer Ha–Tza'ir," Silberstein and Silberberg, under the direction of their teachers, David Lederman and Eliezer Berenholz (now Bar Chaim, who lives in Israel, in Haifa).

The appropriate lighting, with multi–colored little bulbs, was arranged by the Halberstam firm, together with Mr. Shmuel Domb (who lives now in Israel).

The province, too, took part with goods, especially Makabidm with its living stock of 5 doves and a large hen, which from time to time would make a noise…and amuse the hall. Everything at the bazaar was sold and the entrance fee alone brought in more than3000 zlotys, more than a third of the year's budget for the Siedlce Jewish National Fund. I was then in charge of the bazaar and was given the honor of cutting the ribbon. A great deal of help in the bazaar was given by Miss Bella Finkelstein, who devoted so much energy to it.

[Page 368]

Others helpers in the bazaar were Velvel Lev (living today in America), D. Pasawski (now in Israel), Yehoshua Eckerman, Chava Domb, and Mrs. Miriam Czibucki.

Sadly, scores of those who worked at the bazaar did not survive to see the fulfillment of their ideals – Eretz Yisroel. My heart breaks at their terrible deaths.

[Page 369]

The Ger Prayer House

by A. Friedman
(from my memories)

In Siedlce there were Chasidim of all stripes. The number of such Chasidim amounted to over a thousand. Mostly these were Ger Chasidim, who numbered over 500.

At the time of the "Sfas Emes" [the Chasidic rabbi Yehudah Aryeh Leib Alter, 1847 – 1905], z"l, and later, in the time of his son R. Avraham–Mordechai Alter, z"l, who had the merit of dying in Jerusalem – the Ger prayer house in Siedlce was located at number 9 Pienkne Street and occupied two large rooms with comfortable open spaces on both sides.

On Shabboses and holidays, Jews would relax there. On Yom Kippur, during prayers, many people stayed outside and then traded places with those inside, where the heat was extraordinary.

The building of the Chasidic prayer house was set deeply in the courtyard in order to separate it from the surrounding buildings on Pienkne Street, numbers 7 and 11, with their hotels, drunks, and loose elements.

[Page 370]

The "elite" of the Ger prayer house, one could say, comprised the best part of Siedlce's Chasidic life. It is appropriate to recall their names: the devisor R. Yisroel Mardicks (whose son Shlomo, lives today in Israel, in Ra'anana); the three Siedlce ritual slaughterers – Zalmen Greenberg (whose son Mordechai, who lived for a short time in Israel, died there in 1954); Shimon Kleinlehrer (whose son Yisroel–Meir lives in Jerusalem); Yitzchak–Meir Appelbaum. Also in the prayer house were: R. Yisroel Gutgeld, R. Shlomo–Shmuel Abarbanel (whose two daughters Sheyndl and Toybe live in Israel); Henech Steinberg (whose two sons Moshe and a younger one live in Tel Aviv); Yoel Slushni, Ben–Tzion Zucker, Yisroel Lieberman (whose son Shimon lives in Tel Aviv); the brothers Yechiel and Nachum Halberstadt, whose children live in Israel; the old Talmud scholars – R. Chaim Shub, R. Yisroel Sinai (Zeidntzeig), R. Yakov–Baer Arubenshtein, R. Shimon Pursever (a mohel), and the brothers Yoshe and Mottl Mintz.

My father, R. Kalman Friedman, was then a gabbai in the prayer house, and the writer of accounts – the bookkeeper for death records and Simchas Torah hakofos.

This was not a simple thing – on holidays he had to create paper "banknotes" and make envelopes for all those who prayed; and on holidays, when he was not allowed to write, for everyone who purchased the honor of a hakofo or an allya, he had to put the "banknotes" in the proper envelope. [This was a way for synagogues to keep track of donations.]. This had to be done very quickly in order not to delay the purchaser of the hakofo or the aliyah.

Because of the crowded conditions and because of differences of opinion among the attendees of the prayer house, the congregants later divided into three separate prayer houses.

In the circle of the Ger Chasidim there were bitter opponents of Zionism. For them, the thought of Eretz Yisroel or the Jewish National Fund were not kosher.

There were also so–called "pareve" Chasidim who did not totally follow the Ger path and were a bit worldly and had some sympathy for Eretz Yisroel.

It is interesting that from all these "half–kosher" Chasidim, their children are now in Israel, and it is too bad that their parents did not survive to see it with their own eyes; they would to be true citizens of the Jewish state.

[Page 371]

The Activities of "Workers Of Zion" [Po'alei Tzion] in Siedlce

by Yisrael Tabakman (Netanya)

Translated by Theodore Steinberg

In my following memoirs, I will deal with everything I know about the Zionist–Socialist activities in Siedlce before the development of the "Po'alei–Tzion" [Labor Zionist] party and after the Minsk conference, when the Zionist–Socialist groups organized and created the "Po'alei Tzion Workers Association," which was joined by the nationalistically–minded workers who earlier belonged to the "Bund" or to the general Zionist movement. My memoirs cover the period from 1903 until by departure from Poland in 1921.

* * *

In the middle of 1903, a group of young men and women from Siedlce who were dissatisfied with the program of the "Bund" abandoned that movement. The circumstances surrounding that split from the "Bund" were the following:

We were all brought up politically on the Bundist propaganda leaflets, simple booklets, that instructed us about the heroic battle of the Russian proletariat against czarism, about the enormous strikes by thousands and thousands of workers against the capitalists, about arrests, prisons, and death sentences. All of this played on our ethical feelings, and we were ready to fight against czarism and against exploitation. We carried out the battle on the Jewish streets of Siedlce–battles against long workdays, for better pay for better treatment, and so on. But when we encountered our opponents on the Jewish streets, the so–called Siedlce "capitalists," whose workshops were in their bedrooms, when we met at the time of a strike with the laments of the "industrial" women, who pleaded with us: "What do you want from us? On the contrary: get work for my husband so at least I'll have something for Shabbos,–then we began to look on reality with different eyes.

[Page 372]

With our daily practical professional activities among the Jewish workers, our enthusiasm cooled down a bit. Disappointed, we asked, "Is this the same struggle that we read about in the leaflets? Will the Jewish workers lead this kind of class fight for socialism?" New ideas began to arise in our minds. We began to understand that class warfare must employ other methods on the Jewish street, that one must have a different approach to Jewish life. The methodology of the Bund became too narrow for us. The Siedlce "Bund" considered us a foreign element and our group–about ten of us–were expelled from the party. I was already considered an agitator in the Bundist exchange and had an "influence on the masses." It fell upon me to attract from the "Bund" another twenty young people. Thus the thirty of us stumbled around unto we were taken in by the Zionists.

The Rise of "Po'alei Tzion"

But we also found little satisfaction in the ranks of the Zionists. As I recall, in 1903 there was in Siedlce a social and ideological spurt on the Jewish street. There were economic battle. Jewish youth were shaken by the pogrom in Kishinev. Jewish workers were all organized in the already existing parties–"Bund" and P.P.S, general Zionists, in "Ha–T'khiya," and also in minyanim. Many shoemakers belonged to a minyan of young people that had its own "prayer house" where they prayed each Shabbos and celebrated joyous occasions.

[Page 373]

Every event in Jewish life in czarist Russia, and in the whole world, the battles over the Zionist congresses about Palestine and Uganda–all caused reactions among the knowledgeable Jewish workers in Siedlce. In the midst of this Jewish struggle was born in Siedlce, the Zionist–socialist movement. Those who had been expelled from the "Bund," who were not allowed to come to the Bundist center, formed their own center opposed to that of the Bund. We would gather there three times a week to discuss and determine what we should do next. We decided not to split with our comrades and the workers of the "Bund" and to strive to bring them to our side. We had a definite program for agitation that we conducted among the new arrivals. It was an interesting program that we had devised: the Jewish workers had to conduct the class warfare for their day–to–day interests, even though the battle led to totally different results, like for people who had a totally normal way of life. Often the battle entailed having the poor master worker, with his workers, emigrate to America. Other people led the technical development and the battle of the workers for the decline of small undertakings and the creation of large industrial factories where thousands of workers could be concentrated. The masses were "proletarianized" and capital was concentrated in few hands, and that was the path to socialism. Contrarily, the result of the class warfare led by the Jewish workers was emigration. This emigration should have been directed toward Palestine, where a base for class warfare leading to socialism should be created.

With this program we attracted scores of workers to our center. But we were not secure in our intentions and with the way to deal with our problems. We feared the movement that we had called forth. The theoreticians of the new movement were: I and Mottl Koszinicki. Not knowing what to call ourselves, we gave ourselves the name "The New Worker–Zionists."

We decided to send a comrade to Bialystok because we heard that that was the center for such bumbling groups. The lot fell to me to go and determine whether there was such a party and whether they had a literature and whether there was a name for such a party, and, most important–unite with the center and bring back a comrade.

[Page 374]

Meanwhile, there was chaos for us in the city over the new movement. Properly said: with the new center, which on certain evenings drew a good number of workers, most of them boot makers who were employed. In all the parties people spoke about our daring, and it appeared that the Zionists were very interested in us. As I described above, there was at the time a certain dissatisfaction in the Zionist ranks. Zionists with leftist inclinations wanted to unite with our group.

On a certain day I received an invitation to come to Florianske Street to Asher Kramarsz, where a person named Gurewitsch was waiting for me. I quickly guessed what that meant, and I decided to take with me Mottl Kaszenicki. On that evening we went to Asher Kramarsz and there met two people. One introduced himself as Gurewitsch and the other as Kaplanski. Gurewitsch got to the point immediately.

He explained to us that he knew our history and our current work, and he proposed to us that we should join the organization "Ha–T'khiyah," which consisted of workers and intellectuals. The idea behind "Ha–T'khiyah" was to revive the Jewish people on a social foundation. "Ha–T'khiya" had a current program for workers in the diaspora, including: cultural work, organizing self–defense, and so on. After a two–hour long explanation, along with questions and answers, we promised to respond in a couple of days, We said goodbye and left.

After this visit, we were confused b all the new thoughts that had been presented to us. So clearly and logically had he laid out for us the actually situation of the Jewish people in the whole world, especially in the Russian empire, so clearly had he spoken about anti–semitism, emigration, that it was not possible to disagree. Gurewitsch had made a double impression on us–on the one hand as an intelligent person, full of knowledge, reasonable but profound, and on the other hand almost dismissing the class warfare that the Jewish workers were conducting to better their situation. His solution for all the Jewish problems was almost religious, which shocked us a bit.

[Page 375]

We dd not want to dismiss Marxism, but after a long discussion, that lasted a couple of days, we decided to align ourselves with "Ha–T'khiyah" in order to have a roof over our heads and a name.

At the first solemn meeting we sent three people: Yisroel Tabakman [the author of this chapter], Mottl Kaszenicki, and Avraham Silberschein. The whole committee from "Ha–T'khiyah" was there, including: Gurewitsch, Peretz Kamar (a shoemaker), Shlomo Weintraub (a student at the gymnasium), Meir Rozenwasser (who worked in the cigarette trade with his father), Liebe Eisenstadt (a student at the gymnasium), and Mottl Bernbaum (a bookbinder). The meeting was quite solemn. They decided that we would continue our proletarian wok at the center and that we would rent a room for illegal activities, because at the center we only delivered propaganda.

We quickly accustomed ourselves to the comrades of "Ha–T'Khiyah." I felt that the members of "Ha–T'khiyah" were not too happy with not only with the organization but also with their leader Gurewitsch, who got his socialism from the Torah. In the meantime, we became familiar with Zionism. The articles of Her Borochov about Jewish economic questions made quite an impression on me. They were published in the Russian Zionist journal "Yevreioskaya Szizn." We devoured each one. We saw a new world of learning and thinking. From these articles we realized that our program was in agreement with Borochov's articles. We redoubled our efforts, organized a self–defense unit and procured arms, revolvers and daggers, made specially for us. We led individual strikes of the boot makers and their employees that were successful. We also held discussions with the "Bund" on all of Borochov's articles from "Yevreiskaya Szizn"–which we had translated into Yiddish and distributed to the workers, who enthusiastically devoured every word. The whole enterprise was conducted in the spirit of Ber Borochov.

Our comrades numbered in the hundreds. We felt too confined by "Ha–T'khiyah" and we sought a way to free ourselves from their name and from their leader Gurewitsch.

[Page 376]

Gurewitsch took little part in our work, because, as I explained above, he was a bourgeois and could not take part in any illegal mass activities. He also had an official position as a teacher for the Zionists in the Hebrew school and would not take part in illegal gatherings. Consequently he took no part in practical activities. In the city we were already known by the party name of "Poalei–Tzion," though officially we were still "Ha–T'khiyah," until we had the opportunity to organize ourselves as "Poalei–Tzion" in Siedlce.

During the time when we were known as "Ha–T'khiyah," we added hundreds of members. Among the active leaders were: "Yisroel Tabakman, Mottl Kaszenicki, Mottl Teiblum (Mottl Chasid), Menachem (now in Israel, calling himself Menachem Ben Hillel), Nahum Slushny, Moshe Greengold, Avraham Silberstein. We owned quite a library of literature. The latest series of articles by Ber Borochov in "Yevreiskaya Szizn" made quite an impression on us – "The Class Interests and the Nationalistic Question."

We were, overall, Borochov's students. We learned and taught other members at the center. We also conducted our work among the young women. Liebe Eisenstadt brought a whole group of women: Itke Kahan, Itke Slushny, Chana Slushny. All of these members enriched our movement.

At the same time, a party that called itself "Zionist–Socialist" was established in Siedlce. It was led by a certain Boyarski, (a student in the seventh level at the gymnasium. He came from deep in Russia with his sister and brother to study in the Siedlce gymnasium.), Moyshe Zucker, Avraham Nebel, and Zilke Kawa (the registrar's son). They led vigorous discussions. This was at the time of the revolution and the October pogroms (1905). The Jewish masses were in an uproar. The Zionist–Socialists argued that the Jewish people were going under and one could no longer wait for Palestine. We must immediately have our own territory. This called forth in their ranks a large number of workers.

[Page 377]

Our discussions were only with the "Poalei–Tzion," because we did not want to set up an opposition party.

People in Bialystok knew about the existence of "Poalei–Tzion" in Siedlce. From there they sent a man with a monthly journal– "Proletarian Thought." The articles from the journal were truly worth studying. The author gave us practical organizational lessons and left an address where we could reach him. Then he left. At that time there appeared in Siedlce a certain Alter Gottlieb (today in Israel with the name Ben Tzion Yedidiah). He made a true "revolution" in Siedlce. He represented to me that he was from "Poalei–Tzion." His first speech was arranged at the Zionist study beis–medresh, which was then at Itze Maleh's on Pienke Street. The hall was full. The most well–known people from all the parties were there. Such a talk Siedlce had never heard. He gave a three–hour long analysis of the actual state of the Jewish people. Everyone was carried away by his talk.

Gottlieb's departure did not end the discussion. Using the election of two delegates to the sixth Zionist Congress, Yosef Shprinczak (today chair of the Knesset) and Yakov Steinberg, people called a discussion evening for a Friday night. Legally this could not be done. Rusze Lehrer, a member of "Ha–T'khiyah," provided us a place in the new house that her father, Yakov Lehrer, had built on Ogradowa Street. No one lived there yet. The discussion took place there, lasting from Friday night until Saturday night, without interruption. It was attended by all the Zionist factions, as well as the "S.S." The speakers were Gurewitsch, the two delegates, and Alter Gottlieb. In the morning, at the last session, after a short report and a brief discussion, we decided to start a "Poalei–Tzion" party. Thus was established the "Poaleio–Tzion" in Siedlce. Members of the new party committee were: Yisroel Tabakman, Meir Rosenwasser, Gavriel Schlechter, Mottl Teibloom, Mottl Daszenicki, Liebe Eisenstadt, Mottl Berenbaum.

[Page 378]

In the Time of the Revolution (1905)

We grew so much in Siedlce that no political or economic actions were carried out without us. We were represented in the self–defense that had been organized by the "Bund" and the "P.P.S." We divided the city into sections where each night groups watched with weapons. We also sent self–defense groups into the provinces.

The great strike of the business employees in Siedlce was led by the three parties with three designations: "Bund," "P.P.S.," and "Poalei–Tzion," and it was led successfully. It is also appropriate to remember the strike of the shoemakers that lasted for many weeks.

In Siedlce there were several families who were called "Koshetzes." They controlled the business in fruits. They controlled all the fruit orchards, all the kiosks, and the fish business. Their chief executive was Vigdor Koshetz, a tall, broad–backed Jew, who was feared by the whole town. The head of the fish business was Yidl Hol, a tall, well–built man. He was tall, but his shoulders were bowed. Among the "Koshetzes" were two brothers–Shmilke and Itsche, who had shoe factories. They were hit by a strike. Shmilke was the one against whom the strike lasted for weeks. The comrades in Siedlce let them know in Warsaw that these comrades would reckon with Shmilke. At the same time, fights broke out. The "Koshetzes" in Siedlce decided to get even with the workers movement and to eliminate their centers. They especially wanted vengeance against the leaders of the three parties–the "Bund," the "P.P.S." and the "Poalei–Tzion": Shalke Zubrowicz (Shalke Wietrik), Zalmen Burstein (Zalmen Paritz), Yisrolke Tabakman (Srolke the Glazier's) who live now in Israel.

The Koshetze" clan came out with weapons against the centers and dispersed the members, and the three leaders were forced to hide. The city boiled like a kettle. We quickly sent a messenger to Warsaw, because Warsaw always suffered from conflicts. (So it was, too, with the carpenters' strike and others.). A battle began with the "Koshetzes."

[Page 379]

With the help of the organizations in other cities, the fish and fruit merchants were thrown out of the markets and the fish business. The struggle with their forces lasted for weeks. Yidl Hol was beaten up and left without fish. Jews in Siedlce had no fish for Shabbos. Fruits and vegetables became rare in the city. This war lasted for two weeks. A large group of young reinforcements came to Siedlce from Minsk.

The "Koshetzes," seeing that they could not win and that the city was beginning to suffer, since for a second Shabbos there was no fish or fruit, sent messengers to the centers asking for a truce. We went to someone's home and there prepared beer and schnapps; both sides put down their weapons on the table and began negotiations. The upshot was that Shmilke was fined a certain sum–I do not remember how much–and they promised to acknowledge the victory of the strike and persuade the employers to pay the workers for the time during the strike. On our side, we sent letters to all the cities, sealed with our insignias–"Bund," "P.P.S.," and "Poalei Tzion"–that no one should harass the "Koshetzes" and they should be allowed to return to normal business.

Bialystok, becoming aware that the "Poalei–Tzion" movement was growing from day to day, sent us a comrade from Semiaticz, Moyshe Pakhter. There was also a woman, Kaplan, from Semiaticz. We arranged for lectures in the Ger prayer house and at Moyshe Goldberg's. We also had two illegal rooms. One room was on Kolya Street across from the Orthodox Church; we did not know that the "Bund" and the "P.P.S." also had secret rooms there. One day we were spied upon and those rooms fell through. We then decided to hide our literature and our weapons that we had been keeping in the second room on Pienke Street. That night, inspectors came, but there was nothing for them to find.

We also used to participate in illegal demonstrations and to demonstrate with banners. Before the Cossacks could arrive, we would fold up the banners and just walk on the sidewalks. This deception made them murderously angry, so that they killed anyone they encountered.

[Page 380]

But there was no aspect of labor in the city in which "Poalei–Tzion" was not involved.

After the failure of our illegal quarters, we moved to Florianski Street, at Avraham Slushny's, on the third floor. Two of the comrades lived in this illegal room: Meir Rozenwasser and Yisroel Tabakman. From there we organized all our work. We were in regular contact with Bialystok. through a comrade who was available to us, and we knew about the ideological dispute in the Zionist factions throughout Russia and Poland. Different ideologies with different aspirations fought among themselves: the Minsk Poalei–Tzion, practical Palestinians, "Ha–T'khiyah," Saint–Simonists, Sirkin's group, Zionist–Socialists, those who approved of class warfare and those who did not. Ber Borochov ruled over all of them with his evaluations of all the pressing Jewish questions. Siedlce, too, was caught up in the controversies. When Later Gottliev went over to the Saint–Simonists, we immediately cut off contact with him.

In our new room, we called together the first regional conference, embracing 10 cities and towns. At the conference, we devised a uniform organization under the name "Poalei–Tzion." We elected a regional committee. We received relevant literature, monthly journals, pamphlets. We had a full stock of illegal literature. In the building of our illegal room, there were other illegal rooms. The door next to ours led to the room of the "P.P.S.," which was led by Berish Stoler. The first floor was taken by Boyarski and his sister. That was the illegal room of the "Zionist–Socialists."

The year 1905 held for us, "Poalei–Tzion" in Siedlce, many serious responsibilities. The revolutionary events in the Russian Empire did not avoid our city. Our committee decided to organize, separately from the general self–defense, a party militia of volunteers, well armed with revolvers and light Mauser rifles, which we obtained from the garrison in Siedlce.

[Page 381]

In Siedlce there was a regiment of soldiers called the Ostolenker Regiment. The soldiers were selected by a special military committee made up of all the parties. "Poalei–Tzion" was not directly represented but only by the representative of the S.S., Boyarski. He gave us the last shipment of weapons a couple of days before he was arrested. The weapons were, as I recall, six broken–down revolvers and six Mauser rifles, new from the factory but without bullets. On the night when he brought us the cartridges, he was arrested. In the morning we went to Boyarski's and we found everything in chaos: suitcases torn open, bookshelves overturned, mattresses thrown off the beds, the floor covered with papers, newspapers torn up, shredded. Boyarski's sister told us:

When they heard knocking on their door and cries of "Open up," 26 packages of cartridges lay on the table, newly brought from the military storehouse. The younger brother grabbed the packages and threw them out the window that overlooked a field. That is where were had buried our weapons. One package had ripped and many cartridges had fallen on the table. He could not clean them up because they had to open the door. Soldiers came in, and gendarmes with rifles at the ready, and they asked for Boyarski. Among them were Ostrolenker soldiers. They put the cartridges that they found into their pockets, so that the gendarmes could not see. The gendarmes found a military appeal and a stamp from the military storehouse. They showed a warrant for Boyarski. He did not want to go, but they called a carriage and took him away. In the morning we all went carefully into the field and collected the cartridges.

The upshot of the arrest was, as his sister related, that because a son of a gendarme official was involved in the matter of the stamp, the whole affair was hushed up and Boyarski was sent two his birthplace deep in Russia. I believe that was Tiflis. Shortly after, his brother and sister also went there.

The revolutionary events also seized Siedlce. There were demonstrations and strikes. On the first of May, the population was urged to leave their work.

[Page 382]

There were demonstrations in which members of "Poalei–Tzion" predominated. Certain members were assigned particular areas of work. For the province, those assigned were: Yisroel Tabakman and David Orszekh. For the center and for taking care of the illegal literature–Comrade Menachem. For professional worko–Mottl Kaszenicki and Avraham Silberstein, a carpenter who was called Avraham Partzever because when he was traveling with the self–defense force to Partzeve to defend against a pogrom, the police seized him and brought him with the convicts,, so he was given the name Partzever. For agitation and propaganda on site those designated were: Tabakman, Rosenwasser, Schlechter. Responsible for the Bayawka [?] were: Berish (Berish of the lambs), Mottl Teiblum, and others whose names I have forgotten.

In 1906, the Siedlce "Poalei–Tzion" suffered from czarist repression. Many comrades were arrested. Menachem was detained at the train station with a package of illegal literature. I saw him taken away in a carriage and I never saw him again until later, here in Israel. Ignoring those repressive acts, we busily went about our Poalei–Tzion work. We were preparing for our convention, which required us to unite in a single large Poalei–Tzion party. Aside from independent conflicts between workers and bosses, we participated in the great strike of the boot makers. The Poalei–Tzion proposal to the conference that the strike should not affect the poorer bosses but only the larger shoe merchants and the big manufacturers, so that they would open factories and centralize the workers together with the poorer bosses, this proposal was accepted by the whole conference. At the time of this strike, a bomb was thrown. It killed the police chief, Golczow, and several others. The soldiers sot, killing several and wounding others. Arrests were made. But the bloody panic did not stop our work. We continued the strike and were completely victorious. Four large factories were opened, employing 80 workers. The work of Poalei–Tzion was in full force. We were then a party with a name: "The Social Democratic Workers Party Poalei–Tzion" and with a program that was adopted at the conference in Poltawa in March of 1906.

[Page 383]

The repressive actions of the czarist government did not let up. In Siedlce there was resistance. At night, no one left their homes. The dragoon patrols wandered the streets with rifles at the ready. The city was like a war camp where the enemy was expected. However, we were happy with our victory. The factories were working. The shoemakers decided to close the small factories and to concentrate all of the shoemaking work of the smaller bosses in several large factories, but this was delayed until the repressions would cease. But the opposite happened. The repression increased, until the outbreak of the Siedlce pogrom, which Y. Kaspi wrote about in an earlier chapter.

During the pogrom in Siedlce, I was arrested. I was taken to jail where there were hundreds of arrested men, women, and children. We younger men were taken to a second building to a large hall. The warden came and warned us that we were being held for court martial. A little later, Yankel Tenenbaum was brought in with his head bandaged so that he could hardly be recognized. He was taken to a separate room on the second floor.

In the evening, the warden told us what we were being charged with.. The physically weak were guilty of agitating for revolution. I also was charged with this. The healthy and strong young people were guilty of being seized with revolvers in their hands. We were held for a week under threat of a court martial.

At the end of the week we were told that we would be sent to Archangelsk. But on erev Rosh Hashanah, nearly all of us were released. At that time we were informed that we were receiving a "free expulsion," that is, that we had to leave Siedlce gubernia. I decided to leave the country. But until then I remained in Siedlce.

[Page 384]

In the city all the parties had formed an American committee. I represented the Poaleio–Tzion. We fought to come to the aid of the robbed and fallen worker–families and to give them the possibility of getting on their feet. Yisroel Gutgelt and all the other representatives on the committee held that we should reestablish the robbed and burned out businesses on Warsaw Street.

In the meantime, the time for our leaving the country had arrived. I went with a group to Paris, and all the exiles met there. I remember some of their names: two Stalava brothers–one of them, Max, was a leader in the "Bund," and the other was a young man. Two Zucker brothers–Moyshe Zucker, living now in America, then a Zionist–Socialist, Mottl Kaszenicki (Poalei–Tzion), Yenkel Tenenbaum ("Bund"), and the writer of these lines.

After six months in Paris, I became homesick. Individually people began to steal back to Russia and back to Siedlce. The mood at home had begun to settle down. The ruins of the burned businesses were being repaired. The revolutionary movement had been suspended. The party leaders were abroad. Many had become apathetic. Many of them remained at home and interested themselves only with their private lives. The parties ceased to exist. So it was until the Russian powers left Siedlce during the First World War.

Activities during the First World War

When Siedlce was taken by the Germans, community life quickly revived for the Jewish workers. A non–partisan club called the "Workers Home" was established, and, as I recall, the directorship consisted of: Moyshe Menderszecki, Itshe Altshuler, and Henech Saltzman. It soon had many members. Their hall contained a large reading room. At the same time, two Poalei–Tzion committees were established in Siedlce, oblivious to each other. On e committee consisted of Zavl Rosenzumen, Groman, Scherzman, Dovid Greenfarb , and others. The second committee: Yisroel Tabakman, David Arshekh, Yosef Slushny, and Henech Saltzman (who later joined the Bund); the two committees eventually combined.

[Page 385]

The two "Poalei–Tzion" committees met accidentally. We knew that. a representative of the Poalei–Tzion was coming from Warsaw–comrade Yisroel Vesher (Reichman), so we went to the station to meet him. I had already known Reichman for a long time, so I went to wait for him; meanwhile, a member of the other committee also waited for him–he was actually coming for them–and so there we became aware that there were two Poalei–Tzion committees. The first meeting took place in the home of comrade Groman. Comrade Reichman was aware that in Siedlce there was an unaffiliated club called the Workers Home, and he informed us that throughout Poland there were Workers Home societies that were "Poalei–Tzion" clubs, so in Siedlce the Workers Home must also be associated with Poalei Tzion.

Leftist Poalei–Tzion leaders: Yosef Slushny Meir Salzman, Henech Saltzman, Yisroel Tabakman, Reizel Shivek, and Rosezuman

[Page 386]

We began to conduct a secret project around the Workers Home. Thus began a struggle with the "Bund," which wanted to convert the club into a "Tzukunft" organization. The club had about 600 member and had a fine location. The "Poalei–Tzion" party had then in Siedlce active and prominent party members, such as: Slushny, Yisroel Tabakman, Groman, Zanvil Rozenzumen, and others. The arguments over the Workers Home grew heated. Finally the steering committee resigned. In the new election, there were lists from the "Poalei–Tzion" and the "Bund." All the members came to the election. The result was that the "Poalei–Tzion" received twenty–some more votes and was victorious–the first victory in the new era. The Bundists and the non–affiliated would not accept our victory. They held that the hall was theirs and they obstructed our work. It became a scandal. The new steering committee consisted of: Yosef Slushny, Yisroel Tabakman, Henech Saltzman, Dovid Arszech, Groman, Sanvil Rozenzumen, and David Greenfarb. At their first meeting they decided to find a second location and assigned a couple of members to do so. Thus was rented the hall at 41 Agradowa Street, and so began the revival of "Poalei–Tzion" in Siedlce. The number of members in the Workers Home increased. Soon, within the first months, the society numbered 100. We had new people who were active: Melech Heinsdorf (now in Israel), Zanvil Gurnicki, Avrahamele Zikberstein, Meir Saltzman, Shlifke, Rozenzumen, and others whose names I forget. The work was divided up into categories: political (party) activities, economic, professional work, and cultural activities. A specially created cultural committee organized lectures, formed a huge library and reading room. At the first of May demonstration that was organized by the "Poalei–Tzion," speakers from the balcony included: Slushny, Tabakmanm and Zanvil Rozenzumen. Thousands of Jewish workers and everyday people gathered at the Workers Home. The German occupation rulers came too late, when no one was left there.

[Page 387]

Young people from the leftist Poalei–Tzion

The economic committee, led by Melech Heinsdorf, created a people's kitchen where hundreds of workers ate daily, a consumers cooperative, and a bread sale based on [membership or ration] cards, where people could also get other products. The Germans then had a card system for products.

These economic institutions worked quite well. The professional activities were led by comrades Yosef Slushny, Chana Handlasz, and Yisroel Tabakman. The work was very difficult. Unemployment in the trades with which we had to deal, was enormous. All of our economic activities were directed at the unemployed. We let no one go hungry. We tried to create work for the unemployed and we sent people to work in Jewish undertakings and lumberyards and iron works. No one opposed us. You must understand that our activities called forth kindness and sympathy. We also created a war fund and collected money for weapons. The American committee gave us two crates with clothes and other products to distribute.

[Page 388]

All the areas of work grew so much that our hall at 41 Ogradowa became too small and we had to find other locales. Luckily they were also on Ogradowa Street. People in the city said that the Poalei–Tzion was occupying Ogradowa Street. The party was well–liked in Siedlce by both the religious and non–religious.

It is appropriate to recall the following fact: It was before Rosh Hashanah during the time of the German occupation. Unemployment and poverty were enormous. Our social welfare institutions had to remain active. Before Rosh Hashanah, the Poalei–Tzion committee received an invitation from the Siedce rabbi. A delegation comprised of Yosef Slushny and Yisroel Tabakman went to see him. When we arrived at the rabbi's, there was a whole cluster of Jews there, judges and dozors and city officials. They greeted us. One of the crowd approached us: "Here is why we summoned you. Because we know how much you do in the city, helping a great many people who are in need and hungry, you are greatly respected. We ask that you shut down your institutions during the coming holidays, because Ogradowa Street is a Christian street. It would not be seemly for the non–Jews and it would be a desecration of the holy name." Our answer: "If the rabbi and and all the influential people get the bosses to pay the workers for the holidays, we will close up. If you want to avoid such a desecration, the religious must also make a sacrifice. We await your response."

The people of the city approved of our answer. Everyone thought we were right. But there was no answer from the side of the bosses, so our welfare institutions remained open on the holidays to feed the hungry.

Our activities became broader. We were represented in the folk choir under the leadership of Yosef Sonnshein and in the drama group under the directorship of Mr. Heinsdorf. Every Shabbos, the Shtern Sports Club played against other clubs and Jews went to see the competitions.

[Page 389]

The comrades of Polei–Tzion and the activists showed great generosity in working in all of our undertakings. Comrade Hochberg from Sokolow was with us. He led much of the work. The following comrades were active in my time: Yosef Slushny, Hochberg, Yisroel Tabakman, Zanvil Rozenzumen, Gralman, Avrahamele Silbershtein, Melech Heinsdorf, Meir Saltzman, Dovid Aszher, the Mozes brothers, Dor [sic] Greenfarb, Chanah Hanlasz, Shlifke, Shlomo Kainski, and Avraham Yossl Karnicki.

Poalei–Tzion in Siedlce was also in constant constant contact with the province in the district; we organized district conferences and sent comrades from Siedlce to the surrounding towns. The central committee also used many of the Siedlce comrades and sent them to more distant provincial towns. For the first united conference of Poalei–Tzion from Galicia that was held in Warsaw, the Siedlce Poalei–Tzion sent three delegates: Groman, Slushny, and Tabakman, along with scores of guests.

In Independent Poland

At the time of the first city council elections in independent Poland, the lawyer Hartglassm stood as a candidate from the Poalei–Tzion. But he made one condition, that the election list not say "Jewish Socialist Democratic Workers Party Poalei–Tzion," but only "Workers Party Poalei–Tzion." We did not agree. Our list then won six seats on the council: Yosef Slushny, Shlomo Hochberg, Zanvil Rozenzumen, Meir Saltzman, Mozes Greenfarb, and Ch. Shlifke. The Poalei–Tzion constituted a strong faction on the Siedlce city council and fought for workers' rights, for subsidies for the folk school, and for our institutions.

During the Polish–Soviet War, in 1920, when the Red army was in Siedlce and all of the workers' parties participated in the newly created "Revcom" (Revolutionary Committee), the Poalei–Tzion conducted heated discussions about our attitude toward the Bolshevik army and its government. The Poalei–Tzion committee called to a discussion meeting all the representatives from its welfare institutions, professional unions, and considered the situation.

[Page 390]

We discussed whether we could, whether we should, dance after all the other parties and take part in Bolshevik activities in Siedlce. We came to the decision, that no, we should not go along with the game. Each comrade understand and felt the responsibility and what it entailed. We decided to send a delegation to welcome their entry into Poland and particularly into Siedlce and to declare that we were awaiting a decision from our central committee and could meanwhile not take part in any activities. At the same time, we gave full permission to our comrades that they could do what they liked. The delegation consisted of Meir Saltzman, Groman, and Yisroel Tabakman.

It could have been that the Russian comrades would agree to our decision and would leave us in peace. There were, however, two traitors–Mendel Radzinski from the Jewish P.P.S. and Moyshe Altschuler from the Bund–who interfered in the matter. Hearing of our decision, they began to speak out against us, saying that we were involved in sabotage. As things developed, in the morning the military commander ordered up carpenters, locksmiths, and bakers, and our central office was closed down.

Comrade Shlifke, who was then secretary of the central committee went off somewhere. One had to seek private work, but no one wanted to go to work because the workers saw how they were paid–with "money" that one cut with scissors, and no one trusted the system. The conduct of the military was not proper. They besieged businesses, poor dwellings. They bought things, paying or not paying, just as in the days of a new occupation. And the "Revcom" made it seem like we were sabotaging things.

We were informed that we would all be arrested. We called a meeting of workers, explained the situation, and called on them to seek private work, and they complied.

[Page 391]

A day later we were called to a meeting with "Revcom" and we were made to explain why we were sabotaging the labor, why we did not organize the professional unions with the Polish ones, and so on. They said we were in a war time and that we must quickly reorganize the unions. We responded that we were under the control of recent events and that we could not control the situation. One could not reorganize scores of unions on the spur of the moment. We promised to give a definite answer in a few days.

In the meantime, things in the city were chaotic. Everything was fragmented. Soldiers came from all sides. Seeing that people were paying with rolls of papers marked with numbers, people began to hide valuable articles. There was panic in the city. The Polish militia, wanting to appear like communists, seized Jews who were hiding merchandise. The "Revcom" commandeered workers: carpenters, locksmiths, bakers, and they began to hide, not wanting to work. There were rumors that the "Revcom" would arrest all active members of Poalei–Tzion and at the same time rumors spread that the Bolshevik army was entering Warsaw. They were already in Prague. Warsaw would surely be taken that night.

That same evening there came from Moscow highly placed people. They took over Warsaw Street, where "Revcom" was located. Soon there was an order that representatives of all parties must come to a "conference with the guests from Moscow." The delegation from Poalei–Tzion (comrades Saltzman, Groman and Tabakman) were also summoned to the conference. Warsaw Street around the directorate was besieged by Jews. It was a very to evening. The windows of the directorate were open, so that on the street one could hear every word. When we arrived, the great hall was already full. We were summoned to a long table, where all the parties had their places, as well as the guests from Moscow. Then the speeches began. The guests from Moscow spoke about the freeing of Poland, which was not free of the capitalists, and of the necessity of uniting all of the professional unions.

[Page 392]

The comrades from Poalei–Tzion took part in the speeches. Saltzman would speak in Russian, Groman in Polish, and Tabakman in Yiddish. Then I, in the name of the Poalei–Tzion party, greeted the Polish revolutionary government and wished them success. About the professional unions I said: "We cannot all at one time merge with the non–Jewish unions. That would be a blow to the Jewish workers in their daily struggles. Even if we decided in favor, it could not be done at once. It would not be healthy for both sides. It would cause more friction. I propose that for the present, the Jewish professional unions should remain separate while the directors of both sides remain in constant contact."

After me, A. Groman spoke in Polish. He described our position until today. "Tomorrow we will certainly have instructions from Warsaw."

After the speeches by the official representatives from the Bolshevik government, the conference ended.

What happened to the Jews in Siedlce after the retreat of the Bolsheviks is well known. The slaughter that the Poles inflicted on the Jews cannot be forgotten, even today, after Hitler's massacres. Comrade Groman was surely shot after a trial by a Polish court martial when he could not prove that he and his comrades had cooperated with the Bolsheviks.

In the same year as the Polish–Bolshevik War, weary by all our experiences, I decided to leave Siedlce and go to Belgium, Brussels, and there not to sever my ties with Siedlce and with the party.

[Page 393]

The Leftist Workers Movement in Siedlce

by M. Yudengloibn, Buenos Aires

Translated by Theodore Steinberg

Siedlce, like many other cities in Poland, had no real industry. The small number of workers were concentrated in the leather and needle crafts; even so, the workers played an important role in the revolutionary battle against czarism. Often the battle against czarist absolutism took on a folk character, when the whole population, under the leadership of the workers parties at that time, came out into the streets in the unequal battle for a free and independent Poland.

In 1905, the police chief of Siedlce was killed by a bomb, an act that reverberated throughout Poland, and the innumerable arrests and exiles could not halt the revolutionary advance of the workers, who fought without pause for their economic betterment and political rights.

The workers movement took a new turn in Siedlce in 1916, after Poland was occupied by the Germans and the workers began to organize openly and legally, forming around the "Bund" and the "Poalei-Tzion," who increased their activities with more zest and force in all areas of community political life, This legal opportunity that had opened up gave the Jewish workers toe ability to form an actual workers institution, where all could congregate. This was the "Workers' House" on Ogrodowa Street, where nearly all of the workers became members. This was the site of broad cultural work, which involved allowing each party to bring its own people, its own leaders, to organize talks, discussions, and social events, as the town looked the other way.

[Page 394]

With the rise of the community "Workers' House," political positions began to crystalize in the workers movement. Bitter inter-party battles flared up, and the discussions that took place night after night, often with brutal arguments, increased the schism between the workers camps, the "Bund" and the "Poalei-Tzion." This situation could not long endure, as you can understand. The result was two clearly defined political directions that could not coexist under one roof, so that the "Bund" separated from the "Workers' House" and established its own home, the community workers "Tzukunft," on Dluge Street, where it conducted its activities and began to play a major role among the Jewish workers in Siedlce.

A similar process of differentiation occurred among the young people, among whom both existing parties conducted a broad-based educational program, and each one claimed to have enrolled in its circle of influence a greater number of young people; Both the "Bund" and the "Poalei-Tzion" formed separate educational youth groups, where the young people received a broad proletarian education. In a short period of time, two active youth organizations grew, which included not only almost all of the working youth but also bourgeois youth, so that two youth organizations emerged, the Bundist workers youth organization "Tzukunft" and the "Poalei-Tzion" youth organization "Borochov." Each was affiliated with its older party organization, from which they took their ideals of political orientation.

The political situation after the First World War, the outbreak of the Russian Revolution, brought with it a troublesome development in the International world, in particular, understandably, in Poland as well. The Germans, becoming aware of the revolutionary events in the country quickly left Poland; the country would be independent, and the P.P.S, led by Pilsudski took over the country.

[Page 395]

The Jewish workers in Siedlce, taking advantage of the favorable conditions, established an array of new unions, such as those for leather workers, needle workers, transport workers, bakers, and others. This development in the movement of the professions betokened an improvement in the economic condition of the workers and, indeed, of the entire population.

The leather industry had many branches, and Siedlce would send large shipments of shoes to different cities in the country, and later abroad. One could say that 70% of the Jewish laborers in Siedlce were employed in the shoe business.

The needle craft workers worked exclusively for the same purpose, except for a few second-raters who worked for the fairs.

The professional unions were directed and led by the workers parties; thus, for example, the "Bund" at that time had influence over the leather workers, the bakers, the porters, and hairdressers. "Poalei-Tzion" led the needle workers. As time passed, the unions gained strength: they fought for better wages, and a 46-hour work week was established. Piecework was abolished and overtime pay was established.

[Page 396]

Each union also had a youth division that looked after the interests of the younger workers. Simply put, it was the unions that led the working class, looked after their interests, from young to old and from small to big, and took everything under their control. A particular disturbance in the professional activities of the unions was caused by this who worked for themselves at home. They went beyond the eight-hour workday and therefore served the cause of the bosses; the union found a solution to this scourge; those who worked at home were organized and then contributed to the united workers front that worked in everyone's best interests.

A group of young men from the leather workers union

As for the political parties, they found in the professional unions united strength, and for the masses, on whom they depended in order to cement their status and win new adherents, they brought their best leaders from Warsaw and organized lectures and discussions in the largest halls, which were always packed. More than once it happened that one party had split off from another's gathering to hold special lectures and discussions.

[Page 397]

A consequence of the different lively activities, the reputation of Siedlce grew throughout the country and even played a role in the leading sections of the parties. The workers movement grew, and thanks to its organization, institutions, trade unions, cooperatives, and soup kitchens, where a worker could get a cheap—and when unemployed, even a free—nourishing lunch, it was transformed into a potential powerhouse with which everyone had to contend.

In 1920, stirred up by England and France, Poland entered war with Soviet Russia, forgetting that it had achieved its independence thanks to the Russian Revolution. The government allowed the population to wade in blood, and, you must understand, among the first to suffer were the working masses, a situation which was aided by the hostile attitude of the P.P.S. toward the Soviet Union. The Red army entered entered Warsaw, and thus taking Siedlce, where it created a "Revcom," made up of all the workers parties, to come up with solutions to all the problems that could eventually arise. After being in our city for eight days, the Red army began to move back, and this retreat created a panic, and a large number of workers went with the Red army, many of whom later fell into the hands of the Polish army, where some were shot and some received heavy prison sentences. The whole communal political life was, through the terror of the Pilsudski reaction, wiped out.

A short time later, when peace was concluded between Poland and the Soviet Union, life began to return to normal; on Pienke Street there was a tearoom around which workers began to congregate; they opened evening courses for young people, and later they were allowed to reopen the professional unions, and the working class people came to them. Thus was revived the work of the leather workers, needle workers, and other unions, and in no time at all these unions conducted again their far-flung activities.

[Page 398]

A group of students in the Esperanto course

The working masses in Siedlce learned from past times. They began to understand firmly the meaning of unity and grasped the power of organization; for sure, at that time it was not difficult to organize the working class; rather, this work was strengthened by a hundred percent. The professional unions won their old positions of an eight-hour working day and higher pay. Understand that this did not just fall from the sky; there were a number of strikes that ended in victory, which gave more clout to the professional unions and firmed up the workers movement in Siedlce. One of the most interesting strikes of the leather workers union happened in February of 1926. In Siedlce there were two leather workers unions: one for Polish workers and the other for Jewish workers. Both unions, through pressure from the workers, were committed to go on strike together against the leather bosses. Their demands were: better pay and to be paid with cash, not promissory notes. At that time the leather workers experienced a severe crisis: since there were a large number of not organized people who worked from home, they agreed to be paid for their labor with promissory notes.

[Page 399]

The bosses maintained that if they insisted on being paid in cash, they could not work at all and they would soon have to stop their labor. You must understand that this was simply a maneuver on their part, because they themselves had discounted the promissory notes, subtracting 20% from the amount. This maneuver worked for them, so that not only the workers from home but also the salaried workers were compelled to receive their pay in promissory notes. In this situation, every worker who earned a hundred zlotys actually received only eighty; soon there arose usurers or even family members of the employers who robbed the workers of their meager wages.

The Jewish leather workers union worked hard against the persecutions of the Pilsudski regime; the leaders of the Polish leather workers union (P..P.S) did not want to be in contact with the Jewish union, and they did whatever they could to prevent unity among the leather workers; and the bosses, you may be sure, turned this to their own advantage, to the great disadvantage of the working class. But something happened that no one expected: the. mass of the Polish leather workers at a meeting convinced their leaders to go out on strike together with the Jewish workers. You have to understand that this came as a terrific surprise to the bosses, who soon felt the combined strength of the workers. First they decided not to meet the demands and tried to create dissension among the workers, thinking they could "divide and conquer." They considered the Polish workers as a separate category, that is, they were machine workers, so they could deal with them separately, and they agreed not to deal with either group or to give in to their demands. The strike went on for two months, and the strike committee took advantage of their unity and organized the community's working class, which now felt for the first time the meaning of unity. A central council for all of the unions was created, and it organized the solidarity actions for the benefit of the striking leather workers.

[Page 400]

This was conducted not only on the side of Siedlce's working class but it also received aid from the whole region. The bosses tried to farm out the work in neighboring towns, but they did not succeed because at that time (and this should be noted!) strikebreakers could not be found in Siedlce or in the surrounding area, so that this maneuver failed. The huge mass meetings that took place in the premises of the P.P.S. and the enthusiastic voices of the strikers broke the bosses' unity and a split arose among them, with mutual recriminations. They began to negotiate with the strike committee on the leather workers' demands, and the strike ended in total victory for the leather workers.

I remember a curious fact: at the closing meeting of the strike, the strike committee gave thanks to the heroic conduct of the striking masses and to the feeling of solidarity shown by all the workers of Siedlce, as well as from the whole region, which led to total victory. At that moment, Polish and Jewish workers called out, "Long live the united working class! Long live the united movement of the professions!" But the leaders of the P.P.S. union, trembling at there thought of such unity, asserted that unity between the two unions was not possible, but that there should only be (apparently) contact between the two movements. But the masses, against the will of the P.P.S., upheld the unity between the Jewish and Polish workers until the outbreak of the Second World War.

* *

In the years 1919-1921 discussions began throughout the country of the "21 points" from the Third International, including in our town of Siedlce. The "21 points" quickly won as adherents the greatest part of the "Bund" membership. This same discussion, which occupied every worker's home, also took place among the "Poalei-Tzion," but with a smaller following.

[Page 401]

After several months of "battle" the "Combund" was established. It took about 95% of the Bundist party, and the "Combund" stood by the unions, the professional unions, the premises, and, above all, the workers.

With the rise of the "Combund," the panorama of life changed for the worker class in Siedlce, The combat took on greater proportions and paid no attention to the illegality of the "Combund. From day to day it became stronger and more ideologically secure. The Jewish mass of workers from Siedlce became sincere fighters in the workers' cause and through "Combund" they found the means to their end.

The same process, with the same results, came with the workers youth organization "Tzukunft," and so was formed the "Comtzukunft." The young people, as the vanguard of the newly formed revolutionary movement, moved ahead with their active leading fighters on all fronts, conveying their great organizational strength, though most of them lacked even an elementary education, for which, of course, they were not responsible. They began to develop learning circles that strengthened the cultural and political level of the young people and soon awoke hidden strengths that with their labor and political orientation amazed the central agency.

The "Combund" allied itself with the general communist party because over all there was no ideological difference between them, and the existence of two communist parties would not improve their work, which was hard enough because of the Pilsudski reactionaries. Thus on both sides there were monolithic and strong parties. The same course was taken by the "Comtzukunft." Thus was created in Siedlce the "P.P.K." (Polish Communist Party).

On the other side, however, the reactionary and fascist part of Poland grew stronger from day to day; the communist party was declared illegal and had to go under ground, while the best sons of the Polish working class were thrown into prison. The Pilsudski government, wanted to drown the workers movement in a river of blood.

[Page 402]

They threw themselves murderously on the professional unions, considering that the workers had adopted a revolutionary stance that opposed the welfare of the wealthy and their servants.

The working masses again called forth their own leaders who held fast to the revolutionary Marxist doctrine, and class warfare was everywhere as the goal of the endeavor. This did not please our rulers, who organized what was then known as the "Defense," which could not deter the working masses, led by the Comparty, from the battle for their political and economic rights.

In 1923, at the time of the elections for the Sejm, work for the election preoccupied Siedlce. The communist candidates were arrested, as were their speakers, who were caught in the act. But then the Comparty won so many significant voices that it aroused the wrath of the reactionaries, so that they returned to those who had been arrested and sentenced them to four years in prison.

A special chapter in the workers movement concerns the "Red Help," in which all the workers participated and which took care that the arrested and their families should lack for nothing; the arrested were not concerned about food but only with party responsibilities, a spiritual nourishment, that was smuggled in through the thick prison walls without regard for the great difficulty and disorder. Thus the arrested comrades were not cut off from general party life but could focus on self-education and cultivating their spiritual strength so that they could be good and useful advocates for the working class from the moment when they would be released.

In 1925, in reactionary Independent Poland, there were in Siedlce massive police raids, and many of the leading comrades were arrested, such as Avraham Slushny, Moshe Kaddish, Weinappel, and others. These arrested men could not maintain the revolutionary growth of the working masses in Siedlce.

[Page 403]

The Comparty, which continued to lead the professional movement, exercised its total hegemony, while the Bundists attracted only a small portion of the workers despite their propaganda machine that operated all over: the workers avoided them; and if the Bund appeared here or there and did not disappear completely from the arena—that was thanks to the strength of the "rabbinate," the P.PS. Party and the government that gave it the legal right to operate for the professional unions.

Thus we can see how the worker in Siedlce stood on a high revolutionary plane, and his way of thinking and outlook on the world were Marxist, without regard for the persecutions and provocations from hostile elements. He was always true to his ideals, and in this way he wrote a heroic page in the general labor history of Poland.

[Page 404]

Activity of the "Bund" in the Period Between the Two World Wars

by Getzel Lustgartn

We will write elsewhere about the illegal work of the "Bund" in czarist times. Here we will describe briefly the Bandits activity in the period between the two world wars.

Soon after the establishment of Independent Poland the "Bund" undertook the organization of Jewish workers in Siedlce. Through this party the following workers groups were established: the trade unions, which were located at 14 Warsaw Street; the "Tzukunft" at 20 Dluge, a nursery, a consumer cooperative, and a library. Leading the Bandits organization were the comrades: Moyshe Altschuler,

Yakov Fishman, Dovid Neumark (living now in America), Avraham Slushni, and Shalke Zebrawicz. The "Bund" was a mass movement. In addition, the youth organization, which then was known as the "Social–Democratic Youth Organization 'Tzukunft' in Poland," had grown to about 500 members. The leaders of the youth organization were: Yechezkel Lublinerman, David Koperant (living now in America), Sanne Weinshlbaum, and Alter Noutshitshel (living now in Argentina).

All of these organizations, which were established through hard work and which conducted a broad array of cultural and professional activities, were disrupted at the time of the Polish–Bolshevik War. The Jewish labor activists from Siedlce were sent to a concentration camp – Dombia, near Cracow.

[Page 405]

The leadership committee of the "Bund" and "Tzukunft." B. Kramarsh center

After the war, when Jewish community life in Siedlce was revived, the Bund began to reconstruct its organizations. There were no good facilities. The trade unions and other organizations met at 7 Pienke, near the Ger prayer house, but there was no conflict. Later on were built the consumer cooperative and the library. New organizations were created, such as the Workers Corner, the sports club "Morgenstern," and the "Youth Bund Tzukunft."

These organizations presented a wide variety of cultural activities. Every week there were a number of presentations: lectures, readings, chess evenings, recitations, and other events. The "Youth Bund Tzukunft" contributed to the cultural activities youth from the furthest corners of Siedlce. The young workers felt that their organization was like a second home. The youth organization also had a drama circle whose members participated in the recitations.

A branch of the Tzukunft group was the "SKF" (the Socialist Children's Association) – its members were children from 12 years up, mainly schoolchildren.

[Page 406]

The activities of the "Bund" touched deep roots in Siedlce's Jewish workers. The general professional union, under the leadership of the "Bund," grew in strength and regulated the wages and hours of the shoemakers, garment workers, and bakers. Before the outbreak of the Polish–Soviet War the union had 1,000 members aside from the youth division. Yakov Fishman was the secretary of the union.

The leadership committee the youth Bund "Tzukunft"

[Page 407]

The Polish–Soviet War, and later the terror of the Polish reactionary forces, the economic crisis in the Jewish professions, and also the ideological strife among the Jewish workers destroyed the Jewish trade movement in Siedlce. The most prominent Bundist activists went to the big cities. Finally the Jewish parties found a common language for the trade movement and successfully conducted several economic actions.

In 1927, at the time of the elections for the city council, two Bundists were elected: Binyamin Kramarzh and Rochel Barg. On the council an understanding was reached among the P.P.S, the "Bund," and the "Poalei Tzion," which together comprised a socialist majority. They passed its subsidies for the folks school and social aid for poor Jews.

Also on the health insurance board there were two Bandits representatives: Yosef Rozenzumen and Yakov–Yitzchok Liebman. Liebman was the longstanding secretary of the transport union in Siedlce.

In the Jewish community elections of 1933, the Bund came in second and placed 4 members on the community council: Yosef Rozenzumen, Binyamin Kramarzh, Yosef Barg, and Yakov–Yitzchok Liebrman.

On May Day, the "Bund" often held demonstrations together with the P.P.S.

In 1931, the Bundist organization took over the Siedlce Jewish folk school, which had earlier belonged to the folkist party.

The "Bund" in Siedlce conducted its activities until Hitler's hordes came to Siedlce. The Bundists were murdered along with Siedlce's Jews.

[Page 408]

Jewish Workers of Siedlce after the First World War

by David ben-Yosef (Pasovsky)

Translated by Theodore Steinberg

A collection of memories and facts about the life of Jewish workers in the years 1923-1931—the time when I was a community activist in Siedlce.

Siedlce was not an industrial city, but consequently there grew up a strong small artisanal culture. There were hundreds of workshops of different types. About 3,500 Jewish families lived from such work. There were about 2,000 members in the various unions—a respected laboring mass. A good percentage of Jews who did not live from moneylending, business, or odd jobs, but only from labor, people with calluses, exemplified the biblical passage—"By the sweat of your brow will you eat."

The professional unions were led by: the "Bund," the leftist "Poalei-Tzion," the "Reds" (communists), and partially also the rightist "Poalei-Tzion," which organized the unskilled workers.

The leftist "Poalei-Tzion" also conducted evening classes in the community, led by comrade Yosef Slushny. The evening classes were conducted at 46 Ogradowa Street and 16 Warsaw Street, and concerned cultural activities.

The largest craft, according to the number of workers, was the leather workers: shoemakers, boot makers, bootblacks, and makers of sports equipment. About 500 workers were employed in these professions. They were organized in the leather workers union.

[Page 409]

Second place was taken by the needle workers, with about 400 Jewish tailoring workers.

The professional unions were not only concerned with such labor matters as unemployment, the dead season, social problems, support in the winter, and so on—they were also concerned with cultural matters. They organized different social events, gatherings, lectures, and chess evenings. In the leather workers union, which was influenced by the "Reds," there was also a drama club and a workers chorus. More than once these cultural undertakings were undermined by opponents, who would interrupt and make a commotion until the intervention of the "third side"—the police, who restored order by disbanding the gathering and arresting some of the workers for being communists…

In my days, the head of the leather workers union was the well-known Bundist M. Greenberg, and the secretary was—Friedrich. This union was a 4 Milne, but the workers were known to gather as a group for their heated discussions in the square across from the magistrate's and in the large beis-medresh between minchah and ma'ariv. They did not come to pray but only to discuss and agitate among the Jews about the salvation of mankind.

The service workers and wage earners were miserable: record keeping, for low wages and promissory notes and no social concerns.

In the Clothing Industry

There was a time when the needle workers in Siedlce had a strong professional union that watched out for their interests. But then it happened that the main worker, Yosef Slushny, who had devoted so much energy to the union, passed away.

After his death, a battle broke out among the parties over who should control the workers of Siedlce.

In the union there was a battle among the "Bund," the "Reds," and the leftist "Poalei-Tzion" and there were ideological arguments to draw workers to one side or the other.

[Page 410]

The arguments became violent. There were scandals and intrigues. The union became weaker. There was no money to pay the rent and the needle workers were evicted from the hall of the leatherworkers union on Milne.

The party friction stopped the development of the union and made it impossible for it to care for the interests of the needle workers.

In the Knitwear Industry

The knitwear industry began to develop in Siedlce after the Polish-Bolshevik War. It made great progress until 1930. Siedlce began to be counted as one of the great centers for the knitwear industry in the Polish province. During the season, 60 machines would be in operation twenty-four hours a day.

The knitwear workers were for the most part recruited from the so called genteel circles. A young man who had not succeeded in business and sought a new profession to support himself took up the knitwear industry. This was a job that one could learn quickly and soon begin to earn money.

I recall how these young people in 1927 organized the first strike for better wages. The union was then at 7 Pienke, under the auspices of the leather union. After the strike, the knitwear workers joined with the textile union in Lodz and opened a branch in Siedlce. The textile union was under the auspices of the P.P.S.

In season, the knitwear industry employed, counting also the workers from the small towns around Siedlce, around 800 workers. A number of workers learned the trade and then went to Warsaw or left the country—for Belgium, France, and South America. They settled there with their skill and today occupy honored places in the textile industry.

[Page 411]

There were also in Siedlce many workers in trades that lacked organization, like builders, milliners, carpenters, housepainters, hatmakers, and others. They seldom appeared in the organized professional workers movement. Before the Second World War, a branch of the business employees union opened in Siedlce, led by Chaim Reise.

A special spot in Siedlce was held by the "pioneer" training camps. Those who were associated with these camps learned skills in preparation for making aliyah to Eretz Yisroel, mostly in construction.

Over all, Jewish Siedlce had nothing to be ashamed of in regard to its productive workers. We can only regret that it was all brutally cut short and lives now only in our memories.

* *

The Jewish workers of Siedlce, like the workers throughout Poland, often had a taste of difficult crises, especially in the so-called "dead seasons. In order to complete our description of the lives of Siedlce's Jewish workers, we add a section called "The Dead Season" that was printed in the "Siedlcer Vochenblat."

The "Dead Season"

From early in the morning until after dark you can encounter Jewish workers by the city hall or across from the magistrate's. They stand in groups, long rows stretched out—the unemployed, victims of the time.

Hungry people whose pale faces stare out as if from skeletons. They would turn their hands to work, but no one is interested.

More than one of them has a wife waiting at home with small children in a small dwelling where the wind blows in and the poor children cry out in a single voice: "Mama, bread!"

When night falls, you can still run into many of them in the beis-medresh where they come to warm up. They sit on a long bench by the stove, wiping off saliva, and more than one sighs out the questions, "From whence cometh my help?"

[Page 412]

There, too, in the beis-hamedresh, they sit in groups, like in a club, and speak among themselves about wars, world politics, crises, and so on.

Attention shifts to the Jew in the colorful torn clothing, with his sorrowful face; he tells everyone that in his dwelling are his wife and six children, as well as a son-in-law who lives with him—and he has no income. A year ago, he says, things were a little better. He was helped by the support for the unemployed that was provided by the magistrate and the community. He could afford a little warm food for his children, a bit of coal, wood, enough for survival, but today—there is nothing. No one hears about or sees any help. In such conditions there is nothing left but to die of hunger. "That's for sure"—everyone in the circle around him agrees. A second worker, a younger man, apparently self-confident, directs the whole anger of his starving stomach toward the heads of our busybodies, to our different providers. Even our designated work activists—he says—do not consider this catastrophic situation that comes with the "dead season."

"Yes, yes, the dead season"—another takes over, a strongly optimistic young man who really believes that it will not always be so. "In fact," he says, "all workers should be registered at the labor office for work mediation. Go to our Jewish work providers over whom the awfulness of high taxes hang like a heavy sword."

"But oy, what can one do?" Screams a trembling older Jew, the father of four children, including two daughters. "Where does one get shoes for one's children? They can't go barefoot. And as for bread, potatoes, and other food," he says, wtth tears in his eyes, "everything is cheap. 'An ox for a groschen, but there are no groschen.'"

Seeing this sad picture causes one's heart to ache.

[Page 413]

The Community

by P. Drumy (Popowsky)

Translated by Theodore Steinberg

Before 1926 people called the Siedlce community "The Dozor Prayer House." In fact, that name described the state of the community, because both in its internal appearance and in the operations of its doors, it was like a "prayer house."

As for the internal appearance: a long stable–like room. In the corner by the door sat R. Yitzchak Tenenbaum and recorded the newborn children, giving a notice to the magistrate so that the child could be registered–or to erase it in case of a death (rest in peace). In the other corner of the eastern wall sat his son, Hershel Tenenbaum, the secretary of the Jewish community. When a dozor arrives and wants to know something or when there is a meeting, the secretary's table is used, because there is no room for more than two tables.

The community organization had little effect on the population. Its activity consisted of collecting the community tax and paying the salary of the rabbinate. And this activity was conducted sloppily. The tax was collected, because this was done by the non–Jews, but the payment to the rabbis was always a couple of months behind. The income from slaughtering [there was a tax on kosher slaughtering], which affected the budget, was the business of the slaughterers, who divided the income among themselves. When a rebellion was led by the donor Yisroel Gutgelt, who persuaded the secular authority to help, and the slaughtering became a community issue, because he wanted the Talmud Torah to have a certain percentage of the slaughtering feels, it still seemed like a fiction. The slaughter of fowl seemed to be a kind of in–house business of the slaughterers.

[Page 414]

Each shochet slaughtered them in his home and the money went into his pocket. Although the shochets gave a percentage of the income from the slaughterhouse, they did not consent to slaughter for an agreed upon fee.

The small, puny subsidies for the "Ezras Y'somim" [the orphan home] and "Moshav Z'kaynim" [the old people's home] that were in the budget were collected with great difficulty and were always late.

Also the "Chevra Kadisha" [the burial society] and the "Mourners Society" were particularly unreasonable in serving their own interests. If even a moderately well–off person died and his relatives come to the "dozor prayer house" to get permission to carry out a burial, they had to go to the "Chevra Kadisha" to "complete the deal." This was not so easy. The gabbais of the Chevra Kadisha were always "unavailable." After the interested parties were exhausted from running from one to the other, they were given a price for what it would cost, and if they did not agree, the gabbais again became unavailable until they were informed by the head of the "Chevra Kadisha" that agreement had been reached. Then began the haggling with the "Mourners Society."

The "Mourners Society" filled a real need. Before it existed, people would take the deceased to the cemetery in a wagon. If a rich person died or a big shot, friends and acquaintances would carry him and the wagon would follow behind. At a poor person's funeral, the deceased would go on the wagon and often there were not even ten men, a minyan, at the cemetery. So a group of men established the "Mourners Society." The wagon with the horse was done away with. It was decided that people would carry anyone, with no distinction between rich or poor, a distinguished person or a common person. The "Mourners Society" took their mission seriously. Even in the hardest rains or in frost they carried out their job, or their business, and they gave the dead the "grace of truth."

[Page 415]

If a woman died, one had to go to the women's committee. They also took their work seriously and made no distinctions between rich and poor. For their services the Mourners Society received payment, and the community received no benefit from their income.

The only real source of income for the community–the tax–was not used as it should have been. From 4,000 families that were in Siedlce, only 360 paid the tax, that is, approximately ten percent. Even if we say that everyone in the 4,000 could pay the tax, seventy–five percent could, that is, 3,000. But the dozors did not want to increase the number of the "bosses." The Zionist organization made a strong case the people should go to the community and say that they wanted to pay the tax. And truly, a number of comrades from the Zionist organization in Siedlce went to the "dozor prayer house" and asked that the tax be imposed on them. The dozors did not understand their prerogatives and duties even so far as, for example, hiring a cantor of the Great Synagogue, which was one of their activities. Thus was the cantorial contract for R. Yosef Posowski signed not only by the dozors but first by the rabbinate, and later by the dozors and then by all the taxpayers, although the cantor was hired by the community organization.

The council of the Mourners Society

Seated: Moyshe Shmooklosz, Aryeh Galitzky, Yitzchak Rozengarten, Mordechai Gornicki, Berel Srebrenik
Standing: Moyshe Felshpan, Naftali Koopershmit, and Yerachmiel Levin

[Page 416]

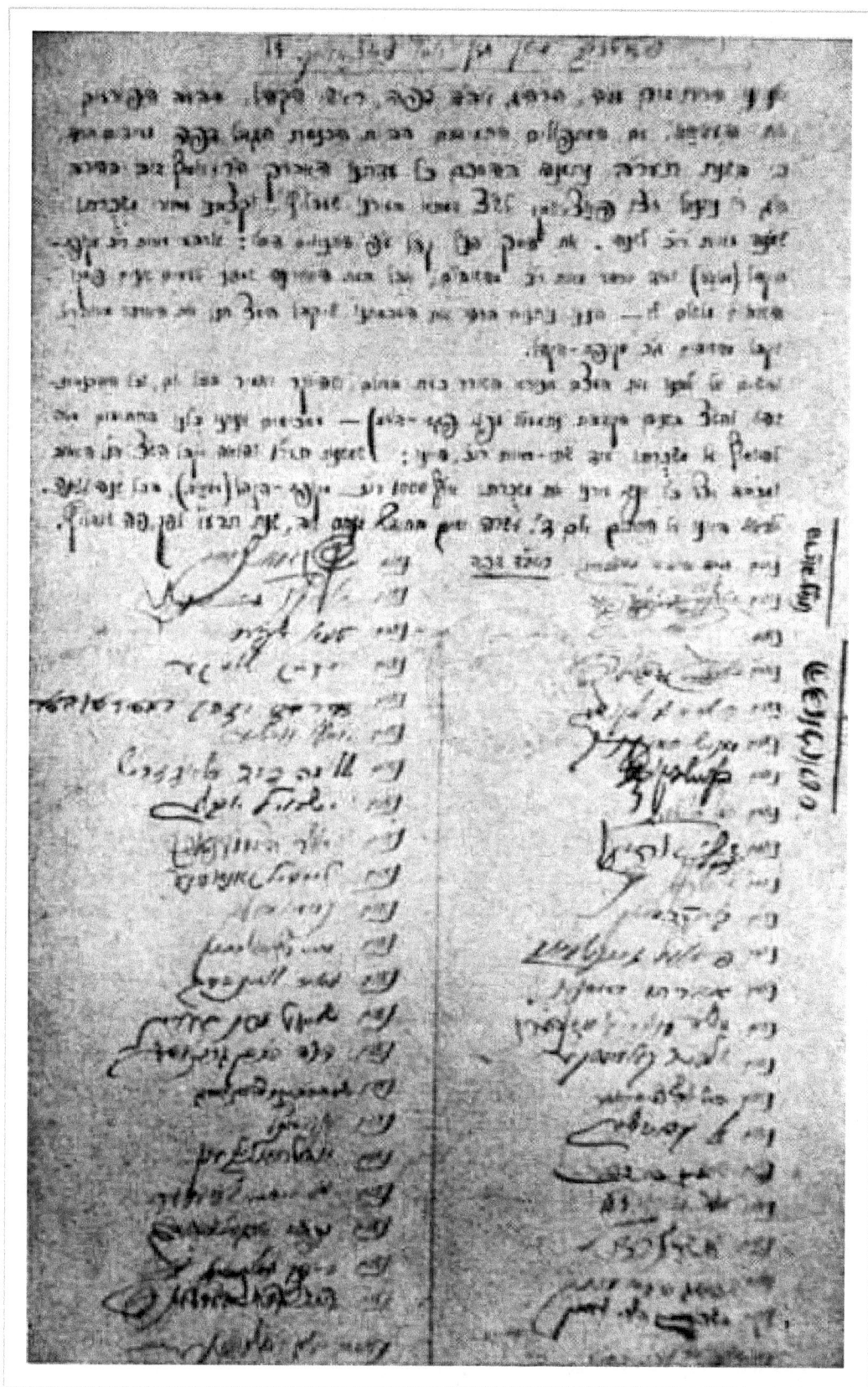

The contract for hiring the city cantor D. B. Posowskyu, signed by the rabbis, dozors, and by the respected, homeowning taxpayers

[Page 417]

Thus had existed the situation until 1926, when elections were ordered for the community. The election ordinance was for the most part democratic. All men over 21 had voting rights, even those who paid no taxes. Women had no voting rights, because the Jewish community was counted as a religion. The following took part in that election for the Siedlce community: Zionists, Mizrachi, Agudah, Folkists, and the artisans. The "Bund" and the "Poalei Tzion" boycotted the election because of paragraph 20, which denied voting rights to the non–religious. The main battle in the election was played out between the "Agudah" and the Zionists. In every Chasidic prayer house and minyan there were calls from the rabbis, who implored the Jews to vote in the election for the "Agudah," in order to prevent the community from falling into the hands of the Zionists, of sinners, who would destroy the Talmud Torahs and yeshivas and who would bring in Reform rabbis.

The result of the election was the following: of the 20 members of the community council, the "Agudah" won 10, 50%, and had no majority. The Zionist list–4, artisans–4. Three of the artisans were friends of the Zionist committee, so there were, in effect, 7 Zionists, and the fourth artisan sympathized with the Zionists. The Folkists and the "Mizrachi" each had one member.

The 20 members of the community council were supposed to elect a 10–person starring committee, and the Folkists and "Mizrachi" had no chance of placing a member on the steering committee, and they had no interest in placing anyone else there. Therefore they took no part in electing the steering committee. Consequently, the "Agudah" received 6 seats and the Zionists and artisans (8 voices) only 4 seats.

The members of the "Agudah" on the community council were: Yakov Szczerancki, Shimon Ridel, Moyshe Shlifke, Eliyahu Tenenbaum, Sender Kantor, Bunim Huberman, Moyshe Zakan, Yisroel Zlotowski, Berish Gurzalke, Yakov Zucker.

[Page 418]

From the Zionists: Y.N. Weintraub, Asher Urzel, M.A. Eisenstadt, and (making a division between the living and the dead) Dr. M Schleicher (now living in Israel); artisan–Zionists were Z.N. Malin, Shmuel Wahrman, Aaron Morecki, and Berl Srebnik. Folkist: Yosef Rosenzumen. Mizrachi: V. Arlavski.

Steering committee members were: From the "Agudah": Yisroel Gutgelt, Ephraim Halberg, Berish Jakubowicz, Tuvia Shiffer, Yoel Slushni, Asher–Moyshe Gelkenbaum; Zionist and artisans: Moyshe Goldb erg, Yehuda Vodeh, Noson–Hersh Gurstein, and (making a division between the living and the dead) Fishl Popowski (now Dromi, living in Israel).

The first open meeting took place with the participation of the of the local official Mr. Kasztliosz. The agenda consisted of a single item: the election of a chair for the community council by the council members and a chair for the steering committee, elected by the committee members.

There were two candidates for chair of the community council: from the Zionists, the old Zionist activist Y.N. Weintraub, and from the "Agudah," Yakov Szczeranski. This time the Folkists and Mizrachi went for our candidate. The result was: ten votes for the Zionist candidate Weintraub and ten for the Agudah candidate Szczeranski. According to the election rules, there had to be another vote. The third time, after a similar result, lots had to be drawn between the two candidates. The local official, Mr. Kasztliosz, who was taking part in the meeting, ruled, however, that since there had been a tie, that Szczeranski, the Agudah candidate, would be chair, and he ordered the election of a chair of the steering committee.

The writer of these words requested a word in order to explain the election. When I started to speak in Yiddish, the official interrupted and asked why I was not speaking in Polish. Was it because I did not want to or because I could not? I responded that according to the rules, only the chair was required to speak Polish. When a representative of the government was taking part, however, the members could speak in Yiddish and the representative could read the speech in the minutes or people could translate it into Polish for him. The audience that filled the hall was very happy with my answer.

[Page 419]

After this incident, I made the following declaration:

"Over the course of years, the Zionist organization has led a cultural war against the character of the Jewish community organization. We are saying that the Jewish community organization should not be solely religious but also secular, that it should embrace the whole of Jewish life, that is, not only supporting the Talmud Torahs but also secular schools, if that is what the community wants. We have said, that the Jewish community should be concerned with all of the religious, cultural and social needs of Jewish society: starting libraries, evening courses, sports clubs, supporting the building up of Eretz Yisroel, and so on. Voting rights should be given to all persons over 18, without regard to gender, whether they pay taxes or not. But the government will not change the character of the Jewish community organization and continues to consider it as a religious organization. They took away from women the right to vote for this Jewish institution. Even though we are unhappy with the voting rules, we decided to take part in the community organization, but we really feel that the Jewish community organization should and must be not only a religious but also a secular institution."

"But seeing the ruling by Mr. Official that violates the rules with the intention of boosting the "Agudah" against the Zionists, I declare that we will not recognize the chair of the Jewish community organization but will consider him as the chair of Mr. Official. We will not recognize his instructions until things are done according to the rules. And as a protest, I declare, in the name of the Zionists and the artisans, that we will not participate in the election for a chair of the steering committee."

Dr. Schleicher translated my speech into Polish, and then he shouted, "I wish good luck to the to the government's nominee!" The official answered that he would send my declaration to the voyevoda . R. Yisroel Gutgelt was elected with six votes from the Agudah. With that, the first open meeting ended.

[Page 420]

The "Agudah," encouraged by the machinations of the official, undertook to ram through their program of "B'yad Khazakah" and in their new budget, supported by their majority, they supported only religious undertakings. Only one option remained for us–Zionists, artisans, and Folkists–to make long speeches and not allow the matter to come to a vote.

This abnormal situation of the community organization lasted for several months. Each meeting was fruitless. We could not vote on the budget, and the work of the organization was as if paralyzed, until there arrived an order from the voyevoda to cancel the nomination from the official for chair and to hold a lottery between the two candidates, that is, between Mr. Weintraub and Mr. Szceranski. An open meeting was called. The lottery was won by the veteran Zionist activist Mr. Weintraub. Most of the Jewish population of Siedlce, even some from the Agudah, received the results happily.

With the conclusion of the chair problem, the Agudah lost the majority on the council. The Agudah members, who were interested in a normal operation of the community organization, primarily R. Yisroel Gutgelt, broke with their prior principles and began to pay attention to our desires. They inserted in the budget subsidies for the Tarbus and Folk schools (admittedly, not as much as for the Talmud Torah), for Hebrew courses, and a subsidy for "Keren Kayames L'Yisroel." Also, my proposal was approved that every pioneer who went up to Eretz Yisroel should receive a grant.

Thus did our Zionist activities in the community organization bring in a bit of worldliness and Jewish nationalism to the legal Jewish institution. On the steering committee it became difficult to tell the positions of the Agudah representatives. The officials from the Agudah often voted for Zionist proposals. How often some of the Agudists were influenced by our Zionist activities can be illustrated by the following:

When the education minister Miklaszewski visited Siedlce, the chair of the steering committee, Yisroel Gutgelt called a meeting and proposed that a delegation from the community organization should greet the minister.

[Page 421]

I was opposed this proposal and I gave the following reasons: 1) We were not invited, and 2) The minister, who had sent Jewish students to Jablona, and he should not be greeted, because greeting him without being bidden would show that we were happy with him, when the opposite was the case. At the time of the vote over my proposal, 2 members from the "Agudah" voted with me, and the proposal to offer greetings was defeated.

The town official, who learned about the vote, was quite let down and said, "What does Popowski think, that he and Lukaszewicz (a former deputy from the minority–bloc) will bring down Poland? I'll get even with those who voted with him." He meant the "Agudah" members. The "Agudah" trustees were frightened, and when the chair called for another meeting to revise the vote, the 2 Agudah members voted in favor of the greeting.

As I have already explained, the election of Y.N. Weintraub as chair of the community organization had created the possibility of progressive work in the community. We began to bring a little bit of order to the life of the Jewish community.

The soldiers under the leadership of Sergeant Zalman Freilich, who lives now in Israel (Netanya)
In the middle is David Popowski, who was in charge of the kosher kitchen

[Page 422]

The community organization took over the supervision of slaughtering as well as slaughtering of fowl, and the slaughterers became salaried workers. Also for the Chevra Kadisha we ordered that people did not have to go around searching for the gabbais in their private dwellings. I must praise the gabbais of the Chevra Kadisha. It was not difficult to persuade them that it was more appropriate and better for them as well that the natter if paying final honors to the dead was centered in the community organization. Understand that they voted to approve what we had assured them that all the expenses of the Chevra would be taken care of by the organization, even the traditional kiddush on the eve of the 8th of Shevat. But things were difficult with the Mourners Society. After long negotiations, we came to an agreement that burials would be coordinated by the community organization. Only the women's group, that was responsible for the care of women who had died, remained independent as a concession. The women's group was led by: Puryah from the Soda Water, the wife of R. Leibele Rosenberg, Chanah Ribawski, Chanah Popowski, and others.

The Jewish soldiers with the committee at the seder

[Page 423]

In the institutions that received larger subsidies there was a representative from the community organization. I was the representative for the "Ezras–Y'somim." At Pesach, the steering committee organized a kitchen for the Jewish soldiers. We also founded a "G'milas–Chesed" [charity] fund where hundreds of people received loans of of up to 200 zlotys without interest. This helped them get on their feet. Small merchants and workers who could not get loans in the banks used the charity fund.

Thanks to these activities in the Siedlce community organization, there began a true Jewish representation that everyone had to deal with. Yisroel Gutgelt, although he had been elected by the Agudah and was one of their leaders, when he saw that we Zionists would invigorate the Jewish community, he would often ask important questions and hold consultations with the Zionist leaders. The Zionists fulfilled their promise that they had made at the first meeting of the Siedlce community organization, that they would institute secular concerns.

[Page 424]

After I left Siedlce at the end of 1932, cooperative work was accomplished by the steering committee members.

At the last election of the organization, there were also Bundists and "Poalei–Tzion" members.

After there was an election for a rabbi, which brought about a battle between the "Mizrachi" and "Agudah" candidates, the cooperation between the Zionists and the "Agudah" came to an end. And so it was until the world war, when the Nazis erased and ended the life of the Jewish community in Siedlce.

[Page 425]

Development of the Jewish Credit System in Siedlce
The Siedlce Savings and Loan Society

by B. Mintz

Translated by Theodore Steinberg

The Jewish community credit system in Siedlce began to develop soon after the revolutionary year of 1905. For Jews, and especially for Jews in Siedlce, that was a difficult and bitter time.

The general situation of Jews in Poland in 1906, the year of the most severe persecutions and suppressions directed particularly toward Jews, afflicted the Jewish community with moral, cultural, and economic destruction–and especially Siedlce in its specific situation, with its lack of rights, its depression, its disorientation, and its despair. The year 1906 appeared to the Jews of Siedlce as a true "vale of tears." The whole of community life felt the burden of having survived the pogrom. The awful images of the pogrom, like dark shadows, clouded over the eyes and filled the hearts with sorrow and pain, with fear and despair.

The young people, out of panicked fear, left their homes in masses and fled to other countries. Whoever could, whoever had the possibility, sooner or later left the city, abandoning their possessions as if they were worthless.

Economic life of the Jews in Siedlce, which had never had a healthy, rational basis, became even worse, more repressive. A fearful indifference, apathy, and hopelessness seized the people and paralyzed their initiative. Some wanted to strengthen community life and to restore to health the ruined economic situation.

[Page 426]

It truly took a great deal of strength, energy and self–sacrifice in order, at that time, to bring to fruition the idea of building in Siedlce and institution devoted to mutual aid built on a foundation of cooperation. The thought of cooperation, the idea of self–help built on economic unity was, at that time, new and not very popular. In the context of Poland at that time (Congress Poland), there were no more than four savings and loan institutions in different cities: Lublin, Radom, Grodna, and Vilna–with small memberships. These institutions had little standing among the Jewish public and had little public support.

It was quite risky to try and establish such an institution in Siedlce. As was well known, Siedlce was always a city where a certain portion Jews with money lived by usury. Since there was no business or manufacturing base and no connection with the industrial centers of he country, Siedlce was always behind in business and manufacturing. It lagged behind a whole array of larger and smaller cities in the Podlosk region. The only homegrown "production" in Siedlce was usury. For a whole layer of Siedlce's Jews, lending money at interest was a stabile source of income and was like a full–time profession passed on as an inheritance from fathers to children.

A particular type of usurer, known as "vochernikes" [means "usurers"] had, for many years, done well in Siedlce, and thanks to there setting up of the savings and loan, they disappeared from the scene. The clients of the "vochernikes" consisted mostly of poor small merchants and workers, particularly when they needed a bigger or smaller loan, for instance to buy a patent or to organize a workshop for their income or in case of a lingering illness. On average, a loan would be for 100 rubles, payable in 50 weekly installments of 2.50 rubles–an interest rate of 50% annually [trans. note: These are. his figures.], which was for the time terribly high.

[Page 427]

The "vochernik" himself would go to the houses and shops to collect the payments–the hard–earned groschen of the Jewish poor. And woe to him who could not fully make the payments. He would become a lifelong Canaanite servant to the "vochernik". The "vocherniks" were hated not only by the poor people, but also by everyone whom they had "benefited." They often met with curses. The whole city regarded them as parasites and treated them with a certain contempt.

This, more or less, is how the general classes of people regarded the community and economic life of the Jews in Siedlce in 1906, on the eve of the establishment of the savings and loan, which later was given the name "Shareholder Bank" ["Bank Udszalowi"].

The First Pioneers and Leaders of the Credit System

The first pioneers, the first community leaders whom we meet at the founding of the saving and loan were: A. Urszel, Shimri Greenberg, N.D. Glicksberg, N. Weintraub, M. Walawelski, St. Sunderland, M.M. Landau, Matisyahu Mintz, A.Z. Mendziszecki, Sh. Zuker, Dr. M Stein, and A. Shlifke. Some of these who were present at the first founding meeting were elected to the lending section of the organization.

Extract from the czarist powers a legitimization for establishing such a society was no easy thing. Even back in 1904, Mr. N. Weintraub, on his own initiative, tried to do so in Petersburg and, despite the intercession of influential parties, was unsuccessful. The matter was not considered to be a legitimate financial undertaking by the governmental offices according to the "local committee for small banks." Only in a certain sense, as through a reform–a thing that in czarist times was considered suspect, as reform led to "sedition," so that a single step was a long way. The request for permission that was subscribed to by all the above mentioned people, was sent by the governor's chancellery to the police division for a thorough investigation.

[Page 428]

And although these men were known as politically pure, or in the language of that time "blagonadioshne," [politically reliable] the police zealously conducted an inquiry, both into this matter and into the individuals.

After great exertion and hardship, they received legalization, dated the ninth of February, old style, 1907, number 11, addressed "to the fully–empowered founder of the savings and loan, Mr. Nachum Weintraub." In the permission it provided that according to the decision of the "Siedlce governing committee for small banking matters," permission was given to open in Siedlce a society under the name "Siedlce Savings and Loan Society," with the emblem of the governmental office at the bottom of the decree from the finance minister, dated August 14, 1905.

Executives of the credit institution

*Seated (from the right): Mendel Liverant, Shmuel Zucker, Y.N. Weintraub, Velvet Bag, Sh. Greenberg, N.D.
Glicksberg*
Standing (from the right): Asher Eisenberg, Agrist, Herzl, Alberstadt

The goal of the society was clear: to provide the opportunity to all levels of the Jewish population to obtain inexpensive credit through accessible means.

[Page 429]

According to its structure, the savings and loan had a restricted field of activity: it had the right to accept deposits and to make loans at a specified level (a maximum of 600 rubles); it could not take part in other banking functions. Because loans were not on promissory notes but only on "reverses," the society could collect administratively and not go through the court. Supervision over the society and its activities belonged to the inspector of small credit, who from time to time conducted an inspection and examined the financial books. The general meeting of the members was the highest authority of the society.

The founding capital of the society included a thousand rubles in cash, which was given by the "Siedlce Committee to Support Those Affected by the Pogrom in Siedlce." The committee held funds from a number of cities and towns in Poland and Russia and in foreign countries, from institutions and from individuals, from Jews and from non–0Jews. Thus the founding capital of the credit society was not local, n to just from Siedlce but, so to speak, "universal," international. This capital was precious, heartfelt, coming from idealistic human feelings, voluntary offerings with one end: to heal, to help, and to build.

April 24, 1907 marked the founding meeting in the hall of the society, in the house of Issachar Levin (5 Proste), with a huge hall full of pledged members. A security committee was elected unanimously: Moyshe Temkin, Shmuel Zucker, Meir Frankel, Moshe Abba Eisenstadt, and Aaron Zelig Mendziszecki; and on the managing committee: Dr. Moritzi Stein, Nachum Weintraub, Shmaryahu Greenberg, Shimon Fidel, and Asher Moshe Gelkenbaum; and on the audit committee: Matisyahu Mintz, Noson Dovid Gliksberg, and Oscar Mintz; as honorary trustee the lawyer Stanislaw Sunderland. Head of the council was Moyshe Temkin, head of the managing committee was Dr. Moritzi Stein.

There maximum loan for a member as set at between 50 and 300 rubles, according to the individual circumstances of the member, with the provision that loans were only for less fortunate people. The maximum payment was determined to be 15 rubles, payable in installments according to the wishes of the particular member.

[Page 430]

The society operated expeditiously. Within a few days it would accept new members and accept applications for loans.

The members were a mixed lot: merchants, small businessmen, workers, and members of the intelligentsia. The managing committee held regular meetings and demonstrated a proper devotion to the institution. Their decisions were all appropriately publicized.

As bookkeeper and office leader they engaged Mordechai Meir Landau, a highly educated man with a fine, subtle sensibility and splendid organizational abilities. He regarded the institution not only as a commercial undertaking built on a cooperative basis, but as a source of self–help, humane mutual aid in financial matters that strove to help the weak, the downtrodden individual. He showed wholehearted devotion. M.M. Landau was also interested in the moral life of the members. He wanted to raise them up, make them more worldly, more concerned with the community. He wanted to proclaim the essence and the goal of the cooperative and to impress them with the awareness that the bank was their own, that they, the members, were its only legitimate custodians.

In addition, M.M. Landau was not as concerned with how many loans were given out as with what they were intended for, whether for business or for funding a workshop, and he was careful not to give loans for so–called "consumption goals"–anything that was harmful either for a member or for a cooperative.

The "loan office" was quickly envied not only by the Jewish population of Siedlce but also widely outside the borders of Siedlce. In many cities and towns the Siedlce "loan office" aroused great interest and gave the local leaders the stimulus to follow the example of Siedlce. Sokolow, Wengrow, Radzin, and Mard were the first to make preparations to found such an office. To that end they sent to Siedlce delegates to investigate.

[Page 431]

The leaders in Siedlce demonstrated a sincere interest in the development of the new institutions and aided the investigators with words and deeds. For these newly established institutions, the Siedlce "loan office" served as a master institution, as a center to which they came for advice and information and with which they conducted a multifarious correspondence. In addition, the Siedlce society gave material aid to the provincial institutions, extending to them larger and smaller credit, as well as helping them to conduct business properly and to improve their techniques in office conduct and bookkeeping.

The popularity of the Siedlce institution grew quickly and led to the interest of the Petersburg chapter of the Y.K.O.–the Jewish Colonizing Association (the Yiddish Kolonistishe Organizatzia). Instructors from the Y.K.O–Messrs. Segal and Ephroikin, were several times sent to Siedlce in order to familiarize themselves with the work methods and growth of the society. In 1912, the president of the Y.K.O., Mr. Kastelianski, who was interested in the situation of the local shoemakers and sought to unite the local Jewish producers and shoe exporters in a single workers cooperative, visited the society. (Unfortunately, his attempt did n to succeed.). The impression conveyed by the Y.K.O. instructors from their inspections was more than enthusiastic. They expressed their appreciation for the current leadership and accomplishments and promised the support of the Y.K.O., which at that time, aside from its many–branched colonizing activities, also supported small–credit activities which at that time were taking shape in Russia and Poland. In 1909, the Y.K.O. gave the Siedlce loan office a long–term credit of 15,000 rubles at 6% annual interest.

On April 27, 1908, the first general meeting of members occurred. From the report of 1907, that was published in a beautiful volume in three languages–Hebrew, Polish, and Russian–we see that for the full year the society had 540 members with a declared capital of 8.019 rubles; 576 loans had been made for a total; pf 56.916 rubles; borrowers owed the society 20,155 rubles; the balance for the year was closed out with a surplus of 292 rubles.

[Page 432]

The continuing development of the loan office moved quickly and soon after its first year of activity it assumed a conspicuous position and earned the fullest trust of all levels of the population.

The location at 5 Proste was not big enough, and in 1908 the office moved to a bigger location–in the house of Shlomo Kahana (17 First of May Street). In 1912, the office of the society moved to a gorgeous six–room building, the house of Ch.D. Lichtenfacht (20 First of May Street). (That was the name of the street before the Second World War.). The yearly balances of the society, from 1908 until 1913, are not known. Consequently we cannot see the gradual development of the society and its growth during this period.

The report for 1913 illustrates this growth through the following figures: number of members–2,542; capital–31,667 rubles; ground and reserve capital–15,055 rubles; outstanding loans, remainder–205,188 rubles; payments—211,501 rubles.

From the profits for this year we can see that the society prospered, even though the interest rate of the distributed loans had been pushed down from 10.3 to 9.3, and then in 1911 to 8%.

The fiscal year of 1908 closed with a surplus of 3,001 rubles, 1909 with 4,062 rubles, 1910 with 4,086 rubles, and 1913 with 4,148 rubles.

In 1912 the society decided to open other branches of the cooperative. To this end, a special fund was created from the yearly profits to purchase food products and heating materials for resale to the members. At the end of 1913, this fund had accumulated 551 rubles. In addition, the following special funds were created: a fund for life insurance for members and a fund for buying a building for the society, for which a percentage of the yearly profits was set aside. These funds showed on January 1, 1913, significant sums.

[Page 433]

In this way, the loan office assumed an important position not only as a credit cooperative but also expanded its activities in other cooperative enterprises.

The culmination of its development was reached in 1914, which saw the strengthening of the financial situation and a growth in the number of loans being given. However, the second half of 1914 stands under the marks of the world war, which had a catastrophic effect on the continuing development of the loan office.

At the outbreak of the First World War, the office had 2,760 members and a capital of 36,000 rubles, with a reserve capital of 20,000 rubles; borrowers owed the office–217,167 rubles.

Community Struggles in the Credit–Society

In order to receive a full picture of he first open, legal, Jewish institution in Siedlce, which was characteristic of other Jewish cities and towns of that tie–it is appropriate to describe the forms of community struggles that erupted in the credit society.

The general meeting of the society were stormy. Siedlce before the war was a backwards community. The savings and loan was the first place where community passions could be played out. For most people it was strange to consider economic questions in a social–community forum. Aside from this, the mass of members lacked the aptitude to know how to approach cooperative problems that were new to them that were new to them, and they had a weak grasp of them. Instead of being quiet and patient with the handling of the details of the agenda, instead of objectively evaluating the activities of the managing group for the coming year and commenting on the working plans for the coming year, such matters came up at the general meetings that were irrelevant to the activities of the society and to cooperation as a community movement.

[Page 434]

The general meetings turned into an arena, into a battlefield for all kinds of private antagonisms and personal ambitions, breaking out in conflicts, Jewish community reckonings, and clannish intrigues. It became as tumultuous as a carnival. One person outshouted another and both ganged up on a third. The atmosphere became strained and heated. The chaos and confusion reached the highest level. Everything was topsy–turvy, with screams and cries, with anger and fury.

The writer of these lines remembers this picture:

In the Folk House, where the general meetings were usually held–stands a member of the council and reads a financial report about the activities of the society. One attendee grabs him tight by the shoulder of his jacket and cries out in a loud voice: "Get out! Get out! I don't want to hear this!" No arguments or shouting help, no intervention helps, whether from the stage or from the audience–the speaker was forced to leave the scene and the report was never completed.

This picture of the general meetings would not be complete if we did not recall the backing and endorsing for offices men who lacked the necessary qualifications, the elementary education and skills, either because they had no income or they were distinguished and belonged to one or another organization, to this or that study house.

For years the ordinary and exceptional general meetings went on in this way with passionate battles over certain people–candidates for positions in the loan society. Usually the meeting divided over two opposing sides, and each side used all possible and impossible methods of promoting its candidate. Ger Chasidim fought for their candidate and Rodzin Chasidim for a different candidate. Eventually both sides succeeded and their candidates took their plates in the society.

We will. Now give a short overview of a few general meetings of the savings and loan and their major decisions.

[Page 435]

The general meeting of April 27, 1908, was presided over by the lawyer St. Sunderland. At this meeting it was decided to raise the membership fee from 15 to 50 rubles, payable over ten years.

At the general meeting of March 25, 1909, presided over by the lawyer A. Hartglass, it was decided to set aside 300 rubles for the benefit of the community "G'milas–Chesed" [charity fund]. Mr. A. Hartglass was elected to the council.

At the general meeting of March 16, 1910, Mr. A. Shlifka presided and the minutes were taken by the lawyer A. Hartglass. Dr. M. Stein resigned from his position and he was replaced as head of the managing committee by Shemaryahu Greenberg.

The general meeting of March 10, 1911, under the leadership of Mr. A.D. Tchotchkes, decided to set aside 100 rubles "for payments to Petersburg with the aim of making efforts to bring a governmental train workshop to Siedlce." It was also decided to set aside 50 rubles for the benefit of poor students in the school of Miss Jadwiga Bartszewska. Other bequests were made years for an array of community institutions: the Talmud Torah, G'milas–Chesed, Bikur–Cholim, and also for poor people at Passover.

Less than three months later, on June 5, 1911, a second general meeting was called, this time an extraordinary meeting presided over by...the Russian inspector Tchaplinski, who had ordered the society to call an extraordinary meeting and to invite himself to preside? The recording secretary is not clear about this. Reading between the lines, it is clear that the meeting was not peaceful, and even the doctrine of respect for the government di don't help. The Jews were not impressed by "the Lord High Inspector" nor by his attempts to quiet them. They fussed and stormed, and they succeeded. They confused the inspector. Over every little point, every detail, they demanded a secret ballot, and Inspector Tchaplinski, a typical czarist bureaucrat, had to follow these legal demands, so that the meeting lasted until dawn, and poor Inspector Tchaplinski could not utter a single Russian curse.

[Page 436]

He had to remain silent. When people spoke, Tchaplinski very prettily said, "Quiet, bearded barons" (or "bearded Jews"!). Over this "verse" the Jews, you understand, did not demand a secret ballot.

The growth in the number of members, nearly 3 thousand, made it impossible to call everyone to a general meeting, which would have resulted in chaos and confusion. –This convinced the management to inaugurate ion 1910 a system of representation. Every hundred members had to elect from among themselves eight representatives who had the duty to represent the bulk of members at the general meetings and to express their wishes. To this end, election meetings were held in the society hall and a hundred representatives were elected as well as twenty alternates.

This system did not work out in actuality, because Inspector Tchaplinski found fault with the election process and he would not recognize the results.

The Credit Institution During the First World War and in Independent Poland

The bloody hurricane which roared over the Polish fields in July of 1914 threw the whole country into a deep cataclysm. The populace descended on the credit institutions to withdraw their savings. There was a chaotic "run" on the banks.

This "run," which was a catastrophe for many banks, did not spare the Siedlce loan society. It shared the same fate as the other financial institutions in the country. It required superhuman effort to control the situation and systematically to distribute the funds all at one time when all sources of money were stopped up and the payments on loans sputtered.

[Page 437]

A mob of account holders daily stormed the society and demanded payment on the spot of their "contributions." There were many moving and tragic scenes. The account holders often threatened the society and its representatives.

The steering committee, despite its best intentions, you understand, was unable to meet all of these demands at once. First they paid out the "contributions" of the reservists who were in the army and their families. Then came the savings of the poorer population and of the middle class. Later they began to make normal payments without such distinctions.

In this way the steering committee operated, paying out over time "contributions" of more than 200,000 rubles in installments of 15,000 because the depositors did not demand the full amount.

It is not necessary to say that during the First World War the pulse of the society became weaker and weaker and its activities consisted largely of paying the depositors and not conducting other business. The staff became smaller. Remaining in the leadership were: A. Slifke, A.A. Kviatek, and Y.M. Saltzman. Things were at a standstill until 1918.

The general meetings during the war years, you understand, lost their whole meaning and attracted little interest in the city. They were poorly attended and several times were not held at all. The members lacked togetherness and contact with the institution. There was one time of election fever, of irritation, of the usual quarrels and arguments: the fight over the custodianship.

In 1918 attempts were made to revive the society, which even received credit in the Siedlce branch of the "Business and Industrial Bank," but because of the uncertain economic situation in the country, each attempt at righting things was bound to fail. Thus at a great mass meeting there was no talk of taking such action.

[Page 438]

Only at the beginning of 1922, when community life began to return to normal, did the question arise of reconstructing the society. This was after the change in the Polish law against cooperatives. The society, on January 25, 1922, once again was registered under the name "Siedlce Cooperative Savings and Loan Society, with Limited Responsibility in Siedlce" and took steps to attract members. The recruitment efforts were led by the steering committee, that consisted of M. Greenfarb, Y. Lichtenfacht, and A. A. Kviatek.

For various reasons and probably because there representatives of the merchants among the representatives, the premises of the society became in the afternoon and evening hours transformed into a temporary merchants' club–a place for meeting and support for a group of Siedlce's merchants. This meeting spot witnessed many comic curiosities. It happened that a member came for a loan and was enlisted as a fourth hand for a card came, On the other hand, if someone came to read a newspaper, he would be dragged in as an over the payment of a promissory note. Eventually the merchants were forced to abandon their free meeting spot, and the premises remained devoted to the exclusive disposition of the loan society.

In 1922, with the help of the society, was founded the "Union of Jewish Cooperative Societies in Poland," centered in Warsaw. With its inclusion in the Union, a "new era" began for the society. It was a recognized member of the cooperative family and had a prominent position in the movement which had to be formed in liberated Poland.

At the end of 1922, the society had 1,500 declared members and conducted normal activities in the area of giving loans. This form of credit (long–term loans), due to circumstances became undesirable, and so a new form was found: giving advances for short–term collection.

[Page 439]

The aforementioned union of Jewish cooperatives was in a stage of organizing. Their chief job was the reconstruction of already existing financial institutions and helping to build new cooperatives, for which the Jewish populace had shown a strong desire. To this end, it was first necessary to create a central credit institution in order to be able to finance the cooperatives and in this way to incorporate them into the union.

The then–existing K.S.K. ("Kassa Spoldzielczego Kredytu"). 1922–1924, which had at its disposal the funds of the Joint and the Y.K.A,, both of which were known for their constructive work in Poland, also played a role in financing the banks and working on instructing them.

The Siedlce savings society was several times visited by the instructors from the K.K.S. [sic], Messrs. S. Galde and A. Shmush, who from time to time conducted audits and showed interest in the pace of activities. Thanks to the efforts of the instructors, and based on their recommendations, in 1923 the society held from the K.K.S. [sic] ten million marks and later–even greater amounts.

The K.K.S. [sic], however, whose duties did not include cooperative work on broader matters, was a rickety creation and had scant influence on the path and development of the cooperative movement in Poland, and in 1924 it considered its activities finished and done with. In 1923, the "Union" received a good audit and it moved toward a narrower affiliation with the Joint and the Y.K.A. The goal that brought together these separate administrative bodies was the necessity of establishing a central credit institution which had to exist under the auspices of the "Union." The existence of a bank called the "Jewish Construction Bank" (Zydowski Bank Odbudowa). The fledgling government of the time, led by Paderewski, promised to legalize it , perhaps out of fear that the Jews would compete in the rebuilding of Poland…The "Joint" then bought out the Russian–Polish Bank (Bank Rusko–Polski) with all of its assets and changed its name to "Bank for Cooperatives."

[Page 440]

In this wawas realized the decision to establish a central bank in Warsaw. At the end of 1923, the savings society had to endure a difficult time. There was constant devaluation and inflation of the mark. From day to day the money became more worthless, and the society was bereft of all its capital and therefore again had to suspend its operations.

The situation created by inflation caused a tumult in the young cooperative movement, and at the beginning of 1924 the "Revised Union" organized a conference of the most prominent cooperative activists in the county with the goal of enlisting members in order to maintain the status that had been established and to work out a plan to actualize the transition to the zloty.

In February of 1924, members were required to make their regular payments in zlotys. These payments in zlotys, along with the 1210 zloty ration cards that had shortly before been obtained by the director, Mr. Malin, now had to serve as the main capital of the society.

Despite all these difficult circumstances, hesitations, and shocks that at that time drove many stronger banks to ruin and liquidation, the society was not harmed and again took up its normal activities.

The Shareholders Bank (Bank Udszalowi)

According to the decision of the general meeting, on July 18, 1925, the name of the society was changed to "Bank Udszalowi," Cooperative with Legal Responsibility in SIedlce."

According to the rules, the bank could conduct all sorts of banking operations, such as loans, discounts, collections of promissory notes, checking, shipping, and so on. The bank also handled deposits and savings in zlotys and in dollars.

The following chart will illustrate the development of the "Bank Udszalowi" and its expansion beginning in January 1925 until the first of January in 1932:

[Page 441]

Year	Capital	Reserve Capital	Deposits	Loans	Surplus	Members
1925	10,212	6,713	9,190	37,960	3,503	715
1926	24,002	10,329	37,960	77,632	2,248	1211
1927	52,202	12,577	218,175	341,659	10,403	1469
1928	81,105	22,981	304,733	499,603	10,130	1506
1929	100,163	33,111	356,887	592,796	2,023	1577
1930	101,113	27,117	237,624	491,891	2,151	1540

| 1931 | 105,226 | 29,432 | 433,452 | 571,501 | 2,261 | 1614 |
| 1932 | 104.745 | 29,432 | 368,945 | 530,345 | not avail. | 1622 |

Census of the Members According to Professions

Small merchants	Artisans	Merchants & Industry	Professionals	Agriculture	Others
593	527	252	132	12	106

[Page 442]

In January of 1926 the "Union" asked the director of the Siedlce Bank, Mr. Malin, to organize a regional conference of all cooperatives in the Lublin Voivodeship with the goal of considering the then current question of whether to decentralize from the movement and especially to run candidates in a group of regional elections.

The building in which the Loan Society was located

The conference, in which 54 delegates from 35 credit cooperatives participated, took place in February, 1926, in Lublin, presided over by Mr. Malin, and they took a number of important resolutions regarding those questions.

The value and popularity of the bank also quite properly influenced the direction taken by the "Bank Polski." The "Siedlce Savings Bank" was the first Jewish cooperative bank in Poland that at the beginning of 1926 received a significantly discounted credit in the "Siedlce Branch of the Bank Polski," from which it profits to this very day.

The bank was also one of the few Jewish credit cooperatives that in 1928 and 1929 profited from the discount credit of the P.K.O. ("Polsko Kasa Oszczendnoszczi" [Polish Economic Bank]).

The growth of the bank in this era and the full–bodied trust in its good reputation among the population are owed in large part to Mr. V. Barb. The head officer of the directorship.

In September of 1925 the bank experienced a new shock because of the sudden collapse of the Polish zloty.

[Page 443]

The dollar went from a head spinning high of 5 zlotys 16 groschen to 13 zlotys, and again the specter of devaluation appeared and presaged a currency catastrophe. The directorship then demonstrated a special agility in handling the crisis, thanks to which the bank emerged from this situation with almost no damage, even though the bank had had large obligations in dollars.

Struggle between the Artisans and the Small Merchants

Parallel with the growth of the bank and its influence over the economic life of the Jewish populace was the quarrel between different classes and groups over representation in the people's organization.

Two economic groups, that is, the artisans and the small merchants, for a long while made a great effort to enlist the bank in their interests and to take over the management through their representatives.

The conflict was more about ambition and show than about practicality and principle. It was more about whether the bank should bear the imprint of the artisan union or of the small merchants thank it was about substantive issues that would benefit either party. The open territory of the bank as a pure economic institution was hidden by the interests of the artisans and of the small merchants. Both sides needed credit, cheap credit, and both sides needed to be interested in creating a calm atmosphere in the bank along with normal operations.

This conflict found its greatest expression at the yearly general meetings of the bank. Already the election meetings had foretold a significant struggle that would break out between the small merchants and the artisans in order to gain control of the bank and to elect their representatives.

That detail–elections–is the central point of the meetings, around which struggle the two election lists: one for artisans and one for merchants.

[Page 444]

The struggle is not equal. The artisans of Siedlce, like a well–organized group, more mature and more oriented toward economic issues, led a broad action in the city and came to the meeting united, as one. On the other hand, the small merchants and commercial people, who always had a limited understanding of organization and who lacked a feeling for community, did not engage their people to stand by them in their struggle with the artisans. The artisans therefore always had the upper hand over the merchants and it was easy for them to seat their people in the most important posts.

But later the situation was quite different, when because of circumstances, more tactical and local that principled, a division appeared in the ranks of the artisans. Twi separate groups of artisans developed with opposing interests, so that two separate artisan unions were formed. Thus the division was between two equal foes, between two well–organized groups, and this split appeared on the grounds of the bank, as an institution for which both unions had the most ambitious aspirations.

As fate would have it, at the head of the bank were two representatives of the artisans from the different unions who considered themselves to be "political enemies." Thus the harmony, the cooperative efforts and the unity of the bank that the members required were destroyed. Each faction of the artisans sought to win for its own representative and one way or another to influence the running of the bank.

So this happened: one person told another in secret, whispering, that promissory notes would be set aside without protest and protests would not be considered and that in the making of loans there were often times when other factors were taken into account. It went without saying that at the same time that certain individuals were favored, dissatisfaction grew in the ranks of the artisans, who suddenly felt abused by one representative or another of the bank.

[Page 445]

If "Reuben" saw, or if it appeared to him, that people were opposed to "Shimon," he would feel himself abused. And this dissatisfaction was not confined to the four walls of the bank. It overflowed to the streets, where it found a broad field for exaggerated rumors. Total untruths, simple fantastic legends, coursed through the city about "terrible" debts owed to the bank by certain artisan representatives, about "stacks" of protests that were lodged. Every detail was exaggerated ten– or a hundredfold.

The "street," which was ravenous for exaggerations and sensationalism, latched on to these versions and immediately spread them over the whole city. It was an open secret that something in the bank was rotten, that it had suffered losses, that the steering committee could not make up the debts, and so on.

The New "Run" on the Bank

At the same time, there came, in the life of the bank, an event that nearly ruined its wholeness and security.

In February of 1929 there was a "run" on the bank, mass withdrawals from accounts and from savings. One wintry morning the aroused account depositors came to the bank and demanded to withdraw their savings. All of Siedlce needed money: one to fill out his daughter's dowry or the groom would leave; another had made a splendid deal and needed the money; a third suddenly had to go to Warsaw on business and certainly had to buy things…

Each one hid his true reason. On the contrary, with a flattering smile on his lips–"Excuse me, Mr. Barg, but what do you think? We have the greatest trust in you and in the bank; we just need the money today. Twenty–four hours from now will be too late. We feel really sorry about that."

[Page 446]

What had happened to make the account owners feel they had suddenly to withdraw their savings? Was this a result of unhealthy politics that swirled in and around the bank, or were there other motives, or was it, perhaps, just pure coincidence? It is hard to pin down the circumstances around the "run." Over all it is better not to try to establish a concrete cause. At that moment it was the psychosis of the crowd rather than something that had been thought through or worked out logically.

How did the steering committee react to this "run" on the "accounts"?

They reacted in a most primitive way, as would be done broadly in cooperative banks. Namely, they brought out great sums of money and satisfied every demand. They paid out accounts that were due and that were not due, large sums and small. They paid out day in and day out, from early in the morning until into the night.

The bank personnel made the greatest effort to satisfy the account owners and so paid out over a short time the hazardous sum of nearly 250,000 zlotys.

Luckily this ebbing of the accounts did not cause the bank any essential damage and did not harm the interests of the members. True, the bank continued its activities in a smaller way and continued to honor loans and credit as much as possible.

After this shock there came a time to take a breath, to calm the spirit, even though it was near the time for the annual general meeting, and those meetings always brought with them an anxious and feverish atmosphere.

At that general meeting in 1929, Mr. Shmaryahu Greenberg was elected chair, and he was later elected as executive officer.

After taking the position as executive officer of the council, Greenberg earnestly committed himself to cleaning up the inner workings of the bank and making an end to favoritism toward any faction, toward any group.

[Page 447]

In this environment of peace, free of worry and committed to methodical work, the bank was headed in a good direction, without distractions and friction. The predicament in which the bank had found itself because of the outflow of accounts became less, as the accounts flowed back in, confidence increased, and the internal strengths of the bank came to the fore.

To conclude, we will recall the people who in their time demonstrated great devotion and trust in the institution. These were the members of the supervisory committee: A.D. Milberg, A.Y. Korniczky, Sh. Wurman, Ch.M. Shapiro, W. Tuchklapper. No one can argue that these men were free of worries about their own jobs, but serving in their offices was for them a community obligation. More than one of them had to put up with all seven stages of crisis, and then how keenly, with what devotion, these men responded to their duty.

What was the "Bank Udszalowi" to Siedlce?

Half of Jewish Siedlce used it: the large merchant, the craftsman, the poor shopkeeper, the woman with a market stall who needed a few score zlotys to buy a bit of merchandise, the worker, the employee, and even not–well–off homeowners–none of them left the bank empty–handed. One with a loan, the second with a discount, the third with an advance of ready cash–it went through the whole city, it was productive and creative.

* *

Aside from he "Bank Udszalowi" which existed for almost 30 years, there were in Siedlce another 3 cooperative banks and a charity fund from the Jewish community organization.

The Merchants Bank was founded in 1924 at the home of Y.N. Weintraub on Pilsudski Street. The founders were: Asher Urszel, Y.N. Weintraub, Yisroel Gutgelt, Dovid Rubenstein, Berish Yom–Tov. In its first active years, the bank developed quickly. As long as it was small, it was in Weintraub's home. In 1927, the bank moved to the home of Mendel Cohen.

[Page 448]

The director was Asher Urszel. Then the director was Avraham Asher Kwiatek. This credit institution served the large merchants and the few industries that were in Siedlce and that belonged to the finest cooperative bank in Poland.

In 1929 and 1930, when the crisis erupted in Poland, it greatly affected the activities of the bank, because in the good years it had extended large amounts of credit, up to 20,000 zlotys and often even more, and because of the crisis it could not collect payments on time–so the bank struggled with its existence. In 1933 it was liquidated.

The "Credit Bank" was founded through the initiative of Monish Ridel (who can now be found in Israel), Mordechai Alfisher, Yisroel Rinecki, Moyshe Mendel Friedman, Yisroel Tsenki, and Eliyahu Tenenbaum. The bank took as its mission to help the small merchants with credit. Monish Ridel was the director of the bank until 1936.

With the growth of the credit institution and then the liquidation of the "Bank Urdszlowi" in 1936, the "Credit Bank" became the only finance institution for all of Siedlce's Jews. Head of its council was Dr. Belfour, vice–chair Yehoshua Ackerman, director after Monish Ridel was Shimon Lieberman. On the central council of the cooperative banks were Yehoshua Ackerman and Shimon Lieberman.

In 1939, when the war broke out, the "Credit Bank" gave up its hall to the Jewish community organization.

The third bank was the "Discount Bank," founded by members of the Agudah: Tuviah Shiffer, Yehudah Aryeh Zucker, Moyshe Zakan, and others.

When the Merchants Bank was liquidated, the Agudah Bank changed it name to Merchants Bank and took over its premises in the house of Mendel Cohen, Chair of its council was Kalman Friedman.

As we have already mentioned, aside from the bank there was also a charity fund in the Jewish community, where an artisan and a small merchant could get a loan without interest for as much as 250 zlotys.

[Page 449]

Activities of "Toz" [Jewish Healthcare] and "Women's Circle" For Child Welfare

by Dr. M. Shlaycher, Haifa

Translated by Theodore Steinberg

In 1923, under the initiative of the writer of these lines, a branch of the TOZ society (Society to Care for the Health of Jews) was established in Siedlce. It had the following duties: 1) to battle ringworm and fungal illnesses, and 2) to battle tuberculosis. Both illnesses had spread especially among children. In the battle against ringworm, the society organized a statistical control over all the children in the schools: Tarbus, the Jewish Folk School, the Talmud Torah, and the Polish-Jewish vocational school. The examinations in the schools were conducted by Dr. Fau. She decided which children needed X-rays for detecting the disease. The X-rays were done at the X-Ray Institute in Siedlce under the direction of Dr. Fau. In severe cases, the children were sent to Warsaw under the auspices of "TOZ" in Siedlce.

The "TOZ" Society in Siedlce influenced the doctors in the Polish schools to take similar measures with the Polish children. When "TOZ" began its activities, approximately 30% of children suffered from these conditions. After three years, the conditions had almost disappeared.

[Page 450]

A large number of children were also afflicted with tuberculosis, having been infected by their parents or other family members. In this case, "TOZ" also carried out practical labors. A file was established for each tuberculosis-infected child. During every winter month, 10 or 12 tubercular children were sent to the "TOZ" and "Health" sanatorium. In addition, lectures were provided for the parents of affected children on how to prevent infection.

The "TOZ" summer colony

Summer colonies also played a big part in the fight against childhood tuberculosis. Every year during the summer break in the schools, hundreds of children participated in summer colonies in the woods and fields. The doctors, along with the Jewish community in Siedlce, were persuaded that organizing these colonies for the schoolchildren was one of the most effective ways of fighting tuberculosis and of insuring the health of the younger generation. Until that time, only the children of the wealthy could enjoy the sun, the air, the woods, and the fields. The needy child spent the hot summer days in narrow rooms or on dusty streets. After their summer breaks, they would return to school weaker than they had been before.

[Page 451]

Also during those summer months many illnesses spread among the poor children.

So "TOZ" created the summer colonies for these children. The colonies brought happiness to the children. The athletic activities for the children out in nature improved their b bodies. Their color improved in the sun that shone upon them. In their colonies the children also learned about cleanliness, about washing with soap, brushing their teeth, and so on.

The colony also taught the children how to live in a community with other children and how to behave in a friendly fashion together. "Half colonies" were also organized for children for whom there was no room in the colonies outside of the city.

From 1925 until the disaster, approximately 1000 children received food in their schools—a second breakfast consisting of a roll and a glass of cocoa. To this end, a "Women's Circle" was formed to help finance the program.

Athletic activities for the children in the "TOZ" colony

[Page 452]

The "Women's Circle" supplied about 30% of the budget and was also responsible for seeing that the breakfast was distributed among all the children without exception.

The "Women's Circle" consisted of the following: Dr. Shlaykher, chair; members Esther Salzman, Felia Urszel, Puah Rabinowicz, Las, Tabakman, and others. In addition, each year the Women's Circle sent to the sanatorium several ailing children, the money having been raised through a variety of social events that they organized.

In 1932, the "TOZ" took over the operation of the Jewish hospital and brought to this healing center the most modern hospital arrangements. A special gynecological section was created under the direction of Dr. Lebel. This section was quite popular among women. Every woman who was about to give birth, whether she was poor or wealthy, wanted to be admitted to the hospital. The good reputation of this department was also known outside of Siedlce. Pregnant women from surrounding towns came to give birth in the Jewish hospital. The division of internal medicine was directed by Dr. Glazowsk. There was also an infirmary made up of specialists.

The budget for the hospital was furnished 40% by "TOZ" and 30% each by the Jewish community organization and the magistrate.

"TOZ" also conducted a prophylactic program among the Jewish populace, teaching disease prevention, how to maintain household cleanliness. Lectures by local doctors were organized and some came from Warsaw: Dr. Walman, Dr. Levin, and others.

The foundation of the "TOZ" budget came from membership dues of about 800 members as well as from admission fees to social events, subsidies from the Jewish community organization and from the central headquarters in Warsaw.

"TOZ" was led by the following people: Chair, Del M. Shlaykher; members, Yehoshua Eckerman, S. Halberstam, Dr. Lebel, Yosef Alberg, Dr. Fau-Halberstam, A. Marttzki, Las, Menashe Czarnabrode, Modl, and others; Secretary A. Englander.

[Page 453]

It should also be noted that Dr. Fau industriously led the medical practice in the ghetto. She provided medical help to all the ailing and occupied herself with th

ose ill with typhus even though there were none of the necessary means of disinfection.

The coordinating committee for the health group "TOZ," with Dr. Shlaykher at the top

Synagogue and Culture Activity

[Page 457]

The Yiddish School System in Siedlce

by Moshe Mandelman, New York

Translated by Theodore Steinberg

In October of 1915, barely two months after the Germans had occupied Siedlce, the first Jewish Folk School opened there, created by the energetic and intelligent young woman—Mrs. Radak. In later years she, together with her husband, worked in Riga's Jewish secular school system, and from there they went to the Soviet Union.

Mrs. Radak arrived in Siedlce as a refugee. She fled with her parents from a border shtetl called Khorszel (near East Prussia). In Siedlce, together with the Siedlce women Tzviah Zubravicz and Rochel Edelstein-Barg, she received from the German school authorities the right to open a school for Jewish children with Yiddish as the language of instruction. This idea—of Yiddish as the language of instruction—belonged exclusively to the above-mentioned Mrs. Radak. She was a teacher from the education courses at the community "M'fitzei Haskalah" [Spreaders of the Haskalah], which were under the supervision of Chaim Fialkow. For a short time she was active as an educator in Warsaw in the newly established nurseries for homeless children, thousands of whom were in Warsaw at that time.

I will never forget the impression that it made on me when my longtime friend Yosef Rosenzumen enthusiastically told me the news: "A Litvak woman, very sympathetic, has come wearing shoes with low heels, and she has opened a school for Jewish children where everything is taught in Yiddish. She speaks Yiddish—it's a pleasure to hear. I myself am studying singing there."

[Page 458]

This information from my friend was a big surprise to me. I was very enthusiastic about what he said, and I decided with him that early the next morning I would go to the school to see and hear with my own eyes and ears this miracle—a Jewish school for Jewish children in Yiddish!

The school captured me. I was bound to it, and I was ready to do my utmost for this educational institution. I sat together with the children and listened with all of my might to hear these new things—they taught natural history, computation, history, and so on—in Yiddish!...Mrs. Radak led the studies in Yiddish, computation, natural history, and history; Rochel Edelstein taught Polish; Tzviah Zurowicz taught crafts, and Yosef Rozenzumen taught singing. Even now I remember that the first song that he taught the children was "Do You Know the Land Where Esrogim Bloom?"

I remember how Mrs. Radak troubled herself to find materials and terminology for all her studies in Yiddish. I brought her some popular scholarly books from the "Yehudia" publishers that came out under the name "People's University," Philip Krantz's "Culture History," and the like. When, after several months, the school moved to a bigger locale, near "Woiskow Place"—I carried the benches on my shoulders in order to cut down on the moving expenses.

[Page 459]

Gradually the school developed and earned a good reputation in the city. There were already four classes with 60 to 70 children—mostly girls. Later on, the school adopted a more private character with the goal of earning a profit. It as called Radak's School. Tz iah Zubrowicz had left. I and my friend Rosenzumen maintained that a school with instruction in Yiddish—something new in Jewish life at that time—should have a community character. Little by little we moved away, until we were entirely separate from Radak's School. But we had already begun to organize a new school on a community basis.

At that time in Siedlce there was also another school for Jewish children where Yiddish and Hebrew were taught. This school was founded and let by the so-called "Brisk Committee."

This was a "self-help" committee shaped by people from Brisk and Pinsk who were "homeless" (as people then referred to refugees). The number of the homeless was not small at all, several hundred families, among whom there were also teachers. This Brisk Committee at the end of 1915 created a school for children from among the Brisk homeless. The teachers were also from among the homeless. About 200 children studied there in two daily sessions. This school was under Zionist influence.

2.

We began to establish the second school by organizing a school committee. Serving on this committee were: Yosef Rosenzumen, David Neumark, Yakov Tenenbaum, Rivkah Burstein-Mandelman, Avraham Zigelwaks, and Moyshe Mandelman. Permission to open the school was given by the German school authorities to three Jewish women who had graduated from a Russian gymnasium and had the right to be teachers. They were: the already mentioned Tzviah Zubrowicz, Royce Tenenbaum, and Minya Gutglick.

The school opened in the summer of 1916. It enrolled many children. In six classes we had 240 students. The following were the teachers: Zubrowicz, Tenenbaum, Gutglick, Rivkah Burstein-Mandelman, Dovid Neumark, Moyshe Mandelman, and Yosef Sonnschein (singing). This school grew quickly and earned a good reputation. Lawyer A. Hartglass (later a well-known Zionist deputy in the Sejm who died in Israel), demonstrated at certain times sympathy for this school with its Yiddish instruction and promoted the institution with the authorities.

The children were recruited from among the poorer classes. You must understand that we took no tuition fees and that the teachers received no pay. They did not need any, because they were for the most part the offspring of middle-class homeowners and did not have to worry about their livelihood. Rent money was just a few groschen because at that time there were many empty apartments in the city, thanks to the evacuation of all Russian clerks, who numbered in the thousands.

In order to pay our small bills, we would offer, from time to time, social gatherings. The member of the school committee, Yakov Tenenbaum, who was just crazy about writing, wrote a three-act comedy with the strange title of "That's No Mouse—It's a Rat," which was produced several times by the drama section of "Jewish Art." Proceeds went to the school.

[Page 460]

A number of students from the Jewish Folk School, with the teachers:
Sarah Czarnebrode, Falle Altshuler, Yosef Sonnschein, Rivkah Mandelman

But again this time we quickly realized that as things were going, the school had to become the private property of the three women in whose name the school license was given. We sought various means to get the school out of private hands. And that brought about an extraordinary political moment.

3.

In the fall of 1916, the Germans announced that the organization and leadership of the Polish school systems would be given over solely to the Poles. Jews then began to demand their right to organize and lead a Jewish school system for Jewish children. It was a great victory when the "People's Group" in Warsaw won the elections to the Warsaw city council.

[Page 461]

This is what led to the creation of the "Jewish People's Party," and its representatives, in the press and at rallies, presented a demand for a school with Yiddish as the language of instruction. Noach Prilucki's speeches made a huge impression in the Warsaw city council, which was considered at that time to be the most important platform in the country. Poles and assimilated Jews watched "with angry amazement" the meetings of the city council in Warsaw to see who was this "Jew" ["Zhid"],who dared from the floor of the Warsaw city council, to ask for "schools" in "Jargon"!…

This was a time of large rallies over educational and cultural problems, where V. Medem, G. Zibert, and other members of the Bund appeared together with the Folkists Prilucki, Hirschorn, Stupnicki, Naumberg, Mendelman, and others.

In Siedlce, too, a struggle began for a school taught in Yiddish. The aforementioned school committee, the newly organized People's Party, and the directorship of "Jewish Art" organized several rallies where political resolutions were taken demanding of the authorities that they give us the right to organize and lead a Jewish school system with Yiddish as the language of instruction, to be supported by the city. Keep in mind that a struggle with Zionists-Hebraists flared up from day to day as the debates about the school question grew more heated, whether in the press or at gatherings.

We organized all of the Yiddishist powers in the city and collected a large number of signatures Fromm the members of "Jewish Art"—the only large cultural institution in Siedlce. We requested from the directors of "Jewish Art" that they should convene an extraordinary general meeting of its members and there consider the question of opening a Yiddish school by the "Jewish Art" society. Our hope was that "Jewish Art" would in time become the Yiddish cultural center where all branches of the Yiddish cultural activity could be found under one roof.

This all required a great deal of effort, because the opposing Zionist-Hebraist side did everything they could to forestall the broadening of Yiddish cultural activities.

[Page 462]

They clung to the argument that it was not the responsibility of "Jewish Art"—according to its by-laws—to concern itself with school building, and furthermore it would be materially quite difficult and the membership would not want to support it. But we were obstinate, so that an extraordinary membership meeting was called. This was sometime in the winter of 1916-17.

This meeting, one could say, was historic. There was laid the foundation for a modern Yiddish-secular school system in Siedlce. The opposing sides had mobilized their best speakers and tried to persuade the members to vote one way or the other. Three evenings, one after the other, were taken up with the meetings. Each side tried, in writing and orally—as if it were a big election campaign—to use an assortment of tricks. There were moments of amazing heat that almost resulted in fisticuffs. Finally our Yiddishist side won. With a large majority of the votes, it was decided that the community "Jewish Art" would open a Yiddish school with Yiddish as the language of instruction.

The school committee wanted to direct that the existing school should be given over to "Jewish Art." When the current owners heard of this plan, they rebelled. They demanded assurances that they would be the teachers in the new school. We did not want to do so in advance. The school committee ceased shaping matters, and the school lost its meager income. A few members from the directorate of "Jewish Art," relatives of the current owners, tried to delay the carrying out of the meeting's decision to open a school. But we were prepared that week and did everything we could to remove obstacles. We saw to it that the whole school inventory should be turned over to "Jewish Art." We received from the German school authorities a charter in the name of the community to open and maintain a Jewish school for Jewish children in Yiddish. The school was set to be open for the new school year of 1917/1918. In order to avoid conflicts with the former teachers, we decided to bring in teachers from Warsaw, even though they would have to be paid.

[Page 463]

Friends from Warsaw recommended as a good teacher Asher Perelman, who had taught for a long time in the Warsaw Jewish schools. One Shabbos, Perelman came to Siedlce. He gave a talk about the goals and responsibilities of a Jewish school. He pleased everyone, and we encouraged him to make arrangements to stay with us as a teacher. We We proposed that "Jewish Art" should engage him as a teacher in the new school.

I should note an interesting fact: at a critical moment, during negotiations between the directorate of "Jewish Art" and Perelman over the school budget, when the directors categorically declared that they did not have the authority to guarantee the full sum that the school would cost per month and that the whole matter should be abandoned, our dear, beloved friend Itsche Altschuler—an enthusiastic Folkist and Yiddishist—said, "I will, out of my own pocket, each month make up the deficit in the budget." He kept that sacred commitment, and for many long months he punctually made his donation, 20 marks each month, I think it was. This was a considerable sum, and Altschuler was not a rich man—his income came from a small sugar business.

4.

When "Jewish Art" had advertised through posters in the city that a Yiddish school would be opening, we enrolled about three hundred children in a few days. We decided to build up a normal school that would grow and develop from year to year, so we agreed to open that year with only two elementary classes. Therefore we chose from among the enrollees only eighty-some children ages 6 to 7.

The school opened in October of 1917. It was located in the premises of "Jewish Art" at 66 Warsaw Street. It had a large hall near the concert hall, which served as a recreation and sports room for the schoolchildren.

[Page 464]

The first teachers were Asher Perelman and Lyalya Konsorowicz. She was later the wife of Yitzchak Gordon and she died in Russia.

The school was precious to everyone. The classrooms were a kind of holy of holies. The walls were colorfully decorated and covered with drawings and childish, primitive writing. When one went through the classrooms, even if the children were not present, one went on tiptoe, quietly, lightly , as if in a sacred spot…

The solemn official opening of the school occurred on December 31, 1917. This act took place with great solemnity. Many hundreds of people participated. For this celebration, from Warsaw came the famous author H.D. Naumberg, who in later years was proud of his first trip to the Siedlce Yiddish school and referred to himself as the "godfather" of the Yiddish school in Siedlce. There were delegates and greetings from prominent institutions, Jewish and non-Jewish, from Siedlce and other cities. The children already demonstrated, after a short time, how to show what they had learned. Among other things, I recall, dressed in beautiful costumes, they presented living "menorahs." (It was, after all, Chanukah time.)

After this official portion, there was a banquet for more than four hundred people. For the whole night, until early in the morning, people socialized and danced. From the ten or so windows of "Jewish Art," lights shone, while singing and joy went out into the night. The happiness can only be imagined. I remember the following incident: Naumberg was greatly pleased with my youthful singing singing of the then popular folksong "Oy Avram"!…I had to sing it a second time. Like someone a little drunk, he had me write on the left side of the published program for the evening the words of the folksong: "Over the attic lies a roof." While writing, he sang it with a deep, raspy, sad tune. Naumberg then explained that people used to sing that very song in Peretz's home, at 1 Tsegliana on Shabbos before sundown, when a group of writers would gather around Peretz.

[Page 465]

The school grew. In its second school year, two new classes opened and a third teacher was brought in from Warsaw, Pearl, who later became Perelman's wife. At the beginning of their third year, they—already with a child—went to the Soviet Union, where he died tragically. His only son was killed by an automobile, and I do not know the fate of his wife. The singing teacher was the director of the choir for "Jewish Art," Yosef Sonnschein (now in Argentina). The teachers showed a great deal of sincerity and love in their work. The school stood out even among Polish folk schools. Every open performance by the children, every children's production was celebrated like a great holiday for the parents, friends, and the children. At the same time, there was great sympathy for community political actions around the question of rights for the Yiddish school and about obtaining resources from the city coffers.

The extent of the school's prestige can be seen in the following:

On Lag b'Omer of 1918, we decided to make a large school demonstration: a march of all the types of Jewish schools around the city and an imposing folk-demonstration near the woods, six kilometers from the city. At that time in Siedlce there were the following Jewish schools: the school for homeless children from Brisk and Pinsk (Yiddish and Hebrew), the Zionists had established a Hebrew school, a private Polish school for well-to-do Jewish children (led by the Halberstadt sisters), two private modernized cheers (led by the Hebrew teachers Goldfarb and Morgenstern), and several Polish city schools for Jewish children, where there was no teaching on Shabbos (and they were therefore called "Shabbesuawkes"). From these schools a special ad hoc committee was formed, and it accepted our worked out plan for the celebration.

This was a school holiday that the city remembered for a long time. Six days before, scouts from the "Jewish Sports Union," led by Professor Mandelstadt [fn.: The Sports Union was founded on my prompting in the summer of 1917. It had its own uniform: hockey apparel and bicycle hats, with green-white bands at the bottom.] went around with trumpets to arouse the Jewish population and announce that there would be a great holiday.

[Page 466]

The meeting spot was in the city garden. The march began at eight in the morning. All of the children wore badges for their particular schools. A large militia—our own and the city's—guarded the route. In the front was the combined committee for the school march. They carried signs with different political school demands and slogans. About three thousand children marched along the route, to sounds of two orchestras—from "Jewish Art" and from the Polish city schools. We marched through the main streets of the city. The grandeur of route aroused great respect among the Poles and the Germans. The streets were full of thousands of onlookers, who called to the marches with joyous voices.

After noon, thousands of people came to the city woods, and the school and children's holiday was transformed into a people's holiday. Rallies were held. Scores of groups came with a variety of games and entertainments. Songs, music, joy, and laughter were everywhere.

This holiday concluded with an orderly march back to the city. The route was filled with thousands of teenagers and children who sang lusty and happy marching songs. Later in the evening the route was illuminated with torch lights.

5.

Community political life in Siedlce became more turbulent. Political differences—clear and outspoken, especially under the influence of the Russian Revolution, at the beginning of 1917, added to the Jewish workers movement. Within the ranks of "Jewish Art," two new workers organizations developed—the Bundist Workers Home, at 22 Dluga Street, and the Poalei-Tzion Workers Home on Agradowa Street. Without regard to the persecutions of the German occupiers, both parties conducted multifaceted professional and cultural activities. Also the "Jewish Folk Party" grew significantly. An artisan's union was established as well as a small merchant organization.

[Page 467]

These organizations formed the backbone of the Folkist Party. The problems of the Yiddish school system and other cultural responsibilities were daily concerns. Each political faction undertook to shape substantial responses in these areas.

At the end of 1918, when Germany was defeated militarily, Poland became independent and the revolutionary uproars reached a peak—a sharp political struggle flared up on the Jewish streets for general and nationalistic rights.

In the newly-elected Siedlce city council, the adherents of secular Yiddish schools were prominent. The "Folk Party," the "Bund," and the leftist "Poalei-Tzion," as well as the representatives of the artisans, fought a battle on the floor of the council for the rights of Yiddish schools. They also fought for city subsidies of various sorts that would allow the school system to grow.

At the beginning of 1919, there were three separate school administrations: Dinezon (Folkist), Medem ("Bund"), and Borochow (Poalei-Tzion). The Dinezon administration then had fully under its influence and guardianship the school of "Jewish Art," which was now in a new location at 61 Warsaw Street. There were now four classes with a large number fo children, and at the beginning of 1919, they opened a second school and a nursery. The Dinezon school system took over an entire building of 14 rooms. The "Bund," too, and Poalei-Tzion created nurseries in the names of Br. Groser and B. Borochow.

Regarding the school demands, the three administrations were united. Even about certain practical matters they spoke together. The division of funds that had been collected by a Jewish-American aid committee was conducted by a coordinating committee.

No one wanted to take tuition money from he parents. On the contrary, the children received two meals a day at the school, and, from time to time, also a piece of clothing or a pair of shoes. The Dinezon administration had a large budget and still had to seek new sources of income.

[Page 468]

To this end, the "Folk Party" created a consumer-cooperative whose entire income was devoted to the school system. At that time, when the cost of living was so high, the profits from the cooperative were substantial.

But in the midst of this boom, the whole project was disrupted. In 1920, the war between Poland and the Soviet Union broke out and had, especially in SIedlce, a devastating effect on Jewish life. The wild hooliganism of the Polish reaction during the war and afterwards, buried the Jewish workers movement. Vexations and decrees were unceasing. So it was in the whole country, but it was especially awful for the Siedlce Jewish population. The Bolshevik forces were in Siedlce for only ten days, but we felt the devastation that came with the arrival of the Polish army for many years. Hundreds of young men fled in order to avoid the vengeance of the Polish reaction. Hundreds of people were imprisoned, beaten, and tortured, and some were even shot in accordance with rulings from military courts.

With particular brutality the Polish soldiers robbed and destroyed the premises of "Jewish Art." All of the expensive furniture— hundreds of chairs, tables, wall hangings and curtains, scores of expensive musical instruments, theater decorations and costumes all disappeared. The years-long archive of "Jewish Art" was vandalized and destroyed. And on top of all this, the whole place, seventeen rooms, was requisitioned. As if by a miracle, the library was saved, several thousand books, that were stored for a long time in the cellar of the consumer-cooperative.

The school system, too, was totally ruined. The teachers left for Warsaw, the students were scattered, much of the school property was destroyed, and some of the classrooms were requisitioned by the military leadership.

The Dinezon administration—the oldest and largest school board in Siedlce—did not succumb to the battle conditions. It returned to its work.

[Page 469]

6.

With renewed strength and intent, they undertook to rebuild the schools. The school directorate consisted of: Itsche Altschuler, Menashe Czargabrode, Yosef Tirin, Yakov Schlechter, Yosef, Rosenzumen, Chaim Mendelman, and Moyshe Mandelman. They engaged new teachers, mostly local. These teachers were: Esther Levenstein—who was later the director of a "Shabbesuawke" [a school where there was no teaching on Shabbos]—Polye Friedman-Altschuler, Rivkeh Mandelman, Dinah Friedman-Hochberg, Dovid Neumark, and Yosef Sonnschein.

They had to maintain both schools and the nursery. The "Bund" and "Poalei-Tzion" also reopened their nurseries, but they were soon closed due to lack of funds.

The Dinezon administration struggled with all kinds of obstacles. Especially difficult were the material struggles. Their bills grew, while income declined. The teachers did not receive even their meager pay on time or in the full amount. Fund raising events were impossible to stage, and there was no central body to appeal to. The directors and the teachers,, with full understanding, assumed the burdens and the needs in order not to abandon their school positions. They bore their needs, but they went on believing in their work, with the hope of finding a smoother and more secure path. There were. Hopes to incorporate parents directly in the work of the school, but in hindsight that did not succeed.

The income from he first school conference, and from the conference alone, brought a revival to the work. People were full of hope for new growth and development. The problem of the school was back on agenda of the Jewish street. At this conference, the Dinezon administration was represented. From Siedlce there were also delegates from the "Bund" and "Poalei-Tzion." Our delegation belonged to the independent faction, which played an eminent role at the conference, like a strong force.

[Page 470]

When "TZISHO" (The Central Jewish School Organization) was founded, we submitted, organizationally and pedagogically, to their directives and regulations.

For the new school year of 1921-1922, which again began with a hail of persecutions on all of the Jewish school systems in the country, thanks to the socialist resolutions of the school conference, we were compelled to combine the two school systems in one. We did, however, maintain the nursery, as an actual base for the school. Our school and nursery were then the only modern, community, Jewish school facilities in the city.

We began to demand tuition from the parents, which was new for them. The students' parents were for the most part poor, and each expense hit them hard. Our actual financial base was then the monthly subsidies from "TISHO." We also had a bit of income from the cooperative. We received no help from the city coffers. So the school life went, one year better, one year worse materially—until the school year of 1925-1926.

Every year we had to struggle with the persecutions and vexations from the school authorities. In order to maintain our annual city budget, we had to conduct bitter struggles in the city council for subsidies for our school. When once they agreed to set aside a certain sum, the administrative overseers would come and eliminate it. But at the same time there would be visitations from the school authorities who demanded strict adherence to the school rules. We had great difficulties and worries with our premises. For many years, the military had requisitioned two rooms, but eventually the requisitions were eliminated.

The school grew. We now had 5 or 6 classes with two hundred children, and we were very crowded. We had to institute early morning and afternoon class sessions, which caused bitter conflicts among the teachers and also were not good for the children. We should also note that on the matter of requisitioning schoolrooms, there was a bitter fight.

[Page 471]

Deputy Noah Priludski several times in his speeches in the Sejm illustrated the government's handling of the Jews by using Siedlce as an example. He even brought in a special statement, with signatures of many Polish deputies about the matter. Since this matter also had to do with the War Ministry, this battle lasted for five or six years. Finally, however, we won—we received back the two room and rent for the past years.

The school was several times on the verge of being dissolved, but still it survived, mostly thanks to the teachers' readiness to make sacrifices and the actions of several members of the directorate, whose numbers had decreased. During the years 1921-1925, the active teachers were: Krusman—later the manager of the Peretz School in Lublin—and his wife Miadownik, Aaron Shenicki,, who began his teaching career with us, still wearing his student hat and later for many years was the director of the Borochow School in Warsaw and a member of the board of "TZISHO." He died in Siberia as an exile from his home and country; H. Borenstein—later a well-known translator of many books from Polish and other languages into Yiddish.

The Jewish Folkschool, with the teachers:
Borenstein, Flam, Friedman, Y.F. Greenberg, Shenicki, Miodownik

[Page 472]

One of the most critical moments, when the school was on the verge of going under, was the summer of 1925. The new school year was on the threshold and there had been no refurbishing of the premises. The few members of the directorate seemed to have given up. The teachers were owed many months' pay. We owed hundreds on rent and the outlook for subsidies from "TZISHO' was not good. It looked like it was all over. There was no way out. I proposed that we should make the following attempt: we should call and extraordinary meeting for all the parents where we should lay out the situation and together seek a way to save the school. Such a meeting was called for, three days before the beginning of the school year. We were given the task of speaking to the parents who had gathered.

At this meeting, I set forth to the parents in full detail and clarity the question of "to be or not to be" for the school, and I said clearly: "You are not doing us any favors by sending your children to our school. On the contrary, we are hitting our heads against the wall, we are wrestling with all sorts of difficulties, political and material, all in order to provide your children with a good menschlich-Jewish education. So you have to be partners with us. You have to make material sacrifices. You must each pay tuition, naturally all according to their means. It all depends on you today whether we will open the school for the new year. The tuition must amount to 40% of the school budget. If you agree, we, the directors, are ready to go forward and worry about the other 60% of the budget." As expressively as I could, I demanded from the parents a clear, straightforward answer. Their decision was surprising. The gathering unanimously accepted the proposal for tuition that would amount to 40% of the budget. A parents committee of 5 people was chosen who would work with the directors to establish the tuition for each child.

That same evening we held a meeting for the directors with the local teachers, and we decided to open the school and to proceed urgently with the necessary repairs. I had to assume the onerous duties of the secretary and actually worry about the community-financial aspect of the school.

[Page 473]

With everything decided and agreed upon, I gradually carried out the principle that all parents should pay a minimum tuition (a zloty per month was the minimum). Although I ran into many unpleasant aspects, I maintained that the most important thing was to create a solid financial base for the school and, in addition, to to involve the parents directly in the work of the school. This effort paid off. The tuition over the following years amounted to 5-6 thousand zlotys per year, which was about 40% of the whole school budget. For the first time in the history of the Siedlce school system we had set aside a firm foundation for a normal, steady income. The parents gradually learned that they had to make sacrifices in order to give their children a modern Yiddish education.

A second important accomplishment:

The school license was in the name of three people, so it was a kind of private business; however, it had no legal community force that would enable it to demand its rights and defend it against grievances. I therefore immediately created a chapter of the "Yiddish Folk Education League" (a school and cultural organization founded by the Jewish Folk Party in 1922). During the 1925-1926 school year, the school license was put in the name of that organization. This also benefited the fate of the school, because as a school of the Folk Party it was treated better by the government, like the schools from the other radical parties. The chair of the central committee of the "Folk Education League" was Noah Prilucki, who was for a long time the Sejm deputy, and he therefore knew better how to defend the institutions that were under his influence. But the "Folk Education League" was not only of political help to us. We benefited materially as well in the fleeting school year of 1925/26. But even in this school year, the financial situation of "TZISHO" worsened, and, in line with the prevailing practice of distributing subsidies, our school received almost nothing for the year.

[Page 474]

The "Folk Education League" central group still had a bit of money. With personal intervention with Deputy Prilucki, I arranged a monthly subsidy of 300 zlotys, and—it should be noted for praise—in that year we received from the central "Folk Education League" 2,600 zlotys for the whole year. This constituted 25% of our school budget. It also fell to me in that year to get from the central board of the Jewish small merchants union in Warsaw a one-time subsidy for the school in Siedlce in the amount off 300 zlotys.

You should also understand that community support for the school grew stronger. With the cooperation of "TZISHO" in Warsaw, it fell to us to enlist the "Bund" and the "Poalei-Tzion" as active helpers with the work of the school. We formed a membership that brought in 150 zlotys monthly. We also distributed among friends of the school, in private homes, about 200 school pushkes. [collection boxes], on the order of the traditional pushes. Once each month we would empty the pushes, and we would collect about 80-100 zlotys a month. On the traditional Jewish holidays, when Jews give money for various causes—Purim, Erev Yom Kippur, and Hoshannah Rabba—on these holidays we would raise funds among individuals. These collections brought in up to a thousand zlotys a year.

From time to time we would arrange large school celebrations, where the children would demonstrate their preparation in learning and education. In order to bring education to the parents, we created a lecture series for the parents, led by the teachers. There were lectures of a pedagogical and community nature, and, from time to time, collective celebrations for the parents, children, and teachers.

The school in that year advanced pedagogically, because we won as a teacher Mordechai Gilinski (Batka), who was in later years known in the county try through his work in the "Medem Sanatorium." He was among the newly graduated seminarians from the famous Jewish teachers seminary in Vilna.

[Page 475]

He came to us directly from Vilna, not yet having even passed the official examination. One could say, without exaggeration, that "Batka" brought the spirit of life into the school with what he had absorbed in the teacher's seminary, and his overwhelming love for the children was not in doubt. And the children responded the same way. Such love from students for a teacher—the love of our students and later of the hundreds of children in the Medem Seminary for Batka—is seldom encountered. In this way, a great number of people were mobilized to secure the school legally, financially, pedagogically, and in the community. In the following years, this work became even broader.

In 1925, on the tenth anniversary of the death of Y. L. Peretz, a huge march was organized in Warsaw to Peretz' grave. Scores of thousands participated. There were delegates from the whole country. Our school, too, took part. On my initiative it was decided to commemorate Peretz' memory in Siedlce by naming the school after him. From then on it was called "The First Yiddish Folk School in the name of Y.L. Peretz" in Siedlce. At a special ceremony on this occasion a school pennant was unfurled, made of expensive green damask, on which was embroidered with silver threads the name of the school.

7.

With the arrival of the 1926-1927 school year, we resolved to improve the schools in all aspects. The teaching staff was especially strengthened. These teachers arrived: Karol and Mina Weisberg—both licensed teachers. We now had seven teachers whose work raised the prestige and pedagogical level of the school.

The number of children increased and we soon decided, at the beginning of the school year, that it was time to hold our first graduation from the school. We had to give the school, we said, the tradition of a graduation. Although we never had in a year more than six classes, we then decided to make a graduation from the sixth class. The studies were specifically planned so that the students in the sixth class—there were about seven of them—should get special care.

[Page 476]

This decision proved to be important. The graduation ceremony was held in a big hall in the city. Each of the students showed off one aspect of the school subjects—Yiddish, Hebrew, Polish, history—Jewish, general, and Polish—natural science, and so on. Because these demonstrations were direct results of the year's studies, the graduation made a great impression on the parents. The school thus rose in their estimation. At the end of this school year there was a grand children's production of Oscar Wilde's famous symbolic story "The Happy Prince." The costumes and the settings, as well as the fine performances of the children, enchanted everyone. It was performed three times in the city's summer theater to full houses of children and grown-ups. The local press praised it highly.

At the same time, we conducted important political campaigns for the rights of the school, both internally and externally. We made great efforts to obtain subsidies from the magistrate and from the Jewish community organization.

During that school year there were elections for the city council and for the Jewish community organization. In order to hav our voice heard in the election campaign, we created a weekly paper, "The Word." This was no outspoken party organ. It was edited by a committee: Yakov Tenenbaum, Menashe Czarnobrode, and myself. This was a paper that published radical Yiddishist thought. At that time the Zionists had their self-produced weekly, the "Siedlcer Vokhenblat," and the "Agudah" also had a weekly paper, "Undzer Veg." In our paper we had the possibility of informing the community about the inner workings of the school, of clarifying and convincing, and simultaneously fighting our opponents.

As difficult as it was for us not to be receiving a subsidy from the city, it was far more bitter to have to force through in the Jewish community organization what was absolutely controlled by the "Agudah." We had only a single representative in the community-council—Yosef Rosenzumen. On the board, however, there were representatives only from the "Agudah" and the Zionists. Still, we could exert more pressure, because we enlisted in our struggle the students' parents, among whom were many workers and craftsmen.

[Page 477]

In addition, the organized workers movements "Bund" and "Poalei-Tzion" were on our side in the struggle.

In the city council, where the "Bund" and "Poalei-Tzion" were represented, with the help of those factions who had a significant influence with the magistrate, we managed to get a subsidy commensurate with the number of children in the school. There were times when we received about 3,000 zlotys a year.

The battle with the community council lasted more than two years, and we triumphed thanks to the local Polish official. This is what happened: At every meeting of the community council, we would arrive highly organized and seeking ways so as not to allow the budget to be passed in favor of the "Agudah." The chair of the council was Mr. Nachum Weintraub (for many years a prominent community activist dating back to czarist times) and we had to work through him. I, even though I did not belong on the council, wanted an exception made so that I could speak and establish our right to be supported by the council. And so it happened. At the next meeting I was given a chance to speak, although the "Agudah" strongly protested. Understand, however, that we had come to the meeting well-prepared and organized. When I had finished speaking, the vice-chair, the Agudah representatives Y Czeranski, stood up and and called out in a loud voice," And I say 'No,' with a capital N." This had the effect of an explosion. There was a rush toward the podium, the barrier was broken, the electricity went out, and there began a melee with screaming and shouting that disturbed the whole neighborhood. The police soon arrived and there began a close investigation. But we declared that we would not give up. Our school must be supported by the community council. A new Polish official had just arrived in the city. When he learned what kind of scandal was taking place in the Jewish streets, he assumed the role of a peacemaker. The next meeting of the council came at the behest of the official, on his premises, and he persuaded the "Agudah" to agree that our school should be subsidized on the same principles as the Talmud Torah and the "Tarbus" school. After that, the school, received two thousand zlotys annually. Thus in the following years, 1927-1929, the school budget was almost fully covered.

[Page 478]

Our freedom from material needs made it possible for the school to be inwardly stronger, and the pedagogical preparation in those years was obvious. This was confirmed by the frequent visits of the "TZISHO" teachers Rosa Simchowicz, D. Police, Ch. Sh. Kaszdan, Sh. Mendelssohn, Y. Pat, and others. Also, the official visits from the school authorities. Thanks to the objective, favorable reports of the school inspectors, we received subsidies from the magistrate. These reports we attached to our official applications for subsidies. It is worth noting that that thanks to such favorable reports from the school administration, we also received funds from the national subsidies that "TZISHO" once distributed.

8.

In the years 1927-1929 the school achieved its highest level. We strengthened our community outreach, both written and oral. In those years we had seven full classes with about 250 children. There was a kind of crystalisation—the parental element in our school became more ideologically conscious.

In time the financial situation of "TZISHO" improved. B. Michalewicz' visit to America brought in considerable sums for the Yiddish school systems. That gave us the opportunity to accomplish much. I obtained from TZISHO a special large sum to completely renovate the school. We made the school more comfortable and fixed up the appearance of the classrooms. The monthly "TZISHO" subsidies reached a hundred dollars (800-900 zlotys). In addition, we received about a hundred dollars a month for feeding the children in the school. For this purpose we arranged for a kitchen in the school with all the necessary appliances. All the schoolchildren ate breakfast in their classrooms together with their teachers. This had great educational benefit.

[Page 479]

Incidentally, the children themselves helped serve at mealtimes, where they served two rolls with a glass of milk or cocoa.

At the end of the 1927-1928 school year—on the tenth anniversary of the school's founding—we created a number of school celebrations. Over the course of two weeks, among all the organizations and institutions where we had any influence, thee were extra school rallies and gatherings. In one of the largest halls in the city there was an imposing performance by the children. There was a march by the school through the streets of the city, by children, parents, and friends. And to top it off—a wonderful exhibition about the school that took up all seven classrooms. For the opening of this exhibition, Yosef Leszczinski (Khmurner) from TZISHO and Deputy Noah Prilucki (Folk-Education League) came from Warsaw. The exhibition, which was the result of a year's worth of work, represented all the areas of study and made a great impression on all who attended. The exhibition was open for two weeks. In that time it was visited by more than five thousand people. Among the visitors were representatives of the school administration, a number of teachers and professors from the Polish folk school and gymnasia, many of whom reacted with great praise and attention. In the visitors book there were many interesting entries in Yiddish, Polish and Hebrew from numerous Jewish and Polish circles who expressed amazement at the great pedagogical education in our school. Some of the designers of this exhibition in 1929 were at the international school exhibit in Locarno, where TZISHO had its own hall.

In 1928-1929 we had our first graduation from the seventh grade. This solemn occasion occurred in the presence of a large audience. There were delegates and greetings from various groups and from abroad. This graduation publicly demonstrated the great educational preparation of our school. For this special occasion, we distributed a one-time publication in which students from different classes published their work on a number of subjects. The year 1928-1929 was also a record year, because this was the only year in which the teachers received their full salaries for all twelve months.

[Page 480]

The school also had a fine library for teachers and one for children—run by the children under the supervision of a teacher, a selection of important laboratory equipment for experiments. The crown of our educational work was the student club, which, during the year, promoted education in independence and character building for hundreds of students.

9.

In the summer of 1929 I was working in Warsaw, for a short time in the Medem Sanitarium, and, from the fall of 1929 until the outbreak of the Second World War in 1939—as a community instructor for TZISHO. M. Gilinski (Batka) was also away, permanently, working in the Medem Sanitarium, where he was active as a teacher until the Hitler catastrophe. Also my friend Rivkeh Mandelman had accepted a job in the newly established school in Kutna. These developments did not have a good effect on the continuing existence of the school. Things were made worse by the general world crisis that also affected Poland and almost entirely ruined the Jewish population of Siedlce. Jews were simply impoverished—left without anything.

The school existed until 1933. It struggled in its last years with all sorts of obstacles-chief among them, financial problems. TZISHO was again in a bad way financially. It made heroic efforts to maintain the school system in the country, and it gave special attention to the school in Siedlce. From time to time TZISHO sent special envoys to conduct local school activities and to reinforce certain people there who did not want to relinquish their positions. In addition, the subsidies from the magistrate and the community organization collapsed, so that necessarily the teachers' wages were decreased.

The few members of the directorate were worn out. The whole burden of the school was borne by Menashe Czarnogrode and Mottl Friedman. In the school's last years, representatives of the "Bund" and "Poalei-Tzionn" joined the directorate. Binyamin Kramosz worked hard.

[Page 481]

He was the secretary of the school until the end. The crisis became worse and worse. It was one of the most bitter years in the history of TZISHO. The "slaughtering knife" of need made one cut after the other, and the school in Siedlce fell under its blade. The teachers suffered from hunger, the burden of rent for the school increased over the year and the landlords threatened eviction. The two leaders of the directorate could not persevere and the school was no longer opened. Even in that year, when we should have been celebrating the school's fifteenth anniversary, it quietly gave up the ghost...

The landlords went through with the eviction. The school furniture and everything else was put out onto the street. For a little while it was stored in a warehouse. Finally the school inventory received a reprieve—it was transferred to the Yiddish school in neighboring Mezrich.

In later years, when the situation of TZISHO improved, especially after 1936, when there were attempts to improve political conditions in the country, when the Jewish public became much more active in reaction to the reactionary governmental attitude toward the Jews—even in those years, throughout the country, interest in the problems of schools increased. There were again attempts to renew the school activities in Siedlce. After much effort, a branch of TZISHO was opened, and concrete plans were made to open a nursery and a first grade of a school. Funds were even gathered amounting to a hundred zlotys. Sadly, these plans could not be carried out. The shadow of the anti-Semites grew greater and darkened the Polish skies until—Hitler's hordes took over and in a few days Jewish life was destroyed. The German beasts burned and destroyed everything which we had with so much love, faith, and devotion built up over 25 years in Poland.

When I ask myself what resulted from all this work? Was it worth all the effort?

[Page 482]

What did we achieve with all that money and human energy? I answer wholeheartedly—Yes! It was worth it! The understanding of oneself as an individual and as a member of a people that we planted in the students of our secular Yiddish school played an important role in the heroic struggles of young Jewish workers in Poland in the ghettoes against the Nazi enemy. They are the ones who wrote the hero chapter of Jewish history in our tragic time; they are the ones who sanctified the name of "Jew" and the Jewish people in the world! The small number of survivors, former students of the TZISHO schools are today, spread across the whole world, the enthusiastic fighters and builders for a renewed Jewish life in all its forms!

A class from the Polish government folk school

[Page 483]

The Hebrew School System in Siedlce

by P. Dromyk–Popowsky (Tel–Aviv)

Translated by Theodore Steinberg

Usually people maintain that the Hebrew school system in Siedlce began in 1927, when the first Tarbus school opened. But that date is mistaken, because actually a Hebrew school already existed in Siedlce in 1904 when through the Zionist minyan the teachers Gurewitch and Kaplansky were brought to Siedlce. They, together with Akiva Goldfarb and David Morgenshtern, founded the first Hebrew school in Siedlce.

The school was located at 10 Pienkne, on the whole second floor, and about 180 children were students there.

The children were almost all from Zionist families, who supported the school all by themselves, without outside support. The school was considered a great success among Siedlce's Jews.

People began to hear Hebrew in the Jewish streets. The school ran evening courses for adults, led by Gurewitsch and Kaplansky. Understand that the lessons were in Hebrew. Later, when Gurewitsch left Siedlce to become director of the Hebrew gymnasium in Vilna, Akiva Goldfarb and David Morgenshtern continued the school. The first Hebrew school lasted a good while and hundred of children learned Hebrew.

In 1917, M.M. Landau opened a Hebrew–Yiddish school called "Da'as." But it did not last long.

[Page 484]

Aside from Goldfarb and Morgenshtern's school, there existed "Chederim M'tukanim" of David Adler and Shmuel Moyshe Jabkowitsch. The "Cheder M'tukan" of Prizent and Berkowitsch later became a Mizrachi school called "Yavneh."

There was also a school called "Torah v'Da'at." The teachers were Bernzweig, Greenberg, Javerbaum, and Sonnschein.

In 1920, the Zionist committee opened a kindergarten. Among those who were active in it was the teacher Chanah Keyser, who lives now in Haifa.

When the law was passed in Poland for compulsory education, the school of Morgenshtern and Goldfarb was divided up and each part became a "Cheder M'tukan." Children seven years of age came to the school before they were subject to compulsory education or in the afternoon when they had finished their studies in the government schools. Many parents, even wealthy ones, sent their children to the "Talmud Torah", which was not recognized by the government, so that their children would study Jewish subjects.

For a long time there was a question about opening a Tarbus school in the Siedlce Zionist committee, but the truth is that, unfortunately, it had to wait for another time, because when it came to the practical matter, they did not have the first hundred zlotys that were necessary at the start.

Once at a meeting of the Zionist committee, in the summer of 1926, when the question again arose of opening a Tarbus school in Siedlce and there was again a question of where they would get the first couple hundred zlotys to secure a place and get school desks, a writer, who at the time worked for the central office of Keren Kayames as an instructor and who had just arrived from Warsaw–took out of his pocket 500 zlotys, laid them on the table, and said: "I'll lend you my month's salary so that you cannot blame a lack of funds for not opening a school."

The comrades accepted it and decided to form a special committee with the responsibility of opening the school. The committee consisted of the following comrades: Levi Gutgeld, Moshe Yom Tov, Yehoshua Ackerman, the writer, Avrahamtshe Altenberg, and Meir Tenenbaum as secretary. For a long time after he served as secretary to the school.

[Page 485]

Early the next morning, they went to Warsaw to engage teachers for the school.

As director the engaged comrade Yosef Okun who would hire the teachers. He remained in Warsaw to engage them. A few days later he arrived with the teachers Shalita, Wein, and Fried, and we called together a comprehensive meeting, which obligated older comrades to become active so that the school could be opened. There was not much time before the beginning of the school year. It was decided to form several committees: 1) for finance 2) to secure a facility for the school 3) to consider furnishings 4) for persuading people to send their children to the school.

The finance committee consisted of: Asher Urszel, N. Weintraub, Dr. Schleicher, Shalom Zaltzman, Henoch Riback, Fishl Popowski (now Dromy). The committee truly succeeded, thanks to Asher Urszel. In a short time they came up with more than 2,000 zlotys. This was then a sizable sum. In addition, the committee to secure a facility, under the leadership of Y.T. Ackerman, succeeded quickly in finding a location in a house at 17 Florianski, from Itsche Schwartz. The committee for furnishings also quickly did its task.

The schoolteachers and the executives with the leader Mr. Okun

[Page 486]

On the information committee, Levi Gutgeld was particularly notable. He wrote for the newspaper, spoke at meetings of young people and old. Working energetically along with him were Fishl Popowski, Yehoshua Ackerman, Altenberg, and Yosef Ukon. There were also visits to houses, notably by Yosef Gutgeld, Yehoshua Ackerman, and Moshe Yom Tov. They were helped in this project by "Ha–Shomer Ha–Tza'ir" and "He–Chalutz Ha–Tza'ir."

In this fashion, the Hebrew school became a factor in the Jewish life of Siedlce. In the first school year there were three classes in the school with over 100 children. In its first year of existence, the school won the full trust and sympathy of the Jewish population of Siedlce. Fully involved in this success were the director Yosef Ukon, the education professionals in the school, and the lay leaders, who worked with outstanding enthusiasm.

In subsequent activities, a smaller school committee was selected to replace the earlier one. On the committee were: Asher Urzhel (chair), Henoch Riback, Yehoshua Ackerman, Moshe Yom Tov, Fishl Popowski–Dromy, Shalom Saltzman, Yosef Gutgeld., Meir Tenenbaum (secretary), Levi Gutgeld, and Avrahamtshe Altenberg.

The Tarbus school committee, with Asher Urzhel, chair, in the middle

[Page 487]

In the second school year, 1927–28, two new teachers arrived, Kushlian and Horowicz. The number of children went up to 200.

In the third school year, 1928–29, more new teachers arrived–Heller and Mlashn. The number of children increased, approaching 250. The building on Florianski was too small and so they rented a place on Pienkne in the house of Sukenik. The school's success exceeded all expectations. It was considered to be among the best schools in Poland. It grew from day to day and earned the affection of all facets of the populace: Chasidim, comrades in the "Bund," and even parents who were communists sent their children to the Tarbus school.

The Lag B'Omer celebrations of the school became a popular holiday. The celebration would begin in the evening, the night before Lag B'Omer, with a parade through the streets. In the morning there was an excursion for the schoolchildren in the woods that belonged to Yitzchak Nachum, Weintraub. The trip to the woods included children from other schools and also grown–ups, who celebrated the Jewish children's holiday.

The faculty and some students

[Page 488]

Schoolchildren at a Lag B'Omer celebration in the woods

Levi Gutgeld wrote an article about the significance of the Hebrew school for the "Siedlcer Vochenblat."

The following lines from the article show what a large role the Tarbus school played in the Jewish life of Siedlce. Levi Gutgeld wrote:

"Tarbus" began four years ago with a hundred children. There were problems about a location and with finances. There was no lack of pessimists. The generosity of the directors and the parents, however, triumphed. Last year the school enrolled more than three times as many children. It seldom happens that a committee of parents works so hard, which is a sure sign of their happiness with the school and is the best advertising.

It should be known that despite the school's difficult financial situation, there are fifty children who learn there at no cost, while most of the children pay a minimal fee–while the school has outstanding personnel that any school in Poland would desire. They adopt a parental attitude toward the children, while an exemplary harmony exists between the teachers and the parents. These are the secrets to the present reputation of the "Tarbus."

[Page 489]

Along with the growth of the school's reputation, there was also growth in its deficit. It was like "the waters come to my soul" (Ps. 69:2, that is, as if drowning). There was a time when the teachers were not paid for several months. We were compelled to appeal to the banks, and the school personnel received money as loans–until things improved. The landlords of the facility demanded their rent or they would throw us out. We thought thought that the school would soon have to close.

The matter was considered at a meeting, which was attended also by a representative of the teachers. Several proposals were considered, but no concrete action was decided on. A moment arrived when everyone just sat quietly.

Suddenly Yossele Gutgelt called out, "We will not close the school. We'll go to Yitzhak Greenbaum in Warsaw. He will give us a loan." And thus it happened: With Greenbaum's help we got a loan of 4,000 zlotys and the school was rescued. It was not closed. Just the opposite–it became even bigger and from year to year new classes were opened. The Tarbus school could actually support itself. Many poor working–class children learned in the school, as well as children from the orphanage "Ezras Y'somim" who could pay no tuition. We had to conduct long, difficult combat with the community directorate until they were willing to provide subsidies.

Then we had to fight with the custodians of the "Agudah," who were ten of the twenty directors, and the director of "Mizrachi," who was part of "Agudah" and stood with them against the subsidies. That added up to eleven of the twenty directors.

After a long, exhausting fight by our comrades in the community–Urszel, Schleicher Popowski, Velvl Barg, Weintraub, and others– we overcame the opposition and we received a subsidy, though not as much as the Talmud–Torah received.

If we had to battle in the community organization with the "Agudah," in the city council we had to fight not with the non–Jews but with the Jewish representatives of the "Bund" and the leftist "Po'alei Tzion," who held that the Hebrew school was designed for "Palestine" and catered to wealthy children. Naturally, because the Jewish labor representatives spoke this way, the representatives from the "P.P.S.," who, together with the labor representatives constituted a majority, said: "We cannot speak out against the wills of our Jewish comrades."

[Page 490]

It thus fell to our energetic comrades–Dr. Schleicher, Asher Urszel, Rubinstein, to make a breakthrough. They were helped by the representative of the "Agudah," R. Yisroel Gutgelt. Our representatives on the city council demonstrated that the greatest majority of the students in the "Tarbus" school were the children of workers, as were the children from the orphanage, and they paid almost nothing in tuition. Our arguments worked. It was finally decided that they would provide a subsidy.

Understandably, thanks to the subsidies from the community and the city, our financial burden was relieved. At that time, Mr. Okun left Siedlce and went to Bialystok, and his place as principal was taken by Tzvi Bokser, one of the best teachers of the time. Also the secretary, Meir Tenenbaum, left his position and was replace by Zev Lev, who lives today in America.

The school head Bokser with a group of students

[Page 491]

The school committee was joined by M. Yudenglauben, Wladowski, M. Ratbein, Yakov Yom Tov, Mendziszeczki and, for many years, Mrs. Genia Vyman and A. Feinzilber. In 1930–31, we had our first graduation.

In 1931, we celebrated the introduction of a banner for the school. The "Siedlcer Vochenblat" put out a special issue dedicated to this event. We will present excerpts from articles from this special issue of the "Siedlcer Vochenblat" written by teachers and activists in the "Tarbus" school

Principal Bokser wrote in an article: "The 'Tarbus' school is the creation of the people, for the people, and grounded on firm roots. It is a bridge from the past to the future." And he concludes his article: "Even though this emblem belongs to a school for children, everyone–everyone who raises his eyes to the banner–sees that it is a blessing for everyone." The former principal, Mr. Okun, wrote: "A banner for a 'workshop' in Siedlce–the symbol will speak of its accomplishment and of its will. One does not inscribe on the emblem the story of the school's difficulties–on the banner, everything is bright and shiny. From a distance, with tears in our eyes, like a mother standing by her child's crib, we remember the first steps of our school. My wish for you in this 'workshop,' in the school, is that everything for you will be full of light and joy."

Hartglass: "I will not write a whole article, only about what should be written on the banner. Whoever has been in Eretz Yisroel and seen how children conduct their lives in the Hebrew language must come to the realization that the Jewish people lives and will live and will ultimately succeed; therefore I propose that the banner of the 'Tarbus' school should be inscribed with the words 'Am Yisroel Chai'–'The People of Israel Live.'"

Levi Gurgelt: "The foundation of the Tarbus experience lies in the fervor of education. We are now, therefore, in the depths, in the deepest parts of the earth, but under our feet we do not feel the ground, only lessons, not like new heavens under the earth. This should also mark a return to the question, why are we celebrating the unveiling of a banner. Hard times! Bitter times!–But yes, yes, certainly *de profundis* we must create the illusion, and right away, to raise our eyes and celebrate at least a banner."

[Page 492]

On Shabbos evening, there was a celebratory symposium at the city club to honor the unveiling of the banner of the "Tarbus" school. The hall was packed. Many people were turned away because the hall was too small to hold such a crowd.

The symposium opened with the Polish and Jewish anthems, led by a specially chosen choir under the direction of Mr. Garbarcz, accompanied by an orchestra under the direction of Mr. A. Shpielpidel.

Mr. A Urszel, chair of the "Tarbus" school curators, spoke in Hebrew to open the celebration and greeted the guests from Eretz Yisroel and from "Tarbus" headquarters. Dr. Tzvi Zohar, the president of the friends from outside of Siedlce–Mr. P. Eisenstadt , the former leader of the school–Mr. Okun, who returned especially for the celebration, and also the president of the city council–the councilmen Mr. Szeliegewski and Mr. Zaplatowsky and the representatives of the community, of the merchants, of the craftsmen, of the "Urdszalowi Bank," of the "Toz," of the "Ezras Y'somim," of the teachers unions, et al. Mr. Zelikowicz greeted the assembly in Hebrew on behalf of the community and on behalf of the parents' committee–Mr. Henoch Riback, and on behalf of the teachers' council–the principal Mr. Tzvi Bokser, with a long greeting in beautiful Hebrew, on behalf of the students there was D.Y. Meneszeczki, a student from the seventh grade, and on behalf of the graduates of the school there was Moshe Vyman, who lives today in Israel. The last speakers were Mr. P. Eisenstadt from Warsaw (today in Israel) and Mr. Yisroel Ridel on behalf of the merchants.

Levi Gutgelt also reported on written greetings (almost all in Hebrew) from Tz. K. from the Zionist organization in Poland, the directors of the Keren Ha–y'sod, directors of the Keren Kayames, from the Zionist organization in Siedlce, from Mizrachi, from Hatahadot, from Ha–Shomer Ha–Tza'ir, from He'Chalutz, from He–Chalutz Ha–Tza'ir, from Beit"R, from the Hebrew evening courses, from "Toz," from "Ezras–Y'somim," from the women's club for Eretz Yiasroel, from the teachers union from the community schools, from the sports club "Kadimah,", and others. Also from a group of friends of the school, among them the lawyer Hartglass, Moshe Gordon, and from E. Yosselewitcz (all today in Israel).

Dr. Tzvi Zohar offered a longer greeting in Hebrew on behalf of the "Tarbus" movement in Poland. He spoke also in Polish to the appointed representatives of the City Council, describing for them the achievements of the new Jewish culture in Eretz Yisroel and the significance of the Hebrew school.

[Page 493]

Dr. Tzvi Zohar was honored by the presider Mr. A. Urzhel with the celebratory act of unveiling the banner. The banner was raised high and Dr. Zohar cut the cord to shouts of "May it endure." The gorgeous blue and white appearance of the emblem drew great delight in the hall. To the cries of "Go up to Zion," the students of the school paraded before the emblem.

After a brief pause came the ceremony of hammering silver nails into the supports of the banner. More than a hundred people took part in this ceremony. Nails were also put in on behalf of an array of friends of the school on lived in America, South Africa, London, Argentina, Germany, Denmark, and elsewhere. As they inserted the nails, most of the guests promised specific sums for the welfare of the school.

After a short talk about the work and accomplishments of the school, the former principal, Mr. Y Okun, came forth (He lives now in Israel.) and spoke with great enthusiasm, prompting a long ovation.

Then Dr. Tz. Zohar delivered a longer talk in Yiddish on "The Jewish People for the Hebrew School." He spoke broadly about the current idea of "Tarbus" and the foundation of the modern Hebrew school in connection with the structure of the Jewish people and the efforts for a Jewish renaissance in Eretz Yisroel. The audience thanked Dr. Tz. Zohar for his interesting talk with great applause. At the end of the celebration, the choir sang, accompanied by the orchestra, "Rise Up, Zion" and "Sing." Mr. Fishl Popowski spoke about the material situation of the school, calling on the gathered associates to bear the yoke of the budget. The crowd left the hall singing "Ha–Tikvah." After the formal celebration, in the school itself there was a gathering for tea, attended by the guests and the members of the parents' committee, the board of directors, and the teachers.

* *

In the last years before the Second World War, the school continued to grow and found a great location at 60 Pilsudski. It had tern classes and a kindergarten, and ten teachers. The school had a wonderful library, a dramatics section, and a chorus. The dramatics section put on productions with biblical and other themes.

[Page 494]

In those last years a new principal came to Siedlce–Barnsteen, because Bokser became an inspector for the "Tarbus" schools in Poland. People planned on opening a Hebrew gymnasium, but that plan was never carried out. The Hitler massacre arrived and destroyed all plans.

* *

The "Tarbus" school in Siedlce, during its thirteen years of existence produced brave heroes and national battles. The names of several of them have been inscribed in the history of Israel's fight for independence. Let us recall their names. A number of students who graduated from the "Tarbus" school went to Eretz Yisroel. They quickly became involved with the "Hagganah." They were still quite young. These were the sons of: Vyman, Popowski (from the cantor Popowski), Steinberg, Levinstein, Lieberman, and others. At the time of the Second World War, they were in the ranks of the Jewish Brigade and in other units, in Egypt, Tripoli, Italy, Belgium, Germany. Together with the armies of the democracies, they fought against the Germans.

The students in the school courtyard

[Page 495]

With special reverence we remember the names of 6 students who demonstrated outstanding heroism and sacrificed their young lives. They were: 1) Ephraim Vyman, 2) Ziskind Rozenbaum, 3) Yisroel Zucker, 4) A. Bagagan, 5) Yehuda Konski, 6) Henoch Szelaznagora. We should know of their lives and their heroic deaths.

Ephraim Vyman

Ephraim Vyman was born in Siedlce on April 27, 1920, the ninth of Iyar, to Gittl and Dov Vyman. When he was 4 years old, in 1924, he, his parents, and his brother went to Eretz Yisroel. In 1927, the Vyman family was compelled to return to Poland, to their hometown of Siedlce. The 7–year–old Ephraim was enrolled in Siedlce's Tarbus school. There he received his earliest education. He studied in the national Hebrew school for a total of 5 years, and it played an important role in shaping his character and aspirations. The foundations of Judaism and Zionism that he obtained in the Tarbus school, made him a proud Jewish young man who never bowed to outside influences. And the longing for Jewish independence in a Jewish land formed the goal of his life.

When Ephraim Vyman in the seventh grade and it was time for the celebration of the pennant of the Tarbus school, he wrote in the special edition of the "Siedlcer Vochenblat": "From the time that I entered the school, I have sat within the four walls, that seem silent and abandoned, but these walls carry a secret, which is known only to us, but now I will reveal the secret: it is linked with my knowledge of Eretz Yisroel."

[Page 496]

"When I came to this schoolroom, my mind was full of thoughts about Eretz Yisroel, and my heart was full of longing for the Jewish land. Such a secret cannot penetrate the hearts of young people who do not attend a Tarbus school. We, the students of the Tarbus school, think that there is no other school like it in which students learn about the heroes of our people. We learned to endure and suffer like our great brothers and to resist all temptations. Anyone who has not attended a Tarbus school does not know what Eretz Yisroel means to us. And now, after six years of struggling for the existence of our school, we have merited to arrive at this joyous moment of celebrating the pennant of our school. This pennant will remind us of the four walls within which we have learned to persevere."

"When we graduate from the Tarbus school, which is dearer to us than anything, we will each go our own way. But our hearts will be bound up with the school. Our highest aspiration to get to that spot that the school showed us, and all of the temptations that will get in our way we will overcome and make Aliyah, even if we have to fight for it."

And Ephraim kept his promise:

In 1932, he and his family once again went to Eretz Yisroel. Ephraim quickly became acclimated in his new environment, and when he was fifteen he joined the Hagganah. Ephraim attended a middle school in Tel Aviv. When the events of 1936 occurred, the young man was in the seventh class. He left school and went to border of Jaffa in order to defend the settlement of "Tirat Shalom."

In the summer of 1937, after finishing school, Vyman was sent by the Hagganah to care for the petroleum storage in the Jericho desert and from that moment on he was involved in a standing guard unit that carried out its duties around the country.

In 1938, the eighteen–year–old Vyman was mobilized in a division of railroad guards and achieved the rank of sergeant and Instructor on the Hadera–Jaffa line and in the Signal Corps.

[Page 497]

In this period, Vyman was particularly concerned with organizing military signal corps and creating, in different parts of the country, courses for this military specialty.

In February of 1941, Ephraim left the military guard and prepared to enlist in the British army, but there was a clause that prevented the young hero–the Palmach was preparing for its first major war undertaking, namely, seizing the oil refineries in Tripoli and Syria, which then were controlled by Vichy France. Ephraim Vyman enlisted in the group, which was preparing this act of sabotage.

On May 8, 1941, after appropriate training, 23 young men, including Ephraim Vyman, left in a ship from the Haifa coast and headed in the direction of Tripoli. Vyman never returned from this mission. He fell in battle at the age of 21.

Ziskind Rosenbaum

Ziskind Rosenbaum was born in Siedlce in 1918. His parents were Sarah and Yosef. He was the grandson of Itzl Czibucki. He received his education in the Tarbus school. At the time of the German occupation, Rosenbaum, together with his friends Yisroelik Zucker and Berl Begagan, who were the same age as him, established a partisan group that stayed in the woods. The group conducted a variety of raids agains the Germans, killed Hitler sympathizers, and took their weapons. They also performed acts of vengeance against Poles who betrayed Jews to the Germans or who had themselves murdered Jews. Their attack on the rich Polish merchant Paciarkowski and on the German police made a huge impression on the Christian population.

[Page 498]

This happened after the liquidation of the small ghetto, when no Jews were left in Siedlce. Ziskind, with his comrade B. Begagan, came to Siedlce by various back roads, went to Paciarkowski in order to get the money that Ziskind's uncles–Shlomo and Berl Czibucki– gave him when they felt that they were facing their last days. The Czibuckis asked him that if someone came from their family, he would turn over the funds. Since no one from the Czibucki family remained in Siedlce, aside from Ziskind, he asked for the money. (In Israel there are two grandsons from the Czibucki family–Yonah and Fishl Popowski.)

Paciarkowski told them to wait and went into another room that had a back door, went out to the street and brought a policeman. Ziskind and his friend did not wait for the policeman to arrest them. They took out their revolvers and shot the policeman and LPaciarkowski. The policeman fell dead on the spot. Paciarkowski was taken to a hospital in Warsaw, but he died on the way.

Ziskind and his friend decided to return to the forest. Together with their comrades they conducted other partisan activities. Once, on a hot day, the group went to a little river to bathe. A Christian noticed the group and alerted the Germans. The German police came immediately and shot at the group while they were in the river. Soon the river was red with the blood of the four young heroes. One of the group remained alive. He merited taking revenge and seeing the downfall of the Nazis.

[Page 499]

Yehuda Kanski

Born in Siedlce, the only child of his father, a tailor, who was religious and Jew who longed for Eretz Yisroel. Yehuda was a handsome young man with black eyes and curly hair. From childhood on he had absorbed from his father's stories the heroic atmosphere of the Galilee and the heroes of Tel Chai. He learned in a "Tarbus" school and showed special talent in art and singing; he excelled at organizing social evenings. He was one of the most active comrades in the Siedlce chapter of "Gordonia"; he organized and led a dramatics club; in school productions and later in the movement, he always played the leading roles; he organized artistic undertakings and evenings and recruited new comrades. He did not sever his relationship with life in Siedlce even when his parents, in 1939, just before the outbreak of the war, moved to Warsaw. Then in wear he soon became a leading figure in all the celebrations and artistic undertakings. He really wanted to travel to Eretz Yisroel together with his teacher in the movement–Henia Goldberg (now in Kiryat Anavim), and when she departed, he asked her to write letters to him until the arrival of his anticipated Aliyah.

When the time came for fighting in the Nazi period, he devoted himself entirely to the struggle. He was an agile, efficient young man with many ideas and much initiative; a member of the fighting division of "Gordonia" and for a short while its commander. A month before the revolution of April 19, 1943, he was captured–together with his friend Shimon Leventhal while negotiating to buy arms. It appears that the Gestapo had spread a net and the arms dealer was their man.

[Page 500]

The arrest took place in the Schultz factory on Nowolipie Street, in the neighborhood of the ghetto. That was the meeting place with the intermediary. During the Gestapo's interrogation, Yehuda was tortured barbarically by the well–known German sadist Brand. But they could not break him and he revealed nothing. He died from his tortures–he was twenty years old, and when his body was returned, he was black all over and his fingers were a mashed up mass of bloody flesh. His name and be found in the list of the fallen in the Warsaw Ghetto uprising. (The list of Allen also contains the name of his lifelong friend Leah Korn; his parents and sister were killed in Warsaw).

(From the book: Destruction and Revolt in the Warsaw Ghetto" by M. Neustat)

Henoch Szeloznogora

He was born in Siedlce, in 1913, to a poor family. He studied in the "Tarbus" folk school, but after the death of his father–Henoch was then twelve years old–he had to leave his studies and go to Warsaw. There he began to work in a glass factory and support his mother and his younger sister. He undertook self–education in the "He–Chalutz Ha–Tza'ir" organization, among whose first members he was in 1931, when he was thirteen. [Trans. note: This math does not work out.]. Every free evening that he had, after his hard working day, he would come to the branch office, but he would not take part in conversations. He showed dedication and in 1933 he was elected to the local committee and was also named as mentor of an educational group. With his simplicity and generosity, he was loved by everyone. In 1938 he participated in a He–Chalutz seminar in the Warsaw suburb of Volya; he spent some time in the He–Chalutz Forde in Grochow and from there he went to Vilna for the preparatory agricultural course and he worked for the movement. (His older sister Sarah was active in "He–Chalutz," and his younger sister, Ettl,–in "He–Chalutz Ha–Tza'ir"; she was killed in Bialystok.)

[Page 501]

When the war broke out, he was in Vilna and quickly went to the Soviet Union because he wanted to live in a socialist environment. But he did not stay there long. He returned to his comrades in Vilna and had a position of authority in the movement. He was active in the Chalutz underground. At the end of 1941, with the first expulsions from Vilna, he left for Slonim and then, in 1942, for Bialystok, where he became secretary of the collective. He often left the confines of the ghetto, disguised as a non–Jew (he was tall, with a pale face, and did not look Jewish), in order to bring food and other goods to his friends and also to smuggle weapons into the ghetto. The collective also served as a school for fighters, and Henoch was one of the leaders. Even before the war he had taken courses in self–defense and learned to shoot with a rifle and throw grenades. He was active in the Jewish fighters' organization and a commander of a group of fighters. He had no illusions that all of the Jews in Bialystok would not be killed nor about the results of his fighting. At the communal gathering of the collective in Bialystok on February 27, 1943, he said that no one should have any illusions, not about the uprising and not about escaping to the woods. There were two ways to die, and one should die with honor. This faithful comrade of the movement remained at his post until the very end. He died in the revolt in the Bialystok ghetto.

(From the book: "Destruction and Revolt in the Warsaw Ghetto" by M. Neustat)

[Page 502]

My memoirs from Siedlce
(A speech that was not given)

by Yosef Okon

Translated by Mira Eckhaus

I will not mourn or arouse ghosts: Is it possible that this handsome couple, Levi and Yosef, are gone? And Joshua, the king of peace and hope, would not shake off the dust all at once and will be resurrected? And the wise old men, Weintraub and Orwitz - did they don't have the witty ingenuity to ward off the demons? And this excellent person from the followers of Gur, that was great in the Torah, Rabbi Israel Gutgeld, who walked slowly like the water of the Shiloach flew, can it be that he is no longer among us? No, it can't be! Siedlce will not be wiped out! It is still in front of us, with its ancient and glorious being, and pours out a vision on its sons-builders that are scattered from Eilat to Hanita.

Morning in Elul, 5687. Early autumn mists covered with a veil the treetops of the Linden and the oak. The golden domes towers of the houses of awe dip dimly in the damp air. From the old Beit midrash, in contrast, emerges the Shofar sound calling for repentance. Children with schoolbags walk fast to the various schools. Today is the first day of school. About 20 toddlers gathered in the center in Kilinski street for the announcement regarding the opening of the "Tarbut" school in Siedlce.

After a short festive conversation, they started singing and dancing and into the stormy circle of dancers, parents and youth were swept, and Levi was in the middle. The number of students grew day by day. They prepared a special place and equipped it with school furniture. Joshua was in charge of the work; Levy – was in charge of the finance and propaganda; Fischel, may he live long life, was in charge of collecting donations from the public. And as to the tuition fee – There is a tough competition with the government schools and with "Talmud-Torah", in which the study is for free, and no one in Siedlce had to recognize the term "tuition fee". The only source for building and maintaining the "Tarbut" school was through donations and contributions.

[Page 503]

18 Elul. The school has been approved by the Polish education authorities. The assimilated, the followers of the "Povshikhna", were defeated. Chol HaMoed Sukkot, the school holds (a small one but all about pure Hebrew). In the city there are talking: the sound of Hebrew is charming, the Sukkah is a great thinking, alluring. Bereshit Saturday evening. Dr. Shleicher, who is now famous among the physicians of Greater Haifa, then served as chairman of the Zionist Organization and as the official principal of honor of the "Tarbut" School. He opened the 100-anniversary party - a hundred students in "Tarbut" - with the verse "Who are those who come as fast as the clouds and like the doves that fly to their nests"? Our nests? Sharp Nishri-Orzel is saying: is your daughter also in "those" Dr.? - Of course, Dr. Shleicher answered in Polish, when she will grow up!

The year of 5689. The school has 240 students in two rented buildings. It has already gained a reputation and income beyond the ordinary. It is still not enough to cover a meager salary for teachers. The branch became entangled in dead-end debts. An emergency meeting of the Zionist Organization, the Hachalutz branch and the "Tarbut" branch was held. All the options are gone, the credit in the local banks has been fully utilized. The annual fundraising fee has run out and it is not known where the funds will come from for the current budget. Teachers are entitled to a six-month salary, where will the help come from? - Suddenly Yossele stood up and his small eyes were on fire: The school will not be closed! We should turn to…turn to…to whom shall we turn to? A painful question for everyone. To Greenbaum and he will get us a loan at the public banks in Greater Warsaw.

This is indeed an idea! We are all responsible! And immediately 4,000 gold bills were signed and a delegation of three was chosen: Levy, Fishel and myself.

The sun of Tammuz fired fire spears at the capital. Everyone left to the forests of Otwock. The streets are deserted and sweaty. We are standing in front of the door of Itzhak Greenbaum's house. We divided the issues between us: a request, an explanation of the situation and the nature of the responsibility and the bills we have. Levi rang the bell and we entered. Greenbaum appeared in a pioneering shirt: What happened! The first one starts talking. Greenbaum stops him: I understand, a difficult situation, what can I do?

Levy: A bank loan. And Fishel, meanwhile, is spreading the notes on the desk.

Greenbaum: Such a large sum, how? - Levy: It's impossible with less than that. And he starts to talk about our budget affair.

Greenbaum: I see, but … and what do you think, Popovsky? I will not suffer from it?

Popovsky: No!

Greenbaum: And you Gutgeld, do you also suggest I will sign?

Levy: Sign, there is no other choice!

Greenbaum rolls up his sleeve, takes a large pen from the table and signs one after the other. And I, the little one, was left with no need to say my speech.

[Page 504]

"Group of Lovers of the Language of the Past"
The Hebrew Evening–Courses of R. Akiva Goldfarb

by David ben Yosef (Pasovsky)

Translated by Theodore Steinberg

The name "Group of Lovers of the Language of the Past" was chosen by a group of young men and women who were 16 and 17 years old who themselves organized Hebrew evening courses in the private school of R. Akiva Goldfarb at 22 Warsaw Street.

It was in 1924, after a break of several years in the Hebrew evening courses of the Zionist organization, which stopped at the time of the First World War. They felt the need to study and hear "a Hebrew word." These Jewish national young people themselves, not driven by any organization or institution, felt it as a definite fact–so they got together with Mr. Akiva Goldfarb, the well–known and beloved Hebrew teacher, and opened in his school evening courses and enrolled in them.

The instigators were the following: Sarah Kleinlehrer, Tovah Barbanel, Mordechai Gottesdiener, Yisrael Yom Tov, my brother Levi Pasovsky, and myself. We had one goal: to spread knowledge of the Hebrew language among the Jewish young people in Siedlcer.

At our first session with Mr. Goldfarb, a financial question arose: how to manage the budget of the evening courses. This was a big expense. But Mr. Akiva Goldfarb, who believed that teaching Hebrew was a sacred responsibility, agreed to teach without renumeration so that the courses could go on and Jewish young people could learn Hebrew.

[Page 505]

In a short time the evening courses developed and enrolled scores of students, young men and women from all levels of the populace. The Hebrew evening courses became a community focus for the Jewish youth in the city. From time to time there were interesting puzzle evenings and literary conversations in Hebrew on various themes. The well–known Zionist activist and educator Mr. Levi Gutgelt gave talks about the Tanach and drew great delight from his audience.

At a general meeting of the students, it was decided that they would speak Hebrew among themselves at every opportunity. I can picture it now: groups of young people gathering in the evening at the pharmacy on Warsaw Street and speaking Hebrew aloud among themselves, openly and without shame. Although the Hebrew spoken by the group was Ashkenazic…the group of Hebrew speakers attracted the attention of the passers–by.

The Hebrew evening courses of the "Group of Lovers of the Language of the Past" took a great deal of time and were a source of educational skills for the Zionist youth pioneer organizations such as "Ha–Shomer Ha–Tza'ir," "He–Chalutz," "He–Chalutz Ha–Tza'ir," "Ha–Oved Ha–Tzioni" and others.

A group of students from the Hebrew courses led by the teacher Goldfarb.
Among the students is the Poalei–Tzion leader Mordechai Kaznitzky

[Page 506]

The Library and the Society "Jewish Art"

Moshe Mandelman

Translated by Theodore Steinberg

When, at the time of the First World War, the German occupied Siedlce (August 12, 1915), there were only two Jewish cultural institutions in the city—the "Jewish Library" and the "Jewish Art" society. The library dated itself back to 1901, when the Siedlce maskil Y. Goldvasser had maintained a shelf of books in his home. He did not even know who the readers were, especially people who would distribute the books and meet in secret. Several years later the library became legal. It existed as a private concern in the name of the well-known Zionist Mordechai Meir Landau (may his memory be a blessing), a son-in-law of the conspicuous activist Yitzchak Nachum Weintraub, the long-time head of the community under tzars rule and later in the days of Poland. The library operated under Zionist influence. The person who was responsible for handing out the books was Asher Liverant, who simultaneously took care of the National Fund and other Zionist matters.

At that time the library was not properly organized. There were no real rules and the catalogue was disorganized. It was difficult to find the book one sought.

[Page 507]

The "Jewish Art" society—its full name was "Literary-Musical Society Jewish Art"—was established in 1910, at a time when in many cities and towns in Russia, various sorts of literary societies were founded under the names "Ha-Zamir" [literally "The Nightingale], "Lyre", "Harp", "Dramatic Art," and so on. Especially popular at the time were the Warsaw and Lodz "Nightingales." In Warsaw, Peretz then led the famous educational "game evenings, while in Lodz there were huge musical-literary activities. In Siedlce, therefore, people also called "Jewish Art" by the name of "Nightingale" [Ha-Zamir]. Most people, for convenience, got rid of the "Ha" from the beginning and the "r" from the end and called it "Zame." "Don't go to the Zame!" was the name of one-man comedy written by the Siedlce author Yakov Tenenbaum that was often performed under his direction.

You should be aware that both the library and the "Jewish Art" operated under the watch of the tsarist police. For example, one had to present to the police a copy of every newly purchased book, even if it had been published legally, so it could be censored and approved for lending to general readers. Similarly, one had to present to the governmental counsel a full program, with translation, for every innocent literary-musical evening.

The police were often "guests" both at the institutions and at the activities of individual members. A whole array of activists knew when they had to take actions to avoid arrest. This was usually just before the first of May or other unlucky days.

In addition, in the Jewish context, people opposed each young man or woman who dared to enter the library or who took part in discussions at the "Zame," where people smoked cigarettes on Shabbos and men and women danced together, "God help us...". No broad enlightenment work was then possible in the depths of the Jewish masses. Consequently, the number of active doers was also small and these institutions led a dismal existence. The library seldom bought a new book and could not repair the old ones.

[Page 508]

Also, "Jewish Art" around 1912 found itself in a kind of paralyzed situation, on the verge of liquidation. In this hard time, a group of young people arrived, straight from their Gemaras, and with youthful enthusiasm and Chasidic fervor took a bold step—to unite both organizations. After much effort, it was possible to incorporate the library in "Jewish Art." The group—still in their Chasidic long coats—took eagerly to this job. They created a library group consisting of: Avraham Huberman, Velvet Friedman, Asher Liverant, Dovid Eisenberg, Mshe Mandelman, and later Berl Czarnogrode.

They took charge of the books, instituted a regular time for borrowing and returning them, conducted a census of readers, and so on. They also created a Polish section (where earlier there had only been Hebrew-Yiddish and Russian). A group of young women who became part of the library group took special interest in the Polish section. They were: Rokhel Edelstein-Barg (in later years a recognized teacher in the vocational school and in the Polish years was for a time a Bundist member of the Siedlce city council), Golde Halberstam (who died at a very young age), Tirzeh Zucker (tortured by the Nazis in Paris), Bracha Shapiro, and Bronya Goldberg-Glazowska.

We, the co-workers in the library, were, you must understand, also the readers. We fell thirstily on the treasures of the books; with trembling and fear that we would be seen, we would steal into the library, and behind locked doors devour the books. We completely forgot our surroundings and lived in other, fantastic literary worlds.

We all worked with great devotion, and every newly purchased book marked for us a holiday. During the few years before the German occupation, the library grew rapidly. Hundreds of books in Yiddish, Hebrew, Russian, and Polish arrived. It still remained for us to collect hundreds of rubles in cash that we later used to build up the status of "Jewish Art."

* * *

[Page 509]

At the time of the First World War (1914-1918), the Jews in Poland regarded the Germans as liberators. The edicts and accusations from the czarist military gang, the pulling up by the roots of old, established Jewish communities and settlements, the expulsions of tens of thousands of Jews, young and old, men and women, from their homes to who knows where, the kidnapping of prominent Jewish community activists, the ongoing nightmare of pogroms, of physical and spiritual oppression, the theft of Jewish property and goods—all in case the Germans should be welcomed. But people breathed more freely. The young people felt as if chains had fallen off their hands—we truly felt free! There was also an immense change in the religious Jewish way of life. With the discarding of the long caftan, we cast off the ancient image of Yiddishkeit, and, in our naïveté, we spread our hands as thought the world was ours.

In the days right after the Germans marched in, we rented a large space at 66 Warsaw Street for "Jewish Art" and the library. It had been an officers' club. We immediately began to organize the large area. Our goal was to create a major Jewish clubhouse that would consist of the following divisions: literary, dramatic, musical and vocal, library, and reading room. During the course of several months, the association had about 450 members. The aforementioned divisions undertook intensive work, and from day to day their activities increased, so that in several months we could rent the whole three-story building. We then had seven large rooms, including two huge halls that could contain several hundred people.

At that time, private homes were often cold and dark, but "Jewish Art" was half lit by gas and at least was warm and friendly—it bustled with life and activity. On Friday evenings, Shabbos, and Shabbos nights there was a variety of literary, musical, or dramatic evenings with hundreds of attendees, members and non-members. The current German authorities—both civil and military—respected our work. High-ranking Germans were frequent visitors at our evenings.

[Page 510]

They conducted themselves properly and with great respect. There were occasions when the governor or another high official would send warm greetings for our undertakings. A ticket for an event at "Jewish Art" served as a pass so that one could go out on the streets after the curfew. Such were the Germans at the time of the First World War, before they were influenced by the Hitler SS.

The good reputation and influence of "Jewish Art" also affected Polish society, and through certain historical-political acts, "Jewish Art" assumed an important position. Let me present two more facts.

In 1916, after almost 150 years of servitude the Poles were allowed to celebrate their national holiday—the Third of May the holiday commemorating the constitution of May 3, 1771. To this end the city formed a community-wide committee of Poles and Jews to organize the celebration for the participation of the whole population. "Jewish Art" was among the most active participants. On the program was a celebration and a street demonstration of the whole population of the city and the surrounding areas and also delegations from the religious, cultural, and community organizations. Representing "Jewish Art" was a delegation of six people: Yosef Rosenzumen Avraham Zigelwacs, Avraham Greenspan (who was shot on false charges during the Bolshevik invasion in 1920, sentenced by a Polish military tribunal), Shoal t—who is now an engineer in the Moscow State Electrical Station—Yechiel Yablon, and Moshe Mandelman. We wore blue and white armbands on which was emblazoned a Magen David and, in Yiddish and Latin letters, the name "Jewish Art."

The magnificent demonstration, which consisted of tens of thousands of people, with holy pictures and banners moved from the New Church on Dluge Street, led by the highest church leaders and the Polish aristocracy. It had been planned that the procession would pass the Jewish cultural center "Jewish Art." The procession halted there. On the balcony stood the great chorus and on the other balcony was the orchestra.

[Page 511]

They played and sang the Polish hymn Boze, cos Polske" [God Save Poland] and the so-called "Ha-zamir" March, "Zamru, zamru." Truly on that day, as the words rang out—Jews and Poles felt like brothers. In the speeches, special emphasis was placed on the commonality of fate that united Jews and Poles on Polish soil over hundreds of years.

In the fall of 1916 for the first time there were elections for the city council in Siedlce. The elections ran on a system of various levels. The last level, the sixth, was for the common people.

There were no sharp political differences then. We all had the same goal—to elect as many Jewish representatives as possible—so we formed a community-wide election committee that included Zionists, Bundists, Folkists, and Orthodox members of all stripes. The committee consisted, I think, of twenty people. It met at "Jewish Art"; often enough Ger and Kotzk Chasidim met there with the Zionist Harrtglass and Bundists like Neumark and Fishman and Folkists like Altschuler and Mandelman.

The members of "Jewish Art" worked on the elections enthusiastically. We divided the city into five areas and we mobilized hundreds of people. Our victory was sensational: out of 24 council members, we elected 14 Jews. In the midst of the election, Hartglass came out of the election bureau and told us (in Polish): "Gentlemen, you can stop. We already have enough!" But we wanted to show the Poles, and our politicking did not stop until the last minute, when we had an absolute Jewish majority—14 of 24 council members.

You must understand that such acts helped to establish our importance among Jews and non-Jews. It was not then possible to think of such an outcome whether from a Jewish or a community-wide perspective without our participation and encouragement. It was no wonder, then, that the reputation of "Jewish Art" in Siedlce spread through cities and towns throughout the country.

[Page 512]

There was not a single noted writer, artist, or singer, who did not want to be at "Jewish Art," and we received all of them with great honor.

On the dais of "Jewish Art," the famous columnist Sh. Y. Stupnicki (murdered in the Warsaw Ghetto), gave a series of lectures in which for the first time he laid out the theoretical foundations of the Jewish Folk Party. Later these lectures were published in a book called "The Way to the People." Hillel Zeitlin (killed in the Warsaw Ghetto), over the course of several Shabbatos, gave lectures of a religious and philosophical character. Know, too, that H.D. Naumberg, Noach Prylucki, Dr. Yehoshua Gottlieb (the last two killed in the Soviet Union), Yosef Heftman (now in Israel), Shlomo Mendelssohn (died in America), and a host of others were often our guests.

M. Kipnis and Zimra Seligfeld (both killed in the Warsaw Ghetto) popularized Jewish folk songs (at that time a novelty) in a series of concerts. The famous Jewish composer Bensman for several years led the musical-vocal division. He fit right in.

I am reminded of an interesting episode that I should relate: one Friday evening, when Y. Stupnicki spoke with youthful enthusiasm before a packed hall in "Jewish Art" about "Parties and Inclinations in the Jewish Street," the well-known Polish writer Leo Belmont (a convert), entered. He was then in Siedlce, where that evening he was supposed to speak about the Russian Revolution. In the street he noticed the announcement of Stupnicki's lecture. He said to himself: Let's see how one deals, among Jews, in jargon [as people referred to Yiddish], with such matters. For a long time he listened attentively to the talk and to the discussants, including Dovid Neumark (from the "Bund"), Dovid Greenfarb ("Poaelei Tzion"), Mordechai Yaffe (Zionist), and Yakov Tenenbaum (unaffiliated). After the lecture, Belmont came backstage introduced himself to Stupnicki, warmly clasped his hand, and said that he understood everything, that he was astounded at the high level and the deep grasp of the problems. He would never have believed that among everyday people there could be such a cultural debate about community political problems, especially in "jargon."

[Page 513]

He invited Stupicki and some others to attend his lecture "Czardom and Revolution" (this was during the Russian Revolution in 1917). We accepted his invitation, but his lecture did not succeed with us.

In 1917, "Jewish Art" also took upon itself the burden of building and maintaining a secular Jewish school. We described our goal— "Jewish Art" was in fact the Jewish cultural center, where all cultural forms were concentrated under one roof and one leadership.

The Siedlce educational system consisted of four categories of schools: the Talmud Torah, which had about 300 students; a Yiddish-based school; and a "Tarbus" school. And finally more than a thousand students studied in a government school, in Polish. This was called a "Shabbos-away," because the students who studied there did not attend on Shabbos. A limited number of Jewish students also studied in the government middle school.

M. Kaspi has written about the Talmud Torah elsewhere.

The literary division consisted of Yakov Tenenbaum, Pani Radak, Dovid Neumark, Yakov Fishman, Yehiel Groman, and Moshe Mandelman. It conducted a systematic, fine operation over many years. The musical-vocal divisions grew even more. The chorus contained about 50 people. Yosef Zogshein was the director. Musical activities also increased. We formed a string orchestra and two orchestras of wind and mandolins, altogether about 120 people. These orchestras would provide free concerts during the summer in the city garden. The conductors were Eliyahu Shpielman and, after his death, Aaron Shpielfidel and a little later, as I already mentioned, the famous composer Bensman.

The drama division, under the direction of Yakov Tenenbaum, developed wonderfully. At first they presented short one-act plays, but a bit later they put on a number of large three-act dramas and comedies. This division had about 30 people. Over time they assembled a large number of costumes and fine theater sets.

[Page 514]

Even in the Warsaw newspapers there appeared several favorable reviews of of plays by the Siedlce dramatic division of "Jewish Art."

Thus, from year to year the activities of "Jewish Art" became broader and deeper. The prestige and activities of "Jewish Art" spread across the country.

These many-branched cultural activities lasted until the outbreak of the Polish-Bolshevik War in the summer of 1920. In another section of this anthology will appear chapters on the destruction that the Polish reaction and hooliganism wrought on "Jewish Art" and other Jewish cultural organizations in Siedlce.

In 1921, "Jewish Art," together with the library, moved to a smaller location—the corner of Dluge and Sondowa Streets. The smallness of this place did not permit us to carry on broad cultural activities. Still, the library grew a bit. In 1926, people made a big celebration in order of the 25th anniversary of the library's founding. We organized, in a separate location, lectures by the most noted writers in Poland, as well as mystical concerts of the highest quality with the best musicians and singers.

The musical-vocal and dramatic divisions of "Jewish Art" of the Ha-zamir Society
At the top: Yakov Tenenbaum, Avraham Zigelvacks, Aaron Shpielfidel, Yosef Zonshein, and director-members Popowski and Zucker

[Page 515]

In 1933 when the Jewish school was dissolved, "Jewish Art" rented the school building at 62 Warsaw Street. There "Jewish Art" became a club for games and entertainment. But the library remained strong. It lacked not a single new book in Yiddish and Hebrew and the newest books from the Polish market could be found there.

* * *

Exactly what happened to "Jewish Art" and the library during the "Third Destruction" I do not know. Certain it is that their fate was the same as those of all other Jewish cultural treasures in Poland—they were consigned to the flames…

[Page 516]

The Orthodox Newspaper "Our Road"

Rabbi Mayer Schwartzman (Winnipeg, Canada)

Translated by Theodore Steinberg

Having arrived in Siedlce in 1922, I found this capital city of Podlachia to be a lively, singing place, full of vigor and energy. Every tendency, idea, and party affiliation had sunk deep roots in this old community.

The religious part of Siedlce was sidelined, full of Chasidism, with Chasidic prayer houses everywhere beit-midrashim, fellowships, minyan; on almost every street could be found Chassidic prayer houses and synagogues. Three Ger prayer houses on Pienke, Dluge, and

Shul Streets. Aside from them, there were other prayer houses: Alexander, Strikow, Lukow, Kolobiel, Parisow, Amshtinow, and others; the synagogues: the Great Shuo, the beis-hamedresh, the Butcher's Beis Hamedresh, the "Mikra" Chevra, "Parkhei Shoshanim," Yisroel Levin's bets hamedresh, and others. Their leaders tried to attract a host of Jews: Rabbi Avrahamele Morgenshtern—the Lomzher rabbi, a grandson of Kotzk; the Partzev rabbi—a grandson of the Holy Yud; the Koszenitz rabbi, Rabbi Yechieo; the Byale rabbi, Rabbi Yehoshuale and the Lekech-Bekerin's son-in-law. Siedlce also had fellowships: "Linas Ha-tzedek," "Visiting the Ill," women's and men's welfare societies. At the head of the rabbinate was the Righteous Gaon Rabbi Chaim Ginsburg. Also active were the judges Rabbi Alter Eliezer , his son Rabbi Yisroel Mardiks, and Rabbi Itschele.

[Page 517]

In the above-mentioned souls, beis-midrashim, and prayer houses people not only prayed, but they also studied. Chasidim studied the principles of Chasidism and advised young men that they should go to this or that rabbi, Rabbi LKeibsh Feivel, Rabbi Mordechai Shar, Rabbi Mottele Chaim the Shochet's, kRabbi Avrahamtsche Goldberg, Rabbi Moyshe Aaron Hochman—were the pillars of the Ger Chasidim. They recruited new and developing Chasidim from the younger generations.

The Talmud Torah, the yeshiva, the adherents of Mussar looked after education in a traditional Jewish way. This involved the Siedlce Jewish community in all the virtues and failings of other large communities and cities in Poland.

When Poland "arose from the dead" after the First World War, a storm of worldly winds began to stir things up even in the most remote communities and towns, so understandably, in Siedlce as well. Zionism arose from the fanciful novels and started to become real., The Folkists and the "Bund" began their work at enlightenment and cultural activities. They distributed books, brochures, and newspapers. The "Ha-zamir" library in Siedlce took on new life.

Only the Orthodox was happy to sleep its old, sweet sleep. Then the "Agudas Yisroel" awakened the Orthodox part of Judaism.

The "Agudas Yisroel" quickly sank roots in all of Poland, including Siedlce.

From the old world they called forth the most famous and enlightened Chasidim: Rabbi Yakov Shtshereinski, Rabbi Yiusroel Gutgeld, Rabbi Ben-Zion Zucker, Rabbi Sender Kantor, Rabbi Yiusroel Lema Lieberman, Rabbi Berish Jakubowicz. And from the most ardent young people: Rabbi Shalom Yellin, Rabbi Pesach Rosen (later a judge in Lukow), Rabbi Yisroel Mayerr Kleinlehrer, Aaron Nelkenbaum, the writer of these words, Rabbi Bunim Huberman, Rabbi Shmuel Ginzberg, the young man Yehudah Aryeh Zucker, and others.

The Orthodox work of enlightenment in Siedlce could not be satisfied with the Jewish press in Warsaw. The stormy community life of Siedlce and its surrounding towns required its own organ to defend the interests of the Orthodox awakening. The secular schools, Tarbus, the Folkist school and all the others, ripped away parts of the old Talmud Torah.

[Page 518]

The parties and organizations had spread a net to hook the young. We had to begin to fight with the same tools as the modernizers—through our own press organ.

On Friday, May 16, 1923, the first number of "Our Way" ["Undzer Veg"] was published in Siedlce, our Orthodox weekly. The official editor was Berish Jakobowicz, who was aided by his colleagues: Shalom Yellin, Mayer Schwartzman, Yehudah Aryeh Zucker, Aaron Nelkenbaum, Yisroel Mayer Klenlehrer, and Shmuel Ginzberg.

The first issue had a high, earnest tone. The paper defended Orthodox community politics, discussed the education for boys and girls, urged the founding of a "Beis Yakov" school, awoke and encouraged the upholding of the seal of traditional Yiddishkeit, and called for work on behalf of Eretz Yisroel. There were entries from "Agudas Yisroel" and "Tz'irei uPo'alei-Agudas-Yisroel" in Siedlce, Lukow, Sokolow, Biale-Podlosk, Mezritch, Garvolin, Volin, Radzin, Kotzk, Czemernik, Statzk, Szelekhow, Vengerow, and others. "Our Way" spread Torah knowledge, Chassidus, and above all, Yiddishkeit among the broad masses, not only in Siedlce but in the whole district.

Understandably, when it was time for elections to the Polish Sejm, to the Siedlce city council, or within the Jewish community, "Our Way" sided with "Agudas Yisroel" and found for its candidates.

"Our Way" also led the election work in Lukow, Sokolow, Biala, and elsewhere.

In quieter, more peaceful times, "Our Way" would publish stories, novels, poems, opinion pieces, and longer articles, notes from writers and well-known Jewish columnists, such as: Rabbi Samson Raphael Hirsch (z"l), Rabbi Dr. Mayer Lehman, Rabbi Dr. Y. Weinberg, Gedalyahu Bublik, Dr. Noson Birnbaum, Rabbi Asher Rubin, Eizik Baer Eckerman, Yehuda Leib Orleon, Alexander Zishe Friedman. The regular staff were: Shalom Yellin—the editor, Yehudah Aryeh Zucker, and the writer of this piece who used to write under a variety of names such as Mayer Schwartzman, Baal-Shem, Baal-Shacharis, "Emes," "Rabbi Nechorai Sofer." "Avrahaml" of Mezritch used to publish his poems in "Our Way." And A. Zonschein would submit his poems.

[Page 519]

"Our Way" was read by the most noted rabbis from Ger and Radzin, from Sokolow and Strikow, by hundreds of rabbis from our district in Poland, as well as Volin and Galicia.

With limited financial means, "Our Way" existed without interruption until 1930. The newspaper defended Orthodox thought admirably. It was the factual messenger of the Orthodox Jewish part of Siedlce and of the Orthodox in the greater Polish province of Podlachia.

When we look today at the complete corpus of "Our Way," we see a part of the history of Jewish Siedlce and of Jewish life in Podlachia in the era between the two world wars.

In "Our Way" from the 19th of Av in 1926, I see a notice to all "Agudas Shelomi, Tze'irei uPo'alei Emunei Yisroel" in the Podlachia region. They are summoned to a regional conference on Sunday of parsha Shofetim, the 25th of Av, in the hall of the city club in Siedlce. "Representatives of the following cities will take part in the conference: Lukow, Sokolow, Biala, Vengerrow, Mezritch, Kaluszin, Minsk-Mazowieck, Garvolin, Levertow, Parcew, Wlodawa, Radzin, Szeliebow, Konstantin, Janow, Porisow, Kosow Telaki, Stozk, Lumaz, Laszic Sarnak, Mord, Kotzk, Monkobid, Sterdin, Vohin, Mrozi, dJadomowi, Lusebik, Rike, Buczacz, Slawatic, Wisznic, Ostrow-Siedlecki, Terespol, Sobalow.

"Our Way" concerned itself not only with political matters, but also with city interests, like the "Ezras-Y'somim," loan offices, and different banks, welfare institutions like "Bikur Cholim," the hospital, seders for soldiers and prisoners, "Toz," and so on.

The newspaper mirrored Jewish life in Siedlce.

[Page 523]

Memories of Writers, Types and Images

Poland
(To my mother, may she rest in the garden of Eden)

by Mordechai Temkin

Translated by Mira Eckhaus

Poland, my homeland, my root and origin,
I left you when I was young,
As a bird that was left, in the isles of the sea I searched for a place,
In the landscape of the ancient land, desolate and poor.
How, my homeland? The biggest crises of my life
Have covered you like see waves.
But even when the sea is stormy, the azure islands are visible,
The past days I experienced in you illuminate me from afar!

Not as a leaf in the wind I was pulled from my homeland,
Not to the greatness I took off and left my nest.
The desire to an ancient homeland was in me,
So, I was torn with pain from my root like the turn from a mother's womb.
Even my soul disgust of your false land
And like a bee, pursued by the smoke of enmity,
I ran away from you with my loot,
Because you wanted to take more and more!

Oh, Poland, my homeland, my origin and my ancestry,
Together with you in the pit of captivity I dreamed my dream of a return,
A return to my country, in its disobedience and glory;
Ah, how I envied and was angry that you were redeemed first,
And with pride and redemption you despised my people!
But now, in your distress, with all my anger,
Can I mourn on you like a homeland that was lost,
When I'm full of contempt and non-consoling love? !

[Page 524]

Peretz in a Pogrom City
in the Period Between the Two World Wars

by Yoyl Mastbaum (Tel Aviv)

Translated by Theodore Steinberg

In the winter of 1906, shortly after the pogrom in Siedlce, Jewish notables from Petersburg, Odessa, and Warsaw began to visit the beleaguered city. Their intent was to gather facts and materials about the criminals in the czarist government, led by Stolypin, who organized the pogrom and carried it out by means of the colonel of the dragoon regiment Tichonowski. I do not remember who came from Odessa; from Petersburg came the young student from Petersburg University—Prilucki (later a famous activist, writer, and linguist, Noah Prilucki, z"l), who was already known then in Poland through his letters in the Warsaw publication "Undzer Veg." He inspired everyone with his vigilance and agility with the incriminating evidence and the way he proceeded with love and sympathy for the victims,, whom he trusted and encouraged. At the same time, the Warsaw newspaper "Undzer Veg" announced that Y.L. Peretz would come to Siedlce, and as I recall, the announcement spread like a flame.

Siedlce's Jews prepared for Peretz' arrival as if it were a great holiday. The city went topsy-turvy. The newspaper with Peretz' picture was grabbed up by everyone, and twice a day people went to the train station to wait, in case he would arrive, even though his arrival time had been announced. The older donors gathered together and compiled a report about the pogrom and an accounting of the damages to give to Peretz so he could make known to the world the guilt and the responsibility for the killed, the wounded, and the robbed Jews.

[Page 525]

To welcome Peretz there were two amateur troupes who played "Hertzele Meyukhes." The main players of both troupes wanted to show off for Peretz…

Also the students in the eighth level of the gymnasium, who mostly knew Nekrasov, Nadson, Pushkin, and Lermontov, learned to recite their poems in order to perform that evening which the young people had prepared for Peretz.

Our city had its share of writers, as I recall, a whole minyan of them. I will mention the most well-known: one of the writers was my friend, a semi-professional doctor, who had written a treatise about Nietzsche. He was prepared to show his manuscript to Peretz.

A second writer, Dovid Fleytist [flautist], a young man in a green shirt who wore dark glasses like a blind person, had learned to play the flute and spent his days writing poems.

With a third writer I had formed a deep friendship. In my younger years I was a clerk in a fabric business. My boss's grandson wrote sketches in Yiddish and he persuaded me to write "essays" on Tolstoy's teachings in Russian; as we proceeded with our daily labors, we switched roles: I began to write sketches in Yiddish and he—essays in Russian. Later there came a break in my writing life—my relatives, who were involved in revolutionary circles, asked me for proclamations and revolutionary announcements. I threw away my essays and sketches and turned toward insurrection.

On the day of Peretz' visit, a mass of people filled the streets. I remember that gray winter day. A sudden unrelenting snowstorm hit Warsaw Street, a quiet street of merchants.

Jews milled around in the street; hands were stuffed into sleeves as people looked out for the sleds that would bring people with news about the reparations for damages. And what did they expect from Peretz?

[Page 526]

Be assured—that he would certainly help them get back on their feet. Suddenly a sleigh appeared with people with upraised arms. Who were they?—Hometown friends who had seized the sleigh and brought Peretz.

Peretz was first out of the sleigh—"Let's go by foot," he said to the young people. And where? It made no difference, right or left, to the little orchard or to the bigger park. It appeared that our guest was familiar with the city. He knew that Siedlce had a "Yatzik," a copper statue with the globe on its shoulders, and he began to speak about "Yatzik"; he knew that Siedlce had a gymnasium for nice young women, and he began to ask where they were, these students, and so they quickly appeared. Like butterflies around a light they began to circle him , all the nice young girls of the city, students and part-time students, romantic young men with their beloved prima donnas who acted in the theater and random girls and women wearing astrakhans and muffs and galoshes up to their knees, covered with frost.

"Welcome to you, Y.L. Peretz."

"We love our guest."

"Long live Peretz."

Peretz, as he always did, felt alive and vigorous in the company of young people. A middle-sized, well-built figure with a big, bronze-like head. On his broad shoulders was a heavy coat, half-fastened at the neck. He stood there and with his large, laughing eyes, which could hardly be seen under his broad-brimmed hat, he looked at the young people around him. Peretz spoke to them in Polish, Russian, and Yiddish. It depended on whom he was addressing: to the beautiful, graceful gymnasium students he spoke Russian, to the housewives he spoke Polish, and to the young people, Yiddish.

I was seeing Peretz for the first time. He did not make the impression of a person who was so imbued with Yiddishkeit, with Jewish spirit, with Jewish popularity. You would have thought that before you stood a Polish nobleman, a gentleman who spoke Yiddish, but his sparkling eyes betrayed him and spoke their own Yiddish language.

[Page 527]

In the meantime, the circle of people around Peretz grew bigger. The doors arrived with their sons, daughters, and sons-in-law. Peretz was invited to the home of the oldest door, Nahum Weintraub, whose family were old Zionists. But Peretz preferred to go to the Hotel Angelski, where a room awaited him with two silver samovars and enough glasses for a large number of people to drink tea.

Peretz' private secretary, who looked like a puppet with deep blue eyes, had remained in the sled and had already departed with Peretz' luggage for the Hotel Angelski.

The snow was falling and the whiter the earth appeared, the blacker and darker appeared the broken windows, the broken up and ruined houses—open wounds that remained from the pogrom.

Traversing the streets, Peretz stopped women, old people, and children, and asked them if soldiers were in their houses (seeking verification that the pogrom had been an organized event). He was particularly interested in the chief leader of the pogrom, Tichonowski. Around the ruined houses were a glazier, a tin worker, and other craftsmen. Peretz conversed with them, inquiring about the number of damaged dwelling places, ruined buildings, and broken furnishings.

Finally we came to the Hotel Angelski. There Peretz retired from the crowd for fifteen minutes, noting things down. Then he went to his secretary, to the handsome young man with the deep eyes, and gave him the papers on which he had written. The crowd, meanwhile, had expanded. People came to give Peretz accounts of what had happened.

After having heard the crowd, he took a brief rest and then had a light conversation with the young people, among whom were some writers. He called for manuscripts, put his pince-nez on his thick nose, read over them and returned them immediately with his comments. His judgments were short but severe: "Burn this," "A waste of time," "Put it in the fire," "Look for other work." He was like a shochet who kills chickens and flings them away.

[Page 528]

I escaped from this "slaughter" for a simple reason:

I had withdrawn. I was helped by that young man, Peretz' secretary, whom I had known some years earlier. In 1902, in Brisk, where I worked as a ceiling painter and he was writing his first poems under the name "Menachem" (later—Menachem Borisho). Seeing me standing there in perplexity, he tugged at my sleeve and told me to wait until the morning, because today Peretz was "on fire." I followed him—and thus I was rescued.

On the day after the "slaughter," Menachem arranged for me to meet with Peretz in the Hotel Angleski. I showed him one of my poems, and he recommended that I publish it in "Undzer Veg." I later published it in "Neie Tzeit."

I need to recall a few words that Menachem Borisho wrote to me years later about our acquaintanceship in Brisk and later in Siedlce in the Hotel Angleski.

"Do you remember the streets of Brisk?—The officers, the young men of the gymnasiums, the young women of the gymnasiums with the brown bows in their hair, the external students and those who lived at home who were dressed in their student uniforms. Do o you remember on the street a painter with pants covered with whitewash who had come to work in Siedlce and there became a comrade?

"Later, after a long while, we met again in Siedlce at the Hotel Angleski, I, a person with a writing career of a whole two months and you, a beginner even more than myself. It was a pleasure for me, after those Brisk days, to help you enter the literary world."

The three of us spoke for a long time. It is difficult after so many years to convey what that conversation entailed. Peretz was sitting in a well-upholstered chair from the Hotel Angelski with a fat cigar between his fingers. He had already finished with the materials about the Siedlce pogrom. He now spoke of the young men and women of Siedlce, about the writers, speaking in a soft Peretz tone.

[Page 529]

The conversation involved an elusive theme that interested us neophyte writers: what literature should a young writer read: lyric or epic works? Menachem held that a young writer, first approaching should read everything without being choosy; Peretz, however, had a different idea: "No, not so, Menachem. Reading a book is often like a cure, and when one needs a bromide for his nerves, he shouldn't take castor oil for his stomach." They conducted a lively debate in which I dared not take part. I just asked Peretz my particular question: what should a person like myself read?

Menachem answered for Peretz: Read what you want.

Peretz repeated his earlier words: If you need a bromide, don't take castor oil.

I worked up my courage and asked Peretz:

Nu, and Maeterlinck and Wispianski? Peretz answered with his ironic smile: Wait a while for them. Read epic works.

I looked at Peretz with great surprise. It was well known that Maeterlinck and Wispianski were Peretz' pillars of fire and that he wrote under their influence. Peretz revealed his belief that people should read long novels, descriptive, with a realistic background. It appeared that he, the lyrical writer, surely loved what he himself lacked. He cited examples from Greek literature, mentioned insightful ideas, brought out analogies, seeking to convince young Menachem, but all of a sudden the door opened and a group of young men and women entered. They wanted to hear Peretz' thoughts on Zionism, about Eretz Yisroel, where they had decided to go. But none of them dared to open their mouths, until Peretz himself began.

"What can I do for you young people?" Peretz inquired.
They answered with one voice, like a group of children: "We, we want to go to…"
"To Eretz Yisroel, eh?" Peretz interrupted. "Good. What will you do there?

"Study, Mr. Peretz. We will study there."

"Study what/".

"Art."

"What art?"

[Page 530]

They all exclaimed, "In the Bezalel School."

"Oh, Bezalel?" Peretz inquired.
He tried to dismiss the matter with a joke.
"You ask, 'Where?' Go to Vienna. It's true. If you want to study art, Vienna is better."
He soon dropped that tone and began to talk about famous Zionist leaders, especially Dr. Herzl. I do not know how Peretz then felt about Zionism, but he spoke about Herzl with great enthusiasm. From Peretz' words about Herzl and his accomplishments, one could tell that he was among a group of young Zionists. They all began to sing the popular song of those times "There Where the Cedar"— and the most prominent voice was that of Peretz himself.

* *

It is good now when almost fifty years separate us from this magical man to ask the question: what constituted this man's great strength? How did he so beguile us that we still talk about him, comment on him, study him, translate him. I have already given the answer. In the first days when I met him in Siedlce, Peretz belonged to the people, who were led by a deep intuition. Peretz inspired more than he spoke, sang more than he described. In comparison with Mendele and with Sholem Aleichem, he seems fragmented, but his fragmentation is a kind of wholeness. He was totally intuitive, extemporaneous, improvisatory. It is no wonder that he had no spiritual crises, that the secular in him did not conflict with the spiritual, that optimism and pessimism could happily coexist in his soul; and the master, who with so much light and Shabbos holiness forged the golden chain, could lead us in the darkness and profanity of "Night in the Old Market."

I remember his words from 45 years ago in Siedlce, in the city theater, and I see in them a prelude to the two contradictory works.

It as a dark evening. The streetlights burned darkly and our hearts were heavy. On the stage of the half-destroyed theater stood two men: the younger, good-looking Menachem Goldberg (Borisho), who recited Peretz' "The Watchman," and the great master, who improvised a wonderful speech about the destruction in Siedlce, which he concluded with these words:

Know, my dear Jews, that destruction is a bitter passage, but a momentary one; but the world is not headed for destruction. It is headed for rebuilding, for exaltation, for light. Let there be light.

[Page 531]

[Page 532]

My homeland
In the first horrors

(Chapter from a story)

by Mordechai Ovadia

Translated by Mira Eckhaus

The days of the World War II arrived.

The children returned from the Heder in groups with flashlights. They were afraid to look up to the sky. Terrible signs of fire were seen in the sky. At home, they whispered full of fear and their hands shook while holding the newspapers. At the end, they locked themselves in the houses and the women were forbidden to cry. After a night of frequent and horrific shootings, the Austrian Germans came. The streets were filled with infantry and car corps. Loud shouting filled the air: Cigaretten! Cigaretten! Cigaretten! The locks in the gates creaked and the sidewalks became full of people. Clever Jews tried to speak Yiddish. And suddenly, within all this noisy and crowded environment, shootings began, one after the other – people started running full of terror and fear, as if frightening rocks were falling from the sky. Dad grabbed Menashe in his arms, and his hat fell to the ground. Menashe turned his head away. Next to the hat, a man knelt and fell. It reminded him the "kneeing" at Yom Kippur pray – but when he noticed the red puddle near the man that fell, he started crying…

In the days that followed, hunger raised its head, spread and caused illness.

The storefronts of the city shops offered shiny and fatty herrings while the children of Israel blink and swallowed heinous saliva. Raphael, Menashe's cousin, became ill and died. Menashe is from the seed of the Cohanim, and is not allowed to enter the cemetery, yet he did not know how this sight engraved in him, when my grandfather went out of the cemetery, plucked weeds and throwed them behind him. The sight was engraved in him as a symbol of horror: a man's conversation with death lurking behind his back for every step of his life in the world.

The tragedy affected the whole being of the boy, he who prayed three times a day and recited "Shema" with intent with his eyes closed. His entire hope was lost.

[Page 533]

He did not want to surrender to the dark necessity, he did not want to die. Then, for the first time he looked at the people of the house, at the adults, begging for mercy, a little mercy for a delusional frightened boy who does not want to die.

After a short time, Grandpa died. He went as a man in a hurry to a pre-determined path for him; In the morning he defecated, prayed Shacharit and went to bed to rest forever.

The adults, stood crying and lost too. Menashe recalls the sight again: a man's conversation with death lurking behind his back for every step of his life in the world, and he grasps a secret, the horrible amongst secrets.

And the Germans vigorously ordered cleanliness, and boiling disinfection boilers buzzed all day in the streets. And first of all, to "clean" the buffet in which only the rotten bread that is mixed with bran, blackened. In those days my mother's brother, who was a single, was taken to forced labor, to distant places and the people at home were very gloomy because everyone liked him. After a long year with a gloomy winter, he returned home, very skinny and ill, and with his field bottle in which he ate all day potato peels soaked in water.

For many hours the boy was with the young, pale uncle and listened to his frightening horror stories.

In the meantime, many things were banned from trade and even eating, and the Jews were forced to bribe for a living and starved to death. The distress has increased greatly and in the Beit Midrash people who spoke about Israel and Darshanim calculated the end and added gematria and the boy still expects a salvation as it should arrive soon.

One cloudless morning, proclamations were displayed in the open air saying: The Polish people have been liberated on their land! And here and there the last of the poor German officials are expelled with their hands on their heads. And the day after, the Polish Legionnaires were all over the land.

And before they can tell the wonders about the Maccabi Pilsudski to the Polish people, and here is a new legend approaching the country, the Bolsheviks are attacking the country.

Now, when the boy heard slippery, fragmented things, his heart pounded in his chest like a clapper in an agitated bell. Pale and frightened boys of Israel, who grow up every day and every hour under the wings of terror, kissing the mezuzah every evening and giving in their soul to the Creator in supplication: "until the next day, a merciful Father in heaven, until the next day", were spreading the rumor about the Bolsheviks, the "red" Bolsheviks, headed by the Jew Rabbi Aryeh Trotsky, and members of the ten tribes, the "red Jews" beyond the Sambatyon, who will bring redemption to Israel and the world.

But the bitter disappointment was not long in coming. As a herd, the "saviors" raided the shops and in exchange for "tickets" took everything they could.

[Page 534]

They were taking old Jews from the city's dignitaries to sweep the city streets, and they are sturdy guys, their hands in their pockets, smoking fine cigarettes and saying: "Napliavat", "Borjzoim"…

A few hectic days have passed and again cannons roar up near; in the middle of the night the Bolsheviks ran for their lives, and in the early morning the Poles returned, drunk with victory and lust for revenge and murder.

A slight horror accompanied the Jewish boy everywhere, at home, in the Heder and on the street, the horror from the Creator, and in contrast, of the Yetzer Ara that spreads its net at every step, and here came the horror itself and the soul of the Jewish boy fluttered like a dove in the hawk's claws.

Oh, those long, black nights, the howl of the winds and the trembling of the window glasses and floors to the sound of the thunder of the cannons without darkness, without darkness … and into the morning- into the morning a pale, weak universe peeks, and the heart is full of pity for people, flesh and blood, there, in the killing fields … and he jumps from his place with fear to any sound in the door and in the wall.

Now they have stopped whispering. A certain Jew bursts, a brother of a tormented and precious fate and the fear peeks out of his trembling beard, and he tells in panic about dozens of Jews that were hanged on the forest trees and were smeared with tar and burned alive, and others who were killed along to the sound of the harmonica. Red-faced peasants spit on their palm and strike with a sickle on heads and necks, to the beat of wild dances and a strangled "Shema Israel". Once Menashe saw with his own eyes how two soldiers hit in the street a Jewish with a wide white beard, beating him alternately, systematically, until blood flowed - finally they spat and let go of him …

The horror danced and stuck its crooked nails in the terrified soul of the boy…

[Page 535]

Memories from the Gymnasium Days

by Dr. Chaim Lifshitz

Translated by Mira Eckhaus

My happy youth years are related to the city of Siedlce, to which I arrived from the capital Warsaw, in 1909, to study at the Gymnasium. The memory of the pogroms days that were carried out by the tsarist armies at the end of the first failed revolution, was still alive at that time at the Jewish residents. The grocer from the grocery shop, who was a direct victim of the pogroms, was telling me details about the pogroms. But in the city, the life of the Jewish youth, that was swept away by the wings of the resurrection, was already fermenting. Those were the years in which Adv. A. Heartglass' "assistant" was walking on the sidewalks of Siedlce, on his way to the court. While us, the members of the youth movement Hanoar Halomed, who were already heading Zion, accompanied him with awe: he was one of Helsingfors conference heroes!

In the boarding school of the students, on Sankiewicz Street, counselors and tutors have found the youths of Siedlce and the nearby towns, whose souls longed for secular pursuit. "Hazamir" ("the nightingale") was still the sole legal center, around which the Yiddish public nature was concentrated and where the girls from Sloshny's families dominated in the splendor of their manners and in the pleasantness of their voices.

Certainly not many survived that Pre-Zionist period in Siedlce. Levy Gutgeld and his Zionist generation were still youngsters, and the Zionist cell I remember is the Landau's home - one of the Mintz brothers' bank employees. The immigration, especially to Belgium, has taken almost all of the vibrant youth out of the town.

Only few of the locals learned in the gymnasium: out of the six Jewish members in my class, only one was born in Siedlce. I will also mention Elhanan Levin, who was known in Siedlce as a prodigy, who became several years later one of the leaders of the Revisionist movement in Warsaw. Maybe there is still someone who remembers the student who luckily won one day a large sum of money and Levi Gutgeld's father handed him a bag full of gold coins in the presence of a large crowd. It was a farewell gift from Siedlce before I left it in 1913. The years of the First World War passed and after the Russian exile I returned "home" to Warsaw. After a short time working for the central committee of the Zionist Organization in Poland, Levi Gutgeld was also in the group of collaborators with me.

[Page 536]

There was a special closeness between us. I remember Siedlce with the kindness of my youth. When I visited it, I found only a few of the past - the war scattered them all over the world, but I willingly shared myself in the life and worries of the Zionist movement in Siedlce.

And for those who still remember those days I will say: we did not imagine the bitter and hasty end that came upon our dear and glorious communities in Poland. However, we also did not imagine that we would be privileged to live in the State of Israel. We were not asked if we were willing to pay that price. But many of those who did not arrive to Israel, took comfort in their last moments that this is how it will be in the far distant future.

[Page 537]

Types and Figures from Siedlce of the Past

by Y.N. Weintraub

R. Mannis, the City Preacher

Translated by Theodore Steinberg

Reb Mannis lived in an earlier time, before the time of Rabbi Eliezer Shalom Pietrkover (who was called "Petrkover" because he was later on the rabbi of Pietrkow). The city shul was at that time made of wood, as opposed to the beis–medresh, which was made of bricks and stood on the spot of the current township administrative office.

In that very beis–medresh, the city preacher R. Mannis spent all his time, day and night. He was a great scholar and a very poor man. For his words of Torah in the beis–medresh he received a stipend of eighty groschen a week, but not in coin. Rather he received this stipend only in goods: from the baker he received bread and from the grocery kasha and lights.

Aside from his public words of Torah, he also wrote his insights on the Torah. He did not receive enough money in his stipend to buy paper, so he used to use different scraps of paper that people had used as shopping lists. These insights remained in their manuscript form with R. Mannis' grandson, R. Asher Gedalyahu Goldberg.

These manuscripts also contain R. Mannis' calculations about his living expenses. When he exceeded his 80 groschen per week, he tried to make up the "deficit" by fasting. He fasted often, many times from Shabbos to Shabbos.

[Page 538]

Despite his poverty, he always took care to have fish for his Shabbos meal in order to honor Shabbos. The manner of buying for Shabbos in those days was different from today, when everyone goes to the store to buy fish. At that time, two owners of inns sold cooked fish to the whole city for 5 or 10 groschen per serving. But not everyone could indulge in this "luxury."

One of the two inns belonged to Etke Kaweh, the mother of the later community activist Rokhel Etkes. From her, R. Mannis would buy fish for 5 groschen to honor Shabbos. But Etke wanted to have the merit of having R. Mannis eat her fish at no cost, so every Friday she would sent fish with her daughter Rokhel, who was at the time a young girl. The young Rokhel Etkes was, you can be sure, could not easily prevail on R. Mannis to accept the gift. Every time that that Rokhel Etkes brought fish to R. Mannis, he would give her a blessing.

People had that time maintained that R. Mannis had a holy soul: when he met a Jew, he soon saw into that person's soul. The Seer of Lublin, the Jews would say, rebuked R. Mannis a bit: he wished that his holy soul should be more transparent, so that whatever he knew, he should not keep to himself.

Among the many stories that people told about R. Mannis, it was also said that at that time there lived in Siedlce R. David Weinschenker and his wife Royze. Once, their daughter, a young bride, was ill with typhus. They sent their son–in–law Naftali to R. Mannis so that he would pray for the sick girl. R. Naftali ran quickly to R. Mannis, who had just come home from the beis–medresh to rest a little. R. Mannis said they should take the engagement agreement and lay it on the sick girl's head and she would recover. But, he added, she would not live long. And so it happened–in a short time, the sick girl passed away.

People also said that the aforementioned R. Naftali Neuman, wanted to marry for a second time and came to R. Mannis for his advice. R. Mannis ordered R. Naftali to write down the woman's name.

[Page 539]

"Why?" R. Naftali responded. "I'll just tell you."

"No, write down the name," R. Mannis answered. The result was that R. Naftalki Neuman complied. R. Mannis took a look and quickly told him what she looked like and even what clothes she was wearing.

Even though R. Mannis was a fervent misnagid, and even though the Chasidim and misnagdim of the time had terrible disagreements, the Chasidim told stories that praised him. Thus, for example, the Chasidim would tell that once the old rabbi of Kotzk was traveling through Siedlce. Arriving at Warsaw Street, the rabbi got out of his coach and went into the beis–medresh for a couple of minutes. R. Mannis was at that moment deeply engrossed in a Talmudic passage and did not notice the rabbi. Only later, when the rabbi had already departed, R. Mannis clapped himself on the head and said, "There was a fire in the beis–medresh. A great man was here." When he began to inquire who that man was, people told him that it was Rabbi Mendel from Kotzk. R. Mannis ran out of the beis–medresh and ran a couple of versts [almost a mile and a half] outside of the city until he caught up with the wagon and greeted the rabbi.

R. Mannis, even as a committed misnagid, maintained a strong friendship with one of the famous Chasidim of his retime in Siedlce, R. Kalman Areles.

R. Mannis died in Siedlce in 5605 [1834–35] and he lies now in the cometery there. From the inscription on his tombstone we can see that before he was a preacher in Siedlce, he was a rabbi in Ostrow.

* * *

Since I have mentioned the Great Shul, I will tell something about it. After the great fire on Hoshana Rabba of 5611 [1840–41], when the wooden shul was completely burned down, people began to collect funds for a new shul. Five years later, in 5617, the foundation was laid for the brick shul. The stones for the foundation were sold at auction. The laying of the first stone was purchased by D'voraleh the Lubliner, the wife of Rabbi Moyshe Greenberg, for a thousand zlotys. With this mitzvah, she honored the then rabbi, Rabbi Shalom Pietrkower.

[Page 540]

In the Siedlce fire that broke out in 5630, the roof of the shul burned, along with the Aron Kodesh. That Aron Kodesh was a work of art. Work on it took two years, and according to the inscription on it, it was completed in 5621 by Y. Zwibak and his two sons. At the time of the fire, only parts of the Aron Kodesh could be saved, and they were used in the current Aron Kodesh.

R. Eliezer Shalom Pietrkower

Rabbi Eliezer Shalom was a diligent worker on behalf of the congregation. With the permission of the current dozors–R. Mayer Nissan Nussbaum, R. Gedaliahu Saltzman, and r. Noson Zilberzweig, he created a fund for ransoming prisoners, redeeming Jews who had been arrested. They also declared a tax on the yeast and salt sellers; the sellers then passed the tax on to the whole community. No one dared to sell salt or yeast aside from those approved of by the community court and the doors.

R. Eliezer Shalom used to collect pledges. People say that he once came to a community bigwig, one of the oldest residents, R. Mayer Orszel, to collect a pledge for ransoming prisoners. R. Mayer Orszel at first wanted to lower R. Eliezer's evaluation. R. Eliezer, in protest, went to the bookcase, took out a volume of Gemara, and sat down to learn. When R. Mayer Orszel asked the rabbi what it meant to protest in such a fashion. He responded: "'Love upsets the natural order'" [quoted from Genesis Rabbah], by which he meant to say that he considered the mitzvah of charity to be so great that sometimes he must lower his honor before it.

R. Eliezer Shalom went after those merchants who raised their prices. At that time, the trade in fish for Shabbos had begun. There was a story that a visiting Jew, from Sokolow, had brought fish for Shabbos to Siedlce. The fishermen resented this and they damaged the fish. The Jew ran with a complaint to Rabbi Eliezer Shalom.

[Page 541]

R. Eliezer Shalom soon came to the fish market (which was then in Pszeyozd Street, which was also called R. Berl Hershke's Street). R. Eliezer Shalom looked at the fish of the local fishermen and said: "Your fish are not kosher, because they have worms in them." Soon the report spread through the whole city, and no one wanted to buy fish. So it was for a couple of weeks, until the fishermen came to the rabbi and made an agreement that they would no longer raise prices.

Rabbi Eliezer Shalom left Siedlce under the following circumstances: The holder of the option to sell yeast–one of the Siedlce big shots at that time–adulterated the yeast. Consequently, on Shabbos the challahs did not turn out well, and there was dissatisfaction in many homes.

There were some people who wrote "complaints" about R. Eliezer Shalom. When the government got involved, R. Eliezer Shalom decided to leave and Siedlce and become the rabbi of Pietrkow.

R. Eliezer Shalom was known as a great scholar, and people used to say about him that he was the kind of scholar of whom it was said [quoting the Talmud], "Who is a real Torah scholar? He who thinks about Halacha at all times."

The Greenberg Family

One of the first Jewish families that began to play a role in Siedlce in the second half of the eighteenth century was the many–branched Greenberg family.

The patriarch of the family was R. Chaim Greenberg. He was in his time quite rich. He owned many houses and locations in Siedlce, like the locale of the beis–medresh of R. Yisroel Greenberg (a great–grandchild of R. Chaim Greenberg), buildings number 14–16 on First of May Street, a few houses on Puste, Teatralne, the location of what are now numbers 13–165 on First of May Street, and the whole of Sondowa Alley from Pilsudski 16 (the numbers of the buildings and the names of the streets–as they were before the Second World War).

[Page 542]

In the Siedlce records there is a will of R. Chaim Greenberg's written in Hebrew in 1790 stating that he gives to his eldest son David 10,000 zlotys via the magistrate for a site that he had sold. It appears that this concerned the sites on which now stand the buildings of the district court.

R. Chaim Greenberg had two sons: R. David and R. Avraham, and one daughter. David Greenberg was also called Dovid Weinschenker. In the building at the corner of Teatralne and First of May, which once belonged to R. Shmuel Brukarsz (peace be upon him), he ran a tavern [in Yiddish, a "weinschenk"]. R. David Greenberg served as a door. With his own money he bought a spot for a cemetery. This is the cemetery near the Jewish hospital.

The above–mentioned properties R. Chaim Greenberg gave to his son R. Avraham. R. Avraham was the son–in–law of R. Yisroel Chelemer, who was known as a great scholar and knew many languages and other secular subjects.

At that time in Mezritch there was a blood libel against thirteen Jews, accusing them of killing a Christian child and using his blood to make matzos. The trial of the thirteen Jews was held in the district court in Lublin. The authors of the blood libel had, you understand, no evidence that the Jews had murdered the Christian child, but they insisted that the Zohar said that Jews use Christian blood for religious purposes. The court needed a Jew who could translate the Zohar into Polish. But in the whole area, they could find no one except R. Yisroel Chelemer, who lived in Siedlce. Thanks to his clarifications, the Jews were spared a great misfortune.

The Greenberg family, it appears, was the first to grasp that a child should learn the local vernacular. According to the "Official Journal of the Podlasie District" of 1824, on the list of students who finished the vocational elementary school is the name of Miss Hinde Greenberg of Siedlce, who received a certificate for excellent studies.

Chaim Greenberg's daughter married R. Kalman Chasid.

[Page 543]

Avraham Greenberg had five sons: Mottl, Shimon, Yechiel, Yitzchak, Moyshe, and two daughters.

Yehiel Greenberg was the father of Yisroel Greenberg, who established a beis–medresh that was called by his name, "R. Yisroel Yehiel's Beis–Medresh." He also left a will establishing a Talmud Torah (this is the Talmud Torah building on Brawarga Street). Moyshe was the husband of Dvorah from Lublin and the father of Malia Miendziszecki, who was known in Siedlce for her wine business and especially for her righteousness. Moyshe, Chaim's youngest son, was connected by marriage to the then rabbi R. Zishe Plotzker.

Among Avraham Greenberg's five sons, Mottl and Yitzchak were well–known Kotzk Chasidim. The war between Chasidim and misnagdim was fierce. At that time the rabbi in Siedlce was R. Moyshe Hersh, a fervent misnagid. The Chasidim persecuted him terribly. People say that once when R. Moyshe was at the third Shabbos meal, someone threw a dog through his window. It appears that one of the people responsible for this trick was R. Mottl Greenberg.

One time Mottle convinced his brother Yehiel, who was a solid misnagid, that he should go with him to Kotzk for Rosh Hashanah. R. Yehiel was a great scholar and did not know much about Chasidic customs. He thought that he could go there to study and pray. But in Kotzk he found that no one studied and no one prayed as he was accustomed to. He was very upset, and immediately after Rosh Hashanah he returned to Siedlce. When he arrived at home, Yehiel had his brother summoned to the religious court and accused him of ridiculing the Torah. Mottl Greenberg was a happy man and always made other happy with his Chasidic tunes and Polish songs that he had learned.

In addition to being a devoted Chasid, R. Mottl Greenberg was also a diligent worker for the needs of the community and was particularly taken with collecting pledges for social welfare. When R. Mottl once came to collect a pledge from his uncle R. Alter Greenberg, who was known as an important member of the community, he did not want to give as much as Mottl had expected.

[Page 544]

Mottl therefore played a trick and took from a shelf an expensive Chanukah lamp. When Alter Greenberg realized what had happened, he did not hesitate to take R. Mottl to court. The court ruled that Alter must swear that he suspected Mottl of stealing the Chanukah lamp. This oath had to be made in the shul. When Alter was ready to swear, the current rabbi, R. Yisroel Meizlisz, arrived and would not allow the oath, but he ruled that Alter Greenberg should give 150 zlotys to charity and pay the court costs and R. Mottl should return the Chanukah lamp.

One of Avraham Greenberg's daughters, Feige, married Yitzchak Eizik Rapaport. This was at a time when not everyone employed family names and people were called according to their fathers' names. Later, when the rule was made that everyone must use family names, those who had already been using family names had the right to change them. R. Yitzchak Eizik Rapaport then changed his family name to Czarnabrode. The Czarnabrode family in Siedlce stemmed from him. Yitzchak Eizik had two sons: Dovid (who was referred to a Dovid Eizik's) and Paltiel, and four daughters.

R. Yitzchak Eizik Rapaport–Czarnabrode

Yitzchak Eizik came to Siedlce from Kortszow, a shtetl near Otwoc. He was a great scholar and a God–fearing man. He was noted for his good works and he always pursued righteousness. He also knew how to write Hebrew and Polish. While R. Yitzchak Eizikl spent all his days studying Torah and praying, he had no idea how to make a living. His wife ran a business. R. Yitzchak Eizik had a dyeing business. In those days, such a business was, in a real sense, limited. In order to have the right to run such a business, one had to take a test. Yitzchak Eizik took the test and received permission to conduct a dyeing businessl.

Yitzchak Eizik was often took an interest in Kabbalistic books, and he knew well the Zohar.

[Page 545]

Although he was a misnagid, he would go several times a year to the Koszenicz Magid.

Yitzchak Eizik can also be counted as the first "lover of Zion" in Siedlce. The idea of "love of Zion" was not then as widespread as it was later, at the time of the "Bilu" [an agricultural movement for Palestine]. But Yitzchak Eizik longed all his days to go to Eretz Yisroel. Since he was a descendant of R. Yehuda HaChasid, he wanted to create a committee to buy the ruins of Yehuda HaChasid's synagogue in Jerusalem as well as the surrounding area, which was then in Arab hands, forlorn and filthy. Yitzchak Eizik wrote about this to many rabbis and important people of that time, in order to collect money for that purpose. All of this came to nought, and he was left exhausted.

But the idea of buying the ruins of R. Yehuda HaChasid in Jerusalem allowed him no rest, and he turned to R. Moses Montefiore in London. R. Yitzchakk Eizik, who knew Hebrew, wrote a letter about the whole matter. This letter made a great impression on R. Moses Montefiore and he sent his representative to Jerusalem and bought the whole area around the ruins and rebuilt the shul that had been there. He also established a Jewish neighborhood. This neighborhood is even today called "The Tent of Moses and Judith" in honor of R. Roses Montefiore and his wife. This whole venture cost R. Moses Montefiore a lot of money.

Yitzchak Eizik, aside from spending all of his days in the beis–medresh absorbed in Torah and prayer, also diligently looked after the needs of the community. He strengthened the "Mishnayos" Society and the Talmud Torah. The Talmud Torah did not have its own location, so that the students had to learn with the children in the beis–medresh or in other spots, like in the women's beis–medresh or in the women's shul or elsewhere. The Talmud Torah was being neglected. Every Friday, Yitzchak Eizik would go by himself to collect money in order to pay the teachers. He would bring to his home the Talmud Torah children and himself clean them and wash them.

[Page 546]

Those who had nothing to eat, he would feed.

Aside from these good deeds that occupied him, he was a gabbai in the beis–medresh and in the Chevra Kadisha, and he sent money to Eretz Yisroel for the Jews who lived there.

R. Yitzchak Eizik was loved by everyone in Siedlce. In the year in which he died, many people named their newborn children after him.

R. Yitzchak Eizik had two sons: Paltiel and Dovid, and four daughters. Dovid was called by his father's name–Dovid Eizik's. One of his daughters was the wife of Moyshe Friedman, who was known as Moyshe Reb Eizik's. He was noted for his learning and was a student of R. Eliezer Kharlap of Mezritch. In his later years, R. Moyshe was blind, but he would always sit and learn with others. A second daughter was the wife of Hersch Leyzer Rubinstein, who was also one of the greatest scholars in the beis–medresh.

The Rabbi Reb Moyshe Hersh Weingarten

We don't have any certain dates for when Rabbi Moyshe Hersh came to Siedlce. The only thing we know is that R. Moyshe Hersh was the rabbi before R. Eliezer Shalom. Before arriving in Siedlce, he was the rabbi in Sokolow.

From the time when R. Moyshe Hersh was the rabbi in Sokolow, a number of legends were told about him, as they were about many great rabbis. I will relate one, a typical story, that illustrates R. Moyshe Hersh's greatness.

At that time in Sokolow there was a Jewish informer, who used to inform to the police about young people who were then taken by the "kidnappers" [those who seized Jewish young men for the army]. R. Moyshe Hersh sent for this informer and warned him that he should no longer do what he had been doing. But the informer did not want to obey the rabbi and continued in his work. Suddenly he became ill. He began to fail and could no longer be an informer. Everyone was amazed that someone who had seemed so healthy had suddenly become so ill.

[Page 547]

Meanwhile, people became aware that at the time when the informer became ill, R. Moyshe Hersh had gone somewhere, but no one knew where. Later they understood that RT. Moyshe Hersh was staying in a cellar and had made a golem in the form of a bird; the bigger the bird grew, the sicker the informer became. He saw in his illness a punishment for not having obeyed the rabbi, R. Moyshe Hersh, and he told this to the police. The police wanted to start a legal proceeding against R. Moyshe Hersh, so the rabbi left Sokolow and became the rabbi of Siedlce.

In Siedlce, R. Moyshe Hershe was not only rabbi but also the city preacher and every Shabbos he would teach Torah lessons for everyone. And every day he would teach a lesson for the young men.

The rabbi R. Moyshe Hersh was a great scholar. He wrote many books, commented on the whole Torah and offered revisions on the Talmud and on the four parts of the Shulchan Aruch. All of his books remained in manuscript and were later deserted at the time of the fire, with the exception of "Mars Tzvi," which was published with the assistance of his son R. Baruch Rodzhiner, who also wrote an

, but from this book, too, there remain only excerpts.

On the first Pesach after R. Moyshe Hersh arrived in Siedlce, people say, he called for a batch of kneidlech to be made in his kitchen, and he put them in the window so that everyone could see. He wanted to show that the matter of "gebrochts", that the Chasidim held to be forbidden at that time, was not a law given to Moses at Sinai, and that people could make kneidlech to celebrate the joy of the holiday.

R. Moyshe Hersh had four sons and two daughters. Three of his sons became rabbis. The oldest, R. Aaron, was a rabbi in some foreign land; the second, R. Yosef–in Pilev; the third, R. David, was the rabbi in Kharszel; the fourth son, R. Baruch, who was married in Rodzin, although he was an ordained rabbi, did not want to serve as a rabbi and preferred business dealings. R. Moyshe Hersh would say about his son R. Baruch: "Although it state in the Torah 'The balances of deceit are in his hand' [Hosea 12:8], that is not true of his son, who is an honest businessman." R. Baruch Rodziner was also known as a great scholar and a righteous man, and the rabbi of Rodzin, R. Gershon Henich, showed him great respect.

[Page 548]

In his later years, R. Moyshe Hersh's vision deteriorated and he was almost blind, but that did not stop him from learning Torah. He decided issues and learned, as he had always done. One time the rabbi of Warka, Rabbi Yitzchak z"l, was passing Siedlce and visited the rabbi. When R. Yitzchak noticed that R. Moyshe Hersh had vision problems but still answered religious questions and sat there learning, he asked him about it; R. Moyshe Hersh answered that when it came to learning or answering questions, he felt that "his eyes were illuminated by the Torah" [from the siddur] and could see everything.

Although R. Moyshe Hersh was a misnagid, he was a mystic adept in the Kabbalistic books. He would fast from Shabbos to Shabbos, awaken every night at midnight, immerse in the mikveh, and then pray for the restoration of Jerusalem.

When he was older and he felt that he was weak and his vision no longer served him, he withdrew from rabbinic work. The job was taken by R. Eliezer Shalom. R. Moyshe Hersh died in 1857. His grave was for a long time deserted and almost lacking a monument. Some years later, R. Yisroel Sinai Zidenzweig a"h passed away. He was a relative of R. Moyshe Hersh. He was buried near the rabbi's grave. R. Yisroel Sinai's children later put a double monument over the two graves.

The Chasidim persecuted R. Moyshe Hersh because of his opposition to them. As the Chasidim later recognized R. Moyshe Hersh's excellence, they felt remorse and became reconciled with him. This quarrel between the Chasidim and Misnagdim could be called "a quarrel for the sake of heaven" that has "lasting value," because both sides were seeking the truth and later on reconciled.

It is worthwhile to remember a fact: "R. Moyshe Hersh's son, R. Baruch Radziner, became connected by marriage with Mottl Greenberg's son–in–law. Mottl Greenberg had been one of R. Moyshe Hersh's opponents and persecutors. Mottle later felt strong remorse over his persecution, land when he learned that his son–in–law would be connected to R. Moyshe Hersh's son, he encouraged the match and felt close to R. Moyshe Hersh, who was no longer alive.

[Page 549]

It is also appropriate to recall one of R. Moyshe Hersh's daughters, who was a great scholar, both in Talmud and commentators as well as in secular subjects. She often demonstrated her scholarship to her father in deciding ritual issues. Leah Liebe was married to Meir Kroyshar from Warsaw, the son of Yisroel Kroyshar, a well–known family in Warsaw at that time. When she was 90 years old, Lea Liebe maintained an interest in Yiddish books and with Yiddish literature: Sholem Aleichem, Peretz, and Mendele. Leah Liebe spent her last years with her children in Siedlce, where she passed away.

Meir Nissn Nussbaum and R. Kalman Chasid

At the same time that R. Mannis was the city preacher, R. Meir Nissn Nussbaum was the president of the Jewish community council [in Yiddish, "parnas–chodesh," leader of the month]. That was the title that was then given to the dozors, because each month one of the three served as leader.

Meir Nissn Nussbaum was an educated man. He knew Hebrew and Polish (and had translated into Polish the book "B'Khinas Olam"). He was a great scholar and would learn every day with the Talmud Society. Professionally he was a contractor, in addition to which he owned an inn. R. Meir Nissn was in great favor with the government of the time, and they had the greatest confidence in him. When R. Meir Nissn represented the Jewish population on a draft board, he was enough for him to say that he knew someone was weak for that person to be excused from military duty.

Although R. Meir Nissn Nussbaum was one of the most fervent misnagdim, he was friendly with one of the greatest Chasidim in Siedlce at that time, with R. Kalman Chasid, who was his neighbor.

R. Bunem would often stay with R. Kalman Chasid; he would come on business, even before he was known as R. Bunem. He was employed by the well–known woman Temerl from Warsaw, who used to supply materials to the military, and he, Bunem, would frequently come to Siedlce.

[Page 550]

When R. Kalman introduced R. Bunem to R. Meir Nissn Nussbaum, they, too, became friendly. They engaged in discussions and played chess.

One time, while they were playing chess, R. Bunem made a bad move. He asked R. Meir Nissn whether he could take back the move. R. Meir Nissn responded, "What's done is done."

"You're right," R. Bunem said. "A person has to be careful not to make mistakes, lest it happen that that he make mistakes that he cannot correct." The rabbi R. Bunem would correspond with R. Meir Nissn Nussbaum about Chassidism, faith, and other subjects.

R. Kalman Chasid was one of the greatest Chasidim in Siedlce. Many rabbis would stay with him. The following shows how much he was respected: One time R. Kalman was at a bris. Also there was the Stoliner rabbi, R. Asher. The baby's father honored the Stoliner rabbi by making him the sandek, and he gave another honor to R. Kalman. This surprised many people and they commented on it to the father, that he had given a smaller honor to R. Kalman than to the Stoliner rabbi.

R. Kalman studied day and night. But he was not occupied with making a living. His wife tended his business. Early in the morning it was R. Kalman's custom to bring for his wife in the store a piece of bread spread with butter. When his wife once asked him the meaning of this custom, he said, "It is written in the marriage contract that I gave you, 'I will work for you and provide for you as Jewish husbands do.'" But if I do not provide for you, I do not fulfill this obligation." R. Kalman learned all day with a group of boys and young men.

R. Kalman Chasid's son–in–law, R. Yitzchak Gad Kornblum was the only person in Siedlce who spent the whole year in Danzig and came home for Pesach.

Yitzchak Gad was an employee of the firm "Fayance," which sent grain and wood from Poland to Germany via the Vistula.

[Page 551]

This firm was the first to send barges on the Vistula. R. Yitzchak Gad was well known in the firm where he worked for his excellence.

One time, his manager, in a conversation with another merchant, stated that he had no finer employee. The other merchant bet that he could undermine R. Yitzchak Gad. Later, when R.l Yitzchak Gad came to that merchant to buy grain, he set before him a lesser product and promised him a reward if he accepted that. R. Yitzchak Gad rejected this proposition. Then the merchant said to him, "You should know that your persistence has cost me a great deal of money."

R. Yitzchak Gad stayed with the "Fayance" firm for his whole life. When he was older and could no longer work, the firm made him an emeritus. In 1900, when he was 70, R. Yitzchak Gad departed for Eretz Yisroel–at which time the firm gave him a great sum of money. He lived there in a home for old people and died in 1905.

The City Preacher R. Yisrolkele

After the preacher R. Mannis (this must have been in 1908), the city preacher was R. Yisrolkele. He came to Siedlce from Wengerow, together with R. Yizchak Goldman, who's settled here. The preacher R. Yisrolkele wrote many treatises, and R. Yitzchak Goldman served as his amanuensis for 3 groschen per sheet.

R. Yisrolkele was a great scholar and was considered a miracle worker as well. He would expel dybbuks, give spells, and write amulets. R. Yisrolkele wore a caftan made of parchment. Every time that he had to write an amulet, he would cut a piece of parchment from his caftan and write the amulet upon it.

R. Yisrolkele was a fervent misnagid, so that the Chasidim would persecute him and harass him.

[Page 552]

One of the Kotzk Chasidim once fooled R. Yisrolkele at the third Shabbos meal. The leading man among the Chasidim was then R. Mottl Greenberg, who was entitled to wear the clothing of a clergyman. He was sitting at the head of the table wearing a shtreimel. When the preacher R. Yisrolkele entered the prayer house, he was seated near R. Mottl.

In order to make fun of R. Yisrolkele, the Chasidim acted as though R. Mottl was the the Chasidic rabbi. They proposed that the preacher should say a few words of Torah. R. Yisrolkele said some words of Torah, but they were not, you understand, in accordance with Chasidism, and the Chasidim were not happy with what he said. They began to go after the preacher. From all sides they began to poke him with pins. It was then dark in the prayer house and he could not see who was poking him, so he began to shout, "Rabbi, they're poking me!" R. Mottl did not know that the Chasidim had fooled the preacher. He thought that the preacher had just come to discuss Torah, so he called to the preacher: "If one will speak of Torah before Chasidim, one must also receive with love their pins. They poke me, too," said R. Mottl, " if they don't like my words of Torah." The preacher saw that he could not win, so he left the prayer house and ran away.

But that did not end the Chasidic persecutions of the preacher. They created other woes for him. One time a Chasidic young man came to him and said that there was someone through him a dybbuk was speaking, and he asked the preacher to go and exorcise the the dybbuk. The preacher accepted the invitation. He was taken to the Kotzk prayer house. There he found a young man who pretended that a dybbuk was speaking through him.

The preacher said some spells, made a circle of chalk, took a lulav with an esrog and shook them in all directions. The dybbuk, however, did not budge. Then the preacher called for them to bring a barrel of water, and he ordered the dybbuk to come out and into the barrel of water. When the dybbuk would not be roused to do what the preacher said, the preacher became discouraged, because he did not know what else to do and he wanted to leave. But the Chasidim took him and dumped him into the barrel of water.

[Page 553]

Another time the Chasidim inscribed a cross on the preacher's reading stand in the soul. They also did not hesitate to spread slander about the preacher's wife, that she went with strange men, which would have prevented the preacher R. Yisrolkele, who was a kohen, from living with his wife. His wife was deeply embarrassed. She was taken to the magistrate so that she could be sent, according to the laws of the time, to prison. But a couple of prominent citizens were found who knew that the whole thing was a slander and so it was dismissed.

The preacher R. Yisrolkele led a yeshiva. One of his students was the aforementioned R. Yitzchak Goldman, a Jew, a Torah Jew, who learned night and day. R. Yitzchak always told a variety of stories about R. Yisrolkele.

The Chasidim of that time never gave any rest to the preacher and he decided to flee from Siedlce. He fled on the night of Hoshana Raba in 1911. When he was outside the city limits, people say, he put a curse on Siedlce that it should be burnt. In the morning, indeed, in the morning the great Siedlce conflagration broke out, as is known in the history of Siedlce, and the Great Synagogue and many houses were burned down.

All the people who took part in persecuting the preacher, people say, came to a bad end. They regretted the indignity to which they had subjected him.

Over all there was a time off quarrels between the Chasidim and the misnagdim, during which one side would do things to the other. Among the stories about such pranks is the following:

At that time in Siedlce there was a person called R. Leibl Kaveh (or R. Leibl Etkes), the father–in–law of Rokhel Etkes and the founder of the Kaveh family in Siedlce. R. Leibl Kaveh was a religious and upstanding Jew. He lived in the same house where Rokhel Etkes lived later.

It was R. Leibl Kaveh's custom before dawn, when it was still dark, to don his tallis and tefillin in his home and then go to the beis–medresh.

[Page 554]

He was careful not to go through Warsaw Street, where there were stores but only through Kosze Alley. He did this with the intention of not giving the evil eye to Jews who were taking in money. (At that time people used to open their stores before dawn.)

R. Leibl Kaveh insisted that he would encounter the divine spirit. Since he knew that the divine spirit required seclusion, he shut himself up in his house in a special room and had no dealings with the outside world. He occupied himself only with Torah and prayer.

When the Chasidim became aware of this, they could not leave it alone. Since R. Leibl wanted to encounter the divine spirit, they decided to make sure that he would not. Once they came to him when it had been almost four weeks since R. Leibl had secluded himself and they started to knock on the door. R. Leibl did not want to open the door for any reason, but they attacked the doors furiously. R. Leibl became angry. Thus the Chasidim achieved their goal, because they had made him angry and they knew that the divine spirit would not come to him because of the line, "The divine spirit will not settle on one whose heart is not joyous."

R. Leibl throughout his life resented the Chasidim because they stood in the way of the divine spirit.

R. Matisyahu Rubinstein

R. Matisyahu Rubinstein was one of the remnants of the old generation, one of the old Kotzk Chasidim and recognized scholars in Siedlce.

He was a man with a sharp mind, a great memory, and knew many stories about old SIedlce, from the time of Russan domination onwards. If anyone wanted to know anything from those days, he had to ask no one besides R. Matisyahu. It was fascinating to speak with him. In speaking, he would use scholarly witticisms and beautiful proverbs. His shop in Papszetszne Alley, which was also where his home was, always served as a gathering place for wise people.

R. Matisyahu Rubinstein knew a great deal about astronomy; I was convinced of this more than fifty years ago when we studied Rambam together, the laws of the new month, in which R. Matisyahu showed great proficiency.

[Page 555]

He also studied Kabbalah and was deeply immersed in Torah and prayer. His prayers, by himself in the beis–medresh, lasted several hours every day.

Even with his profound religiosity, R. Matisyahu was not overzealous and was tolerant of the younger generation, and he attempted to understand their aspirations and their demands.

In the last two years of his life, R. Matsyahu Rubinstein became quite feeble, but he was still diligent in Torah and prayer. Even three days before his passing, he went to pray in the beis–medresh, and, as was his custom, he prolonged his prayers.

He lived for 84 years.

His funeral was attended by a large crowd from every level of Siedlce's populace.

[Page 556]

Avrahamele Rosenberg

by Hersh Abarbanel (Buenos Aires)

Translated by Theodore Steinberg

Yizkor…When we remember with reverence and veneration our intimates and near ones from our home town of Siedlce, who were killed in the time of the Hitlerian cataclysm, when we call up the characters and images of our destroyed shtetl, who shared in the bitter fate of European Jewry—in order to commemorate and eternize their memory, it is also appropriate to remember an earlier epoch and

Avrahamele Rosenberg

to recall the figure of Avrahamele Rosenberg, who, with typical Jewish earnestness, took up the unequal battle—the battle of the Jew without rights under the czarist regime, with a willful police chief and a governor, who were at that time like the sole rulers over the domain of Siedlce.

Russian Jewry under the czarist powers had to withstand a succession of persecutions and pogroms, discrimination, degradation, and violations of rights. Jewish Siedlce was no exception. Siedlce shared the fate of all Russian Jewry.

* * *

In the nineties of the previous century, the governor of Siedlce was a certain Sabatkin; the vice-governor was Liaskowski, who had a Jewish wife, and a young 22-year-old police chief, Semientowski, whose uncle was a minister in the Russian government.

[Page 557]

The characters of these three rulers, in whose hands lay the fate of Siedlce Jewry, were quite different. The governor appeared to be a milksop and entirely under the control of the brutal young police chief. Even when the police chief had an illicit relationship with the governor's wife, and it was an open secret, the governor either did not "see" it or was powerless to react.

The vice-governor was largely independent of the two of them and often did good things for the Jews, very often under his wife's influence. However, the police chief was a bitter hater of Jews and with sadistic glee caused them many misfortunes.

In addition to the vexations and persecutions of Siedlce's Jews, which the police chief oversaw with brutal glee, he extracted bribes from them and demanded money arbitrarily in the form of weekly or monthly payments. Even Moyshele, the synagogue sexton, who also led the morning prayers, he oppressed.

One Friday evening before Kabbalas Shabbos, he came into the shul and threw him out. Only after Moyshele gave him 300 rubles as a bribe did he say to him, "Nu, now you can go say "Ha-melech.""

One Yom Kippur he entered the Ger prayer house and dragged out a couple of Jews. He put them in a carriage and drove them around the city, cutting off the beards of Jews and cutting away the hems of their kaftans—such was a frequent pastime for this brutal police chief.

* * *

Avrahamele Rosenberg, or "Dear Sir," as he was known—because that was how he addressed everyone—was a Jew about whom people said, "He wouldn't let anyone spit in his kasha" [an old phrase that means he would not take abuse from anyone]

[Page 558]

He did not seek adventures and he was not ostentatious, but in a confrontation where Jewish honor was at stake, without hesitation he took up the challenge and with all his strength he fought for Jewish honor.

Avrahamele Rosenberg's name was a byword in Siedlce and its surroundings. People spoke about his extraordinary courage with respect and appreciation. Avrahamele Rosenberg also took up the fight against the infuriating police chief and defeated him.

* *

Avrahamele Rosenberg once entered a bakery to buy pastry. He paid with a large bill and received change. At that moment the police chief entered and seeing him standing over the cash register without acknowledging the chief, he yelled at him, "Scabby Jew. Don't you see who is here? Why haven't you moved?" Avrahamele Rosenberg's response, that he had not seen him, did not satisfy the police chief, who smacked him on that head.

Avrahamele answered sharply, and the police chief was infuriated and arrested him.

After a few days of detention, he ordered Rosenberg be brought to him and asked: "How did you dare answer a police chief like that?" Avrahamele even then did not hold back, and he answered him sharply. More time in detention he could not command, so he freed him. From that moment on, Avrahamele Rosenberg waged war against the police chief.

Avrahamele knew that complaining to the governor would be wasted speech, because he was so close to the police chief, so he complained to the vice-governor and told him all the troubles the police chief had caused for Siedlce's Jews. The vice-governor listened attentively, but he could not help him.

[Page 559]

One Friday, the police chief was a guest at the governor's summer house in Stok, a village near Siedlce. On his way there, he encountered a Jew—it was Berl Glazer—who was returning to Siedlce for Shabbos. The police chief stopped his carriage and ordered him to kiss his horse's behind.

Berl Glazer refused to go behind the horse, so the police chief beat him murderously with a stick, leaving him bleeding and beaten up in the middle of the road, until a peasant came by and helped him to the city. "Where are you going?" he asked the peasant. "To the home of Avrahamele Rosenberg," he told Berl.

Avrahamele Rosenberg immediately took him to the vice governor in order to tell him what the police chief had done. The vice-governor, upset with this brutality, sentenced the police chief to seven days of detention. Hearing of this sentence, he went right to the governor, who rescinded it.

Thus began the war between the governor and the police chief on one side and the vice governor on the other. So vicious did the war become that the police chief put forbidden literature in the vice governor's office. Then the police understandably made a search and "found" the prohibited literature.

At that time, Avrahamele Rosenberg sent a complaint about the governor and the police chief directly to the emperor, but the complaint did not make it to the emperor, because the police chief's uncle—the minister—saw to it that the complaint would be misdirected. People advised Avrahamele to send it via Germany,. Avrahamele did so, and the complaint finally went directly to the emperor. The emperor sent the complaint to Warsaw to the governor general with a command to investigate the matter.

One day an order are for Avrahamele to appear before the governor general in Warsaw. Losing no time, he went immediately to Warsaw and hastened to the governor general, who immediately received him and inquired about the whole affair.

[Page 560]

Avrahamele told him everything, with all the details, and the governor general sent him to the chief prosecutor; the prosecutor received him in a friendly way, spoke with him for two hours, and said he would take care of the matter.

In the highest sphere of Warsaw s commission was named to go to Siedlce and there to investigate the matter.

The good brothers [?] soon transferred the governor and the police chief. The latter, who had ties to the underworld, hired a fellow named Tuviah Kashetz, for 500 rubles, to lure Avrahamele to the city, where the police chief would "set him to rights."

Tuviah, however, was not stupid. He understood that after doing this bit of dirty work, the police chief would seem to be free of him so that he could not testify against him. Having already taken the 500 rubles for his job, he reconsidered and returned the money to the police chief.

The governor had prepared to receive the commission in a more respectable way. He called to himself all of the important Jewish citizens and warned them: if any of them spoke out against him, he would "teach" all the Jews of the city.

Having taken care of them, he sent for Rosenberg. Avrahamele knew well that he was not being summoned for anything good and that in the palace of his enemy, the servants could break his bones and no one would say anything. But one could not refuse to go when the governor called, One could not be boorish. He came up with a plan. Instead of speaking with the governor alone in the palace, he went to the police club.

It was a Friday, when all the commissioners from the surroundings used to come to the club on Langer Street. The governor was their leader. Avrahamele went to the club, observed the carriages that were standing outside, and seeing the governor's coachman in the carriage of his master, he knew that the governor was already inside. He went up to the doorman and gave him a coin, asking him to notify "his highness the governor" that the "Jew" Mr. Rosenberg wanted to speak to him. The governor called for him to be allowed in.

[Page 561]

Avrahamele went into the club. Around the table were sitting all the commissioners with the governor at their head. Seeing Avrahamele, the governor yelled in front of everyone that he should immediately and without delay withdraw the complaint against him, and if not…And he told the commissioners that if he had to leave, they would all lose their positions.

"Distinguished lord," Avrahamele cold-bloodedly asked, "I sent three complaints. Which of the three arrived where it was supposed to I have no way of knowing. So which complaint should I withdraw?"

"I'll read them to you," answered the governor, and he pulled out from his briefcase a copy of the most recent complaint, which his colleagues in Warsaw had sent to him, and began to read it. Coming to the spot where it said that he was old and operated under the influence of the police chief, he became embarrassed in front of the commissioners and tried to mumble. Avrahamele did not allow this and urged him to read it again clearly and distinctly. The governor had to read aloud about his weaknesses, at which all the commissioners laughed to themselves, knowing that this was the truth.

After the reading, Avrahamele announced, "To my regret, I cannot withdraw the complaint, because then I would have to face a trial for bringing frivolous charges against government officials."

Controlling his anger in the presence of his subordinate, and recognizing that Rosenberg was a tough nut to crack, the governor invited him to the palace for an intimate talk, speaking in an unintimidating tone.

Avrahamele thought to himself, " When one goes to war, one has to smell gunpowder," so he went, with trepidation, to the palace.

First the governor politely extended his hands and asked him to take a seat. On the table were a variety of beverages. Seeking to frighten Avrahamele, the governor reproached him by asking why he had written in the complaint that he was old.

"I'm old? Look at this!" And the governor, with wild Fury, threw the cupboard that contained the glassware onto…the floor.

[Page 562]

At the shattering of the glass, several servants came running in, but the governor dismissed them with a real Russian "blessing."

"Now you can see," said the governor to Avrahamele, "that my strength is undiminished."

Avrahamele's teeth were chattering, but he took heart and responded, "Even a goy in sandals can break glasses. One expects from a governor that he would have enough strength of character to be in charge and to direct his own way."

* * *

The upshot was that the commission came, called on Avrahamele, called on other Jews, investigated, and returned to Warsaw.

Avrahamele told the whole truth about the wickedness of the police chief and the incompetent rule of the governor. The other Jews, however, being afraid, decided that "silence is golden," and therefore did not tell of the chicanery and inflictions of the police chief.

The sentence later came down that the police chief would be demoted. Out of shame at being defeated by a Jew, he threw himself under a train and died. Siedlce's Jews had taken vengeance on their Human, thanks to the fearless fighter Avrahamele Rosenberg.

But Avrahamele himself came to sorrow for seeking justice. Because the vice-governor became the governor of Kielce, the governor of Siedlce now had a free hand, and he used it to take vengeance on Rosenberg. With the help of the court, he arranged to have Rosenberg banished from Siedlce as an undesirable citizen.

Thanks to the intercession of Rochel Etkes, his mother-in-law's mother, people succeeded in having the governor allow Avrahamele choose where he would go, and he chose Kielce, where his protector Liaskowski was already the governor. He lived there for three years, during which he exhausted his resources, and died in his birthplace a poor man.

The governor of Siedlce felt some respect for his former courageous and upstanding enemy, so every Pesach he would send him a gift for the holiday.

[Page 563]

When Avrahamele Rosenberg had gone to his eternal rest, the "Siedlce Vochenblat" wrote:

"This past Sunday, at the age of over 68, Avrahamele Rosenberg died. He was known as "Dear Sir", one of the most interesting characters of the older generation. At the time of the well-known villainous Russian police chief Semientowski, the deceased showed the courage to battle with him openly, even to the point of open confrontation with the then governor Sobotkin, for which he earned banishment to Kielce for three years."

So by us in Siedlce, as in other Jewish communities, lived proud Jews, who like righteous people from the prophets, would not make peace with their corrupt, tyrannical surroundings, and in a world of wickedness and injustice fought for justice and truth. They would not bow their heads to those who were more powerful and they believed in the ultimate triumph of righteousness.

[Page 564]

Yisroel Rosenblum
– The Head of the "Beis Lechem" Synagogue

by Dovid ben Yosif

Translated by Theodore Steinberg

People from Siedlce remember well the small shop in an old wooden building at 67 Pienke. It belonged to Yisrael Rosenblum, the head of "Beis Lechem."

The "Beis Lechem" members were old–style Jews for whom the notion of charity had not taken on a modern character. They all undertook to make a hot meal on one day of the week, Shabbos, for a hungry family. They themselves went with their baskets to the courtyards to collect challah, bread, and other foodstuffs and then carry them into the flimsy homes of the needy and the hungry.

The center of the "Beis Lechem," the control center of this organization, was its head, Yisrael Rosenblum. His family always contended that the Beis Lechem took up ore of his time and labor than did his own children – his own home. And all of it was centered in his shop.

Since Beis Lechem worried most of the time that hungry families should have a hot meal on Shabbos, in Rosenblum's shop on Friday afternoons the "real carnival" began. A notable woman would enter, looking as if she had just finished busying herself with Shabbos matters, and she would engage in quiet conversation with the head of "Beis Lechem." She had come to ask for something to eat on Shabbos for someone else. Soon the head of "Beis Lechem" would ask another member to buy a couple of challahs, bread, herring, and then to take it to a particular address.

After that, every Shabbos, those for whom the woman had interceded would be visited by the "foodbearers" with two challahs, bread, sugar, and other food. And then he himself was in that situation. The number of needy, of hungry people, increased, and even more, the number of donors decreased–lamented the head.

Erev Pesach was in Rosenblum's store the high season, when an oppressed person, an anguished person, who has been driven to the extreme and has no hope of celebrating Pesach, comes to Mr. Rosenblum and pours out the bitterness of his heart. And he, the head of "Beis Lechem," says nothing. He has pushed through walls so that he would not allow that any Jew should, God forbid, have to celebrate the "season of our freedom" in hunger and have an empty table instead of a Schulchan Aruch [a set table, but also the title of the Code of Jewish Law].

In later years, Yisrael Rosenblum was feeling oppressed. He complained that the hearts of our "righteous ones, sons of righteous ones" had become hardened. No one was touched by another's need, another's sorrows. No one was moved that his neighbor on the other side of the wall was languishing from hunger. Each one was satisfied if he had provisions, if he had what he needed.

Yisrael Rosenblum never complained about his own situation. He never said that his shop barely provided him a living. He worked always for the poor of Siedlce who needed help – that is the kind of Jew that Yisrael Rosenblum was.

[Page 566]

Reb Yitzchok "Eisner"

by Yisroel Winograd (Buenos Aires)

Translated by Theodore Steinberg

One of the most remarkable characters that Siedlce lost under the horrific rule of the barbaric Nazis was, without doubt, the person everyone in Siedlce knew as Yitzchokl, or, as he was called, Yitzchok "Eisner."

Who does not know Y.L. Peretz' story "If Not Higher?" in which the Litvak discovers that instead of ascending to heaven, as the Chasidim believed, the rabbi of Nemirov on the night of Selichos goes into the woods, chops some wood, and carries it to a poor, sick widow, where he himself tends to the stove while saying the Selichos prayers?

Exactly such a remarkable person was this Yitzchok "Eisner," who had the nickname "Eisner" because he owned an Iron business. But he was not the one who dealt with customers. It was she, his wife, who was the breadwinner and took care of their home. Yitzchok "Eisner's" labor, however, was important: he came into the business every Passover eve, at the search for chametz, or on a Friday market day and fall on the floor, even in the presence of Christian customers, prostate himself on the ground, and say to his son or to his wife: "Look! This is the lot of humankind – man comes from dust and returns to dust. When a person dies, people take him out and give him his due; so why worry about income? He who gives life provides food! Is it not better and finer to imitate the ruler of the world – "As he is merciful, so should you be merciful to others!"

[Page 567]

And Yitzchok "Eisner" never thought about or worried about his profession. His job was to the hospitals or to the homes of the poor where there were unfortunate sick people whom people did not know to visit, and he did whatever he could to lighten their sorrows, because it was simply not a question for him about doing so.

It had been known to happen that his wife made Yitzchok "Eisner" a new overcoat for the winter, but he would meet on the street a poor man who was shivering from the cold, so he would immediately, on the spot, take off the new garment and give it to the poor man.

So this, we see, was his way of life: for the whole day during the week he would go to the sick and unfortunate and help them, some with personal help using his own money and some with words of comfort that gave the helpless the strength to deal with their physical ills. And on Friday nights, however many people in the Ger prayer house where he prayed needed meals, he would invite them to his table.

More than once he was asked: Reb Yitzchok! If you did not take all these guests, they would eat on Friday nights at a richer person's house. So why do you take everyone to yourself?" But for Reb Yitzchok it was not a question; he was only afraid that those people would have nowhere to eat.

Early on Shabbos mornings he would wake up and take a basket and go around calling: "Good Shabbos, Jews! Bread in the basket!" And he procured bread for the "Beis Lechem" – organization that distributed food to the poor for Shabbos. This was the Reb Yitzchok's custom: not to think or worry about himself.

Once, his wife experienced a deadly shock, because the police were seeking her husband. And when they found him, they wanted to give him a heavy sentence because of a Communist love…

And here was the story: There was a secret love between a Jewish girl and a Christian boy and the Jewish girl was prepared to go to a Catholic Church to convert, but in the meantime not wanting to lose any time, she became pregnant and bore the Christian a baby boy. This mother lay in the hospital without any marriage ceremony, to be sure, the hospital by the market, and took great pride in her son. Reb Yitzchok "Eisener," who came to the hospital to help a sick person, heard about there whole "wedding" with no celebration and decided to do something for the young mother.

[Page 568]

No sooner said than done: He began to visit the woman often and bring her snacks and he often put a couple of zlotys under her basket along with other little things, and he played with the newborn as if it were his own child. Gradually he gained the confidence of the mother, so that on one particular morning, when the Christian boy was supposed to take the woman home that evening, he played specially with the baby and danced with him. While dancing, he danced with the child in his hand into the neighboring room, where he had already put a mohel, and as quickly as it takes to say "Shema Yisroel," he had circumcised the child. Reb Yitzchok returned the circumcised child to his mother with a mazel tov and quickly disappeared. When the Christian boy learned that night about the bris and the Jewish godfather, he rejected both the young woman and his now damaged Jewified offspring.

The police, you understand, looked everywhere for Reb Yitzchok "Eisener" the benefactor, but thanks to three things – money, funds, and riches – this scary story ended well.

* * *

Aside from having devoted himself to the sorrowful and suffering, he was also very humble. When he was learning and would encounter a difficult passage or an obscure comment in Tosafos, he was not ashamed to ask even a bright young child for an explanation saying: "Don't look at the pitcher but at what is inside the pitcher."

On Simchas Torah, no one could approach R, Yitzchok: he would assemble a large number of children or young men, as many as he could find, and he went out into the street with them in a rapturous dance in honor of the Torah. His ecstasy was like the spreading of rain, as if he were entirely freed from the vanities of this world and had become something heavenly that rose higher and higher, if not higher! And if one wanted to awaken him from ecstasy and otherworldliness, it was enough to say: "Reb Yitzchok, there are sick people around who need a prescription, who need your help," and he would leave his ecstasy and run off to help the ailing, forgetting about his otherworldliness.

[Page 569]

In "Beside the Dying" [a story whose literal title is "At the Head of the Death Bed"] by Y.L. Peretz, the Angel of Light tells Nachman. of Zbarash: "Come with me to the Garden of Eden, where you will not hear of any ill or helpless and you will find yourself among those radiant with God's grace, with golden crowns on their heads." Nachman replies, "But what will I do there, where there are no unfortunates and sufferers who need aid? No, I will not live only for myself! Better I should go to Gehenna to help the weak and tired, those who are lost, accursed, and forgotten by God so that I can share in the sorrows of my fellows – my place is there." So, too, was Reb Yitzchokl:

always running from rest and tranquility and working only to alleviate the troubles of those who are in need. But it is clear that the dark fate of world Jewry as a whole and of our brothers and sisters in Siedlce in particular could not elude the holy personality of that dear excellent Jew who was known as Reb Yitzchakl "Eisener."

May his memory be blessed!

[Page 570]

The late Hazan Yosef Pasovsky

by M.S. Gashuri

Translated by Mira Eckhaus

On 12 Menachem Av, 5711 - The day the Zionist Congress convened in Jerusalem, the capital of the State of Israel, the Hazan of Siedlce, Rabbi Yosef Dov Pasovsky, left us. In Orthodox Jerusalem, he acquired sympathy and a place of honor. So far, friends and acquaintances have not recovered from his death. Indeed, since the death of the renowned Hazan, Rabbi Bezalel from Odessa, in Jerusalem of more than sixty years ago, the place has remained empty of veteran Hazanim, with inspiration and control in the traditional Hazanut, until the Hazan Y. D. Pasovsky from Siedlce in Poland came and established his seat in Jerusalem.

He belonged to the same small number of Hazanim, presenting themselves at the first appearance in full force, and his respectable majestic appearance added much to his great personality.

He was born in 1882 to his father, Rabbi Netanel, the rabbi of the town of Zietela, Grodno, the author of the books: "Meshivat Nefesh", "Emunat Atchi'ya", and "Gan Hadassim". At the age of 13, Yosef Dov was accepted as a student at the well-known Yeshiva Novarduk, where he studied poetry at the time from the local Hazan Boyarsky. Until the age of twenty, he studied in various yeshivas in Lithuania and received authorization from Rabbi Mordechai Salonimer. But his heart was drawn to Hazanut, and he learned Hazanut from the Hazan of Smorgon, Zimmel Mashvitsky, and with him he systematically learned to read and write musical notes, the vocal scales, and received good musical-technical training. In 1904 he was admitted, while he was still young, to the synagogue in Bobruisk as a poet and the second Hazan (the famous Aryeh Leib Rotman was the first Hazan there). For a long time, he was singing for famous Hazanim in southern Russia and had many successes.

[Page 571]

After he has married in 1907, he was invited to pass in front of the box in the municipal synagogue in Slonim and in 1912 he was accepted as the urban Hazan in the Great Synagogue in Siedlce, where he was preceded by artists Hazanim, such as Zeidel and Yaakov Rovner and Tikotinsky. He served as the Hazan 23 years, until he made an Aliya to Israel. He had a lyrical baritone voice with a color and he was a great prayer and an excellent Hazan. In his pleasant prayer he always attracted a large audience and even on winter Saturdays. When he prayed in front of the pillar, the synagogue in Siedlce was at full capacity. He arranged a choir for him, and the audience enjoyed its performances very much, but due to lack of budget it was scattered.

In Siedlce he was liked and respected very much, because he was a Torah scholar, knew Hebrew, knowledgeable in ancient and modern Hebrew literature and also knew Russian literature, a polite man and a wise student with no flawless in his clothes. From the disciples of P. Minkovski from Odessa, who knew the traditional Hazanut and Hazanut literature founded by David Novkovski, Shlomo Kashtan and their friends. His figure in front of the box was most convincing in his upright posture, in his precise movements, and he especially captivated his listeners with the tensed soul that had reached in him to achievements. He knew by heart pearl creations that were written by the gifted creators: Weintraub, A. B. Birenbaum, and more; And he designed the sung works as if he were the author, with the power of inspiration and joy of creation that excite the audience from the beginning of the prayer till its end. He continued the glorious golden chain of Hazanim and poets in Israel who passionately illuminated the darkness of Diaspora life.

And then he decided to put an end to the life in exile and to make an Aliya to the Holy City of Jerusalem. The Jewish community in Siedlce held a glorious farewell party for him, and all the people of the city attended. On the day of the trip, all the people of the city gathered in the halls of the train station and greeted him with a blessing of "safe trip". He was a member of the association of Hazanim and conductors in Poland, attended a national conference in Warsaw and was elected as a member of the National Council.

His appearance in the Eretz Israel in 1935 made an impression. He passed in front of the box in the "Ohel Shem" Hall in Tel Aviv and in large synagogues in Jerusalem, appeared on the Hazanut songs program at "Kol Yerushalayim", was a member of the council of conducting Hazanim and lovers of religious poetry in Israel, and almost never missed visiting the Hazanim club in Jerusalem and participated in the discussions held on the problems of the Hazanut in Israel and around the world. In his house he had a library of the best Hazanut literature of A. B. Birenbaum, whose works were very popular with him, especially the Talmudic Rhapsody "Bema Madlikin", and of the works of Little Yeruham, Nissan Belzer and others, and even created his own recitations for prayers in the traditional spirit. The Hazanim in Jerusalem saw him as a creative and vibrant force, who embarrassed the young ones, he was a nice conversation man and it was interesting to hear his stories from the world of Hazanut and the lives of the great personalities who served as Hazanim in Russian cities. He even placed young Hazanim in the traditional Hazanut, and many of his students hold prominent positions in the Jewish communities in Brazil, Argentina and more.

[Page 572]

It was a great privilege to see almost all his family members in Israel involved in Torah and work life and in the resurrection of Israel, and always when he remembered that he was lucky to make an Aliya and sit in Jerusalem, he blessed "She'hecheyanu". During his long illness, he was often visited by music lovers and Hazanim that spent hours with him in a pleasant conversation on topics of building the country and reviving the Hazanut in the country.

[Page 573]

R. Yisroel Gutgelt

by M. Dromi

Translated by Theodore Steinberg

He came from a rich, scholarly Chasidic family – Gutgelt from Grodzisk. R. Yisrael married Sarahle in Siedlce, the daughter of Yossele Enzeles, an important man, a merchant and a great philanthropist who every week donated to many honored families as well as supporting a variety of organizations.

R. Yisrael Gutgelt, as soon as he arrived in Siedlce, showed an inclination for business activities. He was always busy. He would sit and study in his well – furnished personal library, whose walls were covered with shelves stacked with books: the Talmud, religious texts, commentaries, Chasidic books, and works by various authors. In his library Gutgelt found spiritual satisfaction. Outside of that, he conducted businesses in salt, kerosene, and herring. In his later years he was also a lumber merchant. Despite his profitable businesses and his spiritual life, he found time to deal with community affairs. There was hardly a community organization to which he did not belong: the bank, merchants organizations, the "Ezras Y'somim," the "Briyos," the hospital, the governmental evaluation commission, the city council, several years as a dozor in the religious community. Also in 1926, when the religious community was given a broader foundation, R. Yisrael Gutgelt became the chair of the community council.

He devoted much time, energy, and money to the Talmud Torah. He was totally dedicated to it. While he was dozor, he worked so that ritual slaughtering would become a community function so that the Talmud Torah would receive a percentage of the income.

[Page 574]

In the Talmud Torah he established a locksmith workshop so that the young men who graduated from the Talmud Torah would have a place to learn a trade. He insured that on the board of the Talmud Torah would be people who understood how to improve religious education. One of them, R. Henech Steinberg–Kalushiner, made a revolutionary proposal regarding teachers. R. Henech moved that in hiring a teacher for the Talmud Torah, they should see whether he could teach children, whether he was capable of explaining things, whether he was totally suited to be a teacher, because it was customary in the Chasidic prayer houses that a young man who had gone through his dowry became a teacher, with no regard for whether he was capable of doing it. R. Henech fought this system. He was regarded as a subversive.

Another exceptional member of the Talmud Torah board was R. Shlomo Shmuel Barbanel, a great scholar who came to the board because of R. Yisrael Gutgelt.

R. Yisrael Gutgelt was much loved by the Jewish populace as well as the Christian. They would call him "Zhid wierny" – loyal Jew. When he walked down the street, he never waited for anyone to say "Good morning. He greeted everyone – young or old – first. Officially he belonged to the Agudah, and in many organizations he represented the Agudah. He was a Ger Chasid, and in his heart he was a Zionist and spoke with real love about Eretz Yisroel. Perhaps his home influenced him. His home was purely Zionist. His two sons, Levi and Yossele, whom we have discussed elsewhere, and also his three daughters were Zionists. Even his wife was always collecting money and giving to Keren Kayames. To an extent he was influenced by the Zionist leader Hartglass. R. Yisrael Gutgelt often told me that Hartglass made him understand that Zionism had saved the Jewish young people from going over to communism or abandoning Judaism. But more than anything he was affected by his warm Jewish heart.

In secret he would give Hartglass, from time to time, sums of money for Keren Kayames.

[Page 575]

I also received money from him for Keren Kayames. When he gave it to me, he said, "I trust your discretion," but he knew that I was putting it in the Keren Kayames pushke.

Yitzchak Greenbaum came to Siedlce to begin a campaign for Keren Ha'yesod and there was a gathering of the merchants' organization. R. Yisrael Gutgelt, chair of the organization, greeted Greenbaum and wished him success. After the meeting, Greenbaum proposed that Gutgelt should contribute to Keren Ha'yesod. Gutgelt's answer was: "I would gladly give, but I am not allowed to. Still, since people should not say that I don't give because I want to hold on to my money, I will give a certain sum to the national council." And truly – the next morning I received a large some of money from him for the national council.

In the last years before the outbreak of the Second World War, he lost most of his possessions and was in dire straits.

He died on the night when the Nazis burned the Great Synagogue and beis–hamedresh.

[Page 576]

In Memory of the late Levi Gutgeld the 14ᵗʰ

by Baruch Yaffe

Translated by Mira Eckhaus

Friends asked me to raise some lines in memory of Levi Gutgeld, a friend, who did not get to see the fulfillment of his dream and who perished in the Diaspora by the oppressor.

About 35 years passed since we first met. We have been a short time together but after that we parted ways. But this period was unique; both in itself and in our lives, and its signs did not wipe out.

Shortly after the outbreak of World War I, the Russians expelled the Jewish inhabitants from Brisk, Lithuania, a fortress town. A group of Brisk refugees then moved to Pinsk, and after it was occupied by the Germans, they were transferred to Siedlce, Poland. In this group there were also some young people caught up in Zionism from an early age.

The meeting of these young people with the Zionist youth group in Siedlce was almost a two ends meeting. And perhaps that is precisely the reason why these two were attracted one to the other. Differences of origin, environment and tradition – were all piled up together in this case. The Brisk people from Lithuania came from an environment that was full of "opponents" whose Hebrew education was a combination of the education of the Beit Midrash, the new Hebrew literature and the external influence of the realistic Russian literature. From the Jewish political point, the members of this group were under general Zionist influence, which was strong in their hometown, with tendencies towards Tze'irei Zion" (Zion youth) who then began their first steps to establish a special organization. While the members of the Zionist group in Siedlce, their environment was entirely "Hassidic", their Hebrew education was the education of the Hassidic "Stiebel", and to the extent that there was an external influence, it was the influence of the romantic Polish literature.

From a Jewish political point of view, Siedlce had a tradition of tendency towards the "Bond" and Yiddishism. And here these two groups met at a critical hour, during a clash of worlds and views in Poland.

[Page 577]

With the German occupation, the possibilities of a legal organization for political action opened up before the Jews of Poland. The Polish Zionist organization (then still undivided and undefined, in which all the Zionist parties participated) was established on the one hand, and the Agudat Israel movement, which was especially supported by the occupation authorities (or by its advisers on Jewish affairs, who were members of extremist Orthodoxy in Germany) on the other hand.

The merged group developed a feverish action: founding a Zionist association, a Zionist club, evening Hebrew classes, organizing a Zionist school, science lessons for adults, assemblies and lectures, attacks on the fortress of the Yiddishism - "Agudat Hazamir" - and attempts to conquer it for Zionism and Hebrew, active participation in the general politic life from the Zionist aspect, etc. The living spirit in all this action among the Siedlce youth group was Levi Gutgeld.

* * *

So, I see him in my mind as if it was the first time I saw him: short, blackish, with shiny eyes, curly hair, wearing a capote and a small Hassidic hat. When we became closer and started a joint operation, I discovered that he is all lively and boiling, tireless, full of initiative and vigor, ready for any work and any idea of a new action. With literary tendencies and delicate aesthetic taste. His writing style was original, with a tendency to linguistic and conceptual surprises.

At the time we met, Levi Gutgeld was particularly influenced by two older local Zionist figures: the late M. M. Landau, and may he live long, Heartglass, who nowadays lives with us in Israel. Landau was a Torah scholar, an educated Hebrew Zionist, with tendencies as one of the people, gentle-minded and good-natured and avoided daily political activity that involved friction and clashes with various people. He was sickly and died shortly afterwards when he was very young. Heartglass was already known at the time, a sharp Zionist publicist, but was entirely immersed in the Polish culture and still did not know Hebrew nor Yiddish. The possibility of his action among the Jewish masses was, therefore, very limited. Beside that, due to his general public activity and in connection with his appearances on various occasions, he was suspicious in the eyes of the German occupation authorities and had to compel himself to abstain from political-Zionist action. The common ground of these two, is that although they did not participate in the day-to-day action at the time, their impact on our behind-the-scenes action was enormous, and their share of advice and guidance was enormous.

Dozens of episodes from Levy Gutgeld's action in those years come to my mind. I will mention only two: one from the period of the German occupation and the other from the period of the German defeat and the period of independent Polish rule.

I mentioned above the German advisers on Jewish affairs. One day, Dr. Carlebach and Dr. Cohen came to Siedlce and held a public meeting, in which they conducted propaganda for the Agudat Israel.

[Page 578]

But they did not know how to separate their role as members of the "Aguda" from their official role as advisers to the government. Our group, led by Levi Gutgeld, treated them as members of an opposing political organization, and when they began their attacks on the Zionists, we started interrupting them. When they saw that the crowd was mostly against them, they remembered their official position and called the German military police. As a result, we found ourselves a few days later, before a German interrogator as accused of harming the representatives of the occupation authorities. We claimed our claims and probably also the German interrogator understood how ridiculous the matter was and let us go.

The other episode belongs, as mentioned, to the second period. In the elections for the Polish Sejm, appeared in the town of Biala that is near Siedlce, as a Zionist candidate, Adv. A Heartglass (which was born in our town) against the candidate of the writer A. D. Numberg, that represented the Folkists. The Siedlce group was called in to help the Zionist candidate - both because of the physical proximity and because the candidate was a city resident. And again, Levi Gutgeld was the living spirit in the successful propaganda operation and organization. (As a funny episode of the propaganda of those days, I will mention one story. Heartglass, who was a delicate person, refrained from appearing in assemblies for his own benefit. Noah Prilotsky, the head of the Folkists, who appeared at the assembly in favor of Numberg, used the following argument: "Do you know, Jews, why the Zionist candidate himself did not appear before you? Because he does not know how to speak to you in your language, because he does not speak Yiddish."). In the argument that followed this speech, one from our side (Dr. late Esther Mengel) responded: Mr. Prilotsky told you that our candidate does not know how to speak to you in Yiddish. You will probably be interested to know that the Folkist candidate does not know how to speak at the Sejm, because he does not speak Polish … ").

* * *

After a while we parted ways. I left Siedlce and moved to Warsaw, to work in the secretariat of the Central Zionist Committee. We continued to meet for joint work at conferences, etc. I left Poland and moved to London in 1920, as a delegate to the Zionist conference on behalf of Tze'irei Zion, "Hapoel Hatzair"; I did not return to Poland anymore and made an Aliya to Israel in 1921.

For years we were still in touch by letters. While I was in London, Levi Gutgeld notified me about a newspaper in Yiddish that he is publishing in Siedlce and at his request, I published letters from London in this newspaper. When I made an Aliya to Israel, the letters relation between us became more and more loose until it stopped completely.

Maybe others will talk about the last period in Levi Gutgeld's life. But I'm sure that if he was asked, he would have said that the period I tried to describe was the most important and interesting period of his life.

[Page 579]

Mordechai Meir Landau

by Levi Gutgeld

Translated by Theodore Steinberg

Mordechai Meir Landau was a quiet, intelligent Jew whose mind contained European ideas and whose soul contained the subtle Jewish beauty of a Torah scholar, and from that combination emerged acuity and good humor.

Every Jewish institution in Siedlce was bound up with the name of Mordechai Meir Landau. He devoted a great deal of time, effort, and energy to the Siedlce Jewish library. Thanks to him it existed from 1904 until 1912. What it took in those years to bear the responsibility for a Jewish library – a community one, at that – under a Czarist government, how many dangers that involved – is difficult to grasp today.

Mordechai Meir Landau was born in Brisk in 1876 to very observant parents. At ten years old he was already proficient in the Talmud. At fourteen Mordechai Meir began to study in the city's beis–hamedresh, where hundreds of growing boys studied. Among them were some who had sampled the Haskalah. Mordechai Meir met them, and soon he began to hide "forbidden" books under his copy of the Gemara…

Secretly he undertook to learn languages and mathematics. But he did not leave the beis–hamedresh. The Haskalah did not tear him away from the past, for which he had deep feelings.

[Page 580]

His modest, self–effacing bearing made him beloved by everyone, and even the strict supervisors in the beis–hamedresh overlooked his "apostasy." The young student had a stepfather who helped Mordechai Meir in his secular education. He got him language teachers, particularly French and German.

In 1900, Mordechai Meir Landau arrived in Siedlce. He became the son–in–law of Y.N. Weintraub. In Siedlce, Landau became interested in community work, especially with Zionism. In 1904, the Jewish community library became legal under his name. In 1907 he created the savings and loan bank, later called the Udzhalow Bank, which we will describe elsewhere. He was also active in the Jewish business organization for mutual aid and on the relief committee after the pogrom.

In 1914, at the time of the First World War, Landau created the relief committee and worked with it in the city's citizens committee that existed during the German occupation. Later he took advantage of a public position on the city council. Landau always looked carefully after the interests of the Jewish population. Everyone paid attention to his speeches, and he even got the attention of his anti–Semitic opponents.

In 1915, Landau helped to create the Hebrew evening courses. A year later he established the local Zionist committee and in 1917 the educational organization "Da'as," which, during the First World War, conducted a Hebrew–Yiddish folk school and Jewish evening courses for young people,

When he returned from the Second Zionist Congress in 1917, his health declined. Nevertheless, at the end of 1917 he attended a meeting in honor of the Balfour Declaration. When he came to the words "Zion, will you not ask" [the opening words of a poem by Yehuda Halevi], he cried so hard that he could not finish his talk. People immediately took him home, and he never recovered from his illness.

Mordechai Meir Landau died on the thirteenth of Sivan in 1918. All of Jewish Siedlce took part in his funeral.

[Page 581]

Kalman Galitzky

by Y. Goldberg

Translated by Theodore Steinberg

— 1 —

A highly sympathetic appearance, especially favored by his pince-nez, aristocratic manners, and a ringing voice.

He was the son of a poor teacher. As was the custom, until he was 18 he was crowded onto a bench in the beis-medresh. Later he threw himself totally into the Haskalah and philosophy. He became a teacher and set up a private school.

In his school he was both the principal and the teacher. He gave lessons in Russian and Hebrew. After a hard day of work, he would sit until late into the night over philosophical texts of Kant and Hegel, Schopenhauer and Spinoza, Rambam and Ranek, swept up into higher worlds, occupied with the immortality of the soul, the meaning of life, and other sophisticated world problems.

He was greatly persecuted for his free thinking, almost to the point of excommunication. He was strongly opposed by the then rabbi of Siedlce Rabbi Dov Her Analik. The Russian government gymnasium wanted to hire Galitzky to teach religion, but the rabbi strongly opposed him to the government, not wanting to allow such an apikoros to teach religion.

A circle of the enlightened (maskilim) and young people formed around Galitzky, people who had been "caught up in the story." Quietly and in secret they would talk to him a bit about higher matters. He would help them with books from his well-stocked library and give them advice.

[Page 582]

Kalman Galitzky was one of the those who wanted to found in Siedlce an "Agudas Achim" society on the order of of Achad Ha-Am's "B'nei Moshe," whose purpose was to raise the morals of the Jewish youth and, in hindsight, to influence the older generation. In "Agudas Achim," Galitzky gave lectures, to which many people paid close attention. He was also among the founders of the organization "Jewish Art," and he spent a great deal of time there as chair.

In 1915, during the First World War, Galitzky left Siedlce along with the evacuated Russian gymnasium. He set himself up in Chernigov (Ukraine), where he experienced several terrible family catastrophes, which left him a broken man.

Once, in the middle of a talk, standing on the dais, his heart failed. He was 61. Far from his home and in foreign surroundings, he gave up his soul.

— 2 —

Yitzchok Moykher-Sforimnik

Translated by Theodore Steinberg

Yitzchak Lipietz, with his bright, homey face, good-natured, smiling eyes, and white, patriarchal beard, was known among the Jews of Siedlce as Yitzchok Moykher-Sforimnik [which means Yitzchak the Book Dealer].

Lipietz received the name "Moycher-Sforimnik" not because he dealt in books but only because he had a library and gave books to readers. He was the first librarian in Siedlce, during czarist times, before a legal library had been established.

At that time, Jewish Siedlce belonged to the most conservative and fanatical city in Poland, where maskilim suffered all kinds of persecutions. Not only was learning worldly subjects unacceptable, but learning Tanach was accounted a sin. If a young man wanted to take a look at a book of theory or to read a secular book, a "piece of uncleanness," as the religious called it, he could not be sure of his life.

Yitzchok "Moykher-Sforimnik," an idealistic maskil, ignored it all.

[Page 583]

He set up a library of Hebrew and Yiddish works, such as: "The Guide for the Perplexed," "The Kuzari," "The Wanderer in the Paths of Life"; Yiddish Maskilic books, such as: "The Black Young Man," "The Jewish Eve of Passover," Goldfaden's poems and theatrical works, Peretz' "Holiday Stories," and other current anthologies and journals.

Yitzchok Moykher-Sforimnik needed no canalogue. He knew all the book in his head and could find them in the dark. This peculiar librarian had his own system and order in relation to his readers. He loved to lose himself in conversation with his readers, to philosophize, to interrogate them about their reading, and to distribute to each one reading materials appropriate to that person.

"Yitzchok Moykher-Seforimnik" was an outstanding scholar, an expert in the Talmud and its commentators, and he was simultaneously familiar with Hebrew and Yiddish literature, sitting day and night "before the Torah and his work," digging in the detailed, faded lines of old books and inscribing his fine handwriting from cover to cover in his notebooks. Lipietz was himself and author of books. He wrote in Hebrew and in stylized Yiddish—from fables to prayer books, pious prayers, and "Yehi-Ratzons" ["May it be His will] that would draw forth tears from righteous women," a "G'dolos Moyshe" that God-fearing women would would say on Simchas Torah with great joy, inscriptions on tombstones, and so on. Yitzchok Lipietz was himself a religious, careful Jew, but his religion did not prevent him from partaking in the Haskalah and getting readers for his library.

The following compositions came from his pen: "Chanukat Ha-Chashmonim," "Im L'mikra U'l'msorat," "Pach Ha-shemen," "Mishlei Avot," "M'ta-amim," "Ve'haya Mishneh," "Binat N'vonim," "M'ta-amim Ha-chodesh," "Shivchei Knesset HYisrael," "Succat Shalom," and others. Despite the scores of books that he published, which enriched the publishers, the author lived all his life in poverty; he also did not concern himself with whether readers paid for the books they borrowed or even whether they returned them.

Early on, Yitzchok Moykher-Sforim loaned his book secretly. Later on, all of Siedlce's Jews knew that R. Yitzchok "ruined" young people with his books, but respect for him was so great that even the most religious people did not want to take action against him.

[Page 584]

Yitzchok Lipietz was truly the pioneer of modern Jewish culture in Siedlce and the first distributor of Jewish books.

Yosef Rosenvasser

Translated by Theodore Steinberg

The Jewish national revival movement at the end of the nineteenth century resonated broadly among the Jewish youth of Siedlce. Interest in national problems and in community action increased.

The nationally inclined young people organized themselves in a Zionist group, at the head of which stood the temperamental and elderly Yosef Rosenvasser, or, as he was known—Yossl the Cantor's Son.

Yosef Rosenvasser had invested tremendous effort in organizing the Siedlce library, which was later taken over by the "Yiddishe Kunst" organization.

When the library was beginning, the great question was—where to get books. There was no money to buy them. They therefore had to seek private donations. Rosenvasser applied himself to this work, and he even approached a Russian baron, an officer from the local Russian garrison, Baron von Kleist, asking him to give books from their collection for the Jewish library.

[Page 585]

How did Yosef the Cantor's Son come to the haughty Baron von Kleist?

Rosenvasser's acquaintance with the officer stemmed from the cigarette business. Yossl was a specialist in making cigarettes. He learned the art of fixing different types of tobacco to satisfy the taste of the Russian officers.

Baron von Kleist became friendly with the Jewish cigarette maker, and in conversation proved himself to be a friend of the Jews and a believer in Zionism. Rosenvasser told his Russian friend about the Jewish library that the Zionist youth were establishing and about the dearth of books. Baron von Kleist quickly gave to the library a significant sum and a large number of valuable books in Russian and German. His example inspired the manufacturer Feigenbaum, who donated a large number of Polish books by famous authors.

These foreign-language books formed the basis for the library. Yosef Rosenvasser and his Zionist group organized a fundraiser and bought Yiddish and Hebrew books.

In 1900, when the library was in operation, Rosenvasser was satisfied with his work and and was happy that he had been allowed to lay the foundation for the Jewish library in Siedlce.

[Page 586]

The Feldsher A. Gron

by Yakov Tenenbaum

Translated by Theodore Steinberg

[A "feldsher" was an unlicensed medical person, rather like the old–fashioned "barber–surgeons" who may be familiar from eighteenth–century novels.]

The feldspar A. Gron never graduated from a university; I guess he never had a middle–school education. Still, he healed sick people and was loved by his patients. People told wonderful stories about him, as for example: "Doctors had given up on my life, but Gron came, cure, and the illness disappeared as if by a wave of the hand."

Gron knew how much confidence his patients had in him, but that did not encourage him…he was anything but pleased. Gron really hated his vocation. He loved medicine as a form of knowledge, but not as a profession from which to earn an income.

A good friend of his once confided to him that he would take an exam to be a feldsher. Gron warned him not to undertake such foolishness because he would regret it for his whole life. And here is what was amazing: He himself was at the top of the local feldspar organization, where for many years he was the vice–chair and secretary, fighting tooth and nail for the interests of feldspars, even though in his private life he opposed the feldsher vocation. "Doctors without 'titles'" – he would say – "should not exist…People ask of us even more than they ask of doctors, and that makes the attitude and treatment of the society of feldshers so miserable…Our misfortune is that we do not have a free hand. Although we are open to all approaches, we lack independence. On the one hand we are exploited and overused by the community, while on the other hand we are hated by the doctors for the competition that we give them."

[Page 587]

Gron was quite capable of standing at the top of his vocation, so that he could be compared not simply to a bad doctor, he knew anatomy as well as he knew the fingers of his hand, and he often loved to interrogate young doctors in the hospital. He would pose questions to them that none of them could answer…He also used to say that doctors could have no love for an intelligent feldsher.

Gron also had a poetic spark and used to write a great deal. Most successful is something he wrote about his own death: He describes an early morning…A lament comes from the house at Pilsudski 48 (where he lived for a number of years). A Jewish woman goes by with a basket of rolls and wonders why people are crying. They answer, "Gron the feldsher has died." "Oh! Vay! Vay! He healed everyone and couldn't help himself!" He did not finish the sketch. And why not? He said, "Life itself will complete it…"

And so it was: He died shortly thereafter.

[Page 588]

Hershel Tenenbaum, of Blessed Memory

by F. Drumy (Popovsky)

Translated by Theodore Steinberg

I met Hershel Tenenbaum one evening in 1916 through a Hebrew course. After that, I saw him at all the Zionist meetings and social events. He always sat quietly and listened. He never took part in the discussions, and when action was decided upon, like collecting funds or taking political action, he participated quietly and modestly, earnestly and precisely.

He was also very exacting about work in the Jewish community, and even at the time when his father, R. Yitzchok, was the secretary and he, the son, helped him in his work, he tried to a certain extent to improve his father's work, although his father was responsible and not Hershel.

When he became the official secretary of the Jewish community and was in fact responsible for the work, he showed no partiality to anyone. Even from his father he expected more precision in observing his work hours, and he gave him advice about his daily work.

In 1926. when he was selected as a member of the community board, I began to work more closely with Hershel Tenenbaum. I saw in him a man who was trustworthy and responsible in keeping his word. He took care that the decisions of the board or the council should be carried out, even when he was not happy with them because they were not in accordance with his convictions,.

[Page 589]

At the time, the Agudah had a majority not he community board. He used to say: "What's done is done – we have to carry it out."

So quiet, peaceful Tenenbaum, who lived to carry out all the decisions of the higher authorities, did not carry out the decisions…

As Siedlce Jews who survived the Holocaust relate, there were instances when the "Jewish council" did not pay the full tribute [demanded by the Germans] or when they did not fulfill the orders of the Germans. The Gestapo summoned Hershel Tenenbaum and asked why the "Jewish council" had not carried out the orders exactly. Hershel always responded that he was guilty and not the "Jewish council." "I," he would answer, "cannot carry it out." He received blows from them, but that did not persuade him to blame anyone else.

Thus did the quiet and peaceful Zionist soldier take on his responsibility for the Siedlce Jewish populace in normal times and demonstrate energy and national pride when the danger of the German murderers hung over his head.

He was tortured to death by the Germans along with his wife and two children.

[Page 590]

My Teachers

Y. Goldberg

Translated by Theodore Steinberg

My teachers were each men of distinction. Not as pedagogues, heaven forbid, but in another way. Aside from teaching, each of them had a vocation, a specialty from which they derived a bit of an income. To this day I do not know which was more important to them, their teaching or their craft. Let me memorialize several types of Siedlce's teachers.

Itzele Boich [Paunch]

My first teacher, who first showed me the clef-beys, was—the elementary teacher Itzele, or, as he was known to us, "Itzele Paunch," because for a teacher, he had a large stomach. He had a scratchy voice, like a chazan after Ne'ilah. This hoarseness gave him a certain respect. The city considered him the best elementary teacher, and all the highest class people thought it was required to send him their children.

As I later came to realize, he did not know more than a little Hebrew, and as to the meanings of words—not at all. Still, after teaching us the syllables, he jumped right to Chumash. But Chumash meant not Genesis and not Exodus, but Leviticus.

The cheder consisted of a big room with a low beamed ceiling and two windows that looked over the courtyard. The walls were grey, though every Pesach they were whitewashed, and the floor was washed when it was not Pesach, and also when the "director" would come, once a year, to examine "Russian language" and to give out "awards."

[Page 591]

This room was divided by a thin wall, behind which was the rabbi's "bedroom." That same bedroom bordered on the kitchen and the baking oven, under which was a storage area in which to put chickens and with which they used to frighten the children by saying they would be put there if they misbehaved. Opposite the door there were a washtub and a bucket for cleaning and next to those a bed.

Behind the wall, in the "bedroom," lay the rebbetzin, who was lame and moaned. When the rabbi was not in the room, the children would carry on and make a mess. This would upset the ailing rebbetzin, who, wanting to get even with the "delinquents," would call with a weak voice to one or two of the students and, taking them by the hand, use her skinny fingers to give them a sharp pinch on the arm, which they would not soon forget. Thus would she quell her anger.

Boys and girls learned together. The boys were in cheer from eight in the morning until nine in the evening, and the girls would come for a few hours. At the head of the table would sit Itzele with his greasy hat on his head. In his right hand—the "pointer" and by his side the whip with its rawhide. With his hoarse voice he would say quietly: "Kametz alef—o. Kametz beis—bo." Across from the rabbi said Avraml, the assistant, who liked to pinch the girls while they were learning. The second assistant—Chaim—would bring the children to school and take them home and take care of their needs.

When someone would bring food for a child, the rabbi would take the parcel, examine the portion, nimbly put a part of the cutlet in his sleeve, and then divide the rest in pieces, saying to the child: "You see? I made a lot for you. so give me a littler for my Moyshele." Naturally he would not wait for an answer, and he took a sizable portion for his son. Two or three times a day we would study with the rabbi and his assistants for five or ten minutes a time. But we were kept busy the whole day.

[Page 592]

At R. Itzele's we made a certain kind of "goat". that would be sold at the fair on market days. Each child would receive a piece of dough from which to make little goats. They were made in the following way: one took a piece of dough and rolled it out in his hands. Then one formed two horns on top and four legs on the bottom. Then it was baked until it turned a light brown. People in the market bought them for a groschen each. For this "labor," the rabbi allowed us to play for a couple of hours each day, a nd some would get a pinch on the cheek for being a good boy.

Chaim the assistant had the job of making Chanukah dreidels, graggers and Haman-noisemakers, pennants for Simchas Torah and bows [presumably for Lag B'Omer], and we would help. Once, I remember it clearly, he lacked some red paint for making the stripes on some bows. Without thinking, he pricked his finger and used the blood to make the red stripes on the bows.

In addition to being a businessman, the rabbi was a bit of an entrepreneur. He dealt with fowl, which would lay eggs in the storage area, and with a goat, which provided milk for the ailing rebbetzin. Sometimes when there rabbi would ask a student, "Nu, what sound does kametz alef make?' the chickens would answer, "Cu-cu-ri-cu!" And the goat would add, "Mehhhh!" In this way the chickens and the goats grew up with the children of the wealthy, and we would often wonder what kind of reincarnations they were!

Before we left for home, the rabbi would station himself by the door, allowing the children to leave one by one, saying to each of them: "For God's sake, tell them at home that you learned with me three times, that you ate your whole meal. If they ask if anyone struck you, you must say no."

"Good night, Rabbi!"

"For God's sake, come early tomorrow!—good night and good year.

[Page 593]

Yoshe Nose

From Itzele Paunch the elementary teacher, I went on to Yoshe Nose, the Gemara teacher. His school was near the cemetery, not far from the shul. Altogether there were 10-12 students there.

This rabbi got his nickname because he had a flat nose and spoke very nasally. Instead of a beard, he had only a few yellow hairs, He looked a lot like a Chinese person without the pigtail that the Chinese used to wear—instead he had two pigtails, one either side of his face—two braided side-curls.

His rebbetzin was a tall, thin woman with red-circled eyes. She was always occupied. She ran a big business with geese. Whole carts with wooden crates would come to the door of our school and then disappear down the road that led to Warsaw. But always running around in the courtyard of the school were scores of fat white geese that there rebbetzin each week would sneak away and transport to the wealthy homeowners.

These flocks of white geese, around whom we worked, took on fantastic forms in my childish mind, and when it came to there Talmudic legend of Rabbah Bar Bar Chana, it seemed to us that we saw the "white geese" with our own eyes. [Rabbah Bar Bar Chana was involved with a number of fantastic stories, including one that included giant geese.]

With Yoshe Nose we studied Chumash, Rashi, and Gemara. Sometimes when we were learning, we would play a game or play with "buttons," and when the rabbi noticed us, from anger he would shove a dirty finger into his mouth and bite until it bled. More than once, he would unbutton our pants and swat us, counting "one plus one, one plus two" until we assured him that we would no longer do it. Aside from whippings, we also were subjected to "packages." The rabbi would choose a student who had misbehaved, unbutton him, take out his shirt, bind his arms, and put heavy things on his shoulders, things like boots, for example. The student would have to stand in this way for a couple of hours. Meanwhile moisture would leak from his eyes, from his nose, and from his mouth.

[Page 594]

During our learning time, there was often a black "kozele" (named for a fragrant resin) in the shape of a lump of sugar, about the size of a half of a finger. This "kozele" the rabbi had bought in the pharmacy for a few groschen each and stood it on a glass of water that was covered with a piece of paper. When the "kozele" was lit, it smoked for a long time, until it burned through the paper and fell into the water. Later the rabbi would take it out, let it dry out, and then use it again. It was a kind of disinfectant against evil spirits that arose during the lesson…in order to determine who was guilty, the students would often touch their noses—and woe to that student who had a warm nose…During the break, we were put out in the courtyard and turned over to the geese.

I left Yoshe Nose in the following circumstances: One Shabbos, after napping, the rabbi came to hear my lessons. My father chose a Talmudic passage and called on me to recite it. My recitation did not go well. Suddenly I felt a sharp pinch on my leg that felt like a burn on the thick part of my leg, and I jumped away. My father was surprised and did not understand what had just happened. When my recitation ended, I told my father about that vicious pinch that the rabbi had given me. This story caused my father to reprimand the rabbi strongly and take me away from him.

Avraml Koshke

This teacher belonged to the same category as the earlier one that my father had exchanged for Yoshe Nose. He was called Avraham and came from More.

[Page 595]

Because everyone from that town was known to us as Koshkes—he was known as Avraml Koshke. Avraml was no sleepyhead. He was a modern person. He had worked for "noblemen." He was always telling tales and wonders about "Russia."

From that period I remember several students. One, a butcher's son, was an only child whose mother had gotten him with the help of a "good Jew" and who, when he was born, his father "paid for him" with gold coins that he had vowed for sacred needs.

The boy wore white linen clothing for his health, and he was quite nervous. They were always bring things to school for him to perk him up. In school we always worried about him, because he was wild and daring. so it was dangerous to provoke him.

The rabbi really suffered because of him. He used to pour tobacco into his grits, so that the rabbi would choke, and he would direct strong curses at the rebbetzin. When the rabbi napped, he would glue his beard to the table with sealing wax. When the rabbi awoke, he would tear out part of his beard. Once when Rabbi Avraml wanted to punish him, he took out a "gypsy" knife and slit the rabbi's trousers from top to bottom so that the rabbi stood there in his underwear.

The rabbi had a student who was cross-eyed. His eyes seemed to be angry with each other: when one eye looked to the north, the second, as if in anger, looked to the south. Furthermore, he couldn't properly pronounce many letters of the alphabet.

One afternoon he interrupted our class and cried out, "Priends. My mother had a pig. It dave a swill when it was scored, so they shot it." [This is an attempt to render the gibberish that the author presents. He adds that in actuality the boy's mother had given birth to a deformed child. *Translator's note:* this is a really distasteful story about a child who obviously had some physical problems.]

[Page 596]

The study day began as we busied ourselves with "fritters." That dish was traditional with all teachers from time immemorial, though in other schools only the rebbetzin made the fritters. In addition to the fritters, each child patronized the "bean woman," as we called there Jewish women who sold peas and beans and cherries.

The rabbi himself was always occupied with some kind of business. He had to get things ready for the rebbetzin, who had a "stall" at the market. The rabbi was a specialist in making paintbrushes. And we assisted him in this work. We would lay out the individual bristles for the brush, get them all ready, cut the wooden handles, and the rabbi would bind the brushes and with a sharp ax he would even them out.

When we finished this task, we would take a turn at learning. But while we were learning, the rabbi always had other work. He would take pieces of copper, put them on an iron form, and hammer out "three-ers," (coins worth three Russian groschen), perfect and round as the real thing, and with these "three-ers" he would buy cheap tobacco and other necessities. He would take a box of matches and split each match into two or four pieces and twist them up in blotting paper like cigarettes. They had the habit of extinguishing themselves all the time.

Tuesdays and Fridays were market days. The rabbi would help the rebbetzin at her stall and then come home after half a day. Each time he would leave, he would tell us that we should review our lessons. But as soon as he had closed the door behind him, we played games like "kama-kama-tir" and "sharde-barde," and we would give each other potches. The students knew all kinds of tricks. The spoiled kid specialized in rolling back his eyelids and frightening everyone. A second kid specialized in curling his tongue and making four "figs" with both hands. Thus we amused ourselves until the end of the day.

[Page 597]

On Fridays after lunch, when the rabbi returned from the market, while the rebbetzin remained at her stall, he would bring back in his big red handkerchief little fish and prepare them for Shabbos. He would cut the fish as we went over that week's Torah portion. If someone got something wrong, he would grab him by the ear and pinch him until it hurt like fire.

None of this bothered us, because we knew that we would soon be free for half the day on Friday and for all of Shabbos. We were so excited that we quickly forgot the pinches and the Torah melody, the potches and the ear-pullings; and like freed birds we whooped and shouted as we quickly ran through the streets and alleys.

Yoshe Mottl Heshe's

My rabbi was called Yoshe, and with his father's name: so Yoshe Mottl's. But since his wife Heshe was the boss in the house, people called him by the full name Yoshe Mottl Heshe's.

My rabbi was considered the best Gemara teacher in the city. He was not much more than a neglected pauper, like all teachers. He had a proverb or a saying for everything, which he used to convey with a throaty voice.

He had studied in a modern way, with a particular style. He knew how to make clear a bit of Midrash or Tanach with the commentary of Malbim. Sometimes he would come out with liberal idea that had stayed with him from the bygone time of the Haskalah, to which he had been connected.

The rebbetzin Heshe dealt in lime. Mean and talkative, she was always at odds with her competitors, whom she covered with curses and threats. Her wig, which was always sprinkled with lime, used to fall over to one side, and her face was always inflamed.

The rabbi had great difficulty with her, but he always kept silent about it.

The lime, which was always in their place and on the street, often covered the students as well as the rabbi and rebbbetzin.

[Page 598]

People would drive up a wagon of lime. We would have to unload it and then help to prepare it. We would help to pour the dry material, then pour water, mix it with a special tool, filter it, and cover it with boards until it was set.

Understand that our clothes would be covered with lime and our boots would be as white as milk.

Among the students in the school was one who never took part in this labor. He only observed from a distance. He was the son of a rich old wood merchant. So dainty and slim, he was like a newborn. This young man had never tasted butter, schmaltz, milk, eggs, or meat. He had never tasted fruit. He lived only on liquids. He drank tea in an original manner: into a glass full of sugar, someone would pour a bit of tea, which he would drink. With the sugar that remained in the glass, the rebbetzin could make do for the rest of the week.

No one ever struck him, because he was very high-strung. If someone disturbed him, he would scratch his nose until it bled, so that the rabbi would lay a cold key on him, moisten his handkerchief and put it on his nose, and pacify him as one might a small child.

When we studied, we were always so tired that we took naps, and that is how we learned.

Right in the middle of our studies, suddenly there would be a knock at the door and on the threshold there would be a whitewashed non-Jew with a clay dipper who would yell out: "I need lime."

The rabbi would lay his handkerchief on the page and tell us to review our lesson and he would be right back. His sons would go with him. And we—instead of reviewing our lesson—would play word games, like making up nonsense sentences based on the first letters of words.

[Page 599]

[***Translator's note:*** He gives examples of these games which are untranslatable.] We made our own "telephones" from a string with two matchboxes, one on each end.

We also discussed politics, each of us sticking firmly to his convictions. We also knew that the emperor's portrait, which hung in every classroom, was such that when the emperor died, its appearance would change…

Aside from the workman who wouldn't. Buy lime and would interrupt our studies, we were rescued by sundry other people. Thus, we would suddenly be visited by the lottery man. From his red handkerchief he would pull out, as if by magic, a silver Chanukah with lions, an alarm clock with a cuckoo that he would play for us (such a pleasure), a spice box with a tower and a little pennant at its top. Each student would buy a lottery ticket, in the expectation of great luck. Another time we would be visited by a man who placed on the table a model of the "mishkan" that he had made with great skill according to the description in the Chumash. We did not know whether to regard the "mishkan" or the man, who had a head like a government minister and who told us that that had served him well throughout his life. Yet another time we were visited by a man with huge eyebrows and a black tangled beard. For two groschen he allowed us to look into a box that contained beautiful pictures that enchanted our souls.

Avraham-Hersh

Quite different was my last teacher—Avraham-Hersh Assine. If I have described my earlier teachers with a certain frivolity, for Avraham Hersh I have want to express the deepest respect and gratitude.

[Page 600]

Even before the advent of "improved schools," with their new methods, Avraham Hersh understood what people needed to learn. He hated pilpul, hairsplitting, and simplifications. He loved clear learning, learning that was correct and tasteful. My rabbi was then a young man of around thirty. He was tall, with childlike ears. His face was creased and surrounded by a thin black beard.

He was the model of a true, devoted maskil, imbued with that spirit. Earlier he had read the most recent Hebrew and Yiddish books, and he loved to share his thoughts and feelings with his students.

One of his closest and most devoted friends was a young man named Yankl Pigove, a very interesting person. His very name indicated that the young man was an apikoros and an all-around malicious fellow. He frightened all the religious Jews of the city.

This Yankl Pigove was the son of a poor tailor, whose family was referred to by the surname "Gypsy." [***Author's footnote:*** There is an interesting story about this name in Siedlce, but I will relate that elsewhere.]. He was a hot-headed young man who was granted rabbinical permission to study. He knew the entire Tanach by heart, and he quickly learned Russian, German, French, and many other subjects. He also put together a Hebrew dictionary, which a publisher issued with a few changes and called his own. Because of his status as an apikoros, he was as if excommunicated, and even the freethinkers were hesitant to be seen in the street with him. Even so, my rabbi was friendly with him, and although he could have lost his teaching position because of him, this Yankl Pilove was his constant guest.

[Page 601]

Of the four or five students who studied with Avraham Hersh, the rabbi showed special attention to two: myself and Yankl Yoln [fn.—Yoel Mastbaum, the well-known Yiddish writer]. whom he treated with special love and attention after our lessons were over. When all the children left for home, we remained, and the rabbi would read with us books like "Ahavas-Tzion," "Ashmas-Shomron," and "Ayit Tzavua" by Mapu and other Hebrew books.

On those beautiful summer evenings, we three—the rabbi and his two students—went walking outside the city and the rabbi would show us the beauties of nature, where everything is "wonderful, harmonious, and Godlike." He would be delighted with the landscape and with the gorgeous sunsets. Avraham Hersh would enthusiastically study the prophets with us, using a special tune, singing "The vision of Isaiah ben Amotz"…and other verses so that they entered one's soul. And we felt as though the prophet Isaiah stood there on a high mountain with a snow-white beard and spoke to the rebellious children of Israel.

Sometimes a restless spirit that offered no peace would occupy the soul of this man; then he would take up his fiddle—he had an old, broken instrument—and play different Jewish tunes and songs. Sometimes he would paint landscapes and figures.

On the eve of Rosh Hashanah he would be busy painting special new year greetings on pink sheets of paper. On these sheets he would paint lions and eagles, garlands, mosaics in different colors, gold and silver, and in the middle he would inscribe with professional lettering flowery wishes for the new year.

These new year wishes would be bought by young men and women, mostly brides and grooms, who paid well for them. His specialty, however, was woodcarving.

Near our school lived Yidl Sholkis [fn.—First a teacher, then a noted woodcarver, at that time the first and only one in Siedlce]. My rabbi, Avraham-Hersh, would often visit him, to observe his work, which pleased him greatly.

[Page 602]

Not long after, he made the tools he made—actually one that combined functions—and soon he was an accomplished woodcarver and earned some income in that way. While we were learning, there sat on the table the twisted leg of a piece of furniture, a piece of a headboard for a bed, or a cornice from an oak closet—and the rabbi would carve with a chisel while we learned. He would dig away with his pick! We would carve out a half-finished page and make connections between them. And we would divide our attention between the Chumash and the carving.

The rabbi's artwork had a tremendous effect on us students. When we arrived home from school, Yoel would try to paint pictures, while I—tried a variety of activities. I made hourglasses, water machines in which the water circulated and…fiddles. One time, this resulted in a battle between Joel and me. I had made a fiddle and showed it to Yoel for his criticism. Instead of saying anything, Yoel grabbed the fiddle and would not return it. I grabbed his hat and ran into my house. Yoel followed me into the furthest room and asked for his hat back. And I—for the fiddle, which he had broken out of anger. Unable to come to an agreement, Yoel closed the door and said to me:

"You're taking my hat? You won't get away alive," and he showed me a crude knife…

I saw that he was deathly pale, with bulging eyes, with his knife at the ready, so without hesitation I returned his hat.

* * *

Aside from these jobs, the rabbi also wrote essays. He wrote a guide to Hebrew grammar based on the Tanach, accompanied by a simplified translation in Yiddish.

I remember that one time an unknown man ent4red the classroom, an old man with a pack of books. The rabbi picked one up and began to sing.

[Page 603]

What do I see through the window?

They are coming like doves…

[Fn.—These words come from a folk song by Elyakum Zunzer called "Shivas Tzion."]

Later I learned that the old man was an author and that he had translated into Hebrew poems by Elyakum Zunser and Goldfaden. The rabbi was close to him and gave him addresses where he could bring his "merchandise."

The rabbi had a long and difficult war with the rebbetzin. He wanted his son and his daughter to be educated people, but learning did not come easily to them, particularly to the son, so he tried to force upon him Russian grammar and exercises. Consequently, in the school all hell broke loose and the rebbetzin would scream, "Nu! And what if he doesn't know...."Rifmatik. So he won't be a "doctor." I don't care."

So it went for the rabbi. He wanted his son to have what he had been unable to get. Consequently, he acted with us, his students, especially Yoel and myself, more like a friend, generous and faithful. He remains in my memory until this very day.

[Page 604]

Folk Stories of Siedlce

A Siedlce Conversion Story

by Yitzkhok-Nakhum Weintraub

Translated by Theodore Steinberg

The story that I am about to tell is sad, like many other stories from old Siedlce. It is not recorded in any other chronicle. It was told by older people, who kept it in their memories.

It happened right after the revolution in 1863. In the village of Wimishli [?], near Siedlce, lived a Jew named Yitzchok-Yosl who had a lease on the Wimishli mill. Yitzchok-Yosl was a simple Jew and was known as a respectable person. One day, so the story goes, something broke in the mill, so Yitzchok-Yosl brought in a repairman from Germany to fix the mill. Eventually Yitzchok-Yosl could not come to terms with the repairman over the price and they argued. In the course of their argument, the German said to Yitzchok-Yosl, "Just wait. You will remember me for eternity."

From that point on, Yitzchok-Yosl was a different person. He departed from the path of righteousness, began to drink and did other bad things. And of course you understand that he did not take care of his business. It struck everyone that his wife, who was a respectable and modest woman, had to witness his misdeeds.

[Page 605]

Yitzkhok-Yosl had a Jewish servant who noted the change that had overcome his boss, and she mentioned it to his wife. Yitzkhok-Yosl's wife not knowing what to do, wrote to Vengrow, his home town, to his family, saying that someone should come and help return him to his senses. Not long after, Yitzchoko-Yosl's two brothers came to Wimishli. Seeing that Yitzkhok-Yosl had abandoned Jewish customs and crossed himself frequently, they deduced that he had gone crazy; they bound his hands and confined him to a room, hoping that the madness would pass. But they saw no improvement in him; instead he got worse: even when his hands were bound, he would lick crosses on his books.

With a great deal of effort, the brothers persuaded Yitzkhok-Yosl to go with them to the rabbi R. Yitzkhok in Neskhizh. When the brothers came to the rabbi and explained to him about their mission, he answered that there was no hope of recovery. They returned to Wimishli and dropped Yitzchoko-Yosl there. Within a couple of weeks, Yitzkhok-Yosl had converted and adopted the faith of Pravoslava. Yitzkhok-Yosl had two children, 10 and 4 years of age. He took the ten-year-old to convert with him. The younger child fled with the wife to Siedlce where she tried to protect him from conversion.

The apostate was very irritated that his wife had done such a thing, so he went to Warsaw to the current governor general, Graf Berg, and petitioned him. The governor general strongly ordered the Siedlce governor Gromeko and the police chief Modrach that they should see the child who was with his mother and deliver him to the Pravoslava faith.

It was not long before the police chief had, with the help of threats, found the mother and took her child. With the governor's permission, the police chief adopted for himself this child, treating him like his own. He did not know, however, who should teach the child, because Police Chief Modrach had no other children, so he handed him over to a Paroslava barber-surgeon from the quarantine station. The barber surgeon lived at 11 Pienkne Road, in the house of R. Yitzkhok-Gad Kornblum. The child, longing for his mother, screamed and could by no means get along with his new teacher.

The mother would come every day to R. Yitzkhok-Gad to see her child, but the barber-surgeon would not allow it. He maintained that he was responsible for him and that he had been told he should pay special attention to the child and not allow the mother to see him. After great efforts, the mother succeeded in persuading him to allow her to see her son once a day and give him a kiss.

However, after a time the child got used to his new situation and began to speak Russian. At the same time, he was taught to hate Jews. He refused to speak Yiddish to his mother. The mother did not rest, however, and devoted all her energies to figuring out how to get her child out of the Christians' hands. At that time the rabbi of Siedlce was R. Yisroel Meyzlish. The mother came to him every day to see if he could succeed in getting her child.

R. Yisroel Meyzlish gave her a letter for his father, R. Berish Meyzlish of Warsaw, so that he might do something about the matter.

R. Berish said that he could do nothing. It was known that R. Meyzlish had taken part in the Polish revolution of 1863. After the revolution was put down, he was followed by the czarist government, so that he could take no action.

But R. Berish Meyzlish gave the mother advice. If she could accomplish nothing through the administration, she should try through the courts. The courts at that time were Polish. So the mother submitted the matter to the court. As she had been advised, she maintained that the child's father was not her husband, Yitzkhok-Yosl, and consequently he had no right to have the child converted. She maintained that the child's father, was someone else. She found someone else who came to the court as the child's father. Police Chief Modrach, however, maintained that the child was a Pravoslaver and no one else had any rights over him.

[Page 607]

Because of missing evidence, the mother lost the case and the child remained with the barber-surgeon.

Seeing that all of her efforts to regain her child had failed, she went to the Amshinov rabbi, R. Dovid, may his memory be a blessing, a son of R. Yitzkhok Vorker and a comrade of R. Mendel of Kotzk, may his memory be a blessing. She asked his advice. R. Dovid was very active in community affairs and had a good heart. Having heard her story, he promised her to come specially to Siedlce and to consider what could be done.

Indeed R. Dovid came to Siedlce a couple of days later and consulted with R. Yisroel Meyzlish. They realized that there was no legitimate way to succeed, so the only solution was to get the child through trickery. through deceit.

At that time there was a Jew in Siedlce named Kalman Grayanski (the first of that family, who had the nickname "Kosheces"). Kalman Grayanski was a very energetic and heroic Jew, who feared nothing, and R. Dovid Anshinover and R. Yisroel Meyzlish ascertained that Kalman was willing to undertake the job. They sent for Kalman Grayanski and told him about the whole business and promised him that he could earn a spot in the World to Come if he carried it off. They shook hands on the agreement that he would tell no one about their talk. He would rescue the child, and once he had taken the child from the barber surgeon's room, he would take him to R. Dovid in Amshinov.

Kalman Grayanski called together a group of his friends, and each one swore that he would tell no one what they had talked about. Kalman brought the whole troupe to R. Dovid and R. Dovid told them how to proceed.

Kalman and his troupe began to surveil the house where the barber surgeon lived, and they were certain that he had gone to Warsaw for medicines for the quarantine station, so that his wife was alone with the child. They seized that moment to set a watch around the house that night, and they blocked the doors and windows of the neighboring houses, tying them with rope so that they could not be opened.

[Page 608]

They did the same to the doors and windows of the barber surgeon's dwelling. They left only one window free, through which they entered the house. The barber surgeon's wife, seeing this sudden attack in the middle of the night, set up a yell that people were trying to take the Jewish child, and she fought back, wrestling with them. The rescuers, having no other choice, tied her up, stopped up her mouth, and took the child out through the open window, which they then blocked up so that no one could get out.

In the house of R. Yitzkhok Gad, the same house where the barber surgeon lived, they heard the yells of the wife. R. Yitzkhok Gad's tenants, however, could not tell where the screams were coming from because the doors and the windows were shut up tight. Eventually the cries drew the police, who opened up the blocked doors and windows. Seeing what had happened, the police turned on R. Yitzkhok Gad, because he was the nearest neighbor. According to police procedures, R Yitzkhok and his wife were taken to jail. Other nearby homeowners were also arrested, among whom was R. Shimon Greenberg, may his memory be a blessing, about whom the barber surgeon had said that he offered him 1000 rubles for the possibility of taking the child away at night.

The Jews of Siedlce then had some difficult days. Governor Gromeko and Police Chief Modrach were among the most earnest in their offices that Siedlce had ever seen. And while there was no pogrom, still the Jews experienced much trouble. A thorough inquest was begun into those who had been arrested. Eventually all of them were released, except for R. Yitzkhok Gad, who was frequently visited in prison by the investigators, who had R. Yitzkhok beaten to make him reveal who had taken the child.

R. Berish Meyzlish undertook a vigorous intercession to have R. Yitzkhok Gad released, because there was no evidence against him. This intercession succeeded and he was released.

[Page 609]

And what happened with the rescued child? Since the police were certain that the child had been kidnapped, they set up guards at all the roads out of the city and inspected everyone who tried to leave, but they never found the child. He was held in a secure place.

When the watch around the city was removed, the child was taken to Amshinov to R, Dovid, who brought him up. Only a very few knew about this. To everyone else it was a secret, and no one knew where the child had gone.

* *

Some years later, R. Yitzkhok Gad received an invitation to a wedding in Brisk. On the invitation, the representative of the groom's side was listed as R. Dovid of Amshinov. At first R. Yitzkhok Gad did not know who the groom was, but later he understood that the groom was that child who had been rescued from apostasy. The Amshinov rabbi had wanted to please r. Yitzkhok Gad, because he had taken such a large role in the story.

Kalman Grayanski and his friends upheld the oath that no one would discuss the matter. After a time, when people learned about it, people praised them for their devotion and for their willingness to act. It was said about them: "Even the simple men among you are as full of good deeds as a pomegranate."

* *

The fate of the apostate Yitzkhok-Yosl: In his old age he became a beggar and begged for alms at Jewish homes.

[Page 610]

"Devils"
(From Stories of Siedlce)

by Yehoshua Goldberg

Translated by Theodore Steinberg

There was a family by us that was known as the "Devils." They were not evil people or scoffers before whom people trembled. On the contrary, they were quiet people who would not have harmed a fly on the wall. They received their nickname as an inheritance from a father who had an amazing story.

The father was simply named Yossl. People called him Yossl Baker, because he had a shop with baked goods and rustic challah at the end of the marketplace where on Tuesdays and Fridays, the market days, the peasants from the surrounding areas would come with wagons of bread, potatoes, and other produce. They went to Yossl to buy baked goods and the rustic challah, which was baked in big pans and covered with oil and baked onions.

Yossl was a Jew of fifty-something, with small, lively eyes. Because his beard was always covered with flour, one could not tell if it was gray or black. The peasants liked him, because he was a wise man and conversed with them, patted their shoulders, and gave them advice on a variety of matters.

There was one peasant, Antony, a tall, hearty man with watery gray eyes and a blond mustache. This Antony felt close to Yossl and after the market hours he would come around, unbutton his coat, shake all of his receipts out of his pockets and onto the counter, where bits of noodles lay. He counted and counted, but he could never get it right. Yossl would have to help him. Then he would calm down, take a pastry and a glass of tea.

[Page 611]

One time Antony sat with Yossl in the cubicle looking downcast, his hands stretched out and resting on his knees, his eyes looking at the ground, his hat askew. Yossl asked him, "Is Antony upset?"

He did not respond.

Yossl drew nearer, put his hand on Antony's shoulder and asked quietly, "What's wrong? I can see that you're very upset. Are you missing money? Did someone steal from you?"

Antony slowly raised his watery gray eyes, looked around absently, and finally he said to Yossl, "Dear Yossl, I am so unhappy!" And he told him a whole story: Devils had shown up, had tormented him for a long time and made a shambles of his home; they killed sheep, lamed horses, and spoiled the milk of his cows.

Hearing this story, Yossl thought, "It would be a good thing to play a trick on him to make him dismiss such thoughts of devils.

"Truly I see," he said to the downcast goy [sic], "that this is something new for Antony. More than once I myself have had to deal with this bunch, and, dear friend, I got rid of them. But Antony should know: the people have a custom that if they gang up on one and move in with one, one cannot get rid of them with pokers or shovels. One should not give up and see what happens.

These words aroused the peasant and he begged Yossl for good advice for dealing with the demons.

Yossl advised Antony that first of all one should ask if he has perhaps insulted the demons with with a word or curse, so that they have come to get even.

In order to plead with the demons, one should prepare: a bottle of strong whisky, "96", almonds, two eggs, geese and a black hen. One has to take these things into the ruin near the old mill.

[Page 612]

"And as the sun sets," Yossl advised, "one must carry them backwards into the ruin and then wait outside until the middle of the night. At exactly midnight, the Samorad demon will appear. He will converse with you and you will be able to appease him."

This advice really pleased the peasant. He heartily shook his hand and promised to do everything just as he had told him.

On the designated day, Yossl prepared a lantern covered with black paper, that showed only two round lights, that were covered with red paper, and in it he put a little light. He took a fur piece with long disheveled hair, a long paper bag with a hood. and he went to the ruin near the old mill.

He sat there and waited. Then he saw Antony coming in the distance with a loaded wagon, so he hid in a corner. Antony stood there, looked around for a minute until the sun would go down further in the west. Then he took everything out of the wagon, walked backwards into the ruins, carefully put everything on the ground, not daring to look around. Then he sat on the wagon and waited fearfully for midnight.

Sitting on the wagon in this way, he fell asleep. Suddenly he heard a wild purring. He jerked up his head in confusion, and fell from fear out of the wagon. Before him in the ruin stood a monster with a high pointed head and a pair of blood-red eyes. The creature did not walk. It jumped. Its hands and feet shook. His teeth chattered. His eyes went back and forth with fear. He heard himself being called:

"Antony! Antony!" And the cat-like voice asked, "A flask of strong whisky? You brought it?"
Antony gathered his courage and, understanding what was intended, answered with a pounding heart and short breath, "A flask? Brought."
"96?"

"For sure."

[Page 613]

"Two non-flying fliers—you brought?"

"Brought."

"Three almonds—whitish-yellow, all separate—you brought?"

"Brought."

"And all fresh without a drop of blood?"

Antony stood there distraught and did not know what to say. He was afraid to tell a lie…but he did not know the truth. Then the creature came closer and Antony became so frightened that he started to scream in a wild, desperate voice: "O-lo—bogo! O-lo—bogo…"

People came running and found the peasant had fainted and fallen to the ground. Barely able to catch his breath, Antony looked at the looming ruins.

The group of men helped him there. Restored to himself, he wanted just to get away. Suddenly, one of the men detected a movement in one of the corners. When the men approached, they saw a big ball with long white strands of hair. They were shocked. Coming even closer, when they had removed the ball, set it aside, taken off the fur piece, and undone the paper covering, out came Yossl Baker, who was embarrassed at the uproar he had caused…

People gave him a hard time about all of this for a long while. He suffered from their judgments and he and his children bore the nickname "Devils."

[Page 617]

Destruction of Siedlce

Out of the avalanche

by Shlomo Rosen

Translated by Mira Eckhaus

Parts from his book that was published in the series "from the Moked", published by Am Oved, Tel Aviv, 5704, translated by Haim Tratkover. The author fell in a battle for the defense of Kfar Etzion.

The horrible Thursday

A shiver goes through my body when I remember this day.

It was on Thursday, September 7, the seventh day of the outbreak of the war. While I was lying down in my bed, I heard a loud bomb. The bombings got me out from the bed, but I became indifferent to everything that happened. Before I went out, I looked, as usual, at my schoolbag, which was lying in the corner, packed from the moment I was preparing to make an Aliya to Eretz Israel. It was packed and ready for the ride, so I could put it on my shoulder at any moment and hit the road.

More than once I thought that there was no point in holding my belongings in the schoolbag, while I was sure that it was not possible to travel to Eretz Israel. This time, too, I thought of unpacking the schoolbag and forgetting everything that had happened, but this time I postponed it for another day.

Outside, it is said that the Germans are constantly bombing our city, because Siedlce is on the main road of Warsaw refugee escape. It is said that after the evacuation of Warsaw, also the government that was in the city left on its way to Brisk. Siedlce is suffering, therefore, because it is on the main road of the evacuation to the east.

It's about ten-thirty. I stand by a loudspeaker and listen to the news about the status of the war. Suddenly I heard a noise of aircraft engines and the crowd fled in panic. Only after all the people have been hidden, who is in the shelter and who is in the house, the alarm signal was heard in delay.

[Page 618]

I could find a shelter behind the concrete gate of the house, where the radio speaker was, but it was a small, one-story house, and I wanted to hide in a big house. The few houses that were destroyed by the previous bombings at the back of the city were all one-story or small wooden huts and I was tempted to believe that a big house was a better shelter. When a bomb falls on a large building, you have time to escape through the lower floors, until the upper floors begin to collapse. So, I ran to a large house, at 44 Shenkovitz Street, and hid in the hallway. There were about 15-20 people there with me. I remember the young woman with the baby in her hands and the black chimney sweep, that a rope was wrapped around his waist. The chimney sweep, a young Christian, was known to me from his visits in our house to clean the chimneys. He stood and I could watch his movements. I remember: he came running to the hallway, where we all stood, looked at the ceiling and moved aside, so he will not be beneath the iron beam that held the ceiling. I realized his concern and thoughts and I looked at the ceiling as well, as if asking for a safer place. At the end I decided to stay where I was, in the middle of the hallway, in the first floor, while my hand is holding the back rest because I thought in case a bomb will fall on the house, I could run away to the exit in front of me. I did not have time to finish thinking about it when hail-bombs slammed around and before I managed to understand what is happening, - Bang! - A bomb fell on our house. Neither I nor anyone else could escape though my senses kept clear, but I did not have the power to do anything, or even to move from my place, because within one moment the whole house collapsed on us and all of us were in a stifling darkness. I saw nothing around me. I just felt a terrible dust and my hands felt fractures of bricks and wooden planks and other non-recognized materials. My hands tried to look for the exit but without success. I struggled to get rid of what was blocking the path ahead of me but I could not move a thing. All my work was for nothing because darkness was all around me. Everything my hands touched could not be moved. I was about to faint and after a while weak voices reach my ears.

Someone was shouting: "Help!". Another voice shouted "Shema Israel!". A woman was weeping and shouting loudly: "My children!" and the voice of a gentile was heard:

"Jesus, for God's sake!". A baby cried in fear, a hoarse voice repeated a name, probably of a relative or of a child. And the voices mingled within the living tomb and reached my ears as if they were across the wall. I realized that all the people that were in the hallway were covered in an avalanche just like I was. What should I do? Despair strikes me. Everything around is pressing on me and there is no space to move around. I will be buried here; I will die alive under these ruins. My whole life passed before my blind eyes, and I asked myself: Is this really the end of my life? Did I leave my friends and relatives before I made an Aliya just to be buried alive in a living grave?

[Page 619]

Did I receive permission from my group to make an Aliya for this purpose? I did not understand anything and together with the general choir of cries for help of all the people, which the avalanche covered, I also whispered words that expressed my bitter feelings at that time. Just as unintentionally I came to the people, which were covered by the avalanche on 44 Shenkovitz Street, the same way my redemption arrived. Something moved above my head and suddenly a small hole opened near me, through which I was able to see the daylight again. I felt like a blind man whose eyes were suddenly opened to see, someone in front of me was moving, climbing and crawling to the side from which the light came. It was the window in the corridor next to the stairs, where you go up from the concierge's room to the first floor. Through this window, apparently, someone saved himself, and when he came out, the rescue door opened for us as well. I helped the person that was before me and blocked the way, to climb and get out and after he cleared my place, I moved too. I climbed over objects I did not know what they were. A mix of brick fragments and wood, various soft things, maybe limbs of dead or injured people, my head bumped into something, my hat fell as a result. I didn't want to look for it from the fear of dragging something that would cover me again. I was drawn to the hole, from which the light came, another climb, a foray and I was rescued. I do not know how long I was under the avalanche; I guess ten minutes, because more than that I could not live without air. When I came out alive, I did not know what to do. First of all, I ran with all my strength as far away as possible from the place of destruction. I passed the passageway of 44 Shankvitz Street to Pinkana Street, and from there I crossed the alley Shpitlana, and only then I heard and realized that the bombing was still going on and houses around me were collapsing. I did not know what was better for me, whether to run on or hide again by "a protective wall" as before. I have seen people rushing like forest animals, their eyes protruding and their faces were strange and all looking like savages because of the layer of material on them and on their clothes. Suddenly an explosion was heard from the hospital street. I saw: Some people are lying on the sandy ground in the street (it was at the time the roads were repaired), I was also lying with my face down, not to see the bomb fall on me, but rather to die immediately. Someone at the gate calls us and demands that we'll enter and not lie down in the street outside. A tall man, who was hiding in the same gate, shouts at us in a loud voice, in a "true" Polish, with lots of curses, to hide in the entrance of the gate. I run into the gate and from there to the yard, outside, because I'm afraid of the "shelter" that the house will provide me, if a bomb falls on it. They do I not let me stand outside again. I tell them what happened to me. In the yard I see few more people with black and terrible faces just like mine. They probably also escaped from some ruin that covered them. Jews bring me water from their house. I wash the dust over my head and wash the wound on my leg, a light wound on my right leg, bleeding, and I did not feel it at all.

[Page 620]

I drink from the water that is mixed with the dust in my mouth - the thirst and the suffocation in my throat made me unbearable burning. At the gate howls of people who have fled here. A Polish woman falls into the officer's arms and whines hysterically: "Where is my husband? Did he escape from the taxi? Where is he?" I am told that the officer, the woman and her husband stopped here from their trip from Warsaw; their taxi was near the town hall; a bomb fell and the taxi turned into a broken box and no one knows where the passengers went. An injured person tells how and in which house he was injured. I see a Christian guy whose face looks like a real demon's face: his eyes are prominent and his wild hair is full of dirt and dust. I must have looked the same before I washed my face with the water the Jew had brought me from his house. From the same apartment water is also being brought to all the other wounded. Meanwhile the bombing has stopped and I leave the yard heading to the places where my friends and relatives live. Walking on the sidewalks is impossible, because you come across white mountains of bricks and dirt from houses that collapsed. Out of these houses rise heartbreaking cries for help. There is no one who can help them because everyone runs like a crazy to save his family and relatives. Everyone desires to see someone they know, and it gives them the power to run and enter inside the ruins of a house, in spite of the danger that the rest of the walls, which were damaged by the explosion, will collapse as well. Rescued people pounce on each other's necks while bursting into tears and excited shouts. They no longer believe that the brother is alive. We arrived at the house on S. Street where the members of the G. family live, a friend in our group and R., another member of our group. From the side, the house did not appear to have been destroyed, but immediately at the entrance to the courtyard, the destruction caused to the house by a bomb dropped on it was noticeable. It was a two-story house and now turned into an avalanche, its roof fell down and mixed with the bricks, planks, furniture fragments and other things that were in the house. From this mess, which was once a house, we see an old Jewish head, adorned with a white beard with blood all over him. His apartment was upstairs, on the second floor, and the old man did not have time to go down and crashed with the whole house. On the side were parts of flesh, shapeless, a mix of hands and other limbs of human beings.

The entire avalanche mound was piled up at the front, at the entrance of the corridor. The back of the house and the rooms of family C. were not harmed. Only the ceiling beams were displaced from their place on one side and were hanging in the air, threatening with the collapse of this part as well. The danger did not stop me and I entered through the window into a half-destroyed room. Out of a basement pit came weak strangled human voices, from the kind of voices I already knew. With the rest of their strength, women begged in a hoarse voice for rescue. Next to me were two men looking for their relatives and we immediately started the rescue work. Any touch we touched could have endangered our lives and the lives of those inside the avalanche, and among the ruins shouted people that were buried alive.

One woman wants to serve her, into the pit, some water - to save her fainting child in her hands. Another woman we managed to get out was so tired and weak from screaming and fearing death that she lost the power of speech and only her lips moved strange movements - she asked for water.

[Page 621]

Another woman we could not rescue in any way. Her head and most of her body were already out, but one of her legs was stuck and pressed and all efforts to rescue her did not succeed.

I saw my friend A. He cried because his grandmother and her children were covered in the avalanche there. He knew nothing about my friend.

The people we rescued could not give us any information, they had not yet recovered and did not know what world they were in. With the rest of my strength, I helped pulling and saving more people. All that time the danger of the collapse of the second part of the house hovered over us. Finally, I learned from the young man G. that his brothers and sisters and the rest of my friends who live in this house are alive. They were among the first to be rescued here. He showed me the place. They were sitting in the garden opposite. I felt like I was being reborn. There was no limit to our happiness. God's supervision set us one destiny and we were very close to death. We might have died under the ruins, without anyone knowing the fate of another.

There was a plane noise again and I waited until it was quiet. We sat under the tree and told each other briefly what had happened to us. When it was quiet, I gathered the rest of my strength and ran home, to see if there was destruction there as well. On the way I met my friend A. with his mother and his little sister and I was relieved to see him alive. In general, when acquaintances met, they considered each other as returning from another world.

Horror images of destruction were seen everywhere in the city center. Just a half an hour earlier large and beautiful houses were standing here. Half-dead people are now shouting from their ruins. As a side story, Yosef told me that his apartment, which was on the top floor, under the roof, was destroyed and "flew" downstairs due to a strong shock caused by a bomb that fell on a nearby house. Luckily, there was no one in the apartment and the whole family survived from death, but they no longer have an apartment to live in. Now they are running out of the town, to wait in a garden until the end of the bombings, which do not stop at all.

I continued on my way home. Near the passage gate on Pinkana Street, I asked some of my acquaintances about what was happening at our house, they answered me that in this part of the city a fire was burning and probably also our house was full of flames, I ran fast, I see the fire in the distance and cannot access. I am forced to bypass and approach the house from another side. All the fences are destroyed. And I'm by the house. It is impossible to enter it through the door because of the strong fire burning in the wooden house opposite. Through some nearby window I enter to our apartment. It is empty. There is no one there. Part of the linings and the cloths were taken out.

[Page 622]

Through the open window a heat was blowing from the fire in the house opposite. In the hallway there was a large puddle of human blood, but there was no sign for a human being. A neighbor was saving his movables and taking them out from the house. I asked him: where are my relatives, where is my grandmother, her daughter and the whole family, are they still alive? The neighbor calms me down and says: they are alive, nothing bad has happened to them, they were just worried about me. Where are they now? He does not know.

* * *

I hurried to the window again and entered the room and I did not know what to do. I'm like a crazy, I do not know what world I am in. Should we save the rest of our belongings in the room, or perhaps pour water here, so that the fire on the other side will not be able to grip our house? Or maybe run again - although my feet are heavy - until I find a member of my family? I'm standing confused. But when my eyes see that my neighbor takes things out of his apartment - I do as he does. I save my Tefillin, I pull outside my schoolbag that this morning I wanted to unpack. I took out some household items, and I hear a neighbor calling me out loud, that it would be better if I bring water and help people wetting parts of the house near the fire. If I do so, I will not have to take objects from the house. I listen to him and I start carrying water from the well to the house. Neighbors from distant homes helped us. I put water in through the window and when I left, I took things with me from home. Then I hear the same neighbor shouting that I better hurry to fetch water and not take objects outside. And I did not know what to do. I did not know what was more important. I even sat on the first-floor window and helped pouring water on the small wooden warehouses nearby, which were about to be eaten by the fire. I was sweating from both the work and the great heat. We finally walked away in despair because the fire was already gripping the logs of the wood warehouses and the goose and chicken coop. Then, when the house had already turned into a hill of ashes, I watched and saw that we did not do very well. First, I could save more objects from the house; Second, we had to call few more people for help to dismantle the wooden warehouses and the fence that ran from the scene of the fire to our house. This way it was possible to save the house from the approaching fire. However, the good thoughts were late to come. Neither I nor the other people who came to save the house thought about it.

I learned that my old grandmother and her family were now in the yard opposite and I immediately went there. I found them all alive, they were worried about me very much and did not think they would see me alive. Now they did not let me go to the place of the fire. Despite that, I went there to move the belongings here. Then I looked at my new "apartment."

[Page 623]

Lots of people that were saved from the fire were sitting here, on the bedding that were saved, just on the ground, leaning on a tree, and each one sighs while reporting to himself what was lost and who died. People talk about who they still hope to see, but do not know where they are. One mourns for a son who was killed by a bomb, and one mourns for the silver lamps or the like that he left in the house. Among the survivors of the fire are also people who have not had anything bad happen to them so far. They took some of their belongings out here. The fire is still far from their house but they are crying that their house is about to be burn. A sickly old woman lay on a stretcher and sighed. She used to have a house where she could lie sick and now, she has been taken out of there, she has to lie down in the open air. Her apartment is on fire. There was a sound of geese that were rescued from the coop and later a bad dog, that did not let anyone get close to where he was tied up, barked. All this together with the groans of the people that survived the fire and the victims of the bombings joined to one shocking commotion sound. Everyone was miserable, even those whose house was still standing and existing. The fire brigade arrived. They could easily extinguish the fire in our small house but they did not go there, because the house was internal and they thought it would be wiser to save the large houses, those in the front, such as those of Rabinowitz, Gutgeld, Kirschenbaum, Skorzitki, Kokbaka and others, even though there was no hope to save them. All the windows were already on fire and there was no way to save anything. But these homeowners, and especially Herzl Halberstadt, promised the fire brigade commander a large payment in exchange for rescuing their property from the fire, and this apparently had an effect.

The old woman was still lying on the stretcher and sighed, there was no one to take care of her, she would serve her something, because everyone was in their troubles. Her son-in-law arrived. When he saw that she will probably die here and could not be buried properly (because the city is full of dead victims from the bombings of today, and no one knows how to bury them, because all members of the "Red Cross" and "grace and truth" have tons of work to deal with despite the help of others), he decided to take her to the hospital where she would be treated both her life and after her death. He offered me a payment to assist him moving her to the hospital in Starvish. I went with him and we carried the old lady to the hospital. On the way to the hospital, there was another attack from the air. People fled like mice from their holes. I did not run because I already knew that no matter if I hid in the house, in the shelter or stood with the old woman on the street, the result would be the same, because the bombs hit everywhere and anyone who is sentenced to be killed or injured would not benefit any shelters in the world.

I did not care what was done in the world of the Blessed One, I stopped thinking about it. After I rested a bit, I carried her again even though it was at the time of the attack. There was no obligatory to defend against attacks.

[Page 624]

Whoever wanted to hide – hid and whoever wanted to stay on the street - stayed on the street because most of the "violators of discipline" were among the people who had already suffered from the bombings: one lost his son, the other lost a family member; the home of another was destroyed and all the property of that person was burned, etc., etc. My heart did not think I should keep safe from the airplanes above. I continued to walk with the old woman. When we arrived at the hospital, a military car had just arrived and a wounded man was taken out, wearing civilian clothes, apparently one of the new recruits, who had not yet received his army uniform, had not yet had a rifle and was hit by a shell that caused his current condition: wounded, with a deformity that might kill him due to blood loss. I did not think much about him and hurried - I entered the hospital yard with the old woman. I was immediately reprimanded by those who carried the military wounded: "Don't you know – they read aloud – those soldiers have a priority in receiving help before everyone else?" I said I didn't know which was the truth as indeed I did not know. We both put the old woman in the waiting room which was a spacious hall full of stretchers with wounded. There were covered stretchers and I did not know if dead were lying there or wounded enjoying "sweet sleep". Again, I saw people there, that seemed to me like a picture from a hospital for surgery according to Remark's descriptions rather than a reality. I think that among everyone, I have seen the familiar face of a Jew with a beard and he had a bandage where there should be a hand. And more sights. I was afraid to look at what was going on in the waiting hall and quickly escaped. Outside I looked at the coin I had received as a reward for taking the old woman to the hospital. I struggled with myself and was angry for being paid to transfer the woman to the hospital so she would not die in the street. Is it allowed to bind together a despicable coin with the salvation of a living soul? I was disgusted with this money but I did not throw it away because I remembered I don't have an apartment where I can stay, nor money to buy bread to stay alive in the first days of my measurable life without an apartment. With these thoughts I came to my "new apartment" among those who survived the fire in the fruit tree garden, on 29/13 Shankvitz Street. I did not have patient to sit there for a long time and when I saw that there were no more airplanes in the sky, I went to visit Rachela at her "new house" in the garden opposite, a place where the survivors of that house lived. They, the neighbors of the same house, meant to go to Makavada or other villages in that area until the bombings of the city will stop. Here they had nothing to lose after their house had been destroyed and each family had victims. Every soul wanted to escape from the place of disaster on this bitter and horrified day.

Rachela and her mother prepared for the journey. I said goodbye to her out of a feeling I would not see her soon. On the way back from her I met my friend Danziger, a member of a pioneering kibbutz in Lodz. He was in the kibbutz for about 4-5 years. His Aliya to Israel was also approved and he prepared himself for the illegal journey.

[Page 625]

I was about to set off before him and now we were both in the same situation. His house was destroyed by a bomb, so he decided to walk, after Shabbat, to Pinsk. His girlfriend was living there and he could live in her house, too. He said he was looking for friends to join him for the march and I could accompany him if I wanted. I told him I don't know what I will do after Shabbat and I cannot guarantee that I will join him. When I walked away from him, I thought that maybe it is wise to join him. I had no clear plan where to go and for what purpose but I really, really wanted to run away from the place of the destruction.

I told my family about it and immediately they disagreed. "You want to get out of here," my grandmother said, "and it doesn't matter what will happens to me? Where will I be with my daughter and her small child?" My claims were blocked, because I knew that I could not help them here either and I could not prove her mistake, because I also did not know what benefit would my wanderings do to me and how far I would reach if I had no money to live on.

I was hungry after a whole day without eating and after experiences that exhausted all my strength. During the whole day I did not think about eating. When I took the things out of our apartment, I saw bread there and it never occurred to me to take it with me, because it was unnecessary in my opinion then. The reason for it is unclear to me until now. Later on, I learned about the blood puddle in our house. In the morning, before I left the house, my neighbor, the carpenter Zalazni, asked me to help dig the shelter at Kokabka in the garden opposite our window. He, who was in charge of defending against air strikes in several houses, was responsible for this work, in the same yard. I told him that I thought the work was unnecessary because there was not enough space for a shelter. If a bomb falls there, all the wooden fences and all the wooden houses that are around the shelter will fall and cover in their fall all the people who will seek refuge in the shelter and they will die.

I did not help with the building of the shelter and went on. After 15 minutes, when the horrific attack came from the air, bombs shrapnel hit the people that dug the shelter. Some of them were injured and they were put in the hallway of our house, one of them lost a lot of blood which created the puddle I saw.

[Page 626]

I Survived the German Extermination of Jews

by Herztel Kaveh

Translated by Anita Frishman Gabbay

Edited by Theodore Steinberg

Donated by Dana Szeflan Bell

The Outbreak of the War and Bombing of Siedlce

Friday, September 1, 1939 came as a total surprise. Everyone in Siedlce immediately felt the disaster of war was imminent, but no one could predict the threat and the annihilation of the Jewish people. Groups of between 1 and 10 airplanes appeared in the skies. We began to discuss: some said they were ours(Polish), others said they were German. Meanwhile they didn't touch Siedlce, but the panic intensified. We began to prepare food essentials, but shortly afterwards many shops were out of basic products.

In a period between Saturday and Sunday, the German planes were circling over our city. Monday they returned, dropped bombs next to the city and they left. Tuesday, they returned. Several bombs were dropped, the target happened to be a peasant village and again they left. On Tuesday they returned, dropped several bombs, hit a peasant wagon, and left. The enemy reappeared over the city with a large fleet of airplanes. The bombardments started at 10:15 in the morning and continued until 3 in the afternoon. When it became quieter, we emerged from our hideouts. Terrible pictures unfolded before our eyes: broken houses, deep craters where the bombs had fallen, close to homes. Many families found their dead under the rubble, and from the destroyed homes came cries for help.

[Page 627]

After the bombardments, thousands of people prepared themselves to leave the city. They left not knowing where to and to whom. Small children in their arms, bundles on their backs, they departed on their journey. The terrible bombings lasted 4 days. In these same days the Germans already began their routine-murders early in the morning ending at night. At night everyone was fearful: from a distance Siedlce looked like it was burning from all directions. Black [underworld] elements took advantage of the situation, looting and robbing. The bombs fell mainly on Jewish homes. There were at least 1500 dead. Sixty percent of the homes were destroyed.

Life Until the Ghetto was Established

On September 12 the Germans marched into Siedlce. Trembling and a panic arose in each one of us. There were rumors, all the men will be shot. The second day of Rosh-Hashana they caught men to be sent to East-Prussia for labor. Three days later it began again. At three in the afternoon, we suddenly heard shooting. We want to see what happened, but it was forbidden to go outside. We are chased back through our gates. We understood immediately what this meant. Several men hid but others were too scared to do this, because the first time when they caught them [the ones that hid] the Germans shot them immediately.

Every gate was manned with a German soldier so no man was allowed to leave. At the same time German officers with revolvers went from house to house and ordered the men to reveal themselves. When we asked what was happening, we were told the shootings came from the Jewish homes. You could see the men being led outside. A thorough search took place everywhere. They searched pockets. Worthwhile items were taken or thrown away. Conditions in the Siedlce prison were awful. People had to run with their hands held high. Whoever couldn't were badly beaten.

[Page 628]

At the prison-gate we were beaten with rifles, studded clubs and leather belts. Many of us were severely wounded. Night fell. A room that was meant for 2-3 people was crammed with 15-20 people. There wasn't an inch to move. Who even speaks of lying down to sleep. Those that didn't have a place in the cells, remained in the courtyard of the prison. Holding us for more than a day, they remembered about feeding us and we were given a piece of stale bread.

Wednesday morning, September 21, they ordered us into the courtyard. In front of the prison women waited with packages to say their farewells, thinking they were never to see their loved ones again. With bitter tears and heavy-hearts we left in the direction of Mordy or Mazowiecki. Passing through Polish villages, the peasants wanted to give us water, but the Germans did not allow them to approach us. Several of us managed to escape, others were shot escaping.

We were more than 8000 men, Jews and Gentiles. 40 soldiers watched over us, some on horseback others in automobiles. We arrived at Wegrow at night. Many wanted to escape now, but it was almost impossible. They brought us into the center of the city and ordered us to lie down. Exhausted and beaten from this long journey everyone dropped like a "dead person" and fell asleep, not even noticing the rain. Early morning we searched for places that were not heavily guarded. Lucky for some, such places were found and we started running. We had to climb over a fence 2 meters. Until the Germans realized what was happening, dozens of men were already on the other side. Also, my father and myself ran. I think, I was among the last ones, as shooting was heard from behind. In Wegrow and its surroundings no one was captured. When they brought water, also dozens of men escaped from the square. The remaining men were led further on their journey to Ostroleka. At the same time an order came to free all the men.

[Page 629]

The Germans settled in and the Gestapo arrived in the city, together with gendarmes, Volk-Germans and also—new protocols against the Jews. Those Jews with shops(enterprises): each Gentile who pledges allegiance to the Germans and proves himself worthy, can take the shop; it didn't take long and he received it. Many times the Jew did not even have time to take his merchandise out and had to hand everything over.

The evening visits were frightening. Suddenly, a knock on the door, an order to open! German gendarmes entered and turned the house upside down, destroyed whatever they wanted, and whatever pleased them they stole. The evening guests appeared very often.

Jews started arriving from the outskirts, territories that were now in the Third Reich. We received these refugees with welcome arms and provided them with our limited means. A "Judenrat" [Jewish Council] was established, led by Dr. Leibel. Belonging to the Judenrat were: [Icchak] Nachum Weintraub [chairman], who was an outstanding citizen of Siedlce for many years, Hershel Tenenboim as the secretary and others [Hersz Eisenberg, vice-chairman]. Life became somewhat "normal". We had to greet every passing German, and those who mistakingly forgot or didn't notice the German, were beaten severely. The Germans burnt our beautiful synagogue on Christmas.

On December 31 an order was issued that Jews must wear a blue-white arm band with a "Magen-David", and from this day on, life for the Jews grew worse.

Erev Shavouth slave laborers began river-improving work on the River Liwiec. Polish engineers directed the work together with Polish overseers.

Ziskind the book merchant with the armband

[Page 630]

Every overseer received a group of 15 men. The work wasn't difficult and food was still cheap, easy to obtain and a few "groshen" still remained in your pocket [inflation had not yet set in]. Nice weather—all things together made life bearable. The people called this work—"summer dacha(vacation). But this did not last long. One day the Gestapo arrived. They got out of their cars, inquired how the work was progressing and pressured the Polish overseers to report those who worked slowly. The Gestapo, with their rubber and spiked clubs arranged themselves in rows, approached those Jews who were pointed out, berated them and beat them with their rubber whips on their naked backs over and over. 15 bloodied and wounded individuals were led to the hospital. These unwelcome guests came every few days. The work dragged on until winter, and then the deportations to the work camps in the Siedlce-Trzeszanov (Lubliner province). Several never returned from these camps.

Beginning March 1941, someone threw a grenade and a German soldier was wounded. This was a provocation against the Germans. Shortly after, they blamed a Jewish girl that she did it. The Germans started a "pogrom" in the city. In the middle of the night they organized groups, broke down doors, tore out windows, shot and beat women and children, whoever they found. There were dead and wounded and it took the "Judenrat" several days to restore order and appease the Germans, by paying a large bribe [100,000 zlotes]. Inflation creeped in day to day. A kilo bread cost 17 zlotes and a kilo potatoes 3.25 zlotes; our survival became harder and harder.

There was a large celebration when the German-Russian war broke out. We believed our liberation was close-by. Quickly we realized our mistake. At the end of August a new edict was issued: all Jews must live in designated places which will be for Jews only.

[Page 631]

Two ghettos were formed: a large and a small. The large one, with the streets, a part of May 1st. until Aslanowitche, Brawarna, the Jatkowa Street [Butcher street], Okupove, Stary-Rynek [Old-Market Square], one side of Bane-Ligne(train station street), and 3 houses of 11th November-Street. In addition there were 2 gates, one at Pilsudski's memorial, the second—end of Aslanowitche and 11th November Street.

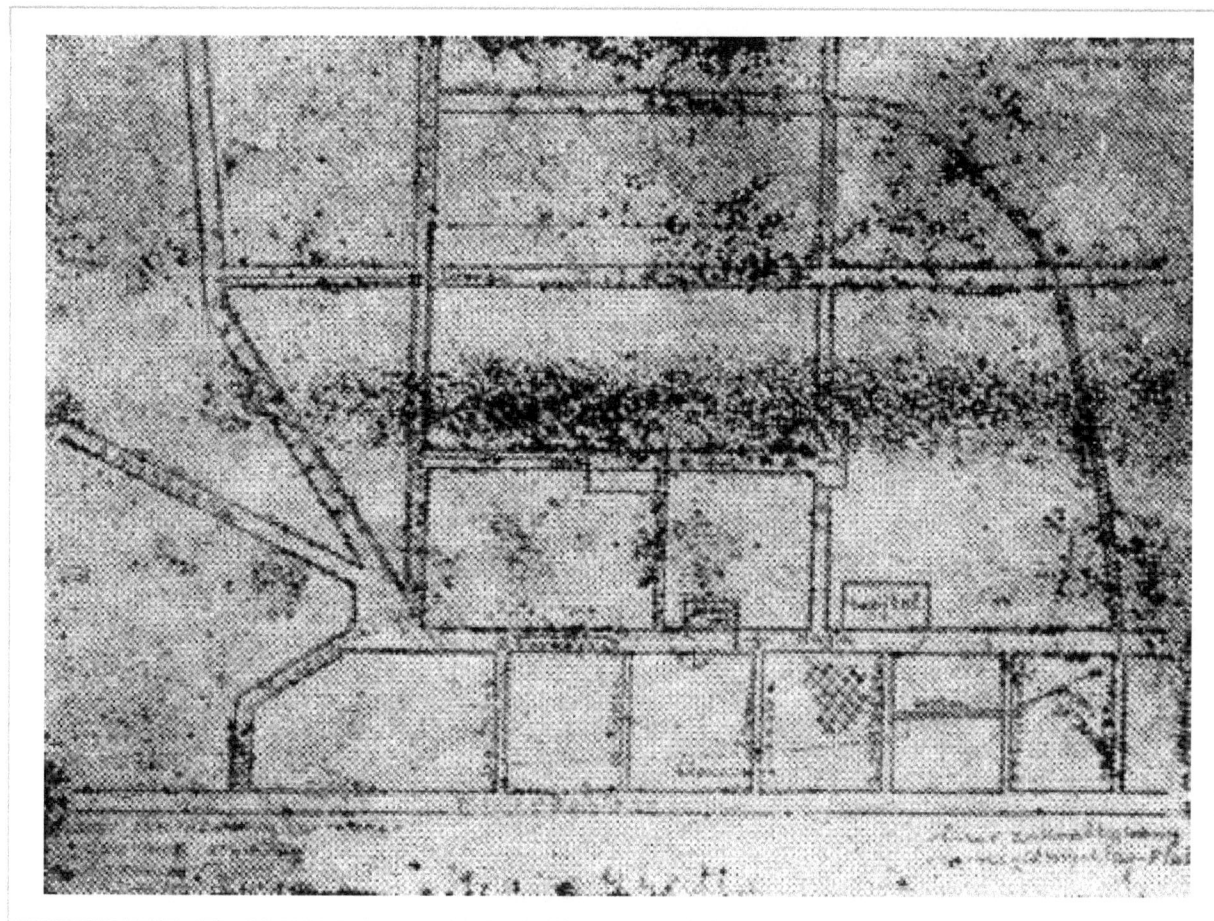

The map of the ghetto
The second ghetto, called Dreiek, was bordering these streets: A small section of Sokolower-Street, Aslanowitche and
11th November with a gate across from the gate of the large ghetto—Aslanewitche 11th November
(Drawing of the artist Ben)

A gate of the ghetto

[Page 632]

The writing on the gate

Life in the Ghettos

By September 15, 1941, we already lived in the ghetto. Whoever had the means bought food for their families, with extra provisions for worsening conditions. It was clear to everyone, life in the ghetto will get worse. The Jewish police already existed. Their mission was to control life in the ghetto, to guard the gates and other duties. Erev Yom Kippur both ghettos were locked. With heavy hearts everyone awaited Yom Kippur. We wanted to cry, to scream, but this was also difficult. In a room meant for 2 people, 10-12 people were crammed. This led to the outbreak and spread of various diseases.

Day in, day out, they caught us for various jobs, despite the fact that the Judenrat provided more than 3000 workers. Siedlce became a source for Jewish workmen. Those with permission slips from the Germans could leave the ghetto. Those Jews slightly improved the lives for the others in the ghetto. They managed to smuggle from the Polish side important food items:

Bread, potatoes and other life-saving basics. Small children and women were used to ease the situation, some carrying 25 kilos of potatoes on their backs. Neither woman nor child escaped paying with their lives. It was enough when we were on the Polish side to be detected and denounced as a "Jew" to be immediately handed over to the Gestapo and beaten to a bloody pulp. At night they brought him [the injured one] to the ghetto and told him to crawl through the barbed wire. When he arrived into the ghetto he was met by bullets from these hooligans. Each day brought us sacrifices. The difficult winter also added to our misery: frost, cold, starvation. Typhus broke out and hundreds died.

We couldn't endure any longer the sacrifices of the slave-labour. Neither day, nor night, no Sabbath, no Sunday; work continued non-stop. So many people changed that they became unrecognizable.

[Page 633]

The ghetto gate guarded by Jewish policemen

[Page 634]

Many cried it was so difficult to see one's own father in such a condition.

The rations became fewer and smaller. We received 100 grams of bread daily. Whoever still had things to sell, sold them and bought more bread. Most of the people starved. [Soup] kitchens were opened for the most needy. Life continued to deteriorate. There were times when the living envied the dead.

At Pesach another rumor circulated: the Jews of Lublin were deported. Where to we didn't know. One July day, in 1942, the Gestapo informed the Judenrat that the train needs workers with wagons. This was immediately organized, not knowing for which train-line. They brought the workers to several closed railroad cars and ordered them to open them. A "black sight before their eyes"; this terrible picture unfolded: dead bodies, dressed in new clothes, new shoes. We saw they did not have a long journey. This was a Radomer transport and the first time the Jews of Siedlce laid their eyes on such a scene.

Later more transports with closed railroad cars went through Siedlce which took Jews in the direction of Treblinka. The death-camp was 60 kilometers from Siedlce. We in Siedlce started to feel the threat which was approaching. Some believed that the Jews of Siedlce will meet a similar fate, even though they contributed thousands of workers. With this idea we lived until August 22, 1942.

The First Action

August 22, 1942, at night, many rumors in the Siedlce ghetto spread. One was, something was taking place in Minsk-Mazowieckie; exactly what, we didn't know. But soon everyone understood that it was about the deportation of the local Jews to Treblinka. The representatives of the "Judenrat" tried to lie to us that this was about the Jews of Minsk. I believe, part of them knew the details what happened there. The catastrophe didn't take long to reach us as well.

[Page 635]

At two o'clock at night the 2 ghettos were surrounded by gendarme and Polish policemen. Shooting began from all directions, a panic broke out, fear paralyzed us. Next morning we left our homes to see what occurred. We knew immediately the ghettos were surrounded and no one was leaving for work. Everyone understood what lies ahead. But we still couldn't believe that the leaders of the "Judenrat" didn't know, at least some hours ahead of time what lies ahead of us? I blame these men for turning a blind eye. All that was needed was to give us a warning so hundreds of our young people could escape the ghettos and perhaps would have survived. I turn back to this dark Shabbos day!

As it became clear what lies ahead we ran to each other. Perhaps we can save ourselves by preparing hiding places. Not everyone wanted to or was able to do this. We needed courage and the will to continue with our struggle. Understandably, people who lived in fear and in such conditions for almost 3 years were psychologically and physically exhausted. In the early morning the Jewish police appeared house to house advising us to be ready at a given hour. Those that didn't leave their homes were forced with their belongings, by the Jewish police out onto the street, some in their work clothes, others in their "party" clothes.

The Gestapo chased us into the street. Those who lagged behind had a shorter distance—they were shot. This is how they chased us to the former cemetery in the Synagogue-street. There they combined the Jews from both ghettos. My family consisted of my mother and 2 sisters. My father was in the hospital at that time. We needed to sit among the tombstones. Thousands sat squeezed together. Watched by Volk-German and Polish policemen, we couldn't dare raise our heads. Who even thought about standing up?

[Page 636]

The Gestapo and other hooligans were jovial. They walked over to us, shot at us and beat us. At this critical moment the will for revenge awoke! We needed to do something, to spill some blood of our enemies, but our hands were paralyzed.

At 11, before noon the, "death-squads" arrived led by the Gestapo-leader Feivish. They took charge of us. A squabble began between the leader of the German command and the death-squad of Treblinka. The first one wanted the artisans to remain, the second one wanted as many as possible for the death camp. People fainted for a lack of water. The murderers didn't allow us any water and with their sadistic laughter on their faces instilled fear in us.

At two in the afternoon an order came: men aged 16-40 should come forward. We didn't know what this meant. A small number of men didn't move from their spot. I can't imagine how children left their parents. Men—women, bidding farewell with their dearest and departed for a designated place in the Synagogue street. With tears in my eyes I kissed my beloved mother and sisters and with force I was torn from them. My mother spoke the entire day with me and assured me that I will remain alive. Her prophecy came true.

The murderers were waiting for us in the Synagogue-street, standing on both side with sticks, rifles and revolvers. The selection started. Who will be selected for work and will return to the former spot. Everyone had to pass through this street. Those who were sent to the right were chosen for work. Left, back to the cemetery. Broken-hearted and defeated, they returned to the cemetery. Those chosen for work were told to sit on the grounds of the hospital, the former Polish "Red-Kreitz [Red Cross]". We were told the Gestapo leader will speak to us. He arrived at 5 in the evening and made a speech. He informed us we were the lucky ones, to have remained alive and everything will be fine.

[Page 637]

You will work. We are giving you 3 houses in the small ghetto.

At the same time the gunshots at the cemetery intensified….and they led us to the 3 houses. The walls between the rooms were destroyed and broken, unrecognizable.

That evening Saturday to Sunday was a miserable one for us, the survivors. The shooting of the Jews continued non-stop throughout the night. Sunday morning we saw wagons passing by carrying the dead and half-dead. The Polish overseers were removing the clothing, shoes and other items from the dead bodies. The remainder in the cemetery were shot during the night from Shabbos to Sunday.

Saturday evening many were taken to the train. The road from the cemetery to the train station was a difficult one. The Polish townsfolk were overjoyed to witness this.

Siedlce Jews on their last road to the gas chambers of Treblinka

A transport of Jews to the train, among them Pinchas Konopne, Melech Radushinski

[Page 638]

Very few of them had regrets. Broken hearted, thirsty they arrived at the train. There they waited for the railroad cars that were transporting them. Several hours later, covered railroad cars with barbed-wire windows arrived. 40-50 people were shoved into a railroad car.

I will describe the road between the train-station until we reached 3 kilometers from Treblinka.

The painful journey was told to me by my cousin Shloime Kaveh, who was transported to Treblinka and at the gate of death escaped from the train.

The floor of the cars were covered with a layer of quicklime. The train stopped at a designated spot, which everyone knows very well. Families remained together. They didn't want to separate. They wanted to die together. The lamenting, the screaming cannot be described. The heat in the wagons became unbearable. The quicklime was suffocating, many fainted, some undressed because the heat was so unbearable. One request—a drink of water before death. There were cases, when some drank urine. The train stood to the side, 3 kilometers from Treblinka. Each incoming train did not go directly into the camp. This was specially orchestrated, so people could not hear the cries from the camp. This happened to our transport of Siedlce Jews. An entire day, Sunday, the transport waited by the side rail-way line.

At 12 in the evening, the train moved to the line to Treblinka. A small section arrived in the death camp. Amongst them was my dear mother and both sisters. Many escaped when the train was on the way to Treblinka, also my cousin. Many were shot or killed during the jump. My cousin survived intact. They brought him to another passenger transport, also destined to the death camp. He jumped again from this train.

[Page 639]

After the First Action

We, those remaining in the ghetto, awaited our impending destiny. At this time many of those that were hidden reappeared including women. We numbered about 1500 people.

On Monday at 12 noon, we heard shooting again. The hospital wasn't spared. In cold-blood, they first shot the sick and then the personnel. Among those shot was my dear father.

On August 25, Tuesday morning, many arrived to select workers for different places. People were running from place to place. We thought the other place would be better. I was sent to do train-work. Several people including the aged and women remained in the small ghetto. The large ghetto burned down and we couldn't enter.

They sent us to a place about 2 kilometers from the station. They gave us a barrack to rest our "parcel of broken bones", no beds, boards of wood with a few pieces of straw. A kitchen was opened for us railroad workers. The kitchen personnel were made up of those individuals who hid themselves from work. The food was not sufficient to keep us alive. A quarter kilo bread and some black coffee in the morning, at night a watery soup. Some did not settle for this. Those that had money had an opportunity to buy other things. There were some other food products, but the staff sold it for their own profit instead of putting it in the food they were cooking. The train workers were divided into groups, some to unload the coal, some to load sand. I was sent to a Polish workshop.

The workshop performed various services for the Germans. We were a group of 20 men. Amongst them was Nelkienbojm and Liwerant. Going alone between the railroad track risked being shot. To and from work we were escorted by a Polish foreman. It was an order, one time they caught 3 workers on their own between the tracks.

[Page 640]

The German train-police brought them to us and shot them in front of us. The unwelcome guests often visited us during the night. They rushed us outside, kept us there for a long time, beat us, yelled at us and left. At the time I was still at work. None of us wanted any altercations with the Germans. The engineer of the workshop was a man over 50 years. He was a quiet, decent and good-natured person. He spoke with kind words to us. He told us, our work was essential and confidentially speaking, in short order all the workers will be shot. He told us to prepare warm clothing and boots and quietly leave. His words reminded us to think of our destination [plan].

There were some Italians stationed in Siedlce, in railroad cars on the railway line, and their job was to unload the cargo coming for those doing business with Italians. In those times, Italian soldiers fought on the Russian front and many of them drove through Siedlce. Liwerant had an idea—perhaps the Italians can be of some use to us. The plan had to be implemented by Yablonafski, who worked closely with them. He believed it would be a good opportunity to carry out the plan. Involved in this were Liwerant, Nelkienbojm, and Yablonavski who badly wanted to succeed.

Very few knew about this plan. On a given day I went to Liwerant and Nelkienbojm and asked them to include me in their plan. We agreed and the next step was how to implement the plan. We couldn't waste time. We saw Italian trains passing through to Warsaw, not knowing where these trains were going. These were Italian transport trains with Italian soldiers, who abandoned the Russian front. Sometimes they stopped for an hour or two, or even an entire day in Siedlce. Then we decided to act on our plan, be prepared at any given moment. For several weeks we all went to work with 2 kilos of bread and a flask of coffee. This was until October 23, 1942. The night before I told my cousin about our plan and begged him to join us.

[Page 641]

He refused and said he had enough and wished me success. This was the same cousin who jumped from the train to Treblinka.

Friday, October 23, 1942, going to work like any other day, we had the feeling that something "good" was awaiting us. We had to cross 3 kilometers of railroad to reach our work. On our way we noticed one Italian train waiting on one side, another further away. We continued so as not to arouse suspicion. We quickly made a decision between us: if one train leaves the station before noon, we will leave at lunchtime and take the second train. And if both remained until noon, then we still have time to execute our plan after work. To our good fortune neither train left the station, the whole day.

Restless, we awaited the right minute. Half past six maybe we bid our friend goodbye and left the workplace quietly. With determination and with heads held high we marched to our train. Ten past seven we passed the Siedlce train station. The German train-police that were standing there observed us but we continued on our way. This strengthened our will and with a quicker pace and stronger determination we continued. When we reached the train we looked for the best possible way to board. On either side stood 2 German trains with the Italian one in the middle. We went from wagon to wagon looking for a small window, a crack into which we could squeeze ourselves. Every minute seemed like an hour. In the last car we found a spot to climb in. One by one we climbed in and we held our breath until further developments. We didn't know where this transport was going. This we left for uncertain destiny.

[Page 642]

The Road from Siedlce to Italy

Friday evening, October 23, 1942, the train moved and we left Siedlce. When the train passed the city we looked around to see where we were. Shortly afterwards, we opened a flask of shnaps and made a "L'Chaim". This was a transport train, but it was well equipped inside with some benches to sit on. In the corners there were 2 small iron ovens with 2 wooden boxes, which could serve as kindling wood.

In the same evening we passed Praga [suburb of Warsaw]. Saturday, 8 in the morning, the train stopped. We were lying on the bench when the wagon was opened by a Polish train-worker and then closed it immediately. To our good fortune he didn't notice us. We saw him. This was in Skerniewicz. After this we looked for places to hide. The fore-mentioned wooden crates were useful for two of us. The third one found a place in another car under heaps of cotton, which were in the car. We could pass from one railroad car to another. From time to time we left our hiding places and met up to see where we were heading. We passed Pietrikow.

On Sunday mid-day a soldier on patrol found one of us. They tried to communicate between themselves in sign-language, finally the soldier understood that he was a watchman who was guarding the merchandise in the wagon. At night we emerged from our hiding place which was cramped. We were hunched over all day long and couldn't feel our feet. We had enough bread. We did not have enough to drink. We had reached the German territory, passing German towns: Coltbus, Glogau, Munich and others.

Monday night a soldier found us all. He was drunk. From him we learned several things. He spoke a few words of German. It was possible to speak with him. We told him everything, including our goal. We begged him not to reveal this to the commander.

[Page 643]

He assured us he would not to inform on us. From him we learned that in 8 hours we will reach the Italian border.

I had several rings and a 10-zlote silver coin which I pressed into his hand. He didn't want to take it. This took place in the Austrian Tyrol. We went back to our benches to rest.

Thirsty, broken-hearted and dirty we waited impatiently with the news the Italian soldier brought.

Tuesday, 6 in the morning the train suddenly stopped. The wagon was opened and immediately closed. Again they didn't see us. We understood something happened. We couldn't reach our hiding places because they could hear our footsteps below. They came and took us off the train. We immediately saw we were on the border town of Bienner. They brought us to a cabin of the border-police. They took good care of us, gave us water, apples, cigarettes. Shortly they advised the commander of the train about us. The commander approached with 2 soldiers. He heard we came from Warsaw and gave each one of us a pat on the back, said something and was very generous with more cigarettes. When it got lighter outside, they brought us to the commissar of the city, a middle-aged man, and very gentile. He interrogated each one separately and took our finger-prints. One of the last questions was if we want to return to Poland or if we want to remain in Italy. The answer was quite clear for everyone. The commissar told us the papers will be sent to Rome to the Italian Minister and they will decide our outcome. We received food, which we ran out of weeks ago. In the evening they brought us to Vifitene, a town 17 kilometers from the border, a beautiful district where they put us in their local jail. This was a pass-through jail for people who smuggled and other things. We were well treated in this jail.

On December 5, 1942, a telegram arrived from the Italian Interior Minister, we will be sent to "Ferramonti". Where this is and what awaited us we didn't know. But it was sufficient, as long as we were in Italy.

[Page 644]

In the pass-through jail, in the town of Vivitena, [Varena] we stayed for 40 days. The town was 27 kilometers from the Brenner Pass. The jail personnel were from an Italian family which took care of all of our needs. I want to emphasis my thanks to this family, who greatly helped us, knowing that we were Jews.

December 6, on the 40th day in this jail, 3 carabineri [policemen] came for us and put us in handcuffs and then bound us together with another chain. The trip took us on several different luxurious trains, passing through beautiful villages, fruitful landscapes, valleys and hills filled with vegetation: Bologna, Verona, Napoli, until Calabria. We got along very well with our greeters. They collected money for us. From their faces we could feel their sympathy.

The trip went rather quickly. It took 2 days. We arrived at Terasa [Teramo or Teranto [unclear] on the 8th, a station for Ferramonti and from there we went by foot. We arrived at noon at Ferramonti. All formalities were dropped and we were treated like the locals. Bernstein, from Warsaw, took interest in us and helped us to settle in. We cut our hair, shaved, changed our clothing and felt like we were reborn. We became a sensation in Ferramonti. Everyone knew that 3 young lads arrived from Poland.

The first weeks we didn't get any rest—invitations, sight-seeing. A woman named Natanson befriended us; she provided and worried for us the entire time like a mother. I am very thankful to her for the great attention that we received.

[Page 645]

Ferramonti [Di Tarsia], Internment Camp Near Calabrian Town of Cosenza

Ferramonti is situated in Calabria, in a valley between hills. There was an internment-camp which was home to citizens of different countries, also Christians. We didn't have to work. Everyone was given a ration and we were able to do whatever we wanted with it. The personnel consisted of a director, local officials and the militia [Black Shirts] which guarded the internees. They treated us fairly.

We acclimatized very quickly, made new friends and companions. There was a group of young people who went to work outside the camp in the woods, about 6 kilometers away. We were interested in obtaining this type of work, so Nelkienbojm and I joined the group. This work was good for one's health, especially for us. Also economically it was worthwhile. We were able to procure more food. Our rations were small.

Life in the camp was friendly, sanitation was not bad. Families lived together in small homes, singles--in larger barracks. We led a cultural life and we waited here for the war to end.

Life was uncertain for awhile. When news arrived that our friendly armies landed in Sicily and will soon be arriving in Calabria, we sensed the day of liberation was near. At the same time we were afraid that the fleeing German army will take this road that was so close to us. The Italians removed the barbed wire and gave the means with which we could leave the camp. Most of us left for the mountains and waited there until liberation. The German army actually retreated using this road close to our camp.

After several days in the mountains we became aware that officers of the liberation army arrived in the camp. We could now consider ourselves free… leave and return.

One day an automobile arrived in the camp with a "Magen-Dovid" [Jewish-star].

[Page 646]

Soldiers from Eretz Yisroel were in the car. A "Simcha", long awaited joy overcame us. We saw liberated Jews and also Israeli Jews. Many cried for joy. We didn't want to separate from them, we wanted to stay with them. We wanted to hear news from home.

The Israelis came to visit more often.

Then Nelkienbojm and I left the camp so we begin to inquire inquire how to make Aliyah to Eretz Israel. We arrived in Bari, where Israeli soldiers were stationed in the neigbouring area.. We approached the mayor of the city, Mayor Sacharov, the current police-commander at that time [I. Sacher]. We had a long conversation with him, recounted our tribulations about our escape and internment and our goals. the Mayor showed great sympathy towards us. In the middle of our discussion, a sergeant entered, who later was our leader.

It didn't take long and we joined his group. The sergeant who took great interest in us, he was Yechiel Teiber [one of the Teiber brothers]. We started work immediately. Our first job was to help the cooks. Shortly after we became independent cooks. Liwerant arrived several weeks later and went to work with us. This new life was very interesting.

Weeks went by, months, and rumors began that a transport to Israel will soon leave. We didn't have to worry, we knew someone that would arrange this for us. In the mean-time Pesach arrived. A Seder was prepared by the military. Hundreds of civilians and the entire military partook—this was very uplifting. We felt like home. It was well organized and went through the night. Singing and dancing ended the Seder.

The day of our departure was approaching. The staff prepared an entertaining evening for us. Every person drank a" L'Chaim" with us and spoke some kind encouraging words.

May 29, 1944, we boarded the ship in Taranto. This was a Polish luxury boat "Batori" and brought us to Alexandria. There were also hundreds of English soldiers. The trip was very comfortable.

[Page 647]

The sea was calm, the atmosphere very sophisticated. Everyone had awaited this day that they could be in the "land". The first day, at noon, we arrived in Alexandria and then continued our trip by train. As we got closer to the border our happiness intensified and the singing was filled with joy. In the morning we passed the control and found ourselves in Eretz Israel and danced a hora. The train continued until we arrived at Atlit—some went to relatives, others to the synagogue and our new life began.

Translator's note: Names and places often misspelled or unknown. The train ride from Siedlce through the Austrian Tyrol to Italy, Ferramonti denotes some unfamiliar or mispronounced names.

[Page 648]

The Destruction of Siedlce

Ida Yom-Tov (Tenenbaum)

Translated by Theodore Steinberg

The Arrival of the Germans and the First Suffering of Persecution

On September 12, 1939, Siedlce was seized by the Germans, who arrived from East Prussia. In the first days of the month of October, the Germans began their murderous work—they seized Jews, and even non-Jews, and with beatings with clubs and sticks, without food and without a drop of water, forced them on foot to Wegrow. Those who thus suffered, young and old, were forced to go with their hands held high. In Wegrow the Germans left the older people and forced the younger further, to the camps in East Prussia. The year 1940 was filled with kidnappings for labor and people being sent to the camps, with forced "contributions" and enclosures, along with other kinds of oppression and suffering.

At the beginning of 1941, the S.S. man Fabish was named as commissar of the city. He was a bandit, a murderer, and a madman rolled into one. If we lived in orderly terror until 1941, now life literally hung by a thread. Fabish's first undertaking was the establishment of a ghetto. With others of Hitler's "highly-placed personnel," one could sometimes bargain with money, jewelry, furs, and beautiful clothing for their wives and girlfriends. But one could not discuss anything with Fabish. As far as that German was concerned, the Jews were not living creatures. Jewish property he held as his own, and under the pretext of the government's requirements, he stole whatever he wanted.

[Page 649]

Jews also were forced to set up a brothel, at their own expense, located in a Jewish house at 11 Pulaski Street.

At the beginning of November, 1941, the ghetto was established. Leaving the ghetto was punishable by death. Hunger ruled in the ghetto, along with typhus, which spread easily because of the crowded lodgings. Just as people were kidnapped for work, so the fear of death seized all hearts. Terrible news about barbaric deportations and murders reached us, but it was not believed. People comforted themselves with the thought that the Germans would not destroy such a reservoir of laborers as occupied the ghetto.

Every day, 1500 workers left the ghetto, aside from the regular workers who had personal permissions to leave—they labored at specific jobs. Siedlce was truly a center for transport to the Russian front. The need for workers grew every day. Workers were brought in from surrounding towns, which strengthened our hopes of remaining alive. Meanwhile, though, the terror increased. The Gestapo became more severe. Every day at the gates of the ghetto there were executions.

Terror, Murder, and Death-Wagons

Whoever fell into the hand of the Gestapo, for whatever reason, never returned home alive. First came examinations with the help of rods. After "guilt" was "established," a sentence was issued, though the condemned were not informed of it. In the evening, between 10 and 11, the condemned were led to the gates of the ghetto, at 11 Listopad, or Torgowa. They were told to run toward the gates and were shot from behind. Every evening, those who lived in the neighboring houses were disturbed by shots, and early every day the Jewish police gathered up the bodies.

Fourteen thousand Jews were shut up in the Siedlce ghetto, and the bosses over life and death for the Jews were:

[Page 650]

The city commissar—S.S. Man Fabish; head of the Gestapo, Dube; and the work chiefs Zorga and Sonntag.

On August 20, the Jewish Council received an order from the Work Office to send several score of workers to offload a train in the station. It could go no further because of a burned axle. Rumors spread in the ghetto that in the wagon there were Jews from Radom. The only Jew from Radom in the ghetto was among the workers—Heniek Adler. The picture that confronted the the workers was a portent of the fate that awaited the Jews of Siedlce in the near future. This wagon was part of the "death train" that took Jews to Treblinka, but because of the burned axle, it could not proceed to its destination.

When the workers opened the wagon, they confronted a hundred dead bodies, squeezed together, one on top of the other. All had died from heat, from lack of air, and from the smell of lime that was spread out across the wagon's floor.

Under the clubs of the S.S. convoy, the workers had to unload the wagon. The corpses were taken to the Jewish cemetery and buried. Heniek Adler from Radom recognized among them many whom he had known. This incident firmly undercut the rumors that the Germans had spread that those tortured in the wagon were prisoners who were being taken from one prison to another.

Consequently the fear of the inevitable end grew in the ghetto. Reports that arrived from other cities showed the Germans were carrying out a barbaric extermination of the Jews. On Friday, August 21, 1942, we heard about the aktion that took place in Minsk-Mazowieck, 40 kilometers from Siedlce. We already knew about the liquidation of the Warsaw Ghetto that began on July 22, but the liquidation of Minsk-Mazowieck caused a terrible panic for us.

The Jewish Council, headed by Dr. Henryk Loebel, reassured people that in Siedlce "it would not happen."

[Page 651]

A big Jewish center like Warsaw could not be sustained, but Siedlce would be spared because of its great work productivity (3,000 workers were employed daily)—in this way the Jewish Council repeated the lies of the Germans in Siedlce. Even on that terrible day, when the liquidation of the ghetto in Siedlce began, August 21, 1942, the people on the Jewish Council assured us, in the name of the Germans, that nothing was happening. There was then an order from Himmler not to proceed with the destruction of the ghettos. This stratagem worked to pacify the ghetto for several hours.

The Extermination Aktion Begins

In the evening, the workers who were employed outside of the ghetto returned to their homes, bringing the news that the Polish police, the so-called grenade police from Pilsudski faction, who worked for the Germans, were called to an assembly at 3 in the morning. The news spread like lightning throughout the ghetto and left no one with any illusions. We all knew what that meant. The distress and panic grew larger in the ghetto every minute. Some people sought hiding places. Some packed their bags, under the delusion that they could escape. Most people, however, were resigned to the fact that the situation was inescapable—we were all condemned to death.

That night—this was Friday night, the 21st to 22nd of August, the ghetto was surrounded by thick squads of Gestapo, gendarmes, special service men, and Polish police. Soon shots were heard and the first victims fell—people who had tried to get out through the fence around the ghetto. In the morning, the shooting increased. At 7 in the morning, as usual, the Jewish police gathered in order to receive their "daily orders." Gestapo men arrived. They were delighted with the orderliness of the police and issued a command: to gather in the square of the burned synagogue all the Jews, without regard to age or illness. Whoever did not obey by 9 o'clock was condemned to death. The Jewish police carried out the orders of the Gestapo. They spread through the ghetto and called out the orders of the Germans.

[Page 652]

The burned synagogue

In the square by the burned synagogue the Jews gathered. Many came with baggage. They believed that they were being sent elsewhere. At the same time, the various German bandit groups—S.S. men, special services, extermination squads, Germans, Ukrainians, and Lithuanians robbed and murdered every Jew they encountered in a dwelling. Pszetsszecki and Goldblatt were shot in their own homes. The number of Jews in the square grew larger. New groups arrived with panic in their eyes, driven on by the Germans who attacked their victims with shots and whips. Dead bodies of teenagers and children lay on the sidewalk. Living children also lay abandoned on the sidewalk. Across from the Umschlagplatz [assembly point] was the building of the Jewish hospital. The dead were left lying as a warning to others. The wounded had a different fate. Commissar Fabish said the hospital and the doctors would remain and take care of the wounded.

[Page 653]

Suddenly the number of people in the square increased. There were now about 12,000, but that was not everyone. The Germans, with their helpers, ransacked the homes, spreading death and destruction and driving people to the square with whips. The Jews from the so-called "Three Corners," from that part of the ghetto composed of the following streets: 1th of November, Sokolow, and Oslonawicz—were gathered into a courtyard by one of the houses and shot by the "special services."

In the square itself, where the 12,000 Jews had gathered at the command of the Gestapo, the Germans carried out bestial murders. Several Gestapo men sat on the sidewalk and occupied themselves by shooting—at Jewish heads. Whoever raised his head got a bullet. Other Germans sought out old Jews with beards, dragged them out of the crowd, and made them sing, dance, jump around , and then struck the heads of their unfortunate victims with the handles of their revolvers or shot at them—such sadistic entertainment the Germans had at the Jews's expense as they led them to death. Dr. Henryk Loebel arrived at the square, the Elder of the Jews. He was also the chief doctor in the Jewish hospital. The Germans wanted to leave him so that he could stay at his post in the hospital, but he refused and came to the square so that he could accompany the members of his community.

The Jews stayed in the square for three hours. They had to remain lying down. Anyone who raised his head was shot. There were about 300 dead, aside from the wounded. The Germans ordered the Jewish police to accompany them to Jewish dwellings to see if there were any Jews. The police carried out the Germans' commands. In the afternoon, the commander of the Jewish police received an order to prepare lunch for 15 people. Each one should get a chicken with wine. The Jew murderers would eat lunch, while those condemned to death had to serve them. Soon after this order, the Obergruppenfuhrer" of the S.S. arrived and ordered that he should be given two pairs of silk socks. He was quickly given this gift.

The "Umschlagplatz," where 12,000 condemned to death lay, and near them hundreds of the murdered and wounded, was transformed into a macabre entertainment. On the other side of the fence, on Pilsudski Street, stood many Poles who watched the slaughter of Jews.

[Page 654]

Germans entertain themselves by pulling the beards of Siedlce's Jews.
In the middle is Shachna Rubinstein (from Sokolow).

[Page 655]

Nachum the water carrier, Sholem
Bronfnmacher's son-in-law

#1—Yisrolke, the chazan and mohel.
#2—Yidl Tzenerkop.
#3—Yehoshua-Feivush, the sexton of the Tailors'
Shul.

Among the Germans there was a special group whofilmed this Jewish spectacle. In the middle of the street, the mass murderers set up a table and, in the midst of the dead and the half-dead, celebrated a cannibalistic meal. The photographers and film makers brought their equipment close up to the unfortunate victims so that their images would be precise.

The Selection for Life and Death

The head of the extermination command called Dr. Loebel and ordered him to distribute this order: "All able-bodied men from 15 to 45 years of age must present themselves and run the gauntlet." Dr. Loebel delivered the order and all the men presented themselves and proceeded through the ranks of Germans, who hit each one with the butts of rifles, with sticks, and with whatever else they had in their hands. They were especially fierce with Jews who tried to identify themselves with work certificates or with passes for German work projects. Whoever showed the smallest scrap of paper received murderous blows until he expired. The only passport that earned going to the right, that is, to the working groups, was—torn clothing and hands with calluses.

Without any process, "the elder of the Jews," Dr. Henrik Loebel, and the leader of the work office of the Jewish Council, Ezriel Friedman, passed through. A few days later, the head of the Gestapo, Dube, shot Dr. Loebel together with the hospital personnel and Friedman at a gate at the corner of First of May and Torgowa Streets. Among those being sent to Treblinka, the Germans placed the long-time clerk of the Jewish community organization and secretary of the Jewish Council, Hersz Tenenbaum. As secretary, Tenebaum had saved not a single Jew from the claws of the Gestapo. In the name of the Jewish Council, he also obeyed every German command

and satisfied their needs. Now, at the selection for who would live and who would die, everyone envied the Jewish Council secretary, because his familiarity with the Germans would "save" him. The Gestapo put him on the first transport to Treblinka.

[Page 656]

At the time of the selection it became clear to everyone that older men and women and children were beyond the bounds of life. Some ended their lives right on the spot. Mrs. Dr. Pfau poisoned herself with potassium cyanide. Others cut their wrists and waited to bleed to death. There was no end to the suffering of the unfortunates. Every couple of hours, Fabish ordered the firemen to spray the square full of people.

At 5 o'clock, the group of about 1500 chosen people was herded into a demarcated "triangle," which was guarded by the "special services," Polish police were prepared to take over the "selected." A minute after the work-group departed, the shooting began with redoubled force. Dr. Loebel had not gone into the "triangle," but into the hospital, which was a hundred meters from the Umschlagplatz and had been ready to help the people. The hospital aides, dressed in white, gathered together the wounded and also the unwounded. They put white uniforms on some and thus saved them. Finally, permission was given to the Jewish police to give drinking water to the unfortunates. Despite all these efforts, very few people were able to leave the square.

In this outhouse, they shot the rabbi from the butcher's beis-medresh. Nr. 1—The crate containing the rabbi's body. Standing are Yontl Goldman and two Polish children. Note: Our fellow citizen Yontl Goldman took care of the burial of the murdered in Siedlce. In this way he served many.

Throughout the night from Shabbos until Sunday, the Germans went wild in the ghetto looking for those in hiding, robbing, and burning.

[Page 657]

During that night they shot in the ghetto 200 people whom they rousted from hiding places. The German associates of the "special services" shot 30 who were hidden in Yankel's bakery. Among those shot were the family of Yankel the baker. On the premises of the mikveh, about 50 people were shot. In the office of the Jewish Council about 20 were shot, and under it the family of Ephraim Zelnick.

Early on Sunday they began to clear the dead from the street. The "selected group" from the "triangle" conducted the work under the leadership of Rubinstein, the commander of the Jewish police. The collection of the dead proceeded in the following way: two people were hooked up to a wagon and dragged it through the streets, while others piled up the bodies. When the wagon was full, it was taken to the gate of the ghetto and there Polish wagoners transferred the dead into their wagons and and took them to the Jewish cemetery. In this terrible work, a few hidden people managed to escape. They came out from their hiding places, ran to the wagons, and after doing the work, went with the others to the "triangle, which was already called "the little ghetto."

For two days and two nights the unfortunate ones lay in the square. During the day they were tortured by the heat and the constant fear of death from the infernal shooting. First thing Monday morning, the Gestapo took the first group to the baggage station and there packed them into the death wagons. The route for the death train was short: Siedlce to Treblinka, 35 kilometers. So it went for two days. On Monday and Tuesday, there was transport after transport. The last left on Wednesday morning. In the wagons, covered with uncollected waste, 100-120 people were packed. The packing of the wagons was aided by rifle butts, axes, and other blunt instruments. Many fell by the wagons. Shmuel Leviton was struck in the head with an axe by a Ukrainian. The Polish police did not hold back from beating and robbing. Many dead were taken from the wagons to the cemetery and buried there in a single grave—the dead with the wounded who were still alive.

[Page 658]

The last road to the baggage station.
Nr. 1—Binyamin Kramarsh.

On the transport there was no one bold enough to jump from the wagons. Later on, people jumped from the transports. People broke boards from the wagons and jumped out. The German guards who escorted the train shot. Many fell dead or were wounded and later were beaten either by the police or by the peasants. The train line from Siedlce to Treblinka was littered with the dead and wounded. A few people managed to get back to the city and fled to the "small ghetto."

In the "Small Ghetto."—The Shooting of the Hospital Personnel

In the "small ghetto" the "selected" workers took to organizing their lives. A strong Gestapo unit guarded the ghetto. On Monday the "extermination unit" left Siedlce. In the now-emptied large ghetto, the German army continued to go wild: they searched for hidden Jews and emptied out the dwellings. Due to the large reduction in German strength and the bribing of Polish police, a few hidden Jews managed to get to the "small ghetto."

[Page 659]

No women were allowed there, only men. The rescued women, therefore, dressed in men's clothing. Many spent all their days in the attics, fearing that they would be recognized by the Gestapo, who kept close watch on the "small ghetto." Their fate in the future was a tragic question: what would happen if the German army would capture them: would they be "stood up against the wall" or would they be allowed to continue their painful lives?

Despite their horrible, bloody Gehenna, despite the pools of blood in the streets and the constant traffic to the Jewish cemetery of the shooting victims, and although their lives had lost all value—the inhabitants of the "small ghetto" wanted to live. Things went so far that several small children who had been brought into the "triangle" were suffocated because their existence could betray the women who were hidden there and could lead to the liquidation of the rest of the "selected ones."

By Wednesday, the large ghetto was still not completely empty. Found there were: the Jewish hospital with 60 patients, 4 doctors, 2 surgeons, nurses, aides, and those rescued from the Umschlagplatz—altogether about 100 people. Aside from the hospital and those people whose existence was permitted by the German powers, there were also in the ghetto some hidden people. Cut off from the world, lacking food, and living in fear of death, they waited with faith—perhaps they could be eventually be rescued.

After sending out the final transport to Treblinka, a unit of Ukrainians came to the hospital courtyard under Fabish's command. He gave an order calling all hospital personnel immediately to the courtyard. All came: Dr. Henryk Loebel with his wife and son; Dr. Leon Glazowski, Dr. Shoal Shwartz, Dr. Shlomo Tenenbaum; two old and veteran surgeons—Josef Alberg and Yankel Tenenbaum; the oldest nurses—Fella Friedman and Edusha Alberg; the laboratory personnel—Lola Saltzman with her mother and sister; the staff, among whom were Tzesha Temkin, Dora Goldblatt, Sala Rabinowicz, and Bronka Shoferman.

[Page 660]

After this order to the hospital personnel, the S.S. men shot the patients who lay in their beds, including some newborns. Later on, the S.S. murderers shot the hospital personnel with handguns. The first to be shot was Dr. Loebel with his wife. Their son tried to escape in the hospital garden, and he found a hiding place. He hid for a year and a half, but finally he was discovered by the gendarmes and was shot. After Dr. Loebel, all the other hospital workers were shot. Their warm bodies, in their white and bloody hospital coats, were taken through the streets to the Jewish cemetery. Their blood dripped from the wagons and showed the path that they took.

Besides the doctor's son, from the hospital personnel the lab worker Lola Saltzman also escaped. She was lightly wounded by the shots and lay with the dead bodies of her mother and sister. When the murderers were gone, she left the hospital courtyard and snuck into the "small ghetto."

In the small ghetto, a "normal" life was established. The hard reality, the tragic conditions, and the difficult labor so dulled the people that they could not think about nor imagine anything else.

The wagon taking corpses to the cemetery

[Page 661]

Hard Work, Suffering, and Death

The Germans encouraged the illusion that people would be allowed to live. Commissar Fabish gave assurance that if people went regularly to their labor, the "small ghetto" would be sustained. To reinforce the illusion, the women who had hidden in the large ghetto were given an amnesty. The women were given a special task: to go every day into the large ghetto. There they would go through the empty houses and put the things they found in order. The next day, 30 women were led under the watch of Polish police to their job. In the evening they were taken by cars to the Jewish cemetery and there were shot on the pretext that they had stolen clothing from the abandoned homes and put them on. Among those shot was the wife of the lawyer Landau. She left behind two small children.

After this mass murder of women, Fabish assured people that if the women would not steal, they would face no danger. But this assurance reassured no one. The women refused to go to this labor. The police sought them out and forced them to go. After a couple of days, when the women returned from the work alive and they were permitted to bring with them leftover items from the empty houses—the women were reconciled with doing the work.

The wall where they shot the 30 women.
Yontel Goldman points with his finger to the wall.

[Page 662]

Several German undertakings took their workers from the "small ghetto." They put them in barracks and established for them communal kitchens. Thus it was in the area of Siedlce, so that it was like several score of small work camps, among which the smallest numbered several persons, and the largest, several hundred. The living conditions in the larger and smaller camps were not at all alike. They depended on the direction of the overseer of each camp.

Life in the camps was generally difficult, but in comparison to the lives of the workers in the "small ghetto" it was an "oasis" of peace and well-being. In the "small ghetto," each person, after a hard day at work, came home dead tired and had to scrounge for food. No one could even think about regular meals. There was no official supply of food in the ghetto. The powers in charge and the employers gave no thought to that. The food that people smuggled into the ghetto went for such high prices that only those who had been paid could afford it. So people starved; the starving people lay down to "sleep"—that is, they stuffed themselves into a corner and wrapped their collars around their ears so they could not hear what was going on.

People had long given up on a good night's sleep. The terrible crowding and the constant shooting at the ghetto fence did not allow it. The victims of this "sport" were collected each morning by the police. The crowding in the dwellings was so bad that on the average there were 20 to 30 people in a mid-size room. The room would be full of people—no beds, cots, or bedding were available. The attics, stairways, and basements also served as living spaces.

[Page 663]

The whole small ghetto consisted of wooden houses, only two of which had a single story. In the "small ghetto" there were also Roma. The Germans put them into two buildings, one with one story and one with two. The Roma stole from the Jews their last bits of poverty that they had brought from the large ghetto and they informed on the Jews to Fabish and to the Gestapo.

Commissar Fabish and Dube, head of the Gestapo, often visited the ghetto. They came every day. Their visits ended either with sadistic beatings of "chosen" workers or with the seizure of people who a few hours later would have to be buried by the Jewish police. When Fabish summoned Jewish police, they brought with them spades and shovels, because they knew what Fabish wanted of them.

Hunger and need so weakened the people that they had no strength left for work. The Germans therefore ordered seizures. Early every morning, at about 5:30, a group of police, soldiers, and special service men would fall upon the ghetto and the hunt would begin. Dragged to the courtyard were the old, the young, the healthy and the ill. They were beaten and tortured, and even the women were not spared.

The Jewish Council in the "Small Ghetto" and Its Activities

In the "small ghetto," the Jewish Council organized itself. At its head was the former vice-chair of the Jewish Council in the large ghetto—Hersz Eisenberg. His associates were the leader of the workers' office on the Jewish Council, Moshe Rotbejn, and the provision director, Anatol Goldberg. The first task of the newly-formed Jewish Council consisted of collecting several thousand zlotys for Commissar Fabish. He ordered this as a reward for the firemen for their work in spraying the Jews with water while they lay in the "Umschlagplatz" awaiting the transport to Treblinka. Further, the Jewish Council was occupied in organizing a constant supply of bread at normal prices and supplying the ghetto with the necessary medications and first-aid equipment. Soon these matters were taken care of.

[Page 664]

This quick settling of the concerns of the ghetto was one of the tactics of the German extermination program. They had to blind the eyes and distract the attention of the Jews, whose end would come through death in the gas chambers. Through intervention with the directors of the Jewish Council, Fabish had ordered the city leaders of Siedlce to distribute ration cards to the inhabitants. The head of the Gestapo had given all three members of the Jewish Council permission to move freely around the city. Thanks to that, it was possible to establish contact with the bakers, who every day produced bread. There was an agreement with the pharmacists, who dealt with the medications. They were also allowed to purchase necessities for the ghetto, such as: lights (there was no electric lighting), matches, laundry powder, and so on.

Because of the hunger, filth, and hard labor, a variety of illnesses flourished in the "small ghetto," producing many victims. Aside from those being shot, every day, people died of illnesses. The "mortuary" was found in a stable in a muddy courtyard in the center of the "small ghetto." There the dead were laid directly onto the ground. Most were set down there completely naked, covered with flies. Once a week, an open wagon came, onto which the dead were hastily thrown and taken to the Jewish cemetery, where they were buried in a common grave.

A great addition to the mortality rate in the ghetto came from the German firm Reckman. The firm's headquarters were in Berlin. Its main concern was building train cars and train stations for freight. Here they employed several hundred Jews, who had to work until they dropped. For the slightest detail they were beaten unmercifully. The rations that the firm provided for the Jews consisted of a little dish of watery soup in which there swam a few bits of wilted greens and potatoes. In such conditions the people had to work until late into the night unloading the wagons and laying new tracks for the great number of military transports that were going to the east.

[Page 665]

Seldom did a worker last more than two weeks. Sending a person to work there amounted to sending him to a painful death. It was no wonder that no one wanted to work for the Reckman firm. The guards from the firm, together with the foremen, therefore each day ordered raids in the ghetto and later also kidnapped women for this difficult work.

Each day a supply of men who had fallen from weariness was brought back. There was a horrible procession: several score ragged and exhausted Jews dragged the train car, on which lay people with yellowed faces, swollen, with guards behind them. Thus did the Reckman firm send home Jews who had fallen from mistreatment at work. At their return to the ghetto, those incapable of work were taken out of the wagons. They were left lying on the ground. Sometimes someone snuck them a piece of bread or a bit of water, and thus they lay there until they expired. Among the unfortunate victims were many who had "escaped" to Siedlce from other ghettos that were liquidated earlier. The Reckman firm, through its labor system, helped the Germans carry out their extermination program while extracting large profits from the unfortunate doomed slaves. Despite the whole horrible and desperate situation, people quickly adapted to the sad reality to the extent possible.

Gradually in the "small ghetto" there was a change for "the better": the Roma were taken out, and the buildings that they had taken were divided among the Jews. This reinforced the feeling of security. People were comforted with the idea that nothing would happen during the winter. People began to prepare food and heating. Thus things went during September and October, and then the month of November arrived.

[Page 666]

The Germans Assemble the Jews for the Final Extermination

On the first of November the Germans issued an order to create five large ghettos. There they would settle all the Jews from the whole Government General. Siedlce belonged to the selected cities with a "Jewish ghetto." By the first of December, all the Jews from the surrounding towns, within about 40 kilometers had to assemble in the "small ghetto" in Siedlce.

The inhabitants of the "small ghetto" had various opinions about this order. Some took it as a good sign; others held that the danger was not obvious and they surmised that the Germans simply wanted to gather together all the Jews in the ghettos, those who remained alive and those who had been hidden, so that they could later easily send them to Treblinka. A few days later, the German authorities issued an order that the ghetto would be called the "Gesi Borek Labor Colony." This colony was three kilometers outside the city and consisted of three resident blocks in the middle of a field which were to be inhabited by the unemployed. The motive for moving the ghetto was announced—the danger of the typhus epidemic in the ghetto could have been transmitted to the Aryan side.

The move was supposed to begin on December 27, early. People were only permitted to take with them what they could carry in their hands. An extraordinary panic broke out. People feared the fate of the several score of children who had been smuggled into the ghetto and they were uneasy about the fate of the old and the ailing who could not make the several kilometer trip. Those people who over time had managed to get a bit of clothing, food, a sack of potatoes—it was hard for them to part with their few goods. A few days before the transfer, people managed to smuggle the things they had to leave behind outside the ghetto to Poles whom they knew. Not far from "Gesi Borek" was a glassworks, in which there labored several scores of Jews.

[Page 667]

The Jews lived there and people secretly took the smuggled goods to them. In the last two days, there were even wagons bearing goods. The Gestapo and the gendarmes closed their eyes so that they would not see what the Jews were doing. Naive people rejoiced that they were fooling the Germans. The last evening before the transfer to the new ghetto, people secretly took to the glassworks several score of people—among them, the old and ill. They were put in a nearby barn. In the morning they were supposed to be taken to the residential blocks. The last night in the "small ghetto" was sleepless and frightening. People thought: "Isn't 'Gesi Borek nothing more than a German joke, when in fact we will be taken to the station and from there sent to Treblinka?"

It Will Be "Good"—A "Free, Unfenced Ghetto"

In the morning, all assembled for the march. At 9 a.m., Fabish and the head of the Gestapo arrived. They looked over the lines of people, gave the final orders, and informed the Jewish Council that for transporting the ill and the weak there were wagons. In fact, soon enough several wagons appeared, sent by the magistrate. People loaded some packs and the ill on the wagons. At around noon, with sighs and weeping, people left the "small ghetto." The long column headed in the direction of "Gesi Borek." No one was ganged up on, shot or beaten. The trip lasted about 2 hours and ended with no one having collapsed. Again the hangmen pretended to drop their vigilance, but only the totally naive believed that the Germans had become better and had good intentions. People with deeper insight looked with dread at everything they saw and asked—what lay behind these German machinations?

"Gesi Borek" was a type of open ghetto, not surrounded by fencing. Jews felt free there and soon after their arrival at their new dwelling place they began to purchase food from the local peasants and even thought about straw for bedding. Things seemed good, but for how long?

[Page 668]

They did not have to wait long. Soon, in the morning after the arrival at the new ghetto, the labor office ordered all Jews who lived at their places of labor to move into the ghetto. Outside of the ghetto, only those Jews who had special permission could remain. Soon after, thanks to the Gestapo, they began to bring transports of Jews to Gesi Borek from the surrounding area, and one block of residences was given to the Roma. It began to grow hot. The storm was imminent.

The Jews from Loszitz, 30 kilometers from Siedlce, are brought to the Siedlce ghetto

People received no bread from the city. The single well could not supply everyone with water. There was another well in the courtyard of the Roma, but they would not spare the Jews any injustices. The crowding in the dwellings was again horrible, and on top of this another 1000 people arrived in the ghetto. Leaving the ghetto was forbidden upon pain of death. In the nearest village, several Jews who had gone to find food were shot.

The Final Liquidation of Siedlce's Jews

This situation did not last long. On the night between Shabbos and Sunday, from November 30 to December 1, "Gesi Borek" was surrounded with a heavy cordon of gendarmes, Polish police, and specially brought-in Ukrainian police. They called everyone out of their homes and beat everyone murderously, ordering them onto the ground near the houses.

[Page 669]

After a couple of hours sitting, they were commanded to get up and march. Soon there was an announcement that there were no wagons at the station. They were ordered to go into one block and not to stir from the spot. They were not even permitted to go from one room to another. Even without that command, it would not have been possible to go from one room to another because of the crowding. In the small room of the single-storied brick building there were about 3,000 people.

So there we sat, crowded together, for all of Sunday. During the day, the various German employers brought their Jewish laborers and delivered them to the hands of the Ukrainian police. The following businesses retained their Jewish workers:

1) Gravel pit mines "Kisgrube"—200 people; 2) trains—100 people; 3).camp for army welfare—150 people; 4) agriculture syndicate—30 people; 5) glassworks—about 60 people. There were two firms whose names I do not remember that presented their Jewish workers.

The condemned sat there for a whole day without a drop of water. There was unbearable shooting. People who looked out of the window were shot. In the square between the houses they shot: the head of the Jewish Council Hersz Eisenberg with his wife and one-year-old daughter and the commander of the Jewish police—Avraham Ressler. He was killed by an older Polish policeman with whom he had had personal difficulties.

In the evening there was a terrible wind and a snow storm. It became completely dark, so that one could not see. The darkness encouraged a few bold ones to jump out of the windows. The guards began to shoot blindly and constantly. Scores tried to escape and two hundred were shot.

Early Monday we were taken outside and arranged in columns, then taken to the "Falmin" train station. There were no wagons there. We were forced to sit in the snow and wait. Meanwhile, the Gestapo men walked among the columns and took from the unfortunate people their last bit of money, rings, earrings, and so on.

[Page 670]

A couple of hours later, the train arrived and they began to load the Jews. The Jewish police ripped off their insignias and wanted to board with everyone else. But the murderers would not permit them to. For their fidelity and service during the whole time the ghetto existed—the Jewish police received a privilege—a wagon all their own.

The last Jews of the Siedlce ghetto walk to the loading station on their way to Treblinka

Around 4 in the afternoon the train moved in the direction of Treblinka. The "passengers" were not ignorant of their fate, which had already overtaken hundreds of thousands who had gone on the same route. All aspects of that treacherous and awful "death mill," Treblinka, were already well known. Three months after the first aktions, during the time of the "small ghetto," people who had through some miracle escaped from the flames of the crematoria took refuge in Siedlce, which was almost always their first place to rest. They told the truth about Treblinka. No one believed the German assurances that they were being taken to labor in the eastern areas, and they therefore sought the possibility of avoiding the death wagons.

As soon as the train started to move, people in many of the wagons sought a way to create openings. The well-known Siedlce locksmith, Szymka Wilk, brought tools with him with which one could open locked wagons. When the train was fully in motion, Wikl opened his wagon and many of the condemned leapt out.

[Page 671]

Also many jumped out of the wagon carrying the Jewish police. The majority of those who leapt out were shot on the spot or captured. Those who managed to escape the bullets ran back to the area of Siedlce and went to the work centers where there were still Jewish workers. Although these Jews lived with the fear of death and had no security from hour to hour, they accepted into their barracks the escapees and protected them from the guards. And these workers did not hold out for long either. Anticipating the danger, a portion escaped from the work camp into the woods. Others forged Aryan papers and lived in various towns. Those who could not, or who feared running from the work camp, were taken out to the Jewish cemetery and shot. They were taken out in groups—each day a separate group. The last were the Jewish workers from the train, and gravel pit firms.

The Jewish possessions were liquidated in the following way: the best and most expensive things were taken by the Germans. The rest were sold for groschen to the Poles. They went off with wagons full. Peasants in particular loved buying Jewish items. They would stand for several hours in lines in order to get some. Everything that remained in the "small ghetto" and "Gesi Borek" was given away to the Roma.

In 1943, Siedlce was "Judenrein." From time to time a Jew would be captured in the area, but he would be shot on the spot.

Thus did Hitler's murderers obliterate a center of Jewish life that had numbered 17,000 souls, a center that had glittered with a rich cultural and community life.

Some people survived the liquidation of the Siedlce ghetto by means of Aryan papers. The escapees joined underground organizations that fought against the enemy. A number of them were killed anonymously. I know a little about four Siedlcers: the dentist Dr. Stanislaw Gilgun was killed in the Warsaw uprising; brothers Anatol and Stanislaw Goldberg lived under the names Stanislaw and Antoli Gurki. They were taken in Warsaw and tortured by the Gestapo; Kuba Levin fell in Lublin fighting for freedom.

[Page 672]

A number of Jews from Siedlce with Aryan papers were sent to Germany for compulsory labor, along with other Poles. There they suffered hunger, destitution, they worked hard in war industries, and in the spring of 1945 they were liberated. I was among them.

Yontel Goldman prepared the bones of the tailor Sosnowicz, who was beheaded by his Polish neighbors in Roskosz. His neighbor stands nearby. Yontel's brother is also there. The young woman fled from Bonn, going to Treblinka.

Yontel Goldman puts into a crate the bodies of Friedman's daughter (from the dry goods shop), with her small child and her uncle Chanina Rafal, whom the Germans killed in Hopelia (near Siedlce).

Yontel Goldman puts into a crate the bodies of the Rafal family: a woman, her two children, and her mother-in-law, shot in Hopelia (near Siedlce)

The execution of 18 Jews, among them Zebrowicz. They were murdered shortly before the liberation, November 10, 1943

[Page 673]

On the fourth yahrzeit of the last Jews from Siedlce being sent to Treblinka, a small monument made of pieces of grave markers is set up in the Siedlce cemetery.
Under the monument is a common grave in which lies also the rabbi of the butcher's beis-medresh.
Standing by the monument are: 1. Velvel Goldfinger. 2. Shmuel Alberstadt. 3. Moyshe Alberstadt. 4. Simchah Levin.
5. Monish Ridel.
6. Yontel Goldman. 7. Eli Kishilinski. 8. Chaim Rizo. 9. Gwiazre. 10. Raphael Kishilinski from Hopelia.
11. Yidl Rozowikwicz (Lidl Kessele).

[Page 674]

My Survival During the German Occupation

by Rokhl Shmukliasz-Vainshtain

Translated by Theodore Steinberg

When the war broke out I lived in Kotzk with my husband Mendel Wishnieh. Desiring to see my parents, Aaron Shmukliasz and Ratze, and my sister and brother, I took a chance and ignoring the fact that no Jew dared be seen in the street or traveling by train, I went to Siedlce in order to see my relatives. In Siedlce, on March 15, 1941, in the Jewish hospital I gave birth to my daughter Batya, with the help of Dr. Lebel.

In the hospital, the whole Jewish intelligentsia cooperated in order to escape being killed. Among them was my former teacher Edzia Alberg, my former drama director from the drama club in "Ha-Zamir," Yakov Tenenbaum. Eight days after the birth of my daughter, that is, on March 23, 1941, a terrible pogrom began in Siedlce, led by the Germans. The moans and cries could be heard in the highest heavens. They threw women and children from the balconies. Berl Wengrowskiy and others whose names I do not remember, were shot in the mouth. Children were stabbed with bayonets. The Germans tried to drown out the screams and cries of the victims with the noise from truck engines, motorcycles, and other machines.

Thanks to the extraordinary efforts of my husband, I was able to escape from that Gehenna. I managed to get back to Kotzk safely with my child. Despite the great hardships, I was able to stay in contact with Siedlce. I learned that my father, on his way to work, had been hit on the head by an SS man, which caused an infection. His foot had to be amputated. His soul departed in the Jewish hospital.

[Page 675]

Siedlce was devoid of Jews. My mother and sister had to flee from Siedlce and stay with a Christian, Barkowski, in the village of Shmiari. Not wanting to be separated from me, they came by back roads to Kotzk, where we were together for three weeks.

In Kotzk, people had already begun to speak of an "action" that signified the liquidation of the ghetto. My relatives advised me that I should flee with with my child to Warsaw, using Aryan certifications. Following their instructions I decided to leave Kotzk. Parting from my relatives was tragic. I truly did not want to leave them, preferring to die together with them. But my beloved mother reassured me and gave me courage and hope that we would soon see each other because they would come to me as soon as possible. Finally, I left.

Traveling by train to Warsaw with my fourteen-month-old child, the Christians recognized me as a Jew. They stabbed me with their poisonous words, and not wanting to be taken by them, I decided to throw myself under the train with my child. But suddenly one Christian grabbed hold of me and would not let me jump from the train.

I can still hear his words: "I hate Jews, but I feel pity for a mother with a small chid"—and he rescued me from certain death.

The Pole's actions affected all onlookers in the car. They left me in peace, and so I arrived in Warsaw. With my Aryan papers, I managed to fit in among the Poles, always in a panic. I lived with my child in constant fear of death, and thus I survived the war.

[Page 676]

About the Final 2000 Jews of Siedlce

by Dov–Ber Blechstein (Jerusalem)

Translated by Theodore Steinberg

I will offer a collection of memories about my experiences in Siedlce in those black autumn days of 1943.

In those days there were already a number of cities and towns in the General Government of Poland that were "cleansed" of Jews. Most of them had already been killed. In Warsaw, Siedlce, and in a few other cities, as well as in the labor camps, a small number of Jews remained. Hitler's killers worked slowly, with German efficiency and diligence; the Jews had to be exterminated until the very end–made to "disappear," so the "actions" were conducted frequently. The plan also involved using the physical labor of the Jews. So the Jews were crowded into the diminished ghettos and labor camps.

This is how I survived the "actions" in Warsaw and in Otwock. In Otwock, after the bloody "action," a few hidden Jews remained. On the morning after the liquidation, the houses were searched. Those who were found were shot on the spot. I was in a group about to be shot, but suddenly there was an announcement: "Let us have no more to do with the Jews. What we have done will not find favor with America."–So said the Polish police who were guarding us. So the group of us, around 60, were taken by transport to Kolbiel, where there was a "permanent ghetto." From there I was taken to Kaluszyn. In Kaluszyn I was seized by the SS and taken to the Siedlce labor camp of the "Richard Reckman Engineering Company."

The name "Reckman" was a well–known horror in Jewish Kaluszyn.

[Page 677]

I, along with some others, was led to this hellish place. When we had gone a couple of kilometers from Kaluszyn, the transport stopped. Soon an SS officer appeared. He took us to his small car and said, "Work hard and in two weeks you will be able to leave on furlough." We formed a column. Along the way I often saw Jews with shovels in their hands that were intended for the work. Finally we arrived at the area of the train station.

In "Reckman's" Gehenna

When we got out of the car, it was pretty dark. We were met by Germans, A Jewish young man told us in Yiddish and Polish that any skilled laborer should identify himself. I identified myself as a joiner. Soon we were led into the barracks. Hungry and tired, we fell fully clothed onto the ground and kay on the muddy, filthy straw. The night was half gone and soon we were awakened. We had to stand up immediately and stand in a thousand–person line in order to receive a little cup of chamomile tea and a tiny piece of bread with marmalade. It was still dark. Fog still hung in the air. Hundreds of electric lights shimmered, lighting up a huge area of railroad tracks, buildings, and building materials. We were given a while to eat. Standing there, the little bit I ate wore off and I began to feel hungry.

Later there was a roll call. The German overseers called for their former and newly selected workers and led them to work. Fear was palpable. Men were transformed into working animals who were beaten with whips. Some were torn open, barefoot, bloody. I understood that they would beat you bloody. I became acquainted with the German with the "Red Sling." He was there terror of the prisoners. Every day he had to have a bloody victim. The groups went off to their daily tasks, to shoveling sand, to working the concrete, mostly to digging, carrying, and so on. The skilled workers worked in their crafts. We went gratefully to the joinery and to the cross–saw.

[Page 678]

At noon there was a signal and we all stood in a row, which from day to day grew longer. In charge of our lunch was a Pole who held a thick stick. Without provocation, he struck out to the right and to the left. People said that this stick–hero was the former teacher Zayancz. Anyone who had a bowl and a spoon could eat a half–liter of chestnut soup, in which one could sometimes find a potato. Once I noticed that in the kitchen worked Jewish girls from Siedlce and a couple of men. For such good jobs they must have paid a lot, but they were not to be envied. One fellow was beaten to death there. Standing in line lasted a long time, so that often there was not enough time to finish the little bit of soup.

The Polish train officials and workers had their own kitchen, where soup could be bought for a zloty. This is what was left over after the meat and the other substantial elements were removed. One had to sustain himself with this little bit of purchased food. The German civil officials at the train station had brought their families from Germany–wives and children. German children used to walk through the work area and mock the Jews, striking them with sticks. Woe to those whom they found with a bowl of food near the Polish kitchen. I myself was well beaten by a teenaged "Hitler youth." I could barely get away, and defending oneself meant certain death through gruesome means.

Horrible were the days and painful the nights. For sleeping, we were treated like cattle in a stall–all the time in a different spot. For a short while my group slept about two km. from the workplace. We were awakened by the German overseers and the Jewish enforcers– the well–known Jewish ghetto police. In our stall there was much anxiety that if one had to go out at night, he would no longer return to the place where he had previously lain. Therefore it often happened that one lay in his own urine, even when it became frosty…

[Page 679]

Every morning the roll call was repeated. Then people went off to their unbearable compulsory work; again there were long lines of exhausted, bloodied Jews and again the question arose: what else could happen?

One Jew, a heavy fellow, bloodied, whose clothes consisted of a sack around his loins, threw himself into a pit full of water, trying to kill himself. Merciful Jews pulled him out of the water and he again was forced to stand for the roll call. Someone pointed out that this was an unsuccessful suicide attempt and he should be given easier labor. To this the "Red Sling" responded, "It's too bad you rescued him. Now he'll have to die gradually." Meanwhile, the SS people appeared in the camp and shot the weak, who could no longer work quickly. In the morning, at the roll call, the work commander said: "Do your job so that you don't end up like they did yesterday." People continued to seek a bit of hope, and more than one thought, " We are not the guilty ones…"

The Nights of Horror and Terror

A short time passed. For a week I slept outside the city. My companion was a wagoner from Kielce, a good soul. He worried over me and took care of me. One time I had to sleep nearer to our workplace, in the area of the train station near the bridge. That was a night of horror and terror.

In the middle of the night, someone pulled my sleeve. Friends awakened me. We were formed into a work detail that had to bury the dead in the middle of the night. So half dead, verging on death ourselves, we went to bury those who were already dead. We found some taleisim, I don't know how. We buried the martyrs in deep silence and respect near the foundation of the building we had worked on that day. The workers from Siedlce made a mark near their fellows' grab, so that anyone who saw it would know that this is the resting place of those who had been killed.

[Page 680]

That night I could sleep no more. I was fated to have more terrible experiences.

From the train area came bitter laments and cries. Once before, in Otwock, I had heard such desperate sounds. Every hour the overseer would turn on his electric light. Then I saw around me the exhausted sleeping men. Only one young man was not lying down: he was standing and praying. Twice more by the glow of the watchman's light I saw him swing in prayer, and when dawn arrived, I saw him in the same position. When people were commanded to stand–he had finished his prayers. I suddenly realized that this had been the night of Yom Kippur…

The Polish railway workers told us that at night people had transported the Jews of Kaluczne, and that news spread through the camp. The Nazi hangmen always used the Jewish holy days to carry out their bestial murders.

Yontl Goldman looks over the bodies of the murdered in the train station of Siedlce. He holds 500 zlotys that he found on one of the murdered

***Yontl Goldman lays out one of the murdered, who was found
by the station without documents***

[Page 681]

I was dumbstruck–I had left my family in Kaluczne. I tried to say that it could not be true. I had been sending cards to my relatives inn Kaluczne that a Polish worker had been taking into town and mailing. It had only been a couple of days since I received back my last cards with the inscription "Address does not exist." By that time I understood German refined, sinister perfidy. I knew about gas chambers in Treblinka. Already in Kolibiel I had encountered a Jew from Warsaw, a porter, who had loaded up in Treblinka the clothing of those who had been gassed. He hid himself in the piles of clothing and got out in one of the wagons. He escaped and told me everything. The inscription "Address does not exist" gave me no rest for days and nights.

The arrival of new Jews in the camp unfortunately indicated that the "Actions" had increased. At roll call the Germans told us: "There have been cases when people escaped from the camp, but where can they go? Your families no longer exist; there are no longer Jews in the cities; so work hard–those who work, live!" This refrain I heard many times in different places.

Things went worse and worse for me. I kept thinking about the fate of my dear ones, and more than once I thought it was better to be dead than alive. I became apathetic. But now my companions began to give me strength. They helped me to eat, especially the Siedlce blacksmith, who often gave me a piece of bread. Thus passed several days.

Early one morning, when I went to get my work tools, not far from the bridge, I saw a new "institution" in the camp: a foreman had opened a chamber and I saw before my eyes a detention chamber. The foreman called out the detainees, but no one moved. They hid in their miserable straw. The watchman fired a shot, and only then did I see wild faces with glazed over eyes. In the chamber had been confined people ill with fevers or injured from the labor. This was the home of the ailing inmates.

[Page 682]

Brotherly Help from the Afflicted

On Sundays people generally did not work. The directors–Germans and Poles–had to rest. We only had to work if there were interior matters. On these free days, those from Siedlce, under guard, went into the ghetto. For providing an escort, the work leaders received packs of cigarettes. One had to have permission to go. I dreamed about visiting the ghetto, and I regarded the Siedlce ghetto as a Garden of Eden.

First of all, I wanted to get a shirt there. My shirt was all torn up and full of lice. But I had received no permission for that. I went into the city with the carpenters to take in boards, and on the way we showed our companions the Jewish quarter. This was near a Gothic church with two tall towers. I took note of these.

I became familiar with the area and its appearance. My companions from Siedlce decided to help the foreign Jews after they heard about my experiences.

The privileged skilled craftsmen, to whom I did not belong, in the meantime received a new place to sleep in a stone building. They slept on wooden bunkbeds with straw mattresses. It was crowded. A few lay on the ground and they found a spot for me as well. I took advantage of the new sleep arrangement for a couple of nights. At night the group cooked and roasted potatoes. They generously gave me something to eat. Sundays were always an opportunity for more food, because the Siedlcers brought some food from the ghetto and then shared it with others. When I met someone new on a Sunday, he would give me a hand with my work and often bring a bit of food of his own.

When I remember the fellowship in that vale of tears, there swims up in my memory the generosity of the Italian soldiers. A number of them walked or drove through the work area.

[Page 683]

They threw us their fresh rolls and cigarettes. One of them took off his neckerchief and gave it to me. The Germans looked at him with contempt. One of the Germans called out to the Italians, "You don't understand anything."

Those more "merciful" days in the carpenter shop soon ended. I soon became superfluous there, and at the roll call I was assigned to carry railroad tracks. The work in the carpenter shop had been for me a pleasure, although there had also been difficulties. I worked really hard until my strength gave out. I was often beaten without provocation.

One time, the foreman threw at me an enormous board. I moved aside and avoided being killed. Another time, the foreman left me on my own for a short period, near the cross–saw, which was near the border of the work area. A German civilian who was going by was suspicious that I was escaping and he led me away to be shot. On the way, he beat me with my own hammer. My foreman returned an freed me from my assailant. One time a German stopped me, a train official. He told me to move back three steps and then he asked my profession. I answered that I was a carpenter. "Sure," he said. "You were a carpenter. You had a furniture store and you swindled Gentiles." Then he beat me with a board that he ordered me to give him–and this was the good stuff.

Now I became part of a group that was carrying railroad tracks. I could barely hold up for half a day. We carried tracks that were nailed to the ties. In each opening between the ties was placed a man who held the rails in his hands, stood up, and started moving. In the afternoon, I had to stand at the end of the track. I could no longer hold on to it. At first I walked bent over, and later I could not carry it at all. The overseer took me out of the line and started to beat me. I fell down and could not stand back up. He never stopped beating me. A second German came by and kicked me.

[Page 684]

Then he put his revolver to my temple. I was lying on the ground and thought I was seeing the last moments of my life. I did not care. Let death come–the redeemer. Suddenly there was a tumult, chaos, around me. The wagon driver lifted me up and put me in the middle of the line among the rails. He himself took my previous position at the end, the most difficult position, and he worked there for a good hour until night fell and work ended.

In the evening, I could not even go after a piece of bread and chamomile tea…I barely dragged myself to the dormitory of the craftsmen. There I collapsed, beaten and battered. I did not know what went on around me. My companions tried to cheer me up and later gave me a bit of boiled potato. Slowly I came to consciousness. They lay me down in my bed. Each of them came to me and advised me that early in the morning I should flee to the ghetto. Otherwise the overseer would beat me to death. My whole body ached and I was woozy. I could not think clearly. I thought that my end was near. At best they would send me to the "sick ward" that I had seen and I would suffer for a couple of days. The Siedlce ghetto seemed like a deliverance, but to get there I had to escape from the camp and sneak through the Aryan streets, which were full of deadly dangers. I thought it all over and decided that running to the ghetto is the best way out. Beaten and exhausted, I slept deeply. In the middle of the night I was awakened by a noise in the room. Something terrible happened.

In the night shift, Jews worked at finishing up sewer connections. A huge mountain of sand had collapsed and injured many of the workers. Our weary companions ran to rescue these unfortunates. I tried to get up, but I could not. I felt terrible and thought that I could not get to the ghetto. I fell back asleep. I was awakened by the noise of my friends returning. All of the injured ones were still alive. My companions did not allow me to go back to sleep.

[Page 685]

One brought me water so that I could wash myself. Another shaved me. They did all this so I would not look like an inmate on the Aryan side. The Jewish badge I had gradually stopped wearing, like the others. Recently there had been an order to wear a "band of shame." Some had made them out of paper, but generally people did not pay attention to it.

I washed up. This was one of the last times that I washed in the camp. Washing had a good effect on me. Day was beginning. No one spoke, but I sensed my companions' good wishes.

I left the building, which was near the street, and went by the train bridge. I turned left and went a fair distance. After a while, I found myself by train tracks. I knew that I had gone too far. I ran back to the bridge and there went to the right. Soon I saw the well–known church towers. I went quietly in that direction. I saw no one in the street except for one guard, who was sweeping. Soon I saw the barbed wire of the ghetto. I went along the fence until I found a wide opening. There was still a distance to the gate. I looked around and then crawled through the fence.

In the "Small Ghetto" of Siedlce

I finally reached my destination. By the fence stood an old, partially collapsed building. I decided to go in because I was afraid that someone might have noticed me. I entered a room with trepidation. A couple of women were in the room. Their husbands had gone to work. I briefly told them about myself and the women immediately gave me food and drink. After a short time there was suddenly some confusion: men were seized for labor. A man came in from outside and hid himself in a dresser in a dark corner. I did the same.

[Page 686]

For a good hour I lay there in an uncomfortable position. This was my introduction to the ghetto.

When I left my hiding place, I ran into a small Gypsy boy. [Trans. Note: "Gypsy" is a pejorative term, but it is the term that was used, so I retain it for authenticity.]. In the Siedlce ghetto, the Germans used Gypsy children to search for people who were hiding in the buildings. The child spotted me and I was seized for labor. I was placed in a work detail and sent to the train station to unload coal. So I found myself back at the station, but this time on the other side of the viaduct, opposite "Reckman's." I began to pour out coal, but it did not want to go. With me was a Jew from Vengerov whom I had known in Kalusze. He stood before me and told the German that I had had typhus and was just out of the hospital. The German ordered me out of the wagon so I could pick up coal from the ground. How this could have happened I still cannot explain, because the same German beat everyone else mercilessly with a cane. In the afternoon, another German came to guard us, and he shot a well–known dentist from Siedlce, Gelbfish. The coal was loaded into dump trucks. When the work had ended, we were taken in the same vehicles to unload the coal. It appeared that we were at the Siedlce land administrator, for whom the coal was intended. It was dark and cold. My comrades put me under a staircase and they unloaded and unloaded without stop through a hole in the cellar. It was quite dark when we were led through the ghetto gate. The man from Vengerov took me with him to eat in a kind of restaurant. I ate some and then I could not stand up. I must have had a fever, because everything became hazy. A young man from Otwock came over to me. I had traveled with him to Kalusze, and he cared for me, took me by the arm and led me through courtyards and up steps until in the darkness we arrived at an attic room, whose floor was covered with people who were lying down. The young man cleared a place for me and we both lay down to sleep.

I was awakened by the call, in German, "Time to get to work." I now observed the people lying there. They were asleep in their clothing.

[Page 687]

They stood up and went down. Only the ailing remained. I could not move, and I thought, what will be will be. The young man had left. As he went, he said to me that he would be back in the evening. He would consult with a group of Chasidim and see how I could be helped. In the meantime, I found myself in a hovel, on the first floor of which was a hospital and infirmary, which was run by Dr. Belfor.

The Hospital in the "Small Ghetto"

I knew the doctor from "Reckman's." He came there often–for what? I do not know. It seems that later on he had to stay at "Reckman's." They found a corner where he could sleep in the barracks. I stood in line for the hospital doctor. After a wait of several hours, I was admitted. I told him what had happened to me the previous night. He told me to undress, examined me, and told me that he had never seen such bruises in his life. My body was totally covered with red and blue welts. What could the doctor do for me beside recommend that I stay in the hospital?

I lay down with someone else on a straw mattress and covered myself with my summer jacket, which I wore earlier when I thought I would die. After some time, for the first time I could take off my clothing.

The "hospital" consisted of a hall, a kitchen, and a large room. Where I lay there were three beds near the wall. Opposite, a pair of straw mattresses on the bare ground. A variety of sick people lay there–with typhus, dysentery, tuberculosis, and other ailments. The one who lay with me had been shot while leaping from the death train. He had to return to the ghetto. In another bed lay an old Jew who in "Reckman's" was assaulted every night. A rock had broken his foot. In the third bed lay a man who had been beaten. Opposite us– these patients: a woman and a few men. Near the door stood a bucket where we all, men and women, had to do our private business.

[Page 688]

The stink was terrible, but even worse were the bedbugs, the lice, and the flies.

The Jewish Council provided the hospital with black bread and black coffee. In the kitchen was a worker who emptied the bucket. For a small fee he brought a little soup when it was allowed.

Among the hospital personnel was a young woman, formerly a teacher, who every morning washed the floor. Her whole family had been sent away and she was sick and unhappy. The Jewish Council had assigned her there to spare her from working for the Germans. In the "hospital" there was also a room where the doctor saw patients. As became clear to me later, there was behind the reception room a hidden room where they kept people when work seizures occurred.

Throughout the day there was activity in the hospital: sick people came to the doctor, and others sought a hiding place. At night, too, people came looking for a little place to sleep. People also came to visit the sick.

I also had guests. The young man from Otwock sought me out and came to me. He was happy that I had found a place. Among those who passed through to the next room, I recognized a friend from my childhood whose name was Ratofel. He was happy to see me and was quite moved. He gave me 100 zlotys, saying that money will not fail me. Eventually I got to know almost all the ill and the well in the hospital. These were the remainder of the Siedlce intelligentsia. Among the others there was a young medical student. He worked as an orderly. At night people gathered around my bed and talked. One of them always had something to eat. He would begin to eat and would treat us as well.

I could no longer stay in the hospital. Also, it was becoming dangerous. An SS man appeared and sought people for labor. My childhood friend disappeared. People said that he had gone to Warsaw. The young man from Otwock introduced me to the Rodziner Chasidim, who were prepared to help me.

[Page 689]

After leaving the hospital, I again began a time of wandering. I knew the ghetto well, all of its nooks and crannies…It was a quadrangle drawn among two ruined wooden buildings and a pair of not much better stone houses. Of the walls between the houses there was no trace. The whole thing comprised a single place. People could go from house to house. Where there used to be an entrance only from the street, people had knocked down the walls. The entire area of the ghetto had become a large courtyard of rubbish. Wherever you turned, you saw the barbed wire that surrounded the Jewish quarter. People lived where there was only a hole: in cells, on landings, and laundry rooms; almost on the street, in cold and frost, I saw sick people lying on beds. In these horrible, crowded conditions, a pair of rooms were reserved as barracks for outside workers and underground workers. Aside from the hospital, there were three rooms for the Jewish Council and the ghetto police, in a wooden, one–story little house near the ghetto gate. From the gate, through the barbed wire, one could see an already destroyed street–that was the former ghetto. Now it was empty and dead, and when one looked at it, one shuddered at the slaughter of thousands of Jews who had been killed a couple of months earlier. In the shrunken ghetto lived about two thousand Jews, men and women. I do not remember any children.

The nicest four–story brick house had belonged to the Gypsies, a couple hundred of whom lived in the ghetto. They seemed privileged. For leaving the ghetto, a Gypsy was fined, while Jews were beaten to death. The Gypsies wore a sign on their arms. The Gypsies were an additional plague on the Jews in the ghetto.

People in the ghetto lived in extraordinary fear. Each day there were new victims, and the inhabitants trembled. There were many strangers in the ghetto. At first I wondered where these Jews came to this distant, sealed ghetto, but later it became clear to me.

[Page 690]

These were fragments of the three million Jews: in the hardest times of the German extermination, people set aside their lives and traveled to acquaintances and relatives; from the ghettoes, Jews were sent to different camps. Many jumped from the death trains and wandered to a Jewish "settlement"–some such were in the ghetto of Siedlce.

Someone told me that a well–known Otwock property owner had died. I went to pay my final respects. I was taken to the mortuary. That was a large, half–ruined hall. There lay a number of corpses, covered with their clothing. Some were half–naked. In the hall, sitting and standing, were weeping mourners. I don't know any of their fates. The dead were taken to the gate, where a Gentile waited with a wagon. The dead were handed over to the Gentile, and he took them to the cemetery. Jews could not accompany them.

This is how I lived. I ate soup in the "restaurant." A fine Jewish woman, who was destitute, tried to make a living: she made soup for purchase, or she stood in a corner with foodstuff. There for the first time I saw pages from the Gemara used as wrapping paper. I do not know why, but I was quite surprised. In Warsaw I had sold books to the purse–maker–he took Yiddish books, but he would not buy Hebrew books. There in the small ghetto of Siedlce things had come to such a pass!…Indifference to life had led to indifference toward the sacred.

One time I was passing near the window of the Jewish Council. A good–natured older Jew with a red beard called to me. I later got to now him. He was Ephraim Zelnick. He gave me 30 zlotys. Despite my deplorable situation, I was ashamed to take money from a stranger. But he told me to take it and buy myself a shirt. He gave me soap and soap powder from the Council warehouse. Such was Ephraim Zelnick. I remember him always for his goodness.

The Jewish Council also saw to the mail. Somehow I had by chance a form from the "Red Cross," from the Germans, from the time when I was a clerk in the Jewish post office.

[Page 691]

Zelnick took from me a short letter that was addressed to my relative in Eretz Yisroel. Our only shreds of hope were always bound up with longing for Eretz Yisroel. In later years I wondered if the letter through the "Red Cross" arrived. The Nazi extermination machine did everything it could to stop the outside world from knowing that Jews still existed.

I continued to sleep in the attic, on the bare floor. I had nothing to cover myself with, although it was winter. I was nearly barefoot. I had left my former ghetto dwelling near death, in August, with a pair of summer pants with holes in them. It was awful. I also became more fearful that I would be seized for labor. I had no idea what would happen until the young man from Otwock, the Rodziner Chasid, appeared again. He was now working in the labor camp, in the "field building office of the Luftwaffe" in Novo–Siedlce. On Sunday he came with a number of other workers, under guard by the camp watchmen–Ukrainians whom the Jews called "Yagdes" because of their black uniforms. The man from Otwock advised me to go to the camp, where I could survive. People there slept in barracks on straw mattresses. There were also enough straw mattresses that one could cover oneself. One could wash oneself. The work consisted of loading building material. I had earlier admired his wisdom and resourcefulness, and I trusted him. At least I would have a place to sleep. There was another motivation for me to go to the camp: I could take the place of another Jew and receive a pair of shoes and 200 zlotys.

That same day I marched with others into the "field building office of the Luftwaffe" in my new shoes. The shoes were big and uncomfortable. I stuffed them with straw and paper. It was hard to lift my feet. But I was not cold in them. It was already evening when we arrived in a large hall. By one wall there were two layers of boards on which lay the straw mattresses. There was also a table, washing utensils, and faucets. The hall was weakly illuminated with electric lights.

[Page 692]

I was amazed when I soon saw a minyan of Jews saying the afternoon and evening prayers. In my state at that time it seemed like a redemption and it sent me into a rapture. Later on, people gave out pieces of bread with marmalade. They ate at a table. The prayers were quite mournful and tragic sounding. After being there for a couple of hours, I found that I was among broken men: widowers, orphans, broken pieces of destroyed families. I discovered that a few days earlier there had been a pogrom in the barracks. The Gestapo had searched everywhere for money and valuables that might have belonged to the people of Siedlce. This search culminated in theft and human sacrifices.

That night I did sleep on a straw mattress and under a straw mattress. Near my bed I found a little prayer book. I took it was such joy and surprise, as if I had discovered something in an archeological expedition from a world that had disappeared long ago. I had already gone such a long way from the time when a normal Jewish world had existed.

I was among the last to get up. I ate the little bit of bread that remained from the evening before, which had to serve for two meals. I had not been able the night before to master my hunger and I ate too much, more than half of the bread. Soon a Polish foreman arrived and we went, under the surveillance of a "Yagda," for about six kilometers to the workplace. There, every day, there was a roll call. My name had already replaced that of the previous worker. The change had not cost me much. The young man whom I had replaced had discovered that his brother lived in another camp and he did everything he could to reach his brother.

I again passed myself off as a carpenter. Together with other carpenters, none of whom was a true craftsman, we made crates. Our hands grew tired of sawing and hammering nails. At the midday break we ate soup, which I devoured like a wild animal.

We didn't always do the same work. Every couple of days we were assigned to other labor. I packed electrical equipment in crates, arranged and carried heavy boards and beams and did all kinds of hard work.

[Page 693]

Then came heavy frosts. The snow lay deep on the ground. All day we spent outside. It was not possible to grasp anything, and it was as if we were in "Reckman's" death camp. But through all that need and suffering, we still had our human companionship–together we carried, together we rolled, together we loaded. At work, one companion would help another, give a piece of bread, or share a carrot he had found.

It was a privileged group of craftsmen who lived at the building material place. Among others, there were shoemakers and tailors who worked in the workshop. When the cold was so terrible, at lunchtime we could go in and warm ourselves. Among those workers, I met a young man named Kirschbaum. He worked in the metal depot. Also with us was another young man, a melancholy fellow, who always called out for his wife and child. Kirschbaum always took risks for him and every day asked for his help in the depot. Kirschbaum dreamed of Eretz Yisroel as the only solution to our woes in exile.

I grew weaker and could barely get around. I grew worse and worse. Again I started to be beaten with sticks and boards. Mostly I was beaten by the Polish foreman Derkocz. He also beat others. Once we were filling sacks with potatoes for the Aryan workers. Derkocz had given another Pole a stick for beating Jews, but the Pole did not use it. Derkocz chewed him out with the words, "You should be ashamed. Are you not a Pole?"

We took the sacks full of potatoes in wheelbarrows to the gate. I overturned the load twice. Behind me a young boy was pushing a wheelbarrow. He had a small sack. He stopped and said, "Let's trade. I'm afraid they'll beat you to death"…While unloading the potatoes, I put a couple of potatoes in my dish. On leaving the workplace, the gatekeeper, an older "Yagda," noticed.

[Page 694]

He struck me with his whip. For a long time I could not catch my breath. With great effort I got to the barracks. The next morning, there was no way I could get to work. After a day of rest, I managed to get back to work.

At that time, a soldier came to the barracks from the agricultural area and chose several workers to work in the courtyard for a couple of days. I was among them. We traveled there and I managed to rest for a short time. Every day was a treasure. But as soon as I got there, I was dead tired from the work. In the yard we loaded bundles of hay onto trucks. With us was the Siedlce hairdresser Yedidah Schwartz. From the yard it was about a kilometer to the kitchen, from which people traveled to the Luftwaffe supply area in a wagon and ate there. We would go there and have our soup.

Then again there were days of pain and torment. It was impossible to sleep in the hall because of the cold. They took us to a neighboring stone building. One morning a few of us remained in the hall in order to bring the mattresses and other things to our new quarters. When we came back to our former places in the evening, the "Yagdes" ordered us to go to the stone building. I did not have much to do. My bowl and spoon were with me. All that remained was a sack, in which were my old pants, a reminder of the dear hands that had bought them; a tablecloth, soap, and bicarbonate that I had received from Zelnick, and the prayer book I had found. The building where we were located had a few rooms on the first floor and a few on the second. In the room where I was were two levels of cots, on which lay blankets. There were 13 of us in the room, among them Yontl Goldman and his nephew. This was the only time while I was in the camp that I encountered two people from the same family. Yontl took good care of his nephew. They slept next to each other. At work, he looked after him.

[Page 695]

The evenings were easier–tolerable. People brought coals and heated the oven. We sat up until late at night. Some people cooked and shared with strangers. With us in the room was a young man from Sokolov who was known as "the Sokolover." He was nearly naked. The group got together and at night had the tailor make him a warm coat. The companionship in this new spot was even much stronger, and despite the fatigue from such hard work, there were close ties among the inhabitants of that house. I became acquainted with many men, and I learned that with us were Jews from a second camp called "Flieger–Horst." In the group I recognized a university friend–the lawyer Tchornobrodo

Time passed. I could not bear the difficulties, and I saw no end to them. Most of the laborers went to the ghetto, but I could not even think about marching so far. There was a difficult Sunday when everyone had to go to work. But this time there came a Pole, an anti–Semite, with a whip in his hand. Terror fell on everyone. He led us to what was called the "tobacco–monopoly." This was a couple of kilometers from our quarters. There we loaded into wagons beams, boards, crates, barrels. The frost was oppressive. We worked under the gaze of SS men and the Pole. Our overseers beat and pummeled us. I fell off my feet. The worst part was rolling the barrels. My fingers were numb from the cold. They turned black before the evening. Suddenly rain fell. I was totally without strength and had nothing to lose. I left my work and stood next to a building where there was little roof. Suddenly I heard a shriek from a worker on whom a heavy beam had fallen. It was already eleven o'clock when we were called to go into the barracks. We found something that served as a makeshift stretcher on which they put the injured man so they could carry him. Every few minutes they took turns. In order not to shake him up, they took a longer route. Only a few, weak and ill, went as they had in the morning–through the fields. It was so dark that we could barely see each other.

[Page 696]

That night I hardly ate anything. I lay on my bed, weak and worn out. In the morning, I again did not go to work. And I was not the only one. In our rooms lay a good number of dead from the previous day, including the man who had been injured.

On the following days, too, I did not get to work. People started to say that those in the Siedlce ghetto would be sent to "Gensze Barky." I did not know what that meant. Once again the oppressed voices of my companions had an effect on me. They all had someone in the ghetto. The ghetto was a support spot for the camp workers.

I continued to lie there and started to become increasingly swollen. I noticed that my companions were concerned about my condition. Yontl Goldman brought in parsley, boiled it in water, and gave me the water to drink. People said this was a cure for kidney disease that had made me swell up. The tailor among us sewed all night. He had just about finished up a roll of thread and discovered that the thread had been wound around a 20 zloty banknote. They all decided that the money belonged to me and that they should rescue me. They bought food for me to eat.

From day to day, there were more people ailing in our rooms. One night, a young man came to us, a twenty–year–old SS man. He looked around. Someone was smoking in his presence. This was a great impertinence. The SS man took out his revolver. The Jew shouted, "Shema Yisroel," almost like a scream, but the one with the "death's head" did not shoot. He asked me why I was lying there. I responded that I was very tired. I was afraid to tell him that I was ill. The young German laughed and said, "They'll be burying you somewhere," and he left us.

[Page 697]

The matter of "Gensze Barky" arose again; "Gensze Barky" meant something terrible.

In the morning it was announced that the ill and many of the other workers would be sent back to the ghetto. There was an uproar and lamenting. People sought protection so they could stay in the camp.

I was indifferent to all of it. I lay there for a couple more days. Lying there was legally allowed for the ailing. For the moment, one could breathe free.

In the middle of everything, we had guests. About twenty of our comrades arrived from the other work camp. They had been working at the "Luftwaffe field house." Most of them were candidates for the ghetto. In the morning we were all taken out to the street. A number were divided out to go to the ghetto. The "lucky ones," those who stayed behind, went to work as usual.

We left the place, and under the watch of the "Yagdas" we went in the direction of the small ghetto.

The Small Ghetto is Liquidated

Those who returned to the ghetto went to friends and relatives. But I stood there alone. I had no one. To whom could I go? My first steps took me to the room that was familiar–the waiting room of the Jewish Council and the ghetto police.

When I was near "Reckman's," a Jewish policeman smacked me in the face because I did not get into the line. My cheek immediately swelled up. The policeman was a former hairdresser, but not all of the Jewish police were like that. Among them were some who recognized the ugly role they were playing and felt bad about it.

In Otwocs, a Polish and a Jewish policeman had led me to execution. The whole way, the Jew cried and embraced me.

[Page 698]

He said, "Oy vey iz mir. I'm taking you to your death." One time a Jewish policeman threw me a 20 zloty coin, and when I wanted to return it to him, he said that it was not his. So I went into the police department with the hope that I would find there someone with a human heart.

I sat for a while in the police department and looked around to see what was going on. There I learned that at the end of the November, the Germans had announced in the "New Warsaw Courier," on placards on the Aryan side, and also through notices in the ghetto that a new ghetto was being prepared where Jews could settle freely until December 1.

But where should people go now? On the second floor of the same house lived the Itzkowitz family, whom I had known earlier. The doors were still open to anyone. I went in and sat there quietly. I wanted nothing but to sit. Both in the room and outside there was a commotion. Along the fence stood Jews and tried to sell things at low prices to the Poles. But at each moment there were fewer buyers. Why should they pay even the smallest price when on the next day they could take anything in the ghetto for free?

Dejection was everywhere. Everyone had packed up. Everyone still had a little hope for life. Hitler's beasts had ordered that the ghetto had to be cleaned out and handed over, but that in "Gensze Barky" everyone would be able to survive the war. So why could we not remain in Siedlce? People seized on the word "must," as if the word signified a necessity that was not totally comprehensible and so seemed conditional.

The whole day wagons passed with beds, bedclothes, and other things for "Gensze Barky." Anyone who had money and protection could transport these necessities. The Jewish Council also sent their storehouse of bicarbonate, soap, and basic medications. The Germans allowed all this and thereby showed that they had "no bad intentions," only that the ghetto had to be cleared out.

Everyone packed up. Early in the morning, everyone had to leave the ghetto carrying only hand luggage.

[Page 699]

The noise and commotion were terrible, and meanwhile night had fallen. It was already quite late when the voices quieted down and the tired populace all lay down to spend their last night in their birthplace, where their ancestors had lived for generations and where they themselves had grown up, now to be displaced by the Germans.

That night I had no worries about where to sleep. I stayed with the Itzkowitzes. I had material to make a bed–on the next day, everything that remained would be worthless. The Itzkowitzes were always good to me. When I awoke, the elder Itzkowitz was standing in his tallis and tefillin, praying. He was weeping. New people arrived in the house–relatives who had been sent from different work camps and had been assigned to go to "Gensze Barky." People were packing until the last minute. We also ate. I put wood on the fire and roasted potatoes, as much as I wanted, since we could not take them with us. The potatoes belonged to no one, since the "Aryans" did not want to buy them.

Finally I was ready for the unknown road. I put a few potatoes in my bag, since I was not strong enough to carry too many. It was very cold. In the room remained tablecloths, pieces of clothing. I could ask no more questions. I wrapped a tablecloth under my coat, put some things on my shoulders, wrapped up my neck–something in addition to the scarf that I had received from the Italian soldier. I put my bag on my back and I was ready for homelessness. Everyone else had already left the room. I was the last, like a forgotten dog…

Soon the gates of the ghetto were ordered open, this time on the other side of the house, where the Jewish Council and ghetto police were. This lasted a little while. It seems there was an order not to rush. No Germans could be seen, only Polish police.

Finally the sad, dark mass of people began to trudge over the white, snow–covered streets.

[Page 700]

Again I was among the last. People went so slowly. There were many who were old and ill. On the sides of the streets, on the sidewalks, the Polish police watched us. We approached the street of the church. Curious and happy Aryan Poles came out to the street to watch the parade.

That parade was awful. Men and women walked (as for children, I do not recall any) with burdens on their backs and in their hands. Some made sleds from a pair of boards and dragged their baggage through the snow. Behind the Jews came the Gypsies. From time to time a cry was heard, when the Gypsies wrested a bag away from a Jew; soon it became still again–after all, what did that signify in the sea of Jewish woes?

When we were outside of the city, I noticed about 18 meters from the road I saw a gendarme in his brilliant yellow uniform and yellow boots. He was probably in charge. He was proud. and silent.

We arrived at "Gensze Barky." A few three–story houses of red brick stood in the form of a letter "chet" near the street. In the middle was a large courtyard with two pumps. The area was surrounded by barbed wire, but there were open spots. Rolls of barbed wire lay around for finishing the job.

I could barely drag myself to the new Jewish living area, and I had only one desire–impossible though it seemed, to lie down under a roof. Many people had already been in their living quarters, which the Jewish Council had assigned; others were seizing dwellings. The anxiety in the rooms was extraordinary; the rooms were small, for single people, built for the unemployed. Straw lay on the floor. There were no beds and no cots. I saw divided rooms on two floors. The Gypsies were given preference–they took over a whole building. Soon people had barricaded themselves in, fearing an "invasion" of strangers.

The frost was unrelenting. The attics and stairways filled up.

[Page 701]

Two of my acquaintances from the campo arranged themselves under a stairway…they welcomed me there, but I turned them down, because there was not even space there to sit and it was as cold as out on the street. I continued to look for a place in a room, but I became totally desperate and hopeless. After a while, I saw people crowding into an empty room. This spot was reserved for the Jewish Council as an office and a storeroom. But in the meantime, it was packed with a score of people. At first everyone was standing, but later–and I do not know how–most began to sink down and all lay down, pressing into each other. Night fell. Half–standing and half–sitting, I fell asleep. So I slept through the whole night in this mass of people, awakened frequently by my neighbors who, in their sleep, fell upon one another. When day came, many left the room. Now I could stretch my bones, but I could not remain for long in this asylum. People came to claim the room for the Jewish Council and we had to leave. I thought that now would come my hoped for death that I could not impose on myself–the easy death of freezing…

After the awfulness of the previous day, life got a little better. I was happy when I ran into the medical student. He told me that the Jewish woman who had sold food and made the soup was still carrying on her "business," and he took me to her location. It was a wonder that in the building there was a kitchen, a stove, and a dwelling. The crowd there was unbelievable. I ate some soup and stayed there as long as possible. When I was outside on the street, I returned to the room of the Jewish Council. There I met Zelnick and his son–in–law, the lawyer Eisenberg. He greeted me. It appeared that he knew about me. I told him that I wanted to return to the Warsaw Ghetto. Zelnick invited me into his room. His wife served me a dish of soup and then another dish of soup. I sat there for a long time, eating the soup and not thinking of courtesy. In their dwelling were a couple of relatives, who were quite nervous.

[Page 702]

While I was sitting there, hungry people continuously knocked at the door; people gave each of them a piece of bread. More people came into the room, and I clearly understood that I had to leave, so I stood up. As I was leaving, Zelnick told me that I could spend the night in the Jewish Council room, where he would lock me in. I suffered through another couple of hours until it was night. I waited for Zelnick. Finally he arrived and let me into the room. He left me a light and matches. I found a bit of wood and made a fire. Sitting at the table, I slept for the night. In the morning, Zelnick let me out. I ate more soup and paid with the potatoes that I had in my bag and went out again into the cold.

In the courtyard there was a huge commotion. People had lined up at the pump to get some water. A little further on there was a burial for those who had frozen during the night because they had had nowhere to go. A policeman led about twenty people to work in the city–work was now a privilege.

My savior Zelnick came to the Jewish Council. A crowd of men came up to him. These were refugees from other cities who, according to the decision of the Jewish Council, should receive 10 zlotys and an identity card. Zelnick had spoken to me earlier about this and he had assured me that I would get a greater sum. He kept his word and stuffed into my hand some papers. I counted later: he had given me 40 zlotys. An "identity card" he had given, but without the German stamp and only for Kaluszyn and Rembertow. Not for Warsaw. Zelnick squeezed my hands in farewell.

The gates of the new ghetto were not guarded, and the fence had not completed.

My feet were terribly swollen; I was nervous about going. But I had already decided, long ago, to go to the Warsaw Ghetto. I went on the path to Kaluszyn and met up with a group of Jews. My feet were so heavy that I remained walking behind.

[Page 703]

How I dragged myself to Kaluszyn, Minsk, and later to Warsaw, that is a separate chapter that does not belong to the story of the destruction of the Jews of Siedlce.

I arrived at the Warsaw Ghetto shortly before the uprising. I was interested in the fate of the last Jews of Siedlce who had been taken with myself to the "Geszne Barky." I learned that the last Jews of Siedlce had been taken to Treblinka.

The committee of the great city shul

Standing: Y, Kleinwechsler, Akiva Goldfarb, A. Kirschenbaum.
Sitting: Dovid Rubinstein, Eliezer Shlipke, Chazen Pasowski and Nachum Halbershtam

Overturned pieces of gravestones

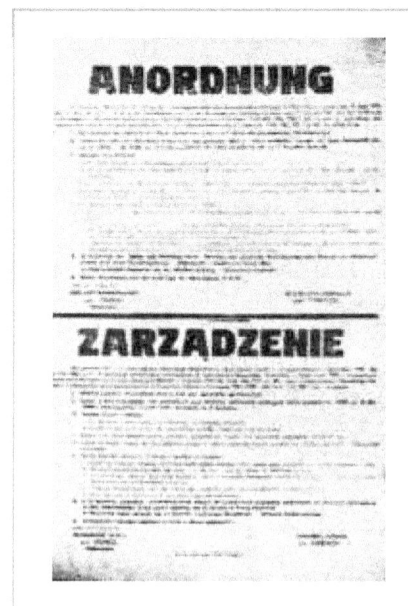

An order concerning Jewish behavior

Cows graze among monuments in the Jewish cemetery

Because of a mechanical oversight, we are printing these pictures together here because of their importance for this book.

[Page 705]

Number of Jews in Siedlce at the time of the War's Outbreak and in Different Periods of the German Occupation

Translated by Theodore Steinberg

In the quarterly of the Jewish Historical Institute in Poland, "Historical Pages," volume 4, number 2, figure 10, is the following statistical accounting of the number of Jews in Siedlce from the beginning of the war until liquidation.

Date	Number of local Jews	Additional Refugees
Sept. 1, 1939	15, 253	——
Dec. 1940	around 13,000	March 15–1,201
March, 1941	12,000	——
July, 1941	11,674	——
June, 1942	11,700	——

As we can see from this chart, the number of Jews in Siedlce declined during the German occupation, as is recorded in the German murder–record, due to epidemics and a growing death rate from hunger and privation.

Dates of Jewish Martyrdom in Siedlce

Translated by Theodore Steinberg

September 7, 1939 (23 Elul 5699), Thursday morning–The Germans began their air assault on Siedlce, focusing on the Jewish streets; the bombardment lasted, with short pauses, until Monday (9/11/39) at night. During those days about 2,000 people were killed, mostly Jews.

[Page 706]

September 9, 1939–Hoping to escape with their lives from the barbaric air assault, the whole civilian population left the city, abandoning their dwellings with their property and their goods. The city was in flames. During the chaos, hordes of peasants came from the surrounding villages and plundered the Jewish homes and businesses.

September 11, 1939 (27 Elul 5699), Monday night–The German army arrives in Siedlce.

September 15, first day of Rosh Hashanah–People are taken from their homes and taken to the military barracks and on Shabbos morning sent to East Prussia via Sokolov–Vengerov.

Simchas Torah. During prayers–A group of German soldiers entered the shul and beat the Jews murderously, ripping their taleisim from them shooting at those who jumped through the windows; shot was Yosef Rubin. Throughout the night bands of armed Germans plundered the Jews's homes and businesses. They dragged people from their houses and led them to Vengerov.

End of October, 1939–A group of German soldiers burst into the shul and the beis–medresh. They took the Torah scrolls out of the ark, ripped them up and stomped on them.

End of November, 1939–The Gestapo arrived and issued an order for a Judenrat of 25 people. This Judenrat was ordered by the Germans to pay the sum of ten thousand zlotys.

December, 1939–The Judenrat received another order to pay 20,000 zlotys.

December 24, 1939–In the middle of the night, the Germans set fire to the shul and to the beis–medresh. Many Jews were burned, wounded and killed in the flames.

April, 1940–Registration of all Jewish men aged 16 to 60.

[Page 707]

June 12, 1940 (first day of Shavuos)–A group of savage, armed Germans attacked Jews and shot the iron merchant Asher Hertz.

November, 1940–The Judenrat received orders to pay another ransom, this time for 100,000 zlotys.

December 31, 1940–A German command that every Jew above 12 years old must wear a arm band with the inscription "Jew" and a Magen David. Also Jewish businesses must be marked with a Magen David. During 1940, Jews were thrown out of the apartments and businesses, which were turned over to Christians.

March, 1941–The German army in Siedlce conducted a pogrom against the Jews that lasted for three days. The Germans plundered and murdered. Six Jews were shot and many were wounded. The pogrom began with a provocation when on the streets Jews were shot. After the pogrom, the Judenrat was ordered to pay another 100,000 zlotys.

Spring, 1941–Jewish homes are burned by order of the German ruling commission.

August 1, 1941 (Erev Tisha B'Av, 5701)–An order is published by the German army ordering the Jews of Siedlce into a ghetto.

October 1, 1941 (Yom Kippur, 5702)–The ghetto is closed off, enclosing the following streets: on the right side–Kochonowske (Shpitalne), Stary Rinek, Berek joselewicz, Mala, First of May as far as Sandawa; on the left side: Pusta, Oslanowicz (Prospektowa), Tornowa (Jatkowa), Browarga, Okopowa, Blonya. After the ghetto was shut up, epidemics and illness increased. Deaths increased.

December, 1941–The Germans demanded that the Judenrat deliver all the fur coats belonging to Jews.

January, 1942–The Germans imposed a fine of 100,000 per month on the Jews.

[Page 708]

March 3, 1942 (Purim, 5702)–The Germans seized ten Jews and took them to Stok–Latzki, a village near Siedlce. By order of the head of the government council for labor, they were shot on the pretext that they had refused to work. The Judenrat was compelled to issue a proclamation that the Germans were correct in their decision to execute the ten Jews.

June, 1942–The Germans ordered the Judenrat to send a variety of craftsmen, with their tools, to a work detail. The selected Jews were sent to an unknown destination. Later it was learned that they had been transported to Majdanek for extermination.

July, 1942–Thirty Jews were arrested on the pretext that they were "laggards" from work. They were tortured in captivity for several days, after which they were led back to the ghetto and shot.

August 22, 1942 (Shabbos, 9 Elul, 5702)–Liquidation of the ghetto. In the middle of the night, the ghetto was surrounded by Germans, Ukrainians, and Polish police. In the morning, all Jews were assembled in the old cemetery by the shul. A selection was made according to suitability for work. A so–called "small ghetto" was formed in a triangle of these streets: Sokolower, Oslanowicz, Torgowa. Five hundred Jews were led in. About 1500 Jews snuck into there "small ghetto." In the cemetery, several thousand Jews were shot.

August 23–About 10,000 Jews were taken to the train station.

August 24–Liquidation of the ghetto hospital. A group of Germans and Ukrainians, led by the city commander Fabiash, besieged the ghetto hospital on Dluge Street, shot the ill in their beds, including newborn children, as well as the doctors and their assistants. The nurses and the rest of the hospital personnel were led to the courtyard and shot.

[Page 709]

August 26, 1942–Thirty young Jewish women were taken to work in the emptied ghetto, working on sorting and packing the stolen Jewish goods. At night the women were taken to the cemetery, lined up against a wall, and shot.

November 25, 1942 (16 Kislev 5703)–Liquidation of the "small ghetto." About 2,000 Jews taken to Genshe–Barky.

November 28, 1942–In the middle of the night, Genshe–Barky was surrounded by German, Ukrainian, and Polish police.

November 30, 1942–The last 2,000 Jews of Siedlce and the surrounding area were led from Genshe–Barky to the train and transported to Treblinka. Thus ended the four–hundred year history of the Jews in Siedlce.

[Page 713]

Inhabitants of Siedlce in the entire world

Inhabitants of Siedlce in Israel
Participation in the Wars and in the Building of the State

by David ben Yosef (Popovsky)

Translated by Theodore Steinberg

The aliyah of people from Siedlce to Eretz Yisrael began along with the general aliyah and Zionist revival more than fifty years ago. From the individuals from Siedlce who came at the beginning of the twentieth century, in 1924 there was a small "family" of several score from the city. With the growing tide of the Third, Fourth, and Fifth Aliyahs and with the last Aliyah before the Holocaust, there are now in Israel about 2,000 Siedlcers.

Jewish Siedlce went through all the stages of the aliyahs to Eretz Israel. Siedlce pioneers, builders of the land, went through all the suffering and pain of acclimatization, of sinking roots, and of establishing their positions in the building of our homeland.

The first pioneers who came to Israel from Siedlcer were: Kaddish Goldstein, L. Rosenberg, Meister, G. Gutgelt, Menachem ben Hillel, Dr. Moshe Temkin, the writer Mordechai Temkin. After the First World War, the young idealistic pioneers came to the land: Melech Heinsdorf, Simcha Atman, Yakov Morgenstern–Shachar, Mordechai and Yechiel Korona; later Moaz Huber, Yehuda Tenenbaum, Edah Barg, the Reinman family, the Nosowski family, the Vyman family, Chaim Rosen, Moshe Glikman, Avraham Altenberg, Rotberg, Y. Ch. Rotstein, Yitzchak Orzhel, Mordechaiu Greenberg, z"l, and others arrived.

A small group, a limited group of Siedlcers were then in the country, but they lived like a single family; they prepared the way for many other Siedlcers who arrived in later aliyahs. Among the Siedlcers there was a strong sense of togetherness and mutual help in word and deed, both in work and in getting accustomed to the land. There were friendly, comradely gatherings in evenings of entertainment or for the third meal of Shabbat or even at various family celebrations.

[Page 714]

The chief "ambassador" from Siedlce was then Mr. Melech Heinsdorf. If one had to organize people for fork, in 1921, one had to go to Melech–entirely, overall, Melech.

In 1921, the Siedlcers established a brick factory that over time became a whole construction enterprise, which dealt with various building trades such as trenching and foundational work. This was during the first days of "prosperity" in our land, so they did not lack for work. Whoever came from Siedlce was already working in the brick works and earning a living. The leadership of this undertaking involved an agreement with Mr. Shvergold, the owner of a cafe on Allenby Street, that every Siedlcer who came with a badge from the factory would be allowed to at on the account of the brick factory. This was a real accomplishment.

People from Siedlce in Israel in 1924

[Page 715]

Later on this factory expanded and became a cooperative under the name of "Hadadyot." This was also the first cooperative of the Histadrut in the country and became the foundation for the greater cooperative movement in Israel. At the head of this cooperative and also of other cooperatives was Boaz Huber, who was a long–standing member of the central committee of the cooperative movement of the workers' Histadrut. People from Siedlce who came to Israel had no worries about making a living. They had work as well as food and lodging. Every Siedlcer's home was an open hotel for a newly arrived pioneer. The Siedllcers in Israel were masters of care and brotherly mutual aid.

At the time of a crisis in the country, of unemployment, people knew that the "ambassador" would look out for work. One knew that in a cooperative–the master of advice in labor matters was Boaz Huber.

This idealism and brotherly community life among the Siedlcers in the country lasted until 1933. With the general development of the country and with the arrival of greater numbers of pioneers from Siedlce and other immigrants to Israel who lived in different cities and villages the traditional Siedlce brotherhood weakened.

The brickworks of the Siedlcers in Israel in 1924

[Page 716]

At the same time, there arose in the country community advisory bodies and institutions to look after new arrivals. This situation prevailed until after the Holocaust. The Holocaust and the obliteration of our dearest and most loved ones again created a sense of unity, a feeling of family, among the "refugee remnant" of Siedlcers in Israel.

Siedlcers in Israel also assumed a leading role in the general dynamic developments in the building of the country. They were active in a variety of professions and army positions, in undertaking work in the moshavahs, in maritime activities, in digging for sandstone, and later in sport fishing. They had to resist strong opposition from the Arabs, who did not want them there. During the various organized Arab periods of unrest, when the whole Jewish settlement took up the required battle positions, Siedlcers were active in the special voluntary police aid, in various Haganah groups, armed and ready. Let me recall here our comrade Tzvi Brenner from the kibbutz "Afikim"–a young pioneer from Siedlce, who came here from America, where he had gone with his mother. He was a member of the kibbutz, and in the unrest of 1936–1938 he was one of the chief aides to Lord Wingate. In the War of Independence, sadly, he was badly wounded and was left an invalid.

Today our Siedlcers are all over the country, from Dan to Eilat and from Sodom to Methullah; one encounters Siedlcers in all kinds of professions, in important positions and in everyday life, in cities and in villages.

We have already discussed the first brick factory and first cooperative that were created by Siedlcers; in addition, the modern Grand Hotel in Tel Aviv on Allenby Street was established by Siedlcers; furthermore, Siedlcers were members of eminent industries, construction companies, members of kibbutzim, state officials, and notable contributors to community institutions, police officials, officers in the army, and so on.

[Page 717]

In the years of unrest and Arab terror, many Siedlcers fell and sadly did not live to see with their own eyes the fulfillment of their dream–the establishment of the Jewish state. Among the fallen was Yakov Morenstern–Shachar, a brother of the Siedlce Hebrew teacher Morgenstern, who was brutally killed as the foreman on the train line in 1938 when he traveled with Arab workers to repair a bridge on the Haifa–Tel Aviv line, near Qalqilya. He left behind a wife and daughter. In the Second World War, among the fallen we're Yaverbaum and Greenfarb, Ephraim Vyman, a son of Mr. Dov Vyman. He set out on a boat with about twenty men. They were on a secret mission for the Haganah and they never returned. Until today the whole affair remains a secret, but it caused his parents terrible heartache. In the battle for independence conducted by the national underground, A. Kna'ani fell in a battle with the English. He was the son of Mordecai Kna'ani–Kramasz.

The only son of Dr. Bergman, the Siedlce Zionist activist Yakov Bergman, fell in the battle for our independence in the Negev as an officer in the Jewish army. Zvi Charney–Shachor, who entered the country illegally in 1939, became a member of the "Ha–shomer Ha–Tza'ir" kibbutz "Yad Mordechai," worked in fishing, fell guarding his kibbutz. In the War of Independence, Sh. Fuzen fell in K'far Etzion, Jerusalem.

Simcha Yaverbaum　　　*Tzvi Shchori (Charney)*　　　*Avraham Kramasz–Kna'ani*

[Page 718]

A whole array of Siedlcers have distinguished themselves in actively fighting for our freedom, such as: Tzvi Brenner from kibbutz "Afikim," Vyman's son, the son of P. Dromi, D. Lederman, Israel Brenner, his brother Ben–Yosef–they were active in the defense of Jerusalem and other Siedlcers fought in other parts of the country.

Siedlcers were soldiers in the Jewish Brigade in the World War.

In the decades of building and development of the Land of Israel, there have been many changes–arrivals and departures. There were Siedlcers who could not adapt and acclimatize in the country and, unhappily, left, returning to Siedlce or going to other parts of the world: to America, to Argentina, to Brazil, and elsewhere.

The hundreds of Siedlcers who remained in the country became firmly established, planted deep roots, and are happy and fortunate to find themselves in the Jewish state. But the people of Siedlce cannot forget the great destruction of their old home.

The dias of the memorial meeting in 1952 on the tenth yahrzeit of the destruction of Siedlce

From the right: Cantor Zifuwicz, Kleinwechsler, Rochel Shmukliarsz, P. Dromi, Dr. Heller, Ben–Yosef, Hersh Barbanel from Buenos Aires who was at that time in Israel, and A. Friedman

[Page 719]

The attendees in the hall–for the tenth yahrzeit of the destruction of Siedlce

The attendees in the hall–for the tenth yahrzeit of the destruction of Siedlce

[Page 720]

The yearly memorials and gatherings of the Siedlcers in Israel are transformed into traditional days of mourning and of brotherly gatherings of the "remnant of refugees." In these meetings, much time is devoted to private, personal conversations. Each person recalls a bundle of memories about their old former home, and there is much to recall…

The Siedlcers are organized into an association headed by a committee led by the following: Fishl Dromi Popowski, D. Ben–Yosef Popowski, Yitzchak Kaspi, D. Vyman, Moshe Steinberg, Mordechai Kna'ani, Melech Heinsdorf, Yitzchak Orszel, Yakov Shkliarsz, Tchatchkes, Y. Mendelssohn, Sara Czarnabrode, in Haifa the Histadrut activist A. Bar–Chaim, Esq., Kleinwechsler, Dr. M. Shleiber, and others. In Jerusalem–Y.M. Kleinlerer, who is a member of the Jerusalem city council.

The Siedlcers are also proud of the Siedlce writers group, cultural leaders such as: the noted writer Yoel Mastbaum, the Hebrew writer Mordechai Temkin, his brother Dr. Moshe Temkin, the young Hebrew writer Mordechai Ovadiah, formerly Gottesdiener, who has been popular since the time he served as Bialik's secretary, H.M. Feinsilber, who published a documentary volume on the destruction of Siedlce, Y Akun–teacher and educator, Rabbi Kalman Frankel among the leaders of the Mizrachi, and many more Siedlcers who hold an honored place in the cultural life and creation of Israel.

[Page 721]

Organization of Siedlce Townsmen in Israel

by Y. Kaspi

Translated by Theodore Steinberg

Until the Fifth Aliyah, in 1931, no attempt was made in Israel to organize a townspeople-circle because each aliyah maintained that it had come to the the country to fulfill a historical mission and therefore it had to break with the past, with the exile. Organizing such a circle would mean being bound to the exile. At the time of the Fifth Aliyah, when immigration from Siedlce grew and making arrangements for it involved huge expenses, the thought arose to establish a townspeople-circle for mutual aid.

On March 2, 1933, a conference was held calling for the shaping of a "organization of immigrants from Siedlce in Israel," issued by a committee.

According to the record, the organization would have the following tasks: to organize all Siedlcers in Israel into a single unit; to gather and consider statistics concerning the economic situation of Siedlcers in Israel; to find a site for a club for Siedlcers and for the offices of the elected committee; to stay in contact with the major national organizations in Siedlce for mutual help, especially with instructions and advice for new arrivals in the country and for those who were preparing to come.

In order to realize this plan, the organizing committee decided to make inquiries of all Siedlcers in the country.

[Page 722]

After all the responses had been received, the statistics were studied and concrete plans were made for a general gathering.

This gathering actually took place. The newly selected committee organized a Purim Ball. A small sum of money was gathered and was sent to the "Tarbus"-shul in Siedlce. Then the organization ceased to exist. No more activities were forthcoming.

In the midst of the World War, as appalling news arrived from Poland, and particularly from Siedlce, I. Kaspi, along with P. Dromi, took on the responsibility of renewing the Siedlce townspeople-circle. We believed that Jews remained in Siedlce and that after the war it would be necessary either to bring them to Israel or to support them.

After an exchange of reports, on April 18, 1944, a conference was held in which it was decided to reorganize the organization of immigrants from Siedlce under a name that fit the times: "Organization of Immigrants from Siedlce." It as also decided to make a collection of funds.

The first general gathering and a memorial for the martyrs of Siedlce came on the 9 Elul, 5704. It was well attended. Siedlcers from every corner of the country came. From then on, every year there was such an assembly and a memorial.

The concrete help provided by the "Organization of Immigrants from Siedlce" consisted of the following:

While the war was still going on, fifty packages were sent to the refugees from Siedlce who were in the Soviet Union. It was a real help for the unfortunate refugees, who were scattered in the far corners of Greater Russia, when they received clothing or a pair of shoes.

[Page 723]

The new immigrants, who arrived naked and lacking everything, were given money so they could get apartments or earn a living. Certain sums were given as loans, which were repaid. Monetary support was also offered. There was no pressure on repaying the loans.

Siedlce was rid of the Nazi murderers on June 22, 1944. After that, the committee made a variety of efforts to connect with the city. Letters were sent and telegrams to those in charge of the city, to the postal officials, to the Jewish committee in Lublin, and to similar authorities.

In February of 1944 the committee from the Organization of Immigrants from Siedlce took on the responsibility of organizing the people from Siedlce throughout the world in order to devise ways to help the Jews who remained in Siedlce itself and the refugees in the Soviet Union. No one realized that the disaster had been so enormous.

Letters about this initiative were sent to Canada, Argentina, Cuba, Mexico, Australia, and South Africa.

In Israel itself, 175 people pledged to contribute to the general sum of 932,200 pounds. By March of 1945, 303,453 pounds had been raised. The distribution of packages that had been sent cost 87,167 pounds. The supervising committee received no support for its relief work aside from 100 pounds that had been sent from the Argentine Siedlcers.

The committee played a definite role in reuniting families. It gathered addresses from the Siedlcers in Israel, who were being sought by refugees from Siedlce through the auspices of the Jewish Agency in Jerusalem, the Joint, and HIAS.

[Page 724]

When contact was established with the "remnant of the refugees" in Siedlce, the Tel Aviv committee sent a transport of matzah for Pesach, a large sum of money packages of clothing, and a special sum to create a park by the cemetery and to erect a monument in memory of our martyrs. Nothing came of the last plan.

In recent times, the Organization of Immigrants from Siedlce in Israel undertook to publish the Yizkor Book, which required a great deal of work until it was completed.

The editorial team for the Yizkor Book

From right to left: David Ben Yosef (Posowski), Wolf Yosni, Fishl Dromi (Popowski), and Yitzchak Kaspi

[Page 725]

Jews of Siedlce in the Diaspora

by Y. Kaspi

Translated by Theodore Steinberg

The economic backwardness of Siedlce provided little possibility for even an average material life; the accompanying growth of anti–Semitism, which brought with it pogroms economic boycotts, and thuggish attacks–this difficult Jewish life gave birth to the realization that there was no place in the city for Jews. At the end of the nineteenth century, Jews throughout the whole czarist territory were caught up in two powerful emigration movements: "Am Olam," which led to the United States and to South America, and "Chivat Tzion," which led to Eretz Yisroel; that barren Jewish land could take in only idealists who were prepared to act selflessly while building a Jewish homeland. Consequently, there was also a large Jewish emigration to South America, and among the emigrants were a large number of Jews from Siedlce.

The first Jewish emigrants from Siedlce to the United States we find in 1895. The number of emigrants from Siedlce was still small, because at that time Jews in Siedlce considered emigration a sin. There were families who were ashamed of their sons and daughters who had gone to America, just as one might be ashamed of a convert in the family. There were cases when young people, fearing their parents' opposition to emigration to America, snuck away. The parents only found out later. People would joke about this kind of emigration; they would say that so–and–so son of so–and–so had gone to America when he just went to close the shutters. There were cases when parents went into mourning and sat shiva and said Kaddish for a son who brought on such disgrace by fleeing.

[Page 726]

Quite different was the case of someone who went to Israel. Such a person was treated with honor.

According to reliable sources, the first Siedlcer to go to America was R. Moshe Fuchs, a watchmaker. After him came others but not all decided to remain there. Some returned.

Around 1906, when the Siedlce pogrom broke out there were about 180 Jews from Siedlce in the United States. After the pogrom, emigration from Siedlce increased and continued until the outbreak of the First World War in 1914.

The first person who undertook to organize the Siedlcers in America, in 1903, was Yitzchak Meir Eisenberg. He, together with sixteen other Siedlce Jews, established the "First Siedlce Support Association in New York." During 1904 the number of members increased to about forty. The Siedlce association, under the influence of the new immigrants, joined the "Workers Circle."

Siedlce Branch 53 continued to grow, so that in 1906 it had fifty members. The number of Siedlcers in America at that time was about 200.

The privileges of membership in Siedlce Branch 53 were as follows: a member could use the sick–fund; those with tuberculosis could use the sanitarium. Every ill member was entitled to receive thirteen dollars a week–eight dollars a week from the fun of the "Workers Circle" and five dollars a week from Siedlce Branch 53, for up to fifteen weeks a year; each member could be insured for up to a thousand dollars; in case of illness, each member and his family were entitled to free medical help, which came from the "Workers Circle" doctors. The Siedlce members could use all of the organizations and institutions that the "Workers Circle" had created, and after death they could receive a burial place in the "Workers Circle" cemetery.

[Page 727]

Siedlce Branch 53, as is told in "The History of the Workers Circle," from February of 1904 until 1925, paid out to the ill and needy $2,500; to the victims of the programs and the war $1,000; to HIAS $10 per year; in addition, a one–time payment to HIAS of $500 (paid in installments); and a general payment to a variety of organizations in America of $1,455. [See "The History of the Workers Circle," by A. Sh. Sacks, vol. 2, 1925.]

Over time, friction developed between the founders of the "First Siedlce Support Association" and the leadership of "Siedlce Branch 53, Workers Circle." Finally there was a split: on February 18, 1912, Moshe Garbowin, Chaim Leib Milstein, and David Spiegelman revived the liquidated "First Siedlce Support Association." This organization was later renamed "The Siedlcer Society." It considered itself to be a mutual aid society, as was stated in the form of a brochure. From this brochure we know the regulations of the "society": they accepted members from 18 to 40 years of age according to the following terms: membership dues–$14.60 per year; for those over 40, $15; over 50, one had to be unanimously approved at a meeting in order to become a member.

The "Siedlcer Society" had a sick–bank. Anyone who was over 50 at the time of joining the society could not use the sick bank. An ailing member could get $9 per week for six weeks each year. If the member were ill for a longer time, he could receive $4.50 for another four weeks. When a member became ill, according to the rules, he had to give written notice. Twice a week, a special committee would visit him to determine whether the doctor's certificate should be accepted so that the member could make use of the sick–bank.

[Page 728]

The "Siedlcer Society" employed a doctor who gave free medical help tot he members' families. When a member sat shiva, he was entitled to receive 49. In case of a difficult financial situation, when a member needed support, a special committee would visit to evaluate his financial situation and designate support. When a member got married, the "Siedlcer Society" sent a delegation to wish him "mazal tov" and to bring a gift of not less than five dollars. In case of death, survivors received an insurance payment of $200. Of this, $100 came from the society's treasury and $100 was raised by the members, not as a donation but as a duty. If none of the survivors accepted the responsibility of erecting a gravestone, the "Siedlcer Society" put up a stone and the expense was deducted from the $200.

The statutes of the "Siedlcer Society" also described a whole list of committees, such as: an examination committee to consider the applications from candidates, a finance committee, an illness and shiva committee, a burial committee, an honor court, and so on.

The rules went into effect on January 12, 1921, but then in 1917 the "First Siedlce Support Association" purchased its own cemetery in the "Bais David" cemetery in Jamaica, Long Island, New York. The Siedlce cemetery was surrounded by a small park that was behind a marble gate, beautifully made, with iron doors and the inscription: "First Siedlce Support Association." The cemetery cost $1,600, and the gate cost more than $1,200.

The "Siedlce Branch 53" and there Siedlcer Society" had two fundraising events: the yearly ball, which was organized every winter by there "Siedlce Branch 53" and the yearly picnic, which was organized each summer by the "Siedlcer Society."

[Page 729]

In 1913–1914, an attempt was made to establish the "Siedlcer Young Men's and Ladies' Educational Club" (a club for young people). It began with about thirty members. This club existed only for half a year, until the outbreak of the World War in 1914.

During the First World War, the Siedlcers created the "Siedlce Relief Committee," whose goal was to help the Jews of Siedlce who were victims of the war.

At the founding of this committee, it was decided to send delegations to "Siedlce Branch 53" and the "Siedlicer Society" to enlist them in the relief effort by sending representatives to the new organization so that it could speak authoritatively in the name of the whole Siedlce population. Both organizations at first were indifferent about the matter, but when the American newspapers began to publish news about the catastrophic lot that befell Siedlce, the indifference disappeared and the "Siedlce Relief Committee" took off.

The "Siedlce Relief Committee" formed an amateur theater group, consisting of: Eliyahu Sonnshein, Louie Altfeder, Max Ridel, A. Levartowski, Wishnia, Sarah Kindman, Aaron Rozen, and Isidor Azet, They put on plays, with the admission fees going to war victims. During one production, Sara Kindman sang the song "Give a Donation" and choir in the wings accompanied her. After all expenses, $500 remained for the relief.

In May of 1917, the "Siedlce Relief Committee" purchased a theater production called "Shema Yisroel" from Ossip Dimov. The undertaking brought in much money. This activity was interrupted on April 6, 1917 when America declared war on Germany. A little later, the "Siedlce Relief Committee" resumed its activities on behalf of Jewish war victims in Siedlce.

With the help of the "Joint," the "Siedlce Relief Committee" sent notable sums of money to Siedlce.

In order to increase its income, the "Siedlce Relief Committee" purchased from Maurice Schwartz art theater a production of Peretz Hirschbein's "Green Fields," which brought in much money. The "Releif Committee" conducted activities until the end of the war, bringing in $5,000.

[Page 730]

At the conclusion of the peace, in 1921 the "Relief Committee" sent Avraham Yablon to Siedlce with $2,000 for various organizations and $5,000 for relatives.

In Siedlce a committee was put together, including: Yakov Tenenbaum, Menashe Czarnobrode, Yitzchak Zeitz, Yitzchak Altschuler(Dromi, living now in Israel).

The liaison committee of Siedlce–in–New York in 1925

Seated: Zeitz, Avraham Yablon, Yakov Tenenbaum
Standing: Menashe Czarnobrode, Altshuler, Fishl Popowski

[Page 731]

The committee, along with A. Yablon, collected the money. When the envoy returned to America, the "Siedlce Relief Committee" was dissolved. From time to time collections were made by individuals in America to support Siedlce institutions, particularly the "Aid to Orphans." From 1921 to 1932, about $1,500 was sent to Siedlce in this way.

The Siedlcers in the United States also did local relief work. Siedlcers in 1920 founded i8n America a charity fund called the "Siedlce Finance Corporation," which had 250 members. Each member contributed $25, and in case of need could get a loan. After a few years, the "Siedlce Finance Corporation" was dissolved.

In 1925, the "Siedlce Society" created a loan fund, which assembled a sizable amount of capital. This fund was active for a long time and contributed greatly to community needs.

On November 19, 1930, the "Siedlce Branch 53–Workers Circle Women's Club" was established, which, for various reasons, was reorganized on November 2, 1931 as the "Independent Siedlce Women's Club," with over 70 members.

In 1952, the "Siedlce Branch 53" decided to contribute funds to the creation in Israel of a building to immortalize the memory of the martyrs of Siedlce. A. Kaddish, a special activist in in "Siedlce Branch 53," pledged a large sum to this cause, and together with the assigned sum, a total of $14,000 was given to the "Workers Histadrut" in Israel. The "Histadrut" took on the responsibility to erect in Acco a cultural center containing a movie theater, a small theater, and amphitheater for the summer, with lessons in Hebrew and rooms for the offices of the local workers council. According to the estimate, the building and its furnishings would cost nearly 80,000 pounds.

[Page 732]

On Chol Hamoed Pesach, 1953, in the presence of a large crowd, representatives of the workers council of "Histadrut" and a committee of Siedlcers in Israel all gathered in Acco, occurred the solemn laying of the foundation stone for the building. All of the speakers emphasized the importance of the building being built in the name of the martyrs of Siedlce and being located in Acco, a city of new immigrants, a gathering of exiles.

Fishl Dromi spoke on behalf of the people of Siedlce in Israel. He emphasized the significance of the great deed of establishing in Israel a remembrance for Siedlce's martyrs who suffered so much in exile.

Fishl Dromi (Popowski) greeted at the laying of the foundation stone

How the Cultural Center will look when it is completed

[Page 733]

הנחת אבן הפינה
לבית התרבות
ע"ש קדושי שדלי"ץ

The sign of the cultural center

France

The emigration of Siedlce Jews to France also began in 1906. After the First World War, emigration increased. The emigrants were mostly leather workers, who suffered from crises in the business and fled from the persecutions of the existing Polish regime, which went after communists and even Jewish socialists.

Around 1925, the Siedlcers in Paris formed a committee to give aid to Jewish communists who languished in Polish prisons and to help the families of the detained. Such help was, in fact, provided. Money was sent to Siedlce. This action prompted other activists to create a Siedlce union to deal with general affairs for all who came from Siedlce.

After the Second World War, the surviving Siedlcers in France returned to their homes. Many Siedlcers were brought to France by the Nazis. The survivors were naked and barefoot. The existing Siedlcer union undertook a relief program for the remnant from Siedlce. The children of Siedlcers, orphans, were taken into protection by the union. The new arrivals to France from Siedlce received support.

The Siedlce union, although it was associated with the Left, defended Israel in the great battles fought by the Yishuv for independence. A sum of 200,000 francs was raised for the Haganah.

[Page 734]

The inscription on the monument with the names of Siedlcers,
murdered and martyred, in Paris

[Page 735]

The procession to the unveiling of the monument in Paris

The following figures illustrate the activities of the union in 1945–1948:

Support for 434 people	699,650 francs
Clothing for children	360,050 francs
Summer dwellings for children	169,650 francs
Housing for children	480,000 francs
"Haganah"	200,000 francs
Total	1,909,350 francs

Aside from the above–mentioned countries, Siedlcers were found in other countries, though not organized in unions–in Australia, in South American countries, in Canada, and in South Africa. Siedlcer Max Kaczynski, one of the greatest South African philanthropists, is there. He donated great sums for the building of Israel. He gave the Hebrew University in Jerusalem many thousands of pounds. In 1934, Kaczynski spent ten months in Israel and learned Hebrew.

Siedlcers in Paris bring the urn with the ashes of Siedlce martyrs for burial

[Page 737]

Jews From Siedlce in Belgium

by Dov–Ber Blechstein (Jerusalem)

Translated by Yisrael Tabakman

The Jews from Siedlce in Belgium have taken on a prominent place in Jewish communal life. There is not a single society or party in which the Siedlcers are not represented or take part in the practical work.

The odyssey of Siedlce's Jews to Belgium began in the years 1927 to 1933. The emigrants from Siedlce actually wanted to go to America, but due to a lack of funds or for other reasons, they were stuck for the most part in France, specifically in Paris, and a small number—in Belgium, mostly in Brussels, with a few in Lieges or Chareroi.

Those Siedlcers who settled in Belgium did not change the professions they had followed in Siedlce. They organized according to their crafts: tailoring, shoemaking, gaiter making. A small number of gaiter sewers turned to "Moroccaneria," that is, to making women's pocketbooks, which was then developing. There were also some bakers, who organized themselves in the provinces.

At the founding meeting of the Siedlce Landsmanshaft in Brussels (I do not remember the year), about 100 people gathered; we estimated then that there were more than 200 families from Siedlce in B Belgium. It was decided at the meeting that all the business of the Landsmanshaft would focus on Siedlce and its institutions.

[Page 738]

The Siedlcers in Belgium, as I have said, were involved in all the local institutions and parties that the emigrants had fashioned. Many were members of the "Solidaritat" Society—an organization of the Jewish communists. A greater number belonged to the "Mutual Aid" Society and worked actively in the Peretz schools of there leftist "Poalei-Tzion." Very few belonged to the "Bund." I will mention several community activists in Belgium whom I knew personally.

When I arrived in Belgium, in 1927, I met Meir Sluszni. When he was young, he belonged to the Bund. There, in Brussels, he ran a printing shop, where he worked all alone. He was an outstanding cultural worker, he spent his free time in that cause. For a long time he as the secretary in the Jewish Central Handworker organization in Brussels. Sluszni was known particularly because of his son, a pianist, who was famous throughout Europe and played in the. Belgian royal court. Several times he was invited to England, France, Switzerland. After the liberation, Sluszni became a member fo the "Poalei-Tzion" and assumed all the cultural labor, in which he is still active.

Avraham Gutnowski came to Belgium with his family in 1928 and settled down in his craft—sewing gaiters. His wife Rivkah—a leading member in the Siedlce "Bund," helped with his work. They had difficulty earning a living. Avraham Gutnowski also wrote poems with a socialist bent. His poems were published in Yiddish papers and journals in France, such as the "Free Press" in Paris and "Our Word" in Brussels. The Gutnowski family suffered terrible misfortunes: at the time of the Spanish Civil War, their eldest son enlisted in the International Brigade and fell at the front in Spain. During the Hitlerian occupation, a second son joined the Belgian partisans. The Gestapo captured and tortured him. The older Gutnowskis survived difficult times in Hitler's years, but they never gave in to the pain and troubles. After the liberation, he continued to write and took an active role in raising the monument in Belgium to the murdered people of Siedlce.

[Page 739]

Meir Tabaktan, born in Siedlce in 1927, left his parents when he was fifteen and after a short time in France came to Belgium. With his Poalei-Tzion outlook, he was one of the most active comrades of the Borochov-youth in Brussels and was later the leader of that group. In the Poalei-Tzion Party he was especially active in the area of sports, and he was one of the founders of "Shtern," the Jewish sport club and he led it to being one of the strongest sports clubs in Brussels. In 1935, Mr. Meir was elected to the party committee and did much important work for them. The war broke out and in 1940 Mr. Meir was one of the founders of the popular organization in our community—"Mutual Aid." The younger community workers threw all their energy into helping Jews returning from France.

In 1942, when Hitler's monsters began to rampage on the Jewish streets in Belgium, Mr. Meir was one of the most active Jewish resistance fighters against the Germans. He came in contact with the leading Belgian personalities in the resistance movement and was named by the Poalei-Tzion Party Committee to lead negotiations about allowing a group from Poalei-Tzion into the partisan movement. At the end of 1942, while on party work in the street, he encountered a police raid, and one of the S.S. men recognized him. Mr. Meir was badly beaten and sent to the Molin [?] camp. When they were preparing the deportation to the death camp, he planned and organized the escape from the deportation train. Mr. Meir worried over the gear to make holes in the floor of the wagon. The plan succeeded . About 200 Jews, including Mr. Meir, escaped from the train. Because of injuries from a bad fall from the train, he had to spend several days in a hiding. When he had healed a bit, he returned to active resistance work. Because he was responsible for the illegal press of the Poalei-Tzion Party, he often kept hundreds of copies of "La Libre Belgique," "Flambeau," "Fran," "Undzer Vort," "Freie Gedank" (illegal publication of the left Poalei-Tzion in the Flemish language).

A short time later our beloved Mr. Meir was captured. Against he wanted to escape, but he could not.

[Page 740]

He was deported on the 22nd transport, and again he jumped from the train. When he returned to Brussels, his friends advised him to remain in hiding, but Mr. Meir would not submit to such a luxury; people had to save Jewish children, Jewish parents. Again he went on party missions. This time he put up posters against the occupiers, calling on the Belgian people to help the Jews who stood with them in a common battle against the enemy.

On January 1, 1943, Mr. Meir was packing food for Jewish children in hiding. They were together with Belgian children, who would also be happy with a "Saint Nicholai" gift. But the Gestapo interrupted his life and life-giving activities. This time a Gestapo man recognized him as one of the escapees, so with a red band on his arm, our Meir was deported to his death.

Aside from those people whom I have mentioned, those active in community affairs in different ways in Belgium were Hersh-Leib and Bineh Srebrnik (now in Israel). Hersh-Leib Srebrnik was an active member in the handcraft club and in other community committees in Brussels. Also his wife, Bineh, was an active member of "WIZO," Keren Kayemes, "Mutual Aid," and of the Peretz School. She was devoted to raising money for all of these organizations.

Feivel Garbiesz (now in Australia) was an outstanding worker in a number of organizations and was generous in community matters, though he had to work hard for himself. Avraham Gutowski (still in Brussels) devoted all his energy to the Siedlce Landsmanshaft and gave tremendous help to the erection of the monument to the murdered Siedlcers in Belgium. One more Siedlcer will I recall from Brussels who is no longer among the living—this is Yekel Gottesdiener. I knew Yekel Gottesdiener in Siedlce when I was young, though then I knew him as "Yenkele Rachtshes," and I would often encounter him at Yakov Moyshe Morchbein (or Greenberg) playing chess. I knew then that he was one of the best chess players, but in Brussels I found a totally different Yakov Gottesdiener, a Jew of stately appearance, a fine European Jew with a broad worldly outlook on all worldly questions, whether related to general party matters or Jewish problems. He was respected in a number of Jewish circles in Belgium. He was a consciously free-thinking Jew, but at home with his family and among his people he was a strongly traditional Jew.

[Page 741]

I will mention another important matter: the activities of the Siedlcers in Belgium to benefit Siedlce itself. In the years 1940-1941, the Siedlce Landsmanshaft was in close contact with Siedlce by sending letters and packages to the Siedlce ghetto, and we operated as the central post office for all Siedlcers in the western European countries; from England through Switzerland and from Switzerland to France and Belgium. Letters also came from America to two addresses that were known abroad: these were my address and, I believe, the second address belonged to Hersh-Leib Srebrnik. Many letters came from lots of foreign countries. The letters contained things to be sent on to families: tea, pepper, month, and questions about whether their families were still alive. In the letters were were international postal coupons and sometimes money. We worked around the clock trying to do what they asked. We had to fix the envelopes, rewrite the addresses accurately over the pepper or the tea or whatever else was in them. And there were hundreds of such letters.

For the Siedlcers, this was among the most sacred work in their daily lives. We imagined that here, in the Siedlce ghetto, we were saving people from death. And the letters we received back, which were not many, we immediately sent on to those who awaited responses. Thus we worked day and night without growing weary until the beginning of the Hitlerian repression in Belgium. We wondered that the Gestapo would leave us in peace so that we could carry on with our work. Many letters arrived having been censored by the Gestapo, but nothing changed.

At the beginning of 1942, when the wild persecution of Jews in Brussels began, Sluszni and I received summonses to come to the Gestapo on Rue Louise; we knew that one had to obey such a summons…but I did not think that Sluszni should go because he was already an older man, so I was amazed when I encountered Sluszni there.

[Page 742]

And when we were taken in to the leader, an ugly bandit, we encountered other Jews who had been summoned. We were summoned because of the Siedlce Landsmanshaft, Sluszni as the chair and me as the secretary, so that we could explain the duties of the Siedlce society. Know, then, that we explained that this was only for Siedlce, to help the institutions there. They suggested that we continue our work. We excused ourselves with the excuse that we were the only two left. When we got back home, our families burst into tears.

Meanwhile I was sure that the Gestapo bandits had "invited" us, that is ordered all representatives of Jewish organizations to come, so that they could be sure who were the representatives of the parties and the organizations in the Jewish community of Belgium. I told them that in Belgium there existed a council of Jewish organizations in which were registered all all societies and parties. On May 10, 1940, when the Germans occupied Belgium, on the second day, all members of the council left Belgium and abandoned the whole archive. They did not even lock the office. The Germans confiscated everything and so became aware of all Jewish movements in Belgium.

Right after my visit with Sluszni to the Gestapo, one morning we received an order to come with another person to the Gestapo as representatives of the "Leftist Poalei-Tzion." My son Meir, too, was appointed the representative of the "Shtern" sportclub.

With the increased repression, when Jews could barely continue living in Belgium and everything was being destroyed, the Siedlce Landsmanshaft ceased to exist.

Shortly after liberation in 1945, there was the first coming together of a few Siedlcers: Sluszni, Tabakman, Srebrnik, Gutnowski, Garbiarsz, Mendel Piekarsz. We were certain that among the 28,000 Belgian Jews who had been exterminated there were more than 100 from Siedlce who were killed. We decided to revive the the Siedlce Landsmanshaft

[Page 743]

. All of our work focused on the plan to erect a monument in Belgium for the Jews of Siedlce who had been killed. The work was quite difficult. Worn out from work in the underground and having the responsibility of restoring the living conditions of the Jewish settlement in Belgium, for whom we had risked our lives, was a bit too hard to devote oneself to a separate task like the monument. And besides, who could even think about it? After such a great catastrophe, when the whole nightmare appeared before our eyes, when the small number of Jews who remained alive in Belgium were bunched together in one spot, in Brussels, without a shirt on their backs, where they needed help every day, like food, clothing, doctors, medicines, a roof over their heads, one would have been regarded as crazy to speak about a monument for murdered Siedlcers; it would have seemed like foolishness. But the Siedlcers decided to erect such a monument, and they carried out the decision. That represented a lot of work. The question was, where to build the monument.

[Page 744]

It was decided to build it in the Jewish cemetery. I was selected to intervene with the Jewish authorities about a place for the monument. On the monument were to be, in addition to the names of the murdered, also their pictures. When I came to the first meeting of the authorities with a plan and asked for a plot of two meters for a monument of black marble with a pedestal, with names, with pictures of the murdered Siedlcers, I was listened to in silence; and then everyone at the meeting addressed me this way: "How can you, Mr. Tabakman, ask that in a Jewish cemetery we should erect a monument with pictures, just like the gentiles?" After a long discussion, they called for a meeting with the Brussels rabbi, and if the rabbi approved, they would allow it.

I wasted no time and hastened to the rabbi (whose name, sadly, I do not remember, though he now lives in Tel Aviv) and delivered my request, explaining to him that if he would approve, then the authorities would allow it. After a long talk, the rabbi said, "Since I know about your suffering in Hitler's time, your untiring work in the present, after liberation, for the welfare of the Jewish community in Brussels, I will approve, with one condition: no photos." He asked that I be satisfied. I agreed and settled things with the rabbi. I drew up a contract with the authorities for a plot of two meters at the nicest spot in the Jewish cemetery of Brussels. I reported this to the Siedlcers, and then began the real work of collecting funds and carrying out the plan. That was hard work, but we did it all heroically. Every Siedlcer was involved and helped turn the idea into reality.

With great effort and work, we were able to eternize the murdered Siedlcers, and the monument stands in the nicest spot in the Jewish cemetery of Brussels. Underneath the monument are buried bones of Jews from Lukow that had been scattered around the city of Lukow and were brought by people from Lukow. There are also names there, particularly of fallen Siedlcer partisans. On the day when this grand monument was unveiled, all of Jewish Brussels attended and filled the whole cemetery.

[Page 745]

This was one of the saddest gatherings that I saw after the liberation. This was my last activity with the Siedlcers before I traveled to Israel.

It is my wish that Siedlcers from the around the world should consider putting up a large monument in the "Forest of Martyrs" in the hills of Jerusalem.

The monument for the Siedlcers in Belgium

[Page 746]

The committee in Argentina that issued the Yizkor Book

Sitting (left to right): Yisroel Vinograd, the proofreader Moshe Konstantinowski, Moshe Yudengloibn, Moshe Federman, Hersh Abarbanel
Standing (left to right): Bunim Finifter, Yitzchak Bistrowicz, Avraham Creda, Feivel Englander

[Page 747]

The Siedlce Landsmanshaft of Buenos Aires

by Moshe Yudengloibn

Translated by Theodore Steinberg

On April 20, 1930, a group of natives of Siedlce gathered together in the home of Mr. Bezalel Rosenbaum. These included: Hershel Levin, Moshe Federman, Shimon Kirshman, Gedaliah Solarsz, Yosef Rosenbaum who was later killed in Poland by the Nazis.

This group of Siedlce natives took on the responsibility of founding a union of emigrants from Siedlce, so that the newly arrived could find a warm corner and not be strangers in a strange land. They would care for the new arrivals, help them in case of illness, and so on.

After a discussion, they decided to establish an association of Siedlce natives, and they elected a committee consisting of Hershel Levin, Moshe Federman, Bezalel Rosenbaum, Shimon Kirshman, and others.

After their first meeting, they put out an announcement to all Siedlcers in Buenos Aires that they should join the group. This appealed to a certain number of Siedlcers, but the majority remained outside the association. The committee made the greatest efforts to publicize and declare the need for such an association. This work paid off a little. For a little while, the association met in the home of Bezalel Rosenbaum.

When the association reached a hundred members, it moved to the premises of the Jewish-Polish Association and began to undertake its activities. They set out to realize the duties they had written down. Different undertakings were organized to attract all the Siedlcers of Buenos Aires, to approach them, to familiarize them, and to create a warm atmosphere for them. The Siedlcers began to feel homier, closer, and they often got together.

[Page 748]

Meanwhile, more Siedlcers came to Buenos Aires. The association was for them, from the beginning, a home. People helped some with a kind word, some with finding work or with a big of advice about what to do. In time, the association grew and began to think about creating a credit union, which was quite necessary at that time. The newly arrived Jews from Siedlce, as well as local residents, needed credit. The local banks required guarantees from highly-placed people, and at that time there were few Siedlcers who could give such guarantees.

At a specially called meeting, the question of forming a credit union was discussed. The gathering showed great interest in the matter. They discussed how to pay for sharess and what the price should be.

It was decided to make the price for a share 25 pesos and a loan limit of 100 pesos. An ad hoc committee was selected to solicit shareholders. Many members signed up for shares, some for one, some for two, and so on. A considerable sum was raised at the meeting, and the committee got down to work.

After much effort, the credit union finally opened and made its first loans. This had a huge effect on the Siedlcers and they became ever more interested in the activities of the credit union. In time, the credit union got credit from the Jewish Folkbank, which allowed it to give even bigger loans. Loan payments started to pour in, so the credit union's activities could grow.

Enough money was coming in that Siedlcers of better standing who needed more money than the banks would allow approached the credit union, and this resulted in a difference of opinion on the committee. Some maintained that the requested sums were not sustainable, because the bank was not yet in a position to give such loans. It needed more time to practice by giving smaller sums, according to the bank's abilities, because in fact the bank had been created to give loans of up to 100 pesos.

[Page 749]

But the second group on the committee (the majority) did not want to take into account the actual situation and decided to give the requested sums as a larger bank. would have. The result was that recipients of the large loans did not pay—the coffer remained empty; they could no longer give even the smaller loans.

A number of Siedlcers began to mutter that there was no money. The shareholders who had shares and had taken no money lost trust and wanted their investments back. Two sides formed, and each side blamed the other. The apathy of the Siedlcers toward the association and to the bank increased, and it went bust. The committee, which had taken money from the Folksbank on their personal responsibility with promissory notes had to come up with funds to cover the loans, because no more money was coming in. The large borrowers were not repaying were deducting the costs of their shares. The coffees were empty. In this situation, it emerged that the shareholders, who had two or three shares, would lose the money for their shares. It must be stressed that at that time the shareholders had nor other funds. The situation led to the collapse of the association and of the bank, leaving a bad taste with all of our Siedlcers.

As time passed, more people from Siedlce arrived. The new arrivals would gather with people they had known at home—in private dwellings, where they could talk, recall their old homes, and think about who they could take away from there. The resident Siedlcers conducted community life in meeting spots, each according to his inclinations: home in the workers movement, others in Zonist circles; each found his own spot. Many remained as they had been in their old homes—apathetic toward everyone; they were interested in nothing, not their fellow Siedlcers, not in the community, and not in their old home. But those who were active in the community of our Siedlcers produced a number of people who were active in the Argentinian Jewish settlement.

[Page 750]

After Hitler's Extermination of the Jews

When the bloody Second World War came to an end and Jews throughout the world knew of the great misfortune that had befallen European Jews, the terrible news came as well to us in Argentina about our home town of Siedlce.

We immediately met and began to assess the situation. The question arose of how to to create aid for our surviving sisters and brothers. The horrible misfortune united all of our Siedlcers. Many of them came prepared to help all who were in need. Immediately a committee was formed to conduct the aid project. The committee consisted of the following people: Avraham Kreda, Moshe Federman, Tz. Rosenbaum, Mosher Yudengloibn, Yoel Levin, Hershel Levin, Mendel Saperstein, Meir Malawnczik Sh. Kirshman, Mottl Sckerrmsan, Itzl Rosenbaum. Our friend Avraham Kreda was elected to preside. The secretary was Moshe Federman, the treasurer M. Saperstein. A women's committee worked alongside the men's.

At the first large meeting, the committee immediately collected money for the aid fund. The committee members were the first to contribute. Everyone followed their example. A large sum was quickly raised.

After the meeting, the committee sought to visit every Siedlcer whose address was known. Thus it was done to broaden the action so that the help would be larger. At that time it was incumbent to amass a large sum of money. Meanwhile, letters arrived letters of a collective nature from the cities of Lodz, Siedlce, and others.

We prepaid six crates of clothing for men, women, and children, of which 90 percent was new, gifts from our comrades. The six crates of clothing were sent on a Polish ship. Later we received a response that they had received them and divided them up.

The certificate making permanent the "Siedlce Kehillah" in the Golden Book

[Page 752]

There were some who asked for help in leaving Poland and whether people would receive them in Argentina or help with their papers. We did for them all that was possible. We helped come to Argentina: a woman with her child, a family of three, and we helped them get settled. We also gave material help to many Siedlcers who could not bring over their surviving families.

A little later, letters began to arrive from the D.P camps asking for help in the form of food packages. We quickly sent packages to wherever it was possible. We also sent 500 dollars to Paris for the Siedlce orphans and material help to the appeals of individuals Siedlcers in Paris. To Israel we sent 100 pounds to the Siedlcer Landsmanshaft , and especially for individuals from Israel who had come to us, we sent food packages.

Also for the Haganah we contributed 1,000 pesos. Thus we conducted our aid work to the maximum and in proportion to our membership.

Thus ended the financial aid.

After this activity there was a pause in the activities of the association. But the committee continued its work. It organized undertakings from time to time, eternized the Siedlce Kehillah by having it registered in the Golden Book on the first anniversary of its origin.

The committee had the idea of issuing a Yizkor Book that would be a monument for our destroyed community. We gathered materials for such a Yizkor Book. The committee went to Siedlcers in many countries asking them to send pictures and newspapers that had a bearing on Siedlce and also to write memoirs. We, on our side, were ready to do everything to see that such a book appeared, but we lacked materials. Finally from Israel came the surprising news that they had the required materials, memoirs, photocopies, and so on, and that they were prepared to join us in issuing the Yizkor Book.

Intensive work began immediately on preparing these materials.

[Page 753]

Siedlcers who attended the announcement of the publication of the Siedlce Yizkor Book and who paid the first installments

[Page 754]

The visit of our comrades Hershel Barbanel to Israel hastened the appearance of the book. He discussed it with our Siedlcers in Tel Aviv and prepared the plans for publication.

Our Siedlce colleagues in Israel deserve the greatest recognition for their true extraordinary work in organizing these rich materials, for which their hands should be blessed. This book should be a great honor to all Siedlcers throughout the world.

יזכור

אֶת נִשְׁמוֹת קְדוֹשִׁים וּטְהוֹרִים
בְּנֵי קְהִלַּת שֶׁדְלֶץ
אֲשֶׁר הוּשְׁמְדוּ בְּמִיתוֹת שׁוֹנוֹת
ע"י הַנָאצִים הַטְמֵאִים וְאַנְשֵׁי בְּלִיַעַל
עַל אַדְמַת הָעִיר שֶׁדְ־לֶץ
בִּסְבִיבָתָהּ בְּגְדוּדֵיהֶם וּבְמַחֲנוֹת
הַהַשְׁמָדָה לְמִינֵיהֶם
תִּהְיֶינָה נִשְׁמוֹת הַמְעֻלִּים צְרוּרוֹת
בִּצְרוֹר הַחַיִּים שֶׁל הָאֻמָּה
נִזְכּוֹר אוֹתָם לָעַד

[Page 755]

Yiddish translations by Theodore Steinberg; **formatting and Hebrew translations by** Mira Eckhaus

---

Remember

The holy and pure souls, members of the Siedlce community, who were exterminated in various deaths by the impure Nazis and evil persons on the land of the city of Siedlce, in its surroundings, in their wanderings and in the extermination camps.

May the souls of the tortured be bound up in the bond of life of the nation.

We will remember them forever.

[Page 756] Blank [Page 757]

For eternal memory

Orzel Family

The honorable man, who was engaged in public needs with faith, Rabbi Asher Orzel;

Moshe Orzel,	Hannah Firster - Exterminated among 29 girls
Playa Orzel,	Basha Orzel
Semick Orzel,	Brunia Pedrovsky
Gute Firster,	
Schindel-Zola	Semick and their daughter
Zeev Firster,	

Esther Shvartz and her husband Shaul and their sons Yagush and Theodore

The mourner:
Itzchak Orzel and his family.

Eisenstadt Family

My dear father, Rabbi Moshe-Abba Eisenstadt, the son of Rabbi Paltiel from Barza,

My mother Itta, the daughter of Yosef-Chaim Zilbertsweig,

My brother-in-law Eliezer, the son of Rabbi Ya'akov Levin

My sister Pola (Pesia) Levin and their two sons, Ya'akov and Tuvia, and their daughter Miriam.

The mourners:
The Paltiel Eisenstadt family

[Page 758]

I hereby mention my father, the dearest, the true Hassid and the extreme scholar, who educated me since my childhood to the love of Zion and Jerusalem. The honorable gentlemen: The late Israel Sinai, the son of the late Rabbi Shmuel, from Warsaw, who died in Siedlce on the 25th of Iyar, 1903, at the early age of 58 years old.

My dear mother, a woman of action, who, thanks to her efforts, saved many people from imprisonment and other troubles, the honorable ladies: the late Mrs. Rachel, the daughter of the late Rabbi David Greenfarb, who died on 28 Cheshvan, 1928, in an advanced age in the city of Siedlce.

My brother, my dear, the distinctly wise student, comfortable with God and human beings, a rare person, the honorable gentleman, the late Mr. Shmuel David, who died in the city of Siedlce on 15 Cheshvan, 1932, while he was 69 years old.

My dear sister, a modest and pious woman, the late Mrs. Nechama, the wife of Rabbi Avraham Abba Frenkel, who died young in Warsaw on the 23 Elul 1911.

And those of my family members who were killed, strangled, or burned alive by the impure Nazis, may they name be blotted out:

(Continued)

My sister-in-law, Mrs. Hava, the wife of my late brother Shmuel David, daughter of the late Rabbi Natan-Neta Bornstein, from Sarcomela, with her daughter Dvorah, with her husband Moshe-Haim Geffen - Brisk Lithuania - with their three daughters and children and their son and his wife and children, the two sons of my late brother Shmuel David, Yechiel Meir and his wife Itke, the daughter of the late Rabbi Moshe David and Kalman, with their two sons, and Avraham-Mordechai with his wife and daughter.

My dear, gentle sister, Mrs. Reisel-Hadas, with her husband, Rabbi Menachem Mendel, the grandson of the Rabbi, the Rebbe from Biala, Rabbi Dobrish Landau, may the memory of the righteous be a blessing, with their two daughters, Esther-Frida and Malka and their husbands and children and their son Avraham and his wife and their children.

My dear sister, the loyal Zionist, the late Mrs. Liba-Sima, with her husband Mordechai Halperin and their son Israel and his wife and child and their daughter Lilka.

My niece, the daughter of my late brother Shmuel-David, Rivka, gentle and pure, devoted to Zionism and Hebrew, with her husband Pinchas Weingerten, the son of the Rebbe of Lubashov, may the memory of the righteous be a blessing, with their two sons.

The wife of my nephew, Reisel-Hadas, the late Mr. Barish Landau, from Losice, with her two sons and their wives and children and her daughter and her husband and her daughter.

The daughter of my eldest sister, Sima, who was to us like a sister, Mrs. Roizla, with her husband, Asher Ashkenazi, with their son, the lawyer Shmuel and his wife and daughter, and their daughter Sima with wise Mordechai, the son of the Rabbi from Bielsk, with their son and their daughter from Brisk in Lithuania.

My dear brother-in-law, my wife's brother, may his light shine, the lawyer Avraham Slava from Warsaw, the son of the late Rabbi Moshe-Aharon Slava from Radom, a member of the Central Committee of the Zionist Organization in Poland, the founder of "Hachalutz" Craftsmen in Poland and more. May their souls be bound up in the bond of life, May God avenge their spilled blood.

The mourner:
Isha'ayahu, the son of Sinai
Zeidenzieg

[Page 759]

We will never forget these

My dear mother, the humble woman, a loyal activist, Hannah Papawski,

My sister Chaya with her husband Zeev Peshanana and their three daughters,

My sister Bracha with her husband Gershon Zilberberg and with the whole honorable family.

The survivor:
Fishel Dromi (Popovsky)
With his family in Israel.

Killed by the assassins of Hitler, may his name be blotted out

For eternal memory

1.   My beloved wife, the late **Esther**, the daughter of Rivka and Mordechai **Rubin** of Pilv (once Lublin).

2.   The beloved daughter the late **Rachel (Rosa)**, the daughter of Yehuda Leib (Leon) Glicksberg from Siedlce and her husband the late Avraham Halberstadt from Lodge.

3.   My beloved son, the late **Aaron (Adalf)**, the son of Yehuda Leib.

4.   My beloved brother, the late Dov-**Ba'arish** and his family from Warsaw, the son of the late Natan David and the late Malka Hadas Glicksberg.

5.   My beloved brother, the late **Meir** from Belgium, the son of the late Natan David and the late Malka Hadas Glicksberg.

6.   My beloved brother, the late **Shlomo** and his family from Vilna, the son of the late Natan David and the late Malka Hadas Glicksberg.

7.   My beloved sister, the late **Felie (Feril)**, her daughter Malka and her husband the late Avraham Kahana from Berdichev.

8.   My beloved mother-in-law, the late **Rivka Rubin**, daughter of the late **Rachel and Mendel Bayer** of Pilv (once Lublin).

9.   My sister-in-law, the late **Felie (Feril)** Kamien and her late son Mendel, the daughter of the late Rivka and Mordechai Rubin from Otwock.

10.   My late brother-in-law, the late Ya'akov, the son of the late Natan Dobrezinski, from Lodge and Leah from the Sheinfeld family.

11.   My sister-in-law, the late **Rania (Rachel)** Dabrezinski, the daughter of the late Rivka and Mordechai Rubin from Pilv.

12.   Their son **Ignash (Itzchak)** Dabrezinski and his wife Sara from the Schatz family in Warsaw.

13.   My beloved uncles, the late **Meir and Ya'akov** Kahana with their families, the sons of Menachem Shlomo and Hannah Rivka Kahana.

14.   My aunt, the late **Itka Mintz**, the daughter of my elderly father Menachem Shlomo Kahana and Hannah Rivka from the Orzel family.

15.   My cousin, the late Sara Rokach, with her 2 daughters, the daughter of the late Meir Kahana and the late Feige from the Ginzburg family.

16.   My beloved brother-in-law, the late Avraham Ben Ya'akov and the late Hodel (from the family of Margalit of Berdichev), Kahana.

Bitters over them and their holy souls.

Yehuda Leib (Leon) Glicksberg of Siedlce
Now in Tel Aviv, 95 Allenby Street, PO Box 1903

[Page 760]

For eternal memory of the Domb family

Mendel Domb	- Died in the ghetto - 22-8-42
Rachel Domb-Shapira	- Died in the ghetto - 22-8-42
Hava Domb Ackerman	|
Joshua Ackerman	|- Exterminated in 22-8-42
Oded Ackerman	|
Yosef Domb with his wife Fanya	- Died in Brisk, Lithuania

The mourners:
Shmuel and Sara Aloni (Domb)
Bella Aloni
Simcha Aloni and his family
Sara Bergman-Domb

Eternal tombstone

In memory of our ancestors, the unforgettable children: The late Rabbi **Naftali Hertz** ben Mordechai **Halberstadt**

The late Yente-Gittel, the daughter of the late Israel-Dov Liebernat-Halberstadt

Who were murdered in the last extermination of the Siedlce ghetto (Poland) on the 20th-22nd of Kislev 5703 (29.11-1.12/1942).

Our late sister Roiza and our late brother-in-law Yosef Citrin and their late son Mordechai.

Who were killed in the liquidation of the Warsaw ghetto on the 13th -19th of Nissan 5703 (18-24.4/1943).

The commemorators:
Israel Halberstadt and his family - in Israel.
Henya (Nolka) Halberstadt-Teitel- in Israel.
Shmuel Halberstadt and his family - in the United States.

For eternal memory!

The graves of our dear and esteemed parents The late Rabbi Feibel-Shraga, the son of the late Avraham Greenspan, who died in Warsaw on the 14th of Kislev, 5698 (18.11/1937), the late Miriam-Sara, the daughter of the late Avraham Zilberzahn-Greenspan, who died in Warsaw on the 18th of Adar A 5696 (12.3/ 1936), our late brother Avraham Greenspan, who was murdered in Siedlce on 11th Elul 5680. Our late brother Ya'akov (Yanek) Greenspan and his family, who were killed in Siedlce ghetto on the 11th of Elul 5702, Our late brother Itzchak (Adek) Greenspan, who died in Siedlce ghetto on the 26th of Tevet, 5702 and his family, who was killed in the ghetto, our sister Perill (Pulia) Greenspan-Zeitlin and her late son, our sister Sheindel (Stasha) Greenspan- The late Herzlberg, our late sister Bluma (Malbina) Greenspan.

The mourners: the only one left alive from the entire extended family
Rachel (Lonia) Greenspan-Halberstadt and her husband Israel Halberstadt with their daughter Miriam in Israel.

[Page 761]

The Halberstadt family

Nahum Halberstadt - Transferred to Treblinka: 25-11-42

Itke Halberstadt from the Rubinstein family - Transferred to Treblinka: 25-11-42

Hirsch Halberstadt - Killed with his family in Warsaw

Israel Halberstadt – Died in ghetto Siedlce: 9-12-41

Dr. Helena Papau – Murdered: 22-8-42

The Goldfarb family

Heinech Goldfarb - Transferred to Treblinka: 25-11-42

Rachel Goldfarb from the Brenner family - Transferred to Treblinka: 25-11-42

Chaya Virtsershol from the Goldfarb family - killed in Warsaw

Lib Godfarb - Died in Warsaw

Sima Ya'akobowitz from the Goldfarb family - Murdered in Warsaw with her husband

Asher Goldfarb - fell in August in the general Polish uprising

The bitter mourners:
**Henya and Moshe Halberstadt
and their sons
Bluma Goldfarb and David
Shedroytski**
Tel Aviv, Israel

[Page 762]

Memorial prayer

We bitterly weep the death of our loved ones, the death of our dear father and teacher, the late Dov, the dearest and modest person, the death of our late sister Dvorah and her family and the death of our younger brother Ya'akov and his family, who were killed and died a martyr's death by the impure Nazi murderers.

Their precious memory will never be forgotten!

Mordechai and Sara Temkin.

The beloved and pleasant in their lives

Our father, the Hassid and honest in man, the chairman of the merchants' bank committee, the late Rabbi Kalman Friedman.

Our mother, the educated and humbled, the late Mrs. Rachel (from the Folman family) who were murdered and burned at Treblinka.

Our sisters, the innocent Feigele, who was an employee of the "Taz" and the hospital in Siedlce, and the young and graceful Dina'tche, who did not want to leave our parents, and was murdered in Siedlce.

Their memory will not be forgotten!

The survivors:
The sons: **Avraham, Menachem and Zechariah and their families** (in Israel)
And the daughter: **Leah'tche and her family**
(Mebila, Greenbaum, in Paris)

[Page 763]

For eternal memory!

The Zelzstein family: Israel, Esther-Malka:

Itzchak (Idel), Tzluva, Levi Gutgeld, Rachel, Sara.

The Weiman family, Bunim - Masha:

Shmuel, Vira, Ya'akov, Aharon, Miriam, Frida, Heinech Vegoski, Mendel, Henya, Yosef
Gutgeld, Feliya, Zaman Rotfeld, Chaya'le, Avraham, Hana'ke from the Frester family.

Herschel Lederman and Masha

Etke and Aharon Gerstein, Simcha, Gittel and the boy.

Bitterly mourn:
The Weiman Dov family,
The Zelzstein Shalom family,
The Ledeman Dov family.

The Mordasky family

My dear and kind father, Rabbi Aharon, the son of Abba Mordasky

My mother Riesel My sister Chaya

My sister Schindel

My brother Ya'akov

My sister Feigele

I will never forget them
Israel Mordasky and his family

[Page 764]

For eternal memory

Our father and grandfather, Rabbi Itzchak Asman, who died in 1931.

Aryeh-Leib, the son of Itzchak Asman, who died with his wife Hannah, the daughter of Dov, in the Siedlce ghetto.

Shamay Asman and his Haim.

For eternal memory

Ya'akov Goldberg, who died in the ghetto.

Mirel Goldberg, who was murdered with her children by the Nazis.

Chaim Goldberg and his family Feivel Goldberg and Moshe Goldberg.

The mourners who survived, and the memory of their loved ones will never be forgotten:

Simcha Asman and his family (in the United States)
Gavriel Asman and his family (in the United States)
Leah Ferfel from the Asman family and her family (in Israel)
Israel Asman and his family (in Israel)
Sara Friedman from the Goldberg family (in Israel)

[Page 765]

Eternal tombstone

In memory of our beloved father, Rabbi Hanoch - Hanich Steinberg, may the memory of the righteous be a blessing, the honest and precious in man.

In memory of our beloved sister, the late Rachel Steinberg (Goldberg),

Who were led to the massacre by impure Hitlerite taskmasters in 5702
(our father from Siedlce and our sister from Warsaw).

Bitterly crying:

Moshe Steinberg - Israel - Tel Aviv
Yehuda Steinberg - Costa Rica - San Jose
Sara Steinberg (Aloni) - Israel-Tel Aviv
Avraham Steinberg - Israel - Tel Aviv

Eternal tombstone

In memory of my beloved and dear parents:
The late Rabbi Ya'akov Stavkovsky
The late Esther Stavkovski

In memory of my beloved and loyal sisters:
Chaya Stavkovski
Itke Stavkovski
Tova Stavkovski
Perla Stavkovski

Who found their death under the impure Hitlerite occupation in 5702 in the city of Siedlce.

Bitterly crying:
Their only daughter and sister
Sima Stavkovski (Steinberg), (Israel, Tel Aviv),
and her husband **Avraham Steinberg**

[Page 766]

A memorial tombstone

In memory of our unforgettable loved ones:
Shraga Ben Yoel-Hirsch Mendelssohn
Rozsha
Moshe
Michal
Chaya

The commemorators:
The Mendelssohn Family (Israel)

A memorial tombstone

Shalom Ben Itzchak-Isaac
Bluma-Male, the daughter of Yechiel
Arie Leib
Chaya'le Morgenstern
Eliezer, the son of Mordechai Kleinlerer
Golda the daughter of Shalom
Menachem Mendel
Shulamit

The Morgenstern family

[Page 768]

Eternal tombstone

In memory of the son and brother Arie-Leib Pasovsky, the son of the late cantor Rabbi Yosef-Dov.

He fell on the Russian-German war as an officer in the Red Army in a battle near the city of Bialystok - in 8 Av, 5701.

He was buried in the Jewish cemetery in the city of Vawkavysk

His family was exterminated in the town of Brinsk.

Their memory will remain blessed!

The commemorators:
The mother: **Zvia Pasovsky**
The brothers: **Dov Ben Yosef and his family**
Daniel Ben Yosef and his family
Netanel Ben Yosef and his family
Michal Ben Yosef and her family
State of Israel

To the eternal memory of my dear and beloved parents, Tov and Chaya-Liebe Finkelstein, my sister and brother-in-law Baruch Surbitz and their child Fridke (from Szambriv), in addition to all of my own relatives and friends – victims of the Nazi regime.

The sole survivor
Dinah Finkelstein (Ranec)
Israel, Ramat-Gan, 12 Medel Street

[Page 769]

To The Memory of Those Who Are Not Forgotten

Tzalel and D'vorah and their children.
The children of Mendel and Rochel Tabakman, who were killed in the ghetto.

Berl Shiwek and Esther and their children;
Chana and her children,
Henyeh and her children
Who were killed in the ghetto.

Hodes and her husband and children, killed in Mord.

The children of Zelda and Mendel Shiwek.

Dedicated by:
Yisroel Tabakman and his Sister Rozenzumen

In Eternal memory!

Rabbi Israel Rosenblum (Birzier), The great and devoted activist for the poor, became famous as chairman of the "Bethlehem" company, was an activist at "Mizrahi".

Hershel Rosenblum and his wife Hannah, Moshe Rosenblum, Rachel Rosenblum (Kotlersky), Reisel Rosenblum, Primt Rosenblum - all were murdered by the impure Nazis.

Bitterly mourners:
Dvorah Kriez, her husband Isaac and the children
In the State of Israel

In eternal memory of our dear family Zlotowski

The parents:	
The father:	Israel
The mother:	Miriam (Maya)
The sisters:	Nechama (and her husband Einech Zinstein and the children)
	Mina (and her husband Ya'akov Kamien and their children)
	Feigele
The brother:	Itzchak

Of blessed memory

Delivered by brothers: David & Avraham
Haifa, Israel
Michal – Paris, France
The sister: - Minsk, Russia

[Page 770]

To the Eternal Memory

My Not Forgotten, Dear and Beloved Family

Parents: Ritza and Aaron-Yitzchak Shmukliarsz – killed in the Siedlce ghetto;

Brother: Elieer Shmukliarsz and his wife Leah and children – died in Siedlce;

Sister: Henyeh Yellen and her husband Dovid and children – killed in Warsaw;

Brother: Dovid – killed in Siedlce;

Sister: Esther – killed in a village near Siedlce;

My uncles: Baruch Mordechai Shmukliarsz and David Shimon Shmukliarsz and their families.

Feyga and Moyshe Bialilev and their children.

D'vorah and Avraham Gersht and their children.

Henyeh and her husband and children.

Moyshe Bergman, his wife Sarah, and their children.

Their survivor and mourner, who eternalizes their memory
Rochel Shmulkliarsz-Weinstein and her husband
Avraham and Children (In Israel)

Memorial Candle

**For the holy memory of my dear family members,
who were murdered by the impure Nazis and their helpers**

The parents: Arie and Alta-Sara Orlansky

The brothers and sisters: Israel, Fishel, Batya, Hannah, Zviya and their descendants

This memorial page is dedicated with admiration and love
By **Yehoshua Orlansky**

[Page 771]

With God's help
In memory of the Kramerzesh families in Siedlce

A.   **Rabbi Zvi Menashe, the son of the late Rabbi Tuvia** Kramerzesh (Rabbi Hershel Tuvia's) from 16 Deloga Street, a great and wise scholar, a Hassid and an activist with faith.
His wife, **Mrs. Miriam, the daughter of the late Rabbi Israel Ya'akov HaCohen**
B.   **The late Rabbi Mordechai Bar-Zvi Menashe Kramerzesh** (Rabbi Mattel Kramerzesh) from 3 Uleina Street, a wise scholar, a Hassid with fear of God, with good virtues, who was involved in rescuing Jews during the Holocaust in Siedlce. (See the poem "The Savior" by the poet Shaul in the book "Lamoed", which was published by "HaMizrachi" in the publishing of the late Rabbi Bar-Ilan in 5707, page 89: "In Siedlce, which was completely bombed, a wall remained and a savior, a wonderful Jew, etc., he saved the others but the savior was not saved").
His wife, the late Mrs. **Figa**, from the Papir family.

May their souls be bound up in the bond of life, May God avenge their spilled blood.

The mourners:
Rabbi Shmuel Menachem Karmesh-Can'ani and his family, Meshek Gvat, Israel. The son of Rabbi Hershel Tuvia's and the brother of Rabbi Mattel Karmesh.
Mr. Yehoshua Karmesh and his wife Hannah Sara from the Riza family, Kiryat Haim, 45 A.B. Street, the son of the late Rabbi Hershel Tuvia's and the brother of the late Rabbi Mattel Kramesh.
Mr. Simcha Bunem Karmesh and his wife Esther Sara from the Lubliner family and their sons, Haifa, 38 Sirkin Street, the son of Rabbi Mattel Karmesh and the grandson of Rabbi Hershel Tuvia's.
Mrs. Mindel Karmesh-Sheinfeld, Givat Aliya and her family, the daughter of the late Rabbi Mattel, etc.
Mr. David Karmesh-Cna'ani and his family, the Ma'agan Michael group, the son of the late Rabbi Mattel, etc.
(The late son Ya'akov fell in 1948 in the War of Independence in the Battle of Tantura, may God avenge his blood).

In memory of the Lubliner family in Siedlce

The late Rabbi Nachum-Ze'ev Lubliner
His wife, Mrs. **Sima**, the daughter of Rabbi Itcha Tabakman
Their children: **Joshua, Abraham, Henya, Chaya** and **Hannah.**

May their souls be bound up in the bond of life, May God avenge their spilled blood

The mourners:
Their daughter and sister **Esther Sara,**
the wife to **Mr. Simcha Bonam**
Karmesh, Haifa, 38 Sirkin Street

In memory of the Riza family in Siedlce

The late **Rabbi Itzchak Aharon, Riza**
His wife, the late Mrs. **Rebecca**
Their children: **Israel**, **Sa'arke** (Finkenkavish), **Toive** (Gingold), **Chaya** (Shmilina) and **Esther** (Guthalf)

The mourners:
Their daughter and sister **Hannah Sara Kramesh**,
the wife of **Mr. Yehoshua Kramesh**,
Kiryat Chaim, 45 A.B. Street

[Page 772]

For eternal memory of our father and his family

Who were exterminated by the impure Nazis in the month of Elul, 1942 in Siedlce.

Bunim Rybak, the son of Avraham-Itzchak.
Meir Rybak, the son of Avraham-Itzchak
with his wife and their children.

Baruch with his wife and their children;
Avraham Shlifke, the son of Itzchak
with his wife and their children.

Meir Shlifke with his wife and their children.

Zalman Shlifke, the son of Itzchak, with his wife and their children.

Bitterly mourners:
**His wife Malka Rybak, their sons and their wives,
grandson and the brothers - the Rybak family.**

For eternal memory of our parents and brothers, who were murdered by the Nazis in the city of Siedlce

Ya'akov-Zvi, the son of Arie Galitsky
Bila-Ides, the daughter of Moshe-Ze'ev
Mattel, the son of Ya'akov-Zvi
David, the son of Ya'akov-Zvi

Bitterly mourners, those who survived:
The boys with their wives
The girls with their husbands
And the grandchildren
– The Galitsky family in Israel

For eternal memory

Our parents

Father: **Haim Bernholtz**
Mother: Sara
Our brother: Moshe
The sisters: Chantshe and Gittel
Mother: **Basha Vishniya**
Brother Shlomo
The sister: **Leah**

Commemorators:
**Eliezer Bar-Haim
(Bernholtz)
Chava Lishniya - Bar Haim**
(Haifa)

In memory of Aaron and Itke Libernat and their children, Sara and Zvi Rubinstein and their children

Dove and Shaul Bernholtz and their children
Israel and Chaya Libernat and their children
Binyamin Libernat

The commemorator:
Gila Binstock
(Haifa, Israel)

My father and my teacher, **Rabbi Avraham-Zvi Serbernik**
Mother: Sprintza Sisters: Desha and Bila

The commemorator:
Israel Serbernik
(Israel)

In memory

Mother: **Rivka Kirshenbaum**
The brothers: Mordechai, Yehoshua and Shlomo
The sister: Figa

The commemorator:
**Chanina David Devani
Kirshenbaum**

An eternal candle

In memory of my father: Itzchak Orzel
Mother: Sara-Shifra
My sister: Dove
My brother: Matityahu

The commemorator:
Reuven Orzeshel
(in Israel)

I will never forget

My brother: **Ben Zion Kamineni**
My sisters: Esther and Rashka Kamineni

The commemorator:
Avraham Kamini
(Haifa)

In memory of my **Mother**
Nehama Binstock

Her sisters: Itke and Yente, Rachel and Herzl
Tiblum and their children,

Hannah and Eliezer Zashirovich and their children

The commemorators:
The brothers
Zvi and Avraham Binstock
(Haifa)

A memorial

For my brother: **Baruch Shapira**

And my sister: Rashka

The commemorator:
Alexander Shapira
(Haifa)

[Page 774]

We will not forget our loved ones forever!

In memory of my father and my
teacher: **Matityahu Obogi**

Mother: Hannah

The sisters: Gittel, Rivka, Hinke,
Chaya and Perl

The brothers: Ya'akov, Leibel and
Yosef

The commemorator:
Yechiel Obogi
(Haifa)

**In memory of my father: Aharon
Drozeshansky,**

My sister: Schindel

Grandfather: Rabbi Mendel

And my grandmother: Rachel

The commemorator:
Israel Drozeshansky
(Haifa)

Tombstone

My father: **Rabbi Avraham Rybak**

My mother: Gittel

My brothers: Herschel and Barish

My wife: Menucha

And my dear son: David

The commemorator:
Mordechai Rybak

An eternal memory

To mother: **Zelta-Esther Mister**

My sisters: Pearl-Hannah, Breindle

My brothers: Ya'akov, Yisha'ayahu

The commentator:
**Menachem Mister
(Israel)**

In eternal memory!

My parents: **Asher Yubiler**
And his wife **Zvia**

My brothers: Moshe, Meir-Shalom and Heinech

My sister: Esther (and her husband Ben-Zion)

The only commemorator that survived from the family:
Avraham Yubiler-Tzoref and his family
(in Israel)

May their souls be bound up in the bond of life

In memory of the saints:

My parents: **Moshe Berenfeld** and **Esther -Piga**

My brothers: Shlomo, Mindel, Hainka, Alteka and all my family

Rabbi Nachman Baranek and his wife Rivka-Pearl

The commemorators:
**David Bernfeld,
Freide Bernfeld (Barenek),
Yehuda Baranek**
(State of Israel)

[Page 775]

For eternal memory

Our father: **Avraham** the son of Shmuel **Tsetskis**

Our mother: Hinda Tsetskis

Our sister: Shifra Tsetskis

Our brother: Shmuel Tsetskis

Our sister: Gittel Tsetskis

Our sister: Brina-Rivka Tsetskis

Our sister: Hannah Tsetskis

The mourners:
**David Tsetskis and his family
Fishel and his family**

In memory of the Yaberboim family

Our father: **Matityahu-Menashe Yaberboim**

Our mother: **Rivka** Yaberboim

Our sister: Leah Yaberboim

Our brother: Isaac Yaberboim

Our brother: Shimon Yaberboim

Our brother: Chaim Yaberboim

The mourners:
**Mordechai and his family
Sara Wolfling and her family**

The Suchozewski family

My father: **Moshe-Meir Suchozewski**
My mother: **Hinda** Suchozewski
My brother: Mordechai (Max) Suchozewski
My brother: Asher Suchozewski
My brother: Baruch Suchozewski

The mourner:
Avraham Suchozewski
(In Israel)

The Nauchichel family

My father: **Hersh-Leib**, the son of Hanna- Shifra
My mother: **Dvorah**
My brother: Ya'akov
My brother: Shalom-Meir
My brother: Avraham-Yosef
My sisters: Sara, Figa

Bitterly mourns:
**Hannah Nauchichel-Tzfoni
with her family**
(Jerusalem)

[Page 776]

For eternal memory

The father: **Isaac Chernibroda**
The mother: **Rachel**
The brother: **Bunim** (and his wife and children)
The brother: **Moshe**
The brother: **Chaim**

Bitterly mourns:
**Sara with her husband
And her son Ya'akov
Cheshka and her
husband**

They were also among the six million

The honorable Hassid, **Rabbi Leib Listik** and his wife, who were murdered in Warsaw

Their son, who devoted all his years to the Zionist idea, Yosef and his wife, who were murdered in the Cititz

Their only daughter Sheindel with her husband and their two children, who were murdered in Warsaw

The mourner: Their only surviving son: **David Listik with his wife and son**
(In Tel Aviv)

For eternal memory

The mother: **Frida Nussboim**

My brother: Shmuel with his wife Esther and the children

My sister: Hannah and her husband, Haim Berg and their son, David

My brother: Simcha

My sister: Mina Spetsiska with her husband and their child Moshe, who were murdered in Baranovich

The one who survived:
Shmuel Nussboim
(In Israel)

In memorial

My father: **Nachman-Neta Sheklerz**

My mother: **Henya-Braina**

My brother: Chaim-Aharon (with his wife Tzitza, from the Sukenik family and their children)

My sister and her husband: Rivka and Nathan Sheklerz

My cousin: Chaya, from the Mokovotsky family

The mourner:
Ya'akov-Zvi Sheklerz and his wife

[Page 777]

For eternal memory

The Zelikovich family

My mother: Frida-Rivka-Rachel

My brothers: Isha'ayahu-Binyamin and his family

Moshe-Zelig and his family, Yehuda-Leib and his family, Pinchas, David

My sister: Zlata-Itke Teiblum and her husband Israel Teiblum and their family

My parents: Ya'akov and Gittel Lubelski

My brothers: Menachem, Shamai and Shalom

The commemorator:
Aliza Lubelski (Alpert)

To The

The Rotberg family

My parents: Elijah-Hinach and Pesia

My brothers: Itzchak and Ya'akov and their families

My sister: Zletke Farbstein and her husband Itzchak and their family

My brother: Avraham, who died in 1937

Eternal Memory

Our dear Chasidic father, R. Moyshe Kleinlehrer, son of R. Chaim Shochet, of blessed memory—who died at the beginning of the struggle in Siedlce

Our clever mother: Itke;

Sisters: Chana and Rochelle and

Brother: Yitzchak

Brother Binyamin and his wife Dova (née Zucker);

Aunt Esther Levin (killed in Paris).

The survivors:
Sarah Kleinlehrer (Mordechowicz) (Israel);
Aunt Rivkah Mandelman(America);
Binyamin's children: **Betty, Moshe** and Esther's daughter **Eva**(in Paris)

To the Eternal Memory

of my beloved wife and children, who were killed in Siedlce by Hitler's Murderers:

Chanah bas Yakov; Yakov ben Simcha, Freyda-Dinah, Yitzchak, Reuven, Sarah-Leah.

In deep sadness, their surviving Husband and father:
Simcha Shlipke(Israel)

Obituary notice

With a feeling of respect and awe, we, who remain alive from all of our families and their entire family members, stand in silent, remembering our dearest and loved ones in life and death, the families:

Doa, Tochklepper, Freilich

Who were murdered and killed in cold blood by the cruel enemy of the people of Israel in Siedlce, our hometown.

The survivors who live in Israel (Netanya):
**Doa Ze'ev,
Chaya Tochklepper,
Zalman Freilich**

[Page 778]

In memory of the Orlovsky family

My father: Zeev Ben Zalman Orlovsky

My mother: Zvia, who died after a severe illness

My brothers: Zalman with his family, Mordechai with his family, Matityahu with his family

My sisters: Yeudit with her family, Sara with her family, Bracha with her family

The mourners:
Shoshana with her husband: Moshe Shmukler
(In Israel)

In memory of our father: Aharon-Eliezer, the son of Menachem-Mendel HaCohen Druzensky

Our sister Schindel

Our brother Ya'akov, who fell in the forests of Russia with his wife Figa

The mourners:
Shlomo and his wife, Israel and his wife

In memory of Nathaniel, the son of Itzchak Greenbaum

His wife, Hannah Rachel and their family

The mourners:
The brother-in-law and the sister-in-law Moshe and Shoshana Shmukler

In memory of my brother: Baruch-Mordechai Shmukler, his wife Figa and their family

The survivor:
Moshe and his wife Shoshana

In memory of my father: Moshe, the son of Kalman Weinstein

My mother: Gittel, the daughter of Leib Friedman

My sister: Chaya-Sara, the daughter of Moshe Weinstein

My sister: Sima Ackerman, the daughter of Moshe Weinstein

The mourners:
Sima-Moshe Weinstein Yaffa Druzensky (Weinstein)

In memory of Aaron- Itzchak, the son of Shmuel-Ya'akov Shmukler, his wife Ratza, with their whole family

The mourners:
Their daughter: **Rachel Weinstein,**
The brother: **Moshe Shmukler and his wife**

In memory of our mother: Rivka Weinberg, the daughter of Leibel Smiatizcki (Frives)

Our brother: Dan Ziskind, the son of Avraham-Moshe Weinberg, his wife: Golda from the Eisenberg family

The grandfather Rabbi Leibel Smiatizcki (Frives)

The mourners:
**Chaya Weinberg-Abramovich
Esther Weinberg-Austria**

David-Shimon and his wife Malka with the family

The mourners:
Moshe and Shoshana Shmukler

In memory of my father: Shlomo Warnerbaum

Yirmiyahoo Wanderbaum

Ziskind Wanderbaum

Hava Wanderbaum Zakalik

Henya Wanderbaum

Levy Miriam Wanderbaum

Fillet Wanderbaum Raphael Gurfinkel

The mourner:
Mina Wanderbaum
(In Israel)

[Page 779]

In memory of

The mother: Rivka, the wife of Rabbi Aharon Ekhoiser

The brother: Shmuel, the son of Rabbi Aharon Ekhoiser and his family

The sister: Esther with her husband and the rest of the family

The mourners:
Shalom, Hannah and their family and Figa

In memory of

Natan, the son of Uziel Kaveh, Rivka with her whole family

Moshe, the son of Uziel Kaveh with the family

The mourner:
Hannah, the daughter of Uziel Kaveh with her husband

In memory of

The father: Chaim, the son of Yoff Zaionz

The mother: Rivka, the wife of Rabbi Chaim Zaionz

The sister: Gila Fishman and her daughter Shenela

The mourners:
Hannah, Shalom Ekhoiser

In memory of

Yosef, the son of Chaim Novchinski

Rivka, the daughter of Yehoshua Novchinski of the Visoki family

Joshua, the son of Yosef Novchinski

Berill, the son of Yosef Novchinski with his family

Ita, the daughter of Yosef Novchinski with her family

Fina, the daughter of Yosef Novchinski with her family

Hershil, the son of Yosef Novchinski with his family

Vellvell, the son of Yosef Novchinski with his family

The mourners:
Chaim and his wife (Israel), **Sara Gerber and her husband** (Canada)

In memory of

Ita Giora, Mandel's wife
Yehuda with his family
Motel with his family
Barish with his family
Meir with his family
Israel with his family

The mourner:
Hannah Peshishtshilina

In memory of

Our father Binush, the son of Nahum Steinberg
Our mother: Frida, the daughter of Avraham Edelstein
Our brothers: Simcha, the sone of Binush and his wife
Luzna Vilnia
Our sister: Hannah Greenberg with her husband and
children
Our brother: Zvi-Hersh - killed in Lodz

The mourners:
Moshe Steinberg and his wife
Mirtza Steinberg and her
husband

In memory of

My father: Ya'akov Tiblum
My mother: Dina Tiblum
My brother: Gedaliahu Tiblum
My brother: Mendel Tiblum
My sister: Ettil Tiblum

The mourners:
Yona Ben-Ze'ev and
his family
(In Israel)

In memory of

Our dear mother: the late Rachel, the
daughter of Shmuel and Leah, who starved
to death in the steppes of Ukraine on the
19th of Av, 5704 (6-8-44)

Her memory will be blessed!

The mourners:
Her sons: David,
Raphael and Frida
(Israel)

[Page 780]

In memory of the Geffen family

My teacher and my Rabbi, the late Shlomo-Zalman Geffen
My mother is my teacher, the late Mrs. Sara-Gittel
My brother: the late Itzchak-Aharon and his family

My sister: Tzipa and her family

My sister: Miriam Sprinza and her family
My brother: the late Yeruham-Fishel
My brother: the late Avraham

The last remnant
of the Geffen family in Siedlce
Shimon-Mendel Geffen (In Israel)

In memory of the Friedman family in Siedlce
My mother: Yocheved, the daughter of the late Shlomo-Zalman Weinberg
My brother: Joseph
My sister: Hannah

The one who Survived:
Moshe Friedman

In memory of the Hertz family

My father: the late Yosef, the son of Nissan Hertz
My mother: Frida, the daughter of Aharon Ekheizer
My brothers: Menashe, Avraham and Chaim

The mourner:
Moshe Hertz (United States)

In memory of the Holtzman family in Siedlce

My father and teacher, the late Rabbi Nissan Holtzman, my mother and teacher, the late Mrs. Pesia-Leah

My brother: the late Pesach-Yona Holtzman and his family, my brother: the late Moshe-David

My late sister Figa and her family, my late sister Rivka-Nechama, my late sister Chaya

The last remnant of the
Holtzman family:
Isaha'ya Holtzman
(Haifa, Neve Sha'anan
neighborhood)

[Page 781]

For eternal memory

The parents: Mordechai Burstein and his wife: Rivka The sisters: Zletka, Frida, Rachel The commemorators: **Mendel Burstein** **Moshe Burstein**	The parents: Nathan Greenberg Mattel Greenberg The sisters: Leah, Yente The brother: Yosef The commemorators: **Hannah Molodonic and her family** **Gute Rinechki and his family**
The parents: Ya'akov Sokolowski RebeccaSokolowski The brothers: Moshe and David The sister: Sara The commemorator: **Asher Sokolowski**	My uncles: Ya'akov Langer - murdered in Danzig Pinchas Langer - murdered in Paris His wife Hannah And their children: Moshe, Bluma and Israel The commemorator: **Asher Sokolowski** (Tel Aviv)

The names of the deceased

The parents: **Moshe Uzik Pesia Uzik**
The sisters: Schindel, Zissel, Figa, Rivka
The brothers: Yosef and Ya'akov

Those who survive and
live in Israel:
Uzik Mordechai
Uzik Zvi

The parents: **Figa-Rosa Altman,
David Dazar**
The brother: Chaim-Leib with his family
The sister: Pessia
The brothers: Eliyahu and Michael
The uncle: Yosef Goldstein and his family
(chairman of the orphanage)

The commemorator:
Shmuel Altman

[Page 782]

For eternal memory

Zvi-David Kava, murdered in Siedlce
The commemorator:
**Israel-Pesach
Kaveh** (Petah Tikva)

The parents:
Shmuel Fischer Reisel
Fischer
The sister: Hannah
The brother: David
The sister: Schindel
The commemorator:
Zvi Fischer

A memorial tombstone

To our dear father, mother and sisters:

**Rabbi Ya'akov, Sara, Leah and
Esther Rosenberg**

Who perished with all the people of Israel while their hearts were belonged to Zion

The commemorators:
**Isser and Zehava
Rosenberg**
(Pines-Hadera Village)

[Pages 757-809]

Names extracted from Obituary section

Transliterated by Gilberto Jugend

א	ב	ג	ד	ה	ו	ז	ח	ט	י	כ
Alef	Bet	Gimmel	Dalet	Hey	Vav	Zayin	Chet	Tet	Yod	Kaf
ל	מ	נ	ס	ע	פ	צ	ק	ר	ש	ת
Lamed	Mem	Nun	Samech	Ayin	Peh	Tzadik	Kof	Resh	Shin	Tav

Family name (s)	First name(s)	Maiden name	Sex	Marital status	Father's name	Mother's name	Name of spouse	Additional family	Remarks	Family name(s) of eulogizer	First name(s) of eulogizer	Relationship of eulogizer	Page
א													
ABARNABEL	Sara Mindel		F	Married			Shlomo Shmuel			ABERBANEL		son	785
ABARNABEL	Idel		M		Shlomo Shmuel	Sara Mindel		children		ABERBANEL	Hesrshel	brother	785
ABARNABEL	Nachum		M		Shlomo Shmuel	Sara Mindel				ABERBANEL	Hesrshel	brother	785
ABARNABEL	Malcha		F		Shlomo Shmuel	Sara Mindel				ABERBANEL	Hesrshel	brother	785
ABARNABEL	Shlomo Shmuel		M	Married			Sara Mindel			ABERBANEL	Hesrshel	son	785
ABARNABEL			F	Married			Levi	children		ABERBANEL	Hesrshel	brother-in-law	785
ABARNABEL	Levi		M	Married	Shlomo Shmuel	Sara Mindel				ABERBANEL	Hesrshel	brother	785
OBOGI	Hana		F	Married			Matatihau			OBOGI	Iechiel	son	774
OBOGI	Rivka		F		Matatiahu	Hana				OBOGI	Iechiel	brother	774
OBOGI	Haia		F		Matatiahu	Hana				OBOGI	Iechiel	brother	774
OBOGI	Iakov		M		Matatiahu	Hana				OBOGI	Iechiel	brother	774
OBOGI	Matatihau		M	Married			Hana			OBOGI		son	774
OBOGI	Perl		F		Matatiahu	Hana				OBOGI	Iechiel	brother	774
OBOGI	Gitel		F		Matatiahu	Hana				OBOGI	Iechiel	brother	774
OBOGI	Libel		M		Matatiahu	Hana				OBOGI	Iechiel	brother	774
OBOGI	Iosef		M		Matatiahu	Hana				OBOGI	Iechiel	brother	774
OBOGI	Hinke		F		Matatiahu	Hana				OBOGI	Iechiel	brother	774
OGIK	Feiga		F		Moshe	Pesia				OZIK	Mordechai	brother	781
OGIK	Zisel		F		Moshe	Pesia				OZIK	Mordechai	brother	781
OGIK	Rivka		F		Moshe	Pesia				OZIK	Mordechai	brother	781
OGIK	Shindel		F		Moshe	Pesia				OZIK	Mordechai	brother	781
OGIK	Iakov		M		Moshe	Pesia				OZIK	Mordechai	brother	781
OGIK	Iosef		M		Moshe	Pesia				OZIK	Mordechai	brother	781
OGIK	Moshe		M	Married			Pesia			OZIK	Mordechai	son	781
OGIK	Pesia		F	Married			Moshe			OZIK	Mordechai	son	781
OTSCHEN	Shifra		F					children		MALOVONTCHIK	Iakov	relative	790
ORZEL	Felia		F							ORZEL AND FAMILY	Itshak		757
ORZEL			M							ORZEL AND FAMILY	Itshak		757
ORZEL	Moshe		M							ORZEL AND FAMILY			757
ORZEL	Asher		M							ORZEL AND FAMILY	Itshak		757
ORZEL	Bashe		F							ORZEL AND FAMILY	Itshak		757
ORZEL	Itshak		M	Married			Sara Shifra			ORZSHEL	Ruben	son	773
ORZEL	Sara Shifra		F	Married			Itshak			ORZSHEL	Ruben	son	773
ORZEL	Matatihau		M		Itshak	Sara Shifra				ORZSHEL	Ruben	brother	773
ORZEL	Dobe		F		Itshak	Sara Shifra				ORZSHEL	Ruben	brother	773
ORLOVSKI	Zeev		M	Widower	Zalman		Tsvia			SHMUKLER		daughter	778
ORLOVSKI	Matatihau		M		Zeev	Tsvia		his family		SHMUKLER	Shoshana	sister	778
ORLOVSKI	Zalman		M		Zeev	Tsvia		his family		SHMUKLER	Shoshana	sister	778
ORLOVSKI	Mordechai		M		Zeev	Tsvia		his family		SHMUKLER		sister	778
ORLENSKI	Batia		F		Arie	Elta Sara		children		ORLANSKI	Iehoshua	brother	770
ORLENSKI			M	Married			Elta Sara			ORLANSKI	Iehoshua	son	770
ORLENSKI	Hana		F		Arie	Elta Sara		children		ORLANSKI	Iehoshua	brother	770
ORLENSKI	Fishel		M		Arie	Elta Sara		children		ORLANSKI	Iehoshua	brother	
ORLENSKI	Elta Sara		F	Married			Arie			ORLANSKI	Iehoshua	son	
ORLENSKI	Israel		M		Arie	Elta Sara		children		ORLANSKI	Iehoshua	brother	
ORLENSKI	Tsvia		F		Arie	Elta Sara		children		ORLANSKI	Iehoshua	brother	
EISENSTET	Moshe Aba		M	Married	Paltiol		Ieta			PALTIEL ISENSTAT			
EISENSTET	Ita	ZILBERTSVEIG	F	Married	Iosef Haim		Moshe Aba			PALTIEL ISENSTAT			757
EISENBERG			F	Married			Zilke	children					809
EISENBERG	Moshe		M	Married			Blima						809
EISENBERG	David		M	Married	Iakov	Dina Reisel	Sonie	children					809
EISENBERG	Zilke		M	Married				children					809

Family name(s)	First name(s)	Maiden name	Sex	Marital status	Father's name	Mother's name	Name of spouse	Additional family	Remarks	Family name(s) of eulogizer	First name(s) of eulogizer	Relationship of eulogizer	Page
EISENBERG	Blima		F	Married	Naftali		Moshe		Naftalis				809
EISENBERG	Gitel		F										809
EISENBERG	Bashe		F	Married			Iosef	children					809
EISENBERG	Iakov		M	Married	Moshe	Blima	Dina Reisel						809
EISENBERG	Freidel		F		Iakov	Dina Reisel							809
EISENBERG	Dina Reisel		F	Married			Iakov						809
EISENBERG	Iosef		M	Married	Iakov	Dina Reisel	Bashe	children					809
EISENBERG	Sonie		F	Married			David	children					809
EICHENBOIM	Sheindel		F	Married			Avraham	children		GOLDESTEIN	Brontshe		804
EICHENBOIM	Avraham		M	Married			Sheindel	children		GOLDESTEIN	Brontshe		804
ALBERSHTAT	Note		M	Married			Ester	their family		PERL	Iudel		809
ALBERSHTAT	Ester		F	Married			Note	their family		PERL	Iudel		809
ALTMAN	Michael		M		David	Figa Rosa				ALTMAN		brother	781
ALTMAN	Haim Leib		M		David	Figa Rosa		his family		ALTMAN	Shmuel	brother	781
ALTMAN	Elihau		M		David	Figa Rosa				ALTMAN	Shmuel	brother	781
ALTMAN	David		M	Married			Feiga Rosa		Dozor	ALTMAN	Shmuel	son	781
ALTMAN	Pesia		F		David	Figa Rosa				ALTMAN	Shmuel	brother	781
OSMAN	Moshe		M							OSMAN			764
OSMAN	Bina		F					her family		OSMAN	Simcha		764
OSMAN	Shamai		M					his family		OSMAN	Simcha		764
OSMAN	Haim		M							OSMAN	Simcha		764
OSMAN	Avraham		M							OSMAN	Simcha		764
AKERMAN	Ester Pashe		F	Married			Iehoshua			AKERMAN	Motel	son	809
AKERMAN	Perl		F	Married			Avraham Itshak	children		AKERMAN	Motel	brother-in-law	809
AKERMAN	Moshe Aharon		M	Married	Iehoshua	Ester Pache	Rivka	children		AKERMAN	Motel	brother	809
AKERMAN	Ioshua		M	Married			Ester Malcha			AKERMAN	Motel	son	809
AKERMAN	Avraham Itshak		M	Married	Iehoshua	Ester Pache	Perl	children		AKERMAN	Motel	brother	809
AKERMAN	Rivka		F	Married			Moshe Aharon	children		AKERMAN	Motel	brother-in-law	809
AKERMAN	Sima	VINSTEIN	F		Moshe	Gitel				VINSTEIN DROJENSKI	Sima	sister	778
AKERMAN	Ioshua		M	Married			Hava			ALONI DUMEV	Shmuel		760
AKERMAN	Hava	DUMEV	F	Married		Rachel	Iehoshua			ALONI DUMEV	Shmuel		760
AKERMAN	Oded		M		Iehoshua	Hava				ALONI DUMEV	Shmuel		760
ERNSHTEIN	Israel Feivel		M					his family				relative	784
ERSHANSKI	Henie		F		Tsvi					RUBINSTEIN VINOGRAD	Ode		803
ASHKENASI	Shmuel		M	Married	Asher	Roisele			Lawyer				758
ASHKENASI	Roisale		F	Married		Sima	Asher						758
ASHKENASI			F	Married			Shmuel						758
ASHKENASI	Asher		M	Married			Roisele						758
ASHKENASI			M		Shmuel								758
ASHMAN	Ester Beile		F	Married			Shmuel Iosef			RAFAEL	Moshe	son-in-law	803
ASHMAN	Shmuel		M	Married			Ester Beile			RAFAEL	Moshe	son-in-law	803
ב													
BAKERMAN	Hava	PERLA	F		Simcha	Golde		her family		PERLA	Moshe	brother	799
BAKERMAN	Rivka Perl		F	Married			Nachman			BORONEK	Iehuda	son	774
BAKERMAN	Nachman		M	Married			Rivka Perl			BORONEK	Iehuda	son	774
BORAK	Hava		F	Married			Hilel	children		BOBIK	Matatihau		803
BORAK	Hilel		M	Married	Moshe Perets		Hava	children		BOBIK	Matatihau		803
BORAK	Ester		F	Married			Shmuel Leiser	children		BOBIK	Matatihau		803
BORAK	Shmuel Iosef		M	Married	Moshe Perets		Ester	children	Israel	BOBIK	Matatihau		803
BORESTEIN	Rachel		F		Mordechai	Rivka				BURSTEIN	Mendel	brother	781
BORESTEIN	Zeltka		F		Mordechai	Rivka				BURSTEIN	Mendel	brother	781
BORESTEIN			F		Mordechai	Rivka				BURSTEIN	Mendel	brother	781
BORESTEIN	Rivka		F	Married			Mordechai			BURSTEIN	Mendel	son	781
BORESTEIN	Mordechai		M	Married			Rivka			BURSTEIN	Mendel	son	781

Family name(s)	First name(s)	Maiden name	Sex	Marital status	Father's name	Mother's name	Name of spouse	Additional family	Remarks	Family name(s) of eulogizer	First name(s) of eulogizer	Relationship of eulogizer	Page
BIALILEVO	Haimel		M		Ieshiau	Bracha				BIOLILEVO	Melech	brother	795
BIALILEVO	Bracha	ERLICH	F	Married			Ieshai			BIOLILEVO	Melech	son	795
BIALILEVO			M	Married			Bracha			BIOLILEVO	Melech	son	795
BIALILEVO	Avramele		M		Ieshiau	Bracha				BIOLILEVO	Melech	brother	795
BIALILEVO	Feige		F	Married			Moshe	children		VEINSTEIN SHMUKLIARTCH	Rachel		770
BIALILEVO	Moshe		M	Married			Feige	children		VEINSTEIN SHMUKLIARTCH	Rachel		770
BINSTOK	Nechama		F							BINSHTOK	Tsvi	son	773
BINSTOK	Ienta		F			Nechama				BINSHTOK	Tsvi	brother	773
BINSTOK	Itka		F			Nechama				BINSHTOK	Tsvi	brother	773
BISTROVITCH	Moshe		M	Married			Lea Dina			BISTROVITCH	Itshak	relative	789
BISTROVITCH	Feigale Libe		F		Meshulam	Ester Golde				BISTROVITCH	Itshak	relative	789
BISTROVITCH	Efraim		M		Moshe	Lea Dina				BISTROVITCH	Itshak	relative	789
BISTROVITCH	Hana Lea		F		Meshulam	Ester				BISTROVITCH	Itshak	relative	789
BISTROVITCH	Ester Golde	KOSHEMACHER	F	Married			Meshulam			BISTROVITCH	Itshak	relative	789
BISTROVITCH			M	Married			Ester Golde			BISTROVITCH	Itshak	relative	789
BISTROVITCH	Lea Dina	SHETSHIKEL	F	Married			Moshe			BISTROVITCH	Itshak	relative	789
BISTROVITCH	Toive		F		Moshe					BISTROVITCH	Itshak	relative	789
BLUSHTEIN	Pesie		F	Married			Shalke			GURGINKEL	Hersh	cousin	794
BLUSHTEIN	Shalke		M	Married			Pesia			GURGINKEL	Hersh	cousin	794
BEN-DET			M		Mordechai	Sima			From Brisk Dlita				758
BEN-DET	Mordechai		M	Married			Sima		Son of rav from Bilsk				758
BEN-DET	Sima		F	Married	Asher	Roisele	Mordechai						758
BEN-DET			F		Mordechai	Sima			From Brisk Dlita				758
BERGMAN	Moshe		M	Married			Sara	children		VEINSTEIN SHMUKLIARTCH	Rachel		770
BERGMAN	Sara		F	Married			Moshe	children		VEINSTEIN SHMUKLIARTCH	Rachel		770
BERENFELD	Pesel		F	Married			Iakov			BERENFELD	David	brother-in-law	808
BERENFELD			F	Married				children		BERENFELD	David	brother-in-law	808
BERENFELD	Leibel		M	Married			Elte			BERENFELD	David	son	808
BERENFELD	Shie		M	Married	Leibel	Elte		children		BERENFELD	David	brother	808
BERENFELD	Iakov		M	Married	Leibel	Elte	Pesel			BERENFELD		brother	808
BERENFELD	Elte		F	Married			Leibel			BERENFELD	David	son	808
BERENFELD	Feige		F	Married			Moshe	children		BERENFELD	David	brother-in-law	808
BERENFELD	Moshe		M	Married	Leibel	Elte	Feige	children		BERENFELD	David	brother	808
BROZSHNER	Isak Itshak		M					brother and sister		BROZSHNER	Shoel		799
BROTT			F	Married			Meir	children					809
BROTT	Zilke		M	Married				children					809
BROTT	Meir		M	Married				children					809
BROTT			M	Married				children					809
BROTT			F	Married			Sender	children					809
BROTT			F	Married			Zilke	children					809
BROTT	Ieheskel		M										809
BERG	Haim		M	Married			Hana			NUSBOIM	Shmuel	brother-in-law	776
BERG	David		M		Haim	Hana				NUSBOIM	Shmuel	uncle	776
BERG	Hana	NUSBOIM	F	Married		Frida Rivka	Haim			NUSBOIM	Shmuel	brother	776
BERNHOLTZ	Sara		F	Married			Haim			BAR HAIM LISHNIE	Eliezer	son	773
BERNHOLTZ	Hentche		F		Haim	Sara				BAR HAIM LISHNIE	Eliezer	brother	773
BERNHOLTZ	Gitel		F		Haim	Sara				BAR HAIM LISHNIE	Eliezer	brother	773
BERNHOLTZ	Moshe		M		Haim	Sara				BAR HAIM LISHNIE	Eliezer	brother	773
BERNHOLTZ	Haim		M	Married			Sara			BAR HAIM LISHNIE	Eliezer	son	773
BERNHOLTZ	Dobe		F	Married			Shaul	children		BINSHTOK	Gila		773
BERNHOLTZ	Shaul		M	Married			Duba	children		BINSHTOK	Gila		773
BERNFELD	Selig		M		Moshe	Ester				BERNFELD BORONEK	David	brother	774
BERNFELD	Mindel		F		Moshe	Ester Figa				BERNFELD BORONEK	David	brother	774
BERNFELD	Leibel		M		Moshe	Ester Figa				BERNFELD BORONEK	David	brother	774

Family name(s)	First name(s)	Maiden name	Sex	Marital status	Father's name	Mother's name	Name of spouse	Additional family	Remarks	Family name(s) of eulogizer	First name(s) of eulogizer	Relationship of eulogizer	Page
BERNFELD	Moshe		M	Married			Ester Feiga			BERNFELD BORONEK	David	son	774
BERNFELD	Eltka		F		Moshe	Ester Figa				BERNFELD BORONEK	David	brother	774
BERNFELD	Itka		F		Moshe	Ester Figa				BERNFELD BORONEK	David	brother	774
BERNFELD	Shlomo		M		Moshe	Ester Figa				BERNFELD BORONEK	David	brother	774
BERNFELD	Hinke		F		Moshe	Ester Figa				BERNFELD BORONEK	David	brother	774
BERNFELD	Ester Feiga		F	Married			Moshe			BERNFELD BORONEK	David	son	774
ג													
GOLDGEVICHT	Davidtche		M	Married	Leib Sheie	Feige		children		GOLDGEVICHT	Dvora	sister	802
GOLDGEVICHT	Feige		F	Married			Shaie Leib			GOLDGEVICHT	Dvora	daughter	802
GOLDGEVICHT	Roshke		F		Leib Sheie	Feige				GOLDGEVICHT	Dvora	sister	802
GOLDGEVICHT	Shie Leib		M	Married			Feige			GOLDGEVICHT	Dvora	daughter	802
GOLDGEVICHT	Velvol		M		Leib Sheie	Feige				GOLDGEVICHT		sister	802
GOLDGEVICHT			F	Married			Davidtsche	children		GOLDGEVICHT	Dvora	sister-in-law	802
GOLDGEVICHT	Gitel		F		Leib Sheie	Feige				GOLDGEVICHT		sister	802
GOLDBLAT	Hanhale		F	Married			Natan	in-laws and children		MALOVONTCHIK	Iakov	relative	790
GOLDBLAT	Natan		M	Married			Hanale	in-laws and children		MALOVONTCHIK		relative	790
GOLDFINGER	Malcha		F						Assassinated 2 weeks before Liberation by	GOLDFINGERRUBINSTEIN	Sara		767
GOLDFINGER	Freide		F							GOLDFINGER RUBINSTEIN	Sara		767
GOLDFINGER	Shlomo Zalman		M							GOLDFINGER RUBINSTEIN	Sara		767
GOLDFINGER	Mishel		M						Died on 9 Feb. 1942	GOLDFINGER RUBINSTEIN	Sara		767
GOLDFINGER	Mashele		M						Deported to Treblinka on24 Aug. 1942	GOLDFINGERRUBINSTEIN	Sara		767
GOLDSTEIN	Berl		M	Married			Ester			GOLDESTEIN	Brontshe		804
GOLDSTEIN	Mendel		M	Married			Dobe	children		GOLDESTEIN			804
GOLDSTEIN	Efraim		M		Iakov	Roshke				GOLDESTEIN	Brontshe		804
GOLDSTEIN	Iakov		M	Married			Rushke			GOLDESTEIN	Brontshe		804
GOLDSTEIN	Dobe		F	Married			Mendel	children		GOLDESTEIN	Brontshe		804
GOLDSTEIN	Ester		F	Married			Berl			GOLDESTEIN	Brontshe		804
GOLDSTEIN	Roshke		F	Married			Iakov			GOLDESTEIN	Brontshe		804
GOLDSTEIN	Blimele		F		Iakov	Roshke				GOLDESTEIN	Brontshe		804
GOLDSTEIN	Leibel		M	Married			Reisil			GURGINKEL	Hersh	cousin	794
GOLDSTEIN	Reizil		F	Married			Leibel			GURGINKEL		cousin	794
GONSHOREK	Hershel		M			Shoshe				FEDERMAN BARSILAI	Tsirel	aunt	787
GONSHOREK	Aba		M		Meir	Shoshe				FEDERMAN BARSILAI	Tsirel	aunt	787
GONSHOREK	Velvol		M		Meir	Shoshe				FEDERMAN BARSILAI		aunt	787
GONSHOREK	Meir		M	Married						FEDERMAN BARSILAI	Tsirel	sister-in-law	787
GONSHOREK	Sashe	DJELIOZNI	F	Married	Haim	Rechel	Meir			FEDERMAN BARSILAI	Tsirel	sister	787
GONSHOREK	Malcha		F		Meir	Shoshe				FEDERMAN BARSILAI	Tsirel	aunt	787
GORBAUZ	Rive	KODJENITSKI	F		Meir Iechiel	Breine Gitel		children		KODCHENITSKI	Mordechai	brother	806
GORNIK	Mordechai		M							MELINSKI GERTNER	Itshak	relative	793
GOTGELD	Iosef		M							VIMAN	Dov		763
GOTGELD	Felia		F							VIMAN			763
GOTGELD	Levi		M							SELTSTEIN	Shalom		763
GOTGELD	Sara		F							SELTSTEIN	Shalom		763
GOTGELD	Rachel		F							SELTSTEIN	Shalom		763
GOTHELF	Ester	RISA	F		Itshak Aharon	Rivka				KARMESH	Hana	sister	771
GOLDBERG	Rachel	STEINBERG	F						Died in 1942	STEINBERG	Moshe	brother	765
GOLDBERG	Moshe		M							FRIDMAN	Sara		764
GOLDBERG	Haim		M					his family		FRIDMAN	Sara		764
GOLDBERG	Mirel		F					children		FRIDMAN	Sara		764
GOLDBERG	Feivil		M							FRIDMAN	Sara		764
GOLDFERB	Hinech		M						Deported to Treblinka on25 Nov. 1942	HELBERSTADT GOLDFREV	Hania		761

Family name(s)	First name(s)	Maiden name	Sex	Marital status	Father's name	Mother's name	Name of spouse	Additional family	Remarks	Family name(s) of eulogizer	First name(s) of eulogizer	Relationship of eulogizer	Page
GOLDFERB	Rachel	BERNER	F						Deported to Treblinka on25 Nov. 1942	HELBERSTADT GOLDFREV	Hania		761
GOLDFERB	Asher		M						Fell during the general Polish uprisingin Aug. 1944	HELBERSTADT GOLDFREV	Hania		761
GOLDSTEIN	Iosef		M					his family	President ofthe OrphansHouse	ALTMAN	Shmuel	cousin	781
GURFINKEL	Miriam	VANDERBOIM	F		Shlomo						VUNDERBOIM	Mina	sister	778
GURFINKEL			M	Married			Rachel	2 children		GOLDFINGER RUBINSTEIN	Sara		767
GURFINKEL	Rachel	GOLDFINGER	F	Married				child		GOLDFINGER RUBINSTEIN	Sara		767
GURFINKEL	Manish		M		Iehoshua	Sara				GURGINKEL	Hersh	brother	794
GURFINKEL	Ieshia		M		Iehoshua	Sara				GURGINKEL		brother	794
GURFINKEL	Reizel		#N/		Iehoshua	Sara				GURGINKEL	Hersh	brother	794
GURFINKEL	Zalman		M		Iehoshua	Sara				GURGINKEL	Hersh	brother	794
GURFINKEL	Menashe		M		Iehoshua	Sara				GURGINKEL		brother	794
GURFINKEL	Ioshua		M	Married			Sara			GURGINKEL		son	794
GURFINKEL	Aharon		M		Iehoshua	Sara				GURGINKEL		brother	794
GURFINKEL	Leibel		M		Iehoshua	Sara				GURGINKEL	Hersh	brother	794
GURFINKEL	Sara		F	Married			Iehoshua			GURGINKEL	Hersh	son	794
GURFINKEL	Haim		M		Iehoshua	Sara				GURGINKEL		brother	794
GURFINKEL	Iente		F		Iehoshua	Sara				GURGINKEL		brother	794
GINGOLD	Tova	RISA	F		Itshak Aharon	Rivka				KARMESH	Hana	sister	771
GLITSKI	Bila Adis		F	Married	Moshe Zeev		Iakov Tsvi			GLITSKI			772
GLITSKI	Motel		M		Iakov Tsvi	Bila Ides				GLITSKI			772
GLITSKI	Iakov Tsvi		M	Married	Arie		Bila Ides			GLITSKI			772
GLITSKI	David		M		Iakov Tsvi	Bila Ides				GLITSKI			772
GLIKSBERG	Dov Berish		M		Natan David	Malcha Hades		his family		GLIKSBERG	Iehuda		759
GLIKSBERG	Ester	RUBIN	F	Married	Mordechai	Rivka	Iehuda Leib			GLIKSBERG	Iehuda		759
GLIKSBERG	Aharon Adolf		M		Iehuda Leib	Ester				GLIKSBERG			759
GLIKSBERG	Meir		M		Natan David	Malcha Hades				GLIKSBERG	Iehuda		759
GLIKSBERG	Shlomo		M		Natan David	Malcha Hades				GLIKSBERG	Iehuda		759
GERTNER	Miriam		F	Married			Leibel			MELINSKI GERTNER	Itshak	relative	793
GERTNER	Haim Iosef		M	Married			Maie			MELINSKI GERTNER		relative	793
GERTNER	Maia		F	Married			Haim Iosef			MELINSKI GERTNER	Itshak	relative	793
GERTNER	Noach		M		Leibel	Miriam				MELINSKI GERTNER		relative	793
GERTNER	Leibel		M	Married			Miriam			MELINSKI GERTNER	Itshak	relative	793
GERSHT	Avraham		M	Married			Dvora	children		VEINSTEIN SHMUKLIARTCH	Rachel		770
GERSHT			F	Married			Avraham	children		VEINSTEIN SHMUKLIARTCH	Rachel		770
GERSHENSON	Baruch		M	Married			Sonie		Died in Brest-Litovosk	BRINEVETSKI	Rachel	son-in-law	806
GERSHENSON	Sonie	BRINEVETSKI	F	Married		Rachel	Baruch		Died in Brest-Litovosk	BRINEVETSKI	Rachel	mother	806
GERSHENSON	Meitele		M		Baruch	Sonie			Died in Brest-Litovosk	BRINEVETSKI	Rachel	grandmother	806
GERSHENSON	Iankele		M		Baruch	Sonie			Died in Brest-Litovosk	BRINEVETSKI	Rachel	grandmother	806
GERSHKOP	Beile		F		Hershel Tsvi			children				Matatihau	803
GEFEN	Dvora	SEIDENBERG	F	Married	ShmuelDavid	Hava	Moshe Haim	3 daughters and their children and their son, his wife and theirchildren		SEIDENBERG	Ieshihau		758
GEFEN	Moshe Haim		M	Married			Dvora	3 daughters and their children and their son, his wife and theirchildren		SEIDENBERG	Ieshihau		758
GEFEN	Itshak Aharon		M		Shlomo Zalman	Sara Gitel		his family		GEFEN	Shimon	brother	780
GEFEN	Sara Gitel		F	Married			Shlomo Zalman			GEFEN	Shimon	son	780
GEFEN	Avraham		M		Shlomo Zalman	Sara Gitel				GEFEN	Shimon	brother	780
GEFEN	Ieruham Fishel		M		Shlomo Zalman	Sara Gitel				GEFEN	Shimon	brother	780

Family name(s)	First name(s)	Maiden name	Sex	Marital status	Father's name	Mother's name	Name of spouse	Additional family	Remarks	Family name(s) of eulogizer	First name(s) of eulogizer	Relationship of eulogizer	Page
GEFEN	Shlomo Zalman		M	Married			Sara Gitel			GEFEN	Shimon	son	780
GROSMAN			F		Shimon	Rachel				MELINSKI GERTNER	Itshak	relative	793
GROSMAN	Haia	RAFAEL	F	Married			Hershel		Perhaps given name Haim is mistaken	MELINSKI GERTNER	Itshak	relative	793
GROSMAN	Sara		F		Hershel	Haia				MELINSKI GERTNER	Itshak	relative	793
GROSMAN	Ester		F		Hershel	Haia				MELINSKI GERTNER	Itshak	relative	793
GROSMAN	Hershel		M	Married			Haia			MELINSKI GERTNER	Itshak	relative	793
GROSMAN			M		Hershel	Haia				MELINSKI GERTNER	Itshak	relative	793
GROSMAN	Shimon		M	Married			Rachel			MELINSKI GERTNER	Itshak	relative	793
GROSMAN	Rachel		F	Married			Shimon			MELINSKI GERTNER	Itshak	relative	793
GERZIVOTCH	Ioshe		M	Married	Heinoch	Gele		children		GERZIVOUTCH	Sara	sister	805
GERZIVOTCH	Heinoch		M	Married			Gele			GERZIVOUTCH	Sara	daughter	805
GERZIVOTCH	Gele		F	Married			Heinoch			GERZIVOUTCH	Sara	daughter	805
GERZIVOTCH			F	Married			Ruven	children		GERZIVOUTCH	Sara	sister-in-law	805
GERZIVOTCH			F	Married			Iesha	children		GERZIVOUTCH	Sara	sister-in-law	805
GERZIVOTCH	Reuven		M	Married	Heinoch	Gele		children		GERZIVOUTCH	Sara	sister	805
GERZIVOTCH			F	Married			Moshe	children		GERZIVOUTCH	Sara	sister-in-law	805
GERZIVOTCH	Moshe		M	Married	Heinoch	Gele		children		GERZIVOUTCH	Sara	sister	805
GRINBOIM	Natanel		M	Married			Hana Rachel			VEINSTEIN SHMUKLIARTCH	Rachel		770-8
GRINBOIM	Hana Rachel		F	Married			Natanel			VEINSTEIN SHMUKLIARTCH	Rachel		770-8
GRINBERG	Menashe		M	Married			Sara			GRINBERG	David	son	803
GRINBERG	Rivka		F	Married			Iakov Leiser			RAFAEL	Moshe	brother-in-law	803
GRINBERG	Iakov Leizer		M	Married			Rivka			RAFAEL	Moshe	brother-in-law	803
GRINBERG	Nuske		M	Married			Mashel			RAFAEL		brother-in-law	803
GRINBERG	Moshel		F	Married			Noske			RAFAEL	Moshe	brother-in-law	803
GRINBERG	Roise		F	Married			Iosef	children		TEIBLUM MOLOVONTCHIK	Feigele	relative	791
GRINBERG	Iosef		M	Married			Roise	children		TEIBLUM MOLOVONTCHIK	Feigele	relative	791
GRINBERG	Lea		F		Natan	Matel				MOLODONIK RINTSKI	Hana	sister	781
GRINBERG	Ienta		F		Natan	Matel				MOLODONIK RINTSKI	Hana	sister	781
GRINBERG	Iosef		M		Natan	Matel				MOLODONIK RINTSKI	Hana	sister	781
GRINBERG	Natan		M	Married			Motel			MOLODONIK RINTSKI	Hana	daughter	781
GRINBERG	Motel		F	Married			Natan			MOLODONIK RINTSKI	Hana	daughter	781
GRINBERG	Hana	STEINBERG	F	Married	Binush	Frida		children		STEINBERG	Moshe	brother	779
GRINBERG			M	Married			Hana	children		STEINBERG	Moshe	brother-in-law	779
GRINSPON	Ieshia		M							KREDO	Iechiel	relative	786
GRINSPON	Iakov Ianek		M		Feivel Shraga	Miriam Sara		his family	Died 1 Sep. 1942 in the Sielce Ghetto	GRINSPEN HELBERSTADT	Rachel	sister	760
GRINSPON	Itshak Edek		M		Feivel Shraga	Miriam Sara		his family		GRINSPEN HELBERSTADT	Rachel	sister	760
GRINSPON	Blima Malvina		F		Feivel Shraga	Miriam Sara				GRINSPEN HELBERSTADT	Rachel	sister	760
GERSHTEIN	Gitel		F							LEDERMAN			763
GERSHTEIN	Aharon		M	Married			Etka	child		LEDERMAN	Dov		763
GERSHTEIN	Etka		F	Married			Aharon	child		LEDERMAN	Dov		763
GERSHTEIN	Simcha		M							LEDERMAN	Dov		763
ד													
DOHA	Avraham		M	Married			Richne	children		HUBERMAN	Sheindel		804
DOHA	Richne		F	Married			Avraham	children		HUBERMAN	Sheindel		804
DOAH								family	Died in Siedlce	DUA	Zeev		777
DOBREZINSKI	Iakov		M	Married			Lea			GLIKSBERG	Iehuda		759
DOBREZINSKI	Lea	SEINFELD	F	Married			Iakov			GLIKSBERG	Iehuda		759
DOBREZINSKI	Ronia Rachel	RUBIN	F		Mordechai	Rivka				GLIKSBERG	Iehuda		759
DOBREZINSKI	Ignas Itshak		M	Married		Ronia Rachel	Sara			GLIKSBERG	Iehuda		759
DOBREZINSKI	Sara	SHATZ	F	Married						GLIKSBERG	Iehuda		759
DUMEV	Iosef		M	Married			Fania		Died in Brest	ALONI DUMEV	Shmuel		760
DUMEV	Fenia		F	Married			Iosef		Died in Brest	ALONI DUMEV	Shmuel		760

Family name(s)	First name(s)	Maiden name	Sex	Marital status	Father's name	Mother's name	Name of spouse	Additional family	Remarks	Family name(s) of eulogizer	First name(s) of eulogizer	Relationship of eulogizer	Page
DEMBOVITCH	Freide		F							GURGINKEL		cousin	794
DROZSHANSKI	Aharon		M					children		KONSTANTINER	Lea		804
DROGINSKI	Sheindel		F		Aharon Eliezer					DROGINSKI	Shlomo	sister	778
DROGINSKI	Feiga		F	Married			Iakov		Fall in the Russian forests	DROGINSKI	Shlomo	brother-in-law	778
DROGINSKI	Aharon Eliezer		M		Menachem Mendel					DROGINSKI	Shlomo	son	778
DROGINSKI	Iakov		M	Married			Feiga		Fall in the Russian forests	DROGINSKI	Shlomo	sister	778
DROZSHANSKI	Mendel		M	Married			Rachel			DROGINSKI	Israel	grandson	774
DROZSHANSKI	Aharon		M	Married						DROGINSKI	Israel	son	774
DROZSHANSKI	Rachel		F	Married			Mendel			DROGINSKI	Israel	grandson	774
DROZSHANSKI	Shindel		F		Aharon					DROGINSKI	Israel	brother	774
ה													
HONDEL	Lea		F							SOIANTZ	Rivka	cousin	784
HUBERMAN	Blime		F	Married			Menache	children		HUBERMAN	Sheindel		804
HUBERMAN	Menashe		M	Married			Blime	children		HUBERMAN			804
HOLTZMAN	Pesia Lea		F	Married			Nisan			HOLTSMAN	Ieshiha	son	780
HOLTZMAN	Pesach Iona		M		Nisan	Pesia Lea		his family		HOLTSMAN	Ieshiha	brother	780
HOLTZMAN	Rivka Nechama		F		Nisan	Pesia Lea				HOLTSMAN	Ieshiha	brother	780
HOLTZMAN	Moshe David		M		Nisan	Pesia Lea				HOLTSMAN	Ieshiha	brother	780
HOLTZMAN	Nisan		M	Married			Pesia Lea			HOLTSMAN	Ieshiha	son	780
HOLTZMAN	Haia		F		Nisan	Pesia Lea				HOLTSMAN	Ieshiha	brother	780
HEIBKOREN	Avraham		M					his family		VISOKI	Berl	son-in-law	807
HEIBKOREN	Ester	VISOKI	F	Married			Velvol			VISOKI	Berl	brother	807
HEIBKOREN	Velvol		M	Married			Ester			VISOKI	Berl	brother-in-law	807
HILLES	Leibele		M						Perhaps father namewas Hilel				809
HELBERSHTAT	Hirsh		M					his family	Died in Warsaw	HELBERSTADT GOLDFREV	Hania		761
HELBERSHTAT	Itka	RUBINSTEIN	F						Deported to Treblinka on25 Nov. 1942	HELBERSTADT GOLDFREV			761
HELBERSHTAT	Nachum		M						Deported to Treblinka on25 Nov. 1942	HELBERSTADT GOLDFREV	Hania		761
HELBERSHTAT	Rachel Rosa	GLIKSBERG	F	Married	Iehuda Leib	Ester	Avraham			GLIKSBERG	Iehuda		759
HELBERSHTAT	Naftali Hertz		M	Married	Mordechai		Ienta Gitel		Died 1 Dec. 1942 in the Sielce Ghetto	HELBERSTADT TEITEL	Israel	son	760
HELBERSHTAT	Ienta Gitel	LIBERNET	F	Married			NaftaliHertz		Died 1 Dec. 1942 in the Sielce Ghetto	HELBERSTADT TEITEL	Israel	son	760
HALPERIN	Israel		M	Married	Mordechai	Liba Sima							758
HALPERIN	Liba Sima	SEIDENBERG	F	Married	Israel Sinai	Rachel							758
HALPERIN	Lilke		F		Israel								758
HALPERIN			F	Married			Israel						758
HALPERIN	Mordechai		M	Married			Liba Sima						758
HALPERIN			M		Israel								758
HOLTZBERG	Sheindel Stosha		F		Feivel Shraga	Miriam Sara				GRINSPEN HELBERSTADT	Rachel	sister	760
HERTZ	Haim		M		Iosef	Frida				HERTZ	Moshe	brother	780
HERTZ	Iosef		M	Married	Nisan		Frida			HERTZ	Moshe	son	780
HERTZ	Avraham		M		Iosef	Frida				HERTZ	Moshe	brother	780
HERTZ	Menashe		M		Iosef	Frida				HERTZ	Moshe	brother	780
HERTZ	Frida	EKOIZER	F	Married	Aharon		Iosef			HERTZ		son	780
I													
VAGOSKI	Mendel		M							VIMAN	Dov		763
VAGOSKI	Henia		F							VIMAN	Dov		763
VAGOSKI	Hinech		M							VIMAN	Dov		763
VOSERSHTEIN	Feige		F	Married			Mordechai						799
VOSERSHTEIN	Mordechai		M	Married			Feige						799
VOKERMAN	Idel		M	Married			Tsirel	children		MELINSKI GERTNER	Itshak	relative	793

Family name(s)	First name(s)	Maiden name	Sex	Marital status	Father's name	Mother's name	Name of spouse	Additional family	Remarks	Family name(s) of eulogizer	First name(s) of eulogizer	Relationship of eulogizer	Page
VOKERMAN		KODJENITSKI	F	Married			Idel	children		MELINSKI GERTNER	Itshak	relative	793
VOKSHTEIN			M	Married			Roise			STOROVIESKI	Iosef	brother-in-law	797
VOKSHTEIN	Roise	PINIETSKI	F	Married		Hana				STOROVIESKI	Iosef	brother	797
VOKSHTEIN	Moshe		M			Roise				STOROVIESKI	Iosef	uncle	797
VOKSHTEIN	David		M					his family			Sale	sister	798
VOKSHTEIN	Blume		F							VOKSTEIN	Sale	daughter	798
VOKSHTEIN	Avraham		M					his family		VOKSTEIN	Sale	sister	798
VOKSHTEIN	Berl		M	Married			Haia Reizel	children					799
VOKSHTEIN	Haia Reisel	VOSERSTEIN	F	Married	Mordechai	Feige	Berl	children					799
VEIMAN	Avraham Simcha		M	Married	Itsel	Iocheved	Freide			VEIMAN	Leibel	son	808
VEIMAN	Gitel		F							VEIMAN	Leibel	cousin	808
VEIMAN	Moshe		M		Avraham Simcha	Fride				VEIMAN		brother	808
VEIMAN	Itsel		M	Married			Iocheved			VEIMAN	Leibel	grandson	808
VEIMAN	Meir		M		Itsel	Iocheved				VEIMAN	Leibel	cousin	808
VEIMAN	Miriam		F							VEIMAN	Leibel	cousin	808
VEIMAN	Freide		F	Married			Avraham Simcha			VEIMAN	Leibel	son	808
VEIMAN	Iocheved		F	Married			Itsel			VEIMAN	Leibel	grandson	808
VEIMAN	Hentche		F							VEIMAN	Leibel	cousin	808
VEISBERG	Haia Sarale		F		Shmuel	Ester				TEIBLUM MOLOVONTCHIK	Feigele	relative	791
VEISBERG	Shmuel		M	Married			Ester			TEIBLUM MOLOVONTCHIK	Feigele	relative	791
VEISBERG	Ester		F	Married			Shmuel			TEIBLUM MOLOVONTCHIK	Feigele	relative	791
VEISBERG	Sara	PINIETSKI	F			Hana		her family		STOROVIESKI	Iosef	brother	797
VEISMAN	Gitel		F		Moshe	Nechama				VEISMAN	Hana	sister	809
VEISMAN	Iente		F		Moshe	Nechama				VEISMAN		sister	809
VEISMAN	Avraham		M		Moshe	Nechama				VEISMAN	Hana	sister	809
VEISMAN	Malcha		F		Moshe	Nechama				VEISMAN	Hana	sister	809
VEISMAN	Nechama	DJETELE	F	Married			Moshe			VEISMAN	Hana	daughter	809
VEISMAN	Moshe		M	Married			Nechama			VEISMAN	Hana	daughter	809
VEISMAN	Neomi	FORBIORDG	F	Married			Hersh Leib			VEISMAN	Moshe	brother-in-law	807
VEISMAN			M	Married			Neomi			VEISMAN	Moshe	brother	807
VINOGRAD	Iakov Moshe		M		Levi					RUBINSTEIN VINOGRAD	Ode		803
VINOKUR	Rivka		F		Hershel	Dina				MELINSKI GERTNER	Itshak	relative	793
VINOKUR	Shaul		M		Hershel	Dina				MELINSKI GERTNER	Itshak	relative	793
VINOKUR	Hershel		M	Married			Dina			MELINSKI GERTNER	Itshak	relative	793
VINOKUR	Dina	RAFAEL	F	Married			Hershel			MELINSKI GERTNER	Itshak	relative	793
VISOKI	Shaie		M					his family		VISOKI	Berl	brother	807
VISOKI	Melech		M	Married			Sheindel			VISOKI	Berl	brother-in-law	807
VISOKI	Moshe		M					his family		VISOKI	Berl	brother	807
VISOKI	Sheindel	VISOKI	F	Married			Melech			VISOKI	Berl	brother	807
VISHNIO	Bashe Miriam		F							SELTSER VISHNIE	Moshe		806
VISHNIO			F	Married			Shlomo	2 children		SELTSER VISHNIE	Moshe		806
VISHNIO	Shlomo		M	Married				2 children		SELTSER VISHNIE			806
VISHNIE	Aharon		M	Married			Sertse Bracha			VISHNIE	Raquel	daughter	807
VISHNIE	Sertse Bracha		F	Married			Aharon			VISHNIE	Raquel	daughter	807
VISHNIE	Hershel		M		Aharon	Sertse Bracha		his family		VISHNIE	Raquel	sister	807
VISHNIE	Shimon		M		Aharon	Sertse Bracha		his family		VISHNIE	Raquel	sister	807
VISHKOVOSKI			F	Married			Haim Hirsh			KONSTANTINER	Lea		804
VISHKOVOSKI	Haim Hirsh		M	Married						KONSTANTINER	Lea		804
VUNDERBOIM	Ziskind		F		Shlomo					VUNDERBOIM	Mina	sister	778
VUNDERBOIM	Iermihau		F		Shlomo					VUNDERBOIM	Mina	sister	778
VUNDERBOIM	Shlomo		M							VUNDERBOIM	Mina	daughter	778

Family name(s)	First name(s)	Maiden name	Sex	Marital status	Father's name	Mother's name	Name of spouse	Additional family	Remarks	Family name(s) of eulogizer	First name(s) of eulogizer	Relationship of eulogizer	Page
VORANE	Rachele		F		Leibel	Hana				IAKOBOVITCH PUGOVI	Golde	relative	808
VORANE	Beile Rivka		F		Leibel	Hana				IAKOBOVITCH PUGOVI	Golde	relative	808
VORANE	Reizel Pesele		F		Leibel	Hana				IAKOBOVITCH PUGOVI	Golde	relative	808
VORANE	Leibel		M	Married			Hana			IAKOBOVITCH PUGOVI	Golde	relative	808
VORANE	Hana		F	Married			Leibel			IAKOBOVITCH PUGOVI	Golde	relative	808
VORANE	Natele		M		Leibel	Hana				IAKOBOVITCH PUGOVI	Golde	relative	808
VORANE	Leibel		M	Married			Hana	5 children		SOIANTZ	Rivka	cousin	784
VORANE	Hana		F	Married			Leibel	5 children		SOIANTZ	Rivka	cousin	784
VEINGARTEN			M		Pinchas	Rivka							758
VEINGARTEN	Rivka	SEIDENBERG	F	Married	Shmuel David	Hava	Pinchas						758
VEINGARTEN			M		Pinchas	Rivka							758
VEINGARTEN	Pinchas		M	Married			Rivka		Son of rabi from Lubshov				758
VIMAN	Aharon		M							VIMAN			763
VIMAN	Bonim		M	Married			Masha			VIMAN	Dov		763
VIMAN	Miriam		F							VIMAN			763
VIMAN	Iakov		M							VIMAN	Dov		763
VIMAN	Vira		F							VIMAN	Dov		763
VIMAN	Shmuel		M							VIMAN	Dov		763
VIMAN	Frida		F							VIMAN	Dov		763
VIMAN	Masha		F	Married			Bonim			VIMAN	Dov		763
VINBERG	Dan Ziskind		M	Married	Avraham Moshe	Rivka	Golda			ABRAMOVITZ ESTREICH	Haia	sister	778
VINBERG	Golda	AISENBERG	F	Married			Dan Ziskind			ABRAMOVITZ ESTREICH	Haia	sister-in-law	778
VINBERG	Rivka	SAMIOTITSKI	F		Leibel		Avraham Tsvi		Private	ABRAMOVITZ ESTREICH	Haia	daughter	778
VINSHTIN	Haia Sara		F		Moshe	Gitel				VINSTEIN DROJENSKI	Sima	sister	778
VINSHTIN	Gitel	FRIDMAN	F	Married	Lib		Moshe			VINSTEIN DROJENSKI	Sima	daughter	778
VINSHTIN	Moshe		M	Married	Kalman		Gitel			VINSTEIN DROJENSKI	Sima	daughter	778
VOITSERSHUL	Haia	GOLDFREB	F						Died in Warsaw		Hania		761
VISHINIA	Lea		F			Bashe				BAR HAIM LISHNIE	Eliezer	brother-in-law	773
VISHINIA	Bashe		F							BAR HAIM LISHNIE	Eliezer	son-in-law	773
VISHINIA	Shlomo		M			Bashe				BAR HAIM LISHNIE	Eliezer	brother-in-law	773
T													
ZAIONTZ	Nutke		F		Ioel	Hanatche				SOIANTZ	Rivka	sister	784
ZAIONTZ	Hanhatche		F	Married			Ioel			SOIANTZ	Rivka	daughter	784
ZAIONTZ	Ioel		M	Married			Hanatsche			SOIANTZ		daughter	784
ZAIONTZ	Haim		M	Married	Iuf (perhaps Iosef?)		Rivka		Perhaps father name was Iosef	EKHOISER	Shalom	son	779
ZAIONTZ	Rivka		F	Married	Haim	Rivka				EKHOISER		son	779
ZALTSMAN	Nate		M	Married			Hietsche			AKERMAN		brother-in-law	809
ZALTSMAN	Haietch		F	Married	Iehoshua	Ester Pache	Nate			AKERMAN	Motel	brother	809
ZONSHEIN	Sime		F							GURGINKEL	Hersh	cousin	794
ZONSHEIN	Motel		F	Married			Haim David			SONSHEIN	Motes	son	799
ZONSHEIN	Haim David		M	Married			Motel			SONSHEIN	Motes	son	799
ZONSHEIN	Iosef		M		Haim David	Matel				SONSHEIN	Motes	brother	799
ZONSHEIN	Berl		M	Married			Miriam			RAFAEL	Moshe	nephew	803
ZONSHEIN	Miriam		F	Married			Berl			RAFAEL	Moshe	nephew	803
ZAKOLIK	Hava	VANDERBOIM	F		Shlomo					VUNDERBOIM	Mina	sister	778
ZONSHEIN	Nechama	ZLOTOVSKI	F	Married	Israel	Miriam	Hinech	children		ZOLOTOVSKI		brother	769
ZONSHEIN	Hinech		M	Married			Nechama	children		ZOLOTOVSKI	David	brother-in-law	769
ZEIDENTESIG			F	Married			Avraham Mordechai			SEIDENBERG	Ieshihau		758
ZEIDENTESIG	Kalman		M		Shmuel David					SEIDENBERG	Ieshihau		758
ZEIDENTESIG	Itka		F	Married	Moshe Aharon		Iechiel Meir			SEIDENBERG	Ieshihau		758
ZEIDENTESIG			M		Kalman					SEIDENBERG	Ieshihau		758
ZEIDENTESIG	Hava	BORENSTEIN	F	Married	Natan Nate		Shmuel David			SEIDENBERG	Ieshihau		758
ZEIDENTESIG			M		Kalman					SEIDENBERG	Ieshihau		758

Family name(s)	First name(s)	Maiden name	Sex	Marital status	Father's name	Mother's name	Name of spouse	Additional family	Remarks	Family name(s) of eulogizer	First name(s) of eulogizer	Relationship of eulogizer	Page
ZEIDENTESIG			F		Avraham Mordechai					SEIDENBERG	Ieshihau		758
ZEIDENTESIG	Avraham Mordechai		M	Married						SEIDENBERG	Ieshihau		758
ZEIDENTESIG	Iechiel Meir		M	Married	Shmuel David		Ietke			SEIDENBERG	Ieshihau		758
ZILBERPODEM	Motel	KODJENITSKI	F		Meir Iechiel	Breine Gitel				KODCHENITSKI	Mordechai	brother	806
ZILBERSTEIN	Pesach		M		Kopel					SILBERSTEIN	Miriam	cousin	800
ZILBERSTEIN	Mendel		M		Moshe Aharon					SILBERSTEIN	Miriam	cousin	800
ZILBERSTEIN	Shlomo		M		Avraham Itshak	Hava Iosefe				SILBERSTEIN		sister	800
ZILBERSTEIN	Elihau Haim		M		Moshe Aharon					SILBERSTEIN	Miriam	cousin	800
ZILBERSTEIN	Velvol		M						Teacher	SILBERSTEIN	Miriam	cousin	800
ZILBERSTEIN	Hava Iosefe		F	Married		Sara Bracha	Avraham Itshak			SILBERSTEIN	Miriam	daughter	800
ZILBERSTEIN	Haim Kopel		M		Avraham Itshak	Hava Iosefe				SILBERSTEIN	Miriam	sister	800
ZILBERSTEIN	Elihau Zilman		M		Avraham Itshak	Hava Iosefe				SILBERSTEIN	Miriam	sister	800
ZILBERSTEIN	Iehuda iosef		M		Avraham Itshak	Havalosefe				SILBERSTEIN	Miriam	sister	800
ZILBERSTEIN	Avraham Itshak		M	Married	Moshe Aharon					SILBERSTEIN	Miriam	daughter	800
ZILBERSTEIN	Gedalihau Pinchas		M		Avraham Itshak	Hava Iosefe				SILBERSTEIN		sister	800
ZILBERSTEIN	Mendel		M		Avraham Itshak	Hava Iosefe				SILBERSTEIN		sister	800
ZILBERSTEIN	Tova		F	Married			Beinish			SILBERSTEIN	Miriam	cousin	800
ZILBERSTEIN	Beinish		M	Married	Moshe Aharon		Tova			SILBERSTEIN	Miriam	cousin	800
ZILBERSTEIN	Iosef		M		Kopel					SILBERSTEIN	Miriam	cousin	800
ZLOTOLOV	Eisik		M	Married			Tsvia	children					809
ZLOTOLOV	Malie		F										809
ZLOTOLOV	Tsvia		F	Married			Aisik	children					809
ZLOTOVSKI	Itshak		M		Israel	Miriam				ZOLOTOVSKI	David	brother	769
ZLOTOVSKI	Israel		M	Married			Miriam Maia			ZOLOTOVSKI	David	son	769
ZLOTOVSKI	Miriam Maia		F	Married			Israel			ZOLOTOVSKI	David	son	769
ZLOTOVSKI	Feigale		F		Israel	Miriam				ZOLOTOVSKI	David	brother	769
ZELIKOVITZ			M			Frida Rivka		their family					777
ZELIKOVITZ	Moshe Zelig		M			Frida Rivka		their family					777
ZELIKOVITZ	David		M			Frida Rivka							777
ZELIKOVITZ	Frida Rivka		F						Rachel				777
ZELIKOVITZ	Iehuda Leib		M			Frida Rivka		their family					777
ZELIKOVITZ	Pinchas		M			Frida Rivka							777
ZALTSZSCHEIN	Israel		M	Married			Ester Poshe			SELTSTEIN	Shalom		763
ZALTSZSCHEIN	Tsluva		F							SELTSTEIN	Shalom		763
ZALTSZSCHEIN	Ester Malka		F	Married			Israel			SELTSTEIN	Shalom		763
ZALTSZSCHEIN	Itshak Idel		M							SELTSTEIN	Shalom		763
ZELTSER	Haia Ester	ZILBERSHTEIN	F		Avraham Itshak	Hava Iosefe				SILBERSTEIN	Miriam	sister	800
ZECHIROVITZ	Eliezer		M	Married			Hana	children		BINSHTOK	Tsvi	brother-in-law	773
ZECHIROVITZ	Hana	BINSTOK	F	Married		Nechama	Eliezer	children		BINSHTOK	Tsvi	brother	773
ZESHELIOZNI	Rechel	SOKOLOV	F	Married	Avigdor	Sara Freide	Haim			FEDERMAN BARSILAI	Tsirel	daughter	787
ZESHELIOZNI	Haim		M	Married	Hershke Ezros	Eidel	Rechel			FEDERMAN BARSILAI	Tsirel	daughter	787
ZESHELIOZNI	Rivka		F		Haim	Rechel				FEDERMAN BARSILAI	Tsirel	sister	787
ZESHELIOZNI	Hershke Ezras		M	Married			Eidel			FEDERMAN BARSILAI	Tsirel	granddaughter	787
ZESHELIOZNI	Eidel		F	Married			Hershke Ezros			FEDERMAN BARSILAI	Tsirel	granddaughter	787
ט													
TOBOKMAN	Tsiltsel		M	Married			Dvora	children	Perhaps Betsalel	TABAKMAN ROSENSOMEN	Israel		769
TOBOKMAN	Dvora		F	Married			Tseltel	children		TABAKMAN ROSENSOMEN	Israel		769
TUCHKLEPER								family	Died in Siedlce	TUCHKLOPER	Haia		777
TIBLUM	Iakov		M	Married			Dina			BEN ZEEV	Iona	son	779
TIBLUM	Gedalihau		M		Iakov	Dina				BEN ZEEV	Iona	brother	779

Family name(s)	First name(s)	Maiden name	Sex	Marital status	Father's name	Mother's name	Name of spouse	Additional family	Remarks	Family name(s) of eulogizer	First name(s) of eulogizer	Relationship of eulogizer	Page
TIBLUM	Etil		F		Iakov	Dina				BEN ZEEV	Iona	brother	779
TIBLUM	Mendel		M		Iakov	Dina				BEN ZEEV		brother	779
TIBLUM	Dina		F	Married			Iakov			BEN ZEEV		son	779
TIBLUM	Hertzel		M	Married			Rachel	children		BINSHTOK	Tsvi	brother-in-law	773
TIBLUM	Rachel	BINSTOK	F	Married		Nechama	Hertzel	children		BINSHTOK	Tsvi	brother	773
TEIBLUM	Itshak		M		Haim Iosef	Roise				TEIBLUM MOLOVONTCHIK	Feigele	sister	791
TEIBLUM	Haim Iosef		M	Married			Roise			TEIBLUM MOLOVONTCHIK	Feigele	daughter	791
TEIBLUM	Roise		F	Married			Haim Iosef			TEIBLUM MOLOVONTCHIK	Feigele	daughter	791
TEIBLUM	Israel		M	Married			Zlote Itke	his family					777
TEIBLUM	Zlote Itke	ZELIKOVITCH	F	Married		Frida Rivka	Israel	her family					777
TOKMIN	Iakov		M		Dov			his family		TOMKIN (BROTHER)	Mordechai	sister	762
TOKMIN	Dov		M							TOMKIN (SON)	Mordechai	daughter	762
TENENBOIM			M		Israel	Elte				TENENBOIM		aunt	785
TENENBOIM	Haia Hades		F	Married			David			TENENBOIM		daughter	785
TENENBOIM	Shlomo		M	Married	David	Haia Hodes	Pese	children				sister	785
TENENBOIM	Pese		F	Married			Shlomo	children		TENENBOIM	Alte	sister-in-law	785
TENENBOIM	Israel		M	Married	David	Haia Hodes	Elte	children		TENENBOIM	Alte	sister	785
TENENBOIM	David		M	Married			Haia Hodes			TENENBOIM	Alte	daughter	785
TENENBOIM	Elte		F	Married			Israel	children		TENENBOIM	Alte	sister-in-law	785
TCHUDNER	Hanhale	LEVIN	F	Married	Ioel	Feigel				LEVIN	Haikel	brother	807
.													
IAGODJINSKI	Shaie		M	Married			Dvoshe			MELINSKI GERTNER	Itshak	relative	793
IAGODJINSKI	Shaul		M		Shaie	Dvoshe				MELINSKI GERTNER	Itshak	relative	793
IAGODJINSKI	Dvoshe	RAFAEL	F	Married			Shaie			MELINSKI GERTNER	Itshak	relative	793
IAGODJINSKI	Shepsel		M		Shaie	Dvoshe				MELINSKI GERTNER	Itshak	relative	793
IAGODJINSKI	Ester		F		Shaie	Dvoshe				MELINSKI GERTNER	Itshak	relative	793
IAGODJINSKI	Sara		F		Shaie	Dvoshe				MELINSKI GERTNER	Itshak	relative	793
IAD	Beile		F	Married			Moshe Mordechai						809
IAD	Moshe		M	Married			Beile						809
IBERBOIM	Shimon		M		Matatiahu Menashe	Rivka				IBERBOIM VOLFLING	Mordechai	brother	775
IBERBOIM	Rivka		F	Married			Matatihau Menashe				Mordechai	son	775
IBERBOIM	Itshak		M		Matatiahu Menashe	Rivka				IBERBOIM VOLFLING	Mordechai	brother	775
IBERBOIM	Matatihau Menashe		M	Married			Rivka			IBERBOIM VOLFLING	Mordechai	son	775
IBERBOIM	Lea		F		Matatiahu Menashe	Rivka					Mordechai	brother	775
IBERBOIM	Haim		M		Matatiahu Menashe	Rivka				IBERBOIM VOLFLING	Mordechai	brother	775
IUVILER	Tsvia		F	Married			Asher			IUVILER	Avraham	son	774
IUVILER	Moshe		M		Asher	Tsvia				IUVILER	Avraham	brother	774
IUVILER	Asher		M	Married			Tsvia			IUVILER	Avraham	son	774
IUVILER	Meir Shalom		M		Asher	Tsvia				IUVILER	Avraham	brother	774
IUVILER	Hinech		M		Asher	Tsvia				IUVILER	Avraham	brother	774
IUDENGLOIBEN	Iosef		M	Married			Haia Sara			IUDENGLOIBEN BORCHOVSKI	Moshe	son	784
IUDENGLOIBEN	Avraham		M		Naftali	Libe						relative	784
IUDENGLOIBEN	Libe		F	Married			Naftali					relative	784
IUDENGLOIBEN	Meir		M		Naftali	Libe						relative	784
IUDENGLOIBEN	Haia Sara		F	Married			Iosef					son	784
IUDENGLOIBEN	Naftali		M	Married			Libe					relative	784
IUDENGLOIBEN	Miriam		F		Iosef	Haia Sara						brother	784
IUDENGLOIBEN	Ester		F		Iosef	Haia Sara						brother	784

Family name(s)	First name(s)	Maiden name	Sex	Marital status	Father's name	Mother's name	Name of spouse	Additional family	Remarks	Family name(s) of eulogizer	First name(s) of eulogizer	Relationship of eulogizer	Page
IUDENGLOIBEN	Lea Rivka		F		Iosef	Haia Sara						brother	784
IUDENGLOIBEN	Moshe		M		Naftali	Libe						relative	784
IELEN		SHMUKLIORDG	F	Married	Aharon	Ritsa	David	children	Died in Warsaw	VEINSTEIN SHMUKLIARTCH	Rachel	sister	770
IELEN	David		M	Married			Henie	children	Died in Warsaw	VEINSTEIN SHMUKLIARTCH	Rachel	sister-in-law	770
IAKOBOVITCH			M	Married			Sima		Died in Warsaw	HELBERSTADT GOLDFREV	Hania		761
IAKOBOVITCH	Sima	GOLDFREB	F	Married					Died in Warsaw	HELBERSTADT GOLDFREV	Hania		761
כ													
CAHANA	Avraham		M	Married						GLIKSBERG	Iehuda		759
CAHANA	Avraham		M	Married	Iakov		Hodel			GLIKSBERG	Iehuda		759
CAHANA	Hodel	MARGALIT	F	Married			Avraham			GLIKSBERG	Iehuda		759
CAHANA	Polie Pril	GLIKSBERG	F	Married	Natan David	Malcha Hades	Avraham			GLIKSBERG	Iehuda		759
CAHANA	Iakov		M		Menachem Shlomo	Hana Rivka		his family		GLIKSBERG	Iehuda		759
CAHANA	Meir		M		Menachem Shlomo	Hana Rivka		his family		GLIKSBERG	Iehuda		759
ל													
LOV	Rivka Zlote		F	Married			Tsvi						809
LOV	Tsvi		M	Married			Rivka Zlote						809
LANGER	Bluma		F		Pinchas	Hana				SOKOLOVSKI	Asher	cousin	781
LANGER	Pinchas		M	Married		Hana			Died in Paris	SOKOLOVSKI	Asher	cousin	781
LANGER	Moshe		M		Pinchas	Hana				SOKOLOVSKI	Asher	cousin	781
LANGER	Israel		M		Pinchas	Hana				SOKOLOVSKI	Asher	cousin	781
LANGER	Iakov		M						Died in Danzig	SOKOLOVSKI	Asher	cousin	781
LANGER	Hana		F	Married			Pinchas			SOKOLOVSKI	Asher	cousin	781
LANDAU	Avraham		M	Married	Menachem Mendel	Reisel Hadas		children					758
LANDAU	Reizel Hadas	SEIDENBERG	F	Married	Israel Sinai	Rachel	Menachem Mendel						758
LANDAU	Menachem		M	Married			Reisil Hadas		Grandson of Rabi Dobrish from Biola				758
LANDAU			F	Married			Avraham	children					758
LOFT	Itshak		M	Married			Tsvia	children		LEIBMAN	Sara		807
LOFT	Tsvia	LEIBMAN	F	Married			Itshak	children		LEIBMAN	Sara		807
LEDERMAN	Hershel		M	Married			Masha			LEDERMAN	Dov		763
LEDERMAN	Masha		F	Married			Hershel			LEDERMAN	Dov		763
LUBLINER	Sima	TABAKMAN	F	Married	Itcha		Nachum Zeev			KARMESH	Ester	daughter	771
LUBLINER	Ioshua		M		Nachum Zeev	Sima				KARMESH	Ester	sister	771
LUBLINER	Nachum Zeev		M	Married			Sima			KARMESH	Ester	daughter	771
LUBLINER	Henia		F		Nachum	Sima				KARMESH		sister	771
LUBLINER	Avraham		M		Nachum Zeev	Sima				KARMESH	Ester	sister	771
LUBLINER	Haia		F		Nachum Zeev	Sima				KARMESH	Ester	sister	771
LUBLINER	Hana		F		Nachum Zeev	Sima				KARMESH	Ester	sister	771
LUBLESKI	Shamai		M		Iakov	Gitel				ALPERT	Alisa	sister	777
LUBLESKI	Iakov		M	Married			Gitel			ALPERT		daughter	777
LUBLESKI	Gitel		F	Married			Iakov			ALPERT	Alisa	daughter	777
LUBLESKI	Shalom		M		Iakov	Gitel				ALPERT	Alisa	sister	777
LUBLESKI	Menachem		M		Iakov	Gitel				ALPERT	Alisa	sister	777
LEVIN	Henia	VANDERBOIM	F		Shlomo					VUNDERBOIM	Mina	sister	778
LEVIN	Tuvia		M		Eliezer	Pola Pesia				PALTIEL ISENSTAT			757
LEVIN	Iakov		M		Eliezer	Pola Pesia				PALTIEL ISENSTAT			757
LEVIN	Pola Pessia		F	Married	Moshe Aba	Ieta	Eliezer			PALTIEL ISENSTAT			757

Family name(s)	First name(s)	Maiden name	Sex	Marital status	Father's name	Mother's name	Name of spouse	Additional family	Remarks	Family name(s) of eulogizer	First name(s) of eulogizer	Relationship of eulogizer	Page
LEVIN	Miriam		F		Eliezer	Pola Pesia				PALTIEL ISENSTAT			757
LEVIN	Eliezer		M	Married	Iakov		Pola Pesia			PALTIEL ISENSTAT			757
LIBERNET	Haia		F	Married			Israel	children		BINSHTOK	Gila		773
LIBERNET	Israel		M	Married			Haia	children		BINSHTOK	Gila		773
LIBERNET	Itka		F	Married			Aharon	children		BINSHTOK	Gila		773
LIBERNET	Aharon		M	Married			Ietke	children		BINSHTOK	Gila		773
LIBERNET	Biniamin		M							BINSHTOK	Gila		773
LEIBMAN	Iakov Itshak		M	Married			Haia			IAKOBOVITCH PUGOVI	Golde	relative	808
LEIBMAN	Haia		F	Married			Iakov Itshak			IAKOBOVITCH PUGOVI	Golde	relative	808
LEIBMAN			M		Iakov Itshak	Haia				IAKOBOVITCH PUGOVI	Golde	relative	808
LISTIK	Lib		M	Married					Died in Warsaw	LISTIK	David	son	776
LISTIK	Iosef		M	Married					Died in Zatish'ye	LISTIK	David	brother	776
LISTIK			F	Married			Iosef		Died in Zatish'ye	LISTIK	David	brother-in-law	776
LISTIK			F	Married			Lib		Died in Warsaw	LISTIK	David	son	776
LIPOVITCH	Simcha		M		Asher	Rivka				STEINBERG	Aharon	uncle	809
LIPOVITCH	Sarale		F		Asher	Rivka				STEINBERG	Aharon	uncle	809
LIPOVITCH	Asher		M	Married			Rivka			STEINBERG		brother-in-law	809
LIPOVITCH	Haimel		M		Asher	Rivka				STEINBERG		uncle	809
LIPOVITCH	Rivka	STEINBERG	F	Married	Itshak David	Elte Nechama	Asher			STEINBERG		brother	809
LEVIN	Iakov		M	Married			Golde			LEVIN	Hersh	son	801
LEVIN	Golde		F	Married			Iakov			LEVIN	Hersh	son	801
LEVIN	Ioel		M	Married			Feigel			LEVIN	Haikel	son	807
LEVIN	Malcha		F		Ioel	Feigel				LEVIN	Haikel	brother	807
LEVIN	Leibel		M		Ioel	Feigel				LEVIN	Haikel	brother	807
LEVIN	Feigel	PERETS	F	Married			Ioel			LEVIN	Haikel	son	807
LEVIN	Feivil		M							LEVIN	Iakel	cousin	799
LEVIN	Haia		F							LEVIN	Iakel	cousin	799
LEVIN	Sheine Kavka		F					her family		LEVIN	Iakel	cousin	799
LEVIN	Shie		M							LEVIN	Iakel	cousin	799
LEVIN	Getsel		M	Married			Shoshe Rachel			LEVIN	Iakel	son	799
LEVIN	Dvora		F							LEVIN	Iakel	cousin	799
LEVIN	Sara		F		Getsel	Shoshe Rachel				LEVIN	Iakel	brother	799
LEVIN	Sashe Rachel		F	Married			Getsel			LEVIN	Iakel	son	799
LEVIN	Ester		F						Died in Paris	MANDELBAUM			777
מ													
MALOVONTCHIK	Avraham Haim		M	Married			Rivka			MALOVONTCHIK	Iakov	son	790
MALOVONTCHIK	Reizel		F	Married			Moshe	children		MALOVONTCHIK	Iakov	relative	790
MALOVONTCHIK	Moshe		M	Married			Reisil	children		MALOVONTCHIK	Iakov	relative	790
MALOVONTCHIK	Rivka		F	Married			Avraham Haim			MALOVONTCHIK	Iakov	son	790
MOLIN	Avramele		M						Family name unclear	BISTROVITCH	Itshak	relative	789
MOLIN	Iosel		M						Family name unclear	BISTROVITCH	Itshak	relative	789
MOLIN	Sarale		F						Family name unclear	BISTROVITCH	Itshak	relative	789
MOLIN	Itke		F						Family name unclear	BISTROVITCH	Itshak	relative	789
MOLIN	Tevol		M							BISTROVITCH	Itshak	cousin	789
MOLIN	Ides		F						Family name unclear	BISTROVITCH	Itshak	relative	789
MANDELBOIM	David		M	Married			Perl	children		TEIBLUM MOLOVONTCHIK	Feigele	relative	791
MANDELBOIM	Perl		F	Married			David	children		TEIBLUM MOLOVONTCHIK	Feigele	relative	791
MANKEBOTSKI			M	Married			Hana	children		MELINSKI GERTNER	Itshak	relative	793
MANKEBOTSKI	Ite		F							MELINSKI GERTNER	Itshak	relative	793
MANKEBOTSKI	Moshe		M	Married			Rachel			MELINSKI GERTNER	Itshak	relative	793

Family name(s)	First name(s)	Maiden name	Sex	Marital status	Father's name	Mother's name	Name of spouse	Additional family	Remarks	Family name(s) of eulogizer	First name(s) of eulogizer	Relationship of eulogizer	Page
MANKEBOTSKI	Rachel		F	Married			Moshe			MELINSKI GERTNER	Itshak	relative	793
MANKEBOTSKI	Hana		F	Married				children		MELINSKI GERTNER	Itshak	relative	793
MARICHBEIN	Nachman		M	Married			Mindil	children					809
MARICHBEIN	Mindil		F	Married	Iakov	Dina Reisel	Nachman	children					809
MOKOVOTSKI	Haia		F							SHKLOZ	Iakov	cousin	776
MORGENSTERN	Haiele		F							MORGENSTERN	Family		766
MORGENSTERN	Shalom		M		Itshak Aizik					MORGENSTERN			766
MORGENSTERN	Arie Leib		M							MORGENSTERN	Family		766
MORGENSTERN	Bluma Male		F		Iechiel					MORGENSTERN			766
MORDESKI	Haia		F		Aharon	Risel				MORDESKI	Israel	brother	763
MORDESKI	Feigale		F		Aharon	Risel				MORDESKI	Israel	brother	763
MORDESKI	Rizel		F	Married			Aharon			MORDESKI	Israel	son	763
MORDESKI	Aharon		M	Married	Aba		Risel			MORDESKI	Israel	son	763
MORDESKI	Iakov		M		Aharon	Risel				MORDESKI	Israel	brother	763
MORDESKI	Shindel		F		Aharon	Risel				MORDESKI	Israel	brother	763
MINTZ	Itke	KAHANA	F			Hana Rivka				GLIKSBERG	Iehuda		759
MISTER			F			Zelta Ester				MISTER	Menachem	brother	774
MISTER	Ieshiau		M			Zelta Ester				MISTER	Menachem	brother	774
MISTER	Perl Hana		F			Zelta Ester				MISTER	Menachem	brother	774
MISTER	Iakov		M			Zelta Ester				MISTER		brother	774
MISTER	Zelta Ester		F							MISTER	Menachem	son	774
MISHLER	Minke		F	Married			Simcha	children					809
MISHLER	Simcha		M	Married			Minke	children					809
MELINSKI	Rivka		F		Mordechai	Haia				MELINSKI GERTNER	Itshak	uncle	793
MELINSKI	Mordechai		M	Married			Haia			MELINSKI GERTNER	Itshak	brother	793
MELINSKI	Haia	MONKEBOTSKI	F	Married			Mordechai			MELINSKI GERTNER	Itshak	brother-in-law	793
MELINSKI	Ite	RAFAEL	F							MELINSKI GERTNER	Itshak	son	793
MENDELSON	Haia		F							MENDELSON	Family		766
MENDELSON	Moshe		M							MENDELSON			766
MENDELSON	Shraga		M		Ioel Hirsh					MENDELSON	Family		766
MENDELSON	Michal		F							MENDELSON	Family		766
MENDELSON	Rudja		F							MENDELSON	Family		766
נ													
NAUTCHITCHEL	Feiga		F		Hersh Leib	Dvora				TSFONI		sister	775
NAUTCHITCHEL	Shalom Meir		M		Hersh Leib	Dvora				TSFONI	Hana	sister	775
NAUTCHITCHEL	Sara		F		Hersh Leib	Dvora				TSFONI	Hana	sister	775
NAUTCHITCHEL	Iakov		M		Hersh Leib	Dvora				TSFONI	Hana	sister	775
NAUTCHITCHEL	Hersh Leib		M	Married			Hana Rivka	Dvora		TSFONI	Hana	daughter	775
NAUTCHITCHEL	Avraham		M		Hersh Leib	Dvora				TSFONI	Hana	sister	775
NAUTCHITCHEL	Dvora		F	Married			Hersh Leib			TSFONI	Hana	daughter	775
NOVTSINSKI			M		Iosef	Rivka		his family		NOVTSINSKI GERBER	Haim		779
NOVTSINSKI	Rivka	VISOKI	F	Married	Iehoshua		Iosef			NOVTSINSKI GERBER	Haim		779
NOVTSINSKI	Iosef		M	Married	Haim		Rivka			NOVTSINSKI GERBER	Haim		779
NOVTSINSKI	Eta		F		Iosef	Rivka		her family		NOVTSINSKI GERBER	Haim		779
NOVTSINSKI	Velvol		M		Iosef	Rivka		his family		NOVTSINSKI GERBER	Haim		779
NOVTSINSKI	Hershil		M		Iosef	Rivka		his family		NOVTSINSKI GERBER	Haim		779
NOVTSINSKI	Feiga		F		Iosef	Rivka		her family		NOVTSINSKI GERBER	Haim		779
NOVTSINSKI	Ioshua		M		Iosef	Rivka				NOVTSINSKI GERBER	Haim		779
NOSBOIM	Shmeril		M	Married		Frida	Ester	children		NUSBOIM	Shmuel	brother	776

Family name(s)	First name(s)	Maiden name	Sex	Marital status	Father's name	Mother's name	Name of spouse	Additional family	Remarks	Family name(s) of eulogizer	First name(s) of eulogizer	Relationship of eulogizer	Page
NOSBOIM			F							NUSBOIM	Shmuel	son	776
NOSBOIM	Ester		F	Married			Shmirl	children		NUSBOIM	Shmuel	brother-in-law	776
NOSBOIM	Simcha		M			Frida Rivka				NUSBOIM	Shmuel	brother	776
O													
SALAUTCH	Kalman		M		Efraim Iakov	Sara		his family		SOLORTCH	Gedalia	brother	796
SALAUTCH	Aharon		M		Efraim Iakov	Sara		his family		SOLORTCH	Gedalia	brother	796
SALAUTCH	Sara		F	Married			Efraim Iakov			SOLORTCH	Gedalia	son	796
SALAUTCH	Pinie		M		Efraim Iakov	Sara		his family		SOLORTCH		brother	796
SALAUTCH	Efraim Iakov		M	Married			Sara			SOLORTCH	Gedalia	son	796
SALAUTCH	Shmuel		M		Efraim Iakov	Sara		his family		SOLORTCH	Gedalia	brother	796
SOFIRSHTEIN	Hama		F		Israel Itshak	Haia				SOPIRSTEIN	Mendel	brother	792
SOFIRSHTEIN	Iosef		M		Israel Itshak	Haia				SOPIRSTEIN	Mendel	brother	792
SOFIRSHTEIN	Haia		F	Married			Israel Itshak			SOPIRSTEIN	Mendel	son	792
SOFIRSHTEIN	Feigele		F		Israel Itshak	Haia				SOPIRSTEIN	Mendel	brother	792
SOFIRSHTEIN	Malcha		F		Israel Itshak	Haia				SOPIRSTEIN	Mendel	brother	792
SOFIRSHTEIN	Israel Itshak		M	Married			Haia			SOPIRSTEIN	Mendel	son	792
SOFIRSHTEIN	Sara		F		Israel Itshak	Haia				SOPIRSTEIN	Mendel	brother	792
SOKOLOV	Avigdor		M	Married			Sara Freide			FEDERMAN BARSILAI	Tsirel	granddaughter	787
SOKOLOV	Sara Freide		F	Married			Avigdor			FEDERMAN BARSILAI	Tsirel	granddaughter	787
SOCHOZBSKI	Baruch		M		Moshe Meir	Hinde				SOKOZBSKI	Avraham	brother	775
SOCHOZBSKI	Hinda		F	Married			Moshe Meir			SOKOZBSKI	Avraham	son	775
SOCHOZBSKI	Mordechai		M		Moshe Meir	Hinde				SOKOZBSKI	Avraham	brother	775
SOCHOZBSKI	Moshe Meir		M	Married			Hinda			SOKOZBSKI	Avraham	son	775
SOCHOZBSKI	Asher		M		Moshe Meir	Hinde				SOKOZBSKI	Avraham	brother	775
SOKOLOVSKI	David		M		Iakov	Rivka				SOKOLOVSKI	Asher	brother	781
SOKOLOVSKI	Iakov		M	Married			Rivka			SOKOLOVSKI	Asher	son	781
SOKOLOVSKI	Rivka		F	Married			Iakov			SOKOLOVSKI	Asher	son	781
SOKOLOVSKI	Moshe		M		Iakov	Rivka				SOKOLOVSKI	Asher	brother	781
SOKOLOVSKI	Sara		F		Iakov	Rivka				SOKOLOVSKI	Asher	brother	781
SORBITZ	Baruch		M	Married							Dina	brother-in-law	768
SORBITZ	Fridke		F		Baruch						Dina	aunt	768
SORBITZ		FINKELSTEIN	F	Married			Baruch				Dina	sister	768
STOROVIESKI	Sender		M							STOROVIESKI	Tchipe	sister	797
STAVKOVSKI	Tova		F		Iakov	Ester			Died in Siedlce in 1942	STABKOVSKI STEINBERG	Sima	sister	765
STAVKOVSKI	Iakov		M	Married			Ester		Died in Siedlce in 1942	STABKOVSKI STEINBERG	Sima	daughter	765
STAVKOVSKI	Haia		F		Iakov	Ester			Died in Siedlce in 1942	STABKOVSKI STEINBERG	Sima	sister	765
STAVKOVSKI	Itka		F		Iakov	Ester			Died in Siedlce in 1942	STABKOVSKI STEINBERG	Sima	sister	765
STAVKOVSKI	Perla		F		Iakov	Ester			Died in Siedlce in 1942	STABKOVSKI STEINBERG	Sima	sister	765
STAVKOVSKI	Ester		F	Married			Iakov		Died in Siedlce in 1942	STABKOVSKI STEINBERG	Sima	daughter	765
SALBA	Avraham		M	Married	Moshe Aharon				Lawyer. Member of				758
SAMOLER	Haim		M	Married				children		BERENFELD	David	brother-in-law	808
SAMOLER	Toive	BERENFELD	F	Married	Leibel	Elte		children		BERENFELD	David	brother	808
SAMIOTITSKI	Leibel		M						Private	ABRAMOVITZ ESTREICH	Haia	granddaughter	778
SERVEI	Idel		M	Married			Rivka Frimet	children		BISTROVITCH	Itshak	relative	789
SERVEI	Rivka Primet	BISTROVITCH	F	Married	Meshulam	Ester	Idel	children		BISTROVITCH		relative	789
SPATSISKA	Moshe		M			Mina			Died in Baranowicz	NUSBOIM	Shmuel	uncle	776
SPATSISKA			M	Married			Mina		Died in Baranowicz	NUSBOIM	Shmuel	brother-in-law	776
SPATSISKA	Mina	NUSBOIM	F	Married		Frida			Died in Baranowicz	NUSBOIM	Shmuel	brother	776
SACOROSHETSKI	Tsirele		F		Iakov	Mintche				FEDERMAN	Moshe	uncle	787
SACOROSHETSKI	Israel		M		Iakov	Mintche				FEDERMAN	Moshe	uncle	787
SACOROSHETSKI	Iakov		M	Married			Mintche			FEDERMAN	Moshe	brother-in-law	787
SACOROSHETSKI	Mintshe	FEDERMAN	F	Married			Iakov			FEDERMAN	Moshe	brother	787

Family name(s)	First name(s)	Maiden name	Sex	Marital status	Father's name	Mother's name	Name of spouse	Additional family	Remarks	Family name(s) of eulogizer	First name(s) of eulogizer	Relationship of eulogizer	Page
SARBRANIK	Avraham Tsvi		M	Married			Shprintsa			SARBRANIK	Israel	son	773
SARBRANIK	Shprintse		F	Married			Avraham Tsvi			SARBRANIK	Israel	son	773
SARBRANIK	Bila		F		Avraham Tsvi	Shprintsa				SARBRANIK	Israel	brother	773
SARBRANIK	Desha		F		Avraham Tsvi	Shprintsa					Israel	brother	773
SARBRANIK	Beile		F	Married			Moshe Iosel	their family		PERL	Iudel		809
SARBRANIK	Moshe Iosil		M	Married			Beile	their family		PERL	Iudel		809
ע													
ENGLENDER			F	Married			Asher	children	Died in Brest-Litovosk	ENGLENDER	Mordechai	brother-in-law	788
ENGLENDER	Asher		M	Married	Iosef			children	Died in Brest-Litovosk	ENGLENDER	Mordechai	brother	788
ENGLENDER	Iosef		M	Widower						ENGLENDER	Mordechai	son	788
ENGLENDER	Malie		F		Iosef					ENGLENDER	Mordechai	brother	788
ESIKMACHER	Eliezer		M							SILBERSTEIN	Miriam	cousin	800
EKHOIZR	Shmuel		M		Aharon	Rivka		his family		EKHOISER	Shalom	brother	779
EKHOIZR	Rivka		F	Married			Aharon			EKHOISER	Shalom	son	779
פ													
PAPOVOSKI	Hana		F							DROMI POPOVESKI	Fishel		759
FAKTCHOR	Lea		F	Married			Avraham	children					809
FAKTCHOR	Avraham		M	Married			Lea	children					809
FARBESHTEIN			F		Iakov	Hana				MELINSKI GERTNER		relative	793
FARBESHTEIN	Hana	KODJENITSKI	F	Married			Iakov			MELINSKI GERTNER	Itshak	relative	793
FARBESHTEIN	Iakov		M	Married			Hana			MELINSKI GERTNER	Itshak	relative	793
FARBESHTEIN	Zlotke	ROTBERG	F	Married	Elihau Heinech	Pesia	Itshak	her family					777
FARBESHTEIN	Itshak		M	Married			Zlotke	his family					777
PEDROVSKI			F							ORZEL AND FAMILY			757
FUGOVI	Zlote		F	Married			Avraham Shmuel			IAKOBOVITCH PUGOVI	Golde	daughter	808
FUGOVI	Hanhatche		F	Married			David			IAKOBOVITCH PUGOVI	Golde	sister-in-law	808
FUGOVI	Avraham Shmuel		M	Married			Zlote			IAKOBOVITCH PUGOVI	Golde	daughter	808
FUGOVI			M		David	Hanatche				IAKOBOVITCH PUGOVI	Golde	aunt	808
FUGOVI	David		M	Married	Avraham Shmuel	Zlote	Hanatsche			IAKOBOVITCH PUGOVI	Golde	sister	808
FURMAN	Henich		M	Married	David	Haia		children		FURMAN	Iakov	brother	802
FURMAN			F	Married			Henich	children		FURMAN	Iakov	brother-in-law	802
FURMAN	David		M	Married			Haia			FURMAN	Iakov	son	802
FURMAN			F	Married			Berl	children		FURMAN	Iakov	brother-in-law	802
FURMAN	Haia		F	Married			David			FURMAN	Iakov	son	802
FURMAN	Berl		M	Married	David	Haia		children		FURMAN	Iakov	brother	802
FIGOVI			M	Married			Zlote	grandchildren		SOIANTZ	Rivka	cousin	784
FIGOVI	Zlote		F	Married				grandchildren		SOIANTZ		cousin	784
FEINHOLTZ	Nate		M	Married			Zisel			MALOVONTCHIK	Iakov	relative	790
FEINHOLTZ	Zisel	MALOVONTCHIK	F	Married	Avraham Haim	Rivka	Nate			MALOVONTCHIK	Iakov	uncle	790
FEINHOLTZ	Hindele Mai		F		Nate	Zisel				MALOVONTCHIK	Iakov	relative	790
FINIETSKI	Berl		M	Married		Hana		children		STOROVIESKI	Iosef	brother	797
FINIETSKI	Leibel		M	Married		Hana		children		STOROVIESKI	Iosef	brother	797
FINIETSKI			F	Married			Leibel	children		STOROVIESKI	Iosef	brother-in-law	797
FINIETSKI			F	Married			Berl	children		STOROVIESKI	Iosef	brother-in-law	797
FINIETSKI	Hana	BROKODJ	F						Died 7 days after war start	STOROVIESKI		son	797
FINFTER	Shifra		F	Married			Israel Itshak			FINFTER	Shlomo	son	805
FINFTER			F	Married			Zod			FINFTER	Shlomo	brother-in-law	805

Family name(s)	First name(s)	Maiden name	Sex	Marital status	Father's name	Mother's name	Name of spouse	Additional family	Remarks	Family name(s) of eulogizer	First name(s) of eulogizer	Relationship of eulogizer	Page
FINFTER	Israel Itshak		M	Married			Shifra			FINFTER	Shlomo	son	805
FINFTER	Zod		M	Married	Israel Itshak	Shifra				FINFTER	Shlomo	brother	805
FINFTER			M		Zod					FINFTER	Shlomo	uncle	805
FINKELSHTEIN	Haia Libe		F	Married			Dov				Dina	daughter	768
FINKELSHTEIN	Dov		M	Married			Hana Libe				Dina	daughter	768
FIENKNOVITCH	Serko	RISA	F		Itshak Aharon	Rivka				KARMESH	Hana	sister	771
FIRSHTER	Hana		F						Killed together with other 28 girls	ORZEL AND FAMILY	Itshak		757
FIRSHTER	Zeev		M							ORZEL AND FAMILY	Itshak		757
FIRSHTER	Gote		F							ORZEL AND FAMILY	Itshak		757
FISHMAN	Iakov		M	Married			Roise	children			Sheindel		804
FISHMAN	Roise		F	Married			Iakov	children		HUBERMAN	Sheindel		804
FISHMAN	Shenla		F			Gila				EKHOISER	Shalom	uncle	779
FISHMAN	Gila	ZOIONETZ	F		Haim	Rivka				EKHOISER	Shalom	brother	779
FISHER	Shmuel Leizer		M	Married			Reisil			FISHER		son	782
FISHER	Reizel		F	Married			Shmuel			FISHER	Tsvi	son	782
FISHER	Hana		F		Shmuel	Reisel				FISHER	Tsvi	brother	782
FISHER	David		M		Shmuel	Reisel				FISHER	Tsvi	brother	782
FISHER	Shindel		F		Shmuel	Reisel				FISHER	Tsvi	brother	782
FOLKSBORD	Moshe		M	Married			Etel			BISTROVITCH	Itshak	son	789
FOLKSBORD	Etel	MELNIK	F	Married			Moshe			BISTROVITCH	Itshak	son	789
FOLKSBORD	Sime		F						Family name unclear	BISTROVITCH	Itshak	relative	789
FEDERMAN	Noach		M	Married			Sara Dobe			FEDERMAN	Moshe	son	787
FEDERMAN	Sara Dube	SHOSTOK	F	Married			Noah			FEDERMAN	Moshe	son	787
PERLA	Hershel		M	Married	Simcha	Golde		children		PERLA	Moshe	brother	799
PERLA			F	Married			Hershel	children		PERLA	Moshe	brother-in-law	799
PERLA	Simcha		M	Married			Golde			PERLA		son	799
PERLA	Golde		F	Married			Simcha			PERLA		son	799
PEREL	Enie Lea		F							PERL	Iudel		809
PEREL	Iosil		M							PERL	Iudel		809
PAPAU	Dr. Helena		F						Died on 22 Aug. 1922	HELBERSTADT GOLDFREV	Hania		761
FRIDMAN	Kalman		M	Married			Rachel		Died in Treblinka	FRIDMAN GRINBOIM	Avraham	son	762
FRIDMAN	Dinatche		F		Kalman	Rachel			Died in Siedlce	FRIDMAN GRINBOIM	Avraham	brother	762
FRIDMAN	Feigele		F		Kalman	Rachel				FRIDMAN GRINBOIM	Avraham	brother	762
FRIDMAN	Rachel	FULMAN	F	Married			Calman		Died in Treblinka	FRIDMAN GRINBOIM	Avraham	son	762
FRIDMAN	Beile	ROSENBOIM	F	Married	Alexander Ziskind	Lea	Hershel	children		ROSENBOIM	Betsalel	brother	807
FRIDMAN	Hershel		M	Married			Beile	children		ROSENBOIM	Betsalel	brother-in-law	807
FRIDMAN	Hana		F							FRIDMAN	Moshe	brother	780
FRIDMAN	Iosef		M		Shmuel	Iocheved				FRIDMAN	Moshe	brother	780
FRIDMAN	Iocheved	VINBERG	F	Married	Shlomo Zalman		Shmuel			FRIDMAN	Moshe	son	780
FRIDMAN	Shmuel		M	Married	Moshe Shimon		Iocheved			FRIDMAN	Moshe	son	780
FRIDMAN	Hershel Tsvi		M	Married						BOBIK	Matatihau		803
FREILICH								family	Died in Siedlce	FREILICH	Zalman		777
FRESHTER	Hanhake		F							VIMAN	Dov		763
PICHOTOVOSKI	Roise	VOKSTEIN	F					her family		VOKSTEIN	Sale	sister	798
PICHIMOTSKI	Mashe		F	Married	Iosel	Zelde	Moshe						799
PICHIMOTSKI	Moshe		M	Married			Mashel						799
PICHICHTCHILINA	Motel		M					his family		FASHISHTSHILINE	Hana		779

Family name(s)	First name(s)	Maiden name	Sex	Marital status	Father's name	Mother's name	Name of spouse	Additional family	Remarks	Family name(s) of eulogizer	First name(s) of eulogizer	Relationship of eulogizer	Page
PICHICHTCHILINA	Meir		M					his family		FASHISHTSHILINE	Hana		779
PICHICHTCHILINA	Ita Giora		F	Married			Mendel			FASHISHTSHILINE	Hana		779
PICHICHTCHILINA	Iehuda		M					his family		FASHISHTSHILINE	Hana		779
PICHICHTCHILINA	Israel		M					his family		FASHISHTSHILINE	Hana		779
PICHICHTCHILINA	Brish		M					his family		FASHISHTSHILINE	Hana		779
PESHENNA	Zeev		M	Married			Haia			DROMI POPOVESKI	Fishel		759
PESHENNA	Haia	POPOVSKI	F	Married		Hana	Zeev			DROMI POPOVESKI	Fishel		759
PESHENNA			F		Zeev	Haia				DROMI POPOVESKI	Fishel		759
PESHENNA			F		Zeev					DROMI POPOVESKI	Fishel		759
PESHENNA			F		Zeev	Haia				DROMI POPOVESKI	Fishel		759
צ													
TCHERNIBRODA	Bonim		M	Married	Aizik	Rachel		children		TCHERNIBRODA	Sara	sister	776
TCHERNIBRODA	Eisik		M	Married			Rachel			TCHERNIBRODA	Sara	daughter	776
TCHERNIBRODA			F	Married			Bonim	children		TCHERNIBRODA	Sara	sister-in-law	776
TCHERNIBRODA	Rachel		F	Married			Aisik			TCHERNIBRODA	Sara	daughter	776
TCHERNIBRODA	Moshe		M		Aizik	Rachel				TCHERNIBRODA	Sara	sister	776
TCHERNIBRODA	Haim		M		Aizik	Rachel				TCHERNIBRODA	Sara	sister	776
TSITRON	Iosef		M	Married			Roise		Died in the Warsaw Ghetto on 18 Apr. 1943	HELBERSTADT TEITEL	Israel	brother-in-law	760
TSITRON	Mordechai		M		Iosef	Roise			Died in the Warsaw Ghetto on 18 Apr. 1943	HELBERSTADT TEITEL	Israel	uncle	760
TSITRON	Roisale	HELBERSHTADT	F	Married	Naftali Hertz	Ienta Gitel	Iosef		Died in the Warsaw Ghetto on 18 Apr. 1943	HELBERSTADT TEITEL	Israel	sister	760
TSEITLIN	Peril Polia	GRINSPUN	F		Feivel Shraga	Miriam Sara				GRINSPEN HELBERSTADT	Rachel	sister	760
TSEITLIN			M			Peril Polia				GRINSPEN HELBERSTADT	Rachel	aunt	760
TSELNIKER	Iechiel		M	Married			Golde	2 children		BOBIK	Matatihau		803
TSELNIKER	Golde	FRIDMAN	F	Married	Hershel Tsvi		Iechiel	2 children		BOBIK	Matatihau		803
TSERENFELD	Berl		M	Married			Rivka			FEDERMAN	Moshe	brother-in-law	787
TSERENFELD	Rivka	FEDERMAN	F	Married			Berl			FEDERMAN	Moshe	brother	787
TSERENFELD	Itka		F		Berl	Rivka				FEDERMAN		uncle	787
TSERESHNI	Miriam		F		Iakov	Rachel Lea				GRINBERG	David	uncle	803
TSERESHNI	Iakov		M	Married			Rachel Lea			GRINBERG	David	brother-in-law	803
TSERESHNI	Biniamin		M		Iakov	Rachel Lea				GRINBERG	David	uncle	803
TSERESHNI	Rachel Lea	GRINBERG	F	Married	Menashe	Sara	Iakov			GRINBERG	David	brother	803
TSATSKIS	Hana		F			Hinde				TSATSKIS	David	brother	775
TSATSKIS	Shmuel		M		Avraham	Hinde				TSATSKIS	David	brother	775
TSATSKIS	Hinda		F	Married			Avraham			TSATSKIS	David	son	775
TSATSKIS	Shifra		F		Avraham	Hinde				TSATSKIS	David	brother	775
TSATSKIS	Avraham		M	Married	Shmuel		Hinda			TSATSKIS	David	son	775
TSATSKIS			F		Avraham	Hinde				TSATSKIS	David	brother	775
TSATSKIS	Gitel		F		Avraham	Hinde				TSATSKIS	David	brother	775
ק													
KOVE	Tsvi David		M						Died in Siedlce	KOVE	Israel		782
KOTCHENITSKI	Haia		F			Rachel Lea				MELINSKI GERTNER	Itshak	relative	793
KOTCHENITSKI	Avraham		M			Rachel Lea				MELINSKI GERTNER	Itshak	relative	793
KOTCHENITSKI	Rivka		F			Rachel Lea				MELINSKI GERTNER		relative	793
KOTCHENITSKI	Rachel Lea	GERTNER	F							MELINSKI GERTNER	Itshak	relative	793
KOTCHENITSKI		VIERNIK	F	Married	Motel		Meir Iechiel		Father from Motel Seiger Macher	KODCHENITSKI		son	806
KOTCHENITSKI	Meir Iechiel		M	Married	Aharon Leib		Breine Gitel			KODCHENITSKI	Mordechai	son	806

Family name(s)	First name(s)	Maiden name	Sex	Marital status	Father's name	Mother's name	Name of spouse	Additional family	Remarks	Family name(s) of eulogizer	First name(s) of eulogizer	Relationship of eulogizer	Page
KOTCHENITSKI	Aharon Leib		M						Glazier	KODCHENITSKI	Mordechai	grandson	806
KOTCHENITSKI	Iekel		M		Meir Iechiel	Breine Gitel				KODCHENITSKI	Mordechai	brother	806
KOTCHENITSKI	Haim		M		Meir Iechiel	Breine Gitel				KODCHENITSKI	Mordechai	brother	806
KOTCHENITSKI	Avraham		M		Meir Iechiel	Breine Gitel				KODCHENITSKI	Mordechai	brother	806
KOTCHENITSKI	Iosel		M	Married	Meir Iechiel	BreineGitel			Jews from Zelikel Bliobortch	KODCHENITSKI	Mordechai	brother	806
KOMIEN	Polie Pril	RUBIN	F		Mordechai	Rivka				GLIKSBERG	Iehuda		759
KOMIEN	Mendel		M			Polie Peril				GLIKSBERG	Iehuda		759
KONOPNE	Ioshia		M	Married			Chinke			KONOPNE	Dvora	granddaughter	804
KONOPNE	Rachel		F	Married			Iosef			KONOPNE	Dvora	daughter	804
KONOPNE	Avraham		M		Iosef	Rachel				KONOPNE	Dvora	sister	804
KONOPNE	Iosef		M	Married	Iehoshua		Rachel			KONOPNE		daughter	804
KONOPNE	Chinke		F	Married			Iehoshua			KONOPNE	Dvora	granddaughter	804
KONOPNE	Hirsh Haim		M		Iosef	Rachel				KONOPNE		sister	804
KONIOPNE	Avraham		M		Pinchas	Iocheved				KONIOPNE			806
KONIOPNE	Iocheved		F	Married			Pinchas			KONIOPNE	Iakov		806
KONIOPNE	Pinchas		M	Married			Iocheved			KONIOPNE	Iakov		806
KONSTANTINER	Pesach		M							KONSTANTINER	Lea		804
KONSTANTINER	Avraham		M	Married						KONSTANTINER			804
KONSTANTINER	Meitshe		F	Married			Eliezer	children		KONSTANTINER	Lea		804
KONSTANTINER	Rivka		F		Hana					KONSTANTINER	Lea		804
KONSTANTINER			F	Married						KONSTANTINER	Lea		804
KONSTANTINER	Gitel		F					children		KONSTANTINER	Lea		804
KONSTANTINER	Roise		F			Rachel				KONSTANTINER	Lea		804
KONSTANTINER	Rachel		F							KONSTANTINER	Lea		804
KONSTANTINER			F	Married			Avraham			KONSTANTINER	Lea		804
KONSTANTINER	Iosef		M	Married			Hana			KONSTANTINER	Lea		804
KONSTANTINER			F		Avraham					KONSTANTINER	Lea		804
KONSTANTINER	Hana		M	Married						KONSTANTINER	Lea		804
KONSTANTINER	Avraham		M	Married				children		KONSTANTINER	Lea		804
KONSTANTINER			F	Married			Avraham	children		KONSTANTINER	Lea		804
KONSTANTINER	Eliezer		M	Married			Meitche	children		KONSTANTINER			804
KONSTANTINER	Hana		F	Married			Iosef			KONSTANTINER	Lea		804
KOTSMAN	Leibeke		M	Married			Hadas	children		TEIBLUM MOLOVONTCHIK	Feigele	relative	791
KOTSMAN	Hadas		F	Married			Leibke	children		TEIBLUM MOLOVONTCHIK	Feigele	relative	791
KOROSEK	Hershel		M	Married			Sara			MELINSKI GERTNER		relative	793
KOROSEK			M	Married			Frimet	children		MELINSKI GERTNER	Itshak	relative	793
KOROSEK	Primet		F	Married				children		MELINSKI GERTNER	Itshak	relative	793
KOROSEK	Rivka	GERTNER	F							MELINSKI GERTNER	Itshak	relative	793
KOROSEK	Sara		F	Married			Hershel			MELINSKI GERTNER	Itshak	relative	793
KAVA KOVE	Natan		M		Uziel					KAVA	Hana	daughter	779
KAVA KOVE	Moshe		M		Uziel			his family		KAVA		sister	779
KAVA KOVE	Rivka		F					her family		KAVA	Hana		779
KOTELRESKI	Rachel	ROSENBLUM	F							KRIZ	Dvora		769
KINIGSBERG	Sara	GOLDFINGER	F	Married						GOLDFINGER RUBINSTEIN	Sara		767
KINIGSBERG			M	Married						GOLDFINGER RUBINSTEIN	Sara		767
KIRSHEMBOIM	Ioshua		M			Nechama				KIRSHENBOIM	Hanina	brother	773
KIRSHEMBOIM	Feiga		F			Nechama				KIRSHENBOIM	Hanina	brother	773
KIRSHEMBOIM	Mordechai		M			Nechama					Hanina	brother	773

Family name(s)	First name(s)	Maiden name	Sex	Marital status	Father's name	Mother's name	Name of spouse	Additional family	Remarks	Family name(s) of eulogizer	First name(s) of eulogizer	Relationship of eulogizer	Page
KIRSHEMBOIM	Rivka		F								Hanina	son	773
KIRSHEMBOIM	Shlomo		M			Nechama				KIRSHENBOIM	Hanina	brother	773
KISHELINSKI	Rivka		F							BERENFELD	David	cousin	808
KLEIMAN	Hersh Shonia		M						Killed by a Gestapo man on 22 Aug. 1943	GOLDFINGER RUBINSTEIN	Sara		767
KLEIMAN	Leib		M						Brother in law of Melech Max Rubinstein. Deported to Treblinka on22 Aug. 1942	GOLDFINGER RUBINSTEIN	Sara		767
KLEIMAN	Baruch Mordechai		M						Died on 26 May 1941	GOLDFINGER RUBINSTEIN	Sara		767
KLEIMAN			F						Died in Siedlce on the6 Sep. 1943	GOLDFINGER RUBINSTEIN	Sara		767
KLEIMAN	Leib		M						Deported to Treblinka on	GOLDFINGER RUBINSTEIN	Sara		767
KLEINLERER	Hana		F		Moshe	Ietke				KLEINLERER	Sara	sister	777
KLEINLERER	Itke		F	Widow			Moshe			KLEINLERER	Sara	daughter	777
KLEINLERER	Itshak		F		Moshe	Ietke				KLEINLERER	Sara	sister	777
KLEINLERER	Dobe	TSUKER	F	Married			Biniamin			KLEINLERER	Sara	sister-in-law	777
KLEINLERER			F		Moshe	Ietke				KLEINLERER	Sara	sister	777
KLEINLERER	Biniamin		M	Married	Moshe	Ietke	Dobe			KLEINLERER	Sara	sister	777
KLEINLERER	Menachem		M							MORGENSTERN	Family		766
KLEINLERER	Shulamit		F							MORGENSTERN	Family		766
KLEINLERER	Eliezer		M		Mordechai					MORGENSTERN	Family		766
KLEINLERER	Golda		F		Shalom					MORGENSTERN	Family		766
KAMEIN	Iakov		M	Married				children		ZOLOTOVSKI	David	brother-in-law	769
KAMEIN	Mina	ZLOTOVSKI	F	Married	Israel	Miriam	Iakov	children		ZOLOTOVSKI	David	brother	769
KAMINNI	Rishka		F							KAMINNI	Avraham	brother	773
KAMINNI	Ester		F							KAMINNI	Avraham	brother	773
KAMINNI	Ben-Tsion		M							KAMINNI	Avraham	brother	773
KARMOTCH	Feiga	POPIR	F	Married			Mordechai		Rav Matel Karmotch.Lived at 3 Elieser St	KARMESH	Shmuel	brother-in-law	771
KARMOTCH	Tsvi Menashe		M	Married	Tuvia		Miriam		Rav Herschel Tuvias. Lived at 16 Idlona St	KARMESH	Shmuel	son	771
KARMOTCH	Miriam	COHEN	F	Married	Israel Iakov		Tsvi Menashe		Lived at 16 Idlona St	KARMESH	Shmuel	son	771
KARMOTCH	Mordechai		M	Married	Tsvi Menashe		Feiga		Lived at 3 Elieser St	KARMESH	Shmuel	brother	771
KREDO	Rivka		F		Haim Hersh	Ester				KREDO	Iechiel	brother	786
KREDO	Ite		F		Haim Hersh	Ester				KREDO	Iechiel	brother	786
KREDO	Ester		F	Married			Haim Hersh			KREDO	Iechiel	son	786
KREDO	Dina		F		Haim Hersh	Ester				KREDO	Iechiel	brother	786
KREDO	Ester		F		Haim Hersh	Ester				KREDO	Iechiel	brother	786
KREDO	Shlomo		M		Haim Hersh	Ester				KREDO	Iechiel	brother	786
KREDO	Haim Hersh		M	Married			Ester			KREDO	Iechiel	son	786
ר													
RABINOVITCH			F	Married			Itshak	children		BISTROVITCH	Itshak	relative	789
RABINOVITCH	Beile Hinde	KOSHEMACHER	F	Married			Zalman			BISTROVITCH	Itshak	relative	789
RABINOVITCH			F	Married			Israel Hirsh	children		BISTROVITCH	Itshak	relative	789
RABINOVITCH	Zalman		M	Married			Beile Hinde			BISTROVITCH	Itshak	relative	789
RABINOVITCH	Itshak Asher		M	Married				children		BISTROVITCH	Itshak	relative	789
RABINOVITCH	Israel Hiesch		M	Married				children		BISTROVITCH	Itshak	relative	789
ROSENBOIM	Eidel		F	Married			David Tsvi			ROSENBOIM	Itshak	son	806

Family name(s)	First name(s)	Maiden name	Sex	Marital status	Father's name	Mother's name	Name of spouse	Additional family	Remarks	Family name(s) of eulogizer	First name(s) of eulogizer	Relationship of eulogizer	Page
ROSENBOIM	David Tsvi		M	Married			Eidel			ROSENBOIM	Itshak	son	806
ROSENBOIM	Moshe		M	Married	David Tsvi	Eidel		children		ROSENBOIM	Itshak	brother	806
ROSENBOIM			F	Married			Moshe	children		ROSENBOIM	Itshak	brother-in-law	806
ROSENBOIM	Lea	MADONES	F	Married			Alexander Ziskind			ROSENBOIM	Betsalel	son	807
ROSENBOIM	Alexander Ziskind		M	Married			Lea			ROSENBOIM	Betsalel	son	807
ROSENBOIM	Sara		F	Married			Iosef	children		ROSENBOIM	Betsalel	brother-in-law	807
ROSENBOIM	Eliezer		M	Married	Alexander Ziskind	Lea	Shprintse			ROSENBOIM	Betsalel	brother	807
ROSENBOIM	Shprintse		F	Married			Eliezer			ROSENBOIM	Betsalel	brother-in-law	807
ROSENBOIM	Iosef		M	Married	Alexander Ziskind	Lea	Sara	children		ROSENBOIM	Betsalel	brother	807
RAFAEL	Hanina		M	Married			Nacha			RUBINSTEIN VINOGRAD	Ode		803
RAFAEL			F	Married			Hanania			RUBINSTEIN VINOGRAD	Ode		803
RAFAEL	Berl		M	Married			Rivka	child		GRINBERG	David	brother-in-law	803
RAFAEL	Rivka	GRINBERG	F	Married	Menashe	Sara	Berl	child		GRINBERG	David	brother	803
RAFAEL	Fila	VANDERBOIM	F		Shlomo					VUNDERBOIM	Mina	sister	778
RAFAEL	Haim David		M		Baruch	Sara				RAFAEL	Moshe	brother	803
RAFAEL	Baruch		M	Married			Sara			RAFAEL	Moshe	son	803
RAFAEL	Rivotche		F		Baruch	Sara				RAFAEL	Moshe	brother	803
RAFAEL	Shmuelke		M		Baruch	Sara				RAFAEL	Moshe	brother	803
RAFAEL	Simcha		M		Baruch	Sara				RAFAEL		brother	803
RAFAEL	Sara		F	Married			Baruch			RAFAEL		son	803
RUBIN	Rivka	BEIER	F			Rachel				GLIKSBERG	Iehuda		759
RUBINSTEIN			M		Matatiahu					RUBINSTEIN VINOGRAD	Ode		803
RUBINSTEIN	Tsvi		M	Married			Sara	children		BINSHTOK	Gila		773
RUBINSTEIN	Sara		F	Married			Tsvi	children		BINSHTOK	Gila		773
RUBINSTEIN	Melech		M						Deported to Treblinka on 22 Aug. 1942	GOLDFINGER RUBINSTEIN	Sara		767
RUBINSTEIN	Hena Leiser		M						Died on 31 Aug 1942				767
ROSENBLUM BIRTSIHER	Israel		M						"Macher" from the East(?)	KRIZ	Dvora		769
ROSENBLUM	Primat		F							KRIZ	Dvora		769
ROSENBLUM	Hana		F	Married			Hershel			KRIZ	Dvora		769
ROSENBLUM	Moshe		M							KRIZ	Dvora		769
ROSENBLUM	Hershel		M	Married			Hana			KRIZ			769
ROSENBLUM	Reizel		F							KRIZ	Dvora		769
ROSENBERG	Ester		F		Iakov	Sara				ROSENBERG		brother	782
ROSENBERG	Lea		F		Iakov	Sara				ROSENBERG		brother	782
ROSENBERG	Iakov		M	Married			Sara			ROSENBERG		son	782
ROSENBERG	Sara		F	Married			Iakov			ROSENBERG		son	782
ROTENBERG	Itshak		M		Elihau Heinech	Pesia		his family					777
ROTENBERG	Iakov		M		Elihau Heinech	Pesia		his family					777
ROTENBERG	Pesia		F	Married			Elihau						777
ROTENBERG	Elihau Hinech		M	Married			Pesia						777
ROTFELD	Avraham		M							VIMAN	Dov		763
ROTFELD	Hihele		F							VIMAN			763
ROTFELD	Zalman		M							VIMAN	Dov		763
ROKACH	Sara	KAHANA	F		Meir	Feige				GLIKSBERG	Iehuda		759
ROKACH			F			Sara				GLIKSBERG	Iehuda		759

Family name(s)	First name(s)	Maiden name	Sex	Marital status	Father's name	Mother's name	Name of spouse	Additional family	Remarks	Family name(s) of eulogizer	First name(s) of eulogizer	Relationship of eulogizer	Page
ROKACH			F			Sara				GLIKSBERG	Iehuda		759
RIBEK			F	Married			Baruch	children		RIBAK	Malcha		772
RIBEK	Bonim		M	Married	Avraham Itshak			children		RIBAK	Malcha		772
RIBEK			M	Married				children		RIBAK	Malcha		772
RIBEK	Meir		M	Married	Avraham Itshak			children		RIBAK	Malcha		772
RIBEK			F	Married			Meir	children		RIBAK	Malcha		772
RIBEK			F	Married			Bonim	children		RIBAK	Malcha		772
RIBEK	Menucha		F	Married			Mordechai			RIBAK	Mordechai	husband	774
RIBEK	Avraham		M	Married			Gitel			RIBAK	Mordechai	son	774
RIBEK	Hershel		M		Avraham	Gitel				RIBAK	Mordechai	brother	774
RIBEK	David		M		Mordechai	Menucha				RIBAK	Mordechai	father	774
RIBEK	Brish		M			Gitel				RIBAK	Mordechai	brother	774
RIBEK	Gitel		F	Married			Avraham			RIBAK	Mordechai	son	774
RISA	Israel		M		Itshak Aharon	Rivka				KARMESH	Hana	sister	771
RISA	Itshak Aharon		M	Married			Rivka			KARMESH	Hana	daughter	771
RISA	Rivka		F	Married			Itshak Aharon			KARMESH		daughter	771
RINETSKI	Lea		F							RINETSKI	Neche	daughter	808
ש													
SCHWARTZ	Igush		M		Shaul	Ester				ORZEL AND FAMILY	Itshak		757
SCHWARTZ	Tiodor		M		Shaul	Ester				ORZEL AND FAMILY			757
SCHWARTZ	Shaul		M	Married			Ester			ORZEL AND FAMILY	Itshak		757
SCHWARTZ	Ester		F	Married						ORZEL AND FAMILY			757
STEINBERG	Rachel		F		Itshak David	Elte Nechama				STEINBERG	Aharon	brother	809
STEINBERG	Itshak David		M	Married			Elte Nechama			STEINBERG		son	809
STEINBERG	Dobe		F		Itshak David	Elte Nechama				STEINBERG		brother	809
STEINBERG	Elte Nechama	FEIGUENBOIM	F	Married			Itshak David			STEINBERG		son	809
STEINBERG	Lea		F	Married			Simcha	3 children			Moshe		806
STEINBERG	Simcha		M	Married			Lea	3 children		SELTSER VISHNIE	Moshe		806
STEINBERG	Hanoch Henich		M						Died in 1942	STEINBERG	Moshe	son	765
STEINBERG	Lutsena Vilnia		F	Married			Simcha			STEINBERG	Moshe	brother-in-law	779
STEINBERG	Simcha		M	Married	Binush	Frida	Lutsena Vilnia			STEINBERG	Moshe	brother	779
STEINBERG	Tsvia Hersh		M		Binush	Frida			Died in Lodz	STEINBERG		brother	779
STEINBERG	Binush		M	Married	Nachum		Frida			STEINBERG	Moshe	son	779
STEINBERG		EDELSTEIN	F	Married	Avraham		Binush			STEINBERG	Moshe	son	779
STERENFELD	Dvora	GERTNER	F							MELINSKI GERTNER	Itshak	relative	793
STERENFELD	Malcha		F			Dvora				MELINSKI GERTNER	Itshak	relative	793
STERENFELD	Mordechai		M			Dvora				MELINSKI GERTNER	Itshak	relative	793
STERENFELD	Moshe		M			Dvora				MELINSKI GERTNER	Itshak	relative	793
STERENFELD	Rivka		F			Dvora				MELINSKI GERTNER	Itshak	relative	793
STERENFELD	Avraham		M			Dvora				MELINSKI GERTNER	Itshak	relative	793
SHTASHOPOK	Iakov		M	Married			Mashel	grandparents, aunt, uncle and all the family		SHTSHUPOK MARKUSFELD	Motel	son	805
SHTASHOPOK	Israel Iermihau		M		Iakov	Mashe				SHTSHUPOK MARKUSFELD	Motel	brother	805
SHTASHOPOK	Avraham Idel		M	Married	Iakov	Mashe				SHTSHUPOK MARKUSFELD	Motel	brother	805
SHTASHOPOK	Mashe		F	Married			Iakov			SHTSHUPOK MARKUSFELD	Motel	son	805
SHTASHOPOK			F	Married			Avraham Idel			SHTSHUPOK MARKUSFELD	Motel	brother-in-law	805
SHIVOK	Ester		F	Married			Berl	children		TABAKMAN ROSENSOMEN	Israel		769
SHIVOK	Berl		M	Married			Ester	children		TABAKMAN ROSENSOMEN	Israel		769
SHLIFKE	Zalman		M	Married	Itshak			children		RIBAK	Malcha		772

Family name(s)	First name(s)	Maiden name	Sex	Marital status	Father's name	Mother's name	Name of spouse	Additional family	Remarks	Family name(s) of eulogizer	First name(s) of eulogizer	Relationship of eulogizer	Page
SHLIFKE			F	Married			Meir	children		RIBAK	Malcha		772
SHLIFKE	Avraham		M	Married	Itshak			children		RIBAK	Malcha		772
SHLIFKE			F	Married			Zalman	children		RIBAK	Malcha		772
SHLIFKE			F	Married			Avraham	children		RIBAK	Malcha		772
SHLIFKE	Meir		M	Married				children		RIBAK	Malcha		772
SHMUEL	Feiga Rosa		F	Married			David			ALTMAN	Shmuel	son	781
SHMUKLIORTCH	David Shimon		M					his family		VEINSTEIN SHMUKLIARTCH	Rachel	uncle	770
SHMUKLIORTCH	Aharon Itshak		M	Married			Ritsa		Died in Siedlce	VEINSTEIN SHMUKLIARTCH	Rachel	daughter	770
SHMUKLIORTCH	Ritsa		F	Married			Aharon Itshak		Died in Siedlce	VEINSTEIN SHMUKLIARTCH	Rachel	daughter	770
SHMUKLIORTCH	Ester		F		Aharon Itshak	Ritsa			Died near to Siedlce	VEINSTEIN SHMUKLIARTCH	Rachel	sister	770
SHMUKLIORTCH	Lea		F	Married			Eliezer	children	Died in Siedlce	VEINSTEIN SHMUKLIARTCH		sister-in-law	770
SHMUKLIORTCH	David		M		Aharon Itshak	Ritsa			Died in Siedlce	VEINSTEIN SHMUKLIARTCH	Rachel	sister	770
SHMUKLIORTCH	Eliezer		M	Married	Aharon Itshak	Ritsa	Lea	children	Died in Siedlce	VEINSTEIN SHMUKLIARTCH	Rachel	sister	770
SHMUKLIORTCH	Baruch Mordechai		M					his family		VEINSTEIN SHMUKLIARTCH	Rachel	uncle	770
SHMUKLER	Aharon Itshak		M	Married	Shmuel Iakov		Retsa	his family		SHMUKLER VEINSTEIM	Moshe	brother-in-law	778
SHMUKLER	Ritsa		F	Married			Aharon Itshak	her family		SHMUKLER VEINSTEIM	Moshe	brother-in-law	778
SHMUKLER	Feiga		F	Married			Baruch Mordechai	her family		SHMUKLER	Moshe	brother-in-law	778
SHMUKLER	Baruch Mordechai		M	Married			Feiga	his family		SHMUKLER	Moshe	sister	778
SHMUKLER	Malcha		F	Married			David Shimon	her family		SHMUKLER	Moshe		778
SHMUKLER	David Shimon		M	Married			Malcha	his family		SHMUKLER	Moshe		778
SHMILINA	Haia	RISA	F		Itshak Aharon	Rivka				KARMESH	Hana	sister	771
SHPODEL	Israel		M	Married			Sara	children		VEISMAN	Moshe	brother-in-law	807
SHPODEL	Sara	VEISMAN	F	Married			Israel	children		VEISMAN	Moshe	brother	807
SHPORBER	Ester Beile	LEIBMAN	F					children		LEIBMAN	Sara		807
SHAPIRO	Baruch		M							SHAPIRA	Alexander	brother	773
SHAPIRO	Rishka		F							SHAPIRA	Alexander	brother	773
SHKELRAZ	Rivka	SHKLOZ	F	Married	Nachamn Nate	Henia Breina	Natan				Iakov	brother	776
SHKELRAZ	Henia Breine		F	Married			Nachman Nate			SHKLOZ	Iakov	son	776
SHKELRAZ	Haim Aharon		M	Married	Nachamn Nate	Henia Breina	Tsitsa	children		SHKLOZ	Iakov	brother	776
SHKELRAZ	Nachman Nate		M	Married			Henia Breina			SHKLOZ	Iakov	son	776
SHKELRAZ	Tsitsa	SUKENIK	F	Married			Haim Aharon	children		SHKLOZ	Iakov	brother-in-law	776
SHKELRAZ	Natan		M	Married			Rivka			SHKLOZ	Iakov	brother-in-law	776
SHRAGA			F	Married			Israel			HUBERMAN	Sheindel		804
SHRAGA	Israel		M	Married							Sheindel		804

NAME INDEX

Karnitzki, 121
Karpinski, 13
Karsak, 61
Kartcz, 110
Kashetz, 296
Kashtan, 300
Kaspi, 5, 6, 98, 99, 101, 111, 115, 176, 203, 273, 380, 381, 382, 383
Kastelianski, 229
Kaszdan, 252
Kaszenicki, 200, 201, 203, 204
Kasztliosz, 222
Katczer, 101
Katz, 71
Kava, 429
Kava, 449
Kaveh, 292, 293, 327, 336, 425, 429
Kawa, 201
Kaweh, 285
Kaznitzky, 270
Kelmeson, 24
Khmurner, 253
Khozonovkski, 6
Khrenovitzki, 44
Kimmel, 111, 173
Kindman, 384
King Boleslaw, 9
King Sigismund Augustus, 9
Kinigsberg, 449
Kipnis, 273
Kirschenbaum, 33, 326, 370
Kirshemboim, 449, 450
Kirshenbaum, 417
Kirshenboim, 449, 450
Kirshman, 395, 397
Kirshrat, 168
Kishelinski, 450
Kishilinski, 355
Klatzkin, 152
Klausner, 139
Kleiman, 450
Kleinlard, 156
Kleinlehrer, 114, 198, 269, 275
Kleinlerer, 380, 411
Kleinlerer, 450
Kleinveksler, 114
Kleinwechsler, 370, 379, 380
Klenlehrer, 275
Kna'ani, 378, 380
Knal, 61
Koczinski, 7
Kodchenitski, 434, 440, 448, 449
Kodjenitski, 434, 438, 440, 446
Kokbaka, 326
Kolykov, 96
Komar, 179
Komien, 449
Konigshteyn, 132
Koniopne, 449
Konopne, 449

Konski, 263
Konsorowicz, 246
Konstantiner, 437, 438, 449
Konstantinowski, 129, 395
Koopershmit, 220
Koperant, 214
Korn, 266
Kornblum, 291, 317
Korniczky, 236
Korona, 375
Korosek, 449
Kosakov, 45
Koshemacher, 433, 450
Koshetz, 47, 202
Koshinski, 6
Koshke, 311
Koshlatch, 94
Koszinicki, 200
Kotchenitski, 448, 449
Kotelreski, 449
Kotsman, 449
Kove, 448, 449
Kozhlatch, 95
Kramarsh, 214, 346
Kramarsz, 200
Kramarzh, 114, 216
Kramerzesh, 415
Kramesh, 415, 416
Kramosz, 254
Krapowski, 90
Krasitzki, 67
Kreda, 397
Kredo, 436, 450
Kriez, 413
Kriz, 449, 451
Krosunski, 32
Kroyshar, 290
Kroyt, 125
Krusman, 249
Kukel, 13
Kushlian, 258
Kuzmir, 153, 154
Kviatek, 232
Kwiatek, 176, 237

L

Ladau, 180
Lamdan, 189
Landau, 76, 86, 87, 156, 167, 168, 170, 174, 178, 227, 229, 255, 270, 284, 303, 304, 305, 348, 403
Landau, 442
Landoy, 39, 86
Langer, 44, 296, 428
Langer, 442
Las, 240
Laterman, 102, 169
Latinek, 99
Lebel, 240, 356
Lederman, 197, 378, 408
Lederman, 436, 442

Orlovski, 431
Orlovsky, 423
Orszekh, 203
Orszel, 175, 286, 380
Orwitz, 267
Orzel, 155, 161, 268, 401, 404, 417
Orzel, 431, 446, 447, 452
Orzhel, 375
Orzshel, 431
Osman, 432
Otschen, 431
Ovadia, 282
Ovadiah, 380
Ovadyahu, 144
Ozik, 431

P

Pachter, 168
Paciarkowski, 265
Paderewski, 233
Pakhter, 202
Paltiel, 431, 442, 443
Pankevitsch, 96
Papau, 407
Papau, 447
Papawski, 404
Papovoski, 446
Paritz, 202
Partzever, 203
Pasawski, 197
Pasawsky, 114
Pasovsky, 216, 269, 300, 412
Pasowski, 5, 130, 180, 370
Pat, 252
Paunch, 309, 310
Pawlik, 96
Pawlyuk, 96
Pczedetzki, 94
Pedrovski, 446
Pedrovsky, 401
Pentak, 42, 45
Perel, 447
Perelman, 246
Perets, 443
Peretz, 68, 114, 133, 138, 168, 179, 200, 246, 249, 251, 270,
278, 279, 280, 281, 282, 290, 298, 299, 306, 384, 391, 392
Perl, 432, 446, 447
Perla, 167, 169, 410
Perla, 432, 447
Peshenna, 448
Peshishtshilina, 425
Pesovsky, 156
Petrov, 26
Pfau, 345
Pichichtchilina, 447, 448
Pichimotski, 447
Pichotovoski, 447
Piekarsz, 393
Piekosinki, 149
Pietochov, 59, 65, 66

Pietrkover, 285
Pigove, 313
Pilsudski, 29, 30, 88, 89, 91, 123, 126, 209, 211, 212, 213,
237, 262, 283, 287, 308, 330, 341, 343
Pinietski, 438
Platkowski, 101
Plony, 115
Plotsker, 152
Plotzker, 287
Police, 26, 46, 48, 50, 59, 64, 65, 74, 87, 252, 317, 318
Poniatowski, 12
Popir, 450
Popoveski, 446, 448
Popovski, 448
Popovsky, 110, 111, 158, 268, 308, 375, 404
Popowski, 92, 121, 168, 175, 176, 197, 222, 223, 224, 256,
257, 260, 262, 263, 265, 274, 380, 382, 385, 386
Popowsky, 165, 218, 255
Posowski, 181, 219, 382
Posowskyu, 221
Prezeh, 48
Priesland, 139
Prilotsky, 303
Prilucki, 245, 251, 253, 278
Priluczki, 168
Priludski, 249
Prilutzki, 68, 143
Protopopov, 59
Prylucki, 272
Pszetsszecki, 342
Pugovi, 439, 443, 446
Pursever, 198
Pyetuchov, 74

Q

Queen Jadwiga,, 12

R

Rabinovitch, 450
Rabinowicz, 176, 240, 347
Rabinowitz, 153, 160, 326
Radak, 243, 273
Radashinski, 176
Radzhikovska, 65
Radziner, 290
Radzinske, 195
Radzinski, 41, 48, 176, 207
Rafael, 432, 436, 438, 439, 441, 444, 451
Rafal, 57, 354, 355
Rapaport, 166, 288
Ratbein, 261
Ratbeyn, 124
Ratbine, 193
Ratiinievitsch, 44
Ratinievitsch, 33, 57, 65
Ratinovitsch, 44
Ratinovitsh, 54
Ratinyevitsch, 41, 42
Ratshin, 30

T

Tchistaaka, 65
Tchlenow, 171
Tchotchkes, 53, 54, 61, 231
Tchudner, 441
Tchutchikel, 43
Teiber, 340
Teibloom, 201
Teiblum, 201, 203, 421
Teiblum, 436, 438, 441, 443, 449
Teitel, 437, 448
Temerl, 20, 291
Temkin, 49, 51, 53, 54, 70, 138, 139, 156, 166, 168, 177, 180, 228, 278, 347, 375, 380, 407
Tenenbaum, 169, 171, 173, 204, 218, 222, 237, 244, 252, 256, 257, 260, 270, 273, 274, 307, 308, 340, 344, 347, 356, 375, 385
Tenenboim, 329
Tenenboim, 441
Tenenboym, 34, 77, 78, 88, 110, 114, 115, 139, 141, 144
Teyblum, 57
Tiblum, 153, 418, 426
Tiblum, 440, 441
Tichanovsky, 59, 73, 74
Tichinovsky, 49, 50, 51, 52, 53, 54, 55, 56, 59, 61, 62, 64, 66, 70, 73
Tichonowski, 278, 280
Tidhar, 158
Tigel, 140
Tikhonovsky, 153
Tikoczynski, 158
Tikotinsky, 300
Tilinski, 6, 7
Tirin, 248
Tobokman, 440
Tochklepper, 422
Tokmin, 441
Tomkin, 441
Ton, 135
Tortshinski, 62
Trotsky, 283
Trumpeldor, 146, 159
Tsatskis, 448
Tseitlin, 448
Tselniker, 448
Tsenki, 237
Tserenfeld, 448
Tsereshni, 448
Tsernobroda, 155
Tsetskis, 419
Tsfoni, 444
Tshatchkes, 70
Tshistaka, 54
Tsikholnik, 122
Tsinaman, 181
Tsitron, 448
Tsuker, 450
Tuchklalpper, 173
Tuchklaper, 87, 106
Tuchklapper, 168, 169, 173, 236
Tuchkleper, 440

Tumanov, 80
Tuvklapper, 180
Tzederboym, 31
Tzelnik, 196
Tzeretely, 68
Tzetzkas, 158
Tzfoni, 420

U

Unger, 150
Urszech, 168
Urszel, 195, 227, 237, 240, 256, 260, 262
Urzel, 222
Urzhel, 257, 258, 262
Ussishkin, 171
Uzik, 429

V

Vagoski, 437
Vainshtain, 356
Vaintroyb, 46
Vanderboim, 435, 439, 442, 451
Vayman, 180
Vaynapple, 44
Vaynberg, 150
Vayntroib, 49, 51
Vayntroyb, 39, 49, 114
Vegoski, 408
Veiman, 438
Veinapple, 7
Veingarten, 439
Veinstein, 433, 435, 436, 442, 453
Veintroib, 7
Veisberg, 438
Veisman, 438, 453
Vesher, 204
Vica, 42
Viernik, 448
Vilk, 67
Viman, 434, 437, 439, 447, 451
Vinberg, 439, 447
Vinograd, 395
Vinograd, 432, 438, 451
Vinokur, 438
Vinshtin, 439
Vinstein, 432, 439
Vira, 41, 408
Virgalitsch, 59
Virtsershol, 407
Vishinia, 439
Vishkovoski, 438
Vishnie, 438, 452
Vishnio, 438
Vishnye, 23
Visoki, 437, 438, 444
Vodeh, 222
Vogler, 115
Voikov, 39, 46
Voitsershul, 439

www.ingramcontent.com/pod-product-compliance
Lightning Source LLC
Chambersburg PA
CBHW082006150426
42814CB00005BA/244